The Very Rich Hours of Adrienne Monnier

Translated, with an Introduction and Commentaries, by Richard McDougall

INTRODUCTION TO THE BISON BOOKS EDITION
BY BRENDA WINEAPPLE

UNIVERSITY OF NEBRASKA PRESS
LINCOLN

⊖ The paper in this book meets the minimum requirements of American National Standard for Information Sciences—Permanence of Paper for Printed Library Materials, ANSI Z39.48-1984.

First Bison Books printing: 1996
Most recent printing indicated by the last digit below:
10 9   8   7   6   5   4   3   2   1

Library of Congress Cataloging-in-Publication Data
Monnier, Adrienne.
[Selections. English]
The very rich hours of Adrienne Monnier / translated, with an introduction and commentaries, by Richard McDougall; introduction to the Bison Books edition by Brenda Wineapple.
p. cm.
Translations from Les gazettes d'Adrienne Monnier, Dernières gazettes et écrits divers, Rue de l'Odéon; excerpts from Shakespeare and company.
Originally published: New York: Scribner, c1976.
"Bison Books."
Includes index.
ISBN 0-8032-8227-3 (pa: alk. paper)
1. Authors, French—20th century—Biography.   2. Booksellers and bookselling—France—Paris—History—20th century.   3. Monnier, Adrienne—Friends and associates.
I. McDougall, Richard. II. Title.
PQ146.M6413   1997
848'.91209—dc20 [B]
96-29079   CIP

Parts of this book were originally published in French in *Les Gazettes d'Adrienne Monnier*, 1925–1945, © René Julliard, 1953; *Derniéres Gazettes et Ecrits divers*, © Mercure de France, 1961; *Rue de l'Odéon*, © Editions Albin Michel, 1960. Excerpts from *Shakespeare and Company*, © 1956, 1959, by Sylvia Beach are reprinted by permission of Harcourt Brace Jovanovich, Inc.

The translator thanks Marie Monnier-Bécat, sister of Adrienne Monnier, and Maurice Saillet, Monnier's friend and literary executor, for their generous permission to translate the writings that appear in this volume and for invaluable information as well; Hélène Baltrusaitis, who in memory of her friendship with Adrienne Monnier painstakingly read through his translations and offered enlightening critical comments; Constance Hirsch, of the Translation Center of Columbia University, who recommended his project for this work to Scribners; and Patricia Cristol, his editor, to whom he is especially grateful for discovering the title and the form of the book.

Reprinted from the original 1976 edition by Charles Scribner's Sons, New York.

INTRODUCTION TO THE BISON BOOKS EDITION
Brenda Wineapple

I loved books, that was all.
—Adrienne Monnier

A bookshop is a curious place. A mortuary for the undead, it is a refuge where one stands comforted in front of beckoning shelves, silent, solitary, never alone.

In what will be known as the era before the bookstore supermarket, bookshops often bore the imprint of visionary women: Elizabeth Palmer Peabody, Frances Steloff, and perhaps none more famous or influential than that Paris pair, Sylvia Beach and her Shakespeare and Company (catering primarily to American expatriates), and the shop across the street that spawned it, Adrienne Monnier's Maison des Amis des Livres.

As Richard McDougall notes in the fine introduction to this anthology of Monnier's essays and occasional writings, Adrienne Monnier opened her lending library and bookshop on 15 November 1915 with her father's insurance money after he had been injured in a train wreck. Her business partner was Suzanne Bonnierre, the pre-Raphaelite beauty Monnier had followed to London six years earlier in the throes of first love. But Monnier had no other fixed or burning passion: she was lady's companion, French teacher, and when back in Paris, literary secretary. The bookshop on the Rue de l'Odéon, in Paris's Left Bank, changed all that.

Monnier's bookshop was not a place where books were mechanically swapped without care for book or buyer. La Maison des Amis des Livres was instead a confederacy buoyed by the devotion of its owner, who fervently believed that the world of books is a world of writers and readers linked together by ineffable, almost mystical, bonds. Yet, there was nothing inaccessible about La Maison, which rapidly became a hub of intercontinental literary life, complete with poetry readings, exhibitions, and aperitif. André Gide read from his own work, Valéry read from Poe's, and patrons flocked to hear Joyce and Larbaud recite *Ulysses* in two tongues.

Nor was there anything unworldly about Mme. Monnier. Clear blue eyes peered out of a face as round and smooth as an apple; friends thought she looked like an abbess. Her bent was contemplative, her nature sensuous. A confessed gourmand, simultaneously self-effacing and willful, she strolled up and down the Rue de l'Odéon in her daily vestment: white blouse, sleeveless velveteen waistcoat, and a floor-length gray skirt that swept the street as she passed. She walked over to the markets on the Rue de Buci to select with care the crispest of fresh vegetables for the evening meal. Hemingway, she said, doubted how one with such elevated taste could resist collaboration with the Nazis. The charge was without foundation. Monnier relished good food and conversation but would sacrifice nothing to human dignity.

Most of all, she loved the exquisite heft of words. Her favorite French authors were Claudel, Valéry, and Laforgue. Her favorite Americans were Ben Franklin and Walt Whitman. And of course there was that transcontinental hero, James Joyce, whom Monnier regarded with an abnegation not quite as encompassing, if no less devout, than that of Sylvia Beach. Monnier financed her own review, the *Gazette des Amis des Livres*, by selling her rights to the French translation of *Ulysses*, over which she had fretted with the scrupulous attentions of a novitiate.

If her impulse toward literature was at heart religious, as many have suggested, it also was shrewdly hard-headed. Adrienne Monnier was no shallow enthusiast. She was a canny observer, a keen critic, and a businesswoman presiding over the publication of several journals, perhaps the most famous being the elegant *Commerce*. The first translation of T. S. Eliot's "Prufrock" appeared in her magazine, *Le Navire d' Argent*; she was the first person to catalog all American writings translated into French; she contributed frequently to the *Nouvelle Revue Francaise*, writing poetry, essays, and even film reviews—some of which are collected in this volume.

But time spent on writing was hard-won: "at the moment when our hand sought for pen and paper—somebody entered," Monnier recalled, "other people came afterward, and the faces of the day absorbed the great ardor of the morning." Nonetheless, over the years she somehow managed to chronicle French cultural life with witty charm. The circus, the Revue Nègre, opera, the Folies-Bergère, the ballet, the cinema, photographic art, and film stars: all are scooped up in a reflective, sometimes pungent style, aphoristic, informed, and often slyly to the point.

Early on, Monnier had published her own poetry under the pseudonym Sollier, her mother's maiden name. According to a friend, these poems were highly praised until colleagues learned the author was Adrienne. Then her fans were strangely silent, perhaps considering Monnier the poet less serviceable than Monnier the availing female bookseller. Indignity of this sort could inspire her to Swiftian satire. Women were incapable of loving books—to say nothing of writing them—she sighed in mock gravity, her life a tribute to the very reverse. "The fact of writing in the margins is furthermore specifically masculine," she told a radio audience in 1938 in a talk later published as "Les Amies des Livres": "Yes, it is curious, a man and above all a young man often corrects the author, he underlines, he denies, he opposes his judgment; in fact, *he adds himself to it.* A woman remains silent when she does not like something, and when she detests something *she cuts it out.*"

Monnier lived, as do we all, in a world saturated with gender, and she acutely observed the separate, overlapping cultures of women and men, perhaps all the more so since she, a lesbian in Paris between the wars, guarded her freedom—and that of others—fiercely. Sensitive to the exclusions any minority feels, like Rabelais and Montaigne she was quick to caricature affectation, even of those friends who trafficked her shop. In a series of succinct and telling verbal snapshots, she sized up the great and near-great: Leon-Paul Fargue, from whom nothing came forth that "had not been cooked and recooked"; Apollinaire, who left one with no time to breathe; André Breton, who belonged "to that family of figures you see rearing up at the porches of cathedrals." Of Maurice Chevalier, she wrote presciently that he "made you think of somebody running down a hard road after all the phantoms of fortune." Cocteau's artifice gave her a migraine, and she said she always let the eminent André Gide have the first and last word.

"I live with books more than with people," Adrienne Monnier confessed. "Which is to say that I can easily do without people (there are days when I could easily do without myself), and that in the country of books where I dwell, the dead can count entirely as much as the living."

Yet, Monnier possessed a talent for friendship and spent most of her life surrounded by or living with the women who loved her. Of these, perhaps the best known to an American public is Sylvia Beach.

Monnier and Beach first met in 1917. Herself in desultory search of a vocation, Beach had gone to Europe three years before. Now thirty years old and in no particular hurry to return to her family in Princeton, New Jersey, it was, perhaps, just a matter of time before she found the little gray bookshop of Adrienne Monnier. Hesitating at the doorway, Beach lost her hat to a sudden gust of wind and Monnier, her long skirt swishing, ran from the shop into the street to recover it. In the laughter that followed, a great friendship began.

Two years later, with the ready assistance of Monnier and Suzanne Bonnierre, Beach opened Shakespeare and Company, the Anglo complement to the Maison des Amis des Livres. After Bonnierre died in 1920, Monnier and Beach's professional friendship developed into an intimacy respected, even envied, among their friends. And as if to suggest their attachment, Shakespeare and Company soon moved to 12 Rue de l'Odéon, across the street from La Maison des Amis des Livres and several doors down from Adrienne's apartment at number 18, where Sylvia herself soon moved.

The arrangement lasted over fifteen years, until 1936. By then, both Beach and Monnier had grown friendly with Gisèle Freund, a talented young photographer and Jewish refugee from Berlin. Ordered out of France in 1935, Freund was literally without a country until Monnier arranged for her a marriage of convenience, and hence a visa. But a year later, while Beach was visiting America, Freund moved into the apartment Adrienne and Sylvia shared. Beach returned to France, packed up her belongings, and withdrew to the apartment above her shop, where she lived for the remainder of her life. The love affair over, the friendship nonetheless endured, and often Beach took her nighttime meal with Monnier and Freund.

During the Second World War, Monnier kept the doors of the bookshop open, and she continued to write. In 1938, she publicly denounced anti-Semitism in the pages of her journal. She assisted German Jewish writers Walter Benjamin and Sigfried Kracauer, she sheltered Arthur Koestler, she provided food and refuge and papers, whenever possible, for those escaping the Gestapo. She encouraged Gisèle Freund to flee to Argentina. "Yes, my voyage with Gisèle Freund has been a great adventure," wrote Monnier in 1939, as if anticipating farewell. "I am seized by despair," she wrote in her journal in 1940, published among these pages. "I call upon the gods of Israel and beg them to make themselves known, so that their own may not suffer new wrongs and torments."

Sylvia Beach stayed on in Paris, but Shakespeare and Company had to close in 1941, and Beach herself was interned for several months at Vittel. After the war, in 1950, Monnier briefly considered moving into Beach's apartment. By then, Monnier was suffering from the cycles of exhaustion and pain that were to sharpen dramatically in the coming months. Yet in 1951, although she decided to sell her shop, she continued to chronicle cultural life in her prose: essays on pre-Columbian art, *Waiting for Godot*, the drawings of Saul Steinberg (the "world that he takes for a victim is the one of which he is a victim"), Vittorio de Sica, Shakespeare, and Marlon Brando. She also began to write more ruminative autobiographical pieces that illumine, for example, her first days in London when the city smelled of anthracite smoke or, more recently, the postwar London of gaping wounds where, regardless, she always sensed the presence of an unseen world. There is nothing nostalgic in these reminiscences. There is, instead, a sense of completion.

Rheumatic, she began to experience vertigo, and by 1954, plagued by hallucinatory voices, Monnier was diagnosed with Meniere's syndrome. In the spring of 1955, wearied from years of brutal suffering, she swallowed a stash of sleeping pills. Sylvia Beach found her the next day in a coma. Adrienne Monnier died on 20 June 1955. Heartbroken, Beach said she sometimes wished that she had died as well. Adrienne, she said, "knew what living without her was going to be like. She knew everything—." *

To Monnier, the bookseller is a custodian of taste who serves a small public with love and erudition and who, "without falling into the wrongheadedness of any kind of snobbery, is ready to assist the new truths and forms." There is a timeliness to Monnier's mission. And to her love of books, from their bindings to their paper: "They that love you and that live in your presence know serenity; they already have dealings with the immortals."

Monnier, of course, would admit that books, however precious, are not sacred in themselves; they do not, cannot, exist without us. Thus, to one who spent a lifetime in their presence, fully nourished and sustained, they were like the bright inner vistas inspired by Savoy, her beloved mother's homeland: a magical interior space, she wrote, from which "arises the sound of a bell, the cry of a cock, and the bark of a dog that no other dog answers."

"Before books disappear," said Monnier, "humankind will have disappeared." She who was their vigilant guardian spoke with an unabashed assurance that today still commands attention. And rightly so.

*Noel Riley Fitch, *Sylvia Beach and the Lost Generation* (New York: W. W. Norton, 1983), 411.

contents

The first time I saw the miniatures of Fouquet and the Limbourg brothers at Chantilly my delight was such that my eyes filled with tears. Before *The Hours of Etienne Chevalier* I thought I heard the reds and the blues and the heavenly white singing life and its reasons in a full voice.

Before *The Very Rich Hours of the Duke de Berry* I seemed to perceive as through a magic emerald the very nature of France: our land and its people dressed in bold colors; gestures of work, as pure as those of the Mass; women in flowerlike dresses; fanfares of leisure; living water, branches; desires and loves; beautiful castles in the distance; a comforting sky; our animals near us; our days colored with hope and finely woven.

It is not without reason that the stroke of strong admiration brings tears to the eyes. The sight or sound of perfect things causes a certain suffering. In the case of these miniatures, is it not as if one were burned by a fine rain of fire? Such works are like the focus of a lens that gathers the light of all space into one intense point. With a passionate concentration they draw from the world of forms a kind of jewel, a fairy-thing.

—*Adrienne Monnier*

introduction

Odéonia

The country of Odéonia, of which this book is in large part a chronicle, is one that the reader need never have visited in order to be among its citizens, in order to owe allegiance to it. One may even be a citizen of this country without ever having known of its existence. For though Odéonia once occupied a specific place in time—the Rue de l'Odéon and its two bookshops on the Left Bank of Paris between the wars—it survives timelessly as a country of the spirit, of the spirit that is embodied in and disseminated by books.

Paul Valéry, Valery Larbaud, André Gide, Léon-Paul Fargue, Paul Claudel, Jules Romains, Ernest Hemingway, and James Joyce were among the citizens of Odéonia, while Colette, Rainer Maria Rilke, T. S. Eliot, F. Scott Fitzgerald, Antoine de Saint-Exupéry, Sherwood Anderson, and Ezra Pound—along with many other writers of several nationalities—were friendly passers-by whose visits from time to time to the country of Odéonia also form part of its chronicle. And in a broader sense, through the same spiritual attraction that draws the reader, they too became citizens of Odéonia, for the two bookshops of that country—Adrienne Monnier's Maison des Amis des Livres, truly a "house of the friends of books," and Sylvia Beach's Shakespeare and Company—were the archives not only of the writers who frequented them but of their work as well; and there were those who felt besides, as Marianne Moore was to say about Adrienne Monnier's shop, that they had personally a place there, "even if one were only a shadow there, and never a presence."

As a place, Odéonia was part of a larger world whose frontiers do not conform exactly to administrative boundaries; but for the sake of convenience, if rather arbitrarily, we can say that its limits are those of the sixth *arrondissement,* which was then as now, with its neighboring quarters, the intellectual and literary heart of Paris. The sixth *arrondissement* is bounded on the north by the Seine, its one natural frontier and the one that does, in fact, define a spiritual limit, for the world of Odéonia belongs entirely to the Left Bank of Paris. On the east the Boulevard Saint-Michel divides it from the Latin Quarter and the Sorbonne; near the western frontier stand the Institut de France and the church of St-Germain-des-Prés with its place and the nearby Café de Flore and Café des Deux Magots; its southern border is the Boulevard du Montparnasse.

The Rue de l'Odéon, the main thoroughfare of Odéonia, is a short, straight street that runs directly south from the Carrefour de l'Odéon, a crossroads, to the semicircular Place de l'Odéon; behind it lies the theater from which the place, the street, and the Carrefour took their common name, the Théâtre de l'Odéon, called officially since 1959 the Théâtre de France. To the southwest, beyond the theater, lies the Jardin du Luxembourg, with its great trees in ordered rows, its paths that cross one another at right angles, its octagonal pond set about by parterres and balustrades, its austere palace that was once the home of Marie de Médicis and is now the seat of the Senate—a formal place, in appearance, in which the French spirit of order seems to have imposed itself upon the least leaf, upon the very waves in the pond, but still an open space, the green breathing space of the sixth *arrondissement.*

"That enormous four-square theater with its portico of columns," as Paul Claudel has described it—his name was to be given to the place immediately behind it—is, according to the critic John Russell, who takes his epithet from another citizen of Odéonia, Paul Valéry, "one of the handsomest and best-sited theaters in Europe; and its immediate surroundings are sacred ground for those who prize *Saint Langage,* whether written or spoken, as one of the highest of human achievements." Intended to house the Comédie-Française, the theater was built between 1779 and 1782, and was known at first as the Théâtre-Français; it received the name of Odéon in 1797, after the French Revolution.

The surrounding neighborhood was carefully designed to enhance the theater. Russell writes: "Standing as it does upon the top of a little hill, it offered the opportunity of a noble vista; and this was well taken in the Rue de l'Odéon, which runs up from the

Carrefour. Such was the priestly status of the new theater that the Rue de l'Odéon was awarded two features as yet untried in Paris: pavements, and gutters at the side, rather than in the middle, of the street." With its related streets, including the Rue Rotrou and the Rue Corneille, which run along each side of the theater, and the Rue Crébillon and the Rue Casimir-Delavigne, "the Rue de l'Odéon forms . . . a nucleus of systematic elegance that has never lost its power to surprise and delight." It was opened in 1779 as the Rue du Théâtre-Français; it was given its present name in 1806.

But we are concerned with a much later era, one that began in the second year of World War I, in November 1915, when, as a young woman of twenty-three, Adrienne Monnier, the founder and chronicler of Odéonia—the name is her own invention—opened her bookshop, later to be called La Maison des Amis des Livres, at number 7 Rue de l'Odéon, on the left side of the street going up toward the Place de l'Odéon. "Built in a time of destruction," as she says in her article that takes its name, the bookshop—through what could only have been the sheer courage and intelligence of its owner—endured throughout the war as one of the few intellectual centers of the besieged city, a place where writers—some of them, like André Breton and Guillaume Apollinaire, in uniform—could gather and, at meetings arranged by Adrienne Monnier, read from their own works. And it was here one day toward the end of the war that she was providentially visited by the American Sylvia Beach, who with Monnier's encouragement founded her English-language bookshop, Shakespeare and Company, in 1919—another significant date in the history of Odéonia—at 8 Rue Dupuytren, just around the corner from Adrienne Monnier. In the summer of 1921, when the two women were already close friends, when Sylvia Beach had already undertaken the publishing of James Joyce's *Ulysses*, the proudest adventure of her career, Shakespeare and Company moved to number 12 Rue de l'Odéon, across the street from La Maison des Amis des Livres. The move was as symbolic as it was practical, for the closeness of the two shops was to stand for as well as to further contacts between the French writers who frequented Adrienne Monnier and the English-speaking patrons of Sylvia Beach; it represented as well the enduring friendship between the two women and consolidated the physical region of that country of the spirit.

There may be no better way to approach the Rue de l'Odéon for the first time than to see it through the eyes of Justin O'Brien, the scholar and translator of French literature. Although he was relatively a latecomer to the street, his impressions hold true for the entire period between the two wars. In an article for an issue of the *Mercure de France* that was published as an homage to Adrienne Monnier in January 1956, the year following her death, he writes (to translate from his French):

> For the young American in the thirties, the Rue de l'Odéon was the intellectual center of Paris. On the right side going up the street, he stopped first before the narrow shop window of Shakespeare and Company, which was filled with books in his language, but most often in editions that he had not encountered anywhere else. The volumes by T. S. Eliot, Ezra Pound, Virginia Woolf stood near limited Parisian editions and the enormous paperbound *Ulysses*. . . . Almost opposite Shakespeare and Company, La Maison des Amis des Livres, perhaps even more attractive for him who had everything to know about the French domain, revealed to him the latest Gide, the latest Valéry, the latest Fargue, along with the avant-garde reviews and books thirty or fifty years old, but for him absolutely new.
>
> From time to time, entering one or the other of those welcoming houses, he could see close up—what he used to dream about in New York—some of his gods: James Joyce in dark glasses and with a light-colored moustache, Gide arrayed in his flowing cape, Cocteau with his prestidigitator's hands. Even those whom he did not see there were present, thanks to the fascinating pictures hung on the walls. . . .
>
> La Maison des Amis des Livres was well named, for Adrienne Monnier received there with an equal goodwill all those who really loved books. There was only, in the matter of hierarchy, those who knew from far back the mistress of that salon covered with books and with whom she conversed at length, sitting in front of a big table spread with papers. From the day when she invited the young American to take a place near her, between the table and the stove, her rosy face with its mauve-blue eyes became the symbol of that friendly house. Those conversations by fits and starts, in the course of which Adrienne Monnier informed herself about his readings and suggested others to him with that so communicative enthusiasm of which she had the secret, were a precious initiation for him to all the best that modern literature offers.

To another friend, the German writer Siegfried Kracauer, Adrienne Monnier was so much at home in her house of books, so much its presiding spirit, that it seemed to him, as he says in his own memoir in the same issue of the *Mercure de France*, that "the room was a part of her person and that a bit of herself had been communicated to the volumes." His portrait adds detail to the brief glimpse that O'Brien's description gives of her:

> She listened more than she spoke and looked at you often, attentive, before answering or drawing your attention to an idea that had come into her mind while she was listening. Her eyes, were they blue? I know only that her look came from a depth that seemed to me to be not easily accessible. The brightness of her outer aspect, of the room, and even of her voice, was not an ordinary brightness, but the covering or the form of an inner self that was lost in the shadows. Perhaps it was this interference of a foreground and a background, of a luminous exterior and a secret spiritual ground that thus drew me to her.
>
> . . . I made myself a precise image of her. The character trait to which my veneration and my love went out—it remains forever engraved in my heart—was that mixture of rusticity and aristocracy that Proust never wearied of praising in the old Françoise and the Duchesse de Guermantes. Around those characters there is still the good smell of French soil, and as they personify in their bearing and their language centuries of ancestral traditions, how would it be possible that they were not of an authentic distinction? It is thus that I see Adrienne Monnier before me.

The Lady of the House of Books

Adrienne Monnier was born in Paris on April 26, 1892, the elder of two daughters of Clovis and Philiberte (née Sollier) Monnier. Her father was a native of Jura, her mother of Savoy, nearly adjacent departments in the mountainous region of eastern France. Although she was to live in Paris all of her life, entirely absorbed by the city whose light she magnified, Monnier never forgot her *montagnard* origins; she was especially drawn to her mother's native community, Les Déserts, a group of hamlets situated on the plateau of La Féclaz, "one of our homelands, one of the faces of our soul," as she calls it in her "Sketch of Les Déserts" (see Part Six). Almost every August, from childhood on, she returned there; during her career as a bookseller it was a place for rest and renewal, where she would find contact with the earth again after her year-long labors in Paris.

Clovis Monnier was by occupation a *postier ambulant*, a postal clerk who worked on trains, preparing mail in transit for delivery at various destinations. Her father was a defender of Captain Dreyfus and was modestly but firmly anticlerical. Her mother, Philiberte, was open-minded in her approach to life and culture and was especially interested in literature. Monnier and her sister, Marie, two years her junior and later known in her own right as an embroiderer and illustrator, seem to have had a particularly happy childhood that prepared them in an exemplary way for the parts that they were to play in the cultural life of Paris. In her literary memoir, "Mémorial de la rue de l'Odéon," selections from which appear in this book, Monnier praises her "wonderful parents who had always left me free and even helped me to become so; my mother, in particular, was always ready to go more quickly and farther than myself." And in her "Memories of London" (see Part Six), she tells us that she, her mother, and her sister "lived in a state of perpetual enthusiasm for everything that seemed beautiful to us, in whatever domain it might be."

Her father's duties, she says in an autobiographical sketch that appears in her collection *Rue de l'Odéon*, "kept him far from Paris two days out of four; when he was absent my mother went to the theater every evening, taking her two little girls with her, from the time when they were seven or eight years old." Among the great productions that she saw as a child were André Antoine's *King Lear*, in which he played the title role, and his *Julius Caesar*, in which the Rumanian actor Edouard de Max played the role of Mark Antony; she gives her impressions of these men and of their performances in her "Memories of Antoine and de Max" (see Part Five). Elsewhere she describes her enthusiasm for Claude Debussy's opera *Pelléas et Mélisande*, to which she was taken when she was ten years old, and for Sergei Diaghilev's Ballets Russes, which she saw in 1909, the year of their Paris première.

Philiberte Monnier also encouraged her two young daughters to read. She familiarized them very early, it would seem, with all sorts of esoteric and sacred literatures—with works by Maeterlinck, Emerson, Novalis, and Lao-tzu, and with the *Bhagavad-Gita*, for example. Such readings took the place of religious instruction—although Catholic by ancestry, their parents were not believers—and fortified them against the possibility of any kind of religious crisis at a later age. Although not a Catholic by faith, Monnier "kept a great deal of affection" for Catholicism, as she says in her article on

Pierre Fresnay, and, as we shall see, she practiced her vocation as a bookseller in a spirit that was almost religious, even to the point of adopting a form of dress that resembled a habit.

Monnier made her first acquaintance with contemporary literature in the pages of the *Mercure de France*, the magazine that Alfred Vallette founded in 1890 and that knew its greatest period in the years shortly after the turn of the century, when she was a young girl. Although the *Mercure* particularly favored writers of the symbolist persuasion, it was open to the best work that was being done at the time, regardless of doctrine. In a memoir that has not been translated for the present collection, "*Le Mercure* vu par un enfant" ["*The Mercure* Seen by a Child"], which was published there in December 1946, Monnier describes how she discovered the review when she was about ten years old, "at the edge of the Seine, in the stalls along the quais, which were the bookshops of [her] childhood and adolescence," when she could not afford new books, when she "had to be satisfied with hunting among secondhand books and borrowing books from municipal libraries and reading rooms." It was her enthusiasm for the work of Maeterlinck, especially for his play *Pelléas et Mélisande*, the basis of Debussy's opera, that led her to the review, in which he often published. She recalls reading in it his introduction to an essay on Jules Laforgue, which appeared in an issue of 1896, and his words of praise—"the admirable and transparent *Voyage d'Urien*"—for an early work by André Gide, whom she was to know so well. She was enraptured by Maeterlinck's description of the heroine of Marcel Schwob's *Livre de Monelle [The Book of Monelle]*: "From what hells or from what paradises does she arise, this strange, pitiful, and beneficent Monelle, who speaks, after death, upon the threshold of this book before her sisters come to live in it?" The words of the poet awakened the young girl to the magical potentials of language. "Spellbound, I was spellbound," she says. "That possible equivalence between hell and paradise, and their plural—the faculty of being at the same time strange, pitiful, and beneficent, of speaking after death—and the sisters—the sisters who were going to come to live there, in the book." Words like these come as an initiation for those who will be writers and, however critically they may be regarded later, they cannot be forgotten. Monnier recalls that upon reading Maeterlinck's description she remained transfixed "for a long moment," clasping her forehead between her hands. She loved the *Mercure* so much that she would cut out the texts that appealed to her—prose and poetry—and paste them in a handmade volume to which she "strove to give the appearance of a binding," covering it with "two Japanese prints, very pretty." Its back was of "gold-yellow brocaded silk, an old Lyons silk" that she had found among scraps of cloth belonging to her mother. "It is this volume," she says, concluding her article, "that I clasp over my heart at the moment of paying homage to the *Mercure de France.*"

At the age of seventeen, in 1909, Monnier received her *brevet supérieur,* a degree awarded at the time after the successful completion of secondary studies and which would have qualified her for a teaching career. Shortly afterward, in the fall of that year, she paid her first visit to England, which she describes in "Memories of London," ostensibly in order to learn English, as she informed her parents, but actually to be near a classmate, Suzanne Bonnierre, who was teaching at a school in Enfield, near London. Suzanne, with whom she was very much in love at the time, was to be her partner during the first days of the bookshop. Monnier spent nine months in England: three in London as a lady's companion—she describes this interval in her memoir—and six as a French teacher in a school at the seaside resort of Eastbourne, where she went after a visit home for the Christmas holidays.

After her return to Paris she taught for a while at a private school; then, deciding to become a literary secretary, she studied stenography and typing. In 1912, at the age of twenty, she became the secretary of Yvonne Sarcey, founder of the Université des Annales and editor of *Le Journal de l'Université des Annales.* Sarcey was the wife of the journalist and critic Adolphe Brisson, the publisher of the review *Les Annales Politiques et Littéraires.* Their son, Pierre Brisson, was to become the editor of *Le Figaro.* Monnier remained with Sarcey until about the beginning of 1915, the year of her own establishment, "very attached to her as a person," she says in her autobiographical sketch in *Rue de l'Odéon,* "but little interested in the academicism of the Université des Annales." In her "Souvenirs de l'autre guerre" ["Memories of the Other War"], another article that does not appear in this collection, but which will be amply quoted from in the following pages, Monnier remarks, "In that stronghold of the Right Bank I had made myself no relationship, no relationship that I wanted to keep and maintain. The authors that I loved did not frequent the place. . . . My tastes and my ideas had been formed in complete independence; the milieu had nothing to do with them." Rather, she was attracted by the Left Bank; she felt that her real vocation, whatever it might turn out to be, lay there: "The Left Bank called me and even now it does not cease to call me and to keep me. I cannot imagine that I could ever leave it, any more than an organ can leave the place that is assigned to it in the body." Patrick Waldberg, in an article on Monnier published in the review *Critique* in January 1961, offers a succinct definition of the differences between the two banks of Paris: "The Left Bank, aristocratic and rustic, studious and bohemian, . . . was the elected domain of poets and of writers with a small audience, whose aureoles were visible only to their own kind or to discerning initiates. It was contrasted then, more than today, to the Right Bank, seat of elegance and of pleasure, of luxury and of 'success' literature."

In 1913, while Sarcey's secretary, Monnier paid a visit to the offices of her beloved *Mercure de France* at its Left Bank address, 26 Rue de Condé, near the Rue de l'Odéon, and was introduced to its editor, Alfred Vallette, by his wife, the novelist Rachilde, with whom she had made an appointment. In "Un Souvenir d'Alfred Vallette" ["A Memory of Alfred Vallette"], her brief memoir of the visit (not included herein), she recalls that he and his fellow writers there received her courteously but without deference for her youth. "I was, for these men," she says, "what they were weariest and most disabused of: enthusiasm, illusion." Earlier she writes: "Like all young people, I was absolute and it seemed to me that I was betraying the very cause of literature by staying with people who had succeeded, when there was such a beautiful heavy job *[belle grosse besogne]* to do on the Left Bank. I believe that I would have accepted sweeping the offices of the *Mercure*."

Monnier's opportunity for what was to be a lifelong "beautiful heavy job" was offered to her as the result of a nearly fatal accident for her father. About the beginning of 1914 he was badly hurt in a catastrophic train wreck near Melun, a city about twenty-five miles southeast of Paris. "My father nearly died in it," she says in her *Rue de l'Odéon* notes. "His hip was dislocated and his scalp was torn; he recovered well but remained lame. On this occasion he received an indemnity, which he gave me so that I might establish a bookshop —for I used to dream of being a bookseller on the Left Bank." In "Souvenirs de l'autre guerre" she writes: "My parents committed the wise folly of entrusting to me the little money that they had, that they had ever had." Although it is reasonable to believe that, given Adrienne Monnier's courage and genius, she might have realized her intention in any case, one can only be grateful for their trust and generosity.

Monnier's enterprise was favored by a second and immeasurably greater catastrophe: World War I. "To tell the truth," she says in "Souvenirs de l'autre guerre," "the terrible goddess favored me. . . . Because there was a war there were shops available at reasonable prices in the noble quarter of Study to which I aspired. Competition could not smother me because most of the booksellers were in the army. As life was slowed down, I did not lack the time to learn a profession whose practice I was completely ignorant of. I loved books, that was all." However, the going was not easy: "Because of my inexperience I knew many struggles and trials. But if I had been able to foresee the dangers, I would never have ventured forth."

The shop opened on November 15, 1915, on premises formerly occupied by antique dealers who specialized in Norman *armoires*. Its beginnings, as Monnier describes them in "La Maison des Amis des Livres," the opening article of this book, were very modest. Retrospectively, considering the triumphant destiny of the enterprise, one may be inclined to think that she was favored at the start by the special interest of powerful friends who made the way easy for her and established her reputation. But in fact, she says in "Souvenirs de l'autre guerre," "The truth is very different. Upon arriving in the Rue de l'Odéon, I was unknown." Nor were even the best known among the writers who soon began to frequent the shop as famous at the time as they would be later, while some who were to become famous—in certain cases precisely because of Monnier's help—were at the time completely unheard of, save by a very few. And even many years after, when La Maison des Amis des Livres had become a literary landmark of Paris, Adrienne Monnier could honestly say to André Chamson, as he writes in his memoir in the *Mercure de France*: "I am not interested only in famous personages, the great joy is to discover. And then, you know, famous people, they were not born so. One always begins by being unknown." Chamson continues: "That spinner of glory—of the glory of others—that embroiderer . . . of the literary tapestry of our epoch, granted as much attention to her unknown subscribers as to the most illustrious of her intimates."

Monnier's first concern was to learn her *métier*, her profession. "In establishing myself as a bookseller," she says, "my dominant idea was not to win the good graces of the authors, but those of their books—their books, into which they put the best of themselves and of all of us. I aimed at the kingdom of God, the rest was given to me as a surplus." If she went to the establishments of the *Nouvelle Revue Française* and the *Mercure de France*, it was not to visit their salons but rather their sales offices. She became accustomed to drudgery—arranging books, packing them, keeping accounts. She says: "One even welcomes drudgery with a certain satisfaction: it is a sort of penance, with all the advantages of well-accepted penances." Although she had the privilege of dealing with a spiritual commodity, she realized that "a bookseller, in many respects, is a shopkeeper like any other." She had to learn patience, to resist the temptation to show annoyance when interrupted by "the arrival of an ill-natured or even simply a banal person while I was plunged in a beautiful and good conversation, in a beautiful and good reading." She would tell herself: " 'You must, like those who are really in religious orders, have no preference, or very little.' The spirit of books is a universal smile. So I strove to smile at everybody; it was at first studied and often constrained, but the little victories led to great ones: my smile made me smile."

As she speaks of "the kingdom of God," of drudgery *[la corvée]* as a "penance," of the need to emulate the charity that is demanded of those in orders, of the happy hypocrisy whereby the feigned smile becomes real, one becomes aware of the essentially religious direction of Monnier's vocation. She brought to literature the faith and the dedication that she might, had she been born in an earlier age, have directed toward God. In a poem about herself that appears in her collection *La Figure* (1923), largely a series of portraits of some of the writers who were her friends—of Claudel, Gide, Romains, Joyce, and others—she compares herself to a *religieuse ancienne*—some "nun of other times"—who "established a house" that is "half convent and half farm." So, she says, though she has no God, did she found her bookshop, where she works for the sake of her "brothers." The poem ends with an evocation of herself as a protectress, a hearth keeper:

> The lost traveler,
> I bring him home to me,
> I warm myself by the fire
> I kindle for his sake,
> I blend into his prayers
> My voice full of night.

Jules Romains, who was to become one of Adrienne Monnier's closest friends, says of their first meeting, which took place shortly after the bookshop opened, early in 1916: "I saw in front of me a girl with a round, rosy face, with blue eyes, with blond hair, who, it appeared almost at once, had just entered the service of literature as others decide to enter the service of religion. Even her costume already had some of the features of that graceful austerity, of that monastic elegance, which she was later to cultivate. . . . Already her voice was authoritative and charming; very watched over, very limpid, at once full of music and assurance."

Monnier's dress, though it was far from being invariable—as photographs show—was adapted to her sense of her vocation. Sylvia Beach, remembering their first meeting, says—as others have said—that her attire was "a cross between a nun's and a peasant's." It would have recalled, then, the convent and the farm of which she speaks in her poem. On the day they met, according to Sylvia's description, she was typically wearing "a long, full skirt down to her feet, and a sort of tight-fitting velvet waistcoat over a white silk blouse. She was in gray and white like her bookshop." White, gray, and blue, Monnier herself says in her "Mémorial de la rue de l'Odéon," were her preferred colors.

For a while at the start of her career as a bookseller, and again for a short period later on, Monnier worked in partnership. Her first associate, it has been noted, was her former classmate Suzanne Bonnierre, who appears briefly in "First Encounters with Léon-Paul Fargue" (see Part One), and whose presence is implied in "La Maison des Amis des Livres," where the use of "we" is sometimes more than editorial. In her "Mémorial de la rue de l'Odéon," Monnier describes her as being "always serious, with a melancholy that might be called classic. Her voice is soft, a bit subdued. She has a noble, well-drawn face; she makes you think of a young man of the Renaissance or of the women in the paintings of Dante Gabriel Rossetti. The symbolists would have loved and saluted her as an almost perfect type of the androgyne for which they were in search." There is a similar description of her at the beginning of "Memories of London."

Monnier says of herself that she had "all the appearance of being the boss"; Jules Romains confirms this, saying that Suzanne "visibly submitted to her empire, received her spiritual orders, participated as best she could in that state of mastered exaltation in which literature sustained Adrienne. This companion separated from her rather quickly, in order to go back to those regions of life in which more ordinary emotions and duties prevail; to go back to them briefly, moreover, for she died after a year of marriage." Her husband was Gustave Tronche, at that time the administrator of the publications of the *Nouvelle Revue Française* and a friend of one of its founders, Jacques Rivière; she died in 1919.

In January 1918, a little over two years after founding her bookshop, Adrienne Monnier entered a second partnership, of which not once, in all of her published writings, does she speak; and only once, and then in passing, does she ever mention the name of her colleague. He was Pierre Haour, "a wealthy young industrialist," according to Louise Rypko Schub, the biographer of Léon-Paul Fargue, "a great friend of arts and letters, and of Fargue in particular, who frequented the musical salons dear to our poet." He published at his own expense a small volume of Fargue's poetry, *Nocturnes*, in 1905 and was one of the three people to whom Fargue dedicated the 1912 edition of his *Poèmes*.

Haour and Monnier together founded A. Monnier et Compagnie, and it was at this time that the bookshop, which had been simply called La Librairie A. Monnier, received the name by which it was to be known ever afterward, La Maison des Amis des Livres. Monnier and Haour were publishers as well as booksellers. They put out a series of small volumes *(plaquettes)* under the title Les Cahiers des Amis des Livres. Among them were French versions of Francis Thompson's *Hound of Heaven* and his *Anthem of the Earth* (published separately) by Auguste Morel, who was to translate *Ulysses*, and works by Claudel, Valéry, and Larbaud, which will be identified later in the course of discussing Monnier's friendships with these writers.

Pierre Haour died almost suddenly at the end of 1920, the year following the death of Suzanne Bonnierre, leaving a wife who at once demanded the dissolution of the company. Thereafter, Monnier directed her bookshop alone, and, with some exceptions, gave up publishing books in order to devote herself to her business. The most notable exception, and by far the most important of all her ventures of this kind, was her publication of the French translation of Joyce's *Ulysses* in 1929. By way of dedication, "La Maison des Amis des Livres" carried Haour's initials ("à P.H.") when it first appeared in a limited edition in 1920. Haour's death left a great void in the heart of Adrienne Monnier. Her silence must be taken as the mask of her sorrow and the measure of its depth.

That this void was filled by Sylvia Beach and some others (Sylvia Beach surpassing all the others and from very far back), Adrienne Monnier never made a mystery.

Some Early Friendships

Although her main concern was to learn her trade and serve her patrons, Monnier enjoyed receiving "beautiful visits" from writers and enlightened lovers of writing. The first of these, at the end of 1915, was from the poet Paul Fort (1872–1960), who founded *Vers et Prose* in 1905. This review, which expired shortly before World War I, was sympathetic to symbolism and devoted to the memory of Corbière, Rimbaud, Mallarmé, and Laforgue. However, it was undoctrinal and eclectic in its tastes, and, as its title suggests, it was open to both prose and poetry; it published early works by Gide, Claudel, Valéry, and Apollinaire. Fort, who in 1890 had also founded the Théâtre d'Art (later the Théâtre de l'Oeuvre), which produced dramas by symbolist playwrights, including Maeterlinck, is best known for his *Ballades françaises*, a collection of more than thirty volumes of poems on French themes that combine prose and verse forms. In "Souvenirs de l'autre guerre" Monnier says of him: "Nobody, I really believe, could better represent, in the eyes of a girl coming from the Annales, the poet in person. He had long hair, a hat with a flat brim, florid speech. His life was free, apparently insouciant; he was a real bohemian, a notorious bohemian even." As she notes in "Valéry in the Rue de l'Odéon" (see Part One), Monnier bought from him the complete stock of *Vers et Prose*—over 6,500 copies; he sold them to her, and at a very reasonable price, in order to help his finances, which "were always in a sad state." It was in the fourth issue of the review, for December 1905–January 1906, that she discovered Valéry's *Soirée avec Monsieur Teste*, which she describes in her memoir of the poet. A short while after she accepted the consignment of *Vers et Prose*, Monnier again helped Fort by becoming the sales agent for the eighteenth volume in his series of *Ballades françaises* (1916).

About the beginning of 1916 Monnier made the acquaintance of Jules Romains, to whom she wrote, taking care to conceal her sex: "At 7 Rue de l'Odéon there is a bookseller who loves your works." She had read everything he had written to that date. He came by a short while later and asked to see Monsieur Monnier. "Ah!" she comments, "how happy I was that I had not let my sex be guessed." Romains (1885–1972), born Louis Farigoule, is best known for his *Hommes de bonne volonté [Men of Good Will]* (1932–1947), a series of twenty-seven novels that offer a panoramic view of French civilization in the first third of the century. This series, long as it is, forms only one part of a prodigiously abundant *oeuvre* that includes several volumes of poetry as well as other fictional works. As a young man Romains and several other writers who were his friends—among them were the novelists Georges Duhamel and Luc Durtain and the poets René Arcos, Charles Vildrac, and Georges Chennevière, whose *Poèmes, 1911–18* was published in 1920 by La Maison des Amis des Livres—promoted in their work a doctrine they called unanimism, which Monnier mentions from time to time in her writings. Unanimism was essentially a social doctrine: any group has a spirit, a collective consciousness, that transcends and is more than the sum total of the personalities of the human beings that compose it; individual lives can receive their full value and meaning only as parts of a group. Monnier was strongly attracted to the doctrine: "Unanimism appeared to me to be a great, fecund, truly inspired idea. It was the firmest and the clearest answer, it seemed to me, that had ever been given to the religious question. . . . Yes, Romains greatly influenced a part of my opinions. At the very moment when I was getting ready to form a group, he supplied me with the most useful of viaticums; he gave an armor to my spirit, which turned too much to quietism." She found "astonishing" a sentence from his *Manuel de déification* (1910): "Your greatest God nowadays, it's perhaps your greatest city." She particularly cared for his novel *La Mort de quelqu'un [The Death of a Nobody]* (1911) and his volumes of poems, *La Vie unanime [The Unanimous Life]* (1908) and *Odes et prières* (1913). It was Romains who in 1917 inaugurated the *séances*, or meetings, at the bookshop, reading his poem *Europe* (1916).

About the same time that Jules Romains visited her bookshop, early in 1916, Adrienne Monnier met André Breton there, as she says in "André Breton," (see Part One), her memoir of the poet from the "Mémorial." Their relationship, as she describes it, was antagonistic from the start, and she was to care only moderately for surrealism, of which he became the high priest. At the time of their meeting he was even younger than she supposes, not "about twenty-one," as she says, but just about twenty. Breton was born on

February 18, 1896, in the department of Orne, in Normandy, the son of a shopkeeper. At a very early age he fell under the influence of Paul Valéry and of the symbolists, especially Rimbaud. Breton at first studied medicine and, as Monnier notes, he served as an "auxiliary doctor" *[médecin auxiliaire]* in the army during World War I. Though he devoted himself to literature after the war, he was interested in psychiatry and especially the work of Freud, which influenced him in formulating his theory of surrealism; he visited Freud in Vienna in 1921.

In 1920, in collaboration with Philippe Soupault, Breton published *Les Champs magnétiques [Magnetic Fields]*, considered to be the first surrealist tracts. In his *Manifeste du surréalisme* (1924) he first defined the principles of the new movement. Later in the decade Breton and the other surrealists, among them Louis Aragon, joined the Communist party; Breton was to break away from it in 1935. During World War II he took refuge in the United States, where he found new converts for his movement. In 1942 he organized a surrealist exhibition at Yale University; he returned to France in 1947. Among his other works are *Clair de terre [Earthlight]* (1923), a collection of poems, and *Nadja* (1928), a partly autobiographical novel of a love affair with a woman endowed with psychic powers. His *Second manifeste du surréalisme* appeared in 1930. Breton died in 1966. Monnier's memoir offers a lucid physical and psychological portrait of the poet.

Monnier says in her "Mémorial" that Louis Aragon, who was born in 1897, first came to the shop a little while after his friend Breton. "He was surely the nicest, the most sensitive young man one could have seen. And the most intelligent as well." With him, as not with Breton, one could come to an understanding. "He adored poetry without demanding from it too much that was unusual. . . . He was already a remarkable talker. He could speak for two or three hours with fluency and that slight nasal tone that he has not lost, I believe, and that carries across his ironic manner: the Punch-like challenge, the playful transport. It once happened that Suzanne Bonnierre, who left the bookshop around three o'clock in the afternoon to do some errands, found him again at six o'clock in the same place, standing in the embrasure of the shop window, plunged in his elegant discourse, which had not undergone a stop and which was not marked by any fatigue. . . . We liked him very much, naturally, and we did not doubt for a second that he would become a brilliant writer."

Aragon, when he became a Communist, left the surrealist movement and joined the cause of socialist realism. Before World War II, as an active party member, he served on the editorial staff of *L'Humanité* and was the managing editor of *Ce Soir*, both Communist newspapers. During the war he participated in the French Resistance and edited an underground newspaper, *Les Etoiles*. He has written both fiction and poetry. Some of his early poems were collected in *Feu de joie [Bonfire]* (1920) and *Mouvement perpétuel* (1926). The war provided him with themes for many patriotic and love poems, which were collected in *Le Crève-coeur [Heartbreak]* (1940) and *Les Yeux d'Elsa [The Eyes of Elsa]* (1942), among other volumes. His novels include *Les Cloches de Bâle [The Bells of Basel]* (1935) and *Les Beaux Quartiers [The Fine Neighborhoods]* (1936).

André Breton and Louis Aragon founded the review *Littérature* in March 1919 with the poet and novelist Philippe Soupault, who is less well known than his colleagues. Like Aragon, he was born in 1897, and he was associated with surrealism only in its early years. He published several volumes of poetry, including *Rose des vents [Rose of the Winds]* (1920). Among his novels is *Les Dernières Nuits de Paris [The Last Nights of Paris]* (1928), which William Carlos Williams translated with the help of his mother and published the next year. Monnier met Soupault after the other two editors. "In my memory," she says, "I only see him associated with Breton and Aragon."

Littérature was to become, in 1920, the organ of the Dada movement, which was born during the war in Switzerland, where it was represented by Tristan Tzara and Hans Arp, among others, and in New York, where Marcel Duchamp and Francis Picabia were its transatlantic spokesmen. At first, however, the review was open to all kinds of writing. In fact, "Valéry was its godfather," Monnier says. "Never, truly, has one seen a table of contents as sensational as that of the first number: André Gide, Paul Valéry, Léon-Paul Fargue, almost all the great loves of the Rue de l'Odéon. And also, Max Jacob, Pierre Reverdy, Blaise Cendrars—the dear *fauves.*"

The Dadaist writer Tristan Tzara (1896–1963), who was Rumanian by birth, made his first contribution, a poem, to the review in its second issue and, as Monnier notes, "beginning with number five there was some Tzara in each number." She adds: "One is surprised to find still, in number eleven, Gide with 'Pages du journal de Lafcadio,' and, in number twelve, Valéry with the 'Ode secrète.' " The issue that brought the review definitely to the side of Dada was that of May 1920, number thirteen, which contained the "Twenty-three Manifestos of Dada." The fifteenth issue printed the notorious Dadaist recipe for making a poem by assembling words cut from a newspaper and drawn at random from a hat. "As if exhausted by its frenzy," Monnier says, *Littérature* "stopped after number nineteen, in May 1921, two years after its founding," but in fact there was a number twenty, for August. In March 1922, the review reappeared solely under the direction of Breton and Soupault. From the fourth issue until it ceased publication in 1924 it was directed by Breton alone. "What claimed him . . . was the series of well-known experiments on language and psychic life." He was entering upon his career as a surrealist.

Two other poets whom Monnier met in the early days of her business were Pierre Reverdy, the founder of the review *Nord-Sud*, which appeared between March 1917 and October 1918, and Jean Cocteau. Her memoirs of both, drawn from her "Mémorial," appear in the opening section of this book. She also soon met the poet Pierre Albert-Birot, the founder of *Sic*, another little review, which appeared irregularly between January 1916 and December 1919. Albert-Birot was a close friend of Guillaume Apollinaire, whom he published in his magazine.

Monnier made the acquaintance of Apollinaire himself, the poet of *Alcools* (1913) and *Calligrammes* (1918), some time after he was wounded in battle in 1916. She does not specify the date in her account of the meeting, which appears in "Souvenirs de l'autre guerre," but only that he had returned from the front, "gravely wounded in the head." His injury, by weakening his health, contributed to his death from influenza in 1918 at the age of thirty-eight. He was in the company of Paul Léautaud, at that time the drama critic of the *Mercure de France*. "I had never seen him," Monnier says, "but God knows I had heard him spoken about by Breton. Somebody in the bookshop told me, 'It's Apollinaire.' I looked attentively at that heavy man in uniform, whose head was in the shape of a pear, . . . crowned by a curious little strap of leather. The two men remained for a good moment in front of the shop window, pointing out several books with their fingers and making many grimaces, then they passed by. Three minutes later the door was abruptly opened and our Apollinaire entered, scattering me with these words: 'All the same, it's a bit shocking that there's not a single book by a combatant in this window!' I did not become too disconcerted, and I answered him rather gently that it was really through the most unpleasant bad luck that *Alcools* was not to be found there, that I had sold it the day before and that I was preparing to replace it and put it back in sight. Still, it must really be said that it was not his position as a combatant that counted here, but that of a poet, of a poet strongly admired. We were good friends right away."

In December 1916 Adrienne Monnier wrote to André Gide for the first time, to ask him, she says in "Souvenirs de l'autre guerre," "to make a gift of a copy of *Les Nourritures terrestres [Fruits of the Earth]*, not to me but to my lending library." This work had been in little demand for many years after its first publication in 1897, but by the time Monnier wrote, Gide had no copy to give her. He said in his reply, *"Les Nourritures terrestres,* after having waited for undiscoverable readers is undiscoverable in its turn." So also were his *Voyage d'Urien [Urien's Voyage]* (1893), and *Prométhée mal enchaîné [Prometheus Misbound]* (1899). "Your letter," he wrote in closing, "has brought me a bit of cheer at a time when I had great need of it. I thank you with all my heart." So began an association that was to last until the writer's death in 1951.

One feels that the friendship between Gide and Monnier was above all literary. While Paul Valéry, Léon-Paul Fargue, and Valery Larbaud, as we shall see, became close associates of La Maison des Amis des Livres and personally shaped the particular spirit of the place—and of Sylvia Beach's bookshop as well—Gide stood somewhat apart, cordial but aloof.

It would be extremely difficult, from her few writings on Gide that we have, to say precisely what Monnier's opinion was of Gide as a man and as a writer. He was, to begin with, one of the most complex personalities of his time; his life and his work have met with adulation at the one extreme and rejection at the other, with all the shades of reaction between the two. In "With Gide at Hyères" (see Part One), her private journal of a few vacation days spent with him, her deliberate flattery of Gide, whom she draws as a man of exorbitant vanity and some malice, is in contrast to a view of his work that she confides to Sylvia Beach. In her brief article "Unkindness" (see Part Two)—the title is a translation of the word *méchanceté,* which defies an exact English equivalent—she denies having used that word to describe Gide's *Faux-Monnayeurs [The Counterfeiters]* when it appeared in 1926. Gide, however, as she herself remarks, wrote at the time in his *Journal* that she spoke to him "eloquently about the fundamental coldness and *unkindness* that this book reveals and that must be the basis of my nature." In the course of explaining in her "Mémorial" that she cannot write her memoirs because it is impossible to discuss the living with total sincerity, she casts a doubt on Gide's own sincerity and on his benevolence as well when she explains: "Even the most sincere hardly say what they would like to say. Gide, in his *Journal*, does something that is almost prodigious. I say *almost* because in what he writes there is more politeness, more circumspection, more prudence than appears at first. His cruelty is a favor reserved for certain heads; his prey is well chosen—they are not the most inoffensive, but no more are they the best armed, the best armed in regard to himself."

Shortly after his death on February 19, 1951, Monnier published the following decorous eulogy of Gide in the newspaper *Combat*:

> The death of Gide causes me profound sorrow. I had with him thirty-five years of literary relations that occupy the dearest and the brightest corners of my memory. Nobody in my bookshop, I truly believe, had a personality that was at once so great and so friendly.
>
> We lose an irreplaceable being who lived entirely for and in writing, while remaining very human, with a marvelously original humanity.
>
> Posterity will know better than ourselves the degree of genius that his work attains, but we know that he had the genius of Literature, that he was in his own home there, that he possessed there a discernment that is perhaps without precedent. Never have we seen such a master for apprentice writers as he was—as much through the teaching of his books as through what he gave from person to person with an extreme kindness.

A few of these remarks seem to contradict some of Monnier's earlier observations as they are reported here, but it should be remembered that she herself called in question the accuracy of Gide's *Journal* report. In any case, the occasion of her writing allowed for only praise; had she not basically admired Gide she would no doubt have written nothing. And it is certain that her tribute to Gide as one who had "the genius of Literature"—which seems incontestable—was heartfelt.

Paul Claudel (1868–1955), who was Gide's opposite in many ways—especially in belief, for he was an orthodox Catholic mystic while Gide was a sceptical rationalist of Protestant origins—was himself a friend of Adrienne Monnier for many years, and like Gide he too stands somewhat apart from the Rue de l'Odéon. He was distant in space if not in spirit: Claudel was in the diplomatic service and, from 1893 when he became a consul in the United States until his retirement, he lived for most of his life outside of France—in Boston, New York, cities in China, where he worked for fourteen years, Prague, Frankfort, Hamburg, and several other places. He was ambassador to Japan during the larger part of the 1920s, and from 1927 to 1933 he represented France in Washington. His letters to Monnier are headed with the names of some of these cities; they attest to his attachment to her and her circle. He writes to her from Copenhagen on December 10, 1919: "I often think of our conversations in the Rue de l'Odéon, and it is not Copenhagen that can make me forget them. . . . Your sincerity and your enthusiasm do me good. I love gay, imaginative, and enterprising natures like your own. . . . Adieu, dear Adrienne, think of me, give me the news from Paris and of all our friends and acquaintances. . . ."

Claudel, who was at first only a titular Catholic, became a devout convert to the faith four years after experiencing what he described as a divine revelation while attending a Christmas Mass at Notre-Dame in 1886. Following his conversion, he imbued his work with the spirit of a religious visionary. In her "Souvenirs de l'autre guerre" Monnier says that when she was twenty-one she was troubled by "the enormous presence of the Catholic religion" in his play *L'Otage [The Hostage]*, but that in 1915, while rereading another play of his, *Tête d'Or [Head of Gold]*, she burst into tears "without apparent reason." From that time forward she was devoted to his work and called him "the immense Claudel." She wrote two poems for him, which she collected in her *Figure* in 1923; they show at one and the same time her agnosticism and the emotional, atavistic appeal that Catholicism had for her. Claudel was moved by one of them. He wrote to her from Tokyo on December 15, 1922: "Your first piece would have given me great hopes in former times [before his vain attempt to convert André Gide]. But by now I have become less prompt in hoping and rejoicing. If the seed that is cast by a saint is so often carried away by the birds, what are a few drops of water cast by a poet? The way of salvation is full of wonders, but I understand that it may seem hard and forbidding to the soul that has not set forth on it, and one must resign oneself to being unaccompanied by those whom one would have chosen most gladly."

Monnier was introduced to Claudel in 1919 by his nephew Jacques de Massary upon his return to Paris after a period of service as a minister in Rio de Janeiro. On May 30 of that year she offered a program of Claudel's work at the Théâtre du Gymnase; Marguerite Moreno and Edouard de Max, among other actors, presented portions of two of his plays, *Tête d'Or* and *Le Pain dur [The Stale Bread]*. Claudel himself began the performance with a speech and a reading of his poem "Sainte Geneviève." The speech was published in the series Les Cahiers des Amis des Livres in the following year. A second Claudel *séance*, or meeting, took place at La Maison des Amis des Livres on May 28, 1921. On this occasion Monnier, Léon-Paul Fargue, and Jules Romains read portions of his plays *Protée [Proteus]* and *La Ville [The City]*, while Edouard de Max and the actress Eve Francis read from his *Vers d'exil*.

There is one instance on record of a disagreement between Claudel and Adrienne Monnier: he did not share her enthusiasm for Joyce. In 1929, while he was in Washington, she sent him a copy of the French translation of *Ulysses*, which had just appeared. He returned it to her with a note saying that the book, though he believed it had a "market value," did not have "the smallest interest" for himself. "I once wasted a few hours reading *Portrait of the Artist as a Young Man* by the same author, and that was enough for me." In her "Readings at Sylvia's" (see Part One), Monnier reports a harsher judgment of Joyce by Claudel.

Paul Valéry, Léon-Paul Fargue, and Valery Larbaud

Although Claudel and some of the other writers described became a part of Adrienne Monnier's life, none, it seems, was as important to the life of La Maison des Amis des Livres as Paul Valéry, Léon-Paul Fargue, and Valery Larbaud. All three became friends of Sylvia Beach as well as of Monnier and were visitors to Shakespeare and Company, where James Joyce presided almost from the time of his arrival in Paris in July 1920.

Valéry, of all the poets of Monnier's own country who visited her bookshop, probably stands highest in the esteem of his immediate posterity. He belongs, as Wallace Fowlie wrote some years after his death on July 20, 1945, "to a very small group of French poets: Villon, Racine, Baudelaire, Mallarmé, Rimbaud—whose work is incomparable." From the time of his first visit in the spring of 1917, described in "Valéry in the Rue de l'Odéon," until shortly before his death, he came regularly to La Maison des Amis des Livres. Here, she says in a prefatory note to letters to her from the poet that appeared in "Paul Valéry vivant," an issue of the review *Cahiers du Sud* that was devoted to him in 1946, "he was the most familiar and the most transcendent of the Masters."

Paul Valéry was born in the Mediterranean coastal town of Sète, near Montpellier, on October 30, 1871; his father was Corsican, his mother was Italian, from Genoa. He went to school at the Collège de Sète (now the Collège Paul-Valéry) until he was thirteen, when his family moved to Montpellier, where he attended the *lycée* of that city. In 1888, upon completing his studies there, he entered the University of Montpellier as a law student. He was to receive his degree in law in 1892, but was never to practice the profession. Valéry began to write poetry at an early age; he was destined from the start for a career in literature.

In 1890, while at the university, he made the acquaintance of the novelist and poet Pierre Louÿs, and, through him, of André Gide, who was to be a lifelong friend. At this time Valéry began to publish his first poems in little reviews, including the *Conque*, which was founded by Louÿs. In 1891 he visited Paris for the first time, where he met the chief of the symbolist poets, Stéphane Mallarmé, of whom he became the devoted disciple. What he admired above all in Mallarmé was the rigorous critical intelligence that the older poet brought to the practice of poetry; Valéry despised facility and mystification and rejected the romantic conception of the poet as an inspired being. It would seem, in fact, that poetry itself was not of paramount importance for him, as it was for other poets of his rank, including Mallarmé; and what he told Adrienne Monnier, according to her report in "The Voice of Paul Valéry" (see Part Three), seems to typify a Valérian attitude: "People always believe . . . that I have the same ideas as Mallarmé, but we differed greatly, and above all in our ways of thinking about art; Mallarmé made a metaphysics of it; he thought that the world was created in order to be *represented,* and that the representation—art—was *the thing in itself.* I myself have never given to art, literary or any other, an essential importance, I have never set it above the other manifestations of life; for me it is *a game*." Valéry habitually spoke about poetry with a certain ironic disparagement, but there can be no doubt that if poetry was a game for him, it was one that he played with the utmost seriousness; he produced several poems, including *La Jeune Parque [The Young Fate]*, discussed by Monnier in "Valéry in the Rue de l'Odéon," and "Le Cimetière marin" ["The Cemetery by the Sea"], that have a place among the greatest and most beautiful works of this century.

Valéry, who loved what was difficult, played his "game" of poetry—for his delight—according to all the strict rules of French classical prosody, believing that they posed arbitrary limits that were spurs to invention. Although he must have been as dependent as any "inspired" poet for the sources of his poetry, he gave supreme importance to form; for him, the process of creation, minutely observed, tended to become the center of his attention, rather than the creation itself; this devotion to mental process is one of the characteristics of Valéry's mind.

Even when he was very young, when he wrote a great deal of verse, Valéry was interested in mathematics and abstract thought. In 1892, after a spiritual and intellectual crisis, he decided to renounce the writing of poetry for the sake of cultivating his mind, and for many years thereafter he produced few poems. In 1894 he settled permanently in Paris. Between 1897 and 1900, when he married Jeannie Gobillard, the niece of the painter Berthe Morisot and the subject of several paintings by Degas, Valéry worked as an editor at the Ministry of War. He then became the private secretary of Edouard Lebey, the director of the press association Agence Havas, with whom he stayed until the latter's death in 1922, when he began to live, as he did for the rest of his life, entirely by writing and lecturing.

Valéry returned to poetry in 1912, after André Gide and the publisher Gaston Gallimard persuaded him to assemble a collection of his early works for publication. As he went over his old poems, his dormant powers were awakened and he set about writing new ones, including *La Jeune Parque* (1917) and the poems that were published under the title *Charmes* in 1922. In December 1920 Adrienne Monnier published his collection of early poems, *Album de vers anciens*, in the series Les Cahiers des Amis des Livres. He wrote in the copy that he presented to her: "With the thanks and the best wishes of the author to the most gracious publisher in the world, Adrienne Monnier. Paul Valéry." The *Album de vers anciens*, along with the earlier reading of his work at La Maison des Amis des Livres—described in "Valéry in the Rue de l'Odéon"—enhanced the reputation of the poet, which had been established by the enthusiastic reception of *La Jeune Parque*.

Among Valéry's other notable works are his prose discourses *Introduction à la méthode de Léonard de Vinci* (1895) and *La Soirée avec Monsieur Teste* (1896); his great esthetic and philosophical meditations cast in the form of Socratic dialogues, *L'Ame et la danse [The Soul and Dance]* and *Eupalinos*, both published in 1921; the unfinished play *"Mon Faust"* (1945), which Monnier discusses in *Lust* (see Part Two), and numerous collections of essays. From the time of his early manhood Valéry kept voluminous notes, sections of which appeared in his lifetime. Monnier published two other works of his besides the *Album des vers anciens*: his reflections on writing, *Littérature* (1929), and a collection of aphorisms and observations, *Moralités* (1931), which contains a frontispiece and decorations by her sister Marie Monnier, who married the artist Paul-Emile Bécat. Valéry was elected to the Académie Française in 1925. From 1937 he occupied the chair of poetics of the Collège de France, where he lectured on poetry until shortly before his death.

At the time of his death in 1945 Paul Valéry was regarded by the French as their national poet—it is as such that Monnier hails him in her tribute at the end of *Lust*. His act of resistance during World War II, when he was an old man, was to defend his country by defending its language and the values that its language represented. "So, over the intelligence of our country," she writes, "there reigned such a poet, a sure sign of salvation and victory." He used the gift of language most courageously when he eulogized Henri Bergson— who was Jewish—before the Académie Française, shortly after the philosopher's death in January 1941. After Valéry's own death, Charles de Gaulle ordered a national funeral ceremony for the poet; this took place on July 25, 1945, at the Place du Trocadéro before the Palais de Chaillot, after a night-long vigil during which his body lay in state upon a torchlit catafalque. Valéry was buried in Sète, in the Cimetière Marin. His epitaph, from his poem by that name, reads: *"O récompense après une pensée/ Qu'un long regard sur le calme des dieux"* ["O reward after a thought/ A long look upon the calm of the gods"].

Over a year before she met Paul Valéry, Adrienne Monnier met Léon-Paul Fargue at the house of a mutual friend, May Raynaud.

He came to the bookshop the next day and was thereafter a regular visitor. "Adrienne's library," says Sylvia Beach in her *Shakespeare and Company*, "was Fargue's headquarters." Monnier's "First Encounters with Léon-Paul Fargue," in which she describes their meeting and the early days of their friendship, along with her two other articles about him, "Fargue and Words" (see Part Two) and "Fargue as a Talker" (see Part Three), give admirably detailed descriptions of the poet and his work.

Fargue was a true son of Paris, so much a part of the city of his day that it is impossible to imagine him in any other time or place. He knew it by heart physically and was familiar with all levels of its social life. Although he enjoyed frequenting the salons of high society—the *salons mondains,* where his conversational gifts made him especially welcome—"he felt perfectly at ease in no matter what milieu," says his biographer Louise Schub. "Differences of class did not exist for him—he would sacrifice without the slightest regret a big supper party at the house of a princess in order to go to comfort his former laundress who had just lost her daughter." His speech, as Monnier describes it in "Fargue as a Talker," was often caustic, sometimes cruel, and he imposed no restraint upon himself. "Otherwise," says Schub, ". . . he was a generous man, a good adviser, always able to understand everything, affectionate, fatherly with young people, with an extraordinary presence and radiance, with a fantastic gaiety; everything amused him."

Yet, beneath his extravagant sociability Fargue was essentially a lonely man; his efforts to postpone, every day, the inevitable moment when he must face himself in solitude—for he was an inveterate bachelor and was not to marry until very late in life—made a legendary noctambulist of him, a member, as he himself said, of "the ministry of the night," when he would make his rounds of the city, meeting his friends at their homes or in cafés. He had very little sense of time; he would invariably be late for appointments. Monnier says in her "Mémorial de la rue de l'Odéon": "His latenesses were legendary—when you invited him to dinner he would arrive at the dessert—but as he himself said with good sense: if he was absent in one place that was because he was present in another." There was a story, says Sylvia Beach, that he once arrived "two weeks late for dinner." This "was enough to make any hostess shudder."

In discussing Fargue's poetry, Monnier emphasizes his satirical spirit, which appeared in his speech as well. Fargue was also the poet of memory, of nostalgia, of lost childhood. The critic Jacques Borel writes in his essay "Passé et solitude dans l'oeuvre de Léon-Paul Fargue" ["Past and Solitude in the Work of Léon-Paul Fargue"], which is the introduction to Gallimard's 1964 edition of Fargue's *Epaisseurs [Densities]*: "Everything, in this work, is memory. . . . Fargue is that man with an inflexible, swarming, proliferating memory, who never forgot anything of what he once lived, not even the slightest sensation once felt." The past that is restored by memory, however, "does not truly appear in Fargue as the refuge or the help that it seemed at first it must be," and one does not find in him the "passionate attention" of Proust, which accompanied "the discovery of a reconquered universe." Rather, "there is, in these endless encounters of Fargue with his past, something furtive and as if by chance. . . . To find himself face to face with his past is always, for Fargue, to rediscover his 'sorrow.' " The light shed by these encounters "is felt only as a lack and as the always sharper consciousness of a dispossession."

Fargue was born in Paris on March 5, 1876. His childhood, though he was loved by both his parents, disposed him to an enduring melancholy. The solidly bourgeois family of his father, an engineer who was to found an important ceramics factory, success-fully opposed the marriage of their son to the poet's mother, who was a dressmaker and as such considered socially inferior, until Fargue was thirty years old. He was not legally recognized by his father until he was sixteen. Although his father and mother saw each other constantly and lavished affection upon him, his rejection by his father's family and his illegitimacy saddened him as a child and remained a bitter memory throughout his life. Fargue always remained close to his childhood, the sweetness and the sadness of it. Monnier remarks in her "Souvenirs de l'autre guerre" that "he was at once a man of the world (in the true sense of the word) and a child, as every poet should be."

In 1892, the year he was recognized by his father, Fargue entered the Lycée Henri IV, where he became a close friend of Alfred Jarry, who was to write *Ubu Roi*. Although he was a brilliant student, he did not continue his formal education after leaving the *lycée*, but instead devoted himself to poetry. Plunging into the intellectual and artistic life of the capital, he attended the weekly poetry sessions that Mallarmé held in his apartment in the Rue de Rome, met Debussy and other composers and musicians, frequented the salon of the *Mercure de France*, associated with Vuillard, Bonnard, and other painters—he was for a time very much attracted by painting—and became the friend of Valéry.

Fargue published his first poems in *L'Art Littéraire* in 1893, while he was a student, and in 1895 *Tancrède*, which Monnier mentions in "First Encounters with Léon-Paul Fargue," appeared in the German review *Pan*. In the early years of the century he frequented the literary circle of the novelist Charles-Louis Philippe, the author of *Bubu de Montparnasse*. Philippe's untimely death in 1909 at the age of thirty-five profoundly grieved his friends, who included, besides Fargue, André Gide, Jacques Copeau, Valery Larbaud, and Marguerite Audoux, the author of the novel *Marie-Claire*. Fargue and Larbaud became close friends immediately after Philippe's funeral, and remained on intimate terms until some time before 1924, when Larbaud permanently broke off the relationship after a gradual estrangement that was no doubt caused to a great extent by his irritation with Fargue's erratic habits. The year of Philippe's death, 1909, also brought the death of Fargue's father, a still greater loss, for he loved his father deeply. He inherited the family's ceramics factory—famous in its time for its lighting fixtures. He managed the business with good will but incompetently; it was sold after a long decline in 1926.

From 1916, the year he met Adrienne Monnier, La Maison des Amis des Livres occupied a central place in Fargue's life. In 1924, with Larbaud and Valéry, he undertook the direction of the review *Commerce*, which was founded then by Marguerite Caetani, Princesse de Bassiano, and was managed at the start by Monnier herself. He became at this time a very close friend of her sister Marie and her sister's husband, Paul-Emile Bécat, whose work Monnier praises in her article "The Paul-Emile Bécat Exhibition" (see Part Three). Marie Monnier, who illustrated his collection *Ludions* (1930), is known first of all for her embroideries, which both Fargue and Valéry—whose *Moralités* she decorated, as has been noted— praised exquisitely in articles devoted to her work. In his "Broderies" ["Embroideries"], first published in the *Nouvelle Revue Française* in June 1927 and collected in *Epaisseurs*, Fargue writes: "The idea of time, of the forest, of light, of seasons, presides over these embroideries, which have not tricked it, which have not betrayed it. Some among them have cost Mme Monnier two years of labor. They are garnished, they are adorned, like gardens, like branches. . . . It is beautiful weather, we open the windows upon them." Part of this article served as a preface to a catalog of an exhibition of Marie Monnier's work in the spring of 1927. Valéry's article "Les Broderies de Marie Monnier" was the preface for an earlier exhibition in 1924 that displayed, among other works, illustrations for Valéry's "L'Abeille" ["The Bee"] and "Palme," Rimbaud's "Les Chercheuses de poux" ["The Lice Pickers"], and Fargue's "Féerie." Joyce's *Finnegans Wake* was the inspiration of another work. As he describes it in his letter of September 20, 1928, to Harriet Weaver, it was "a wonderful carpet . . . representing the Liffey flowing through Dublin into the Irish sea. . . ." Finally, note should be made in these parenthetical remarks of the embroidery that was exhibited at La Maison des Amis des Livres in June 1940, which Monnier refers to in her "Occupation Journal" (see Part Eight) and describes in the final, May 1940, issue of her *Gazette des Amis des Livres* as a large piece, requiring three years of work, that represented "a shepherdess sitting in the meadows at the edge of a stream. It is a region in the mountains: a corner of Savoy inspired it. Around the shepherdess, at her feet, is assembled a whole little court of animals, of those animals that shepherd children dream endlessly of trapping or even simply of seeing. . . . We have called this embroidery 'Fable.' "

Fargue was named Chevalier de la Légion d'Honneur in 1925. In 1927 the review *Feuilles Libres* devoted its June issue to homages to Fargue by members of the literary, artistic, and musical world of Paris; Monnier's "Fargue and Words" appeared in it. He received other honors during the remainder of his life, among them election to the Académie Mallarmé; but he was an unsuccessful candidate for the Académie Française, largely, it seems, because he did not manage his campaign adroitly. Fargue lived with his mother until her death at a very advanced age in 1935; in 1939 he married the painter Chériane, whose own mother had been a friend of Apollinaire and was one of France's pioneer aviators. He suffered a grave stroke in 1943; thereafter, until his death on November 24, 1947, he was bed-ridden, though intellectually unimpaired. He submitted to the regime of invalidism with courage, receiving in his room the friends whom he once visited on his legendary nocturnal rounds. In the year before his death he received the Grand Prix de la Ville de Paris.

Among Fargue's collections of poetry, besides those already mentioned, are *Poèmes* (1912), *Pour la musique* (1914), *Banalité* (1928), *Suite familière* (1929), and *D'après Paris* (1931). Also noteworthy are his prose works *Le Piéton de Paris [A Stroller of Paris]* (1939), a series of reminiscences of the city, and *Portraits de famille* (1947), sketches of friends and others to whom he was strongly attached, including Réjane, Mallarmé, Valéry, and Antoine de Saint-Exupéry.

The formal consecration of Fargue as the poet of Paris was given around the tenth anniversary of his death, in November 1957, when the crossing of the Rue de Sèvres and the Boulevard du Montparnasse, the site of the house in which the poet died, was officially named Place Léon-Paul Fargue. His friend André Beucler said on the occasion that he had treated all the inhabitants, all the objects of Paris, "as members of his family and admitted them into his metaphorical intimacy. In return, the City of Paris thanks him today for having loved, sung, questioned, and passed through her to and fro, and . . . places his name upon her walls, that is to say, her flesh, rightly and justly, for she knows how to distinguish her own."

In her peroration to her "Mémorial de la rue de l'Odéon," which was first delivered as a speech in 1946 at the Club Maintenant, Adrienne Monnier recalls that she met Valery Larbaud in 1919, upon his return from Alicante in Spain, where he had lived for some time during and after the war; Fargue, who was already a close friend of hers, introduced her to him. "He became one of the great friends of the house," she says. "Larbaud, all by himself, would call for an entire volume." Unfortunately, Monnier never had the chance to write that volume or even a part of it; still, Larbaud appears here and there in her work, chiefly in her two articles on Joyce's *Ulysses* (see Part One), which, as a critic and as the director of the job of translating the book, he helped to introduce to French readers. Furthermore, her "Letter to Larbaud" (see Part One)—to a great extent about Whitman, whom he loved—gives intimations of her esteem and affection for him.

Larbaud was born in Vichy on August 29, 1881. He was the only son of a wealthy family whose fortune derived from one of the springs for which the city and the surrounding region is famous, the Larbaud Saint-Yorre, owned by his father, who died when he was a child, leaving him to be brought up by his mother and his aunt. Larbaud devoted himself to study and writing very early. He attended various *lycées,* including the Lycée Henri IV, Fargue's school. As a young man he studied at the Sorbonne, from which he received a degree in foreign languages in 1907. Though his mother tolerated his literary ambitions from the start, and even paid for the publication of his first book, *Les Portiques* (1896), a volume of verse in the Parnassian manner, she did not take his work seriously and was opposed to his literary career until he had won solid recognition; she would rather have seen him become an established member of the wealthy society into which he had been born. She also wanted him to marry, and a woman of her own choice; Larbaud, however, although he maintained for many years an intimate relationship with a woman friend, stayed celibate throughout his life. His mother, though generous, was possessive, and she used her wealth as a means of controlling Larbaud, who depended upon her financially in his early manhood.

Despite his mother's domination, Valery Larbaud's situation at the beginning of his career favored his ambitions; passionately interested in European culture, he received money enough to be able to travel widely and to collect an international library of works, which he housed in a lodge on his mother's Vichy estate, where he would stay from time to time, as well as in Paris, when he was not abroad. He loved England, Italy, and Spain, above all, and throughout the active part of his life he often visited the three countries and maintained fruitful contacts with their leading writers. He knew their languages well and was adept in several others: Latin, Greek, German, and Portuguese. As a translator and as a critic he became a central figure in the international literary life of his times.

It would seem that the English language was the one that he loved best after French, and there is evidence that he spoke and wrote it flawlessly. As a very young man he made a translation of Coleridge's *Rime of the Ancient Mariner*, which he published at his own expense in 1901; ten years later, dissatisfied with this early version, he made and published a new one. His rendering of Walter Savage Landor's *High and Low Life in Italy* appeared in 1911 under the title *Hautes et basses classes en Italie*. A study of Coventry Patmore introduced Paul Claudel's translations of the poet in 1912, and in the same year he published his own translation of Arnold Bennett's novel *The Matador of the Five Towns*. His major achievement as a translator of English was to present the larger part of Samuel Butler's work in French, including *Erewhon* in 1920, *Ainsi va toute chair [The Way of All Flesh]* in 1921, and *La Vie et l'habitude [Life and Habit]* in 1922; this last work had occupied much of his time between 1915 and 1919. Larbaud delivered a lecture on Butler at La Maison des Amis des Livres on November 3, 1920; Monnier published it in the same year in her series Les Cahiers des Amis des Livres. Her articles "Joyce's *Ulysses* and the French Public" and "The Translation of *Ulysses*," with their commentaries in this collection, describe the important part that Larbaud played in the presentation of that book. Larbaud was not only a representative of English literature in France but also a spokesman for French literature in England. He lectured and gave readings there, and for a time before World War I he wrote, in English, a literary letter from Paris for every issue of the *New Weekly*, to which his friend Bennett introduced him.

Larbaud was interested in American as well as British writing. He cared in particular for Walt Whitman, whom he discovered at the age of eighteen. He contributed translations of several of Whitman's prose pieces and "Les Dormeurs," his rendering of the poem "The Sleepers," to a collection of the poet's work in French, *Oeuvres choisies [Selected Works]* (1918), for which he also wrote the preface.

Sylvia Beach says in *Shakespeare and Company*: "What brought Larbaud and me together was his love of American literature. It was my job to introduce him to our new writers, and every time he left the bookshop, he carried away another armful of their books. He met there, too, live specimens of the new generation." In fact, says Sylvia, Shakespeare and Company was "the godchild of Valery Larbaud." He gave her "a little china Shakespeare's House, a childhood possession of his," and a set of toy soldiers—collecting them was his passion—representing "George Washington and his staff, mounted on prancing horses of different colors; and a company of West Point cadets." Their purpose, he explained to her, "was to guard the House of Shakespeare." She kept them in a small cabinet to protect them from her "children and animal customers."

Sylvia's portrait of Larbaud in her memoir tends to confirm what one suspects from reading his works and works about him—that he was not only a good writer but also an extraordinarily kind and good man. "Personally," she says, "Larbaud was charming. His large eyes were beautiful and had the kindest expression in them. He was of heavy build; his head was set close to the shoulders. His hands were one of his chief beauties, and he was proud of them. Also, he was proud of his feet, which he crowded into shoes a size smaller than was comfortable. One of his charms was his way of laughing—shaking soundlessly and blushing. And in quoting a line from some poem he liked, he would turn pale."

Larbaud also translated and introduced numerous writers in the Spanish language. One of his friends among them was the Argentine poet and novelist Ricardo Güiraldes, some of whose poems he translated for the review *Commerce*, of which he was for a time an editor, with Fargue and Valéry. Just as Arnold Bennett helped him to become a contributor to the *New Weekly* in England, Güiraldes arranged for him to write regular literary articles in Spanish for the Buenos Aires newspaper *La Nación.*

While engaged in his work as a critic, scholar, and translator, Larbaud created a body of original work that has yet, in the English-speaking world, to be given the attention that it obviously deserves. One of his most interesting inventions is the persona of A. O. Barnabooth, a young South American multimillionaire who travels throughout Europe in search of an education in life. Larbaud presents this character, his fictional alter ego, as the author of a story, a group of poems, and a delectable intimate journal that were collected and published in 1913 as *A. O. Barnabooth: Ses Oeuvres complètes; c'est-à-dire, Un Conte, ses poésies et son journal intime.* Larbaud's *Enfantines*, stories about childhood, appeared in 1918. Also noteworthy is his novel *Fermina Márquez* (1911), whose heroine is a young South American woman in France, and three novellas, *Beauté, mon beau souci [Beauty, My Beautiful Care]*, *Amants, heureux amants [Lovers, Happy Lovers]*, and *Mon Plus Secret Conseil [My Most Secret Counsel]*, which were published together in 1923. The English titles here are bald, literal translations of the originals, which come from poems by Malherbe, La Fontaine, and Tristan l'Hermite.

Like Léon-Paul Fargue, Valery Larbaud suffered a stroke, but earlier in life, in 1935, at the age of fifty-four, and more gravely, for his power of speech and his ability to write were seriously impaired; he never fully recovered, living in semi-invalidism for the rest of his life. He died in Vichy on February 2, 1957, in the Catholic faith, to which he had been converted from Protestantism as a young man.

Larbaud and Fargue became close friends, as has been mentioned, after the funeral of Charles-Louis Philippe, at which Fargue characteristically arrived late. They had met occasionally before at Philippe's home on the Ile Saint-Louis in Paris. According to Larbaud's physician Th. Alajouanine, who edited and collected the correspondence between the two writers, they were attracted to each other in part because of differences in their natures and situations. He says, "Léon-Paul Fargue seems to have been

immediately seduced, not to say entranced . . . by Valery Larbaud's style of life, by the cosmopolitan experience of the young
millionaire. . . . Valery Larbaud, on his side, was strongly drawn
to the multiform personality of Léon-Paul Fargue; he submitted,
one might say, to the attraction of a meteor, in whose orbit he let
himself be swept with delight, captivated by the sparkling fantasy of
the storyteller or by the tender reveries of the poet, subjugated by
his speech with its multicolored facets and trying in turn to
participate in the playful use of language."

Alajouanine says that Fargue and Larbaud shared a "particular
liking for play and a very live and ever-living feeling for their
childhood and for their past, which became transformed into
reveries and dreams." Larbaud, like Fargue, drew much of his
inspiration from his early memories, especially in his *Enfantines*.
Their spirit of play was shown above all in their way with language.
In "Fargue and Words" and "Fargue as a Talker," Monnier gives
examples of his verbal inventions in his writing and his speech.
Larbaud himself, for his own part, had what he described as his
"passion linguistique," which Alajouanine says he likened to "the
passion for games and sports."

In a more conservative way, for unlike Larbaud he was content
to remain within the French language, and, unlike Fargue, within
the rules of classical prosody and conventional vocabulary, Valéry
is related to both men, it appears, in his love for the game of
language. To their names might be added that of Joyce, who was
the most extravagant wordsmith of Odéonia and the friend of both
Larbaud and Fargue, each of whom helped the Irish writer in his
proper capacity, Larbaud as a linguist and Fargue as a prodigal
inventor—Joyce's contemporary French counterpart, in fact.

Love for the game of language and for play itself was an element
of the *esprit* of the citizens of Odéonia, whose motto might well have
been Yeats's lines ". . . wisdom is a butterfly / And not a gloomy
bird of prey." Two words that appear several times in Adrienne
Monnier's writings are *enjoué* and *enjouement*, which are derived from
jeu [play] and can be translated as "playful" and "playfulness,"
though the French terms have a connotation of gaiety that appears
to be missing from the English. In fact, *gai* and *gaieté* are offered as
synonyms for these words in French dictionaries. In "At the Opéra
with Francis Poulenc" (see Part Four), Monnier relates the
enjouement of the composer to the *gaieté* of the French, showing their
near equivalence in meaning in her context. The gaiety of the

French, she says, referring to her own description in "The Nature of France," the closing essay in this collection, "touches faith." According to this definition, *enjouement* or *gaieté* is not at all frivolous but represents a profoundly affirmative attitude toward life. "Poulenc's playfulness," she says in her article about him, "comes from the feeling of Unity. Because of this feeling you are not a child lost in life, you laugh at your own misadventures; all forms of sociability are embroidered upon this feeling."

The spirit of play in Fargue and Larbaud, which they embodied so well in their words, was characteristic of the general sociability of Odéonia itself. In fact, one of the words that they used with great frequency, and that appears throughout their correspondence, became the very term to designate those who, in Odéonia, were regarded as being among the elect—the *potassons*.

The Potassons

The word *potasson* was invented by Fargue. In "Souvenirs de l'autre guerre" Adrienne Monnier says: "It designated, I believe, at the beginning, a nice fat cat as well-rounded as a pot." Alajouanine, while doubting the strict accuracy of this definition, says that it is certain that Fargue at one time owned a cat named Potasson, described by Léon Pivet, a friend of the poet, as "a curious animal whom its master initiated to various games that a daily practice succeeded in making mystical." The term also appears in Fargue's "Chanson du chat" ["Song of the Cat"] from *Ludions*; the cat of the title is addressed as *"mon petit potasson,"* as if the word were not so much the name of a particular cat as that of the species itself; and it is as such that it appears in the correspondence between Fargue and Larbaud. Almost from the start, however, it is also applied to unidentified members of the human species, and on occasion Fargue uses it as his signature. The name is also metamorphosed, as at the end of Larbaud's letter of December 9, 1910: "Greet Messieurs the Potassons. Here the Papotames await you" *["Saluez Messieurs les Potassons. Ici les Papotames vous attendent"]*. Or he will sign himself variously as "Dépotame," "Dépothèse," "Dépopothèse," "Délepothèse," among other names. Fargue rejoins with variants of these and completely new inventions in the same spirit: "Polémon," "Polémard," "Napolémon," "Dilepotargue." Yet other names, as

Alajouanine notes, have a *"résonance préhistorique"* that recalls Fargue's love for natural history and scientific terminology: "Mon vieux Mégatherium"; "Cher Ptérodactyle"; "Archéoptéryx." Monnier herself will be addressed by Fargue as if she were some fabulous prehistoric beast: "Mon cher Belodon."

Monnier offers this definition of *potasson* as the word was applied to a certain kind of person: "Variety of the human species that is distinguished by its kindness and its sense of life. For the *potassons* pleasure is a positive; they are immediately in the know, they have goodheartedness and pluck. When the *potassons* meet everything goes well, everything can be put to rights, they enjoy themselves without effort, the world is clear, they cross it from one end to the other, from the beginning to the end, from the huge animals of the beginning—they have seen them, they were there—until the end of ends when everything begins again, always with good appetite and good humor." She portrays the spirit of the *potassons* most fully in her memoir on Raymonde Linossier (see Part One), the young Orientalist and lawyer, "our good friend Raymonde Linossier," she calls her in "Souvenirs de l'autre guerre," "whom we had the sorrow of losing in 1930, when she was still in the flower of her youth." The "institution" of the *potassons,* she says in her memoir, "knew an extraordinary power and influence from 1918 to 1923." Léon-Paul Fargue was the father—"our *papère*"—and she, Adrienne Monnier, was the mother. While she was "inclined to decorate with the name of *potasson*" everybody who asked her for it, Raymonde, who had the distinction of being "the Youngest *Potasson* in the World," was "much more intransigent." To satisfy her orthodoxy, "an intermediate category" was established, "that of 'Aspiring *Potassons.*' "

"The real *potassons,* there were not many of them," Monnier remarks in "Souvenirs de l'autre guerre"; "but all the same there were a certain number." Besides herself, Larbaud, Fargue, and Linossier, they included, according to her list of *anciens,* or old, *potassons,* those of the institution's heydey: the lawyer Charles Chanvin, a friend and employer of Linossier; Fargue's friend Léon Pivet, an artist who designed glass for the poet's father; Jean-Gabriel Daragnès, a painter, engraver, and printer who illustrated Valéry's *Jeune Parque* among many other works; Charles de la Morandière, a subscriber to the bookshop throughout its career and a chronicler of his native Normandy; Thérèse Bertrand-Fontaine, an eminent physician and one of Monnier's closest friends; Sylvia Beach, who "formed all by herself a class that was a bit wild"; and the composer Erik Satie (1866–1925), "who was to Fargue, if you please, what the Panchen Lama is to the Dalai Lama." Some of the music of Satie is close in spirit to the more playful poetry of Fargue. He wrote melodies for five of the poems of *Ludions*, "La Chanson du chat" among them, and, says Monnier, "composed the march of the *potassons*." In March 1919, the month in which *Littérature* appeared, she sponsored a recital of Satie's symphonic drama *Socrate* at La Maison des Amis des Livres. "That was really an event," she says in her "Mémorial." The work had not been played before except at the house of the Princesse de Polignac, who had commissioned it. "Suzanne Balguerie sang—sang marvelously—the whole score all by herself, which was a tour de force, as the work had been written for three women's voices. Satie himself performed on the piano. Jean Cocteau made the introduction."

These *potassons*, Monnier says, "formed a sort of ministry." She might have added to the list the name of Francis Poulenc (1899–1963), who was a childhood friend of Raymonde Linossier, to whose memory he dedicated his ballet *Les Animaux modèles*, which is the subject of "At the Opéra with Francis Poulenc." In "Raymonde Linossier," referring to one of Kipling's children's stories, she says that when the composer first visited her shop in 1917 he had the look of being "the Elephant Child whose nose has not yet been pulled." Poulenc describes their first meeting in a memoir that was published in the January 1956 issue of the *Mercure de France*, recalling that it was Raymonde Linossier who had him cross for the first time "the threshold of the celebrated bookshop. . . . She knew that Adrienne, as we used to say then, was 'made for me.' In fact, we immediately became a couple of friends. I loved her face like a gourmand nun's and she was amused by seeing me, with my nose in the air, 'sniff' her store."

Paul Valéry is another who should be listed among the original *potassons*. Monnier says in "Valéry in the Rue de l'Odéon" that she no doubt spoke to the poet about the institution at the time of their first meeting. "He must have lent a benevolent ear to my remarks," she says, "as I have a note from him dating back to that same year, 1917, which mentions the *potassons* favorably." This note was printed in "Paul Valéry vivant," the issue of *Cahiers du Sud* that was devoted to him in 1946. It reads:

Thursday, doubtless (1917)

Others prefer the meadows
But the wisest will deny
The roses for your bookshop
O Mademoiselle Monnier.

In testimony whereof I shall come Saturday at eight o'clock more or less something, to dine at your place with such as are *potassons* by right.

Very happy to be one of them.

—Paul Valéry

Monnier takes up the subject of the *potassons* again in her "Mémorial de la rue de l'Odéon," where she presents in more detail the young woman among them who was to become her dearest friend, Sylvia Beach. "This young American," she writes,

> displayed an original and most attaching personality. She spoke French fluently with an accent that was more English than American; to tell the truth, it was not so much an accent as an energetic and incisive way of pronouncing words; listening to her you thought less of a country than of a race, of the character of a race. In her conversation there were neither hesitations nor pauses; words never failed her; on occasion she deliberately invented them, she proceeded then by an adaptation of English, by a mixture or extension of French vocables, all that with an exquisite sense of our language. Her finds were generally so happy, so charmingly funny, that they at once came into usage—our usage—as if they had always existed; one could not keep from repeating them, and one tried to imitate them. To sum it up, this young American had a great deal of humor, let us say more: she was humor itself.

Sylvia Beach

Sylvia Beach was born in 1887 in Baltimore, Maryland, where her father, the Reverend Sylvester Woodbridge Beach, D.D., a graduate of the Princeton Theological Seminary, was at the time serving as a Presbyterian minister. Sylvia gives us the rudimentary facts of her own early life and her family's background in *Shakespeare and Company*. We learn that her father, on his mother's side of the family, descended from a long line of ministers. Her mother "was born . . . in Rawalpindi, India, where her father was a medical missionary." At the age of fourteen, she says, her father and mother took her and her two younger sisters, Holly and Cyprian, to Paris, where the Reverend Beach "had been asked to take charge of what were called the Students' Atelier Reunions. . . . Every Sunday evening, in a big studio in Montparnasse, American students came under home influence." It was at these reunions that Sylvia heard Mary Garden and Pablo Casals and saw the spectacular dancer Loïe Fuller, who was renowned for her experiments with artificial lighting. "During this first interval in Europe," Sylvia says, "I got the few months of schooling I ever had." She and her sister Holly were sent to a very strict school in Lausanne, "where, owing to the curious notions of the two ladies who directed it, the discipline was better suited to a bunch of incorrigibles in a reformatory than to a lot of meek maidens." She was soon removed from the school, but her sister was kept there for a while longer.

From Paris the family moved to Princeton, where her father became the pastor of the First Presbyterian Church, which he was to serve for seventeen years. The Grover Clevelands, the James Garfields, and the Woodrow Wilsons, she says, were members of her father's congregations. Woodrow Wilson and his family became close friends of the Beaches. "Even after the Wilsons moved to Washington, they always considered Father their pastor." The Princeton years were interspersed by visits to France. "We had a veritable passion for France," Sylvia says.

Sylvia spent the years of World War I in Europe. *Shakespeare and Company* is very vague about her travels and her activities during this period. She tells us that she "went to Spain in 1916 and spent some months there," and that she "went on to Paris" in 1917. "For some time, I had had a particular interest in contemporary French writing. Now I wanted to pursue my studies at the source." We are told that for a while later on she worked as an agricultural volunteer *[volontaire agricole]*, picking grapes in Touraine, and that after the war she spent several months in Serbia with the American Red Cross, distributing clothing. She returned permanently to Paris in July 1919. These facts are more or less confirmed by an interview that she granted an American magazine, *McNaught's Monthly*, in September 1926.

Neither Sylvia Beach nor Adrienne Monnier specifies the exact date of their first encounter, which took place in 1917, when Sylvia was living with her sister Cyprian in the Palais-Royal. Cyprian, a great beauty, was in the films; she was famous at the time in Paris for her role as Belle-Mirette in the serial *Judex*, a work by the pioneer film maker Louis Feuillade. "Louis Aragon in particular," Monnier says, "declared that he was much taken with her; he had followed her once to the bird market, where she went every week, for she adored the birds."

By coincidence, the first poet to visit Adrienne Monnier's bookshop after it opened in November 1915 was indirectly responsible for her meeting Sylvia Beach. "One day at the Bibliothèque Nationale," Sylvia writes, "I noticed that one of the reviews—Paul Fort's *Vers et Prose*, I think it was—could be purchased at A. Monnier's bookshop, 7 Rue de l'Odéon, Paris VI. I had not heard the name before, nor was the Odéon quarter familiar to me, but suddenly something drew me irresistibly to the spot where such important things in my life were to happen."

Sylvia implies, it seems, that she was aware at the time that she was being drawn "irresistibly" to the Rue de l'Odéon, but possibly this sense that her meeting with Monnier was preordained might have come to her as she looked back and considered the ideal configuration that it gave to her life thereafter; in retrospect it seemed necessary, and, since necessary, fated.

When she arrived at the shop, Sylvia says, she gazed at the books in the window—Monnier says in "Souvenirs de l'autre guerre" that they were works by Jules Romains—and noticed a young woman sitting at a table. "A. Monnier herself, no doubt. As I hesitated at the door, she got up quickly and opened it, and, drawing me into the shop, greeted me with much warmth. This was surprising in France, where people are as a rule reserved with strangers, but I learned that it was characteristic of Adrienne Monnier, particularly if the strangers were Americans." After rescuing her hat, which the wind blew off as she stood in the doorway, Monnier sat down with Sylvia at the table and they talked about books. Their friendship began at once. Sylvia became a member of the library and thereafter "spent many hours in the little gray bookshop of Adrienne Monnier"; she also attended the readings there.

Excited by Monnier's example, Sylvia considered the possibility of opening a French bookshop in New York that would be "a branch of Adrienne's," she says. "I wanted to help the French writers I admired so much to become more widely known in my country." However, she soon realized that the expenses of setting up business in New York would be prohibitive, and reluctantly she gave up her plan. Monnier then suggested that she open an American bookshop in Paris, for "rents were lower and so was the cost of living in those days"; she promised to advise her and bring her "lots of customers." Sylvia accepted her idea enthusiastically and they set about looking for a vacant shop. It was Monnier who soon found one, a former laundry, on the nearby Rue Dupuytren, a very short little street that runs between the Rue Monsieur-le-Prince and the Rue de l'Ecole-de-Médecine near the point where they converge at the Carrefour de l'Odéon.

Shakespeare and Company—Sylvia says that the name came to her as she lay in bed one night—opened on November 19, 1919, at 8 Rue Dupuytren. With money provided by her mother, she had converted the laundry into a modest but attractive bookshop whose newly installed shelves were stocked with books that had been supplied chiefly by secondhand dealers in London, New York, and Paris. She had found most of her furniture in the Paris flea market. The walls of the shop, which had been covered with sackcloth, were decorated with photographs, two drawings by William Blake that she had acquired from Elkin Mathews, a London bookseller, and several framed "little manuscripts of Walt Whitman scribbled on the backs of letters," which Monnier describes in her "Whitman at Sylvia Beach's" (see Part One). In time Shakespeare and Company became a gallery of writers' portraits; many of them were supplied by the photographers Man Ray and Berenice Abbott, who, says Sylvia, "were the official portraitists of 'the Crowd' "—the friends and patrons of the bookshop. A signboard that carried a portrait of Shakespeare himself by a friend of Monnier was hung over the doorway of the shop. As this was stolen, the same friend painted another, which was stolen in turn. Finally, Marie Monnier painted a third signboard with the portrait of "a rather French-looking Shakespeare," which Sylvia displayed throughout the existence of the bookshop, first in the Rue Dupuytren, then, after her move in the summer of 1921, in the Rue de l'Odéon.

Shakespeare and Company, which opened almost exactly four years to the day after Adrienne Monnier's bookshop, was busy from the start. Sylvia says that "the shutters . . . were hardly removed . . . when the first friends began to turn up. From that moment on, for over twenty years, they never gave me time to meditate."

Quite naturally, Adrienne Monnier's French friends were among the first to frequent Shakespeare and Company, and André Gide became one of the first subscribers to Sylvia's lending library. She says: "I saw Adrienne Monnier coming around the corner from the Rue de l'Odéon escorting him. It was just like Gide to hurry up and encourage me in my undertaking." Gide had good reason to be especially sympathetic toward the venture, for, like Valery Larbaud, he was very much interested in English and American literature. In 1935, when Shakespeare and Company was in danger of financial collapse, Gide, as Monnier recalls in her "Readings at Sylvia's," was among the French friends of the bookshop who came to its rescue. Valery Larbaud, as it has been remarked, was the godfather of Shakespeare and Company. Léon-Paul Fargue, who apparently visited the shop even before it was converted, drew a picture of the stove as it must have looked in the days when the laundry occupied the premises. As for Valéry, Sylvia says that "often, after opening Shakespeare and Company, I had the joy of having him come in and sit down beside me to chat and joke with me. . . . As a young student under the spell of *La Jeune Parque*, I would never have believed that one day Valéry himself would be inscribing my copy, and that he would be coming to bring me each of his books as they appeared."

If Shakespeare and Company was important to French writers, it was indispensable to writers in the English language, especially to Americans, and it was from the first more than a place to buy or borrow books. Sylvia says, "The news of my bookshop, to my surprise, soon spread all over the United States, and it was the first thing the pilgrims looked up in Paris. They were all customers at Shakespeare and Company, which many of them looked upon as their club." Trying to explain the presence of so many Americans in Paris after World War I, she mentions that Prohibition and "suppressions" had made the atmosphere at home intolerable; but she adds, and rightly, that they "were not entirely to blame for the flight of these wild birds from America." The migration to Paris was not only a flight away but a flight to: "The presence in Paris of Joyce and Pound and Picasso and Stravinsky and Everybody—not quite, since T. S. Eliot was in London—had a great deal to do with it." Innumerable other names could be written under that general designation "Everybody"; or, like Gertrude Stein, Sylvia might simply have said that Paris was where the twentieth century was. The City of Light at that moment of history was beyond any doubt the center of Western civilization.

As she shared so much of her life with Adrienne Monnier, many of the English-speaking friends of Sylvia Beach who appear in *Shakespeare and Company* appear in this collection as well. Among them are the composer George Antheil, who lived for a while above the bookshop with his wife Boski; Robert McAlmon, the publisher of Contact Editions; the novelist Bryher, who became a close friend of both women and was for a time the wife of McAlmon; Ezra Pound, who is seen in this collection chiefly as the supporter of Antheil and Joyce; T. S. Eliot, who appears in "Readings at Sylvia's" and "A Visit to T. S. Eliot" (see Part Three); William Carlos Williams, whom Monnier called "the best *man of letters* in the United States at present"—and who poorly repaid her generosity with his distorted descriptions of her in his autobiography and his *In the American Grain*; Ernest Hemingway, whose story "The Undefeated" she published in her *Navire d'Argent*; and, of course, James Joyce. This list is partial and is intended only as a summary enumeration of a few among many friends *de langue anglaise* whom Monnier discusses in her writings, which, it must be said, do not give and were not intended to give a comprehensive survey of her friendships and admirations. About many writers and other artists whom she cared for greatly—Paul Claudel is the first to come to mind—Adrienne Monnier, for want of time and looking forward to time that was not to be granted to her, wrote little or nothing at all.

Sylvia Beach herself liked Ernest Hemingway immensely, as a man and as a writer. Sherwood Anderson gave him a letter of introduction to her late in 1921; but, she says, she had known him and his wife Hadley "for some time before they remembered to produce Anderson's letter. Hemingway just walked in one day." Sylvia introduced him and Hadley to Adrienne Monnier. "Hemingway's knowledge of French was remarkable," she says, "and he managed somehow to find time to read all the French publications as well as ours." As a sports correspondent for the Toronto *Star*, he took Sylvia and Adrienne to a six-day bicycle race and a boxing match, which they found "engrossing." He then introduced them to his work, reading "one of the stories from *In Our Time*." Monnier was impressed; Sylvia says that she remarked: " 'Hemingway has the true writer's temperament.' " Her own response to Hemingway, whom she calls her "best customer," was, or so she would have it seem, one of simple, unreserved enthusiasm. According to the critic John L. Brown, as he wrote in the August–September 1963 issue of the *Mercure de France* that was devoted to her memory (its contents were published in a volume the same year), she never admitted the existence of a dark side to Hemingway's nature, but always, despite the misery of his later years, "remembered the young Hemingway as the 'real' Hemingway. . . . She did not see, she did not want to see, the desperate desolation of Hemingway's world, considerably preferring her earlier vision of a young man full of charm, who was an excellent writer and also a clean-cut, straightforward American type and a good father who brought along his son while still a baby, when he came to choose books at Shakespeare and Company."

Sylvia Beach, in turn, is one of the few people who appear in Hemingway's *A Moveable Feast* toward whom he is unreservedly kind; his description of her is one of the best that we have: "Sylvia had a lively, sharply sculptured face, brown eyes that were as alive as a small animal's and as gay as a young girl's, and wavy brown hair that was brushed back from her fine forehead and cut thick below her ears and at the line of the collar of the brown velvet jacket she wore. She had pretty legs and she was kind, cheerful and interested, and loved to make jokes and gossip. No one that I ever knew was nicer to me."

Above all there was James Joyce, to whose work and well-being Sylvia Beach devoted many years of her life. Adrienne Monnier's "Joyce's *Ulysses* and the French Public" describes how she and Sylvia met the Irish writer shortly after his arrival in Paris from Trieste in July 1920, and surveys the book from a specifically French point of view, while her "Translation of *Ulysses*" touches upon the enormous labor of putting the work into French—a major occupation of the Rue de l'Odéon throughout much of the 1920s. Joyce, whose life was a heroic struggle against many hardships—his early poverty, his growing blindness, the mental illness of his daughter Lucia, the persecution of his work—was fortunate at least in his friendships. Monnier's articles and their commentaries give an intimation of the enormous support—moral, financial, and literary—that he received from those who believed in his work and were attracted to him as a man.

No one helped him more than Sylvia Beach, but Joyce, it must be said, seems to have taken her help for granted, as a necessary tribute to his genius. In her "Great Amateur Publisher," which appeared in the *Mercure de France*'s memorial issue, Janet Flanner writes: "There is no record of any other great writer of English prose in our time inhabited by so monumental a personality as he possessed or with a character so deeply inscribed and carved by his own ego. . . . A part of her [Sylvia Beach's] fame came from her being an amateur woman publisher with the courage to publish so daring a modern masculine classic as *Ulysses*. All of Joyce's gratitude, largely unexpressed, should have been addressed to her as a woman. For the patience she gave to him was female, was even quasi maternal in relation to his book."

We know from her own account in *Shakespeare and Company* that before Random House published *Ulysses* in 1934, following the decision of the United States District Court of New York that the book was not obscene, Sylvia relinquished all claims to the work, though she and Joyce had drawn up a contract agreeing that she would be paid if the work was sold to another publisher. She also gave up her rights to his *Pomes Penyeach*, which she published in 1927. Joyce received a substantial payment from Random House after it accepted *Ulysses*. Sylvia, who received nothing, writes: "I know how desperately he needed the money. . . . I felt an immense joy over his good fortune, which was to put an end to his financial troubles." Her final judgment, concerning both *Ulysses* and *Pomes*, is: ". . . after all, the books were Joyce's. A baby belongs to its mother, not to the midwife, doesn't it?" It should be added that she did receive royalties from a Continental edition of *Ulysses* that was issued by the Odyssey Press in 1932.

Although one occasionally detects a shrewd, ironic judgment at work beneath its apparently bland surface, the general style of *Shakespeare and Company* is one of modesty and self-effacement. The book at all times shows a desire to be kind at the risk of banality. Janet Flanner believes that "Sylvia herself did not have a literary mind or much literary taste, though in time a certain sense of literature rubbed off into her from the people around her. What she instinctively recognized and was attracted to was merely literary genius or flashes and fractions of it, or of tremendous great talent. . . . Sylvia had a vigorous clear mind, an excellent memory, a tremendous respect for books as civilizing objects and was really a remarkable librarian. She loved the printed word and books in long rows. She exerted an enormous transatlantic influence without recognizing it." Archibald MacLeish writes that Sylvia "was a bookseller who cared less for books than for the men who wrote them—whence the title of her shop—and less for the writers who *had* written than for those who might." Certainly, had she herself been a writer she could not have been the director of Shakespeare and Company: personal ambition, jealousy of her own time and talent would have prevented her. Her not being a writer was a requisite for the exercise of her own genius as a promoter and benefactor of others.

As such, she was not at all as artless as a reading of her book would have her seem. Leslie Katz, another contributor to the *Mercure de France* memorial issue, writes in his "Meditations on Sylvia Beach" that she was "as wise as Machiavelli, well versed in the intricate diplomacy of good will. Under the appearance of unassuming simplicity, acute judgments were made, and the relentless generosity acted in silence beyond argument or polemic."

There can be little doubt that Sylvia Beach, of all her friends, occupied first place in Adrienne Monnier's life after their encounter: "Sylvia," she describes her in "Americans in Paris" (see Part Eight), "so American and so French at the same time. American by her nature—'young, friendly, fresh, heroic . . . electric' (I borrow the adjectives from Whitman speaking of his fellow citizens). French through her passionate attachment to our country, through her desire to embrace its least nuances." Her poem to Sylvia Beach in *La Figure* begins: "I salute you, my Sister born beyond the seas! / Behold my star has found your own . . ." *["Je te salue, ma Soeur née par-delà les mers! / Voici que mon étoile a retrouvé la tienne . . ."].*

The fervor of this passage, along with Monnier's straightforward avowal in her "Memories of London" of her earlier love for her classmate and partner Suzanne Bonnierre, as well as deliberate references here and in other writings to the appeal that women had for her, incline one to believe that her friendship with Sylvia Beach, at least in its earlier years, was sexually passionate. The two women lived together from 1921 to 1937 in Monnier's apartment at 18 Rue de l'Odéon, up the street from the bookshops in the direction of the theater. In the latter year Sylvia Beach took up residence in a small apartment over Shakespeare and Company, where she lived alone until the liberation of Paris, when she moved upstairs to a larger apartment in the same house.

Despite this change, the friendship between Sylvia Beach and Adrienne Monnier suffered no decline. They shared a common devotion to their careers and a common life. On weekends they would often visit Adrienne's parents at their home in Rocfoin, a small town near Maintenon on the way to Chartres, southwest of Paris. Sylvia says that "you could see the cathedral across the treeless stretch of fields in the wheat-growing country of the Beauce." The Monniers' house, as photographs show, had a thatched roof. "I was fond of those lovely mauve-gray straw roofs," she writes, "and was teased by the Monniers for my American preference for anything quaint." Their Sundays "were spent in the garden at Rocfoin. A tall elm, one of the rare trees in the region, spread over it like an umbrella. Against the walls grew pears and peaches *en espalier*." In the summer they passed the month of August at Les Déserts, for some years in the home of Savoyard friends and then in a chalet of Sylvia's own.

"Like Some Proud Ship That Led the Fleet So Long"

In the summer of 1921, at the beginning of the greatest decade of her bookshop and La Maison des Amis des Livres, Sylvia Beach moved Shakespeare and Company from 8 Rue Dupuytren to 12 Rue de l'Odéon. By this time—a year had passed since her first meeting with Joyce—she had undertaken to publish *Ulysses* and Joyce was hard at work finishing it. Valery Larbaud's lecture on the work and the reading of portions of it to "the French public" would take place in Monnier's bookshop the following December; the first copies of *Ulysses* itself would appear on February 2, 1922, Joyce's fortieth birthday.

"The new premises, like the old," Sylvia says, "were a discovery of Adrienne's. She noticed that the antique dealer at No. 12 was looking for someone to take over her lease, and came rushing to let me know. I hurried to No. 12. What luck to find a place in the Rue de l'Odéon, and opposite Adrienne's, too." At this time the street "was as restful as a little street in a provincial town. The only time there was any traffic was when the audiences on their way to or from the Odéon Theater at the upper end of the street streamed past."

The cultural life of Paris between the wars was inexhaustibly various and rich. One can only hope at present to describe a few of the important literary activities of the time in which Adrienne Monnier participated to some degree and which she describes in her writings. The first that comes to mind, and the first in order of time—apart from the preoccupation with *Ulysses*—is the publication of *Commerce*, the resplendent literary review that appeared in Paris from the summer of 1924 to the winter of 1932. *Commerce* was sponsored by Marguerite Caetani, Princesse de Bassiano, who was born Marguerite Gibert Chapin in New London, Connecticut. Like the heroine of Henry James's *Golden Bowl*, she married an Italian prince from an old Roman family; Roffredo Caetani, her husband, was a composer. From 1949 to 1960, in Rome, Marguerite Caetani published a second review, *Botteghe Oscure*, which Janet Flanner has called "a distinguished lineal descendant" of *Commerce*. *Botteghe Oscure* published texts in Italian, French, German, Spanish, and English by hundreds of writers of some thirty nationalities, while *Commerce*, although it published translations—beginning with the fragments of *Ulysses* that Monnier discusses in the second of her two articles on that work—appeared exclusively in French.

The review, whose title was taken from a phrase in Saint-John Perse's *Anabase*, *"ce pur commerce de mon âme"* ["this pure commerce of my soul"], grew out of the frequent dinners that the princess gave for her friends at the Ritz and other Paris restaurants and Sunday gatherings at her Villa Romaine at Versailles. These were attended by the literary company of the Rue de l'Odéon and by composers and painters as well—Marie Laurencin, Igor Stravinsky, Maurice Ravel, and Erik Satie among them. Valéry, Fargue, and Larbaud, as mentioned, formed the triumvirate editorial board of *Commerce*, and Monnier was at the start its administrator. Fatigue from overwork forced her to resign from her position, to the distress of Marguerite Caetani, toward the end of August 1924, when the review first appeared. In her "Translation of *Ulysses*" Monnier describes the enormous labor of preparing the first issue of *Commerce*. The burden of translation was borne chiefly by Auguste Morel and Valery Larbaud; Monnier's own cross was placed on her shoulders not by Joyce but by Fargue, who contributed poems that she would take down at night under his dictation, as she writes in her article, even though, according to Louise Schub, "she was exhausted after a long day in the bookshop." There was apparently no other way of getting Fargue to compose. Her health broke down and she was forced to take a vacation, which did her little good, according to Schub. For a time Sylvia Beach and Philiberte Monnier were much concerned for her. Fargue, as incapable of self-criticism as a child, attributed her illness to fantastic causes. After its first issue, the administration of *Commerce* passed on to others.

Until his resignation in 1930 Fargue contributed many times to *Commerce*; Valery Larbaud and Paul Valéry each appeared in the review some twenty times in all. Among the other French writers whose work is represented in its pages are: Louis Aragon, Antonin

Artaud, André Breton, Paul Claudel, André Gide, Max Jacob, André Malraux, Henri Michaux, and Jules Supervielle. *Commerce* published translations of a number of other writers in the English language besides Joyce: T. S. Eliot, William Faulkner, Robert Herrick, Archibald MacLeish, Edith Sitwell, Virginia Woolf, and Thomas Wyatt. Other non-French writers who appeared in translation were: Federico García Lorca, Franz Kafka, and Boris Pasternak.

Commerce, as this cursory look at its contributors shows, was a great European light, and so during its far briefer life was Adrienne Monnier's own review, the *Navire d'Argent*, which appeared monthly from June 1925 to May 1926. The first issue began triumphantly with Valery Larbaud's homage to the city, "Paris de France," in which we find the explanation for the title of the review: the *navire d'argent*—the "silver ship"—is Paris itself. Larbaud takes his metaphor from the emblem of the city, with its Latin motto: *fluctuat nec mergitur*—"it wavers but it does not sink." He begins:

> After four years of a state of siege, of bombardment, of epidemic, . . . we have seen our dearly beloved city of Paris come out of the shadows and resume her beautiful pace as the capital of the continent. . . .
>
> After the storm, after the fluctuation, to verify that we have once more escaped from danger, that we have not sunk, and to look after its working: to repair the tiller and the rudder, to set the sails again to the wind, to hoist the old flag at the stern and the brand-new flame to the top of the mast, and sail our beautiful Silver Ship, that very one that "led the fleet so long" (Walt Whitman, "O Star of France") and that is getting ready to lead it once again.

Larbaud's essay is in large part an attempt to define the place of Paris as "the capital of the Occident" and to answer a question that he asks himself at the beginning: "Are you a real Parisian?" Rejecting all parochial definitions, he magnanimously concludes:

> . . . one is Parisian to the degree that one contributes to the material activity and to the spiritual power of Paris. Once again we are trying to approach, as much as creatures of flesh can do so, the ideal Parisian whom we used to dream about when we were twenty years old: the Athenian Parisian, the European Parisian, and at the same time the Parisian of Paris of France. . . . That does not prevent us from fraternally welcoming the Parisians born outside of France, that

is to say, the foreigners who have been and are able to contribute to the material activity of Paris and to its spiritual power, like Walt Whitman. . . .

Whitman's statement "I am a real Parisian" is one of two epigraphs of the article. "Paris de France" ends with a truly fraternal vision as the writer anticipates a visit that he will make to the riverside at dawn:

> But that great silence of the dawn. Oh! I foresee that it will be a confrontation full of gravity with the landscape of our oldest beginnings of summer and the terrible and inevitable interrogation: What have you done with the time that has been given to you? Courage. You are not the only one to face that question: all those whom you "carry in your heart"—the friends who were here last evening, the absent ones, the dead ones whose memory in you is so living, your foreign fellow-citizens whose return is announced and who would be so happy to see this Paris morning—they will be there, leaning on their elbows next to you, they will behold it with your eyes, next to you and like you under the protection of our saints, men and women, and in the center of our invented or accumulated riches. . . .
>
> However, it would be intolerable if this confrontation were prolonged; we, filled with a clamor of idle words in the presence of Paris mute and full of glory, as in the presence of our guardian angel and of the soul that was so beautiful and that we have loved so poorly. But the mechanical life of Paris and the movement of the crowd that is hardly less mechanical will withdraw us from this contemplation and will recall to us the movement of the crowds of other cities in which we have lived and other summer mornings in other cities. In those other cities the same question, less insistent but as terrible, would be put to us by the assembly of our memories in the brightness of the dawn. To those also we belong a bit, and for us at least they are all situated in the same country and form with Paris only a single city of which Paris is the center. And that not theoretically, but really in us. . . . A Paris increased by ten other great cities in which we have sought for, as here, happiness, and friendship, and love, and solitude, and ourselves.

The *Navire d'Argent* sailed throughout its voyage of twelve months as by the breath of Larbaud's tutelary words. Monnier published the review with the help of Jean Prévost, who would become well known as a novelist, critic, poet, translator, and biographer. At the time, however, he was only twenty-four years old and had published only two articles. "Her choice," he wrote in a reminiscence about their collaboration, was "proof of audacity." Prévost, who was born near Grenoble, in the department of Isère, south of Monnier's Savoy, was a graduate of the Ecole Normale Supérieure. He was a man of prodigious creative energy and physical strength. Sylvia Beach says that he "was extremely hardheaded: I don't mean in a business sense, but literally; his head was as hard as a rock. . . . He was a boxer and said that punches in the head didn't bother him; he didn't feel them. You might as well have punched an iron bar as Prévost's head. That was how Hemingway broke his thumb in the fight I organized between the two champs." Curtis Cate, a biographer of Antoine de Saint-Exupéry, whose "Aviateur" was presented in the April 1926 issue of the *Navire* by Prévost, who was his friend and who introduced him to Monnier, believes that "it was probably the latent peasant instinct within her which caused her to choose Prévost." He writes in his memoir: "I have never participated in a more generous or a more joyous enterprise. Of all those I have known . . . Monnier alone had an influence upon me; she liberated what my surliness hid of joy, health, even social virtues. Faithful, . . . of a loyalty without parallel, this valiant captain found in me an unequal second." In 1926 Prévost married the writer Marcelle Auclair, who appears in "A Visit to Marie Laurencin" (see Part Three). They were divorced near the beginning of the war, during which Prévost served heroically in the Resistance as a maquisard. He was shot to death by the Germans on August 1, 1944, just before the liberation of Paris, in the Vercors, the mountain refuge of the maquis in Isère. Among his many works are novels, critical and philosophical essays, a life of Montaigne (1926), and the posthumously published *La Création chez Stendhal* (1951) and *Baudelaire* (1953).

Besides "Paris de France," the first issue of the *Navire* included, among other contributions, a joint translation by Sylvia Beach and Adrienne Monnier of T. S. Eliot's "Love Song of J. Alfred Prufrock," "La Chanson d'amour de J. Alfred Prufrock." Monnier says in her "Visit to T. S. Eliot" that she and Sylvia translated this poem because it "had seemed relatively easy" to them; she adds that they "would never have dared to attack *The Waste Land*." Eliot, apparently forgetting a rendering by Saint-John Perse of the first part of "The Hollow Men" that appeared in the winter 1924 issue of *Commerce*, remarks in a memoir on Sylvia Beach: "To Adrienne Monnier with *Navire d'Argent*, I owe the introduction of my verse to

French readers; and so I became a visitor to her bookshop and to that of Shakespeare and Company." Perhaps he gave priority to "La Chanson d'amour" as it was the first complete translation of a poem of his to appear in French, and of a major poem as well.

Adrienne Monnier herself, under the pseudonym J.-M. Sollier—the surname was her mother's maiden name—published in this first issue of the *Navire* a short monologue, "Homme buvant du vin" ["Man Drinking Wine"], one of several prose pieces that she collected and published herself in 1932 under the title *Fableaux [Fables]*; another of these is "Commères" ["Old Wives" would be an approximate translation perhaps], which first appeared in the *Navire* for November 1925. Most of the *Fableaux* draw their inspiration from the life of Les Déserts, her mother's native commune in Savoy, and reproduce the direct, robust speech of the country people.

One of the departments of the first *Navire*—it appears in some of the later issues as well—was a Revue de la Critique, a collection of critical comments from various sources. Another section was a serial bibliography of French translations of works in foreign literatures; this was a permanent feature of the review, except in the issue of February 1926. By far the greater part of the bibliography—from June to November 1925—was devoted to English literature, from *Beowulf* to contemporary writers, while the sections for December of that year and January and March 1926 published lists of American works in translation; the last two sections, for April and May 1926, were reserved for German writing. The bibliography of the *Navire d'Argent* anticipates Monnier's project, which was permanently interrupted by the war, to compile a comprehensive bibliography of works on ancient and foreign countries; this was to include their literature in French translation. It appeared for a time in her *Gazette des Amis des Livres*, the more modest successor of the *Navire*, which she published from January 1938 to May 1940.

Every bibliographical installment in the *Navire* was followed by a supplementary section, Pages, which contained a selection or more from work on the current list. Thus, the first part of the English bibliography, "Des origines à la fin de la Renaissance," is illustrated by Auguste Morel's "De sa maistresse allant au lict," his translation of "To His Mistress Going to Bed," by John Donne.

The *Navire* published translations not only in its Pages but also in the main part of the review. The entire issue of September 1925 was devoted to William Blake, apart from the bibliography, where he is listed, in conjunction with that month's installment, which concerned "Le Pré-Romantisme et le Romantisme." Auguste Morel and his collaborator Annie Hervieu presented a series of masterful renderings of the English poet. Among them are "Aux Muses" ["To the Muses"], "L'Agneau" ["The Lamb"], "Le Tigre" ["The Tyger"], "Londres" ["London"], "Oracles d'innocence" ["Auguries of Innocence"], "Le Voyageur mental" ["The Mental Traveler"], and selections from the prophetic books. The issue also contained critical articles on Blake and was illustrated by a portrait of the poet and Sylvia Beach's two drawings by him.

There was one other entirely non-French issue of the *Navire*, that of March 1926, which was given over to American writers: Walt Whitman, William Carlos Williams, Robert McAlmon, Ernest Hemingway, and e. e. cummings. Monnier describes the preparation of this issue in her "Letter to Larbaud," which appeared in it. Among other foreign writers who were published in the *Navire*, whether in the main body of the review or in its Pages, are: James Joyce, William Butler Yeats, Italo Svevo, Alfonso Reyes, and D. H. Lawrence. Joyce's contribution—the first English version of "Anna Livia Plurabelle," from *Work in Progress*, which was to become *Finnegans Wake*—came out in the issue for October 1925. It had been intended for an English review, the *Calendar*, but Joyce took it away from its editor when he was asked to delete a passage that its printers considered obscene.

Monnier published two short poems by herself in the final, May 1926, issue of the *Navire*, a poetry number. The same year saw the appearance of her *Vertus [The Virtues]*, three parts of a long poem, dedicated to her mother, that she never finished. Her earlier collection of verse, *La Figure* (1923), as has been noted, was a series of poems that were for the most part about her writer friends; but one of them, a very beautiful one, was addressed to her sister: "Pour Marie Monnier." Another, which has been quoted, describes her vocation. *Les Vertus* might be identified as a religious poem, though it is certainly not devotional in any orthodox way. The Virtues of the title are feminine, tutelary divinities; one of the work's most moving passages is an address to the Virgin Mary.

Monnier's chief personal contribution to the *Navire d'Argent* was her Gazette, which became a monthly feature of the review in December 1925. Several articles in this collection first appeared in it: *"La Revue Nègre," "The Ballet Mécanique," "Benoist-Méchin," "The Voice of Paul Valéry," "Whitman at Sylvia Beach's," "A*

Letter to Larbaud," "A Visit to Marie Laurencin," and "A Letter to a Young Poet." Monnier did not collect all of her *Navire* articles, nor have all of those that she did collect been translated for this book; several concern personalities and events by now forgotten, while a few others, hardly more than notes, are unfortunately too short to stand alone. One of these is a paragraph from the first Gazette of December 1925, "Arrivée de Paul Robeson" ["The Arrival of Paul Robeson"], which mentions that Sylvia Beach presented the singer to her friends and that he sang spirituals for them on the occasion. Sylvia herself does not refer to the meeting in *Shakespeare and Company.* Another brief article touches upon *The Gold Rush* of Charlie Chaplin, whom Monnier admired—his name appears several times in her work.

Appropriately but sadly the Gazette of the last issue of the review contains a note, "La Fin du *Navire*" ["The End of the *Navire*"], in which Monnier explains that it will be necessary to cease publication—she hopes that it will be only for a while—because of "an effort, an expense, which only people who are doing or have done a review can imagine." She says that she has resigned herself, in order to pay debts incurred by the venture, to sell her private library, "which represents almost everything I possess that is most precious." Perhaps, she says, the money from the sale will allow her not only to pay her debts but also to continue her effort "in one way or another." She mentions her sale and the sadness it caused her in "Rainer Maria Rilke" (see Part Three). Her books were sold at an auction that took place on two days in the middle of May 1926. The auction catalog lists exactly four hundred items—many of them with written dedications to Monnier by their authors. Paul Claudel, André Gide, and Paul Valéry are each represented by some twenty-five books. The catalog alone shows the degree of her devotion to literature.

Both *Commerce* and the *Navire d'Argent*, though French in language, were international in spirit, and were especially hospitable to writers in English through the medium of translation. Other reviews at that time and afterward resembled them in their leanings: for example, *Bifur*, *Echanges*, and *Mesures*. Only with the last did Monnier, as its manager for a time, have a close relationship. *Mesures*, as it appeared between 1935 and 1940, will be discussed in further detail a bit later.

During the years between the wars there were several English-language reviews in Paris, among them the *Transatlantic Review* (1924–1925), edited by the British novelist and critic Ford Madox Ford; *This Quarter* (1925–1932), which appeared under the joint editorship of Ernest Walsh and Ethel Moorhead and was later published by Edward Titus; and *transition* (1927–1938), directed by Eugene Jolas and others. Among Sylvia Beach's colleagues in the venture of private publishing were Robert McAlmon, with his Contact Editions; William Bird, the owner of the Three Mountains Press; and Harry and Caresse Crosby with their Black Sun Press.

Sylvia Beach herself restricted her publishing enterprise solely to Joyce, despite entreaties by several other writers—notably D. H. Lawrence and Frank Harris—who believed that, having had the courage to publish *Ulysses*, she would welcome other forbidden books. She says: "Writers flocked to Shakespeare and Company on the assumption that I was going to specialize in erotica. They brought me their most erotic efforts." They misunderstood her, of course, and they no doubt misunderstood Joyce as well. "He was no specialist," Sylvia says, "but a general practitioner—all the parts of the body come into *Ulysses*. As he himself said plaintively, 'There is less than ten percent of *that* in my book.' " Sylvia was to issue eleven printings of *Ulysses* before relinquishing her rights to it. In 1927, as has been noted, she published Joyce's *Pomes Penyeach*, a collection of thirteen short lyrics in the most chaste and conventional language. Her final Joyce publication—not by him but about him—appeared in 1929: *Our Exagmination round His Factification for Incamination of Work in Progress*, which she simply calls *Our Exag*. The book comprised twelve critical essays of Joyce's *Work in Progress* (to be called *Finnegans Wake*) by as many writers, with two letters of protest, one of which Joyce himself wrote under a pseudonym as a practical joke.

The year 1929 also marked the publication of the French version of *Ulysses*, bringing to a conclusion Monnier's own Joycean enterprise. In the next decade, with some exceptions, she was to publish only her own work: the first part of a critical catalog of her lending library *(Catalogue critique de la bibliothèque de prêt)* and her *Fableaux* in 1932, and, from January 1938 to May 1940, just before the Germans occupied Paris, her *Gazette des Amis des Livres*.

The Thirties and After

By comparison with the preceding decade, the thirties in the Rue
de l'Odéon, although they were by no means inactive, seem
somewhat like an aftermath. The Depression, which hit the United
States in 1929, in time hurt the French economy; furthermore,
many Americans in Paris whose stay there depended upon money
from their own country found their means of support cut off and
were obliged to return home. And then, as Sylvia Beach writes, "It
had been pleasanter emerging from a war than going toward
another one." The existence of Shakespeare and Company was for
a while in danger: "Our business, which, with the departure of my
compatriots, had already suffered, rapidly declined. My French
friends remained, and they might have filled the gap left by my
homeward-going customers but they, too, had been affected by the
Depression." By the middle of the decade Sylvia feared that she
would have to shut up shop. The business was saved by the
intervention of a committee of French writers, André Gide and
Paul Valéry among them, who organized a program of subscription
readings by themselves and other writers at Shakespeare and
Company; the proceeds from these saved the bookshop. Monnier
describes this episode and some of its highlights in her "Readings at
Sylvia's." Despite this help, it was still necessary for Sylvia to sell
many of the manuscripts and first editions that had been given to
her by Joyce and others. These included, according to her own
description, a "set of the corrected proofs of *Ulysses*," "the first
manuscript of *A Portrait of the Artist (Stephen Hero)*," and "the
manuscripts of *Chamber Music, Dubliners*, and *Pomes Penyeach*."

Aside from her work as a bookseller, Adrienne Monnier was busy
during the early years of the decade completing the first part of the
critical catalog of her lending library, which she had been
compiling for several years. According to its subtitle, this part was
reserved for "French Literature and General Culture." She says in
her preface to it that "at the last moment, in order to reduce the
enormous costs of printing," she had to "leave out almost a quarter
of the text" that she had prepared, and that without the help of
Sylvia Beach she would not have been able to publish at all. Like
"La Maison des Amis des Livres" and "Number One," which open

and close the first section of this book, Monnier's preface to her catalog is a statement of faith in her vocation.

In 1934 Monnier undertook the administration of the review *Mesures*, which appeared from January of the following year until 1940. It was founded and edited by Henry Church, whom she describes in "Number One" as "a French-speaking American writer." Church was, in fact, a longtime resident of France. He went to Europe as a very young man at the turn of the century, and, apart from several years that he spent in Munich and Geneva, he lived in Paris and the nearby town of Ville d'Avray. An amateur in the best sense of the word, he was the author of a collection of poems, four plays, and fiction; he also translated several plays into French, among them *Richard III*. The editorial board of *Mesures*, which met at his home in Ville d'Avray, was composed of the critic Jean Paulhan, who was the editor of the *Nouvelle Revue Française*, the philosopher Bernard Groethuysen, the poet and artist Henri Michaux, and the Italian poet Giuseppe Ungaretti.

Like *Commerce* and the *Navire d'Argent, Mesures* gave an important place to foreign writers, especially writers in English. In its issues are to be found translations of works by W. H. Auden and Christopher Isherwood, E. M. Forster, Robert Frost, Gerard Manley Hopkins, and Edgar Lee Masters, among others. Of special interest, in view of his collaboration with Adrienne Monnier on the *Navire d'Argent*, are Jean Prévost's excellent translations of Frost's "Stopping by Woods on a Snowy Evening" and "Canis Major" and selections from Masters's *Spoon River Anthology* under the title "Tombeaux" ["Tombs"]. As Monnier explains in "Number One," she had no part in the editing of *Mesures*; Sylvia Beach, however, was "consulted rather often on the subject of English language texts translated into French."

Monnier left her position on the staff of *Mesures* after its October 1937 issue and thenceforth devoted herself to her own little review, the *Gazette des Amis des Livres*, which she financed with money that she received from the sale of her rights to the French translation of *Ulysses* to Gallimard publishers in 1937. As she describes her enterprise in "Number One," which filled the whole first issue of the *Gazette*, there is no need to speak of it here in detail. She began in it the foreign bibliography anticipated by her lists in the *Navire*. This bibliography was supposed to have formed the second part of her *Catalogue critique de la bibliothèque de prêt*, but it was discontinued two issues before the war put an end to the *Gazette* itself. Her articles in the review—which was written entirely by herself, apart from correspondence and occasional long quotations—represent a continuation of the Gazette section of the *Navire d'Argent*; several of them besides "Number One" appear in this collection. In the meantime, Monnier had published frequently in other reviews, chiefly the *Nouvelle Revue Française*, to which she contributed regularly from 1934 to 1937.

Of Monnier's articles, which she affectionately called her "gazettes," it is hardly necessary to speak, for they will speak for themselves in this volume. The spirit that conceived them, according to the critic Jean Amrouche, was wonderfully free of the urge that he believes compels most writers, which springs from a consciousness of "a yawning abyss between the self and the world, a lack, a fault (the Fault); an incurable wound." He believes that Adrienne Monnier's work arose not from a sense of lack but from a sense of fullness:

> . . . When was she wounded by the sickness (or by the grace) of writing? What discord, what rift was there between her life and the life of all? One did not see it. On the contrary, one admired among the cares, the duties, the pace of her activity an oasis of calm, of silence, of slowness, . . . as if an arc of light [was] between herself, the others, and the world. . . .
>
> Did she feel, as she was, too rich, too full to be content with saying thank you to life? It seems to me that it was certainly the gratitude that she was full of—like some mystics—that forced her to take up her pen. . . .
>
> . . . Nothing in her writings that are known to me is a confidence to herself. Everything in them is addressed to others. . . . She was satisfied with this world, whose natural spectacle she relished with as much pleasure and attention as the spectacles that are staged by men. How well she knew how to read and to turn appearances to account! How well her mind and all her senses knew how to fix themselves, to enjoy until its exhaustion the pleasure of seeing, of hearing, of losing oneself, delaying to the extreme limit the time for reflection and the moment when memory and judgment come into play to re-create what was first of all intensely experienced in participation or in communion.
>
> Her art of telling is in close correspondence with her art of living. Her writings name, point out, evoke, paint, or describe real objects with which she had dealings and which life bore forth to her whose welcome always preceded the offering. It is easy to see how, in her wonderful reports, the imagination is bridled, severely constrained to invent nothing, but to rediscover, to reconstitute in concert with

memory things as they are, to put them back where they were, where they are, so that they may reside *here* in words. *That took place, I saw it the way I am telling it, with the joy that I took in it,* that is what clearly underlies most of the gazettes. The playfulness, the familiarity of the tone, far from masking the seriousness, the gravity of the testimony, on the contrary make them more sensible to the ears and to the heart. *That took place,* and I hear like a distant echo, *so be it.*

Adrienne Monnier was able to continue her *Gazette des Amis des Livres* for a time after the outbreak of the war in September 1939; there were to be two more issues—those of January and May 1940; these, however, appeared without the bibliographical section. With the occupation of Paris, publication ceased permanently. The difficulty of living, the labor of maintaining La Maison des Amis des Livres—the bookshop remained open throughout the war— required all her time and energy. She writes in her "Letter to Friends in the Free Zone" (see Part Eight), which was published in the *Figaro Littéraire* in 1942: "The *Gazette?* I don't even think about it." As she goes on to say, she was helped greatly by her close friend and literary executor, Maurice Saillet, who after the war was the editor in chief of the *Lettres Nouvelles,* for which she was to write some of her finest articles. During 1942 her work appeared frequently in the *Figaro Littéraire;* all of her contributions to the review appear in this collection, including her open letter to the Free Zone and her "Letter to André Gide about the Young" (see Part Eight). It is to these and to the private journal that she wrote just before and during the occupation of Paris that we must turn for a glimpse of her wartime life. They bear witness to one fact above all: calmly and bravely she continued.

Sylvia Beach, for her own part, decided after the outbreak of the war to stay in France. As Monnier says in her "Americans in Paris," she was one of "a small number of her countrywomen who, having settled in Paris, never wanted to leave it. They shared our sufferings and privations with love and underwent a more or less long captivity." Sylvia herself remarks: "I had resisted all the efforts of my embassy to persuade me to return to the United States. . . . Instead, I had settled down to share life in Nazi-occupied Paris with my friends." She was able, until shortly after the United States entered the war in December 1941, to keep Shakespeare and Company open. As an American she was regarded with hostility by the occupants, and especially so because she refused to make any concessions to them. She had at the time a bookshop assistant, "a young Jewish friend, Françoise Bernheim," who had been excluded "by the Nazi laws" from the Sorbonne, where she was a student of Sanskrit. Unintimidated, Sylvia appeared in public with Françoise, who had been forced to wear a yellow star. "We went about on bicycles, the only form of transportation. We could not enter public places such as theaters, movies, cafés, concert halls, or sit down on park benches or even on those in the streets." Françoise, one learns from other sources, was sent to Auschwitz, where she died.

"When the United States came into the war," Sylvia says, "my nationality, added to my Jewish affiliations, finished Shakespeare and Company in Nazi eyes. We Americans had to declare ourselves at the Kommandatur and register once a week at the Commissary in the section of Paris where we lived. . . . My German customers were always rare, but of course after I was classified as 'the enemy' they stopped coming altogether. . . ." Sylvia shut her bookshop—forever, as it turned out—toward the end of December 1941 after a German officer, to whom she had earlier refused to sell a copy of *Finnegans Wake*, told her that her goods were to be confiscated that day. Her first concern was to hide her books, photographs, and other valuables. With the help of her concierge and Maurice Saillet, she quickly moved the contents of the bookshop, including her bookcases, into a vacant upstairs apartment—it was on the fourth floor (the third by French reckoning)—that her landlady put at her disposal without charge. Here the goods of Shakespeare and Company were kept secretly and safely until the liberation of Paris, when Sylvia herself moved into the apartment from the much smaller one on the second floor, where she had lived since 1937. The premises of the bookshop itself were occupied thereafter by a dealer in antiques; Sylvia lived in the new apartment until her death.

From about the end of August 1942 until the following March, Sylvia was interned at a detention camp for British and American women in the town of Vittel, a hot springs resort in the department of Vosges. In the company of some of her best friends, she endured the hardships of imprisonment with a heroic good humor; later, in a memoir called "Inturned," she even tended to make light of them. "After a week of some deprivation," she writes, "we received parcels from the Red Cross and fattened up considerably on their contents: in fact we were far better off than were our friends at home. . . ." Adrienne Monnier and Maurice Saillet visited her in February 1943, about a month before her liberation. She describes in her memoir how she managed to pass some of her Red Cross provisions to Monnier under the very nose of the German officer who was guarding her: "Adrienne was wearing a wide, long cape, her customary costume, and she stowed under it a lot of the contents of my parcels which had been put aside for her. A can of condensed milk rolled on the floor—right under the table at which the officer was seated: I must say, he showed no sign of having noticed it as I picked it up."

Back in Paris—she obtained her release from the detention camp earlier than some other women through the intervention of "various friends at home who were on sufficiently good terms with the Enemy"—Sylvia lived quietly in her second-floor apartment over the premises of what had been Shakespeare and Company and sometimes stayed at the International Students' Hostel, which was directed by her friend Sarah Watson, who also had been interned for a time at Vittel.

After the war it proved impossible for Sylvia to reopen her bookshop. T. S. Eliot writes in his memoir of her:

> Some of us in England, who appreciated the service which Sylvia, at her *librairie,* had rendered to contemporary English and American literature in France, would have liked to see Shakespeare and Company put on its feet again. But the British Council was powerless to help, as Sylvia was an American citizen; and the Americans had no organization comparable to the British Council. Nor were the auspices for such an undertaking so propitious as they had been twenty-five years before. Nor, I suspect, did Sylvia, after the hardships she had endured and the imprisonment which she had suffered, have the resiliency or the physical strength to resume her former role.

Eventually, Sylvia gave five thousand volumes that had been in the stock of Shakespeare and Company to the American Library, a former rival. Although without her bookshop, Sylvia did not languish after the war. She occupied herself with the well-being of her friends and the people of the quarter and began work on her memoirs—which became *Shakespeare and Company*—for Harcourt, Brace and Company. She cordially received students and specialists of the writers who had been or were her friends, but was always careful not to divulge details of their personal lives to the overcurious.

Needless to say, Sylvia Beach and Adrienne Monnier remained

the closest of friends, sharing their life in Paris and visiting Les Déserts together in the summer, as always before. Monnier continued to direct La Maison des Amis des Livres until 1951. She says in her autobiographical sketch in *Rue de l'Odéon*: "I was obliged to retire because of an infectious rheumatism that threatened me with paralysis; it was checked with great difficulty; I have remained very tired and obliged to take care of myself." She sold her business to two partners, under whose management it underwent a slow decline, which she watched without flinching, although she was troubled because the bookshop retained its old name. She hoped that the premises would in time be occupied by a shop dealing in Norman *armoires,* as long ago. In fact, after a further period under the management of a seller of secondhand books, what had been La Maison des Amis des Livres gave way to a surgical appliances store.

Despite her poor health, Monnier continued to write. The articles that she contributed to the *Lettres Nouvelles* in 1953 and 1954—most of them are in this collection—show an undiminished vigor and excellence. Her first illness was followed by a graver one: in September 1954, while descending from the plateau of La Féclaz after her summer vacation at Les Déserts she was stricken by an attack of vertigo and aural disturbances that were diagnosed as the characteristics of Ménière's Syndrome, symptoms of a disease of the inner ear. Her physical health declined radically in the following months and the symptoms became more acute. She was afflicted in particular by the delusion that she was hearing loud noises. She patiently and courageously underwent various medical treatments that had little effect; throughout this time she kept a meticulous journal of her decline that is difficult to read and impossible to quote. On the night of June 17, or early in the morning of June 18, 1955, convinced that her illness was incurable and unwilling to live in the state of total invalidism to which she knew she was inevitably condemned, she took a fatal dose of sleeping tablets; she died the following night.

In the final weeks of her life Adrienne Monnier had secretly and with great difficulty arranged her personal papers. Her final note, which she wrote in May, was found at the head of these after her death:

> I am putting an end to my days, no longer able to support the noises that have been martyrizing me for eight months, without counting the fatigue and the suffering that I have endured these recent years.

I am going to death without fear, knowing that I found a mother on being born here and that I shall likewise find a mother in the other life.

The news of her passing, in France and abroad, was greeted with reverence, sorrow, and love.

Alone, Sylvia Beach in her own last years received the honors that go to survivors, the official consecrations that must always seem in spirit to be somewhat at odds with the spirit of obscure beginnings. From March 11 to April 25, 1959, the cultural section of the United States Embassy in Paris sponsored an exhibition, "Les Années Vingt: Les Ecrivains Américains à Paris et leurs amis" ("The Twenties: American Writers in Paris and Their Friends") at the headquarters of the American Cultural Center in the Rue du Dragon near the Place St-Germain-des-Prés. Because most of the items on display—some six hundred photographs, letters, page proofs, first editions, and the like—belonged to Sylvia Beach and collectively signified her central position in the life of the decade, the show was as much a tribute to her as it was a retrospective survey. In the same year Harcourt, Brace published her memoirs, *Shakespeare and Company*, and in June, during the course of a visit to the United States, she received an honorary doctorate of letters from the University of Buffalo, to which she donated material from her Joyce collection. On June 16, 1962, Bloomsday, the anniversary of the day on which the action of *Ulysses* takes place, she was in Dublin to participate in the dedication of the Martello Tower at Sandycove, the setting of the opening of the novel, as a memorial to James Joyce.

In Paris Sylvia Beach continued to live in her apartment at 12 Rue de l'Odéon above the premises that Shakespeare and Company had once occupied. Here, on October 6, 1962, she was found dead, apparently of a heart attack, "kneeling but not brought down," as the friend who found her said; she had died a day or two before. Her body was cremated at Père Lachaise cemetery and her ashes were sent to Princeton, where they now rest. Her funeral service, which took place in the chapel of the Colombarium in the cemetery, was attended by crowds of mourners, many of them neighbors in her quarter who knew her not as a literary personality but simply as a friend whose kindness was unfailing.

And of Adrienne Monnier herself, what more is there that need or can be said here? Her own life, simple and profound—simple in its purpose, profound in its motives—has the configuration of a heroic legend and even a legend of saintliness. Her simplicity was that of an undivided mind and a whole heart that followed from girlhood on in the direction of a calling that she seems never to have doubted. We can trace this direction by the act, simple in itself, of describing the outward achievements of her vocation. As for the motives of her "whose life was so mysteriously moving," as Katherine Anne Porter has said, those motives that came "from such depths of feeling and intelligence they were hardly fathomable . . . but always to be believed in and loved," to these her work alone will bear witness. For the rest, all one has attempted has been to give back to Adrienne Monnier in the words of another language the gift that she gave so fully in the words of her own.

part one

Odéonia
The
Country of
Memory

La Maison des Amis des Livres

We founded La Maison des Amis des Livres with faith; each one of its details seems to us to correspond to a feeling, to a thought.

Business, for us, has a moving and profound meaning.

A shop seems to us to be a true magic chamber: at that instant when the passer-by crosses the threshold of the door that everyone can open, when he penetrates into that apparently impersonal place, nothing disguises the look of his face, the tone of his words; he accomplishes with a feeling of complete freedom an act that he believes to be without unforeseen consequences; there is a perfect correspondence between his external attitude and his profound self, and if we know how to observe him at that instant when he is only a stranger, we are able, now and forever, to know him in his truth; he reveals all the good will with which he is endowed, that is to say, the degree to which he is accessible to the world, what he can give and receive, the exact rapport that exists between himself and other men.

This immediate and intuitive understanding, this private fixing of the soul, how easy they are in a shop, a place of transition between street and house! And what discoveries are possible in a bookshop, through which inevitably pass, amid the innumerable passers-by, the Pleiades, those among us who already seem a bit to be "great blue persons," and who, with a smile, give the justification for what we call our best hopes.

Selling books, that seems to some people as banal as selling any sort of object or commodity, and based upon the same routine tradition that demands of the seller and the buyer only the gesture of exchanging money against the merchandise, a gesture that is accompanied, generally, by a few phrases of politeness.

We think, first of all, that the faith we put into selling books can be put into all daily acts; one can carry on no matter what business, no matter what profession, with a satisfaction that at certain moments has a real lyricism. The human being who is perfectly adapted to his function, and who works in harmony with others, experiences a fullness of feeling that easily becomes exaltation when he is in rapport with people situated upon the same level of life as himself; once he can communicate and cause what he experiences to be felt, he is multiplied, he rises above himself and strives to be as much of a poet as he can; that elevation, that tenderness, is it not the state of grace in which everything is illuminated by an eternal meaning? But if every conscious person can be exalted upon his calling and grasp the wonderful rapports that bind him to Society, what shall our own feelings not be for us, booksellers, who before every thought of gain and work that is based upon books, have loved them with rapture and have believed in the infinite power of the most beautiful!

Some mornings, alone in our bookshop, surrounded only by books arranged in their cases, we have remained contemplating them for moments on end. After a moment our eyes, fixed upon them, saw only the vertical and oblique lines marking the edges of their backs, discreet lines set against the gray wall like the straight strokes drawn by the hand of a child. Before this elementary appearance that is charged with a soul made up of all ideas and all images, we were pierced through by an emotion so powerful that it sometimes seemed to us that to write, to express our thoughts, would solace us; but at the moment when our hand sought for pen and paper—somebody entered, other people came afterward, and the faces of the day absorbed the great ardor of the morning.

We have often felt that "all grace of labor, and all honor, and all genius," as Claudel says in *La Ville [The City]*, were granted to us; in that work there are many other words besides that seem written for us, and we can say with Lala:

> As gold is the sign of merchandise,
> merchandise is also a sign
>   Of the need that summons it, of the
> effort that creates it,
>   And what you call exchange I call
> communion.

When we founded our house in November 1915, we had no business experience whatsoever, we did not even know bookkeeping, and along with that we were so afraid of passing for paltry tradespeople that we pretended without end to neglect our own interests, which was childishness besides.

It is ordinarily believed that life extinguishes enthusiasm, disappoints dreams, distorts first conceptions, and realizes a bit at random what has been offered to it. Nevertheless, we can declare that at the beginning of our undertaking, our faith and our enthusiasm were much less great than they are today. Our first idea was very modest: we sought only to start off a bookshop and a reading room devoted above all to modern works. We had very little money, and it was that detail that drove us to specialize in modern literature; if we had had a lot of money, it is certain that we would have wanted to buy everything that existed in respect to printed works and to realize a kind of National Library; we were convinced that the public demands a great quantity of books above all, and we thought that we had much audacity in daring to establish ourselves with hardly three thousand volumes when some reading-room catalogs announced twenty thousand, fifty thousand, and even a hundred thousand of them! The truth is that only one of our walls was furnished with books; the others were decorated with pictures, with a large old desk, and with a chest of drawers in which we kept wrapping paper, string, and everything we did not know where to put; our chairs were old chairs from the country that we still have. This bookshop hardly had the look of a shop, and that was not on purpose; we were far from suspecting that people would congratulate us so much in the future for what seemed to us an unfortunate makeshift.

We counted upon our first profits to increase our stock without end. These first profits were above all based upon the sale of new and secondhand books, for we did not dare to hope to find subscribers to our reading room until after several months.

One of the great problems of our commercial beginnings was the construction of an outside display stand for the secondhand sale. This operation required our presence for more than five minutes, during which we were exposed to the looks of the passers-by; we had to carry outside the trestles, the case, then the books and the reviews, which were old things that had come for the most part from family libraries. The first time that we made that display we were aroused to the point of anxiety, and when the last pile had been arranged we escaped hurriedly into the back room of the shop, just as if we had played a bad trick on the passers-by; we looked through a gap in the curtain at what was for us an extraordinary spectacle, the formation of a little group in front of the books; the faces that appeared behind the shop window sometimes made us burst out laughing, sometimes shiver with apprehension; if those people were to come in, address words to us! And here was an old lady who took a volume from the display and prepared herself to accomplish that grave act of becoming our first purchaser; one of us decided to emerge from the back room and stammered a ceremonious good day to the lady, who, with a very natural manner, showed what she had chosen—it was Henry Gréville's *L'Avenir d'Aline [The Future of Aline]*, marked at seventy-five centimes; she had the kindness not to haggle; if she had haggled the situation would have become painful: we would have been torn between the temptation to give her the volume so that the deal might be more quickly settled and the duty of maintaining our really very modest price to show her that we were serious booksellers who did not charge too much. It was necessary all the same to wrap the book, tie it up with string, take the money, give change out of a franc, thank effusively. That old lady at last perceived the extraordinary emotion that she was provoking; she went away more troubled than she wished to let it appear and did not come back.

In order to give people the temptation to take out a reading subscription, we had glued to the shop front a handwritten poster that included our terms for subscription and the list of the authors whose complete works we possessed. This list was a compromise between our likings and those of the public; we considered certain concessions necessary for our success. We were not wrong, so much the less because these concessions were sufficiently limited. Faith gains nothing by being fanatic. Furthermore, the spirit with which a house has been founded acts all by itself after a little while; it is enough not to let the little flame be extinguished.

In the practical domain some ideas had come to us at the very beginning that turned out to be rather good; for example, to cover the books with crystal paper, not to have them bound, not to stamp them, a barbarous custom that made them resemble animals marked for the slaughterhouse.

But the first of our ideas was, and is still, that the true business of a bookshop includes not only selling but lending, and that the two operations should be performed simultaneously. It is almost inconceivable that one can buy a work without being acquainted with it. To declare that everybody of a certain culture feels the need to have a personal library composed of the books that he loves and that these are good and faithful friends for him is to express a general sentiment; would one want to introduce into a circle of proven friends importunate or indifferent ones? That is what one risks doing in buying books that one has not read. It is true that one can always get rid of them, but very often one will keep a badly chosen volume so as not to have the annoyance of reselling it, sometimes at a tenth of the price one paid for it, and also because it furnishes. But after some disappointments of this kind, one puts new works to the side and swears only by the classics.

It will be said that on the whole one never buys a book entirely at random, that the name of the author, the publishing company, are almost sufficient indications, and that a well-read person can, by leafing through it, have a very clear understanding of its value. Certainly, the signature of a work is already a guarantee; furthermore, it is this guarantee that regulates almost the entire practice of bookshops; but it is surely not a good principle, it is the reason why so many authors are obliged to write only one or two good books and can afterward sleep upon their laurels; it is above all the reason for the obscurity in which new productions lie buried, whatever their value may be; it eliminates in a complete fashion the newcomers of literature. One will point out the example of works that found a just and powerful critic at the time of their appearance, but these cases are very rare; party spirit and intrigue count, alas, more than worth.

Everybody knows that Maeterlinck owed his relatively sudden fame to the article of a known writer. But a man like Gide attained a reputation only belatedly; would you believe that eighteen years were necessary in order to exhaust the first edition of *Nourritures terrestres [Fruits of the Earth]*? At the present time Jules Romains seems to us to be far from occupying the place that he deserves; granting that it is necessary to wait a long time, perhaps, before the *Odes et prières* and the *Manuel de déification* can be assimilated by everybody, *La Vie unanime [The Unanimous Life]*, *Europe*, and above all the prose works have not been transmitted to the hundredth part of the public that they could reach efficaciously if the organs of the bookshops were functioning healthily.

Do not believe that this state of affairs is an evil without remedy and that a man of genius must inevitably pass half of his life, or even his entire life, in obscurity. Certainly, even with the help of a bookseller he will not become known as early as his first work, "Such as to himself eternity has changed him," but he will find his public immediately—the elite of whom he is the spokesman and all the young people. At the age when a man still studies, when existence has not imposed a routine upon him, he is a creature of good will, and to a degree determined by the influence of his milieu, the condition of his knowledge, and the capacity of his intelligence, he enjoys a state of grace in which he can understand life and the images of life. For three years we have been giving the young people who come to our place works to read that seem reserved for a small elite; we always see them become moved by the poems of Paul Valéry and Léon-Paul Fargue, by Valery Larbaud's *Barnabooth*, by Charles Vildrac's *Livre d'amour [Book of Love]*, and by Luc Durtain's *Etape nécessaire [Necessary Stage]*, for example, and nevertheless these authors are most often unknown to them when we speak to them about them for the first time.

It is therefore necessary that young people be able to read what is contemporary to them and acquire the books that will remain their great friends through life. For this there is no need to try to create vast impersonal enterprises that are incapable of providing influences, and therefore cannot help people to progress, and that are incapable of receiving any, and therefore cannot progress themselves.

What must be created, what must be assisted are the bookshop-libraries that do not tend to satisfy a large public but rather a group that it may be possible to know individually and to serve perfectly. The ideal would be that at the head of each bookshop there were only one person, helped to the greatest extent possible, but in continual rapport with the public.

It is truly indispensable that a house devoted to books be founded and directed conscientiously by someone who unites with an erudition that is as vast as possible a love for the spirit of what is new, and who, without falling into the wrongheadedness of any kind of snobbery, is ready to assist the new truths and forms.

So we have understood the task of the bookseller, we have applied ourselves to carry it out as best we can, and our results have certainly gone beyond our expectations. It is true that we founded our house in the most studious and the most charming quarter of Paris; we immediately discovered there a public that has love and respect for books, that has understood and assisted our efforts.

Would we have discovered that in other streets, in other cities? We do not dare to declare that we would have. Nevertheless, it seems to us that in no matter what quarter of a city, for every intelligent bookshop based upon the principle of lending and selling there is a public whose taste it is easy to form.

Have confidence in the good will of people, be sure that they will respect and follow everything you shall accomplish with faith, patience, and order; understand them through constant observation, give them as much of yourself as possible, you will see that they are not so different, so far from you, and that, in short, to live in them is to live more fully in oneself.

Here then, built in a time of destruction, is La Maison des Amis des Livres. Adrienne Monnier wrote these pages there in August 1918. Outside, the menace is less great, but here, in the midst of books that guard all living forms like the animals of the ark, she was preserved from revolt and from fear, she acquired the certainty that everything abides and grows beyond the nights of sleep and death, and that everything is faithful to the best will.

From *Rue de l'Odéon*; first printed for La Maison des Amis des Livres (1920).

Valéry in the Rue de l'Odéon

Paul Valéry came to the Rue de l'Odéon for the first time in 1917.

My bookshop was still in its infancy (we were hardly two years old); it was Fargue who had spoken to him about it—Fargue, who had come in 1916 and was already an old friend.

But Fargue was not with him. I believe that it was Paul Poujaud who accompanied him that day of I no longer know what month—May, perhaps, or the end of April: it was one of the year's first days of beautiful weather.

He appeared early in the afternoon, behind the shop window, which he considered a moment from outside while exchanging remarks with his companion. I already knew how to recognize men of letters by their way of looking at the window; Valéry's was the most discreet that I had yet seen: he looked at it like a man who has really "killed the marionette," but his eyes said literature, they said it in a singular manner, even, according to the nature of their rays

—how shall I say it? The Valérian spirit whispers the word to me: cathodic.

Then he entered and named himself: Paul Valéry. What happiness!

I knew the importance of the man who was standing before me. Fargue had often spoken to me about him—Fargue, who knew all the poems of the *Conque* and the *Centaure*, and who had once told me: "Our greatest poet is Valéry, you will see what I am telling you, Adrienne, you know that my nose (he touched his nose) never deceives me." I believed him all the more because I had read *La Soirée avec Monsieur Teste* in the fourth issue of *Vers et Prose*, of which I owned a large supply, having bought the entire stock of the review from Paul Fort.

This text had made upon me the impression that it makes upon everybody: that it is a magic text. Nothing, in my opinion, produces more effects than these pages, which are perhaps unique in literature. Marvelous and profoundly transforming effects: afterward one is no longer what one was before. In it the master of the tribe gives us a supreme initiation. He slaps us and marks upon our brow a sign of dust. His words express a wisdom that is ancient and very modern at the same time. Monsieur Teste circulates in the midst of the sad and hurrying passers-by of a great, besmirched city (one thinks of the first pictures of Bonnard) and speaks like Lao-tzu.

I do not remember what I said to my august visitor. I surely expressed my reverent admiration to him, and no doubt I spoke to him about the institution of the *potassons,* which occupied us a great deal at that time. He must have lent a benevolent ear to my remarks, as I have a note from him dating back to that same year, 1917, which mentions the *potassons* favorably.

About half past three he took out his watch and left, for he had to be at Monsieur Lebey's at four o'clock.

It seems to me that this visit preceded a bit the publication of *La Jeune Parque.* In any case, I had not read the poem when I saw Valéry for the first time; but André Breton had spoken to me about it, after having heard it read by the author himself at Jean Royère's place. Breton said that it was "transparent" and "gray"; he moreover gave a pronounced emphasis to that "gray."

When I had the slim volume between my hands I was at first less enthusiastic than I was baffled.

La Jeune Parque, I saw her, I see her still, as a strange figure, the strangest, in fact, cut not in marble but in a kind of porphyry. Do you know those Roman statues where the face and the visible parts of the body are white, and the clothing is a veined red? Here it is the clothing and the decoration that are white, of a scintillating and icy whiteness, through which in places shows the rose of roses, while the face and the whole body throb and contract beneath impassioned mineral veins.

A poem in which the classic and the baroque are joined together. A work so mysterious that it whets the mind without ever sating it, disclosing as many marvels as the looks one gives to it.

Fargue, who was greatly smitten with this *Jeune Parque*, read it many times over at his friends' houses. He had read it from the proofs at Arthur Fontaine's and Jeanne Muhlfeld's, readings at which I was not present, but of which I had been given accounts. I attended a meeting that took place at Aurel's some time after the publication. This time Fargue delivered a lecture and did not read the poem. A woman performer whose name I no longer remember was entrusted with it. Valéry, who was not present at the opening of the meeting (his business with Monsieur Lebey did not leave him free until after eight o'clock), arrived during the reading. He told us afterward that as he was climbing the stairs he heard the cries that the interpreter was making and said to himself anxiously: "It's not possible, they're murdering somebody—and it was my Fate!"

The first Valéry meeting that we organized in the Rue de l'Odéon took place in 1919: Saturday, April 12, 1919.

We had been thinking about it all winter, and it demanded preparations without end. Fargue had decided to say "important" things in his preliminary lecture. He was going to show the people who would be there what stuff he was made of—"what wood he warmed himself with"—and he intended to have them warm themselves! As a matter of fact, he spoke above all about the elite and their duties. As Daniel Halévy described it in an article that he devoted to us, it was militant, certainly, with a military march— drums beating!

There were four of us, amateur readers—no actors, no! There was Fargue, André Breton, who was wearing a uniform (the war was not over), myself, and Gide.

Fargue had told me: "It is absolutely necessary that Gide be one of us: he reads like nobody else." Gide did not refuse, but he did not want to be announced on the program; he would read only if, if, and if; it was above all the state of his throat, which was worrying him, that throat which even now—

Therefore our printed program announced a lecture by Fargue and readings by: himself, who would deliver fragments of *La Jeune Parque* and *La Soirée avec Monsieur Teste*; André Breton, who would lend his hammering voice to "Eté" ["Summer"], "Le Rameur" ["The Rower"], and "La Pythie" ["The Pythian Sibyl"]; and myself, who had chosen "Aurore" ["Dawn"] and "Le Cantique des colonnes" ["The Canticle of the Columns"].

We had typewritten copies of the poems that had not yet appeared in books and reviews. That was the case of "La Pythie," which had been destined for Gide. But he had given us so little hope that we had thought it wiser to assign it to Breton.

As if by a miracle, Gide was really there, really on time, and simply decided that he would read "La Pythie" himself. He added to it, to crown our pleasure, "La Caresse" and "L'Insinuant." He delivered the latter poem with an unforgettable artistry, as journalists say. His voice still haunts our ears:

> Oh curves, meander,
> The liar's secrets.

He seemed to offer in that manner—with what a smile—an easy quarry for those who would see in him a prince of evil.

I recall that before he began the reading of "La Pythie" he complained about insufficient lighting. In fact, the light fell feebly enough from the ceiling. I did not have a portable electric lamp, and anyway there was no wall outlet. Literally wild, I went in search of a candelabrum that I kept in the room in back of the shop in case of a power failure. I awkwardly extended it to him, and he seized hold of it nervously. While reading he moved it several times from right to left and from left to right, passing it under his nose, lighting from beneath his face that was a prey to that Pythian sybil with her "nostrils hardened by incense." It made one think of some Eleusinian torch, and it was very impressive.

God, when one thinks of it, what a meeting!

From *Rue de l'Odéon*; first published in *Terre des Hommes* (October 27, 1945).

First Encounters with Léon-Paul Fargue

I am trying to see Fargue again as he appeared to me for the first time.

That was in February 1916. I had been a bookseller for only

three months. One of my first customers, May Raynaud, had invited me to her parents' house one Sunday afternoon in order to meet him.

I was ravished by the thought of becoming acquainted with him. I had read his two collections, *Poèmes* and *Pour la musique,* which were numbered among the jewels of the young and so attractive *Nouvelle Revue Française.*

It seems to me that he arrived at an almost normal hour, toward six o'clock. He had put us at the beginning of his round; as on every Sunday, he had a lot of people to see in the evening and late into the night.

His face inspired in me a curious feeling that was warm and uneasy at the same time. Doubtless he was as one might have imagined him, but with so many more things that harassed and outran one's attention.

He appeared to be more than his age (I believe that he was thirty-nine years old) because of a baldness that was not newborn but adolescent. A beautiful fringe remained on each side of his head; an abundant lock of hair had been arranged over a vast forehead, but the pate was already appearing broadly. This state of his hair, which preoccupied him a great deal as I saw later on, hardly changed during the thirty years that I knew him. It was never seen to whiten, it remained always as brown. The arranged lock of hair lost some of its parts, but it remained firm at its post and absolutely opposed the possibility of calling him bald.

So I had in front of me a large, round head, not round like a ball but like a dome. The skull was high and crowned well the broad and circular forehead constructed above vigorous although slender eyebrows. A powerful noodle, no doubt, but sensitive, or rather full of sensitive points. What an imagination! What a memory! The forehead showed neither wrinkles, nor veins, nor bumps, and still it betrayed a sort of hidden life that I am very much at a loss to describe—there were downs, moistnesses, traces, hardly visible swellings that disclosed the presence of trolls.

How difficult his look was to understand! It was more engaging than tender, and like an enemy's. It was slightly squint-eyed, a sign of devilry, but it also showed an astonishing hypocrisy. It was covered, uncovered, covered again. It was enough to put you at your wits' end, as much or as little as you might have of them.

At that time Fargue wore a charming Debussyan beard—I found

it pleasing. One saw little of his mouth; however, it appeared to be firm and rather thin; the lower lip, which was flat and slightly protruding, shone like that of gourmands and liars. His nose was noble, solidly aquiline.

His voice was superb—deep, harmonious, of a beautiful metal. He was the master of it, he regulated it like an instrument, he drew perfect intonations from it. It was his voice above all that he used in order to seduce; it arose from the depths and went to the depths; it had a sort of manual dexterity. In discussion it was insistent and was accompanied by gestures that went contrary to itself—kindly, a little awkward, as touching as the games one teaches babies to play with their hands, imitating the movements of little marionettes.

His hands were as accomplished as his voice, although managed in a completely different way. I never saw them so much as on the day of our first encounter: he gave them to me so that I might read their lines. They were beautiful, rather fleshy, well proportioned; the fingers had rather square tips, their swollen bases were feathered on the outer side by a few stray hairs. Their nails had a remarkable form; they were neither too long nor too arched, they were solid and elegant at the same time. The thumb was that of a good sort, not the least bit jealous or violent. The palm was only slightly lined; the essential lines had a delicate and faint delineation; the head line was broken. The Mount of Venus was medium sized and finely patterned.

His whole hand had an extraordinary softness, it was as if it were made of little cushions. Its skin was unimaginably soft; its palm had that sort of pigmentation that is characteristic of those who are very sensitive—it was covered with minuscule pink, eyelike spots that moved imperceptibly like a carpet from the depths of the sea, like a throng of little lights on the lookout. I have never seen such a thing with anyone else. Here, I could not doubt it, was the sign of his mediumship, the secret of his poetry, which swarmed with the very secrets of nature.

Yes, his hands said almost everything about him. When he held out his palms to me, he asked me: "I'm going to go mad, isn't that right?" "Oh, no!" I answered him, "You're already very much so."

In spite of those hands that were so soft and almost reassuring, I was struck from the first day by his look of being a courtier, a look that he always had in society. His corpulence—he was a bit pot-bellied, although he was big and well built—would have been marvelously accommodated by the beautiful and ample clothing of other times. He would also have done very well as a sultan or as a rajah—with a turban the world would have been his!

Such as it was, the richness of his temperament struck one at the same time as his knowledge and his calculation. His naïveté, as with Stendhal, was accompanied by an excess of study. Nothing came forth from him that had not been cooked and recooked. He did not serve up the live and bleeding heart in his breast without preparations that went from bourgeois cooking to the wildest sauces. Like certain chefs, he imposed his dishes upon you; they were not always those that one would have liked.

I very much regret not having known him earlier. In the number of the *Feuilles Libres* that Marcel Raval devoted to him (the most beautiful number in homage that has ever been published) there is a photo of him, dated 1907, that touches me every time I look at it. He was thirty-one years old. How sympathetic he was then, how direct his look seemed! He was really the man of his first poems. How, in less than ten years, had he managed to change to such a point? To be sure, he had lost his father and Charles-Louis Philippe. After a marvelous period of travels with Larbaud (in which he dissipated all the money inherited from his father), the latter had started out for foreign places, still rich, leaving him poor. He had experienced grave disappointments in his affections. One of his friends, powerful and fortunate, had made game of him, he believed. He had just missed a good marriage. He had lost his sweetheart. The war was on. He had a great deal of trouble supporting himself and his mother. In addition, he had on his back a glassware factory that had done very well in his father's time, but that gave him only worries.

When I knew him he was bitter and habitually ill-natured. He had kept all of his desires but he had no more illusions. His songbirds had been wiped out, as Pichette would say, and as he might have said himself. He had decided to defend himself and make everybody pay for it; if those who ought to pay for it escaped him, he would make up for his losses with the others, those whom he held in his hands like hostages.

He would have sold his soul to the devil in order to be able to avenge certain humiliations—I do not say this lightly.

No, you could not step on his feet any longer. He had never done what is necessary in order to arrive, but he would do it. He would have society with him, that of the salons and the officials. He would be decorated, why not he as much as another? His comrades would no longer snub him. His uncle was going to see if he was a good-for-nothing. His concierge would no longer eye him contemptuously from head to foot, it was he that would eye *him* contemptuously from head to foot.

All that was said and chewed over and over again from the beginning of our relationship, not in friendly confidences but in the monologues of a vilified John Lackland.

The very next day after our encounter at the Raynauds he came to the bookshop. He brought with him a dozen copies of *Tancrède*.

Tancrède was that priceless little book whose existence one knew about, but which almost nobody had seen. May Raynaud, who was a bibliophile, had asked him how it could be procured. He had promised it to her and he had also promised to entrust some copies to me for sale.

Here the thing is: it is a very pretty little book; the cover is white, it is made of thick Arches paper with a coarse grain. The title is golden yellow. Instead of a company name there is simply "Paris," and underneath "1911." Only two hundred copies were made of it. Larbaud paid the expenses and it was printed in Saint-Pourçain-sur-Sioule, perfectly, at Raymond's.

The epigraph reads:

> The conquering captains have a strong odor.
>
> —André Gide

It is curious, in *Paludes* Gide attributes the sentence to his "young friend Tancrède." The mystery received no explanations, neither then nor afterward.

I agreed to sell the copies that Fargue brought for six francs (double the initial price). I would not pay for them until after I had sold them and I would have a fifty percent commission; that was very advantageous, but I wondered to myself if I would ever arrive at placing the dozen. I was wrong to worry. The copies found admirers. A time came even when there were no more of them, and it was at that moment, naturally, that the demand was strongest.

At the time he came to the bookshop, Fargue made the acquaintance of my friend Suzanne Bonnierre, who kept the house with me. There was no sympathy between them. She was not moved by the misfortunes that he told us. He frightened her and often, after his departure, she had fits of weeping. She reproached me a great deal for having collected such a friend, who came every day, at the end of the day, when we were tired, and who remained until ten o'clock, nailed to his chair.

It is true that at the beginning of our relationship Fargue showed very little his already celebrated wit, of which I had had glimpses at the Raynauds. He was only oppressive.

But that somber climate cleared up quickly. After a few weeks Fargue understood that he did not have two sisters of charity in front of him. We could all the less feel compassion because he was in the prime of life. Before him who had lived so much, suffered so much, who had no resignation, we felt our youth (I was twenty-three years old, Suzanne was twenty-five) not as an advantage but as an inferiority.

We belonged to a completely different world—that of the little people who are weighed down by the law of work, while he aimed at being the idle bourgeois, that is to say, the lord. He habitually crushed us with his relationship. I do not know how it came, the day when he understood.

Perhaps, that day, he arrived earlier in the afternoon and surprised us at our functions as booksellers, speaking to the first subscribers to our reading room, exchanging books and ideas.

He saw clearly that I was mad about literature. Suzanne admired Jules Renard and Charles-Louis Philippe above all.

There, he knew what end to start again with.

He knew what friend he must bring in order to make himself understood and loved, to find again, with us, his poet's soul.

He said one morning, a bit before noon—he had made an effort to arrive in the morning—"Ah! how my good Philippe would have loved this house! He would have come here every day."

We broke for the first time the bread of friendship.

From *Rue de l'Odéon*; first published in *Mercure de France* (February 1948).

Pierre Reverdy

Another poet whom I liked a great deal then, and whom I like more and more, is Pierre Reverdy.

He came regularly in 1917 to bring us *Nord-Sud*, the review that he was putting out with so much valor.

Valor—there is a word that is used a lot for new reviews that have short and beautiful lives. In Reverdy's case the word has its full meaning, I assure you.

When I now consider the collection of *Nord-Sud*, which I have carefully kept, it seems to me the model for avant-garde reviews. Its appearance was modest; for reasons of economy there was no cover, it was the first of its sixteen pages that took the place of one. The title stood out forcefully, black upon white, in big letters of the most simple kind. The name of the director appeared nowhere; you only read at the bottom of the cover: "Address everything that concerns the review, 12, Rue Cortot, 18e" (that was Reverdy's address). The price was relatively high: fifty centimes, while *Sic* cost only twenty centimes.

Nord-Sud showed a serious and coherent spirit; it wanted to coincide with pictorial cubism. Its team was well made up, you rediscovered almost the same names in every number: Apollinaire, Max Jacob, Paul Dermée, Vincent Huidobro.

Apollinaire gave to it some of the most beautiful poems of *Calligrammes.* "La Victoire," published in the first number, is a genuine lettrist manifesto in an early form.

It was in *Nord-Sud* that André Breton, Louis Aragon, and Philippe Soupault began seriously (in *Sic* it was not very serious). . . .

The manifestos of *Nord-Sud* were signed by Reverdy, naturally, and by Paul Dermée. Reverdy spoke above all about cubism. It was Dermée who composed the literary manifesto of the first number under the title "When Symbolism Was Dead." They were looking for the formula of a new classicism based upon inner constraint—no development—the emotion caught at its source. Among other things it said: "What efforts do talented actors not make when they want to be moving, so that a beautiful cry may spring from the words of a dramatic speech? Why not for our own part preserve the beautiful cry and sacrifice the speech?"

Nobody realized this program better than Reverdy. His poems brought about a new style of emotion that is in harmony with the cubism of cities: uniform shapes with the neutral, somber colors of public buildings. His black is the black of night. His white: cruel light of plaster walls—snow—cold. His gray, so much gray, is infinite dust. The feminine soul of the poet, a friend of tears, is forever moved by the dust against which women struggle bodily, desperately, every day. Dust that is fatigue itself, before which human beings with their vertical bodies are without defense.

Almost all the poems of Reverdy are tragic, they have a denudation that is without equal.

They have a hallucinatory character that comes from the extreme fixity of the gaze upon the object-sentiment. As in the pictures of Braque, the object has a strong, dark outline and appears with its elementary form and its magnetic charge. This apparition has nothing in common with the phantoms imagined by Bosch or Michaux, which are terrible phantoms but which are also diverting because of their number and variety. No, it is a solitary phantom, surreal, fed by the matter of the object and by the cerebral substance of the seer. One who gazes in this manner is in a trance of fright; panic-stricken, he feels that his energy is leaving him and passing away beyond the human. The phenomenon often has the nature of a nightmare; it can lead to the horrors of a splitting of the personality. There is, with Reverdy, in this sense, a kind of asceticism that he has practiced to the limits of the endurable.

No doubt we must see at the origin of this asceticism the sacrament of misfortune, poverty that is at once imposed and embraced.

La Lucarne ovale, written in 1916 during the war, opens solemnly with these lines:

> At that time coal
> had become as precious
> and rare as nuggets of gold
> and I wrote in an attic
> where the snow, falling
> through gaps in the roof,
> turned blue.

Farther on, in the center of a page, these words alone:

> Winter chased me
> in the streets.

And again this:

> You can no longer
> sleep peacefully
> when you have once
> opened your eyes.

Yes, many of Reverdy's poems, the first ones above all, resemble a room of misery; in the middle is sitting a man who gazes fixedly before him. You have to make an effort to speak to him, he makes an effort to speak to you; he tells you in the manner of the poor: "Won't you take the trouble of coming in?" In fact it is not without trouble that you do come in and confront so much trouble. But if you do, what a communion! That room of misery is like the ancient "fires of misery," in which everything is put out so that the new fire may be relit. . . .

Reverdy had a great influence upon the young of that time. He gave those who approached him a weight of seriousness that they would not have had without him. In short, Apollinaire was the brilliant, lighthearted father, whose successes and escapades one is eager to match. And Reverdy was the humble, obscure mother, living by the very life of the heart. Did he not say of himself in *Le Gant de crin*: "I am obscure like feeling"?

Those devilish children (the future Dadas) infinitely loved and admired him. It was to him that Aragon dedicated, in *Feu de joie [Bonfire]*, his first collection, the poem that tries to be the most beautiful, the longest, the most sincere, the one that he called "Lever" ["Rising"], like the rising of the sun. It was also to him that Breton dedicated, in *Clair de terre [Earthlight]*, the famous "Tournesol" ["Sunflower"], of which he was to make the mysterious pivot of *L'Amour fou [Mad Love]*.

As it stands out from what I have just said, the influence of Reverdy was first of all fundamental, in the full sense of the word. The forms and the plays of forms, all the beautiful little inventions —it was Apollinaire who had command of them.

From "Mémorial de la rue de l'Odéon," *Rue de l'Odéon*; first published as "Pierre Reverdy en 1917," *Les Lettres Françaises* (June 14, 1946).

André Breton

When I became acquainted with André Breton at the very beginning of 1916, he was wearing the horizon-blue uniform of an auxiliary doctor of the army. He was staying in I no longer know what provincial town, but he came rather often to Paris. He did not yet know Aragon or Soupault. He, like the two others, was at first a transient customer, then an assiduous customer of my bookshop.

We had long conversations right away. I really believe that we were never in agreement. Even on the subjects where we should have come to an understanding—Novalis, Rimbaud, occultism—he had exclusive views that bewildered me completely. He was much more "advanced" than I. I certainly seemed reactionary to him, while in the eyes of my ordinary customers I was a revolutionary figure: I had just discovered Romains and unanimism, and I was plunged in the unanimist experience just as others, a few years later, were going to be plunged in the surrealist experience.

Breton was still far from being a leader of a school; he even accepted being a disciple—a disciple of Apollinaire, whom he loved fanatically. He tried hard to win me over to his clan, but instead of shaking my convictions he only reinforced them. Furthermore, we were not exactly of the same generation; I was older than he by three or four years. (Yes, I was twenty-four and he must have been about twenty-one.)

Besides, I felt the need for violent novelty less than he. I did not have to react against the despotism of a bourgeois milieu, having been granted wonderful parents who had always left me free and even helped me to become so; my mother, in particular, was always ready to go more quickly and farther than myself.

Nor did I have to react against society; they did not put me in uniform and they did not send me off to war. I was too young and too taken with literature to feel a solidarity with a world other than that of books, in which I was happy, as long as nobody disturbed me.

Apollinaire, in my opinion, left no time to breathe. Why say, "Let's go more quickly, in the name of God, always more quickly"? Why wish, at any price, for "new sounds" and that "everything have a new name"? Things are new only insofar as there are old things that follow them with their eyes.

The new spirit—but the spirit is always new. It is the forms in which it becomes incarnate and which it leaves behind itself that grow old. Invention without respite heaps up cast-off effects and does not even give surprise the time to be a surprise.

We know very well that the machine is opening a new era and that we must adapt ourselves to it. But we do not adapt ourselves to it by going faster than itself and by throwing to it in advance as fodder what it will not perhaps demand of us.

Otherwise, I was far from being insensitive to the poetic genius of the author of *Alcools*; he was a very graceful genius-cat, very mischievous and very supple; he could throw himself from the seventh floor and land upon his paws, and I believe that he rather liked to see the others break their paws.

At the beginning of our relationship Breton was experiencing the domination of Mallarmé as much as that of Apollinaire. He was fascinated by *La Dernière Mode [The Latest Fashion]*, which he knew marvelously well. Was he not in contact with Dr. Bonniot? I no longer recall. But I know that he frequented Jean Royère, who had already published verse by him in the *Phalange*. It was at Jean Royère's that he heard, in 1917, Paul Valéry read *La Jeune Parque [The Young Fate]*, which was still in manuscript, and he was the first to speak to me about it. To the questions that I asked him on this subject, he simply answered me: "It's transparent and it's gray"— an impression that I did not find when I read the poem myself. Breton was struck by its classicism and I was struck by its drama. Through the icy form I felt the life of the "convulsive," "fixed-exploding" Fate, as the future author of *L'Amour fou [Mad Love]* might have said.

Let us come back to Mallarmé. Breton, then, was charmed and haunted by him to the point that he wrote his letters taking the courteous and precious tone of the Master—very much old France. I was astonished a good deal by that, I who was always simple and familiar. His handwriting also plunged me into revery: studied, even, smoothed out like hair with fine curls. It was, it seems, an angelic handwriting.

His physiognomy went with his handwriting in more than one sense. It was beautiful, of a beauty that was not angelic but archangelic. Let me say parenthetically that angels are gracious and archangels are serious. Angels are always smiling, they are made of a smile, their work is kindly, while archangels generally have heavy tasks: people to banish from paradise, dragons to slay, etc. His face was massive, well drawn; his hair was worn rather long and was thrown back with nobility; his look remained foreign to the world and even to himself—it was not very much alive, it had the color of jade.

Breton did not smile, but he sometimes laughed with a short and sardonic laugh that welled up when he spoke without disturbing the features of his face, as with women who are careful of their beauty.

Yes, he was clearly of the archangelic type, like T. S. Eliot, with whom he has no resemblance except that of belonging to that family of figures you see rearing up at the porches of cathedrals.

The face of the English poet is certainly less impassive; it is more tormented, but with a torment that is potential, petrified.

As for Breton, violence makes a statue of him. He is a sword bearer. He has the immobile diligence of mediums.

How apparent that was when he was in the presence of Apollinaire! I remember one or two truly unforgettable scenes: Apollinaire seated in front of me, chatting in a familiar way, and Breton standing, his back against the wall, his look fixed and panic, seeing not the man who was present but the Invisible, the black god, whose command he must receive.

What I say here may seem curious, but it would seem very natural in the Orient. The Hindus, for example, know better than anybody the mystery of the rapport between master and disciple. Think of the second interview between Ramakrishna and Vivekananda: the latter, simply at the contact of his master's right foot, is seized by a sort of terror. He sees, according to his own account, the walls of the room whirl around and fall down; there remains before him only nothingness, like a gulf in which his self risks being swallowed up.

I do not say that things reached that degree for Apollinaire and Breton. No more do I say that they were saints, although there is a contrary saintliness, and that type is properly in fashion in our epoch, which is, as Monsieur Guénon would say, the extreme period of Kali Yuga, otherwise called the reign of the Antichrist.

Perhaps the most remarkable thing about Breton's face was the heavy and excessively fleshy mouth. Its lower lip, whose development was almost abnormal, revealed, according to the data of classic physiognomy, a strong sensuality governed by the sexual element; but the firmness of that mouth and its delineation, which was rigorous even in excess, indicated a very self-possessed person who would combine duty and pleasure in a singular fashion, or rather would make them overlap.

I was, at that time, very much drawn to the practice of the sciences that are called occult. I did not fail to look at the lines of his hand also. One thing struck me more than anything else about it; that was the oddity of the head line. This line clearly indicated the predilection of the subject for madness and everything that approaches it. I confess that that frightened me a bit, for I was not to be one of the motivating figures of Kali Yuga. Yes, that frightened me and put me on my guard.

And yet what charm and what authority that young man had! His friends later on all submitted to his influence. Jacques Prévert has noted that they loved him like a woman. He really had what Freud would call the libidinous power of the leader. I felt it, I too, but I only took more care to defend myself from it. Yet there was no merit for me in resisting; my resistance organized itself. My merit would have been greater, perhaps, if I had taken a few steps in his company.

But upon reflection, I did take them, those few steps, since I did not hesitate to accept the general stock of the review *Littérature* when it was founded in 1919. The directorship of it was at Breton's address: Place du Panthéon, at the Hôtel des Grands Hommes. The Rue de l'Odéon figures modestly on the back of the cover: "For sales, address La Maison des Amis des Livres."

From "Mémorial de la rue de l'Odéon," *Rue de l'Odéon*; first published as "Un Portrait d'André Breton," *France-Amérique* (June 23, 1946).

Jean Cocteau

God knows that I have affection for Jean Cocteau, and admiration also; I have them even more at present than formerly. He was such a spoiled child! He is a poet, certainly, more in prose than in verse, in my opinion. He has a style that is very much his own, with a false, heady virginity, while in versified poetry his artifices, because they are reinforced by the initial artifice of the verse, are carried to a point where they make one's head ache. Personally, he gives me a migraine. It may be that I am unjust, but from the moment that you have a migraine it is difficult to be just.

So at the time of *Le Cap de Bonne-Espérance*, he had just discovered modern poetry and the fathers of that poetry. He forswore *Le Prince frivole* and *La Danse de Sophocle*, which contained, however, very pretty things. He must be praised without reserve for having thrown himself at the avant-garde; he lost nothing of his natural gifts by doing so and he acquired more than one cockade.

It is never he that first mounts the breach, but it is always he that plants the flag, and to be sure there really has to be someone to do it.

In composing *Le Cap* he probably wanted to plant the flag of *Un Coup de dés*. Mallarmé is at the origin of the typographical explorations of Apollinaire, and of Reverdy above all, beginning with *La Lucarne ovale [The Oval Attic Window]*—Reverdy, who was a proofreader I believe. With Apollinaire the exploration was kaleidoscopic and led to all the fantasies of the ideograms.

With Reverdy it was well thought out and fertile; a long current of influence started from it. Apollinaire had suppressed punctuation, Reverdy reinstated it by means of blank spaces judiciously set in the text, so that each poem might have its special form and reveal "a superior order."

Cocteau did not hesitate to make a long poem by employing at one and the same time this procedure, which was still unknown to the public, and the personage of Roland Garros, who was well known to the public, better than known—enjoying the prestige of aviation and the hero's glory. One could not have more wings! This was to make very visible to the first person who came along that one was "an aviator in ink" who had the right to say: "I tease eternity."

Le Cap, to tell the truth, was an interesting poem. As in everything that Cocteau does, the explorations and the effects were numerous, stunning, and even personal. If he had not at the start put the label "Dante and Virgil" upon Garros and himself (how he must have questioned himself in order to find out which of the two became him better—Dante or Virgil?) we would only have better appreciated the imitation of cocks, swallows, cockatoos, and airplane noises that studded the poem. There was even a lettrist passage that would have been a staggering novelty if Pierre Albert-Birot had not been the first to employ the sound of letters in this way.

And Cocteau read marvelously well, with his famous metallic voice that acts like a megaphone.

I shall say a word or two about the way in which this reading was organized.

Eight or ten days before there had been an avant-garde poetry and music session at the Rosenberg gallery in the Rue de la Baume, that museum of cubism. I no longer remember the program, except for this: that some works of our dear Satie were presented there.

At this session, which took place one Sunday afternoon, there were many personalities, among them Gide, who was the center of attraction of all looks. It was on that day that I happened to perpetrate a witty expression that had such an eighteenth-century turn of phrase that I shall risk relating it here.

As Gide said to me, not without a slight irony, "But there are only geniuses here!" I answered him with a deftness that still astonishes me (for as much as himself I excel in "the wit of the staircase"): "But, dear master, you are looking no farther than the end of your nose!"

Well, upon the departure of this gathering (a departure that was marked, like all very Parisian departures, by the arrival of Fargue), Cocteau joined me and said pretty much this to me, "Gide would like me to read *Le Cap* at the Rue de l'Odéon."

Le Cap, it was being talked about very much. Its author had already read it in several salons. There had been many telephone calls on this subject in order to induce Valéry, in particular, to say something nice.

Good, if that was what Gide wanted, how could I not want it myself?

To Gide our Cocteau hurried to say, "Adrienne Monnier would very much like me to read *Le Cap* at the Rue de l'Odéon in your presence. You will come, won't you?" Gide quite simply agreed.

We saw almost immediately, Gide and I, that we had been hoodwinked. We were less angry than amused by it, and we decided to let it go at that, all the more because it was not a question of a big meeting but of an almost intimate reading, one afternoon, in the back room of the shop. My only vengeance was to ask Cocteau to bring the cakes (each meeting would be followed by a snack with cakes, sandwiches, and port). In general, I supplied everything; this time I was going to provide only the port.

Cocteau had a *bridge* delivered from Rebattet's. The *bridges* of Rebattet's were, if you remember them, wonderful chocolate cakes. This big, extremely soft, velvety cake was not very easy to divide and eat; we would have needed plates and forks, which I did not have at the bookshop (in such cases I always ordered petits fours). We got a lot of chocolate on our fingers, then on our handkerchiefs.

There were easily about thirty of us at this reading. There were the Godebskis, Fargue, and Satie, naturally. Cocteau had asked me above all not to invite society women. There were only a few of them, who were inevitable because of their attachment to the house. On the other hand, he had insisted that I have all the young people possible come. There was no lack of girls, I had invited all my friends, but in respect to young men, apart from Marc Allégret, who accompanied Gide, only Breton and Soupault were to be seen, both of them still wearing their horizon-blue uniforms. They held themselves very straight, radiating hostility. Fortunately the society women were there to cry out "genius."

From "Mémorial de la rue de l'Odéon," *Rue de l'Odéon.*

With Gide at Hyères

September 1921

Thursday the 1st—Morning nine o'clock, Sylvia sees Gide on the beach! Runs to tell me in the bathroom, where I am; I come out as quickly as possible, throw myself upon the balcony: no Gide. Was Sylvia dreaming?—But there he is, notebooks and a book under his arm, making his way toward the bathing cabins—Sylvia goes down quickly to say hello to him; he gives her a very warm greeting, asks her: "Where are *the others*?"

Gide bathes, then goes to settle down on the terrace—I go to bathe at ten thirty with a lifebelt and a cork jacket; he watches me from the terrace—After I have dressed I go to talk to him. [He has the] kindness to tell me that he will remain because we are here, asks me how much time exactly we are going to be here. I tell him that our friends do not know about our stay, that we did not want anybody's company, but that his arrival delights us: we were just rereading *Les Caves [The Caves of the Vatican]*, we were talking about him without a stop; it is prodigious to see him!

After lunch, [visit] to the rooms—In the afternoon he goes to Hyères, comes back with port, oatmeal cakes, cigarettes, melon.

After dinner, conversation. Heap of little questions about Larbaud: [Is he] Catholic? Fargue: Is he hard up? What precisely are his love affairs? Hardly leaves me the time to answer; would like facts without analysis. There are no facts, to tell the truth. Matthey: [Gide] guesses that Fargue put him in contact with Matthey in order to help his affair with Colette X; it irritates him to have been used as a means. He says that Fargue came to see him one day in order to open his heart to him, but he cut him short immediately: that did not amuse him. Fargue a liar who wants to make himself interesting—(Fargue had told me on the subject of this visit that he had run into Gide, that the latter had invited him to come and spend a moment at his place and had provoked his confidences)—We talk again about Cocteau, about the latest Swedish ballets, about criticism—He will spend the six winter months in Rome, where he has rented a house, but he thinks that Copeau will stage *Saül* before his departure.

He talks to us about *Les Faux-Monnayeurs [The Counterfeiters]*, the journal of the book.

Friday the 2nd—[Gide] goes bathing around nine thirty. Sylvia goes down to bathe with him; while he is drying himself in the sun, Sylvia makes a gesture of wishing to leave him alone; he has her stay, asks her to speak English.

In the afternoon he asks her again to let him read English to her and to correct him; he reads some pages from *Tom Jones*, which Sylvia brought to reread here, and it was precisely a passage from the preface to *Armance* that had made her think of it. . . .

After dinner, a literary conversation. He asks me what I think and what the public thinks about Larbaud, about Giraudoux, about Morand—He seems jealous of Larbaud when I speak to him about the latter with some tenderness or admiration, cuts me short; however, I do not show him all of my feeling toward Larbaud; I use infinite oratorical precautions. I do not speak to him at all about Claudel or Romains; besides, he does not ask me anything about them—I had told him some months ago that I had the intention of writing my memoirs one day; he says to me, pretending to forget this remark: "You should write your memoirs." I answer him that I have always had the intention of doing so, but that they will be posthumous, and terrible for myself as much as for the others—He also speaks to me a bit about Joyce, about Butler—

That evening, after having left him, in our room Sylvia and I exchange many reflections: about the habit that men of letters have of asking you a heap of questions and of hardly leaving you the time to answer; they look for facts, raw material; they do not want you to develop, that is their work; they are always afraid that you will discover their tracks—We find that irritating, but we decide, for political reasons, always to let him have the first and the last words: we shall take our revenge when we are his age and have his authority. Poor young people!

We also have a discussion about the influence he has on the young writers. Sylvia thinks that it is he who influences the new generation most. I do not think so. His influence is more superficial than real; they acknowledge it all the more because little trace of it will be found in their works. Besides, it is rather *chic* to like Gide—I discuss Romains to some length.

Saturday the 3rd—I decide to show myself very little; Gide talked so much with us the day before that he will doubtless keep his distance today—I do not see him all morning long. After lunch I go up to write some letters. We take tea in our room (the day before we had taken it with him, he had offered port)—After tea we take a long walk until dinner. But he is not there for dinner. We saw him, however, on the terrace at a quarter to five. . . .

. . . Perhaps he has gone to Toulon, where he will spend the night.

Sunday the 4th—We go down upon the beach at nine thirty. Gide goes bathing with Mlle Van Rysselberghe, who arrived yesterday evening; he had written to her that he would go to spend some days on her farm; she took advantage of an auto to come here to spend Sunday and a part of tomorrow. I am happy to see her (story of [Charles] Chanvin)—Gide is exquisite with us; he says that he was annoyed not to have seen us yesterday; in despair he went to take a stroll in Hyères; bought us some Prince de Monaco cigarettes, gives me a box of them. He plays the young man with the three of us, pirouettes around the handrail next to the cabins, looks for compliments, obtains them in quantity, above all from me. I tell him that his beige bathing suit is a masterpiece; to an allusion [that he makes] to his baldness, [I say] that hair is only an artifice, that I should love to shave my head; that the wart placed between his eyebrows makes him resemble Buddha—

After lunch, conversation on the terrace. Mlle Van Rysselberghe has a Hindu cane that represents a gazelle being devoured by a tiger. I launch some of my ideas about cannibalism. Gide is of my opinion; he says that he has read in a work by a disciple of Darwin (?) that a hare took pleasure in being pursued by dogs; that wild animals stunned their prey before devouring them, so that they did not suffer; which furthermore proved to him the need to think that pain does not exist in nature, that it was only apprehension and memory, fruit of the imagination, etc. *Meat* (personal development).

After this conversation he prepares to take his siesta; lends me the good sheets of his *Morceaux choisis [Selected Pieces]*, which are about to appear, and in which there are some unpublished pages that he prizes; he lends Mlle Van Rysselberghe a curious letter written by a German baroness, the idol of Greenwich Village. Sylvia was familiar with this letter; they even wanted her to undertake handing it over to Gide.

We go to the salon to read what he has entrusted to us; he follows us, sees a piano. I tell him that it has been reported to me that he was an excellent musician—He needs to be asked only a bit before he begins at the piano; plays from Schumann, Chopin, Albéniz—with virtuosity, but without soul; it is true that the piano is bad, harsh—He plays with a grimacing face, with a care for effect, it seems; his manner, the pieces that he plays, it is all very romantic. . . . After a moment he gets up to go to take his siesta.

We get ready to read; but the door is opened: Jules Romains! Great surprise on both sides; he has come to see Gide; he knows that Gide is here through Copeau, who is in Saint-Clair with the Van Rysselberghes. He left Saint-Julien-Chapteuil to come to spend about ten days in his Hyères house. Naturally he has been to pay his respects to Copeau. He has a little auto that he bought before leaving Paris; the auto is on the path, Bibi has stayed inside with Ginette. I run to embrace Gabrielle [Romains]. I tell them about Gide's arrival and ask them to come to the salon with Mlle Van Rysselberghe. There we find Gide, who, in his shirt sleeves, has begun again at the piano—Hello, hello!—They talk about Hyères, about Edith Wharton, about Paul Bourget—(concerning the famous guide in English). Romains tells Gide that Copeau is awaiting him in Saint-Clair, where he has been for only a short time.

Gide, Sylvia, and Mlle Van Rysselberghe go to bathe. Myself, I leave the Romains on the beach in order to read the unpublished pages.

Tea. The Romains invite us to dinner, and Gide and Mlle Van Rysselberghe as well; they refuse, we accept; we shall go to Hyères by bus; they leave us to go to prepare the dinner.

Hyères. Romains meets us at the bus, drives us to his place. The house is built into a body of construction in the old town; it is painted a rather brick red on the outside, with the window rails blue. We go in, we visit almost immediately. It is a real surprise: the furniture is old and pretty; all the rooms are painted red and blue, with a red that always tends toward that of brick, and with a rather bright blue, but the tones are shaded differently according to the rooms. The whole is very gay, very agreeable. The house itself is curious, with its ample stairwell upon which windows open from the rooms in the back. From the windows in the front one has a superb view over the town, the countryside, and the sea. (Some details are open to criticism.)

Dinner. Coffee at the bistro.

As it would be necessary to leave at nine o'clock in order to catch the train, we decide to go back on foot—We leave at ten o'clock, they accompany us very far. Remarks on Gide, Larbaud, Duhamel —Discussion about inversion.

Monday the 5th—We invited Gide and Mlle Van Rysselberghe to lunch. We do not see them all morning long; at half-past twelve they come to the table: they went to the Salins de Pesquier; there [they] saw a village under the pines, very exotic; they are enchanted.

During the lunch a telegram signed Pierre Louÿs: "On this day, the (?)th of Saint Bartholomew's, I am bedecking my house with flags and we are thinking deeply of you." While reading the telegram [Gide] is calm; he pretends not to understand. He asks me what I see in it. I tell him that I think it is Dadaist. He finds that it is certainly in the style of Pierre Louÿs. After a moment, explosion! The Saint Bartholomew's Day Massacre, the Edict of Nantes!

After dinner, coffee and conversation on the terrace. Mlle Van Rysselberghe leaves us at a quarter after two to take her train— Gide's siesta—Arrival of the Romains at three thirty—Bathing. The English critic Roger Fry, who has come here to see Gide, goes bathing with us—Tea. The Romains tell us that this morning they received a letter from a friend telling them that he is coming to spend three days with them, therefore they will not be able to come to see us; we shall meet again only in Paris. It is surely a story: they have felt that we would prefer to be alone with Gide. Unfortunately, Gide, who must have believed that the Romains would be coming now every day, decides to leave tomorrow evening to go to join Copeau. Besides, he must be afraid of offending Copeau by prolonging his stay here, and as he strongly desires *Saül* to be performed—

In the evening Gide dines with Roger Fry.

Tuesday the 6th—In the morning, bathing with Gide. I speak to him about the unpublished pages that he had me read. We dry ourselves on the beach while eating some figs that he bought—

Lunch with Gide, who invited us. Conversation—Siesta—Tea. We talk about Irma, about the meetings. We are planning one at which he would read some pages by himself, following the plan of the *Morceaux choisis,* without the critical part, however, but the amusing pages above all: "The public does not know *where it should laugh,*" he says—But here is the horn of the bus, he says goodbye to us—When he is in the bus I still say nice things to him, he gives me his address until Saturday. He leaves.

From *Trois Agendas d'Adrienne Monnier.*

Raymonde Linossier

It was in October 1917 that I saw Raymonde Linossier for the first time. She was then a student in the School of Law, I myself was a student bookseller in my own school; for two years I had been practicing a profession that I did not yet know much about, except the intoxication of talking with people who loved the books that I loved.

One morning Raymonde Linossier crossed the threshold of the bookshop; she entered not like a passer-by who is only whiling away time, but with the gay and friendly air of a person who comes on a visit. Had she been told about the shop? I do not think so. As I came to know her better later on I saw that she approached everything in that manner, with the most charming urbanity.

She took it on herself to ask me for the address of a printer to whom she could entrust a novel. In pronouncing the word "novel" she smiled mischievously; it had to do with a work, *Bibi-la-Bibiste,* written by the X sisters.

While she was speaking I watched her. She was a girl dressed in black, endowed with the most striking physiognomy.

Her chin and her mouth were very developed, her lips likewise— large and strong, they resembled a wide-open flower.

Dominating that intense and almost savage lower part of her face, her eyes showed all the sweetness, all the discretion, that one expects of beautiful feminine souls; they were of the purest and lightest blue that can be seen, like clear sapphires.

Beautiful eyes that grief and care could never veil, but in which thought and joy passed like the smoke of incense.

The voice of Raymonde Linossier was no less remarkable than

her face—how shall I describe it? It was quivering, subdued, tender. It clung to words lightly like the feet of a bird; it made them flutter with innumerable little wings; it had silken starts and hoverings that at one and the same time were distracted and attentive. As I write these lines I believe I hear it, it weaves itself into my ears, it is as present, as unseizable as the soul of which it was the human sound and the mysterious warbling.

The manuscript of *Bibi-la-Bibiste* was quickly entrusted to me. It was truly a peculiar little work; it was composed of five chapters, the longest of which had twelve lines. Here is the first, which bore the subtitle "Childhood":

> Her birth was like that of other children.
> That is why they named her Bibi-la-Bibiste.
> (This was the childhood of Bibi-la-Bibiste.)

I confess that I was very baffled and that I did not know how to formulate a very clear estimation. The author, furthermore, seemed to await nothing other than my surprise: she was served to her expectation.

I believe that it was in thinking of the review *Sic* (then in full flower), directed by M. and Mme Birot, that we discovered a certain press, Paul Birault's, located at 4 Rue Tardieu, that is to say, in the very heart of Montmartre. We felt that for a work of the Bibi sort we needed a printer who was not at all banal, but as eccentric and wild as possible. Raymonde started on her way one morning and not without effort discovered the printing establishment in question. She did not see M. Paul Birault, who was then in the army, but his wife, a very kind woman who carried out in person, upon a hand press, the jobs that were entrusted to her. No literary or typographical audacity frightened her; she was even the only one, if I remember correctly, who was capable of printing certain ideograms by Guillaume Apollinaire and his disciples. One could not find better. She gave Raymonde the most honest terms and within a short while delivered an elegant and well-finished little book that was printed, according to the wishes of the author, in fifty copies upon imitation Japan paper.

Bibi-la-Bibiste was dedicated to Francis Poulenc, a childhood friend. He had come to see us one day, alone, some time after Raymonde Linossier's first visit. He held in his arms an enormous pot of flowers intended for a woman relative in the neighborhood, and showed his best look of being the Elephant Child whose nose has not yet been pulled. He had asked us, I believe, to procure for him a certain program illustrated by Kisling, which had been used at the last meeting of Lyre et Palette. It was the epoch when Art et Action, Lyre et Palette, and our modest meetings dispensed almost all the intellectual munitions of the capital. Not enough has been said about what was owed to Mme Lara and M. Autant who, during the hardest years of the war, maintained the literary, musical, and artistic avant-garde with much brilliance and valor. It was thanks to them, who had the *Rhapsodie nègre* performed for the first time, that I learned that the person to whom Bibi had been dedicated was the most fortunately gifted of the young French composers.

Bibi-la-Bibiste, when we possessed it in its printed form, was a source of diversion for us. Once we gave it to Ezra Pound, who was very much struck by it and had it reproduced in the *Little Review.*

It must be said that Bibi had given birth to a genuine doctrine, bibism—unless it was the doctrine that engendered the work.

Bibism was a kind of Dada in an early form. It declared a liking for the baroque and for the primitive. It cherished the savage arts and those forms of popular art that are expressed by stuffed toy animals, little boxes ornamented with shells, surprise post cards, pictures composed of postage stamps, constructions made of corks, etc.—Ah! Raymonde Linossier was very much of her time, but she was so as a true precursor, with much boldness, subtlety, and above all much tact. She never gave an excessive importance to her inclinations, she was always the first to laugh at them, and God knows that she laughed in a kindly way, laughed until the tears came to her eyes, really. There where the Dadaists put the tragic, she put tenderness. She loved wailing and toddling forms of art like a mother who knows very well that it will all become grown-up and serious only too quickly, and that nothing will be equal to the games and the jumbles of the start.

What was really astonishing about Raymonde, given her liking for the primitive, was a rare critical sense; she did not confuse values and did not create arbitrary ones; when she had preferences she knew why; her mind was virile in many respects. In literature, music, and painting she was an amateur of the first order, a member of the elite of Paris, and you know what I mean by that.

The poet whom she preferred, without any doubt, was Léon-Paul Fargue. She knew the *Poèmes* before coming to our bookshop, where

Fargue has always been so keenly admired. She often told me that her teacher gave her bad marks and scolded her because she stuffed her homework with quotations taken from the *Poèmes*. Naturally, she made the acquaintance of Fargue a little while after her arrival among us, and they were immediately very good friends. It was the great epoch of the *potassons*—that is, the people to whom one can say: *"O té un janti"* ["Oh you are nice"]. This institution, of which Fargue was the father and I the mother, knew an extraordinary power and influence from 1918 to 1923.

Raymonde was a founding *potasson* with the title "the Youngest *Potasson* in the World." Nobody took more seriously the company of which she was a part and better contributed to its well-being. I often showed indifference or weakness; I was rather inclined to decorate with the name of *potasson* everybody who asked me for it. That was not because I did not believe in the *potassons*, but I told myself that God would recognize his own, that the very act of aspiring to such a rank already showed aptitude, and that the contact of the good would not fail to make conversions. Raymonde was much more intransigent; we decided to establish an intermediate category, that of "Aspiring *Potassons*"; I was able to have a great number of people enter into this category, and Raymonde at her pleasure could keep them there in perpetuity by endlessly postponing their nomination. I really believe that she made an exception only for Charles de la Morandière, whom she admitted rather quickly among the real *potassons*.

You must not believe, however, that we passed our time in playing about. Our *papère* had to earn his living the hard way by placing his famous lighting fixtures in enameled glass; as for myself, business brought me not a little trouble. Raymonde was doing her law—as wholly seriously as her friends Lucienne Astruc and Juliette Veiller—and she was taking courses in Orientalism, with fully as much passion as her friends Sarah Lévy and Marcelle Lalou.

She received the title of lawyer at the age of twenty-four and immediately sought to practice her profession.

I have often been told that it was very difficult for women to arrive at the Palais de Justice, more difficult than in medicine, even, and that the obstacles became almost insurmountable for a sensitive and modest woman. Raymonde had the luck to be able to find a patron in the person of Maître Charles Chanvin, our friend and *potasson*. She helped him in the capacity of secretary for two years and it is certain that, thanks to her personal talents and thanks to him, she would have succeeded very well if Orientalism, which had always greatly occupied her, had not come to distract her, then to absorb her, in the most fortunate manner. She was a member of the Amis de l'Orient and was active with the photographic service of the Musée Guimet from around 1923. She was ultimately associated with the museum toward 1925—which her friends learned not from her but, almost by chance, on the occasion of the publication of *Mythologie asiatique illustrée*, on which she collaborated. In the museum itself she had a beautiful private office in which she worked every afternoon. We went to pay her a visit one day—Gabrielle Romains, Sylvia, and I, and she guided us through the rooms, which we had certainly never seen or appreciated so well.

Raymonde's modesty was without equal. Her sister, Dr. Alice Ardoin, told me that at the time of a brief journey to the United States that they made together last year, she had put herself in contact with the Orientalists of New York and Philadelphia, to whom her French Orientalist teachers and friends had given her numerous letters of introduction. She told her sister that she had been very well received; you can believe, she added, that I had kind letters! But it was discovered through the correspondence exchanged between American and French Orientalists after her travels over there that she had personally produced a great impression and that she had amazed everybody by the extent of her knowledge.

Never did she speak of her works or of her projects. The article that René Grousset published about her in the *Débats* last February was for many—and I can say, of her intimates—a real revelation. Our friend had to be taken away from us so that we might learn that she had the temper of true scholars and that she was "one of the most active organizers of the Musée Guimet."

For she was taken away from us! Is that possible? So young, so beloved of all, so marvelously gifted! And her death was so brutal—carried off in ten days!

Trying to fix an image of her in the course of the pages that you have just read, I set aside mournful thoughts as much as I could. I wanted this portrait, which to tell the truth is only a sketch, to be at least endowed with the colors of life; I have adorned it with the most cheerful memories.

Raymonde—that name, when it stood for our friend, seemed to

be endowed with a subtle energy. Raymonde, we used to say, and it was like a trace of amber, like the wake of a smile, like a grip on the heart. That *monde,* that "world" that ended her name, how far it went, how many meanings it had for us, how many appeals!—To all those, women and men, who weep for her, I should like to say: Do you not feel that that name is still full of life, and that her soul remains within it? By a supremely mischievous and flirtatious sleight, she has pretended to leave us in order to have herself more ardently sought for and found.

From *Les Gazettes d'Adrienne Monnier*; first published in *Les Nouvelles Littéraires* (April 25, 1930).

Angèle Lamotte

Angèle Lamotte came to the Rue de l'Odéon for the first time in December 1922. She lived in Neuilly, quite far from our quarter. Doubtless she made the trip to my bookshop because she was attracted by the fame of our meetings. Paul Valéry, Joyce, and Valery Larbaud had made the year illustrious.

Angèle was then a very young girl, and exceptionally reserved; however, she did not give the impression of timidity—she seemed as free and easy as a bird—but she had an incredible discretion for a person so young and apparently so vivacious. Her reserve seemed founded upon discernment. This discernment, I saw very well later on, was less practical than it was transcendent; she was conscious of all the heavens and hells that separate human beings; very probably perception of that atomic order made her exaggerate the distances and the obstacles. In any case, she never lost her grace and her domination. Her presence alone was a grace.

Nobody has ever so much resembled a fairy. Even the performers best endowed for that role have not been able to surpass her or, in my opinion, equal her. It was because she played only for herself—playful—how really playful she was! Her voice was the sweetest and most melodious that could be heard—fluting, as if borne up by the sound of a flute. Her face and her whole person, which was rather small, were as beautiful and charming as you could hope them to be. I am aware that in speaking of her I naturally assume the tone of Perrault's fairy tales.

For more than ten years I had only glimpses of Angèle, sometimes very infrequent. Two or three times I saw her in the company of friends who did not have the look of being too much at ease by her side. She came to the bookshop to supply herself, without speaking, with the best texts, showing that she was as intelligent as she was beautiful.

Toward 1935 her visits became more frequent and regular—she had come to live on the Boulevard Saint-Michel. It happened that we now exchanged rather extensive remarks and found ourselves in agreement in most of our judgments. I have encountered few women truly as much in love with literature as she.

I saw her draw close. Bit by bit the fairy became a friend. I watched her face, which was somewhat grave, although always enlivened by a smile. Her eyes were superb—her soul spoke freely in them. Her profile was pure; without her hairdo and her hat it might have been Greek. Her well-shaped mouth with slightly drooping corners, like that of ancient statues, expressed melancholy in repose. Well hidden melancholy, for the words that left those lips were always lively and gay; they often questioned with an irresistible childlike grace; and even when they spoke about the sad side of life they had a delicious humor.

Angèle also struck me with her chic. She followed fashion with spirit, while judging it, while being amused by it; she simplified it and kept nothing of it but the most successful caprices. It seems to me that she could have been one of those women who set it, but that would have drawn her into the social world, with which she did not want to be concerned.

In the spring of 1937, after having asked me for an appointment to talk about serious things, she came, sat down right next to me, and confided in me the secret of the forthcoming birth of *Verve*. I did not yet know Tériade; there was no doubt that I had to know him, but he was very unsociable, as contemplative as an Oriental sage, always afraid of disturbing or of being disturbed; it appeared necessary to Angèle to choose the moment of the meeting carefully, for it seemed to her that our friendship would be certain and fruitful if sealed under happy auspices. For the moment, since it was she who was charged with the secretaryship of the review, she asked me for advice on the subject of authors from whom she and Tériade wished to obtain material. Above all: Claudel, Valéry, and Gide, whom she personally enjoyed with passion. But how approach them? They must be, there was no doubt about it, even more unsociable than Tériade. So she asked me to put her in contact with them. Her way of imagining the difficulties of the undertaking made me really laugh; it was then that I saw her astonishing modesty for the first time. After having asked her about the means that *Verve* had at its disposal, I told her that it would be best if she herself wrote to the authors in question on the review's own stationery, printed with its name at the top, showing herself very precise as to the conditions of publication. As Tériade was connected with all of the great painters, and as he had already been put in contact with the literary avant-garde at the time of the *Minotaure,* that would succeed all by itself.

And *Verve* succeeded all by itself, magnificently!

I had the joy of witnessing the preparation of the numbers from very close; I often went to the Rue Férou to see Angèle and Tériade in their office, and my eyes were sometimes the first, after their own, to contemplate the marvels that were going to be published. Angèle told me with tenderness and good humor about what was going on among the painters whose friend she had become. The world of art, thanks to her, was joined to the literary world that was my own. I had never sought to occupy myself with art, at least with the art of the living, so as to distract nothing from the service that I wanted to render to literature, and because of that fact I was a rather backward person.

During the war *Verve* was a heavy burden for her, which she took upon herself with all her faith. Tériade, immobilized in the Midi, could do hardly more than projects and maquettes; doubtless he remained in contact with his friends Henri Matisse, Bonnard, and Rouault. But it was Angèle who, coming regularly to Paris, had all the bother with the management and the manufacture. Thanks to her sister Marguerite, the Rue Férou office was regularly open, and it could not have been better kept up; one could obtain supplies of the *Riches Heures* and the *Nature de France* from her. But for the books by Rouault and Bonnard, which were in preparation—that sumptuous *Divertissement* and those lively *Correspondances*—for the Theocritus at which Henri Laurens was working with so much love, for the albums of Limbourg and Fouquet, it was necessary for Angèle to find paper, very beautiful paper, come to an understanding with the printers, and oversee the so delicate printing of the plates. All the precious materials that *Verve* needed were becoming scarce and were disappearing. We often saw our friend fighting against fatigue and worries, taking the upper hand with a heroic good humor. It was the spectacle of this admirable effort that decided Paul Valéry, who was infinitely touched by Angèle's grace and bravery, to write his preface for Fouquet's *Antiquités judaïques*, although he too was very tired and very harassed.

And now Angèle is no more.

She died on January 15 of this year. One of the cruelest illnesses carried her off after months of suffering.

We could believe last spring that she was saved. We lived through three months of hope and often of happiness.

Angèle saw the Liberation as an almost well person. The first Sunday Paris was free, we spent it together. A bit later, because it was impossible for her to eat, she had to go back to bed. Then began the heartrending weeks of which she made, with the force of her soul and poetry, a sort of enchantment for those who were close to her. At mealtime the table was placed near her bed; she did not suffer from not being able to eat, it seemed to her that she was feeding herself through the mouths of the beings whom she loved.

She always had pencil and paper within reach of her hand, and, when the pain left her at rest, she worked for *Verve*, arranging everything that seemed important to her, advising her sister, who was going to continue her task.

Sometimes the desire to live awoke in her, regret for the festivities of the world in which, young and beautiful, she might have shone. No doubt she had sacrificed many things to an austere life; she caressed for a moment the jewels she had never worn; she decided, if she should ever get well, that she would go out a bit more all the same. Such moments were lived without bitterness, in that music into which the soul plunges and brightens itself at the sources of pleasure.

Verve—that word illuminated the eve of her death, when she still strove to put her ideas and projects in order.

The day when she had to leave, she turned her head toward the wall (she had said that when she turned in the direction of the wall that that would be the sign) and she went to sleep.

From *Les Gazettes d'Adrienne Monnier*; first published in *Verve* (November 1945).

Whitman at Sylvia Beach's

There has been organized in New York, in connection with the Authors Club, a Walt Whitman Committee composed of writers, professors, and publishers.

The purpose of this committee is to have a monument erected to Whitman in New York, where not even a bust of the poet exists. A medal will be put on sale throughout the world.

M. Jean Catel, the delegate to the American Committee for France, has asked us to organize a Parisian group that would have branches in the provinces. M. Jean Catel, who is preparing a thesis on Whitman, is a professor at the University of Montpellier; he is organizing a division in that city, and on his own initiative the Montpellier review, the *Ane d'Or*, is going to devote a special number to the author of *Leaves of Grass*.

We eagerly welcomed M. Catel's suggestion: the Whitman Committee of Paris is now an accomplished thing.

This committee has its headquarters in Sylvia Beach's bookshop, Shakespeare and Company. M. Francis Vielé-Griffin has accepted the chairmanship of it. Its members are: MM. Léon Bazalgette, Valery Larbaud, Henry-D. Davray, Louis Fabulet, Jean Schlumberger, Pierre de Lanux, Jean Catel, and Sylvia Beach—We should have loved to ask André Gide to be a part of it but, as nobody is unaware, he is traveling in Africa.

You know that the poet Vielé-Griffin is American by origin. He translated Whitman in 1892, the first after Jules Laforgue—Léon Bazalgette told us on this subject that when Vielé-Griffin wrote to Whitman to ask him for authorization to translate "To a Foil'd European Revolutionaire," he composed his letter, he, an American, in French. "Monsieur et cher Poète" he addressed Whitman, who did not know a word of French and who had to have the letter translated.

On March 1 a Walt Whitman exhibition will open at Shakespeare and Company, composed of manuscripts, original editions, and unpublished photos and drawings, drawings in Whitman's hand.

Among the pieces to be shown will figure several rough manuscript drafts by the poet, which belong to Sylvia Beach. Here is how she came into possession of these papers: Her aunt, Miss Agnes Orbison, in the company of her friend Mrs. Bertrand Russell (then Miss Alice Smith, the sister of Logan Pearsall Smith, the author of *Trivia*), had gone to pay a visit to Walt Whitman in Camden. The two young ladies found the poet, who was then old and paralyzed, in his workroom, the floor of which was covered with papers. When they took leave of him, Agnes Orbison asked for his permission to gather up some of the papers that were scattered on the ground. The ones that she collected were for the most part envelopes and letters upon the backs of which he had scrawled in pencil what appears to us to be commentaries on *Leaves of Grass*. These little manuscripts are very much crossed out and do not reveal anything new about their author; one of them is written in blue pencil upon the back of a touching letter that reads:

Columbus, Texas,
Feb. 23, 1885.

Hon. Walt Whitman,
    Dear Sir:

          Will you please favor a Texas boy, one who greatly admires your productions, with a memento of yourself in the way of an autograph. Hoping you will favorably receive my request and greatly oblige an humble admirer,
    I am,

    Very Respectfully,

    Willie N. Jones.

From *Les Gazettes d'Adrienne Monnier;* first published in *Le Navire d'Argent* (February 1926).

A Letter to Larbaud

Paris, February 12, 1926

Dear Friend,

Hurrah! We have finished our translations. Whitman's address is finished, and McAlmon's short story is finished! We really believed for a moment that we would never come to the end of our task. We labored for two months on the address. First of all, there was the difficulty of reading it, because it was printed in very small characters, as small as the smallest on the charts of an optometrist. Sylvia had to use a magnifying glass, and in spite of that strained her eyesight quite a bit; she even suffered for a number of days from an obstruction of the lacrimal ducts; I believe that this was caused less by her eyes than by a state of general overwork. But her right eye was very bad and she had to cover it with a patch, so that at Joyce's birthday dinner both author and publisher were Wotans in miniature. She is cured now.

In addition to the difficulty of deciphering, there were all the problems of translation, which you can easily imagine. This address is written in a very familiar fashion, with turns of phrase that were made less to have a precise meaning than to form beautiful periods capable of touching a popular audience; at certain moments Sylvia would say: "He had his own people there." And surely he must have had his own people, and he had us, us as well; we were very much moved; when we reached the astonishing last paragraph our emotion was such that we could not speak a word; I thought of the speeches in *Tête d'or*, and I had to restrain myself from weeping, because I felt that I should have shed floods of tears. The power, the magnetism, the streaming humanity of the poet shakes me like the outburst of an orchestra.

You will tell me that the poems of *Leaves of Grass* would have moved me even more, but as you know, my knowledge of English is very imperfect, and a translation, even when it has the value of Bazalgette's, deprives a poem of much of its resources. And then, in the particular case of the address, which I was translating with Sylvia, I had this really extraordinary chance of holding between my hands the proofs that Whitman had printed himself and that he had begun to correct. A unique vehicle had been given to me, something like a magic carpet that transported me through time and space to the place of eternal communion where the powers of Whitman continue to work for mankind.

It seems to me that it is not unreasonable to think, to feel this way. It is one of the fundamental principles of religion to believe that what saints have touched is miraculous, and that is logical enough; there are many bodies in nature that are endowed with remarkable properties that have a continuous effect: electricity lasts forever in the magnet and in those organisms that have been able to capture it. And the genius of Whitman was particularly electric, by the composition of his nature and the force of his will.

Those who read the address will see very well the reserves of energy it contains; let them think of the poet's hand patiently assembling those miniscule letters, making fourteen millimeters contain his name, Walt Whitman, to which he wanted to initiate the whole American people; let them try to imagine the series of events that kept this address from being published and that put it between our hands.

I recently wrote to M. Jean Catel to ask him how he had discovered it. He replied that he had bought it in a Boston bookshop with a bundle of newspaper clippings. Whitman, it appears, kept all of the articles that pertained to himself; M. Catel tells me that he saw hundreds of them. No doubt the address had remained lost among the clippings, since it does not appear in the complete works. In this matter, M. Catel carefully leafed through the volumes, and Sylvia in turn made another check.

We found, however, something that is related to it in a rather amusing way; it is in *Collect,* an article entitled "Origins of Attempted Secession," in which Whitman discloses with some detachment that he was interested in politics between the ages of twenty and forty. He did not participate in them, he says, but he observed them, and he voted regularly. Further on he recalls, like an already distant time, the years between 1840 and 1860, when the federal convention presented the worst spectacle ever seen in the United States. Seven-eighths of the members that composed it were "the meanest kind of bawling and blowing office-holders, office-seekers, pimps, malignants, conspirators, murderers, fancy-men. . . ." You recognize here all the polite expressions that he heaped on the heads of the politicians in his address. But he makes no allusion to this address. I have the impression that he must even have been a bit embarrassed by having delivered it; it must have been something like a debauch in his life. He must surely have stirred up strong popular feelings that had filled him with a heavy intoxication, then confusion. You will tell me that such feelings were not of the kind to displease him, since he spent his life in the midst of the common people; but exactly, he wanted above all to enlighten them, to uplift them, and he was too wise not to prefer evolution to revolution. In any case, he felt the danger there would be in renewing a similar experience, and how much political struggles could estrange him forever from the powers of the poet.

I do not believe that he can be annoyed because we have found and published his address. He now no longer risks being poisoned by the sulfurous vapors from the lairs of power; furthermore, he can be at rest, for we are not going to *inundate* cities with it; the *Navire d'Argent* is not a daily with a large circulation—far from it.

But don't you think it would have been a great pity if this text had remained unknown? Beyond its literary value it is a very precious document on the life of the poet. Remember that he made this address in 1856, a year after having published *Leaves of Grass*; he was still in full possession of his genius and his manifesto against the abuses of the times was certainly not useless.

I myself shall never forget the extraordinary emotion that it gave me, and that still endures. I was completely plunged in this emotion when at a dinner of the P.E.N. Club the other night I met Louise Weiss, who asked me if I would like to participate in a movement for the women's vote; although I have never occupied myself with feminism, I answered yes, with enthusiasm, and believe me, I do not take it back.

The translation of McAlmon's short story gave us a completely different kind of sport. It is very good, this short story. It seemed to us to form a rather complete picture of one of the most essential activities in the United States. We hesitated for a moment to translate it because it is often written in slang and because it contains certain truths that the French have the habit of expressing by insinuations, not when they speak, but when they write. We know what the conversation of men is like, and thanks to Fargue we are not ignorant of anything at all that can be inexhaustibly said or invented concerning the noble subject of Sex. We thought for sure that we were going to shock our readers, and that in particular our good friend, Mme L., would reproach us; and then there are things that one does not like to write. But Sylvia, after a serious examination of her conscience, cried: "What! I, the publisher of *Ulysses*, should be afraid of one man when a whole regiment doesn't frighten me?" And we bravely launched ourselves into it. We have even, out of an excess of enthusiasm, presented in footnotes the American expressions that correspond to our own. I hope that people will be grateful to us, since dictionaries do not list them, and it is rather difficult to ask Americans for precise details in this matter. American men have the better of it; those who come to Paris can have themselves initiated by *the little women,* but how do you think Frenchmen are going to enjoy themselves in New York? First of all, it would cost them too much, and then it seems that nobody enjoys oneself over there!

As for slang, it is a rather delicate question in literature, but it inevitably plays an important role among a people whose personal language is in the process of formation; look at the place that it occupies in the work of William Carlos Williams, who is, however, the best *man of letters* in the United States at present.

You doubtless know what Whitman has written in "Slang in America"; while looking over the prose works again, Sylvia came across this admirable essay, which had escaped her memory. I cannot refrain from recalling the following lines to you. Slang is

> an attempt of common humanity to escape from bald literalism, and express itself illimitably, which in the highest walks produces poets and poems, and doubtless in pre-historic times gave the start to, and perfected, the whole immense tangle of the old mythologies. . . .
>
> Slang, too, is the wholesome fermentation or eructation of those processes eternally active in language, by which froth and specks are thrown up, mostly to pass away; though occasionally to settle and permanently crystallize.

That is very true, isn't it? It is the slang expressions on the way to becoming crystallized that the dictionary qualifies as "popular" or "colloquial." How interesting it would be to have Valéry's opinion in this matter.

Dear Friend, it is very sad that you are so far away and that we cannot talk over all these questions at our leisure. I hope that you will find the time to write to me at length.

From *Les Gazettes d'Adrienne Monnier*; first published in *Le Navire d'Argent* (March 1926).

Joyce's Ulysses *and the French Public*

It was on December 7, 1921, that Valery Larbaud presented the Irish writer James Joyce to the Amis des Livres.

That was one of the memorable meetings of our house. The first fragments of the translation of *Ulysses* were given a reading there after this warning: "Certain pages have an uncommon boldness of expression that might quite legitimately be shocking" (I quote from the prospectus). As Auguste Morel had not yet undertaken his translation, it was Jacques Benoist-Méchin who had courageously attacked these first fragments; and Léon-Paul Fargue had been especially consulted for the adaptation of the most daring passages.

Joyce was then unknown to the French public. It was not here, however, at La Maison des Amis des Livres, nor with Valery Larbaud, that he found his first welcome. A little while after his arrival from Trieste, his friend the American poet Ezra Pound had taken him to the house of André Spire, who had received him with his customary kindness. It was at André Spire's house that Sylvia and I met him, in the course of a reception at which many literary people were present. I had a little discussion with Julien Benda; he maintained that there did not exist in France, for the moment, any writer capable of great flights. While we were deliberating, Mr. Joyce, who was sitting in a corner, remained silent, his wings folded. Sylvia Beach, who had read his books and even the chapters of *Ulysses* that had appeared in New York in the *Little Review*, and who admired him passionately, had in the course of the evening summoned up her courage to approach him.

For it was an extremely congenial reception: Spire offered us tea and supper at the same time. There was no lack of time to talk and even to think a bit about what one meant to say. This is the way, then, that our relations with Joyce began.

When one recognizes the importance of the symbol in Joyce's work and the constant care that he takes to establish mystical correspondences, one is struck by the fact that the first person who received him in France, and put him in contact with his future publishers, is a Jewish poet—for Joyce had created in *Ulysses* a great type of Jewish humanity, and he was to find with us a place favorable to the appearance of his work and the establishment of his reputation.

So, in 1921 Valery Larbaud spoke in my bookshop about James Joyce, and above all about his *Ulysses*, which had not yet appeared in book form. This lecture, which was published afterward in the *Nouvelle Revue Française*, and which presently serves as the preface to the translation of *Dubliners*, is a unique achievement in the history of criticism. It is certainly the first time, I believe, that a work in the English language has been studied in France, by a French writer, before being studied in England and in America.

Certainly, the presence of Joyce among us had provoked this phenomenon, but if one thinks about the difficulties of a text like *Ulysses* one is astounded by the tour de force that Larbaud brought off. All the more so because his study is and will no doubt remain the most perfect, the most understanding analysis that could be made of Joyce's work. How Larbaud was able to extract from it a substance so clear, so compact, so pleasing, in so little time and without the help of an earlier work—this is what will never cease to amaze us.

I have no intention of trying to imitate such a master, all the less so because I know very little English and do not have the erudition. My task will be more modest and also perhaps more ambitious. I am going to try to express the most essential judgments that French readers have been able to bring to bear upon *Ulysses*, to which I will add on occasion some personal opinions. I was, before becoming its publisher, the first reader of the French translation of this work. I have thought about it a great deal. My reflections were not, at the beginning, much different from those of ordinary readers, but because they have necessarily been more numerous and painstaking, I have arrived at conclusions that are perhaps a bit more pertinent.

And first of all it must be said that we did not lack the appetite as we approached this thick book. We had awaited its publication for eight years, and Larbaud had known how to make our mouths water; he had even forewarned us that "a reader who is not literary or who is only half literary will abandon *Ulysses* after three pages." But we thought, not without reason, that we were literary readers, and that the clarifications he had lent us in advance should spare us any disappointment. Still, it must certainly be admitted that though we read the book to the end, it was not without many temptations to abandon it along the way.

Let us give a summary of our journey:

We like the first chapter very much—we had, moreover, read it already in the first number of *Commerce*. It is a well-paced narrative, marked by an excellent realism, with poetic touches of a surprising vivacity; three or four sentences on the sea, on the old milkwoman, enchant us with their truly novel tonal relationships.

Second chapter—the climb begins. Stephen, our hero until now, resolutely turns his back on us. The tone of the narrative is lost—no more path. The short, cut-up sentences multiply, and the allusions to many things that we know little or nothing about: the history of Ireland, ancient history, philosophy and scholastic theology, the domain of English poetry.

Third chapter—completely ill at ease. It is what appeared in the *N.R.F.* under the title "Protée" ["Proteus"]. The allusions become more and more shadowy, insupportable. Not only does Stephen turn his back on us, but he murmurs unintelligibly, for himself alone. Our company is not wanted. For the first time the book falls from our hands.

We pick it up again after a day's halt, at least. I'm speaking of the bravest. Here we are rewarded. After a title page indicating the second part of the work, we come at last upon the real hero of the book, Leopold Bloom: Ulysses, Larbaud tells us. As we continue our reading we do not find any relationship to the *Odyssey*, but the scrupulous recording of what a man who is very much alive thinks, says, and does. The succession of short, cut-up, exaggeratedly allusive little sentences—it's the celebrated *interior monologue*—still irritates us quite a bit, but we are already accustomed to it, and then the character onstage is no longer that bookish and self-satisfied Stephen.

Mr. Bloom is very sympathetic. He is essentially a man of good will. His mind moves easily about in things, even the most trivial, without lowering itself; it is not that he shows a truly elevated way of thinking, but he has a manner of communicating with events, at first deriving enjoyment from them, then applying all of his limited knowledge to them, while still aspiring toward a slight improvement—which deserves a tender smile from the goddess of Wisdom. He is the primitive of the twentieth century, the man born to Science, the nursling of great vulgarizations. Someday one will say "Bloomism" just as one says "Quixotism" or "Don Juanism."

So we follow this excellent Mr. Bloom through many comings and goings. His walks along the streets of Dublin, his bath, the burial at which he is present, his entrance into the offices of a newspaper, make up the subject of five chapters, which all bring us notable satisfaction.

It is curious, isn't it, this pleasure that one enjoys in the representation of familiar things, that forever unknown country that is the best known to us. It is well rendered, we say, which means that what the gods have given us we have re-created, we have been forced to render it to them—art, well-ordered exchange with the powers above; admission among the Immortals.

But let us return to Mr. Bloom, whom we left at the gate of the museum where he had gone to make a curious little verification.

In the following chapter, the ninth of the book, we lose him and find Stephen again.

We are in the city library with some young intellectuals. It is a rather difficult chapter to follow. Here again, Joyce cares very little about initiating us into the remarks that take place. I imagine that these remarks must seem clear enough to the Irish, and above all to those who, like the author of *Ulysses*, were intimately mixed up in the literary life of Dublin in 1904. We make out their preoccupations somehow or other: Celtic romanticism, symbolism, esotericism. All the young people have read Mallarmé, Villiers de l'Isle-Adam, the *Isis Unveiled* of Madame Blavatsky. They know the classic and modern English writers marvelously well; they have full awareness of their value and importance; their immediate seniors are: Yeats, George Moore, Synge, George Russell. Some among them found the Gaelic League and try to restore the old Irish language. The fame of the "Saxon" Shakespeare sets them to dreaming. In the group, which includes James Stephens and Padraic Colum, Stephen, who is Joyce himself as an adolescent, already shines out because of the breadth of his culture and the originality of his thought. The conversation that is established between him and his comrades centers almost entirely around the life and the works of Shakespeare, particularly *Hamlet*. Their discussions make us strongly aware of our ignorance. We knew from the first chapter—Buck Mulligan had already informed us of it ironically—that Stephen had theories about *Hamlet*; we are present at last at the exposition of these theories, which end up with an already famous definition of the idea of Paternity:

> Fatherhood, in the sense of conscious begetting, is unknown to man. It is a mystical estate, an apostolic succession, from only begetter to only begotten. On that mystery and not on the madonna which the cunning Italian intellect flung to the mob of Europe the church is founded and founded irremovably because founded, like the world, macro- and microcosm, upon the void. Upon incertitude, upon unlikelihood. *Amor matris,* subjective and objective genitive, may be the only true thing in life.

As you see, this definition is likely to arouse endless debates. Let us continue on our way without stopping here, for we should never be able to get out. We arrive now at a very restful chapter made up of a series of little scenes of Dublin life. The tone of these pieces is set by the first character who enters onstage, the very Reverend John Conmee S.J., that is to say, a benevolent man with a quiet mind, for whom the world has been explained once and for all. This is no longer the inquietude of Stephen or the incessant scrutiny of Bloom, but an outlook that is voluntarily superficial. Things are relieved of their inner problems and appear simply with their contours, their colors, their sounds, their movements; this way of seeing them, in passing, makes them more clear and often more real than they are when they serve as a support for an individual interpretation. It is thus that we are witnesses to the instability of the character of Simon Dedalus, Stephen's father, and to the wretchedness that prevails in the family. Joy in the street, grief in the house.

We come across the carefree Mr. Dedalus, the father, at the Osmond Bar in the company of the singer, Ben Dollard, Mr. Bloom, and several companions. Two charming barmaids, Miss Douce and Miss Kennedy, bronze and gold, preside over the place. Music and especially song form the background of this episode. Everything gravitates around Mr. Dedalus and Ben Dollard, who are invited to sing, sing, and have sung. The first two pages of the chapter have seemed, to most of the readers, very *surrealist,* that is to say, composed of capriciously assembled sentences without a logical connection with one another. The truth is that these pages constitute an *overture,* like an opera overture; the action that is about to take place is prefigured by brief calls that are later called again and developed. Onomatopoeia naturally has an important place in the style of this chapter that is dedicated to the art of sounds.

The episode that follows plunges the reader who has not been forewarned into perplexity. One can hardly make out the setting of the scene, which is the tavern of Barney Kiernan, and the characters that occupy it. A certain Citizen, accompanied by his dog, plays a role that is important, it seems, but that remains confused in the obscurity of the whole. However, each page contains admirable burlesque or lyrical developments. One understands nothing, and yet one is enchanted. The most apparent characteristic of the procedure employed here is an alternation of popular slang with the jargon of archaic legend, the daily newspaper, the high-society gazette, law, science, and politics. The events are related in a fashion that is by turns vulgar and idealistic; sentiments are reduced to their lowest motives, then exalted to distortion. Each detail, taken separately, does not present an insurmountable difficulty, but it is impossible to discover the sense of the composition as a whole. It is one of the chapters for which one cannot do without initiation. Once one knows that it corresponds to the Cyclops episode in *The Odyssey,* everything clears up. One understands that the slang represents a trivial, mundane viewpoint, that of Ulysses's companions, who are tied beneath the animals, and that the bombastic speeches are those of the giants. These giants represent, in some fashion, social organizations, commonplaces, traditions, heroes raised to the dignity of demigods by the people. The people themselves, taken individually, have only a gross and limited view, that of their ignorance, of their servitude, which the liberty of their speech relieves; it is like the man who barks with his dog.

After this very difficult piece there is, happily for us, a diversion. We are transported to a beach in the company of three girls; two of them are minding a baby and two little boys, and they behave like little mamas; the third, Gertie, is absorbed in daydreaming. Mr. Bloom, who is sitting not far from them, misses nothing of their manners and their idle words. This chapter, up to Bloom's final monologue, preserves the tone of the articles and famous little announcements of fashion magazines. Everything that the ordinary woman places at her own feet, the whole flattering murmur that a crowd of others like herself produces in her, all the beauty advice, the dictates of fashion, the insipid poetry, the tame mystery, all-purpose religion, recipes, etiquette, and, hovering over all, impregnating the least detail, love like the atmosphere—yes, everything is there; that devil of a Joyce has left out nothing. The masculine public keenly enjoyed this chapter.

We arrive now at an episode that is no less arduous than that of the "Cyclops," and for which it is just as indispensable to understand the particular intentions of the author. It has to do with the episode called the "Oxen of the Sun," which takes place in a maternity hospital. Mr. Bloom comes to get news about Mrs. Purefoy and finds a whole troop of friends in the waiting room, Stephen Dedalus among them.

This episode is composed of a succession of descriptions "in-the-manner-of," going from the earliest Anglo-Saxon writings to modern kinds of slang (including American slang), passing through the works of the fifteenth, sixteenth, seventeenth, eighteenth, and nineteenth centuries. The method adopted here tries to show the development of the fetus by the development of English prose. Here, according to Joyce's own indications, are the writers whose styles he has successively imitated: Mandeville, Malory, Bunyan, Defoe, Swift, Addison, Sterne, Goldsmith, Junius, Gibbon, Walpole, Lamb, DeQuincey, Landor, Macaulay, scientific reviews of the first half of the nineteenth century, Dickens, Thackeray, Newman, Pater, Ruskin, and Carlyle. This represents, as you see, a terrifying virtuosity. If the episode were not very licentious in places it would make an excellent exercise book for schools.

The chapters that follow are the most beautiful in my opinion; nevertheless, they do not present any real difficulties, and there is no need to be initiated in order to enjoy their beauties. The long episode in dramatic form that occurs in a red-light district, and which ends the second part of the work, is, in itself, an incontestable masterpiece.

Some critics have compared this episode to *Walpurgis Night* and to *The Temptation of Saint Anthony*, but these works seem primitive next to Joyce's "Circe." Here the phantasmagoria is no longer external, borrowed—it has an internal, logical truth that conforms to the particular brains of the protagonists, who in the state of hallucination brought on by drunkenness create their own demons, which issue from what is residual or at a larval stage within them. All possible objects of sensation, emotions, and more or less repressed tendencies become embodied and play episodic roles. The association of ideas, like a magician's accomplice, provokes their passage. This presents a spectacle that is no less swarming, ludicrous, repugnant, or terrible than those invented by the people or by the poet in a vein of black humor; but here there is, in addition, a prodigious psychophysiological operation. It is a scientifically established Hell, with the most modern improvements.

The third part of the work opens with a chapter that is worthy of more attention than is generally given to it. We are in a little bar, The Cabman's Shelter, where Mr. Bloom takes Stephen after having picked him up drunk on leaving the brothel. This chapter is written entirely—the sailor's speech apart—in the tone of Mr. Bloom's *external* conversation. One hears him really speaking, with his studied commonplaces, his superabundant politeness, his best general ideas—all the effort of a man who is responsive to others and who does not intend to be just anybody. It is an incomparably successful piece, perhaps the one that best shows the writer's mastery, his power of application, his fidelity to life. Such a piece will count among the literary exploits of the twentieth century.

Nor does the following chapter, written in the form of questions and answers, seem to me to have aroused all of the admiration that it deserves. No doubt, its form is disconcerting on a first approach and its long enumerations are sometimes tiring; but it is perhaps the summit of the work, from a strictly Joycean point of view. I have a good deal of difficulty, personally, in understanding the reservations of some readers. It seems to me that Joyce has found here a kind of stylization that is not without a relationship to Egyptian hieraticism, science being substituted for religion. This gives, at moments, in the most unexpected fashion, prodigious emotional or comic effects. The swiftness of the sentences, their completely scientific development, the immense energy that is summoned and utilized, produce at certain points a sort of luminous condensation which, through a double inverse action, enlarges the particular and diminishes the general. The least nuances of feelings or thoughts are boundlessly projected, while the earth with its myriads is reduced to what it is—a minuscule point in the heavens.

The final chapter—is there any need to speak of it? It is the celebrated monologue of the wife. Everybody has read it and reread it. I have even allowed myself to say that there are people who have read only that. Its particular style will no longer astonish. One knows that Joyce has suppressed punctuation in order to produce an impression of uninterrupted development, something like the rotation of the earth, the world being considered as the great Goddess-Mother, essential femininity. It is matter—"chaos of irrationality"—says Giordano Bruno, "insensible subject around which is produced the vicissitudes of forms," with the forms (and their vicissitudes) being brought in by the male principle.

Forgive me for having commented in such a summary, incomplete manner upon these episodes, which deserve long, learned works. The truth is that I have not tried to give a complete critical report on *Ulysses*, which MM. Valery Larbaud, Stuart Gilbert, Jean Cassou, René Lalou, Marc Chadourne, and above all Marcel Thiébaut have already done excellently. Nor have I tried to make the humanity of it stand out, which Philippe Soupault rightly believes to be the most important aspect.

My principal effort until now has been to isolate somehow or other certain general ideas oriented in a direction that is as literary as possible. I have wanted to bring to light the means of expression apparently utilized by Joyce and the effects that have been obtained by these means. I have deliberately put to the side the method of the interior monologue, which is, however, so important, and which is without a doubt the one that has been most quickly isolated and best studied of all of *Ulysses*'s resources.

I have abstained from utilizing the data coming from initiation, except for two chapters where it was difficult, if not impossible, to do without it: the "Cyclops" and the "Oxen of the Sun."

To sum it up, my purpose has been to discover some of the reflections that might follow the first patient, painstaking reading by a French reader.

Let us suppose that this reading occurred in March 1929, when the book had just appeared and the various authors I have mentioned had not yet published their studies, except Valery Larbaud, naturally.

We are a bit in the state of someone who has come back from a long and often painful journey. We have traveled over great stages without having seen anything, stupefied by fatigue. Thirst, mountain sickness, insect bites have made us suffer in their turn. But we have also enjoyed some good moments; astonishing and memorable spectacles have been offered, something like the arrival at Lhasa, the forbidden city.

One thing stands forth from our reflections first of all: *Ulysses* is a considerable literary undertaking. Its character of being a summa, an encyclopedia, has been underscored many times. All of the areas of knowledge, all of the genres, all of the methods find their place in it; in it all of the resources of expression are deployed in an assault upon all of the possible objects of expression. And here we shall formulate the first criticism that must be expected of us, who are French: Is this encyclopedic breadth not radically opposed to its artistic value? Is there not here, rather than a masterpiece, a superimposition of works that calls to mind the Tower of Babel and seems to invite its fate? Certainly, we are in the presence of a monster "that expands, that deforms in every direction a vain imitation of the immensity of the universe," as Jules Romains would have it, adding, "It is too much overlooked that though art has life for its subject, the work of art in itself is a living body. The miracle of art is not so much to absorb the subject as it is to organize it."

The famous *interior monologue*, for example, does it represent an appreciable literary resource? Upon reflection, no, for if it records the mechanism of the brain integrally its value is purely scientific; if it represents a new convention there is no reason to prefer it to our ordinary methods of analysis. Furthermore, as M. Auguste Bailly has judiciously observed, the integral psychic development, with its superimposed levels, cannot be reduced to the linear transposition that writing necessarily demands. The interior monologue as Joyce employs it cannot escape the arbitrary, and analysis clarifies the motives of an action or of a feeling better than itself, by isolating the essential currents of consciousness.

Let us pass on to other criticisms: Why the devil has he established so many useless and fortuitous correspondences with *The Odyssey*? And why, if the author sets store by these correspondences, has he presented his book without chapter titles, without a preface, without anything that might be able to guide us? The truth is that nobody is capable of discovering all of the intentions with which his book is stuffed; the best works written about him are, in large part, it must be said, based on his own indications; the initiation always comes from himself. We agree that obscurity may be produced, as Valéry says, by "accumulated work," but not by a stubborn desire to make obscure.

The composition of *Ulysses*, when one really thinks about it, seems like a maniac, senseless, taunting thing. It demands of the reader, at every instant, an immense effort that it does not always reward. It proposes to him nothing but riddles, obstacles, mortifications. It is true that life does not treat us any differently, but isn't art, according to its very definition, in opposition to brute nature? It is a part of nature, but it represents essentially the elements of it that are hierarchically ordered—dispensers of harmony and contemplation. Where in *Ulysses* can be found a passage like the one in *War and Peace* where Prince André, alone and wounded, looks at the sky? Where can be found that air of beautiful weather, that temperature of great works that solaces once and for all the tormented heart of man, that justifies his hope?

As Curtius says, "Properly speaking, we can call geniuses only those men whose production reflects something of the divine meaning of the world, whose creation brings about an exaltation of life. A light and a force emanate from the work of genius. It illuminates the spirit and reflection, it purifies and ennobles the passions, it gives birth to images that form our life. Even the highest intensity of the spirit, the highest degree of inventive and descriptive powers do not constitute genius if this work lacks the force that enlightens and fructifies. The work of Joyce issues from the revolt of the spirit and leads to the destruction of the world." He adds: "*Ulysses* unmasks, exposes, demolishes, and degrades humanity with a sharpness and a thoroughness that have no equivalent in modern thought."

Even though coming from a German, these reflections express the essential grievances of French idealists. Furthermore, a great French idealist, M. Charles Du Bos, has mentioned them in a study published by the *Nouvelle Revue Française*.

Yes, have we not suffered, while reading *Ulysses*, not only from its literary obscurity but also from its moral obscurity? Are not the most indulgent pictures of the book those of filth, drunkenness, and debauchery? Isn't everything that we surround with respect and poetry—love, death, religion—*degraded?* That is certainly the word in this cruel work.

But I do not want to expatiate any longer on the faults of *Ulysses*, they are innumerable. Nevertheless, let us not omit, in finishing, the criticism of M. André Maurois, who has written that "*Ulysses* considered as a novel was a checkmate."

Oh well, yes, *Ulysses* is not a work of art, it is not a successful novel, it is not an elevated production. There is nothing beautiful, nothing adroit, nothing sublime about it. And nevertheless, when we have said this, we are not at rest, we feel that we have not passed judgment and that this book that is without height dominates and judges us.

It has been defined as "a human summa." It is true that it is certainly a human sum, that is to say, a possible total of that which, in man, is *of the world*, in opposition to that which is *not of the world*, as Rimbaud understood it.

Confucius used to say to disciples who questioned him about the mystery of death: "When one doesn't understand yet what life is, how can one understand death?" He also used to say to those who asked him about how the spirits and the genii were to be served: "When one is not yet in a condition to serve men, how can one serve the spirits and the genii?"

Joyce seems to have undertaken the task of serving men in helping them to understand themselves wholly.

That is a more unusual endeavor than it seems; to arrive at such ends one never fails to make use of God and the mysteries. One believes that God can explain man, while it is perhaps man who can explain God. The Earth and its functions have never been very seductive to our species. It has always seemed to the best among us a place of passage, an exile. The spirit contained in this bit of matter that composes us draws us beyond, above, it evaporates us, it wins us over to nebulous indulgences. And no doubt there is a tendency here that does proceed toward a real goal. Our aspiration toward God, toward a pure, harmonious, and eternal state is something that is as real as our need to eat. But before attaining this state, which is perhaps, like everything, ideally contained in our expectation of it, is it not worthwhile to give an exact account of the very situation in which we are immersed? If there is a fortunate way out of this passage, does it not depend upon our living well, that is to say, a way of living that is conscientious and conscious? Why not accept, why not appreciate what is *given*? Is it in the order of things that one who is discontented will ever be satisfied, and doesn't joy always catch fire from joy, as flame from flame?

It may seem strange to pronounce the word *joy* in relation to Joyce, whose work seems basically pessimistic to some, because the spiritual remains improbable in it and because only the material is certain in it. But there is nothing pessimistic about this declaration, it is first of all the result of good sense. Certainly, men have always placed their confidence in the spiritual, it is a bank which, it seemed to them, would reimburse them a hundredfold. It does not seem that it has really succeeded for them as yet. It has succeeded, no doubt, for those who expected nothing from the material world, for the sages and the saints, for those who converted all their funds into spiritual values and then never drew upon them. But that is a precious and unforeseeable minority upon whom one cannot depend for the issue of currency. Nothing should be founded upon them. We must know how to do without them as much as they do without us.

A man like Joyce does without them so as not to be deprived of the immensity of the others. I have always thought that the presence of a profound charity was at the basis of his work. The overwhelming task that he imposed upon himself, that invention of a sensible world—an inventory that supposes, that calls for a classification—no doubt has nothing to do with traditional saintliness, but it nevertheless has something saintly about it, even in the Christian sense, which distinguishes it from the ordinary enterprises of philosophy or literature. Does it not show, to the highest degree, humility, abnegation, courage, patience? It does not aim for a perfection that is impossible, contrary to all the laws of life, obtained only by convention or by fraud. It aims for integrity of consciousness. It practices the virtues of an age of science, whose asceticism is no less harsh than that of the ages of religion.

Far from saying, like Curtius, that the work of Joyce issues from the revolt of the spirit, I shall say that it issues from the submission of the spirit. Yes, the submission of the spirit to nature, to matter—matter being understood, in a certain philosophical sense, *as any physical or mental datum that an activity receives ready-made and subsequently elaborates.*

Furthermore, if matter—even as understood in the current sense of the word—tends toward the spirit as toward a superior state, does the spirit not tend toward matter as toward its unique consecration? Ideas, at the highest stage of their evolution, put on a body. Divine principles invest themselves in flesh so as to be manifest, certain, sensible.

"That which is above is like that which is beneath, and that which is beneath is like that which is above." This could be the very epigraph of *Ulysses*. For Joyce, as for all mystics—and he is, himself, a mystic of the human—all is in all, the least reveals the most, each thing produces its opposite, everything is bound together by invisible or secret correspondences, and sometimes the most visible are the most secret. But this state of truth, of unity, that the mystics express by means of the purest and most beautiful images, Joyce tries to express by it does not matter what means, by means of evil as well as good. He chooses, when he does choose, that which has been sacrificed, shamed, cut off, mistreated—that which nobody had ever dared to present as it really was, that which had always been regarded as outside of the law, outside of love. Nothing to him appears useless or unworthy. Everything feeds the belly of his Our Lady of the Underworld.

It is also through spiritual submission to the real, to every physical and mental datum, that Joyce possesses and utilizes so much bookish erudition. The important thing, for him, is not to formulate a personal interpretation of Ideas, of God, which perhaps seem to him to defy all rational interpretation; but rather it is to understand that which has been expressed of them, that which, drawn from their eternal essence, has become embodied in an action, a doctrine, a tradition, or a book, that which has engendered the present. He concerns himself little with the possible truth of a belief, but rather with the power with which the accumulation of twenty centuries has been able to endow it. That makes up a part of the inventory, of the potential estimation of the resources and the reserves of this world. There is in him a kind of *unanimism* in time, as appears in the very plan of *Ulysses*. It is not from Joyce, precisely, that the criticism of systems in power, the shaking of established institutions is to be expected. The purely passive resistance that he sometimes opposes against them even gives them a real consolation, as if he were buttressing them. His mockery, when he shows it, is hardly exercised except at the expense of the pretensions of the present.

Yes, contrary to what it seems, his work aims at neither reform nor satire. He never places himself above what he describes, he never establishes belittling relationships between the effort and the result, he does not accuse, he does not blame in any way at all, he redresses nothing. He is only true, terribly true, and that is the very reason why he offends us.

Certainly, as Curtius says, Joyce exposes humanity; but he does not degrade it. It is itself that is often degraded, less through its dependence upon the laws of nature than through its ignorance and presumption. What he seems to lower, we ourselves have caused to fall by trying to hang it up too high. If love, religion, and death seem, through his work, ugly and dirty, that is because we have scribbled over them without end. He administers to us an excellent auto-vaccination!

From *Les Gazettes d'Adrienne Monnier*; first published in *La Gazette des Amis des Livres* (May 1940).

The Translation of Ulysses

The idea of translating *Ulysses* must have impressed itself upon us almost at once around 1920–21. It impressed itself upon me as soon as Sylvia Beach had spoken to me about the work; upon Valery Larbaud once he had finished reading it; upon Fargue, who, very much interested by what he had heard said about it, had a great desire to see it in French; upon all of our friends who did not know English.

But who would be the translator? The first victim designated by fate was inevitably Larbaud. When Joyce had made his acquaintance and had become aware of his great worth as a writer, as a translator, and, I shall add, as a friend, he had only one desire—that was to see him translate *Ulysses*. First of all, only he was capable of it. I really believe that it was I who, on Joyce's instigation, was the first to speak to him about it. He did not say no. He even said: "Yes." Great tasks did not frighten him. He had attacked the work of Samuel Butler, of which he had translated five volumes, to which were added studies and notes and the corrections of the proofs of the two volumes that had already appeared: *Erewhon* the year before and *The Way of All Flesh* in the spring of this present year, 1921. All that had taken him five years.

In spite of his good intentions, Larbaud did not offer to translate the first fragments of *Ulysses*, which were going to be read in the course of the meeting in December 1921. First of all, I gave him too short notice; he had only a month to write the lecture he was going to deliver on that occasion. This lecture would be nothing less than a survey of Joyce and his work that he had been thinking about for several months; in it he would present *Ulysses*, which he was the only one in France to be acquainted with; he would make an effort to describe it as clearly and as completely as possible. It was a crushing task that demanded all his strength and from which nothing must distract him. I had to find someone to translate the beginning of the "Sirens" and the end of "Penelope," which he wanted to read following his lecture. If necessary, Joyce would give explanations and would review the work himself when it was finished.

I hardly know what I should have done without Jacques Benoist-Méchin, who counted then among the friends of the house.

Benoist-Méchin was a very young man (he was less than twenty years old). He wanted to become a composer and was taking the courses of the Schola Cantorum; we were not in a position to judge his musical gifts, but one thing was clear to us—his very keen liking for literature. He showed so much seriousness and intelligence in his talk that the great men of the Rue de l'Odéon saw him sympathetically and conversed with him. He knew English remarkably well and German almost as well; he could read and appreciate the most difficult works in these two languages. Sylvia had passed on to him the numbers of the *Little Review* in which fragments of *Ulysses* had appeared, and he had been carried away by them. He was in Larbaud's favor: at the time of the lecture on Samuel Butler, he had performed on the piano some Handelian pieces by the English writer, who, as you know, was also a composer and a painter.

So, Benoist-Méchin offered to translate the fragments of *Ulysses* chosen by Larbaud. As these fragments bristled with difficulties, he set up a relationship with Joyce, who behaved exquisitely toward him and granted him an audience every time he desired one.

Joyce, moreover, who had sensed how much Fargue was related to him, set great store by his collaboration. Fargue asked nothing better than to join the work sessions. Above all, he was to give a turn to "Penelope" that was masterful, yet just the same terrified the young man a little; and of course he was going to undertake the bawdy parts.

So things happened with the usual little hitches: to wit, Fargue stood up Joyce and Benoist-Méchin I don't know how many times.

So much and so well that Larbaud did not have the translations until December 3, and even then "Penelope" was not delivered to him until the 5th, as Fargue had not put himself into action sooner. With his lecture finished on the night of the 6th, he had to review the translations in one day without recovering his breath. I have a note from him dated that December 6, the eve of the meeting, in which, speaking of the fragment of "Penelope," he says, "There is still much to clear up, certain passages completely obscure, not *brought out* by Benoist-Méchin." Poor Larbaud! My heart is torn every time I pick that note up again, I can see so well from the handwriting that he is harassed.

This first translation of fragments from *Ulysses*, made in haste, was not published. It was not until 1924, in the first number of *Commerce*, that these fragments appeared, augmented by others that this time had benefited from much more elaborate work.

In the meantime, the problem of translating *Ulysses* had assumed a different aspect: Larbaud had renounced doing it and Auguste Morel had agreed to undertake it.

On March 24, 1922, Larbaud had written me the following from Rome, where he was staying:

> I am sending you a surprising letter that I have received from George Moore. Strictly between you, Sylvia, and myself. Joyce can know about it, but nobody besides him. He pays me a great deal of honor; but I don't want to translate anything more, since I am renouncing translation so completely that I am even renouncing making one of *Ulysses*.
>
> Who is going to translate it? Morel? A small printing of 2,000 copies at 2.50 francs a copy?

(As George Moore is no longer living, it seems to me that there is no indiscretion in giving his name.)

Larbaud's renouncement is abrupt only in appearance. I am convinced that it was preceded by all kinds of reflections. Given the number of authors whose ambition it was to have him as a translator and as a manager (his launching of Joyce must have made many of them dream of it), without counting those toward whom he was drawn by his own admiration, he risked being crushed without respite beneath translations and prefaces, without the possibility of ever accomplishing his own work, if he gave in, if he let himself go. His friends and admirers could only rejoice over such a decision—myself first of all.

And now, who was Morel? This is what Larbaud wrote on the subject to André Gide, January 25, 1921:

> Auguste Morel is a young man (not thirty years old) who was born on the Ile Bourbon, and his translations appear excellent to me. Apart from Claudel I have never seen anyone so good as a translator of English poetry. First he translated "An Anthem of the Earth" by Francis Thompson (published in Les Cahiers des Amis des Livres). Then he attacked that enormous poem of Thompson's, "The Hound of Heaven" (finished), and after having translated some poems of John Donne's he approached the great poem of William Blake, in which he succeeded admirably.

We had known Morel since the beginning of 1920. He had gone to see Larbaud in order to submit to him some translations of English poems, and you can see from these lines what the master thought about them. It was under the influence of such a judgment that I published everything he had done of Francis Thompson: first "Une Antienne de la terre" ["An Anthem of the Earth"], then, the following year, in 1921, "Le Lévrier du ciel" ["The Hound of Heaven"] (accompanied by the poems: "Corymbe d'automne" ["Corymb of Autumn"], "A feu le cardinal de Westminster" ["To the Late Cardinal of Westminster"], "Une Antienne de la terre" ["An Anthem of the Earth"], and "En nul étrange lieu" ["In No Strange Land"]). These were preceded by "Vie de Thompson" ["Life of Thompson"] and followed by "Réflexions" by Morel himself.

I should like to be able to talk about *La Muse angloise* [*The English Muse*]. May it suffice to say here that under this title Morel, in collaboration with Madame Annie Hervieu, had made a bilingual collection of English poets. The remarkable thing about this anthology was that the poems were translated into the French of the period corresponding to the English. All of the poems that I have seen of it have seemed to me to be surprisingly successful. In the first issue of the *Navire d'Argent* I presented "De sa maistresse allant au lict," after John Donne's "To His Mistress Going to Bed." Larbaud tried in vain to find a publisher for this work. I was myself tempted to publish it, but I did not have the means of doing so, all the less so because I had to keep all of my available funds for the publication of the translation of *Ulysses*, which I was planning. It's a pity that this beautiful anthology has not appeared!

As Larbaud had renounced doing the translation of *Ulysses*, it was natural to speak about it to Morel, as he suggested. I no longer remember very well my first talks with Morel on this subject; I believe he was terrified by the task, and, above all, his *Muse angloise* was occupying him a lot. He wanted to finish it and find a publisher for it. He did not undertake *Ulysses* until the beginning of 1924, and then only after he had been given the assurance that he would receive all the help possible from Joyce and Larbaud—it was understood that Joyce would provide him with all the necessary explanations, and that Larbaud would review the work entirely and write a preface.

In the spring of that same year the Rue de l'Odéon was very busy: we were preparing the first number of *Commerce*. In the table of contents for this number were to appear the names of Valéry, Fargue, Larbaud, Saint-John Perse, and Joyce. The Princesse de Bassiano had asked Larbaud to translate an episode from *Ulysses* for her review; in spite of the decision he had made he could not refuse her; he thought of setting to work on the "Sirens" or on "Nausicaa." He was also expected to contribute an article by himself, and that was what we prized the most. He quickly estimated that he would not be able to finish everything. He wrote to me in May that each of the chosen episodes demanded "two months of exhausting labor—and without doing anything else." He added: ". . . Why don't you ask Morel for his translation of the first episode?" Which I did without wasting a minute.

Morel was at one and the same time both happy about the proposition and upset about having to hurry so much. As he said, "The number of pages to be furnished would be nothing without the centers of resistance that they contain." The first episode ("Telemachus") was almost finished, but it was a first version that seemed to him to demand much more work still, and we needed it by the end of the month—in ten days. In short, he was going to do the impossible.

The time available was prolonged by a week, but alas, we were now asking, in addition to "Telemachus," for fragments of "Ithaca" (the episode written in the form of questions and answers). On the other hand, "Telemachus" would not be published in its entirety; we would only present the first two-thirds of it, which would shorten the work a bit in that area. Larbaud had decided to publish passages taken from three different episodes so that the public might have a more complete idea of the work; he much prized the last pages of the final episode, "Penelope," a perfect example of the interior monologue. But he was going to take the responsibility for that himself. He had already been occupied with it at the time of the Joyce meeting—it was feasible.

On June 6 Morel presented me with his translations. He told me at the same time: "I am not very satisfied with my work, but I am satisfied—very—with the passage that has been worked on. Joyce is truly the Whitman of prose, a Whitman who speaks all of the languages of Whitman and then some."

We had rushed Morel terribly. If we had foreseen Fargue's and Valéry's lateness, we would have been able to give him a good two weeks more. Fargue's lateness, let us say, was foreseeable.

On June 8 we had—Sylvia, Larbaud (passing through Paris), and myself—a short work session, which Larbaud recalled in such a kindly way in a letter written on the 17th, that I cannot resist the pleasure of quoting passages from it:

> It was enjoyable, yes, that translation session on Sunday. But I was hardly in good form. Sylvia found the expressions that were most French, and I, dazed by a bad night and the fear of being late at the Gare de Lyon where Ray was waiting for me, I made lamentable efforts to recall some popular expressions that I nevertheless collect in my heart in every country. My Paris housekeeper says, speaking of her concierge, "She's a horror of a woman." Do you see a place where that might go? But Molly Bloom is not as plebeian as Fargue has made her. I believe that the tone discovered by Sylvia is much more exact.

Originally *Commerce* was supposed to appear in June. It was at the end of June that Fargue handed in his copy, that is to say, the poems that I had spent I do not know how many nights taking down under his dictation. It is true that Valéry was even later, and he did not give in his text until the beginning of July.

Also at the beginning of July, Joyce, who meant to remain the master of all kinds of difficulties, suggested that it would be good, for the translation of the fragment of "Penelope," to suppress not only the punctuation, as had been done, but also the accents over the letters and the apostrophes. It was necessary to write to Larbaud to ask him for his advice.

I hurried to write to Larbaud. I was frankly against it, not against the suppression of the punctuation, which conformed to the original text, but against the suppression of the accents and the apostrophes, which was not logical, as English does not include them. It was neither French nor Joyce. Look at the first sentence, for example:

> . . . *le quart quelle heure pas de ce monde jimagine quils se levent en ce moment en Chine peignent leurs queues pour la journee bon bientot nous entendrons les soeurs sonner langelus elles nont personne qui vienne deranger le sommeil excepte un pretre ou deux pour son office de nuit le reveil des gens da cote avec son cri de coq qui se fait eclater la tete voyons si je pourrais me rendormir 1 2 3 4 5 quescequecest que cette espece de fleurs quils ont invente comme les etoiles. . .*

> . . . a quarter after what an unearthly hour I suppose theyre just getting up in China now combing out their pigtails for the day well soon have the nuns ringing the angelus theyve nobody coming in to spoil their sleep except an odd priest or two for his night office the alarmclock next door at cockshout clattering the brains out of itself let me see if I can doze off 1 2 3 4 5 what kind of flowers are those they invented like the stars . . .

To my great surprise, Larbaud replied in a telegram sent from Marina di Pisa on July 6:

"Joyce is right Joyce *ha ragione*."

So it was that way in the first number of *Commerce*, which appeared in the middle of August. It naturally caused a sensation when the summer season was over. It was stronger than Apollinaire and his school. After all, it fulfilled Joyce's intention very well, which was to represent the uninterrupted progression of the earth and its formlessness. Gide had just published *Corydon*; we used to say, laughing, that Penelope was a "hideous female" without accents.

These events took place, we have said, in 1924. The translation of *Ulysses* did not appear in book form until 1929. Five years still separated us from the goal, five years of almost continual difficulties. I do not believe that we would have been able to finish the job to Joyce's satisfaction without the "providential" arrival of Stuart Gilbert.

I am a bit out of breath from telling you about the ups and downs of our first two attempts, not from writing, but from living it all over again. Allow me, dear readers, to recover my breath before telling you the rest.

From *Rue de l'Odéon*; first published in *Mercure de France* (May 1950).

Benoist-Méchin

Now let us talk about Benoist-Méchin. We have known him for six years. He used to come to us when he was a young student at the Schola. We were struck by his seriousness, by his passionate liking for poetry and philosophy. He spoke little about music, and when he did speak about it his voice was a bit choked up. He read Bergson, lost Gide the better to find him again, was enchanted by Giraudoux, supported Proust against myself, let himself be carried away by Jules Romains and touched by Duhamel, remained a captive of Valéry, and gave himself completely to Claudel. He was there when Valéry read us, in a corner of the bookshop, the pages of *Eupalinos*, which he was about to hand over to his publisher. One day he showed us, jubilant, a copy of *Partage de midi [Break of Noon]* that he had written by hand. We saw him translate fragments of *Ulysses* for Larbaud, who was preparing his lecture on Joyce. He had already assisted Larbaud at the time of the meeting devoted to Samuel Butler, and he had played on the piano some of the Handelian compositions by the author of *Erewhon*. No young man was so much the son of the house as he was. No one was more eager in study and in good deeds. I compared him with pleasure to the Disciples at Sais, of whom Novalis speaks; but for him, as for myself, the Master was the several masters who had been brought together in a single ideal face whose features we never ceased to contemplate.

When Benoist-Méchin left for his military service, which he performed at Wiesbaden and Düsseldorf, he did not waste his time. He went to Berlin and to many cities, and there he distributed the books that he loved and spread his admiration and his ideas. When *Charmes* appeared, he had several copies of it sent to him, which he gave to universities and to people with influence. He paid a visit to Curtius. He attached himself to Unruh and decided that he should have the French know about the work of this man, who no longer lived or breathed except for peace. At that moment I criticized him for wanting to become a translator: I told him that it would harm his career as a musician, but much he cared about his personal success! He too, as much as Unruh, had felt the urgent need to bring about the reign of peace, and he intended to sacrifice all his strength to it. When his translation of *Verdun* appeared, the critics—for he had done it in a hurry, as one runs in order to save time—pointed out misinterpretations and attacked it rather strongly. So one often sees generous works poorly rewarded. The gods are demanding, but despite appearances there is no injustice, and no trouble is wasted. What has been inflicted upon the translator will be spared the musician, and the effort that seems vain in one domain will provide stronger wings and more space elsewhere.

A number of days ago Benoist-Méchin performed for a group of friends that included the dearest of our masters, a piano version of *Choeurs pour une exposition coloniale [Choruses for a Colonial Exhibition]*, which he composed for the poems of Jules Supervielle. Everybody was surprised by the fullness and the force of the whole, by the novelty of certain accents, by the truly transcendent beauty of the finales. I believe that Benoist-Méchin, who is only twenty-four years old, is still too full of the seriousness of adolescence; and I could wish him to be less continually high-strung, less abstract. He should, following the example of Claudel, whom he loves so much, have greater contact with the real. But once these reservations have been made, I must say that I am very proud of our son. He seems to me to be protected from pettiness; he does not have that inclination to astonish and amuse in a facile kind of way, which sometimes ruins the most gifted; he has great inspirations, a great deal of patience and craft. Our faith goes with him!

From *Les Gazettes d'Adrienne Monnier*; first published in *Le Navire d'Argent* (January 1926).

Readings at Sylvia's

About eighteen months ago our friend Sylvia Beach was thinking sadly that she would no doubt have to close the beautiful English-language library that she established here seventeen years ago. The economic crisis, from which French booksellers are already suffering so much, made her suffer even more, naturally.

One day she told Gide about her worries, and about the decision she had already made to give up the place. "But that is impossible," he said sharply. "You play a role among us that we could not do without now, you give us invaluable help. Something must be done."

Then the idea came to us to form a group of Friends of Shakespeare and Company who would pay a yearly subscription. It was Jenny de Margerie and Jean Schlumberger who, in the course of a decade at Pontigny, had the excellent idea of readings by authors, readings that would take place in the very setting of Sylvia's bookshop and that would be offered to the Friends.

Schlumberger drew up an appeal. A committee of patrons was formed that included: Georges Duhamel, Luc Durtain, André Gide, Louis Gillet, Jacques de Lacretelle, André Maurois, Paul Morand, Jean Paulhan, Jules Romains, Jean Schlumberger, and Paul Valéry. We should have liked to see the name of our great Claudel appear on this committee, but we did not dare to solicit him: we knew that he did not forgive us for having published Joyce's *Ulysses*. Hadn't he written to us on that subject: *"Ulysses*, like the *Portrait*, is full of the filthiest blasphemies, in which one feels all the hatred of a renegade—afflicted, moreover, by a really diabolical absence of talent." After that—

So, in January this year readings were given at Sylvia's. It was Gide who began them, giving a hearing to fragments of his as yet unpublished *Geneviève*. We know that Gide reads in an admirable manner. His voice moves through a text with a timbre and an authority that awaken a world. It swims with the great stroke of the king of the Nagas in the heart of blessed Hells.

In February, on the 29th, for it was a leap year, Valéry read prose pieces of his *Alphabet*, chosen from among the most graceful. Afterward he read us "Narcisse" (we had told him of our great desire to hear him read his verses). As at a café-concert, several guests asked for an encore: "Le Cimetière marin" ["The Cemetery by the Sea"]. But it was to Joyce, who imperatively requested "Le Serpent," that satisfaction was given. Valéry, who readily declares that he lacks the art of reading, read his "Serpent" in such a perfect fashion—not as an actor, but as an author, yes, the whole author was present—that even now, when we think of it, our hearts beat in our heads.

At the end of March, Jean Schlumberger read an unpublished comedy, *La Tentation de Tati* [*The Temptation of Tati*]. Schlumberger read ravishingly well, in a simple, adept, and gay manner. His own reading more than any other helped us to recover the atmosphere of the salons of the eighteenth century, in which the most enjoyable exchanges of the spirit took place. His comedy, in which the savages have as much to say as Montesquieu's Persians, and who say it as well, seemed made for this delight.

While listening to Jean Paulhan read *Les Fleurs de Tarbes [The Flowers of Tarbes]* at the beginning of May, I thought of a snake charmer. The line of his voice moved toward the idea like the sound of a flute, and the idea, undulating, reared up like a cobra; it sometimes seemed that the idea was about to throw itself upon its charmer. Paulhan quickly arose, stepped away a bit, fixed the creature with a look (the fangs had not been drawn, I assure you), then his voice went on, insidiously.

To crown this first cycle of meetings, the great English poet, T. S. Eliot, came to Paris on June 6 to read us some poems. The poetry of T. S. Eliot passes, and rightly so, for being obscure. Completely grounded in a very profoundly original sensibility, it is full of incommunicable motifs, slight and overwhelming states of grace that the Zen Buddhists call *satoris*. The poet as he reads knows how to pass his trance on to you; he has a pure voice with a reverberating intonation, well assured in its tranquil torment. His face is handsome and curious: that of an archangel who has too much work to do, and so does only half of it, leaving the rest to the North Wind.

In London this winter they played an admirable drama of his with striking success: *Murder in the Cathedral.* This moving work, which is not at all hermetic, should be translated and played here. Why shouldn't Jean de Menasce, who has already put *The Waste Land* into French so remarkably, translate it?

From *Les Gazettes d'Adrienne Monnier*; first published in *La Nouvelle Revue Française* (July 1936).

Number One

This gazette, doesn't it seem to you that it has always existed a little? In 1925, when I spoke for the first time to Paul Valéry about my project for doing the *Navire d'Argent*, he looked at me and then, fixing a point beyond, he said to me, "No, Monnier, it's not a review that you should do, you ought to publish a sort of bulletin."

At that moment the remark was without effect. I do not even believe that it inspired the gazette of the *Navire*, the idea for which came to me only at the end of six months of navigation. To tell the truth, I am discovering it again only now, at the moment when I am getting ready to give reality to what the poet saw in the space of my bookshop, what our gods were already holding out to me.

For three or four years I have been thinking about this gazette; something in my mind fought against it—the second part of my catalog, devoted to foreigners. I often told myself: First of all you have to finish your catalog, you shall do nothing before your catalog is completed. And then I lacked money, as much as for the one as for the other of these undertakings. The last few years have been hard for booksellers, that is to say, it has become more and more difficult to earn one's living; but we shall come back to this question later on; at bottom these last few years do not displease me so much.

One fine day I thought: but why shouldn't I do the catalog and the gazette at the same time? Previously, after the *Navire d'Argent*, I had had the idea of continuing the only personal part of the review —the reports and the bibliography.

But the time had come when the translation of *Ulysses*, undertaken by Auguste Morel, was finished at last and when it was necessary to publish it. I passed the whole winter of 1928 correcting the proofs in the company of Stuart Gilbert.

A bit later the critical catalog of my lending library appeared to me to be, of all my tasks, the most urgent and the most practical. I assembled my materials and, after a year of confinement, my catalog was able to appear in 1932. Like the *Navire*, it was a heavy expense that put me into a long period of distress.

Three years ago, when Jean Paulhan proposed the administration of *Mesures* to me, I was very glad to accept it; five hundred francs a month, that was not negligible. He had the kindness to offer me a bit more, but it was I myself who fixed the total amount at five hundred, estimating that it was sufficient and that it would not spoil me. For sure, the work that it represented did not please me very much; that administration was to include only bookkeeping, management, business correspondence—all things of which I already had more than my requirement at my bookshop. Many people imagined that my administration was a concealed directorship, and the trouble that I took to undeceive them only served, in many cases, to strengthen them in their belief. I had painful scenes with authors, above all at the time of the poetry prize; I even received some unkind letters. Since you see me now free at last in my little review, I am glad to be able to say publicly that *Mesures* was founded by Henry Church, a French-speaking American writer. Henry Church has always had the literary directorship of his review in his hands, in the company of Jean Paulhan, Bernard Groethuysen, Henri Michaux, and Giuseppe Ungaretti. I have never taken part in questions of editing; on the other hand, Sylvia Beach has been consulted rather often on the subject of English language texts translated into French. That's it. As I have now given my resignation as administrator, and as the review will be managed in the future by another bookseller, people will really be forced to believe me.

Last spring something happened to me that in many respects is a windfall; after three years of bargaining and between two devaluations, Gallimard bought the translation of *Ulysses* from me. They paid 22,000 francs for it. For this amount they got the remaining stock of copies (1,400, exactly), the copyright, and the standing type, which was at the printer. They had a good deal, and I consider that I did not have a bad one, since it brought me money in a time of trouble.

Thanks to that deal, I could return to my project for a gazette. But other difficulties were awaiting me. My 20,000 francs or so gave me the illusion of wealth for two or three months, and made me forget the exact state of my bookshop; I was not enough aware that my subscription fees for reading were far from being adjusted to the price of books and to all the surrounding increases. When, upon my return from vacation, I had the idea of doing my accounts seriously, I saw that for ten months my expenses had continually exceeded my receipts. I had a deficit of nearly 3,000 francs—if my employees had received their remuneration, I myself had not received any. I think that in reading this many businessmen will smile at these figures and this declaration. It is customary to hear it said nowadays that people are working at a loss; in general those who say that have a car and servants. For myself, who live almost from day to day, and for most booksellers, to work at a loss for let us say a year means being forced to shut up shop. I therefore had to take immediate steps. If I were to wait a few more months, all of my little reserve would be exhausted and then goodbye forever, gazette!

I laid off my principal employee, whose salary was 1,200 francs (union salary), and decided to run my bookshop by myself, helped by one apprentice. In order to be able to face all of my tasks I resolved to open only in the afternoon; it was necessary, in fact, to reserve at least the morning for bookkeeping, arranging the books, shipping to subscribers, corresponding—and, if it was possible, for a little reading, for continuing my catalog, for the gazette. Ah! my gazette, what was it going to become? Here we are in October, a month filled up with accounts. It is the time of the return to Paris. Without a stop people are coming to change their books, not a second to oneself, not even the time to put some ideas together. October passes. I am getting along very well all alone. The annoyance is being obliged to explain to each person the reasons for the steps that I have taken, which I have communicated to them by circular letter. How could anyone have imagined that with so much patronage I should have a deficit? But they understand. We all know very well that in our times nothing is easy.

October has passed. It's the first week in November. My whole text must be sent to the printer in two weeks at the most, if I want to appear in January. My strength is failing me. I think of Valéry, who is made absolutely ill by the approach of his lectures at the Collège de France. As Fernand Gregh says, with whom I chatted one evening: "He's not a professor, he has to pull it out of his guts." And I, who am only the lady of the house of books, I too have to pull it out of my guts. All this time I have not ceased to prepare my words, am I going to be incapable of expressing them?

Today, Sunday, November 7, I am writing at last, I am beginning to write. I went down to my bookshop to be more at peace. I am sitting at my habitual place, in the heart of the little ark in which I have been sailing for twenty-two years.

Around me, everywhere, books. The light of my lamp runs its silver fingers over the flat crystal of the paper that covers over all the little pressed-together backs. Behind those backs there is a simple and mysterious body, which is that of the human spirit itself, of which the essential is invisible. A savage who had never seen books and who did not understand the secret of writing, on opening one of these volumes would think perhaps of an anthill or of blades of grass, or of the sky riddled with stars. That infinity, which has come forth from us, does it not hold its own with the infinity from which we come forth, which crushes us with its empty looks? Book, interior firmament. Country of Memory, where the Mothers lull us and ever smile at us. Little books made to the measure of human hands, often pressed against our heart. Books upon which we lean our brow, which give our brow its brightness and its weight. They that love you and that live in your presence know serenity; they already have dealings with the immortals. They know that the whole length of their earthly road you will never be wanting. Before books disappear humankind will have disappeared.

But, you will say, are they not in the course of disappearing? Have we not heard it said for a year from all sides that they are menaced, that they are lost; hasn't Georges Duhamel founded the Alliance du Livre in order to try to save them? Aren't authors, publishers, booksellers, in a slump? Cultural crisis, book crisis—that is the subject of one does not know how many speeches, articles, news items. We are going to try to examine the question seriously.

It is certain that for several years the public has been buying no books or almost no books. This abstention, coming after a period of intense consumption, is afflicting, alarming. It has been said a hundred times that the successive increases in the price of books are less than those that other goods have undergone. In short, books are presently at six or seven times their prewar price, while almost all the rest costs eight, nine, or ten times more. That is exact, but it must also be said, and it has been said without fail, that the expensive material life absorbs the resources of most people almost completely and leaves only a very narrow margin for the expenses of the life of the spirit. Material life, whether one wants it to or not, represents a primary necessity; one has to eat every day, one has to have a place to live, one has to dress. All the same, you will say, there are people who have money for books; they have a lot of it for travel, shows, good dinners; France does not exactly present the picture of a country condemned to all kinds of restrictions; in many cases, in many places, people are spending cheerfully. That is true. Oh, people are not irreproachable! But let us put ourselves a bit in their place: how should they have a liking for buying books when they see such a heap of sales among the booksellers? In one place they are offered at a considerable price a volume that has just appeared; elsewhere, if they stroll around a bit, they find the author's copies of the same work, that is to say, in a first printing, for half the price that is marked. So many illustrated works, beautiful slim books, limited editions that were at a premium some years ago are now offered to them for almost nothing. Not enough has been said about the demoralizing influence of the sales. I know that they are worried about it at the booksellers' union, that Mlle Choureau, the excellent president of our union, has many times introduced projects tending to put things back in order again. They have come to nothing, because it is difficult, if not impossible, to stop a flood of such force. It is a scourge, and a just scourge besides, that was called forth by the excess and disorder of postwar literary production.

No, in my opinion the role of the sales in the present book crisis has never been sufficiently underlined. They have preferred to say that people were stupefied by the cinema and the radio, that the French nation was in a state of decadence, that culture was compromised, if not lost, rather than bring to light this simple fact of the bookshop sales.

I have said that the scourge was just and it is true that for several years, even the ones called the years of "prosperity," we all behaved ourselves rather badly. We made books objects of speculation; we made or let be made a *stock exchange* for books. Ah! we have not chased the money changers from the temple! Myself, did I not often propose books, saying that in a month the price would have at least doubled? And it was true. And it was so easy to sell under those conditions. We wanted to play at being bibliophiles. Now, repentance! Ah, it was well done! As if books were not above all objects of love; the care that we take, wanting them to be on beautiful paper, covered with good bindings, is that not only a sign of love? What does their market value matter to us! The essential thing is that it be within our means. Do we not have even more pleasure in thinking that we are the only ones really to appreciate such and such a book and that it is our love that gives it its price?

Speculation will never be distrusted enough. Its principles are not all bad, however; there are grains of intelligence and courage in it. But it is pernicious because the past is wanting. The object of speculation has no past. Genius is not only the fortunate time of a work, it is also the fortunate work of time. Individual creation counts only from the moment it is accepted and assimilated by others. The disciple makes the master as much as the master makes the disciple—following the disciples come the students. And all that is brought forth in its time.

Shall I risk this comparison?—Speculation is like somebody who swallows down big mouthfuls without chewing, and who vomits almost immediately.

Let me be clearly understood, I am speaking here of speculation and not of business in general. I do not call someone a speculator who possesses a just appreciation of the value of things and who knows how to fix their price. I call someone a speculator who does not love to begin with, someone who sees only the possible material profit, who exploits the creator and the amateur at one and the same time, who buys with expediency and who sells with expediency. The surest values crumble when they have become the prey of speculators, and much time and skill are needed to put them in a good condition again. The artist has no worse enemy than the speculator; the latter sooner or later takes his patronage away from him and after a time of deceptive prosperity leaves him in ruin. A thing of the present above all receives its market value from the feeling that it inspires; this feeling is formed, like every feeling, by our unconscious economy. We cannot judge for posterity, because posterity takes views that are more and more disinterested, therefore more and more clearsighted.

The amateur, the true amateur, is not deceived since he follows only his taste. His acquisitions enrich not his pocketbook but his person, they bring him happiness in the true sense of the word.

One who tries to make *investments* is doomed to disappointments. Before taking his ultimate place, and once again it is the work of time, the artist must put up with the decrees of fashion. Fashion is based upon change above all, alternation (like the Chinese *yin* and *yang*). The short follows after the long and the wide follows after the narrow, and do so with all kinds of little eddies. Fashion is made up of a hundred caprices and has one great law only. You are in fashion, willingly or unwillingly, and then you are no longer in fashion. The only thing that counts, that is the love of some, "the happy few."

To come back to the question of sales, let us observe that the punishment is not inflicted on everyone. If authors, publishers, and booksellers suffer from them, the public does not suffer from them, quite to the contrary. With delight it sees a time come back that is completely according to its own likings and habits. A time for strolling, for browsing in secondhand bookshops, as before the war. The French hate to pay high prices, they want real or artificial bargains, they want to give themselves the illusion that the gods love them and do not confuse them with other mortals.

Oh! they are not difficult, they demand only slight advantages; they know that great favors are not without danger. What they want are the smiles of destiny, and the furtive smiles, rather. Like their Latin ancestors, they are anxious about signs, about omens. The book discovered beneath a pile of others, that is not expensive, whose title pleases, the book whose half-opened pages offer sentences that are in agreement with the mood of the day, therefore boding well, there is the book that will be bought without hesitation; all the same, one will pretend to hesitate for the rite of haggling; the few sous that you will knock off, that again will be a friendly wink from a little familiar god. Have you ever thought about that prewar custom: *new* books were sold at three francs instead of three francs fifty centimes, the marked price.

Ah! you French, born clever, you are very kind, but often your slyness costs others and even yourselves dear. Since you want to be rich, your poets must be poor; you will tell me that that pleases them; it is possible—the task of a poet is to create love, even with hate—but that should not please you, you who should be unable to read coldly this dictionary sentence: "He died in misery."

Notice that I do not want to bring you back to the romantic myth about the poet who pretends to steer the ship with his lyre and demands that society support him. Such a poet believes that he is boundless poetry all by himself, he exaggerates. No, I am not asking you to assure the existence of the poet, but simply not to lose interest completely in the material condition of the poets whom you love for good reasons. Toward those you ought to feel an obligation or rather a pleasure in spending. I say *poets* here in order to simplify, but I am also thinking very much about novelists, playwrights, essayists, and also about painters and musicians—about all those who make it so that our eyes see and our ears hear.

I know very well that you sometimes buy *basic* books without stinting too much. Do not trust only in history, do not trust only in the classics. It is the present that has need of you. The past made you, it is true, but it is the present that makes your future.

I wonder how so many good souls have managed to see books in such great and new danger. It seems to me that they have not examined the basis of things, and above all that they have had more or less defective observation posts. Bookselling is doing badly, that is understood, but yet once more, it is coming out of a period of *prosperity* that shattered it and confused its perspectives. All those who are familiar with prewar bookselling know that in spite of appearances we are coming back to a condition that is perhaps normal.

The book business has never been, in France, very prosperous; the French are not good customers for books; only the Italians and the Spanish, among the great European peoples, are less good customers than they. It is a fact of human geography. Sunny countries favor the most concrete and immediate life and expressions of life. Singing, speaking, dancing take the lead over study and meditation. Everybody is a bit of a poet in the surroundings of the Mediterranean, and for that reason the prestige of the greatest is diminished. For the Latin, Near Eastern, and North African peoples writing is an abstract thing; the printed page seems like a winter landscape to them; they do not willingly supply the effort to decipher it. That is not because writing displeases them, they fully appreciate its personal usefulness, if it did not exist they would invent it. It was they who did invent it (on this side of the world), but they certainly would not have invented printing.

Yes, if we consider Mediterranean civilization as a whole, we see in it creative elites surrounded by broad zones of indifference.

Ordinary people have their own ways of being artists, poets, or philosophers; above all, they want to let themselves live, they allow difficulties only if they can overcome them by practice, therefore by habit. They are content with their little crafts.

The poet, the painter, or the saint seek out the hardest disciplines, those to which one never becomes habituated; they conceive a perfection and attach an importance to life only to the extent that they approach it; their spirit crystallizes in sharp points that leave the mass of men far in the rear. It is the long body of Don Quixote made longer by the long lance that he raises inordinately above the broad Sancho Panza.

As I write this I am thinking above all of Spain, of Italy. France is meridional only by half, perhaps only by a third even. She belongs to the North as much as to the South.

The North, shall we try to characterize it? Its groups assuredly have more unity than those of the South. Their members feel themselves more bound up with one another; anarchy has very little part to play. Northern genius experiences a feeling of responsibility toward the masses, it tries less to dominate them than to elevate them. It rarely cultivates form for its own sake, its aestheticism is moral; beauty is given to it by fullness of heart, by power of comprehension. Even when stricken with romanticism, it attacks God rather than Society. It has benefactors and few saints.

Society, in return, does not regard itself free from obligations toward its "representative men." The English, German, Dutch, or Scandinavian (or North American) author can feel himself as protected as a worker in it does not matter what category; he can live by his pen starting from the day that he has shown himself to be an *author*, that is to say, a thinking part of humanity, a part that is bound to its causes.

The French love books, they are always ready to love them; their feeling is reflective, delicate, subject to sudden changes in direction; it is because their spirit wants to embrace all of the contours of truth that it has ups and downs.

They do not let books impose upon them—do they let anything impose upon them? For them a book is a friend or nothing. Their resistance to publishers' boards and bindings is very significant; they do not put up with rigidity except in a book for study. They want books to be paperbound, supple, not too big; it is good to be able to put them in one's pocket and to turn them back a bit, a very little bit, while reading them; they know very well that it is not good for the book, they restrain themselves when the book is new or when it does not belong to them, but when they have the luck to hold in their hands a used book acquired for several sous or a few francs, they treat it without ceremony—it is a secondhand book.

The act of cutting pages does not please everybody. They come in equal numbers—just as there are fat people and thin people—those who love cutting pages and those who are annoyed by it. But in any case, nobody wants a trimmed book: they love crisply cut edges, slightly downy.

The French are very sensitive to the quality of paper; bibliophiles apart, they do not prize either beautiful papers or wide margins; beautiful papers do not put them at their ease, and wide margins seem like an extravagant oddity to them, something like the long nails of the mandarins. But they have a horror of yellowish or grayish papers that show straw or wood, like a wretched epidermis. A good ordinary paper is what they want!

A French person does not lightly engage in the purchase of a book; if one agrees to pay a high price one wants a pleasing volume, without defects, whose paper promises to last. One likes infinitely better to spend a little more and have something suitable. One rarely buys a book to read it, but usually to keep it or to give it away. One does not easily consent, and one is not wrong, to pay for a copy in the original edition, which is more expensive than a copy in an ordinary edition. One considers that if one is among the first thousand who consent to make an outlay of cash, it is oneself who should have the advantage and not the publisher. It seems to me that publishers would be well advised to come back to the question of the first thousand copies not marked with the edition number and to study carefully the question of papers. Poor papers should be plainly reserved for the very cheap editions. As the number of people in France who are inclined to buy books is not very extendable at present, at least in what concerns literature properly speaking, there is a great advantage in understanding those people well and in not discouraging them. For even the French who enjoy the possession of books can experience a certain pleasure in not buying any, a chaste pleasure that is composed at one and the same time of economy and revery. It is often because they have a high and subtle idea of books that they possess only a few of them. Nowhere is quality so much appreciated, so much demanded, as it is among us, nowhere is the critical spirit so strong. Campaigns in favor of books have often been spoken about these days. I believe that these campaigns have often set authors and publishers in motion, but few, very few readers. Because one is either a friend of books and has nothing to learn about the subject, or one is insensitive to books and will not make it a duty to read any. It was, moreover, a gross error to speak of duty; reading is a pleasure like walking with a friend, listening to a good actor, having beautiful clothes, eating roast chicken or cakes; it is the greatest and most lasting of pleasures, that has been said a hundred times and it is pure truth. Even those who read to instruct themselves read with pleasure (I am speaking of adults). There is nothing more *thrilling* than to instruct oneself, when one does not do it on command but through a personal desire for knowledge.

—Study, that word shines like a star, like the lamp of a sage. Study, a word that promises happiness so feebly and that gives it so fully. Study, a word closed like a little room, but that opens the spirit to the infinite. The infinite no longer frightens one who studies, he has only one fear, that of the finite: the moment when he could have nothing more to learn. But happily that never comes to pass and there are always new joys.

Yes, it has been very much a question during this last year, of developing a taste for reading. It has been said that people were reading less or were no longer reading books. The radio, the cinema, or the weeklies have been held responsible. But this is what Maxime Du Camp wrote in 1873, in his *Paris*: "In short, the Parisian public does not care very much for libraries; it hardly reads; its pleasures and its occupations do not leave it the leisure for reading; it is not interested in self-instruction, because it gladly believes that there is nothing more to learn; and then, why should it go lean over a book in order to look for effects and causes there? Has it not, evening and morning, that enormous mass of detailed volumes that are called newspapers? . . ." So one could believe, in 1873, that the book was doomed because of newspapers. And what would one have written a hundred years earlier when the newspaper hardly existed? Diderot declared that not one of the booksellers of his time had an extra suit of clothes.

Furthermore, the judgment of Maxime Du Camp was no longer valid in 1880. In the meantime municipal lending libraries had been created with enthusiasm, a glorious era for reading had been opened. Everybody was reading books. But what did they read? Books, like language, are the best and the worst of things. Have you ever considered what literary production and consumption were around 1900? Then there was certainly the best and the worst. Compulsory education was bearing fruit, fruit to make the branches break. The nineteenth century had provided foods in abundance. Everything had been sown with seed. The Orient had been discovered, some had set out to look for the Mother there—the Mother, true figure of that century covered with breasts like the Diana of Ephesus. The genius of religions, the genius of language had come out of the mists, shaking sparkling tresses. Science had arisen like a god. Never had there been so many beautiful poems, so many good novels, so many excellent essays. Never had great men been at one and the same time so great and so human; never had they better resolved the initial problem of genius, which is to give itself entirely and to keep its secret.

And still, at that end of the century, what a sewer. What a growth of garbage, like the waste products of an enormous digestion. I am not speaking here of realism, although it is not completely outside of the question, but of the senseless mass of filthy, licentious, and depraved writings. No, all that was not realism, it was rather a degraded idealism, you were drowned in sentiment. It did not have to do with seeing clearly and speaking truly, as now; it was the spirit of orgy, of the Black Mass, everything was confused, turned wrong-side out. Think a bit about what was represented by people like Huysmans, Mirbeau, Pierre Louÿs, Jean Lorrain, Willy, Péladan, Rachilde, Hugues Rebell (I am surely forgetting some). And they, they were the princes. On the level below there were Félicien Champsaur, Jane de la Vaudère, and people of whom you have no idea. Bestiality, incest, sadism, inversion, fetishism, vampirism, everything passed by. Inversion— that was too simple still, there were pederast women and lesbian men. Obviously, these books sold. You found them in the bookshops of working-class neighborhoods, in piles, next to copies of *Petit Larousse, Clefs des songes [Keys to Dreams]*, and cookbooks; they were not even sold under the counter, an honor reserved for the *Kama-Sutra* and the sex manuals.

And crowning the lot there were mountains of popular novels in serial form, which caused torrents of tears to be poured, as if it were necessary to produce a great deal of water to wash all that away.

No, really, when I consider my epoch I see nothing like it. Joyce is great scholasticism. Céline is a lark, we do not take him seriously, and he even less than ourselves. Of course, there is the detective story, but consider the progress: it is the detective who has become the hero instead of the villain.

I have been told that the bookseller in a neighborhood near the Boulevard de Sébastopol, who had always worked in the genre described above, wanted to change his stock-in-trade completely and, in response to the desires of his patrons, was going to become serious: scientific vulgarization, world history, folkways and customs of peoples, classics, good novels—the same as those that the middle class reads. I am sure that it will do very well. People of the working class, young and old, like readings that instruct and lead to reflection: literature for the idle—it is idleness that makes sex proliferate—is almost out of circulation.

Yes, I am a witness to it—people have read, since the war, with an increasing application. They have made arrangements to read at the least expense; never have the public libraries been so packed with readers. They have bought books less and less, above all books in new condition, but they have read with great good will. All the recent bookshop successes are serious books. They have read little poetry, that is true, but it was less their fault than that of the epoch, which did not leave them the time to meditate and to take the mental attitude that Jules Romains speaks about in his preface to *L'Homme blanc [The White Man]*. Let us think a bit about all these years in which, for periods varying from three to six months (the time it takes to recover), such grave internal and external events happen or threaten to happen that the public spirit has no stability and rightly throws itself upon the news in the newspapers. It does not come out in good form, as the sportsmen say, and because of that the problems of form touch it little. Before everything else there are the terrible depths of things, those shaken depths that are raised up like an awakening volcano.

Among the causes that hinder not only reading but the spending that might be made on its behalf, must be mentioned the liking for travel, which is very widespread and for which people keep all their small savings. And winter sports—God knows what they cost us.

And then there are the summer months during which we become people of the South, except for those who are overburdened by work and who want to read during vacation everything that they could not read during the year. The people in this category become more and more numerous. When people speak about the progressive indifference of the public toward books, they do not think enough, in my opinion, about the scant leisure that most of the workers in the elite of our society enjoy—doctors, important officials, business executives. Members of the teaching profession are almost the only ones who can find the time to read. A woman friend told me the other day in regard to the men in her circle: "Either they don't have a position and have no liking for anything, or they have one and that absorbs them completely." These people do not forget books, they often long for them, and when they can they go back to them.

Good, but all that does not put the publisher's and the bookseller's position in order, still less does it put in order the position of the author. The author can live only by doing journalism, which is not a bad thing in many cases. What he writes for the newspapers and the weeklies is useful and receives its payment. And it is nothing to be upset about if his copy remains there. It is even satisfying to think that the book form is henceforth reserved for works that have been labored over for a long time and are worthy of being printed without typographical errors.

As for us, the booksellers, we are hardly better off than the bookseller of Diderot. Those who like myself deal not only with the selling but also with the lending of books just pull through; this year there was no means of getting out of the deficit. Without *Ulysses* sold to Gallimard—

Even when things go well the profit is very slight. Do you know what I can earn, after twenty years of work? Fifteen hundred francs a month, on the average. Last year, I mean in 1936, I reached seventeen hundred, I was very proud. I told myself that in 1937 I would doubtless reach two thousand. Yes, yes.

But what I wrote at the beginning of the last paragraph, that is perhaps normal. At bottom, the real French bookseller is the dealer in secondhand books. I have known many girls who wanted to be booksellers and who went for advice to Gaston Zelger, the lamented director of La Maison des Livres. He told them, and that in the middle of a period of prosperity: "Above all, don't have a bookshop only, sell stationery too, that's necessary."

Bookshop-stationery, that makes sense among us in France. How many people prefer, rather than printed paper, white paper over which they can let their own writing flow. We are authors almost as much as we are readers. The South. Once we have read, read much, read well, we want to write. And what is most curious is that we do not write badly at all. There are some works by amateurs that are devilishly difficult to judge; it comes close, very close indeed. It is often necessary to apply oneself to several in order to know what to think. Yes, amateurs abound among us, and "the literary thing" is often very complicated. Because there are publishers who would certainly not act if the author paid his own expenses, but who willingly accept a silent partner.

Look, do you want to know how we are, the like of us French? When we admire a real, a great author, and when that author has just published an important work, to which he has given himself completely, and when he has need of recovering his forces, and when he is anxiously watching for the applause that is due to him at least as much as to an actor, ah well, do you know what happens to him? Oh, he receives letters, heaps of letters, but instead of simply expressing admiration and gratitude to him, people talk about themselves, about what they have tried to do in the same genre as his own, they send him little manuscripts.

It is far from my thought to speak ill of amateurs. They begin by loving and love leads to production, if not to reproduction. There is no difference between the professional and the amateur but a degree of application. What counts is the craft, the craft that has been practiced for a long time, with a sometimes mortal passion. Read the letters by Van Gogh to his brother, I beg you, you will see what the school of genius can be.

Here we are at the beginning of January. My bookshop gave me so much work in December that I could not finish this text before the end of the year, as I should have wished. I spent the two days of Christmas and those of New Year writing. It is certainly the first time in my life that I neglected good things to eat.

And now, I am going to explain to you what I want to do in this gazette, with you, if you really wish.

First of all, I am going to give you my catalog devoted to ancient and foreign writers. It is not without emotion that I am preparing myself to publish this work; I have thought about it, I have worked on it fervently during these last few years. My ambition is to help you acquire an idea of the world that is as living, as complete as possible. For each country you will have a mass of information concerning the history of its ideas and its accomplishments. You will have the bibliography of the existing translations that I have been able to bring together. I shall publish the interesting letters that reach me whether they are in the sense of information or in the sense of criticism. For my plan is too vast for me to be able to fulfill it alone, and at the first try. We shall work on it together, and perhaps we shall come to the point of endowing our country with a cultural instrument that is practical and of great scope.

Even while pursuing our task we are going to try to serve our Letters with the best of our heart and of our intelligence. We have excellent critics, but they cannot suffice for everything; there are many books that they do not speak about, that they have never spoken about, that they do not speak about enough. The contact that I have had with the public for more than twenty years has shown me very well that as a last resort it was itself, the public, that judged and that it judged soundly. Professional critics do not go beyond it except through their talent as writers, and this talent sometimes opposes their function, which is to do justice in the domain of Letters. There is among the French a remarkable freedom of spirit. It was very amusing to hear them in the lifetime of the good Souday, whom they prized so much; they literally used to throw themselves upon the books that Souday had spoken about, and then they used to say, with as much pleasure in the one case as in the other: "He's right," or, "I'm not at all of his opinion. He's let himself be carried away."

So, my dear friends, you are going to write to me on the subject of books. Tell us the books that you love and for what reasons; do not content yourselves with a simple affirmation; look for the causes. Also tell us everything that it seems to you will help the life of Letters practically; if you have personal experience as a bookseller or as a librarian, your advice will be precious to us. In the pages that I am delivering to you today, look for what may provide material for criticism or development. This gazette will reproduce those of your judgments that are clear and disinterested. Will you please give me your confidence? Do not ask me to answer you individually, doubtless I shall not have the time.

To work, my children.

From *Les Gazettes d'Adrienne Monnier*; first published in *La Gazette des Amis des Livres* (January 1938).

part two

The
Country of
Books

Saint-Exupéry and Le Petit Prince

I have just read *Le Petit Prince*. It is a children's book written by Antoine de Saint-Exupéry that was published in New York in 1943.

This book has been with me since last November (Keeler Faus brought it to me upon his return here); I kept it for three months without reading it. It was there, on my table, with its cover illustrated by a pleasant drawing, but a bit insipid, to tell the truth. Nevertheless, I knew through Keeler that *Le Petit Prince* had importance, gravity even; he had given it to me with a certain solemnity, no, not given it, but loaned it. And I, who have such a horror of people who keep loaned books for a long time, I had not been in a hurry to read it; I was waiting to find the leisure and the warmth, to have less things to mend on the shelf and a bit of fire or sunshine.

Then one fine day Eunice Taylor brought me the book as a gift. It was March; the mending still dominated the situation but the heavy cold spells were far away. I was also impatient to read the *Lettre à un otage*, recently published by Gallimard (it also first appeared in New York, published by Schiffrin).

I read the two works one after the other, I no longer remember which one I began with. I only know that the *Lettre à un otage* seemed admirable from the beginning to the end. *Le Petit Prince* disappointed me at the beginning with its puerility—let's say rather that I was disconcerted, for this puerility is extraordinary enough. Even so, I began to sympathize while reading the story about the flower that has four thorns and that tells lies. The tale about the visits to the asteroids, each one occupied by a single inhabitant, pleased me very much: its irony is utterly charming. When the fox came along, the fox that wants to be *tamed*, I was much moved; my emotion grew with every page, until the end, when the little prince tells his friend the aviator that he is going to return to his star and that he will have *a little the appearance of dying*. Ah, yes, by the end I found myself shedding bitter tears.

While I was weeping I asked myself: "Why these tears, really? It's only a story for children." I quickly realized that behind the little prince Saint-Exupéry himself was hiding, and that I was weeping over his death, of which I was becoming aware at the same time as many figures in his life.

I think it will be so for many people, close and distant friends of Saint-Ex.—but weren't all his readers his friends?

When we learned about his disappearance last summer, we were all of us, or almost all of us, like Commander Alias: too absorbed by our problems to feel a death deeply and suffer because of it, all the more so because that death was doubtful. Hadn't Saint-Ex. always come back from dangerous missions?

Now that grief is here, complete. As he describes it to us in the *Lettre à un otage*, we mustn't keep his place at our table; we mustn't regard him as *eternally absent, a guest who will be late for eternity. He will never be present anymore, but then he will never again be absent.* We must make of him, as he made of Guillaumet, *a true dead friend.*

I know, yes, I understand very well why this friendship seems so much alive to me, and as if waiting for that moment. I live with books more than with people. And often enough people disturb me in my dealings with books. That is not because I disdain the company of authors, far from it, I infinitely appreciate it when they are authors whose work I admire, but it is always in regard to their work that I like them, and not in regard to their fame or their good conduct toward me. I am, however, very sensitive about good conduct, and I do not in any way put up with the bad kind; but I accept it as good conduct only if it comes from somebody whom I frankly admire. My sense of hierarchy dominates my need for companionship. My feeling for values such as I experience them in my innermost self makes up almost all of my feeling.

Which is to say that I can easily do without people (there are days when I could easily do without myself), and that in the country of books where I dwell, the dead can count entirely as much as the living.

Nobody has been more present to me these last years than

Melville and Gottfried Keller. I have lived through this war much more with Green Henry and the sailors of the *Pequod* than with the immediate world, and I have found refuge also at Byrd's pole and in the desert of Saint-Exupéry.

While reading *Pilote de guerre* I was struck by this definition of expanse: "True expanse is not for the eye, it is granted only to the spirit. Its value is the value of language, for it is language that ties things together."

The man who wrote those lines could travel in his airplane through the space of the whole planet, but this space had value for him only by reason of his inner life, by reason of the language with which he was able to make it come alive, the language with which he was able to express it.

And language, let us add, finds its highest value and its consummation in books.

The author of a book like *Terre des hommes* could never disappear. He will forever be a living aviator within the expanse of the spirit. He will speak like a father to every child; every father will read to his children this book by a man who was at one and the same time, and in an exemplary fashion, a hero, a poet, and a moralist. Some of his sayings count among the noblest and purest that have ever been written: "To love is not to look at one another but to look together in the same direction." Does that not baptize a new kind of love?

After *Le Petit Prince* and the *Lettre à un otage* I wanted to reread all of Saint-Exupéry's books—only three books, but each one of them of such richness. Opening the volumes I found again with emotion the dedications in which the author always took the trouble to recall that I had published his first pages in the *Navire d'Argent*.

Saint-Exupéry's handwriting—flowing, simple, harmonious. Looking at it I think of grass penetrated by light.

And yes, it was indeed the *Navire* that had that honor. And it was dear Jean Prévost who had brought me this newcomer whom he had found among his friends. Wasn't it Gide who had introduced them?

That first piece, entitled "L'Aviateur," is the sketch for *Courrier sud.*

It is curious, on picking up *Courier sud* again, I found at the end a kind of prefiguration of *Le Petit Prince*—that little prince who, fallen from a star into the desert, where he comes across an aviator, returns to his star by letting himself be bitten by a snake. Yes, it reminds me of the visit of the young pilot to the old sergeant isolated in the sands, a visit that leaves the sergeant *almost a memory of love;* the pilot, *a lost child who fills the desert,* who does not die so much as he returns to *the most vertical star.*

In all of Saint-Exupéry's books, how many stars there are toward which one rises or which one finds in oneself, how many stars painted with the finest gold of the language.

At the end of *Vol de nuit* there are three stars that appear like *a fatal bait at the bottom of a fishnet.* The aviator climbs toward them and cannot come down again.

Again, how can one not be struck by the analogy there is between the little prince's snake and the pursuit plane in *Pilote de guerre,* which *delivers its venom in one stroke, like a cobra.*

The little prince is Saint-Exupéry—the child that he was and that he remained in spite of grown-ups; it is the child that he might have had and that no doubt he wanted; it is also the young comrade who lets himself be tamed and who disappears. It is his childhood and the childhood of the whole world, *stores of sweetness,* found and found again in the beloved desert.

From *Les Gazettes d'Adrienne Monnier;* first published in *Fontaine* (May 1945).

Alice in Wonderland

The two of us, Sylvia Beach and I, went to see the film taken from *Alice in Wonderland.* Sylvia was very excited. We chatted along the way. She said to me:

—You yourself don't know, and you French don't know what *Alice* is. For English and American children it's a summa; the heroes of the nursery rhymes and others even more astonishing have been brought together there in a definitive pantheon. It's as important for them as the stories of Perrault are for little French children, but it's so different.

—Yes, almost all our stories take place on the level of the feelings, even their fairy-tale atmosphere is emotional, while the adventures of Alice are purely intellectual. The creatures that pass through them very much resemble the angry divinities of the intelligence of which the *Bardol Thödol* speaks. It is the intellect and its questions that transform objects and animals into bristling, teasing, vexing, pompous, fickle personages.

—There is a very amusing kinship between Lewis Carroll, the author of *Alice*, and Joyce in his latest manner as the author of *Work in Progress*. Joyce could say, like Humpty Dumpty: "When *I* use a word it means just what I choose it to mean. The question is which is to be master." No, wait, that's not it, Joyce would say rather: "When I use words I let them go wherever they want, in all four directions." For every one of the words of that man goes in at least four directions.

—Don't you find that some of the poems of *Alice*, swarming with neologisms, also make you think of the Fargue of *Ludions* and of the Michaux of *Qui je fus [Who I Was]*? Recite the lines of the "Jabberwocky" to me.

> 'Twas brillig, and the slithy toves
> Did gyre and gimble in the wabe

—Hasn't that been translated into French?
—Yes, and Paul Gilson hasn't done badly:

> *C'etait grilloir. Les souplards torves*
> *Viraient pertuisant dans l'alloux.*

The part of the translation that follows is not as good, but it was very difficult, almost as difficult as Anna Livia.

—And the surrealists. They are also related, in certain ways, to Lewis Carroll.

—They don't deny it. Aragon has translated *The Hunting of the Snark*. They would say perhaps, in their jargon, that *Alice* engages in a paranoiac-critical activity.

—You know that Lewis Carroll was a clergyman, a professor of mathematics at Oxford. His real name was Dodgson, the Reverend Charles Dodgson. He wrote a great number of mathematical works.

—He was a Victorian, I believe.

—Yes, according to an anecdote Queen Victoria, after having read *Alice* with much pleasure, is supposed to have asked for other works by the author. She must have been really surprised when she saw arrive a pile of books that bore titles of this sort: *Notes on the Two First Books of Euclid* or *Formulary of Plane Trigonometry*—What was so nice about Lewis Carroll was his love for children. He adored little girls; he liked little boys much less, he even detested them when they behaved brutally. They've collected a whole volume of letters addressed to his children-friends, as he called them; in it are the names of more than fifty little girls. He wrote to them with a beautiful painstaking handwriting, and his letters were scattered with delightful picture puzzles that he drew with remarkable skill.

The film did not disappoint us. The machinery of Hollywood produced all the wonders that were necessary. Charlotte Henry is a perfect Alice. The slightest roles are played by stars. It won't be understood over here, Sylvia said, why artists of such great fame have taken such little roles, in which they appear hardly recognizable besides under their grotesque masks. It was surely a sacred thing for them, a great mystery of childhood that would bring them luck.

The heads and the costumes reproduce with an impressive fidelity the drawings of John Tenniel, who did the original illustrations, which are forever inseparable from *Alice*.

Obviously, Lewis Carroll's work is far from being represented as a whole; it contains philosophical insights, linguistic fantasies, and strokes of humor that are inevitably lost on the screen. They have made use of not only *Alice in Wonderland* but also of the work that is its sequel: *Through the Looking-Glass*. The episodes are completely mixed together; the work is done with intelligence. At the beginning of the film they have placed the game of chess and the passage through the mirror, which gives a very logical development to the events that follow. This mixture of the two books shocks children a lot. Sylvia conferred at length on this subject with little Diana Jane Mowrer, who was scandalized. You understand, Sylvia told me, when she reported this interview to me, it's a bit as if one were to mix the chapters of the Old and the New Testaments; even with good results it is inadmissible.

From *Les Gazettes d'Adrienne Monnier*; first published in *La Nouvelle Revue Française* (January 1935).

Fargue and Words

It seemed hardly possible, after the *Poèmes* published in 1912, that Fargue could surpass or renew himself, and he himself must have felt so. Had he not found his perfection? What was left for him to express after that book full of intimacy and enchantment, swollen with music, ceaselessly calling music to its aid in order to say "those words of light for which all others are made"?—After that, he could only be still or learn harmony. In fact, he was still for a long time and for a long time found nothing to appease him but the help of the concerts, and of domestic pianos, which, let it be said in passing, he played marvelously well, without ever having been taught.

And then too, he spoke, he *talked*, that is to say, his words produced many effects. His conversation showed a genius that it seemed must remain oral. How was it possible to fix that extravagant lyricism, that comic cosmic spirit, that satire like red-hot shot?—Doubtless he tried under several circumstances to arrest some of those shifting and thundering palaces with belfries on behalf of some friends about whom he was asked to write under pain of death. We had fantastic portraits of Levet, of Proust, of Larbaud, of Léon Werth. Ah! If you asked him for a man, well, he gave you epochs, travels, regiments, drums, bugles, music leading; he mobilized everything in order to immobilize himself a bit.

In June 1924, in this same *Feuilles Libres* that celebrates him today, he had a decisive interview with his muse. *"Enough!"* she said to him through the voice of a spiritualist's table, *"enough of the Cartesian languages, enough of the flexuous languages, enough of the caesura languages, enough of the reasoning languages! We want ideographic signs, figurative writings, palatine words, the new Mexico!—While waiting, the need makes itself felt for an instantaneous stereotype of the erections of the subconscious proper, for a language that discharges our needs for exoneration, for a language arisen from the internal succulence, from the good-natured mystery, sensitive and sensual, of the one-eyed man on roller skates, of force and of France!"* I have quoted it at length because that sentence constitutes a veritable manifesto.

The month of August of the same year saw the beginning, in the review *Commerce*, which had its own beginning at the same time, of a Fargue in the second manner, who was that of his conversations revised and augmented.

In his first poems the poet strolled about, he remained among the things of this world, he passed through or moved around in them, he peopled them with a mythology that was very human—Now he adopts an attitude of rising, the poem is an ascent, a bird's-eye view, an exploration from above, while lifting off the cover. Men, whose feelings he liked to share formerly, no longer inspire in him anything but mockery and scorn, he takes pleasure in imagining circumstances in which the most pitiable human miseries are thrown into the strongest relief, he accumulates the exaggerations. Sometimes he sees men from so high up that they seem to him to be no more than insects, less still, caviar. The gods whom he encounters at the limit of his ascent are grotesque and terrible monsters. And still there is nothing distressing in his universe, suffering itself turns to pleasure; through the effect of his genius he escapes and has his reader escape from strict reason, he involves him in matter and its games, in movement and its raptures.

Like James Joyce, he searches for "the matrix language" of which Cyrano de Bergerac spoke, that language which is "the instinct or the voice of Nature," through which each thing "declares its essence." That experience beyond the intelligence, that exploration of the fringe that Bergson longed for, very few have attempted it on the level of poetry, very few have realized it as well as Fargue; that devil of a man has reached the very goal that the surrealists set for themselves.

Beyond the surrealists, of which he is incontestably one of the masters, he takes after Rabelais, Swift, Scarron, Cyrano de Bergerac, and, closer to us, Rimbaud, Lautréamont, Jarry. He has the astonishing word finds of the first, the cruelty of the second, the burlesque of the third, the fantastic metaphysics of the fourth; he owes a great deal to Rimbaud; but Rimbaud above all raised up great forms that were removed from their natural confines, while Fargue enters into the intimacy of matter. Nor must one fail to relate him to Hieronymus Bosch—a Bosch with the gracefulness of Bresdin—his *Paradis* is close to the *Délices terrestres [Earthly Delights]*. He likewise has ties with Odilon Redon and with James Ensor. It is curious to notice, besides, the tendency of the first poems toward music and that of the later ones toward painting.

Although it seems impossible to define Fargue's technique, or rather his craft, I am going to try to provide some information.

A poem by Fargue, as you know, has neither rhyme nor well-marked beats—the use of these means would hinder him in his searches and in his finds. However, he has composed some very successful versified pieces; in particular, note should be made of "Nuées," in which he has done the rain very well, as much through a choice of appropriate images as through a regular meter of seven feet. But these pieces do not have the brilliant merits of the poems in which he allows himself every liberty. You must not believe, however, that Fargue does not obey any discipline; he has his own laws, he is a mystic, in poetry, in the full sense of the word. Those who have seen him at work know how much effort and attention he lavishes upon his production, from what truly infinite retouches he makes it benefit. He is all by himself like one of those termite hills that he loves so much, he knits his antennae in all directions; his wits, like thousands of busy insects, go searching to the limits of his knowledge, which is very extensive, for the elements necessary to the secretion of his metaphors. Because for him the metaphor is at one and the same time cellulose and the product of cellulose; he extracts it from everything and applies it to everything; with it he builds and cements the system of his poem; no poet seems to me as metaphysical, as inclined to transformation.

In Fargue's work, then, there is first of all the formation of images, then the expression of them through words upon which the greatest part of his efforts is directed. A book would have to be written about the use of words in Fargue's poetry; there above all reside his mysticism and his knowledge; doubtless Jean Paulhan would say that before everything else he takes into account "their veins, their grain, and their particular sort of resistance," and in fact he has a marvelous sense of their origins and of their properties, he knows how to give birth to them or to give life to them again, through them he penetrates into the secrets of things; "the goddesses of language" truly have nothing to refuse him.

Let us note, with more precision, that he makes wide use of technical and learned words—his vocabulary borrows from the domains of philosophy, even the scholastic kind, of medicine, of the physical sciences, chemical and natural, and particularly of mineralogy, entomology, mechanics, and atomic theory. He likewise makes use of craft words; for each object he employs the very word that the man capable of making it would use.

He finds a resource in all the colloquial words that have a figure or that are based on onomatopoeia.

He likes words of recent formation very much, he draws from them all possible elements of surprise and pleasure, he knows perfectly how to put them at their ease, as much through the suppleness of his sentences as through the neighbors that he gives them. A new word, in fact, when one knows how to make use of it, is more intimately applicable to the object that it designates, it has not yet undergone the effects of usage—deformation through extension or shrinking and fading.

He produces great effects with proper nouns, whether he reduces them to substantives when they are illustrious, or discovers them through a sort of divination when they are peculiar.

Let us also note that he often invents words, whether to designate unheard of things—the word in this case has a poetic character—or to give an idea of states that are completely personal to him; he then forms colloquial and comic vocables, often by means of spoonerisms.

And let us say, finally, that he treats ordinary words with humanity when he has need of them.

From *Les Gazettes d'Adrienne Monnier*; first published in *Les Feuilles Libres* (June 1927).

Waiting for Godot

I had read *En attendant Godot* before going to see it acted. The reading had enchanted me, the performance left me lukewarm and even cold. It was, however, a perfect performance; it is difficult to imagine more sensitive or intelligent actors. Roger Blin had entered into the intentions of the author, had taken them up again on his own account, but he had not brought them to life, because they could not be brought to life by virtue of the Beckett principle which demands that when the body moves about the mind lives little or not at all. See *Murphy* (difficult to read, I warn you), in particular chapter six, in which we find affirmations like this one here: "As he lapsed in body he felt himself coming alive in mind, set free to move among its treasures. The body has its stock, the mind its treasures."

So, for myself and some others who had enjoyed the treasures of the mind in advance, this performance was only a long falling away.

Katherine Dudley, who is among those others, had the impression that the play should have been staged in the style of the Frères Jacques. Perhaps, as a matter of fact, the four bowler hats were an indication in that direction on the part of the author. But I don't know—I believe that the realistic interpretation by Lucien Raimbourg and Pierre Latour helped many people to grasp the full significance of the work. For ourselves, who had lived the lamentable story of Vladimir and Estragon in advance, we could only withdraw before the excess. We would have been able to accept the thing as a Mass—a Mass as gray as the dust of the roads, like the old shoes that occupy the center of the stage. So it certainly appeared, more or less, to the spectators who arrived as virgins at the Théâtre de Babylone.

En attendant Godot has had a magnificent press. It has been a revelation for the majority of the critics. Even the tough ones were choked up and harrowed by this work that is clownery and mystery at the same time—the real mystery of a Passion in which man drags himself along under the burden of having been born—an atrocious world in which hope is put out as soon as it is lit, in which there is no respite except in sleep, and where the essential act is a kick.

With Beckett, it seems, kicking is a substitute for spitting. That is because a kick makes a man who has fallen down stand up again and launches him again into the action to which he is condemned. *En attendant Godot* includes many possible symbols—*parallels*, the author would rather say. It is a symbolic play, as much as *Peer Gynt*, but its form is so completely realistic that it puts a sort of prohibition upon the imagination. It is like the world of nutrition, in which one cannot believe that one is eating chicken when one is eating dry bread, while in the world of love—

Jacques Lemarchand, in his excellent review in the *Figaro Littéraire*, has correctly written: "Samuel Beckett does not have the heavy clogs of the symbol manipulators to which we are accustomed: we do not hear him coming and when we notice the place where he intends to lead us, it is too late, we have been taken."

Shall I say that Vladimir and Estragon made me think of an incarnation of the Verlaine-Rimbaud couple? There is one of them who must have promised the other to restore him to his state as the son of the sun. One who assumed toward the other the manners of a young mother, of a beloved sister. Between the two friends there is not the spiritual Father-Son relationship that occupied Joyce so much, but the Mother-Child relationship, the child being physically the weakest, the one who has need of being helped. In this respect the dialogue is marvelous: woven with the commonplaces that accompany a life in common—alternations of vague tenderness, of indifference, of vague disgust; that never goes to the point of anger or hate or love. As Vladimir says: "The air is full of our cries, but habit is a great muffler."

Beckett has put the accents of an unheard-of intimacy into this dialogue; it is an exemplary familiar tone—the "let's see" of Vladimir is exquisite. None of the other books had shown such a power. He is no longer hindered by himself.

After having read the review by Jacques Lemarchand—I had also been told that Max Favalleli had published an article that was full of praise in *France-Soir*—I said to myself: "Good, the right is going along, therefore the left is going to hang back." To my great surprise I saw that Renée Saurel was going along in the *Lettres Françaises*, she too. Her article is very good, very intelligent. It is true that with Lucky and Pozzo Beckett had given them an excellent bone to gnaw on: master and servant—executioner and victim—oppressor and oppressed.

It is curious, the Lucky-Pozzo team did not appear to me to have that meaning. It made me think rather of a body-spirit relationship; the idea of Prospero and Ariel impressed itself upon me. Prospero is the body, which did not cease to prosper until blindness. Lucky is an old plucked Ariel who "formerly" knew how to dance, to leap, to think, and who has become bit by bit ataxic and mute. A very little feather remains to him—"the divine Miranda," who appears at the beginning of his horrible exercise of thought.

We must not conclude from this that Beckett considers that the body and the spirit have degenerated, starting from an age of gold. For him, as for the mystics, everything is always present, whether "potentially or actually." The truth is that he is not so much a mystic as a sort of yogi, but he would no more accept that name than he would any other—he prefers to be the Unnameable. He is a man of extreme modesty, in spite of the obscenities with which he freely sprinkles his books.

In 1929–30 Sylvia Beach and I often happened to see Samuel Beckett. He was then an assistant English teacher at the Ecole Normale Supérieure; Joyce had a great deal of esteem and affection for him. We were struck by his resemblance to Joyce as a young man, of whom Sylvia had photos; he appeared to us like a new Stephen Dedalus—the Stephen of the "Proteus" episode, who walks alone on the seashore. He spoke little and discouraged every advance.

It was he who undertook in 1930 to translate a fragment (the first third) of "Anna Livia Plurabelle," an episode from *Work in Progress*, which the review *Transition* was publishing. To be precise, the first version of "Anna Livia Plurabelle" had appeared in 1925 in my *Navire d'Argent*, and the definitive version had come out in 1928 in a deluxe edition published by Crosby Gaige in New York.

It was a text that bristled with really insurmountable difficulties, but it was perhaps the most beautiful passage of Joyce's new work.

Beckett was helped in his task by his comrade Alfred Perron, who had spent a year in Dublin and was a schoolteacher. I believe that it was Philippe Soupault who had suggested this translation, which he was intending for the review *Bifur*. Beckett's and Perron's work went to the stage of being set in type (I have the *Bifur* proofs, which are covered with corrections), but it did not go to the stage of being approved for printing, for while Joyce was very satisfied with the result when he was consulted, he got it into his head to team seven persons together under his guidance (five in addition to the two promoters). That was to have the pleasure of saying my "Septuagint." Fortunately, the demon of analogy did not push him to the point of wanting seventy of them—with him everything was possible!

In my opinion, Joyce's revision was very desirable, considering his genius for language and his knowledge of French, but it did not appear to me either useful or just to add to those who had done almost all the work—and magnificently, I assure you—five people of whom some, myself for example, were there only as supernumeraries.

When I think about it now, the matter does not appear so important to me, and above all Joyce should not be reproached for the small pleasure that he gave himself there. All the less so because Samuel Beckett has gone quite a way since "Anna Livia" and has himself also become a great man.

From *Dernières Gazettes et Ecrits divers*; first published in *Les Lettres Nouvelles* (March 1953).

A Little Speech Addressed to Victoria Ocampo

Dear Victoria Ocampo,

We are happy, very happy, to have you among us.

You are truly an extraordinary person. I am sure that there is not, in all of Argentina, a woman or a man who is more argentine than you. You are of your country to the point where symbols are born.

And you pay us the honor of preferring our language to your own, of writing your books in French. In the foreword to your essay on Colonel Lawrence (which has appeared in Buenos Aires), you have put these lines:

"I have never stopped writing in French. I have never published anything but more or less faithful translations of what I had written in that language."

In fact, you are a French writer, you, Argentina personified!

There is something that could turn our heads, if we were not an old, sensible people who are weary of adventures. But though we no longer have a liking for material conquests, how can we not be elated by the idea of this—spiritual protectorate? That is the gift of your love for France, which you have expressed so many times in words, and in actions as well—we know something about that here.

You have forbidden me to talk about your books. Good, then, I shall say nothing about them. Besides, your Lawrence is going to appear soon at Gallimard's, and the French public will at last know you better than through the legend that is already forming about you—how can it be stopped?

All the same, I should like to speak a little this evening about your review, about *Sur*, in which for twenty years you have made known in Latin America what is best in contemporary French literature.

It will suffice, I believe, to give the names of the writers whom you have had translated and published:

Antonin Artaud, Julien Benda, Georges Bernanos, André Breton, Roger Caillois, Albert Camus, Paul Claudel, Pierre Drieu la Rochelle, Paul Eluard, René Etiemble, Léon-Paul Fargue, André Gide, Jean Grenier, Valery Larbaud, André Malraux, Jacques Maritain, Henri Michaux, Emmanuel Mounier, Jean Paulhan, Rolland de Renéville, Denis de Rougemont, Jean-Paul Sartre, Jules Supervielle, Paul Valéry, etc.

I have in my hands the magnificent number of *Sur* that you devoted to Paul Valéry in October 1945. This number contains the lecture that you gave after the death of the poet.

Gisèle Freund has told me what that lecture was like, how the public was crowded together in the hall of the Friends of Art in Buenos Aires—a large hall—with many people standing. At the end of the lecture you launched an appeal for solidarity on behalf of our writers. The whole public responded to that appeal and a short time afterward three tons of provisions and clothing were dispatched to France, to my bookshop more exactly, in which I had the honor of distributing them to almost five hundred writers. You have forbidden me to speak about this famous distribution. Let us simply say that it was like a fairy tale—

The number of *Sur* in which your lecture appeared contains the letters that Paul Valéry addressed to you during the war. Astonishing letters that would make us all jealous if we did not love you so much. In fact, it was to you and to you alone that he confided with such abandon the faith that he kept in his country and in himself.

The letter written in June 1940 ends thus:

I embrace you as a sister of my spirit.

After such an homage I have nothing more to say.

From *Dernières Gazettes et Ecrits divers.*

Lust

This month of May was truly loaded with happy events; let us not talk about the peace in Europe, which is naturally the most happy, but let us remain people of letters.

We had visits from our friends the English poets T. S. Eliot and Stephen Spender—Eliot did us the favor of coming on V-Day to take tea with us, an exquisite Chinese tea that he brought himself. How fraternal our meetings with Spender were, and how many strawberries were eaten at them!

Gide came back to Paris and we happily saw him again in better form than ever.

I shall certainly not forget that performance of *The Knight of the Burning Pestle* which we attended with George Dillon and which gave us so much pleasure. The young company of the Mascarilles, directed by Jean Catel, acted the play with a charming good humor; why don't I have the time to devote a report to it!

But this is what I want to talk about, because it is a book and because it is here next to me, like an ideal being with which one can converse at leisure and at length.

It is the *Faust* of Paul Valéry, *"Mon Faust,"* which he puts in quotation marks, adding in parentheses, *Ebauches [Sketches].* The book has just appeared at Gallimard's in an edition that is very beautiful, very expensive, and already very rare.

I have known the text for several years. With unconcealed pride I shall say here that the poet gave a reading of it to us—to Sylvia, my sister Marie, and myself, in September 1940; I shall even say that our own ears were the first to hear it, after Julien P. Monod's, naturally. Our dearly beloved master had just come back to Paris under the Occupation after a summer that he had spent on the seacoast, writing the scenes that compose the present work. Almost all the scenes; I see none that is new but the fifth of the third act, which takes place in Dr. Faustus's library—an excellent scene in which Mephistopheles excites the appetite for Glory of the Disciple, that is to say, a literary apprentice like some we have known in Odéonia (why not think of the young André Breton?). "Courage," says the devil. "Feel that you are the prince of today! Nothing can prevail against the power of negation, scorn, and virgin energy of pride that arise in the heart of an ambitious young man who has not yet done anything." The Disciple, to whom it is completely useless to teach mockery, defines reading thus: "A to and fro of the nose, which walks from left to right and flies from right to left."

But I must tear myself away from the temptation to cite a hundred features that enchant me; as only so much space is allotted to me, it is Lust whom I am going to talk about here. Lust (which in German means joy, pleasure) is the feminine character of the play; it is she, this "Young Lady of Crystal," who gives the title to the comedy that forms the first part of *"Mon Faust"*; the other part being a *féerie dramatique* [dramatic fairy tale] entitled *Le Solitaire; ou, les Malédictions d'univers*. The comedy is three-quarters written and the fairy tale two-thirds. Very regretfully I am going to put aside this *Solitaire*, which seems as marvelous to me as *Lust* and perhaps even more astonishing.

There are no women in Valéry's books, no women, but how many feminine figures: a Young Fate, a Spinner of bygone days, a Helen, Columns with hats adorned with days, a Sleeper, a Venus still at her birth, a Semiramis in all her glory, a Pythian Sibyl in all her fury, Nymphs for Narcissus, a Princess in a palace of pure rose, Vain Dancers, two dancing stars—Athikté and the great Medusa, a Maiden who combs her hair slowly in the sunlight, a Slave with long eyes, a Laura lost in revery, an Anne who is completely naked, a no less naked Eve who is as full fleshed as a Rubens, four nameless Muses, and Ideas, so many Ideas that frolic among and above one does not know how many naked fragments of women. No, there are no women, but there are a great many women in fragments, magnificent fragments, for a museum!

Excuse me for this inventory in the Prévert manner in regard to an admired, a venerated body of work, but this *Faust*, full of the devil, drives one to devilry.

No, there are no women in Valéry's books, for that is how it is with pure poets, who have all the muses that they want, and who furthermore, as Faust says, among others, insofar as they are "superlative persons" are not of "any sex, or are of both."

But yes, even so, there is a model wife: Emilie Teste. And now, with this Faust, here is Lust, a no less model secretary, who enters onstage laughing like a servant of Molière's, the master being this time a "dear Master."

Two living women with bodies and souls, both of them bringing affective modes that are well tolerated by M. Teste and better than tolerated by Dr. Faust.

Two women who are "transparent" in the eyes of their lords and masters, and who consent to be of crystal. As Emilie Teste says: "I am seen and foreseen, such as I am, without mystery, without shadows, without possible recourse to my own unknown self—to my own ignorance of myself!"

Intelligent, both of them, but while Madame Emilie Teste nobly remains a good provincial housewife, Lust, completely involved in Faust's works, is an ingenuous intellectual. She is a spirited, a lively spirited girl, very free with her master while yet very respectful. She is not a "new Marguerite"; what Faust expects of her is not the love that "ends in ruin, in disgust, in disaster." He says so himself: "I want only a sweet presence near my thought." Here again is how he humorously defines his secretary: "a person relatively serious in gaiety and relatively gay in serious matters; relatively tender in work, relatively laborious. . . ."

Faust shows very well his experience of life by being content with the relative—it is the young madmen who demand the absolute.

The originality of the character of Lust is that, very much smitten with her master, smitten with his spirit and with his presence in the flesh, inclined toward love with all her feminine strength, believing in happiness like any other woman, she remains the mistress of herself and is content with the physical minimum that is given to her. The modesty of the girl approaches the wisdom of the master; furthermore, this modesty is only an ancestral wisdom. It happens, no doubt, that she is disturbed at night; she could recite certain passages of *La Jeune Parque [The Young Fate]*, or say like Madame Roland: "An extraordinary ebullition aroused my senses in the warmth of repose and through the strength of an excellent constitution brought about by itself a purification that was as unknown to me as its cause." It is Mephistopheles who says it for her, to her great confusion, or rather it is he who cruelly lets it be understood.

I have said "originality," but, upon reflection, this originality comes only from the art of Valéry. There are many girls and women like Lust, there are many of them in France. This capacity for being smitten with genius and loving to serve it is certainly a trait of the women of our country, even if the genius inhabits an ugly or aged being—in the light of the spirit, beautiful seems the face, and the body is forgotten. Beauty that is only physical leads only to desire—which is the servant of procreation, which mocks us completely. God knows (the devil does not know) if there are any amorous modes possible between two beings besides the one that leads to the famous to-and-fro movement. Eros is not always a "demoniac," although he must be exceedingly and for ever and ever mistrusted. "Watch out for love," that is the advice that Faust gives to the Disciple, who asks him for a supreme precept. He himself, however, who has arrived at the summit of the art of living, can play with fire and draw his energy from love without risking the loss of his soul and his time.

In *"Mon Faust"* Valéry's style shows a rather new manner; he aims at the familiar, as in *L'Idée fixe*, this time with an increased freedom and the whole of his habitual grace. According to his hero's own wish, the poet sought to express "all the modulations of the soul and all the veerings of the spirit." We find in it, as much as in Shakespeare, both sublimity and extreme drollery. There prevails here, mixed with the most clever irony, a Parisian wit that is very suitable for Mephistopheles (that gentleman who frequents the Opéra and lords it over the Boulevard). But everybody in the play hisses and banters as much as and better than the devil, who besides is rather old-fashioned, very out of date—which Faust easily proves to him. Between two flutters of emotion, Lust herself, that dove, darts a little tongue that is slightly forked. We are in the enchanted kingdom of the Nagas. We see undulating and scintillating the most lithe and the most diamondlike forms. The *vis comica* accomplishes stunning turnabouts among words.

It seems that the genius of Valéry has never shown itself with so much life, so much resemblance to something that is personally intimate.

When you think that the work was written at the beginning of the Occupation, when France was in such a lamentable state, and as if without spirit, you are gripped by everything that it reveals of true resistance, of profound strength, of freedom well assured of its time.

So, over the intelligence of our country there reigned such a poet, a sure sign of salvation and victory. We must, as little Lust wanted to do, kiss his hand.

From *Les Gazettes d'Adrienne Monnier*; first published in *Fontaine* (1945).

"Unkindness"

Gide's *Journal* has come out. It covers fifty years of his life: 1889–1939. It has 1,350 pages.

I wanted to keep it for vacation, and then—no way of resisting. I am at page 345. The most terrible thing is that once you put your nose into it you cannot take it out again. I all but missed my *Gazette*.

It was an excellent idea to publish it in a volume of the Pléiade collection. It is good to have it in a single flow.

It is the life of a great river and perhaps its secret. Here it is near its source, leaping like a torrent. Starting off on a long journey. We shall follow all its meanders. But we do not yet know toward what sea it pursues its course—

I am rediscovering reflections that I had read in the *Nouvelle Revue Française* and that seem much more important to me, or much more charming, because they here have their proper contours and their true light.

Gide gains nothing by being compared to others. His writing is too simple, too subtle; it has nuances, inflections that require all of one's attention. If the reader is fully attentive he is completely satisfied; if he is absent-minded he takes up dry bread.

But I do not have the intention of speaking seriously today about the work or about the author. There would be too much to say.

This note: hardly more than to point out that the volume contains an index. It was unhoped for!

And naturally, the first thing one does is to look for one's name in it. Ah, ah, here's my own, in five places if you please.

The first, page 749: he runs into Paul Valéry at the bookshop.

The second, page 827: he notes a conversation with me on the subject of *Les Faux-Monnayeurs*. I tell him that I do not like the book. I speak to him "for a rather long time and eloquently about the fundamental coldness and *unkindness* that this book reveals. . . ."

The devil if I remember that.

That October 16, 1926, I was not really too wicked.

Unkindness—I knew then perhaps what it is. Do I know now? I have too often observed that the people to whom one does wrong provoke it more or less. As the title of a novel by Franz Werfel says, "The guilty one is the victim."

Unkindness almost always stands for the displeasure that one has in oneself.

From *Dernières Gazettes et Ecrits divers*; first published in *La Gazette des Amis des Livres* (July 1939).

Beowulf

I am very willing to bet that Bryher's *Beowulf* is called upon to occupy an enviable place in English literature. As for myself, I should like better to have written it than most of the books that are spoken about. Its present value will appear more perhaps to us French than to the English people who lived through the period of the bombardments at the same time as the author. I could not do better than to compare it to the admirable documentary films that were shown to us a bit after the Liberation. But here in addition there is the art of the novel, that is to say, a transposition into a domain that is more plastic and more rich in spiritual values.

Yes, although Bryher has given to her book, in a manner that is half humorous, half serious, the name of the hero of the Anglo-Saxon epic, it is a real novel that she has written. It is a novel about The Warming Pan during the war. The Warming Pan is a modest London teashop run by two elderly spinsters—Selina Tippett and Angelina Hawkins.

The idea of taking a teashop for the center of the action seems to me most fortunate. The more so because Selina is a mystical founder in the best sense of the word: she is fully conscious of the attributes of the god Tea, she becomes his humble servant in order to identify herself with him.

Doubtless the French are more sensitive to the virtues of wine (on the side of the men) and to those of coffee (on the side of the women); it is not that teaists are lacking among us, but it is curious that although in France tea is the occasion for an urban and feminine ceremony (precisely, it is a ceremony), I have found more real lovers of tea among men first of all, and then in the country. I am writing this preface in Savoy where the mountaineers among whom I live like it a great deal. If they had all they wanted of it they would probably consume as much of it as the people of Asia.

We drink wine and coffee to restore ourselves, as an excitant, while we take tea to relax, to uplift ourselves. After a few swallows of tea our eyebrows slowly rise up and form again the arches that support our foreheads. We judge while drinking tea, we tranquilly judge the things of life; it is a resting place. How many times, alone in my kitchen, taking my tea with milk and sugar (a sect that is much debated), with my two hands surrounding my cup as if it were a Chinese cup without a handle, has it occurred to me to say under my breath this single word, the only one that suits my gentle blessedness: manna.

It is surely as a distributor of manna that Selina Tippett considers herself and fulfills her task. Complete manna, since tea with her is accompanied by perfect toast and excellent pastry. All the passages of the book where it is a question of the great ideal give me joy: those, for example, that express her reflections before the founding of her house, while she is only a modest woman companion "collecting" teashops, meeting friends in them, taking a train to try out a "Farmhouse Tea" that had been recommended to her and, as she says gaily to Angelina, never finding "the toast, the temperature, and the tea," all together.

Her house opened, Selina boasts that nowhere can such "good standard things and so much variety" be found. But alas, the war comes along and with the rationing of butter, eggs, and currants, everything falls in short supply and disappears bit by bit: "She looked sadly at the meagre row; there was something stinted and miserly about it. It was not the bombs that distressed her, awful as the noise was, so much as the lack of loaded trays to make up for the horrors of the night. She detested ration cards, less because she wanted more food herself than because they were a symbol of some poverty of spirit."

After the disappearance of The Warming Pan, Selina makes this admirably simple and kind remark: "I tried to make it a home from home and to give people value for their money."

It is very much as if in their own homes that the episodic

characters of the book appear: the old painter Horatio Rashleigh, who is so touching and so comic; Eve and Joe, sympathetic young people who are very much of their time; Adelaide Spenser, a strong middle-class soul, and her faint-hearted sister-in-law Alice; the servants—Timothy, Ruby, and the cook. Here is Colonel Ferguson, who brightens the book with his noble figure; it is he that makes this speech: "Death is not dissolution, . . . it is the moment when humanity needs our services no longer." I shall add: that is true, those who die before the accomplishment of their task, we call them, we beg them to help us complete their work.

Nearby The Warming Pan there is Mr. Dobbie, a dealer in teas and coffees, the very type of the London shopkeeper, head of the district during the war.

We pass the time of one chapter with Mr. Burlap, a pedantic and pretentious official, and his secretary Miss Rosy Wings, as he is pleased to call her. This chapter, which unfolds in one of the offices of national defense, will give French readers the consolation of seeing that it is not only among us that it is possible for administration to be incompetent and full of red tape.

In chapter five we are with the servant Ruby and her friend Mrs. Gates. Their whole conversation in the bus is superbly droll. Commonplaces occur there naturally and give us the equivalent of what we used to hear while waiting in lines. It is in the mouths of Ruby and Mrs. Gates that we find these paraphrases of the famous "Rule, Britannia, Rule the Waves!":

> "Somehow," she said, pushing a little, for Mrs. Gates had taken advantage of the bus's swaying to grab more than her fair portion of the seat, "I feel nothing can 'appen as long as the sea is round us." . . .
> "You're right, there," Mrs. Gates snorted, "not, mind you, that I'm against them foreigners but it stands to reason they can't be as 'andy as we are, never 'aving no sea to be on."

". . . to grab more than her fair portion of the seat" is worth a long poem, or rather a thick history book. Bravo, Bryher!

Next to Selina Tippett, almost equal in importance, there is her partner Angelina Hawkins.

Angelina is the type of the advanced woman: *"New,* that was a word that meant what heaven, she supposed, signified to most women." She seeks her spiritual way with a somewhat muddled good will. At first attracted by Oriental philosophy, for a while she made great efforts to control her temper; her partner saw nothing to find fault with there, far from it; it is really her study of Esperanto that appears more contestable to her—wasn't it then a question of writing the menus in Esperanto? Angelina is presently in the midst of a passion for communism, which terrifies poor Selina, who finds her more muddled than ever; she is interested only in political lectures, which she attends assiduously. She always leaves them very inflamed: the customers appear to her to be stupid middle-class people whom it is right to scorn.

Nevertheless, it is Angelina the Communist who has the most go and energy; she saves the situation on many occasions. It is she who, in a fit of enthusiasm, acquires Beowulf, "a plaster bulldog, almost life-sized, with a piratical scowl painted on his black muzzle." She insists upon seeing in him an emblem of English tenacity and good sense and it is for that reason that she gives him the name of the hero of the old epic, who was the destroyer of monsters; all the more, she thinks, because Beowulf can be accepted by the proletariat, having fought the dragon, which was "a symbol no doubt for Viking dictatorship."

I admire that Bryher has noted in Angelina's character that the social and literary avant-garde always rediscovers the totems of primitive clans, while conservatives are content with a much more recent past, the past of which they are the direct heirs.

In spite of the real sympathy that is shown for Angelina, it is very obvious that in her heart Bryher prefers Selina, "the Tippett," as some of her customers irreverently call her. She hides nothing of her oddities or ridiculous features, but at the same time she feels an immense tenderness in the face of the exceptional honesty and goodness of the excellent woman, a modest heroine, really the most modest and humble of heroines; the bombardment that destroys her house and shows her in her glory causes her to make this remark: "I do think it is very embarrassing to be bombed."

Before arriving at this remark, which closes the book, Selina has seen Colonel Ferguson lean toward her with a feeling that is exquisitely noted: a mixture of respect, tenderness, and non-irony, as if irony were keeping still. The look that the elderly people exchange is one of the most moving things, in my opinion, that has ever been expressed in literature; at this instant there is a weight of humanity that is like a diamond.

Bryher has a remarkably subtle talent; she excels in seizing all the shades of feelings and above all the kinds of behavior they entail. Her humor is original; doubtless it is in the English tradition, but with her it assumes modes that seem quite uncommon to me. I really believe that nobody has ever shown an intelligence that is at once so critical and so benevolent, which makes her a painter of delicate caricatures of those who are called "the little people"—always funny and moving for someone who knows how to observe them.

The middle-class people are very droll also, in their fashion (nothing escapes Bryher). The conversation of the two sisters-in-law in chapter four, isn't it a masterpiece? It is very cruel, although discreet, it is as sharp as the kind of needle that is used for making tattoos.

Thus *Beowulf* gives us an authentic picture of the middle classes during the war. In this respect the final scenes, which take place in the shelter, are rich in sketches drawn with lively strokes. With the portraits of Selina Tippett and the old painter Horatio Rashleigh, Bryher has reached the level of great creation; these two good people deserve to take a place among the familiar heroes of the English novel.

Shall I note here that love plays no role in *Beowulf?* One would say that most of its characters, principally the women, have never heard it spoken about and so would be incapable of falling in love, as La Rochefoucauld says in one of his maxims. Even the young people do not show that they are disturbed or curious about it.

I have often thought that if half of the population of Tibet lives in monasteries, the English people are almost all of them in orders: social orders.

Society is the real god across the Channel; there is no sacrifice that is not made to him. Moral reserve is not so much natural to the English as it is vigorously taught to them, in view of the best social profit—just as the worker bees in hives are asexual. The names of things in the English language are neither feminine nor masculine, they have no gender, which is much more sensible and restful.

The varieties of sisters and monks that exist in France and in the Latin countries are not to be seen among them. To what purpose, since the great majority of them are citizen-clerics (those who are not belong to the devil's party). They wear their clothes as if they were those of their orders, that is to say, in my opinion, their well-understood tasks. Tailoring is almost a sacred art. Only among them does masculine dress have meaning and beauty.

Here are some reflections that only a perfectly English book could inspire in me, isn't that so?

Well, yes, this new *Beowulf* appears to me to be already a little classic. In addition to its literary qualities it shows an enlightened patriotism that is certainly exemplary. Bryher, who loves France deeply and has proved it a hundred times, has us live through the period of the bombardments with the people of her country. She knows that a lasting entente can be based only upon understanding.

We should try to tell her our own stories; they are much less simple, and to sustain us we had neither so much sea—nor so much tea.

From *Dernières Gazettes et Ecrits divers.*

An Amateur of Surrealism

I would like today to sketch a portrait. Not one of an author, but of an amateur. An amateur of something that I enjoy moderately: surrealism, but that he himself enjoys in a manner that is so sympathetic, so sincere, with so much delight, that he gives me the desire to reconsider the matter. So it is, some allowances being made, with good priests who lead one to religion.

No, Henri Parisot—he is the one whom I want to speak about—is not an author. He recently answered a friend who asked him to do a study on Hoffmann, the publication of whose complete works he is preparing for the Editions Colbert: "But I never write. At the most I happen to put short bibliographical notes at the beginning or at the end of my translations." This answer charmed me like a rare object.

However, I have read something by Henri Parisot. And that was not without interest. In 1938 the *Cahiers G. L. M.* had posed the following question:

> Against every narrow attempt to annex, stabilize, evaluate Poetry, point out to us twenty poems, without restriction as to country or epoch, in which you have recognized the indispensable thing that demands of you not the eternity of your time but the mysterious passage through your life.

Henri Parisot had answered this question (I quote only the first lines):

Poetry—it does not matter what mode of literary or artistic expression—interests me only to the extent that it succeeds in merging with the Marvelous (Dream, Eroticism, Humor, etc.).

This is very orthodox. This love of the marvelous is, in fact, professed in all of Breton's manifestoes, from the first, which appeared in 1924, down to the pages that were published in 1937 by the *Nouvelle Revue Française* under the title: "Limites non frontières du surréalisme."

To this essential assertion Breton has often added others. For example, he has laid hold of politics or he has let go of it, according to the course of events. He has not left off preaching automatic writing, which for him is equivalent to what we call inspiration. I confess that I do not at all appreciate this way of seeing things, for supposing inspiration really does represent a kind of dictation, and supposing automatism comes into play, as in everything, nothing demands more alertness of the mind, and less of what is mechanical, than does a valid inspiration. Inspiration is, if you wish, the fact of seeing the object with light—it then becomes subject—the light being produced by the active relations of our senses. Now, Breton's system demands a complete passivity. It does not bring to light objects of value but what Jean Grenier in his remarkable essay "Le Choix" ["Choice"] has properly called "wastes." It should furthermore be noted that in his first manifesto Breton presented it in the most ironic manner.

I believe that nobody has ever discussed, in connection with this famous automatic writing, a pamphlet by Swift entitled *The Mechanical Operation of the Spirit.*

This pamphlet, aimed at the religious hypocrites of his time, is concerned not with writing but with automatic speech. It recommends swaying, mumbling, and speaking through the nose as means of artificially producing enthusiasm. Breton says nearly the same thing: "Rely upon the inexhaustible character of murmuring." I have found the translation of Swift's text only in the edition of 1767; I do not know if our surrealists are familiar with it, they have never mentioned it, although they have often spoken the name of Swift with praise.

An equally constant assertion in the surrealist manifestoes is that of nonconformism. From the beginning of the movement Breton and his friends have presented themselves as destroyers and even assassins, eager, no doubt, to give reality to Rimbaud's saying: "The time of the assassins is at hand."

This aggressive nonconformism is certainly what most seduces young people, very young people, who are still rallying to surrealism, which for them is mixed up with what has been called "the crisis of juvenile originality." It is the need to escape from family or school authority, the horror of social cogwheels, the desire to assert one's personality. It is on a par with speaking Javanese.

I have wondered of late if there was not something enduring in the surrealist attitude, and if it did not correspond to the *lycée* age (around twelve to sixteen), that is to say, the age when you are not permitted anything and when you have to act in secret. Sartre made very good note of it in *L'Enfance d'un chef [The Childhood of a Leader]*.

Les Nourritures terrestres [Fruits of the Earth] would correspond to adolescence (fifteen to twenty), when you can smoke, read everything, talk about love and even contemplate making it—provided, however, that these adolescents have not gone through surrealism, in which case they do not stop over.

Henri Parisot himself is a grown man and even the father of a family: he has a delightful little boy who is four years old.

As his answer to the inquiry of the *Cahiers G. L. M.* shows, he has dwelt chiefly upon the love of the marvelous. The twenty "book-poems" that he listed as being those in which the marvelous is most in evidence and most intense were:

Heraclitus: *Aphorisms*. John Ford: *'Tis Pity She's a Whore*. Shakespeare: *The Tempest*. Sade: *Justine*. Arnim: *Isabella of Egypt*. Hoffmann: *Master Floh*. Poe: *Histoires extraordinaires [Extraordinary Stories]*. Melville: *Moby-Dick*. Emily Brontë: *Wuthering Heights*. Nerval: *Aurélia*. Baudelaire: *Les Fleurs du mal [The Flowers of Evil]*. Rimbaud: *Les Illuminations*. Lautréamont: *Les Chants de Maldoror*. Lewis Carroll: *Alice*. Jensen: *Gradiva*. R. Roussel: *Impressions d'Afrique*. Kafka: *The Castle*. Chirico: *Hebdomeros*. Max Ernst: *La Femme 100 têtes [The Woman 100 Heads]*. Hans Bellmer: *The Doll*.

It seems to me that this choice could be acknowledged by many well-read people, up to and including Kafka. The nonsurrealists would no doubt strike off the last three names and Sade.

Parisot, if he is not a writer, is a translator and publisher, and he has been of good service to what he loves in those two capacities. We owe him the translation of several of Kafka's shorter works. He has translated a short story by Melville: "The Lightning-Rod Man." Of works by Lewis Carroll, whom the surrealists justly hail as one of their masters (doesn't surrealism represent a counterpart of English "nonsense" in many respects?), he has given "The Hunting of the Snark," *Phantasmagoria*, and "Poeta fit, non nascitur." He has just published at Corti's a new translation, which to me seems excellent, of the famous "Rime of the Ancient Mariner" by Coleridge.

As a publisher he has managed a little collection modestly entitled *Un Divertissement*, which comprises eleven short texts that are signed with the names of: Gisèle Prassinos, Benjamin Péret, A. Savinio, Chirico, Kafka, Hans Arp, Jean Scutenaire, etc. The name of Gisèle Prassinos appears three times in the collection; she is, as he says himself, his beloved child.

Gisèle Prassinos composed her poems at the age of fourteen, and the champions of surrealism consider that nothing better of their kind has been done. Parisot has gathered together the work of the young poet (it would fill a volume of around two hundred pages), Breton and Eluard have written beautiful and generous prefaces, and they are looking for a publisher. The manuscript was entrusted to me; I read it with a laboriously sustained interest—writings of that sort not being bearable except in very small doses—but I had to recognize that nothing, or few things, was so authentically surrealist.

It would be interesting to know to what degree the girl, who frequented the surrealists, has been influenced by them: the idea of mediumship impresses itself upon you, but without destroying the value of the document, since it is a matter of automatic writing. Still, there is a fairy-tale tone in her poems that is very pleasing once you perceive the slightest coherence; you also notice in them the cruelty of children, a cruelty that is generally manifested in actions and not in utterances: it is the physical object—whether animate or inanimate, it is an object because it is perceived as being nonrelated—that first of all provokes curiosity in children and then cruelty as a means of complete investigation.

This little prodigy is now twenty-two years old, she does not write anymore, apparently, and is passionately occupied with retarded children. As you see, everything has turned out well.

From *Les Gazettes d'Adrienne Monnier*; first published in *Le Figaro Littéraire* (1942).

Les Amies des Livres

Dear Listeners,

If this were not 1938 but a hundred or even fifty years earlier the very title of my talk would give rise to objections: who are they, a great number of gentlemen would say—all those who prided themselves on loving books—"les Ami-es des Livres," but they do not exist, of course. Women are incapable of loving books; far from being their friends, they are their natural enemies. And many authoritative voices would rise up in support of this assertion.

Ernest Quentin-Bauchart, the author of a work on women bibliophiles of France in the sixteenth, seventeenth, and eighteenth centuries, would not fail to give us this information, as he did at the beginning of his book: "Many great ladies had books in the past centuries, but almost all of them were ignorant of their contents, and the title of bibliophile is hardly applicable to them. Once the book was acquired, bound, and arranged with more or less method in a luxurious cabinet the effect was produced and there they stopped."

It would seem that the final stroke was given by one of my colleagues, the bookseller Floury, who said in a lecture that was delivered in 1908 at the Cercle de la Librairie: "For many women the bookseller is a kind of enemy. We all more or less have patrons who, having bought and paid for their books, let them board with us while awaiting a favorable occasion to have them enter their homes—a vacation, a ceremony, etc., an occasion that sometimes takes months to come about."

Are there any women's voices that may be raised against such declarations? Alas, no. George Sand made a coy affectation of calling herself a "bibliophobe"; Mme Emile de Girardin declared that her women contemporaries had no books at all: "What can you expect?" she said. "Young women do not read, and—a more terrible thing, alas!—those who as an exception still read a little—write!"

Albert Cim, from whom I am borrowing this little historical report, maintains in his excellent work *Les Femmes et les livres [Women and Books]*, that there are exceptions even so; these exceptions either go back very far in the course of time or come down to our own days. There were, he tells us, in the first centuries of the Middle

Ages, several women in religious orders "worthy of figuring among 'les Amies des Livres.' " The names of Saints Radegonde, Gertrude, Odile, and Wiborade should be mentioned. For Saint Wiborade, virgin and martyr, the baron Ernouf claimed the title of "patroness of bibliophiles." This saint joined to the merit of loving books that of being an excellent embroiderer; nothing pleased her so much as to embroider the fabrics that were intended to cover the manuscripts of the monastery. When a horde of Hungarian barbarians invaded the region and threatened to pillage the monastery, she ran to the monks crying: "Save the books first! Hide them! You can see to the sacred vessels afterward!"

(Imagine, dear listeners, the pleasure I am taking in giving you this detail, I who have the good luck of having for a sister Marie Monnier, the embroiderer, whose art could win the praise of Paul Valéry and Léon-Paul Fargue.)

In our own days there are many women who are friends of books. Women appear to me to be as capable of appreciating books as men. It is a simple matter of education. It must certainly be said that if so many women are ignorant of or scorn books it is because care has been taken to turn their minds against them. Who, in the seventeenth century, put his collars in a thick volume of Plutarch and mocked the learned women of his acquaintance? It was the fine gentleman Chrysale, that is to say, the bourgeois of yesterday and perhaps of always.

Women are asked to take care of their persons and their homes above all; they are praised for devoting themselves to housework and it is not considered proper for them to become lost in books, whether these books be frivolous or serious.

Sainte-Beuve noted that in antiquity the only well-read women were the courtesans, that is to say, free women, released from the cares that weigh upon wives and mothers. It is far from my thought to prefer the well-read woman, whether she is a courtesan or a nun, to the honest mother of a family who never goes beyond the tales of her household; but recognize with me that the men who reproach women for not liking books are poorly founded in their criticism since it is they themselves who keep women in that state of mind.

The first third of this century brought about great changes in the relations of women with books and with culture in general. Compulsory education has played a great role in this evolution, that cannot be denied.

A woman of today, as much as a man, can become a friend of

books. Naturally, she brings to this relationship some particular traits that we are going to try to make clear. It should be recognized first of all that unless she has received a special initiation she is less sensitive to the *form* of books than a man is; above all she enjoys *reading*, in whatever fashion it may be given to her. But if the form matters little to her, she is certainly more sensitive to the spirit of the book; if this spirit can touch her she can love it with rapture. She will not experience the need, like a masculine reader, to own her favorite authors in beautiful and lasting editions—at bottom it is true that she is not a bibliophile in the sense in which this word is generally understood. She will prefer to keep the ordinary editions that were the very ones she read first, and she will surround them with kind attentions: she will cover them with fine patterned paper, she will put in as a frontispiece a portrait of the author that she has cut out of some magazine, she will sometimes slip in a flower. If the book pleases her intensely she will copy passages from it. It is not she who will have that nasty habit of writing in the margins, except perhaps as far as her school books are concerned. The fact of writing in the margins is furthermore specifically masculine. Yes, it is curious, a man and above all a young man often corrects the author, he underlines, he denies, he opposes his judgment; in fact, *he adds himself to it.* A woman remains silent when she does not like something, and when she detests something *she cuts it out.* I know women who are not at all stupid who cannot stop themselves from removing or covering up such and such a displeasing passage of a book; they do that above all for the benefit or to the disadvantage of a work that they admire but that offends them in places, just as they try to suppress the ugly traits in the characters of the men they love. A number of people would consider that practice hateful; person-ally, I see nothing wrong with it, on condition, of course, that the copy thus treated is far from being the only one and that it is the personal property of the lady. A book is not sacred in itself, it is our feeling that makes it sacred.

It matters less to venerate things than to live with them on terms of good friendship.

From *Dernières Gazettes et Ecrits divers*; first broadcast over Radio-Paris (May 1938), then published in *La Gazette des Amis des Livres* (April 1939).

A Letter to a Young Poet

April 1926

Sir,

I thank you for the confidence that you show in me, but I am very much afraid that I cannot help you solve the problems that you pose. You are a poet, you say, and not a poet by accident but a poet by vocation, tormented since childhood to express yourself in a language that is more intense, more liberating than prose, eager to add your voice to the chorus of the great poets living and dead. And why, you ask, is the world so hostile to poets, since it says that it puts nothing as high as they? Where is the public that reads poetry, that judges it, that opens to it the roads of posterity?

Before trying to study these questions, to which moreover I see no definitive answer, let us examine your particular case a little.

Obviously, such problems must appear exceptionally sharp and painful to you. You live in the provinces, without a friend, without an intellectual environment; you are not a teacher by choice but by necessity; there is nothing there that sustains you, that helps you to live, no symphony concerts, no plays, no large museum, nobody with whom you can exchange ideas; only the ideal company of the poets whom you love, their consolation, their appeal. That is a presence, certainly, but it is a presence that the forces of the spirit do not always succeed in securing, and often, isn't it so, after great concentration, great ardor, there is such a *night of the soul!*

Well, here it is!—in a case like your own the best thing then would be to try to assimilate your poetic life completely to a mystical life. Notice besides that in doing this you would be returning to the most genuine source of poetry, all poetic activity being essentially religious more or less. A saint is always a super-poet, but a poet is not a saint: once his work is finished his only preoccupation most of the time is to bring it out and see it applauded; and if he does not reap from others almost all the approval that he lavishes upon himself, he becomes bitter, he becomes obnoxious to his friends if he leads a social life and falls into a real frenzy if he lives solitary. His inspiration gave him intercourse with the Good of the world, his publication turns him into a demon of the most vicious sort. The success of his colleagues, a success that is not always due to merit, makes him extraordinarily venomous. It is said that in the formation of the world the reptiles gave rise to the birds, but in the case that we are considering it is the birds that become serpents.

And what is to be done, my God!

Shall I dare to speak to you about myself? I am, like yourself, for both my happiness and my unhappiness, attracted by poetry. But no doubt because I am a woman, that is to say, passive by nature, accustomed over several centuries to attach little value to my mind and its "paltry productions," as Hroswitha said, I have been granted more detachment, perhaps, than has been granted to most of my brothers. Like you I began writing poetry at the age of nine, like you I suffered martyrdom at about twenty when the reviews to which I sent my poems I shall not even say *rejected* them; that would have been a consolation even so, to receive one of those letters that begin with the formula "I have read your poems with much interest, but . . ." No, like so many others I was not even answered.

I see very well now that the editors of these reviews were not so guilty. I have been directing the *Navire d'Argent* for twelve months, and I have many crimes of that sort on my conscience. We receive so much poetry! And it must be said that there are no more than fifty people who really wish to read the young poets, and then they ask them, and it is right, to supply a new tendency or formula. Obviously, there is an elite—shall we say of three or four hundred people for the city of Paris, a hundred more for the provinces, a hundred more for all the foreign countries (in respect to French literature, naturally). These six hundred people or so (who may seem to be twelve hundred because of the reflections) do not wait until a poet has died in order to find him great; they have, very nearly, eyes to see and ears to hear. In 1913, 1914 they were the readers of Paul Claudel's *Cinq Grandes Odes [Five Great Odes]* and Jules Romains's *Odes et prières [Odes and Prayers]*. But even this elite is not informed about everything. The sorting out has to have been done before by the little society of the fifty who love the little reviews, even and above all if they are obscure, who often subscribe to them, even while knowing that in all probability these reviews will not go beyond a few issues. These fifty people represent, certainly, the very best that humanity can produce; I do not hesitate to proclaim that some among them are superior to the poets whom they choose and promote; they are themselves elected not by men but by the Geniuses of the Earth; the temptation to express themselves comes rarely to them, it is enough for them to contain an exact and ineffable inner standard to which they must relate everything. Furthermore, if they happen to succumb to temptation they quickly lose everything that made them agreeable to themselves and to the Great Gods.

But enough digressing, I was speaking to you about myself, I believe, who have caught only a glimpse of the true glory of the Fifty. I was telling you, then, that I too believed in the Mission of the Poet, I too ruminated over the grievances of de Vigny's Chatterton. But fortunately this error did not persist for a long time, for an error it is to believe that the world owes something to poets; what it owed them it has given them in bestowing inspiration upon them. It is for them to be satisfied afterward with the state of grace in which they have the leisure to live, for them to be gentle and humble of heart, for them to feel guilty when they solicit the praise of others, for them to fill a calling that is like the rest, that is better than the rest because, in short, what is the goal of poetry if it is not to perceive the very essence of things, to understand hidden reasons, to see no matter what action, no matter what object in its felicity. And here we come back to what I was telling you just now: it is easy to assimilate poetic states to mystical states.

You will ask me first of all how I define the mystical state and mysticism in general. The *Littré* gives this definition: "Religious or philosophical belief that supposes secret communications between man and divinity." The *Larousse* says: "Philosophical and religious doctrine according to which perfection consists in a kind of contemplation that reaches ecstasy and mysteriously unites man to divinity." The Reverend Father Poulain, who is an authority in matters of mystical theology and who has written a treatise *Des grâces d'oraison [On the Graces of Prayer]*, defines mystical states thus: "We call mystical any acts or supernatural states that our efforts, our skill, cannot succeed in producing, and not even feebly, not even for an instant." He adds: "The preceding definition is the one that Saint Teresa has given in a very short treatise addressed in the form of a second letter to Father Rodrigue Alvarez. She begins by defining mystical states, employing the synonymous term of *supernatural* states of prayer. 'I call *supernatural* that which we cannot acquire by ourselves, *whatever effort* and whatever diligence we may bring to it. In this respect, *all* that we can do is to dispose ourselves to it.' "

How I love that *dispose ourselves to it!* But doesn't this *disposition* suppose even so a certain personal skill?

Shall I now dare to propose my definition of mysticism? "Tendency to conceive the Good or a supreme Good and to identify oneself with it." It seems to me that this definition reconciles rather well all the ideas that one can have of mysticism, which in any case does not appear to me to belong exclusively to Religion and Philosophy, given the present meaning of these words. One can be a savant with mysticism, a poet with mysticism—Valéry is a mystic, more a mystic even than Claudel, according to a strictly poetic point of view. One can be a grocer with mysticism, as Chesterton understood in an episode of *Napoleon of Notting Hill.* One can be a pederast with mysticism, as Gide amply proves.

Well, you will tell me, then of what use is it for a poet to be a mystic?—Why, it's that he will then be able, almost as much as a saint, to do without the approbation of the world. If he is attentive only to his spiritual progress he will be gladdened to the very extent that he approaches the Good that appears to him to be supreme. He will understand that inspiration is the first or one of the first degrees of ecstasy; it is, in fact, the consideration of things in their relations of identity of principle or effect with ourselves; ecstasy bathes us in this identity. In the state of inspiration the spirit feels the distance that separates it from what it considers, but it also feels the possibility of reaching it and strives toward it while expressing and intensifying its state. In ecstasy the goal has been reached, and so every external manifestation becomes useless. A wise poet will not try to make use of all of his inspirations, since in doing this he chooses only a middling expression that is in no way capable of making him perfectly happy; rather he will often try to *dispose himself* to ecstasy by renouncing every expression and by simply letting the idea of his Good prevail in him.

What I am saying here no doubt has need of development, clarification, examples; it would be necessary to write a whole book about these questions; I do not know if I shall find the time and the patience to do it; in any case, if you still want to ask me particular questions I shall try to answer them.

But, you will ask me perhaps, should a poet not publish at all, should he keep his works in manuscript?—that long, rolled-up manuscript that used to stick out of the pocket of the romantics and the symbolists with their starving faces. You never knew it yourself, and I myself was very little, but around 1898 there was an excellent artist named Heidbrinck; he used to make terrifying drawings about unfortunate poets. I remember one: you saw in some editorial office a downcast fellow with a wretched stovepipe hat on his head and long hair, with the precious old copy in his pocket, and the caption read, "For twenty years now I've been telling myself that beginnings are hard."

Obviously, a poet can and should senc his poems to the reviews, whether to the two or three big reviews that are not insensitive to poetry or to the three or four ephemeral little reviews, unceasingly dying and unceasingly being reborn, which themselves publish almost nothing but poetry. In both cases, even supposing that our poet is gifted, he may fail. If he addresses himself to a big review he risks finding extremely severe and blasé judges who will welcome him only if he shows tendencies that are sufficiently new and a well-formed manner of expression.

If he addresses himself to a young review he risks finding a little cooperative group that will want to undertake expenses, and very legitimately besides, only to support the interests of its members; he has no chance of being welcomed unless he contributes money or takes out twenty subscriptions for himself alone.

Good, I am going to suppose that you fail in both of these cases. You take the matter stoically, you say to yourself what must always be said, that you still have progress to make, whether in the way of expression or of inspiration. The light that is your friend, just as it is the friend of all poets, enters your room in the morning with an even step, on wings without distance; it touches things and bestows a loving permanence upon them, and of what does it not assure yourself? You welcome it with bliss. A housewife has paused at the window of the house opposite, her broom in her hand; she remains motionless, her eyes lost in the sky, and you feel that she too at this moment is a poet.

Some mornings you write.

You no longer have any desire to send your poems to the reviews, your attempts have discouraged you; but even so you suffer from not seeing yourself *in print*, should that be only for yourself alone.

Well then, get yourself *in print*.

Do not address yourself to a publisher who puts out work at the author's expense; that is useless, that is even dangerous sometimes. Do not hope that the public will believe that you have found a publisher, everybody knows what to think about that. No, simply go to any printer at all, ask him to give you an estimate; if you do not know a little about typography bring him as a model some thin volume whose design has pleased you; ask for a printing of fifteen, fifty, or at the most a hundred copies. When the book is finished, and after you have corrected by hand the three or four magnificent misprints that will not fail to embellish it, send it to all the poets, writers, or artists whom you admire, to your friends and acquaintances, to some critics, to the Bibliothèque Nationale and to the municipal library of your town—give it to your mother even if after having read a few pages she should close it with a shrug of her shoulders, as did the mother of a poet I know. Send it, even, as did another poet who is a friend of mine, to your former sergeant, to show him that you have become *somebody* and that you are now permitted to look down upon him. After that, wait for results, hope for nothing. That is a hard moment to get through. It is probable that most of the praises and compliments that some people will feel obliged to give you will discourage you more than they will encourage you.

But at least you will be able to read yourself *in print,* and that is no small pleasure—I know something about it.

If you must remain unknown, you will always be able to hope that fifty years, or a century, or several centuries after your death you will be discovered and put in a place of honor; you will be able to hope for the fate of Maurice Scève, to whom Valery Larbaud has just restored life and fame so completely that through a clever mistake the publisher of Larbaud's study issued three author's copies, in which he put "specially printed for Maurice Scève."

If you must remain unknown, and if you have nevertheless experienced the joys that are reserved for poets, you will find that happy resignation that causes Fromentin's Dominique to say: "To these unsuccessful attempts I perhaps owe solace and useful lessons, as do many others. In proving to me that I was nothing, everything that I have done has given me a standard for measuring those who are something."

On the day you speak such words you will share the communion of the Fifty whom I spoke about above, and there will remain in you no desire that has not been fulfilled.

From *Les Gazettes d'Adrienne Monnier*; first published in *Le Navire d'Argent* (May 1926).

part three

The
Country of
Faces

Rainer Maria Rilke

There are two kinds of poets. There are those who are chosen by others. They have been rightly called "representative men." They are brought to genius by a number of circumstances that are almost foreign to their own selves. They are often the greatest, but they are almost never the purest and most sensitive. The others are poets for themselves. They live first of all. They sing like precious stones hidden in the breast of the earth. And one must search in order to find them. Their work has a kind of aureole about it. It never gives itself completely so that it may give itself inexhaustibly.

Rainer Maria Rilke was among them.

He was truly an angelic poet, an initiate like Novalis, Blake, Rimbaud. But never was there one of them so tender or so human. What happened to Ramakrishna, whose back was marked by the blows he saw given to a poor man, might have happened to him. And in fact it happened to him often, in ways not much different. *The Notebooks of Malte Laurids Brigge* prove it.

Things were so familiar to him, souls were so fused with his own, that his essential stratagem was to withdraw from them, and this was also the ruse that he employed in order to be able to live, in order to remain yet a little longer with us. He that was in the world, so much, he looked for subjects to marvel at, motifs for a change of scene. I imagine that is why he wrote poetry in French. The use of a foreign language must have given him the distance that he needed so as not to be destroyed in the act of living.

I saw Rilke twice. The first time, Pierre Klossowski brought him to my bookshop. The second time, a while later, he came back. I do not remember what we talked about. Only one thing remains: the impression of his extreme kindness.

At the end of June 1926, I was sitting one morning in my bookshop. I was thinking very sadly about the sale of my personal library, which had taken place some weeks before. You know that I was reduced to this extremity by the publication of the *Navire d'Argent*, an undertaking that went far beyond my means and left me rather heavily in debt. So I was thinking with sadness and humiliation about the loss of so many treasures, and just then the postman came in and gave me a little package. I opened it. It contained a copy of *Vergers*. On the title page there was a dedication, and in this dedication Rilke paid me the honor of quoting a phrase from the "Letter to a Young Poet," which I had written especially for the last issue of the review. This is it, the phrase: "To see . . . no matter what object in its felicity." (Rilke also, I learned afterward, had written a letter to a young poet.)

At the bottom of this page that is so dear to my heart, the beautiful handwriting said, "Please turn." I turned the page and saw a poem: "Le Grand Pardon." A poem that I did not recognize, an unpublished poem, yes, really. And it was completely in his own hand. And it was dedicated to myself, myself, who was unworthy of it, who had just sold the precious books poets had inscribed to me.

I fell weeping to my knees.

From *Les Gazettes d'Adrienne Monnier.*

Lunch with Colette

My friends Paulette Gauthier-Villars and Marthe Lamy had told me when vacation time was over—for us a mythical vacation time, as neither they nor I had left Paris—"We're going to take you to have lunch with Colette."

Let me put in a parenthesis to introduce Paulette and Marthe, who have the good fortune to count among the close friends of Colette. They are princesses of science: Paulette is a professor on the Faculty of Medicine, a title that she is the first woman to bear; Marthe, an excellent gynecologist, is a laboratory head. Along with Thérèse Bertrand-Fontaine, who was the first woman to be named a doctor of the Hospitals, they are among my prides. We are old friends: they have watched my bookshop develop, and I have watched them grow up.

Lunch with Colette. How is it that that was going to come about? Colette is a woman who has a horror of being disturbed. For my part, I have a horror of disturbing —a Colette above all. I love to give pleasure, but I cannot imagine how one can give pleasure to Colette when one is not a flower or an animal, a taste or a scent, a color or music. Her world comes before the human or after the human: it is the kingdom of the Mother, with its great primal fire and its final fires. One dreams in her presence of turning into a white cat, but it would still be necessary never to die, to be an immortal creature, like an Egyptian god.

Well, this lunch was enchanting. But let us begin at the beginning. The affair took place in an excellent little restaurant in the Rue de Babylone. Marthe had already invited me there once before. I do not much appreciate elaborate cooking, but at Souty's it is perfect, it is like being at home when everything is going well. And how kind the proprietress is! A great lover of the opera and the *opéra-comique*, she speaks of tenors with as much competence, really, as the lamented James Joyce. And then what a beautiful cat she has, all gray, truly the most beautiful, the fattest of cats!

I, who am almost always late—oh, not as much as Fargue, of course—I had arrived a good five minutes early; then Marthe came; and at the exact time for the rendezvous, Colette stood framed in the doorway with Paulette behind her.

The beautiful, the famous little triangular face is wonderfully like what it always was. But how fierce its look is! At first it is sharp, distrustful, as for a stranger, an enemy; it becomes tame slowly, with little glances, and one is surprised, suddenly, to feel alight upon oneself the warmth of a kindly look, such as accompanies a gift.

At the table the proprietress is eager to please her. "This is the first time you've come here, Madame Colette?" "Yes, it's the very first time." "Don't you know my cat?" And he is lifted up like a fat baby with outstretched arms, the gentleman cat, who is at once admired, adopted, and seated on the banquette, yes, seated with dignity by the side of people.

The menu? Today there are snails. "Ah, no!" says Colette, "it's the only thing I've never been able to eat. I've tried to enjoy them, but nothing goes down except the juice." In my corner I exult, for I have a horror of snails, and I have never even wanted to put one of them in my mouth. "Then," says Madame Souty, "I'll give you a nice hash touched with garlic. And then—I've just received some very fresh eggs—you'll have a good omelette." "Go, go!" Colette interrupts, her voice as surly and tender as a satisfied truckdriver's. "And afterward," Madame Souty continues, "you'll see—" What we saw (it was a day when meat could be served) was a magnificent tenderloin with a lot, really a lot, of well-browned fried potatoes around it.

Naturally, as we eat we talk about food and rationing. "I'm not a meat eater," says Colette. "I'm not like some of my friends who are ill when they don't have meat." "Then what do you like?" I asked her. "Well, vegetables, things that are well broiled, fruit, milk above all, desserts." We agree that pastry and candy have become inedible—where can one find good chocolates?

After these important questions, we talked about houses that have occult powers: Paulette knows of one that causes the death of little children. Colette owned one that she had to sell because of the hostile spirits that presided over it. This house had been, it seems, an ecclesiastical estate where religious processions passed. Under those conditions one understands its intolerance toward members of the laity, whom it might, perhaps wrongly, have taken for pagans—so naïve and so stubborn the spirit of a house sometimes is!

We also talked about fortune-tellers. Colette knew one of them, Madame Elise, who was sensational. As a preliminary to telling the future she had you carry a candle under your blouse next to your skin. At the time of the consultation you took it out and she began to whittle it down into slivers, meanwhile telling you stories—which never failed to come true. It was not mind reading, since she predicted events that were very much unexpected and even incomprehensible at the moment.

(Ladies who are reading me, do not write to Colette and do not write to me asking for Madame Elise's address: she is no longer in this world. She left us even before the war, so that she could not make the slightest prediction touching its end; no doubt she had foreseen the war—one can always foresee a war that is more or less due.)

Our lunch ended, Marthe proposed that we go to have coffee at her place—very nearby, in the Rue Vaneau—real, prewar coffee, preciously kept for important occasions. We accept enthusiastically.

And there we are, strolling along the Rue de Babylone. It is something to be Colette. Everybody knows you, recognizes you. Many young girls were passing on their way to school or the *lycée*, and there was not one of them who did not look with emotion, with ravishment, at the Mother of the Claudine books. Even the dogs knew it was she and wagged their tails joyfully, seeking a look or a caress.

We stop in front of a bistro that carries this sign: "The Foot of the Whip." What is a foot of the whip? None of us knows. When I got home I looked it up in the *Littré*, and I found nothing. Colette ought to know, now. She has it, her foot of the whip!

At Marthe's place, which Colette was visiting for the first time, there is a close inspection of the premises. It is on the ground floor; you enter from the street, as into a shop, and suddenly you are in the middle of an intimate and perfect apartment. Many books, precious objects, some beautiful paintings. The rooms are bizarrely arranged, with corners and meanderings (it seems that a stove repairer was its occupant before our doctor). Colette walks around as if she were in a small wood, nothing escapes her.

Then there is coffee. Two cups with sugar.

I do a little palmistry. You most likely think that there is nothing to teach Colette, but I was curious to see her hands. Their general form is powerful and harmonious. The lines are very good. The head line, on her left hand, shows a tendency toward mysticism that has been combatted to the benefit of reason. Naturally, the line of destiny is superb. The Mount of Venus is very much what one might have expected, it indicates a rich sensuality; with a Mount like that one can communicate with all the things of this world. But the thumb, what an extraordinary thumb for a woman! What violence! "Madame Colette," I tell her, "you have the thumb of a pirate chief." She laughs. "It's true," she says, "I'm terribly violent, I've often had the urge to kill. I love knives, blades, not revolvers—they make an absurd noise—no, a silent blade with a fine taper. Don't you know, it's the handle above all that's important, you must count on that, it has to fit the hand well, have a hollow there, you have to grip it like that—" And her fingers and her palm put into play an imaginary blade, but which she makes visible, in the manner of fakirs. "Well!" I say, "we're lucky that that wonderful violence has gone into your art."

It is three o'clock. Each of us has a task awaiting her. We leave, and there we are in the street, where a fine, light rain has begun to fall, a gentle autumn rain that enchants our great Colette and makes her brighten and shake herself at the same time.

From *Les Gazettes d'Adrienne Monnier*; first published in *Le Figaro Littéraire* (1942).

A Visit to T. S. Eliot

Upon our arrival in London, Sylvia had telephoned T. S. Eliot to ask if it would be possible to pay him a visit. He at once proposed that we come to dine with him, which charmed and flattered us very much. In English letters Eliot enjoys an almost royal prestige—not without giving rise to a certain amount of grumbling. Here, in spite of his Nobel Prize, he is only a poor, translated poet. I do not say this to belittle him: Dante, Shakespeare, and Milton are also poor, translated poets.

It is a terrible trial for a poet (spared the musician and the painter) that he must undergo translation if he wants to be read outside of his country. In no case can he emerge from this trial to his advantage: the fruit of his labor is spoiled, he is stripped of his most precious possessions, he becomes like an emigrant who must start his life over again upon a hostile soil with means that are often uncertain. (Eliot has such a liking for penitence that it is possible that these hardships give him a kind of pleasure.) And that is so whatever the talent of the translator may be. A Baudelaire, a Mallarmé crown with a halo the foreign poet whom they strive to transplant among us, but they do not communicate their genius to him—if they wish to remain translators. As Baudelaire says in the notice that precedes his translation of "The Raven": "In the mold of prose when it is applied to poetry, there is necessarily a frightful imperfection; but the harm would be still greater in rhymed mimicry."

T. S. Eliot, fortunately for us, does not write only in verse. He is the author of admirable critical essays, translated by Henri Fluchère, which seem to lose nothing essential in our language; I have read them with gratification: those that are contained in the volume *Essais choisis [Selected Essays]* and the one that serves as the preface to *The Cocktail Party* followed by *The Family Reunion*. This last, entitled "The Aims of Poetic Drama," is a literary summit. The volumes in question appeared in the Editions du Seuil in 1950 and 1952. In short, at the time of my visit to London I had read only the translations of works in verse: that of *Murder in the Cathedral* by Henri

Fluchère and that of the poems by Pierre Leyris. In 1926 I had tried to decipher *The Waste Land*, translated by Jean de Menasce under the title of *La Terre mise à nu [The Land Laid Bare]*, in the review *L'Esprit*, which put it in its first number. Naturally I had seen the performance of *Murder in the Cathedral* at the Vieux-Colombier; Jean Vilar in the part of Thomas à Becket had, in the author's own opinion, more authority than the English interpreter; his face and his whole person seemed made for this role; his genius as an actor restored to the drama the greatness and the interest that it possesses in its original form. Things went much less well at the Palais de Chaillot, which demands the fresco and sacrifices the portrait. In London, furthermore, the play had been performed in a little theater.

It is not only the brilliance of a great interpreter that can correct the imperfection of a translated work, but also the ardor of an impassioned commentator. So it was that I could enjoy Eliot's poetry through the spirit of Sylvia; she revealed it to me just as she revealed *Ulysses* to me. For the first number of the *Navire d'Argent* we had translated together "The Love Song of J. Alfred Prufrock"; this poem had seemed relatively easy to us. We would never have dared to attack *The Waste Land*.

On a visit to Paris in 1936, T. S. Eliot gave a poetry reading at Shakespeare and Company. On this occasion we had the pleasure of having him to dinner at our place in the company of Gide, Jean Schlumberger, and François Valéry. In the course of this dinner Gide tried to tear apart the spirit of the Orient completely, and in particular certain works that Eliot, Schlumberger, and I myself said that we liked: The *Bhagavad-Gita*, for example, or Milarepa (I have a very amusing letter from him on the subject of Milarepa). Schlumberger let him speak, then he said to him gently: "All the same there is one Oriental work that you have loved very much," and as Gide looked at him with a questioning air he added: "—the Gospels." Following that I tried rather wickedly to prove that Buddha had had a particular attachment to his disciple Ananda and that it was after a disappointment in love caused by him that he had decided to leave the earth.

It was not at his home but in a restaurant in Chelsea that T. S. Eliot had made a rendezvous with us for the dinner. We arrived a bit in advance and were soon joined by the poet, who appeared pushing a wheelchair that carried his friend John Hayward, whose body is almost entirely paralyzed. Then arrived Madame Lys and

Cyril Connolly, who had also been invited. We had a reserved room. The dinner was extremely good; I remember that to begin with there were slices of smoked salmon with fresh butter (which in my opinion is one of the best things in the world) and that afterward they brought us broiled beefsteak fillets accompanied by finely sliced fried onions. To my great surprise they did not serve beer, but an excellent red Bordeaux. After dinner we were to go to T. S. Eliot's house to spend the evening. He lives nearby, in Cheyne Walk, in the house where Henry James lived, not in the same apartment but on the floor below; John Hayward says that there are days when they hear him walking.

Upon leaving the restaurant we found a remainder of daylight and rain, which was falling fine and hard. Fortunately, we all had raincoats. Eliot went ahead with John Hayward; I saw him raise the collar of his overcoat, and smiling, his back a bit bent, move off, pushing his friend's wheelchair. The vision profoundly entered my eyes and my heart: it was an epiphany.

We followed, led by Cyril Connolly and Madame Lys. The house has a lift, which permits the ascent of the wheelchair. When we arrived at the apartment our hosts were there to welcome us. We entered a rather austere living room, a library rather, but very comfortable, with good armchairs and a great wood fire burning in the fireplace. The days were cold at the beginning of that June, as it also happens in Paris. With the beautiful fire, the port, and the cigarettes—and such company!—we were in paradise. Because of myself, who speak and understand English so poorly, the conversation was set up in French, which everyone spoke very well, John Hayward a bit less well than the others. I tried to speak English with him, I became tangled up, but we reached the point of understanding each other. I should never have imagined that a man could dominate an infirmity with so much life, gaiety, and charm. Though he experiences some difficulty in speaking French he reads it marvelously well. He has a great admiration for the poems and the writings of Paul Valéry, who was his friend and whose books he possesses on fine paper with beautiful dedications— his *Jeune Parque [The Young Fate]* is on Japan paper. It is to him that we owe the precious notes that clarify the translations by Pierre Leyris of the poems and *Four Quartets*.

John Hayward has a great deal of wit, sometimes with artless and felicitous insights like those of a child, and also, naturally, some mischief. He told us a little story that amused us a lot, concerning the son of a French writer, a young man who at the time of the story was much younger, that is to say, showing without evasions the little vanities that occupied him. One day among several, this likable youth, for whom John Hayward has real affection, made a display of his worldly relations in front of him. In particular, it was very much a question of Lulu (by this understand Louise de Vilmorin); after a good while of Lulu this and Lulu that, John Hayward interrupted him and asked him, "Which of the two Lulus?" This abashed our young man, for if there were two Lulus, two Lulus whom he *had* to know, then he knew only one of them. It is understood, of course, that the second Lulu was an invention.

During the course of this evening Eliot asked us for and listened very attentively to the news about our literary world: about his friends the elders and the newcomers. Sartre and Camus, whose names were usually coupled, were already enjoying the height of their fame. I do not recall that he issued a judgment on them, but Cyril Connolly liked Sartre very much; he was busy, moreover, in making him known in England. In the number of *Horizon* that he had devoted to French literature in May 1945, he had published, under the title "The Case for Responsible Literature," the first third of the introduction to the *Temps Modernes* (in advance of the review, which did not appear until October), and also a study by John Russell of the existentialist theater, in which Sartre occupied eight pages and Camus three. On the subject of surrealism Eliot found good reasons for criticizing it, and he even deplored that a young man of talent like David Gascoigne had fallen under its influence.

T. S. Eliot is the author of a little book that Sylvia and I are mad about: *Old Possum's Book of Practical Cats*. I do not believe that one can have a complete idea of the poet without this book, which is a collection of poems devoted to cats. The first of these poems has always charmed me beyond words. It is called "The Naming of Cats," and it is a question of the three different names that cats should have. The first is the everyday one, like Peter, Augustus, Alonzo, or James—the second is a proud and bizarre name, a name that can make his tail stand up straight and stiffen his whiskers, something like Munkunstrap, Quaxo, or Coricopat—but the third name is known only by the cat himself and he will never tell it to you; when you see a cat in profound meditation it is because:

Son esprit est plongé dans le ravissement
De la pensée, de la pensée, de la pensée de son nom:
Son ineffable affable
Affablineffable
Profond, impénétrable et singulier Nom.

His mind is engaged in a rapt contemplation
    Of the thought, of the thought, of the thought of his name:
        His ineffable effable
        Effanineffable
Deep and inscrutable singular Name.

Before taking leave of Eliot I spoke to him about this book and about my desire to translate it. A senseless desire, upon examination, because the translation presents insurmountable difficulties. The title to begin with—how would you put it in French? "Practical" alone is a problem; Eliot must have been thinking of the expression "practical joke," which means a trick that is played on somebody. I thought of *"espiègle"* [mischievous]. *Livre du Vieux Possum sur les chats espiègles*, this is what I found to be most approximate. What do you think of it?

From *Dernières Gazettes et Ecrits divers*; first published in *Les Lettres Nouvelles* (June 1953).

Our Friend Bryher

Yes, our friend, for Bryher is not only the friend of the writers whom we care most for, but is also a great friend of France. I am happy to present her here in this *Gazette*, upon which, from the time that it took its first steps, she has lavished so much affectionate attention.

Bryher is English. She is also from that part of the world from which the Pleiades come. To play her role among us she has chosen to be a writer and a publisher. She is really the most perfectly discreet person whom I know, as much in her appearance as in her words and in her writings.

She is small, slender—slender is not the word: you do not come to think about her body. You grasp only certain aspects of it: her hands, which habitually close into little energetic fists from which her thumbs thrust out like thick buds; the movement of her head, always a bit bent as if for study, and above all her eyes, which are sky blue—it is there that you see all the mischief, all the insight, all the goodness of "the happy few" to whom she belongs.

Her dress—impossible to speak about it; it is distinguished by absolutely nothing; everything about it is neutral to an extreme. When I see her I simply want to brush her beret, as for Sylvia.

Bryher's work, as of now, is not abundant—it is true that she is still young. She has published only three books and several essays that have not yet been collected in a volume. Her writings are autobiographical most of the time. In them she tells about her childhood, her adolescence, her travels, her readings. She blends into her accounts many reflections that are enlivened by the most noble human faith, even while they are tinged with a subtle humor. She takes a particular interest in the problems of education and social life. She is very attentive to everything that has to do with the cinema, doubtless because of her sociological concerns.

Her career as a publisher began in 1927 with a review entirely devoted to the cinema, *Close-Up*, which she put out in collaboration with Kenneth Macpherson. This review lasted seven years and was ranked by the experts as the first in Europe—nothing was as advanced or as well informed as *Close-Up*.

In 1935 she resolutely turned to literature properly speaking. She rebegan the London review *Life and Letters*, whose name she changed a bit into *Life and Letters To-day*. About a year ago she incorporated into it two other reviews that are very much esteemed: the *Bookman* and the *London Mercury*. She herself did not undertake the management; for manager she chose a young writer, Robert Herring, who is as passionate as she is about poetry and social science, and who has been a film critic for several years in the *Observer*.

Life and Letters To-day manifests a broadly European spirit: each one of its numbers contains a translation; but it must be said that France is clearly favored in it. Among the French writers who have figured in its table of contents let us mention the names of Aragon, Jean Cassou, André Chamson, André Gide, Louis Guilloux, Henri Michaux, Jean Prévost, Jules Romains, J.-P. Sartre, Jean Schlumberger, Paul Valéry. Some of them were translated there for the first time.

Three years ago Bryher published the account of a journey she made to Paris as a child, during the 1900 Exposition. These memories, entitled "Paris 1900," have been translated by Sylvia

Beach and myself; the *Nouvelle Revue Française* reproduced them in part in its December 1937 number; I had a small book made of them, the appearance of which has been delayed by events and which is coming out now.

A recent number of *Life and Letters To-day* contained an essay by her: "Initiation into French Literature," which Sylvia and I judged to be of such interest that we translated the essential passages of it. Nobody, it seems, has spoken of Mallarmé in such a simple and moving fashion. The sentence in which Bryher says that Mallarmé appeared to her "as bright as a flash of salty spray split from the crest of a wave in the mid-Atlantic" enchanted me.

Here is the conclusion of this essay:

> French for me was not a supplementary study for the purpose of obtaining good marks, but something that I absorbed, that grew in me in proportion to my own development, so much so that now, without even thinking about it, I cannot separate myself from the destiny of France. I do not believe that a more lasting way of international understanding exists—in any case I have not found another. My problems during those years were those of my successors today: to find the creators, not the cautious authors cherished by the academies, but those who understand the adolescence of each successive generation. A friendly bookshop, a little review that appears courageously for half a year and then ceases to appear are worth more for a country than ten thousand books of ordinary propaganda. One has one's whole middle age for the classics and the professors.
>
> For seven years I did not go once to France, I was twenty-eight years old when I found my first French friendship; the war seemed to have cut off contacts and stopped all development in that direction, but my experience of Flaubert, of Mallarmé, of Verhaeren, and of so many others did not cease to strengthen my European education and initiated me into the discipline of art.

These lines, which appeared in May 1940, were also the conclusion of the Gazette des Amis des Livres. *We remained for four years without news of Bryher, or of any of our European and American friends. Once more "the war seemed to have cut off contacts," but our friendship and our faith sustained us during the trial and we met again, after the Liberation, unchanged and joyful.*

From *Les Gazettes d'Adrienne Monnier*; first published in *La Gazette des Amis des Livres* (May 1940).

Fargue as a Talker

Léon-Paul Fargue, it is known, was a dazzling talker. There is not a critic or a chronicler who, having known him, does not mention the fact when speaking about him. His verve, his wit, his fantasy have been praised a hundred times; these are the words, in fact, that impose themselves. I would like to try today to give a more precise idea of these famous conversations.

Fargue's speech was incredibly living and lived—more lived perhaps than living. Fargue lived what he said intensely; he set about speaking as one sets about acting; his body was brought into play as much as his spirit. This animation was not translated by gestures, by a play of his features, or by moving back and forth. No, he did not mimic, he gesticulated rather little, he remained in his chair. It was a completely different thing. He gathered himself together rather, his arms close to his torso, while thrusting his brow forward. The essential movement remained internal, like that of a motor. One perceived a kind of electric perspiration.

Fargue's voice was beautiful, clear, less turned toward the questioner than attentive to its inner circuits. A voice with a deep timbre, with careful intonations, in which the human element seemed written in advance—recorded—and as a consequence more apt to manifest itself.

Fargue's person, then, was rather imperturbable, even when he was agitated. He had not killed the marionette, he had swallowed it, as the whale swallowed Jonah; it stirred about in him with an incomparable drollery.

Drollery in his remarks was manifested above all by the spirit of caricature. With a few sentences, with a few words, he reduced someone to being nothing but an object of derision. It must be admitted that this was very ill-natured. For example, he found in some of his colleagues (whose names I shall be very careful not to give) the look of a fountain pen, or a sheep's foot in *sauce à la poulette,* or a folding seat, or a chicken's rump. Before the photograph of such and such a great poet he said: "He resembles an anemic gendarme, a swimming teacher." There was always an hallucinating resemblance. The person was transformed before your eyes, as if struck by the wand of a magician. There are good examples of these caricatures in *Vulturne.* Remember the "Barrès' sturgeon skull stoppering the hole of a fetid ship's latrine"; the "Ritz and the Meurice, with women who have the mugs of superior candy bonbons for which you pay dearly and diplomats made of ear cotton"?

Such games of massacre abound in the pieces that Fargue wrote between 1924 and 1928 and collected in *Espaces*. I wonder in passing if their style did not influence Céline, whose *Voyage au bout de la nuit [Journey to the End of the Night]* appeared in 1932.

That impetuous style, the most satirical that ever was, springs from his conversations. He spoke that way, and as his speech was much more free and direct than his writings—he took no precautions, the names of his victims were not hidden but proclaimed—you can imagine, can you not, that it frequently led to quarrels.

What made his verve pricelessly funny were his returns to reason, to common sense, to the established order. He then showed a kind of hypocrisy in which the smugly sententious bourgeois gentleman and the tough guy were curiously married. He played the moralist, and even the censor, lavished good advice, reprimands, and severe warnings. When he inflicted you with such preachings it was far from being amusing, but when it was the others who caught it you found it wildly comical.

I shall try now to analyze the substance of his speech, which was like his physical body. Doubtless his manner of speaking resembled his manner of writing, while being less dense and having broader strokes, naturally. He employed fewer precious and precise words in speaking, but more colloquial and slang expressions. His oral discoveries were as abundant as those of his writing, but they were more artless, less forced, and often better sprung. It would occur to him to improvise sentences that had such a delicate assemblage and a movement at once so spellbinding and so perilous that you held your breath, as when watching a trapeze artist.

In the conversations of Fargue it is also necessary to note the presence of a commonplace subject matter that was like an inexhaustible almanac. This marvelously popular subject matter was like the warp of a fabric over which passed and passed again the weft of his personal spirit. It helped him to weave a spell, exactly, without leaving empty spaces, to hold his audience while allowing it to relax after having vigorously strained its attention. It was also the presence, in his "soul of a sentimental truck driver" (the expression is his own), of a world of men from whose mouths issues a world of words.

No traveling salesman has ever known so many and said so many hackneyed stories, old saws, witticisms, puns, tales from restaurant tables and the barracks, bawdy jokes, historical anecdotes, refrains from sentimental and comic songs. He adored the songs of Dranem and the adventures of Colonel Ronchonnot.

Spoonerisms held a great place in his remarks. He played a hundred tricks with them. He truly handled them like nobody else, whether he quoted classics of the kind, *"Dites, j'ai mangé une excellente tourte aux cailles à l'enseigne du Congre debout,"* etc., or whether he invented them by upsetting words, as in Verlaine's famous verse *"Je suis venin, calme orphelu . . ."*

The written work lets rather little show through of these aspects of the life of the party, which he displayed above all in society. Traces are to be found of it in the *Caquets de la table tournante*, which are included in *Espaces*.

There is a writer among us who has the gift of reconstituting Fargue's speech; he is André Beucler, who was one of his best friends. Beucler has written a little book that is called *Dimanche avec Léon-Paul Fargue [Sunday with Léon-Paul Fargue]*; it is the best and the most living portrait that has ever been made of our Léon-Paul— and it is a masterpiece, as true as I am here.

From *Rue de l'Odéon.*

The Voice of Paul Valéry

Paul Valéry paid us a visit the other day—I should like to be able to reproduce his remarks, but I do not feel capable of doing so with exactness. At the most I can remember a parallel between Mallarmé and himself: People always believe, he said, that I have the same ideas as Mallarmé, but we differed greatly, and above all in our ways of thinking about art; Mallarmé made a metaphysics of it; he thought that the world was created in order to be *represented,* and that the representation—art—was *the thing in itself.* I myself have never given to art, literary or any other, an essential importance, I have never set it above the other manifestations of life; for me it is *a game.*

Valéry is a talker. He aims at neither effects nor wit, but what he says awakens and thrills one. He has the gift of raising the listener to himself, he always makes a student of him, imperceptibly. With grace he puts within one's reach the fruits of his intelligence, but his voice tantalizes.

Shall I try to describe his voice?

If one says that it is muffled, like M. Teste's, that does not give an idea of its tonality, which is muffled, to be sure; but one is aware of its metal, like that of muted wind instruments.

It is swift, hardly seizable. It has the short vowels of the Midi, but not the consonants, which it mortifies.

It seems that the term "mechanical sieve" can be applied to it. It makes one think of the machine that separates earth from pebbles in which precious stones are found (I saw this machine at the cinema). It is a heedless sorting out; one sees reflections passing by. He is uninterested in it, the work comes afterward. As if disdaining itself, his voice turns over and over again the matter in which ideas lie embedded; it delivers a still raw mass upon a given subject that it grasps, grinds, and subdues.

From *Les Gazettes d'Adrienne Monnier*; first published in *Le Navire d'Argent* (February 1926).

A Visit to Marie Laurencin

We knock. She comes to open the door herself—it's Sunday, and her maid has her afternoon off—"Hello. Wait a bit," she says, "I'm on the phone with a friend. Do come in."

"Hello! Then you say he beat you?"

. . . .

"Don't let him in."

. . . .

"Ah, yes! He insists; you think he might cause you trouble."

. . . .

"Listen, say that you're ill. Go to bed. See him in bed. Oh! This is an idea—have a doctor come to be near you. You don't know somebody who is strong?"

. . . .

"He's going to phone you back in a little while, you say. Of course, it's difficult."

. . . .

"Under those conditions, see him just the same. Gain time, be prudent."

. . . .

"Ah, well, that's it! I'll call you in an hour from now, or else call me. Goodbye."

She comes back to us and explains: "It's a friend of mine, you know the little woman I was with the other day? She has a boyfriend she'd like to get rid of, a big brown-haired fellow, not bad at all, a woodworker, he was a friend of X—you know, the art dealer, she pinched him from him, but now she's had enough of him. She told him the other day that she had enough of him, she offered him a thousand francs and a dozen beautiful photos that she'd made of him, he tore up the photos and threw the thousand-franc bill in her face. He said to her, 'Ah, no, you made me lose my job, it's not going to happen like that,' and he beat her. Today he insists upon seeing her again. So I told her to see him with a solidly built doctor next to her. Oh, it will be all right. Do you want some tea? Sit down."

We sit down, we turn our heads right and left, five minutes have not gone by and there she is with the tea and a plate of those little salted "collation" biscuits. "This is all I have," she says, showing the biscuits, "the women who come here are all afraid of becoming fat."

We install ourselves around the table. There are four of us: she, Marcelle Auclair, Sylvia, and I. She met Marcelle at the bookshop the other day, she had liked "La Coquetterie guérit l'amour" a great deal, she wants very much to do the portrait that will decorate the volume. "Don't you find," I say, "that Marcelle is much better with her hair drawn back and her ears uncovered?" Let's have a look. She unfastens the comb, she draws her hair back with two firmly placed hands, she uncovers ravishing little elongated ears. "Ah, yes!" says Marie, "she's much better like that, but she's right, it's better for her to hide her forehead and her ears. You see, intelligent women have a certain shape there (she traces with her finger a little line between the jaw and the hollow of the ear) that shows they're not stupid. In order to please men it's better to pass for stupid, I'm the queen of the fatheads."

I reflect that Marie Laurencin sometimes wears her hair drawn back and showing half an ear, sometimes with bangs and her ears well hidden.

"Have you any new things to show us?"—"No, I've sent

everything to Rosenberg. You know what's here. On that big canvas (she points to an oval, absolutely white canvas above a sofa), I don't know yet what I'm going to do."

I myself already see upon that canvas two women with looks that float like a perfume, a tender horse kneeling down, courtly clouds, and a big, bantering ribbon—But, I think, she has already done that painting; yes, but this time one of the women is a bit more heartless, the other is much more resigned, the horse looks elsewhere, and the ribbon does not know what it is saying.

She has Marcelle Auclair visit the apartment. At every step there are cries of pleasure: those shells in a square receptacle of thick glass, that ostrich feather, a bit out of curl, placed like a flower in a Second Empire vase, those porcelain animals, those beautiful little pieces of antique and modern furniture that go marvelously together, the organdy of a curtain, and everywhere, in adorable frames, those women as sad as pleasure who open big eyes as empty and voluble as the sky between the walls, and all those doves that lightly carry, beak to beak, the burden of happiness that is so heavy for humankind.

There are three drawing rooms, each one prettier than the others; two bedrooms, one of which is called "a girl's" and is pink and blue—we do not dare to enter it for fear of spoiling the picture. There is no dining room.

This visit to Marie Laurencin took place on Christmas day. The portrait of Marcelle Auclair is now finished. Marie has covered almost all of her forehead with a big comb, and as for her ears, clever will he be who guesses the form of them; however, Marcelle had arranged her hair in the manner most proper for not *pleasing men.*

Some time ago Marie Laurencin paid me the honor of wanting to do my portrait. "Yes," I said, "but I'd like to know if you'll let me keep my nose. There's not much of it, but that's precisely why I care for it." Marie looked at me for a moment and answered: "I don't see you with a nose." So I preferred to do without the portrait. Now I think that I was very wrong to attach so much importance to my nose. What stupid pride! The rebellious angels were banished from heaven for lesser presumptions—How many things are given to those who do not value their noses too much!

From *Les Gazettes d'Adrienne Monnier*; first published in *Le Navire d'Argent* (April 1926).

Verve

Verve is less a review than a spectacle. Each one of its numbers is mounted like a ballet.

First of all, it's the cover, always different, especially composed by artists such as Matisse, Braque, Bonnard, Rouault, Maillol. These astonishing covers seem like words shot with devilish spirit into the heart of a beautiful and rustling company. The title *Verve* bursts forth more new each time.

Leafing through the pages, you see with a feverish joy more things than you will ever be able to seize hold of—a cave out of the Thousand and One Nights, in which everything gleams, lures, and challenges. A certain time is needed in order to get over it, and you never completely get over it.

That is because there is an electrifying mixture of the old and the modern in it—"shocks of icicles against the stars." *Verve*'s part on old art is magnificent: it shows the treasures of a Europe that is more curious and distant, sometimes, than Asia. The miniatures of our illuminated manuscripts have proliferations that are no less ardent than those of the temples of India, but they are half internal; their colors are like precious stones drawn from the depths of the mind.

What a joy there is in possessing here perfect reproductions, so beautifully adorned that you become a child again—you want to touch them.

Look at the photos next to them—astonishing old photos mixed with ones that are so young they seem to have come from prenatal, protoplasmic regions. And, what always gives pleasure, the photos of artists in their studios.

The texts must be spoken about: they count very much in this review. The lover of literature can take delight in them if he is not dazzled too much by the pictures. It is only after having leafed through *Verve* at least ten times that you can begin to read.

The table of contents of the latest number, which is devoted to that subject of subjects, *the human face*, shines with the names of Valéry, Gide, Suarès, Alain, Giraudoux, Reverdy, Supervielle, Paulhan, Michaux, Jouhandeau, Hoppenot, Sartre, Daumal, etc.

Henri Michaux said the other Sunday, on leaving the *Mesures* garden party, that at least six young writers had asked him to recommend them to Tériade.

Tériade?—I hear you asking: who is that?

It's true, few people have seen him: he does not try to make himself seen. I know him thanks to my friend Angèle Lamotte, who is his collaborator on *Verve*.

He is a fat person like myself, a gourmand, a *potasson*, but he is not very sociable, he is very meditative. A wide-awake dreamer.

I had been told that he was of Greek origin. When I asked him where he was born he answered me with a trace of hesitation and a slight blush: on the island of Lesbos. And as I smiled he added: Oh! that's become very middle-class since.

He has a round head with beautiful eyes whose look is like good, very hot coffee. Because of his Mediterranean hairiness he has the look of being poorly shaven. That does not go badly with him, Saillet even finds that it gives him character. For my taste that lower part of his melancholy face would turn out well with a beard —the pleasing little beard that Greek herdsmen still wear, as you can see in "La Figure humaine" ["The Human Face"].

The sound of his voice transports you to the kingdom of childhood; it makes you dream of milk, flour; it is woolly; it is the voice of a grown-up speaking to children.

He has beautiful plump hands with slender, tapering fingers, like those of people who love the plastic arts.

Tériade is a "poor nabob." He founded *Verve* a year and a half ago, financed by New York publishers who had asked him to make for them "the most beautiful review of art in the world." He therefore began this undertaking with all the money that was necessary. But the people over there were disappointed, it seems; they found the review "sophisticated," not devoted enough to the French eighteenth century; they would have liked, for the photographic part, a larger number of graceful nudes. Tériade hardly saw the means of satisfying them and, after a year of performing his duties, he regained his liberty. With the four numbers already issued he had won a public. He believes now that he will be able to proceed alone. And here we are, we French, with the most beautiful review of art in the world in our arms. It is an honor that we are able to face up to, it seems to me.

I wonder if it is not Tériade who is going to convert me to present-day painting. For I continue to be stubborn on the subject. I try to explain my case to him as to a doctor.

Obviously, I tell him, old paintings no longer give me so much pleasure. I was at the Louvre recently; everything there seemed outmoded, surpassed. I felt that it was necessary to find something else.

That's the way it always begins, Tériade says gently.

I am improving: I have the impression that painters are now doing things that belong to the fields of literature, of music. They reason too much, they throw themselves into metaphysics. They are looking for forms, but forms are given for once and for all; they are those of nature—our bodies, animals, plants, stones. We cannot change them except very slightly. Great changes, as my friend Berthier says, are of a geological order.

Yes, photography is a catastrophe. But they must recover from it, what the devil. Think a bit: before it was only a question of imitating nature; genius was measured according to fidelity, according to the faithfulness with which one embraced the forms that had received life, that is to say, matter consecrated by the spirit.

Should the artist ever be afraid to be photographic? Does he not have his own nature to oppose to nature?

It is by applying himself to reality that he gets to transform it according to his views; he must catch up with it in order to go beyond it with moderation, that is to say, in a way that renews it.

Our present-day artists do not transform, they deform. That gives pleasure to nobody. It changes everything, therefore it changes nothing.

They have a liking for matter, they say, that of Aristotle: unformed, undetermined. But matter, whose virtue lies in its resistance, what does it signify if it is not brought to take on a meaning? In ancient times they made objects of it, that is to say, useful things. There were vases, weapons, jewels, utensils, furniture, clothing, carpets. They were made with moderation, according to natural forms. Deformation came only from lack of skill.

There were also images of the gods.

What the painters are doing today could be of a religious order; but into what limbos, what intestines have they gone to look for their gods?

I know very well that they dream of primary forms, that they want to find the essential Roundnesses, the paternal Numbers, the colors of Ideas. They believe that they are descending to the kingdom of the Mothers, into the regions of the non-born, but in reality what they make us see very much justifies the terror with which Faust pronounces their names.

The Mothers—they are perhaps the great Machines. Might it not be the consideration of machines, perhaps, that causes so many larvae to surge up from the depths?

Oh, well, yes, I see even so one of the justifications for the art of today—revolution, accomplished or to be accomplished. It is no longer a question of beauty, of pleasure. But why still stick to easel painting? That is perhaps the cause of the misunderstanding. The exposition of 1937 justified many of the experiments by carrying them to a large scale, upon the walls of collective—and temporary —buildings.

This is what is happening: it's that the most abstract experiments, the most cruel hypotheses, serve the broadest and most common uses.

Abstract art: a construction site for high fashion, for advertising, for furniture.

Look at the exploitation of cubism by advertising; that was profoundly logical; a product that wants to impose itself upon the masses does well not to have an individualized expression; it can arise from elementary geometry in a rather totemic manner. What a dictatorship, when you think of it!

And this is also what is happening: almost nothing that the painters are doing remains in our hands. People hardly buy anymore except to sell again—that is another story altogether. There are no longer any real amateurs. Nothing is made in order to be loved. Everything depends on fashion. Everything is simply decorative, more or less immediate. Nothing is finished.

The harmony that endures, that consoles us for living, where is it? How can it be reborn?

Look, M. Tériade, when I ask you why one must love such and such a painter, and how he must be understood, you give me a guarantee of *moral order*. You answer me: I know him, he is sincere.

Of some you declare: They are the most intelligent, they are serious.

Tériade says tranquilly: You know that it is a question of returning to reality.

From *Les Gazettes d'Adrienne Monnier*; first published in *La Gazette des Amis des Livres* (July 1939).

The Henri Michaux Exhibition

When Henri Parisot came to tell us five or six weeks ago that an exhibition of gouaches by Henri Michaux was going to be held at the Galerie de l'Abbaye, that he was taking care of it with Betty Fernandez, the owner of the place, we were completely delighted, all the more because it was a matter of the poet's coming to Paris. We had not seen Michaux since the exodus; we knew that he was settled in Le Lavandou and from time to time friends coming from the Free Zone used to tell us: "He misses Paris very much, but as he's Belgian it's difficult for him to get a pass." They also said that he was terribly short of chocolate, that he needed it in order to work, as others needed tobacco or coffee.

The exhibition has been open now since June 12 and Michaux is still not here. It was the charming Marie-Louise Ferdière who brought the latest works painted by the poet, as well as a typewritten manifesto.

It's very precious, this manifesto. It's a pity they did not get it in time to have it printed. It would have greatly helped the visitors to understand the paintings that are exhibited.

Michaux declares in it:

> If I liked *Isms* and being the captain of a few individuals I would really launch a school of painting: phantomism or psychologism.
>
> There is a certain inner phantom that one must be able to paint and not the nose, the eyes, the hair, which are found on the outside and are often like the soles of shoes.
>
> The face has features. So what? I paint the features of the double (who does not necessarily need nostrils and may have a network of eyes).
>
> I also paint the colors of the double. It is not necessarily on his cheekbones or on his lips that he has red, but in a part of himself where his fire is. So I also put, I put blue on his forehead if he deserves it (for I forgot to say that I have been practicing psychologism for some time).

Upon reflection I do not share Michaux's way of seeing and thinking. It is literature that takes the responsibility for the "psychological" red, or blue, or yellow. We say: "a yellow streak," or "to see red," "to be blue," "to be green." If the prerogatives of the muses are mixed up what will it lead to? But what am I saying, what has it led to?

The redskins have neither a written literature nor easel painting, but with their face paintings they have invented something that very much resembles psychologism. Sylvia Beach possesses two magnificent albums that were published in Philadelphia: *The History of the Indian Tribes of North America*. These albums contain a hundred and twenty portraits of chiefs. You should see their headdresses, their jewels, and above all their painted faces. Some of them have broad red strokes that cut diagonally across their faces, like a ribbon on the chest; sometimes strokes underline the wrinkles on their foreheads. There are those who have scarlet laurel leaves on each cheek; with others a whole ear and the part of the head around it have been treated with red lead; still others make themselves a kind of half mask that is the color of buffalo blood. You see as well, above all on the young men, blue, green, yellow, and red stippled lines that are arranged in the most charming fashion on the cheeks and the forehead: lengthwise in a little Indian file, around in a little ring. An Ojibway has black paint around one eye and green paint—brilliantly green—around the other. Some of them have a kind of black or blue hand spread out over their mouths as if to impose silence upon them forever.

Ah, Michaux! If you could see that you would be blue, and green with envy, I dare to say so.

To come back to what I was arguing just now—it is with similar ideas that present-day painting has arrived at God knows what. I shall take care not to speak ill of it, even though it rarely gives me pleasure. In any case, considering what painters properly so called are doing, Michaux would be wrong not to feel at ease. The time is now or never for him to paint. I used to hear people say that what he was doing was the painting of an intellectual, but all painting nowadays—the kind that it is honorable to admire—is intellectual, abstract, even when it flatters itself on having a "subject."

I have been told that before arriving at his syntheses Henri Matisse accumulates substantial studies that he does not preserve. This reminds me of that recipe for *rôti à l'impératrice*, mentioned by Horace Raisson in his *Code gourmand*: you take an olive from which you have removed the pit, for which you substitute an anchovy filet; you put this olive in a lark, which goes into a quail that is enclosed in a partridge that is hidden in the cavity of a pheasant that in its turn disappears into the middle of a turkey whose hiding place is a suckling pig. You roast it all on a spit, and when the cooking is finished you throw everything out the window except the olive, which has become the quintessential center.

As far as I'm concerned, I should prefer all the rest, particularly the suckling pig, rather than the olive.

Yes, in my eyes Michaux's painting is certainly as good as Matisse's, or that of others. I even believe that I prefer it. He knows really very well how to do phantoms—more exactly, they are devils. In the time of the cathedrals he surely would have been the one to be charged with doing the devils.

The day of his opening did not pass without devilry. Let us say first of all that this private showing was very brilliant. To be seen there were: Paul Eluard, Germaine and Jean Paulhan, Gaston Gallimard (very happy about his new young one, Albert Camus, the author of *L'Etranger*), Jean Grenier, Raymond Queneau, Rolland de Renéville, Audiberti, Alix Guillain and Groethuysen, Marcel Raval, Jacques Boulenger, Brice Parain (his wife, Nathalie Parain, was exhibiting on the same day little paintings similar to illuminations, with a charming realism like that of a child who wants to say everything). Fargue? No, Fargue was not there, it appears that he came the next day.

I am coming to the devil of the day.

This devil, or rather his portrait—it was the ugliest of them all—had been put on exhibition in the show window. Around six o'clock several young people, four or five, stopped in front of it and began an argument. We saw them grow hot under the collar and boil over. One of them smacked the window; after a moment the bravest entered and began to shout, "It all stinks, it's a lot of shit." A sentence he repeated I don't know how many times, shouting louder and louder. As you see, his insult did not show much variety —it was rationed like the rest. He gesticulated, threatening the pictures hanging on the wall. Betty Fernandez went up to him and said that nothing obliged him to stay there and that he would be better perhaps outside; she even took him gently by the arm to lead him toward the door. But he shouted louder than ever, "It stinks, it's a lot of shit," adding that the place was public and that he would not leave.

The thing was dragging out and we were worried about the paintings. It was then that Saillet, displaying the general feeling, stepped forward and flew at the devil-possessed ranter, returning his own compliments to him, to wit, that he was the one who stank and that he was full of shit, and that he should do him the favor of leaving immediately if he did not wish to receive his foot somewhere (the warning was formulated in an even more energetic manner). He took him by the shoulders; as soon as he felt himself touched, the other struck and a beautiful hand-to-hand fight followed. Two spectators tried to separate them. Parted for a moment, they continued to abuse each other, which naturally made them fall into each other's arms again, and as it is said in one of Michaux's poems: "I grab hold of you—pow. I grab hold of you again—pow."

We were trembling for their jackets.

The arrival of two policemen was a relief for everybody. The policemen led the combatants away to a nearby station; Mme Fernandez and Henri Parisot accompanied them. When the examination was made it appears that a very civil gentleman was found there to bear witness to the moral character of the person who had caused the disturbance. He stated his last name, given names, and occupation: it was M. Pougheon, a professor at the Ecole des Beaux-Arts. Several people have told me that he was with his students in front of the window and that he had done his best to inflame them.

Naturally, the matter was not serious and the good-natured superintendent had the accused released early in the evening.

From *Les Gazettes d'Adrienne Monnier*; first published in *Le Figaro Littéraire* (1942).

The Paintings of Henri Michaux

When I saw the paintings of Henri Michaux for the first time in 1942, at the Galerie de l'Abbaye, I most certainly did not suspect that I would take such a liking to them. At that time I did a rather ironic review of the exhibition for the *Figaro Littéraire*, not only with regard to Michaux but also to modern painters in general. I said that considering the tendencies of today's painting Michaux was not wrong to enter the lists. From the moment that art takes less account of the body than of the spirit, less account of form than of the formless, less account of the concrete than of the abstract, the man with a literary imagination has the advantage over the man who practices the plastic arts. The latter, if he really has a painter's temperament—a hand that is stronger than the brain—and if he wants to follow the passwords, will turn toward primitive productions as toward the sources of ideas and myths, or will enter the ranks of the cubists so that he may subdue forms, or will try to blend the two experiments. At any rate, it is not the concern of the modern painter to commit himself to the visible and natural world. In these conditions a poet, if he learns how to use a pencil and a brush, can have the advantage—Henri Michaux has learned how to use a pencil and a brush.

Did he paint as early as he wrote? His first attempt, or at least what he showed of it to the public, goes back to 1927. Invited by Marcel Raval to collaborate on the number of the *Feuilles Libres* that was devoted to Fargue, he had responded not with a text but with a drawing. Yes, said Fargue, Michaux doesn't want to write anymore, now he is going to do painting. Let us observe that then, at the beginning of 1927, Michaux had as yet published only two thin volumes: *Fable des origines* and *Le Rêve et la jambe*, both of which came out in Belgium; we had also read some texts in Franz Hellens's review, *Le Disque Vert*, in particular "Les Idées philosophiques de *Qui je fus*." We were expecting a great deal of Michaux; if he had already decided not to write anymore, it was very sad. Now that was what he said, eh?—

To come back to the drawing in question, let me say that it was far from delighting me, it was a kind of scrawl that was vaguely related to André Masson. It seems to me upon seeing it again that Michaux meant to express by this drawing something like the mumbling that often occurs between poets.

It was not until 1936 that we again saw drawings by Michaux. In the meantime, fortunately, he did not give up writing, and we had seven perfectly admirable volumes. Plume was born. His author traveled, he went to the equator and to Asia. He had us go to Grande Garabagne. He became the unique Michaux, the one of whom it can be said, as in a eulogy by Confucius, that if he had not been born we would not have had him.

Well, in 1936 he contributed seven drawings and a frontispiece to illustrate the collection *Entre centre et absence*, which was put out by Matarasso. Among these drawings there was the little horse that flaps in the wind and heavy figures that were very disturbing, but I did not stop there; the texts carried me away beyond them, I said to myself: When one is a poet like Michaux, why want more, or rather why look for less?

The exhibitions of 1937 and 1938 that took place at the Galerie de la Pléiade and the Galerie Pierre—I did not go to them. In 1939 the little volume that includes seven poems and sixteen illustrations was put out by the Editions G. L. M. These illustrations, I was told, were reproductions of paintings that were in the exhibitions that I did not see. Here I began to change sides, most of the pictures were hallucinating, some heads were so terrible that they could hardly be looked at. Only the clown bothered me because it was meant to illustrate a poem that is one of the most beautiful Michaux has written, a poem in which he unites holiness and genius. No matter, I was caught. I saw that Michaux the painter was not to be neglected and that he would have to be reckoned with.

It was in this state of mind that in 1942, under the Occupation, I went to the exhibition organized by Betty Fernandez at the Galerie de l'Abbaye. Michaux had not been able to obtain a pass to come to Paris, and it was his wife who had brought the pictures that were there from Le Lavandou. Henri Parisot had spoken to me about the gouaches upon a black background that figured in the exhibitions before—furthermore, Louis Chéronnet had made an allusion to them in his foreward to *Peintures*. I looked around for them—there were only two of them, they had a light and charming magic; one was already bought, and I hurried to acquire the other. Eluard, who was present, made an acquisition also, of a watercolor, not one of those that I would have chosen.

As black paper had become unavailable, there were watercolors above all at this exhibition. Some portrayed the heads of terrifying idiots; there were many devils and their victims; you saw melancholy grayish brown landscapes in which there sometimes figured two or three minute creatures who were indefinable but peaceful. For the occasion Michaux had written a manifesto in favor of *phantomism*. He said there among other things:

> There is a certain inner phantom that one must be able to paint and not the nose, the eyes, the hair, which are found on the outside and are often like the soles of shoes.
>
> The face has features. So what? I paint the features of the double (who does not necessarily need nostrils and may have a network of eyes).

How debatable these ideas were, how superior the poet was to the painter, that was not the question. The talent that asserted itself in the exhibited works was evident. Michaux had the right to paint—he could not have stopped himself from doing so.

I have seen other exhibitions since, I have not missed any of them: at the Galerie Rive Gauche, at the Galerie Drouin, where the most important one took place in 1948. Each time I have been struck by Michaux's technical progress, by the variety of his means (one year he did some drawings in red chalk that had a tremendous elegance), by his growing power to fix upon paper, through all kinds of formulas that are very much his own, the infernal or fairylike legions that crowd together in his head.

The Michaux manner that I prefer is in gouache or in watercolor heightened by gouache. A world that has emerged from astral regions and asks only to dissolve into them is left too vaporous or too liquid by watercolor alone. Gouache gives a volume that renders the apparition more tangible. I own a painting that portrays a kind of gnome who looks a bit like a guinea pig, who would be invisible without the strokes of gouache, no thicker than heavy white thread, that mark his figure; he also has a semblance of outline in India ink that the paper absorbs slightly, just enough to give a vigorous impression. This little creature appears to me to have slipped out of *A Midsummer Night's Dream*, he comes as a messenger, he says: Hush! Listen!—he himself lends an ear to the sound of an approaching band.

When Michaux told me at the start of the fall season that he was returning to gouache—he had previously made some not very convincing attempts at oil painting—I took it as good news. And in February I rushed to the Galerie de Nina Dausset to see his recent works.

The twenty-seven pieces on exhibition show new motifs and above all attempts at stylization. The manner is less protoplasmic and has a geometrical tendency. The dimension of the pictures is larger. The forms, instead of rising up from the paper, are enclosed in cells, a bit as they were for the Alphabet of *Exorcismes*. They are not linear but fibrous rather, not of a single thread but of many threads—snarled nervous systems, entangled mandrake roots. They seem to represent the painful fixation of states that are lived through vegetable or insect sensibilities—what is human remains humiliated far at the bottom and in the rear. You see sad figures under shattered lattices, snared among rods of reinforced concrete. What I am trying to express here are impressions that have fermented in my memory; most of the pictures, when you are in their presence, say nothing and allow nothing to be said. The colors have no brilliance, they make you think of Hindu silks woven with threads of several hues that are a bit darkened, and that further darken one another mutually.

Not all the pictures on exhibition are in this manner; there are four of them in particular that are connected with the attempts that we had seen in *Mouvements*; I find them marvelous; if Michaux was the man to pursue one vein of expression, I would gladly tell him to continue in this direction.

Mouvements was published by René Bertelé about a year ago; it is a large collection that comprises a long poem, sixty-four drawings, and a postscript. I have the feeling that the importance that it deserves poetically and artistically has not been given to this publication. The poem is one of Michaux's most successful—it has an unheard-of impetus and power. The images—and rarely has a poet shown so many and such diverse ones—have an arrangement that leaves nothing in the mind that is unsatisfied. Never have Michaux's *frantic demons* been so frantic and at the same time so well tamed. Whole pages of drawings in India ink accompany the images of the poem. Drawings? Rather plays of lines and spots. Signs that resemble the first scripts but that stir about and return to the gestures that begot them. Spots that sometimes have the look of squat bodies, sometimes of thin bodies with long legs—all gesticulating, palavering, dancing, running, fighting. You think of archaic terra-cottas, of rock paintings; but these allusions that beset the mind do not extricate us from the world of Michaux, in which the poem retains us with an iron fist. It is not the drawings that illustrate the text, but rather it is the text that illustrates the drawings, that animates them, carries them away, and carries us away with them.

The four gouaches that I particularly enjoyed are like groups of these Movements, but they are arranged in such a way as to make a subject more or less. Looking at them I immediately saw that we were in Grande Garabagne: here are the Rocodis and Nijidus coming to meet us; upon that one we see a violent brawl among Arpèdres; and upon that other one there are Vibres galloping along a beach. It is all done with wonderfully original colors; there is a new *light of day* in Michaux's painting. Happy mortals who own these pictures!

From *Dernières Gazettes et Ecrits divers*; first published in *Les Lettres Nouvelles* (April 1953).

The Drawings of Steinberg

If you could see what was going on in the head of a woman making lace or knitting, you would often be very much astonished. She has only one guardian angel—the one that guides her steady hands, but she has a flock of devils that hiss spite and rage into her ears; they make Margot the Terrible rise up in her. It is then that she takes her revenge, that she constructs for her husband, her women neighbors, their dirty kids, the grocer, her rich cousins—a castle of the Marquis kind in which slaps in the face and insults are the least of things. As concerns knitting women I do not have to give proof of what I assert, the history of France is loaded with it. Concerning lace makers, we now know how it is, almost, thanks to Steinberg.

The drawings of Steinberg, if you wish, are hooked lace. His characters have a simple hook by way of a nose; that does not make hooked noses, properly speaking, rather it makes you think of the bent points of a lace maker's needles; their eyes are elementary ovals that resemble the eyes of sewing needles. These drawings have us penetrate into a country of arachnids in which the thread is at one and the same time the material and the discourse. What distinguishes Steinberg's thread from the line of ordinary artists is his meticulous whimsies, his fashion of taking delight in games that are very much his own, minuscule embellishments, like stories that you tell yourself while all alone, for distraction, but for him it is the better to seize his prey.

The malignity of Steinberg has nothing to do with that of housewives; his spite is neither personal nor cheap. The world that he takes for a victim is the one of which he is a victim; his grievances are those of men, poor men, not especially American men—although his art expresses America and is very much in its place within the framework of the *New Yorker*.

How can the individual defend himself in a city that is too big, too high, too mechanized, too intense, too much given over to women? That city, it is men who made it; those women, it is men who made them also, and wanted them to be at one and the same time abandoned spendthrifts and the stubborn guardians of morality. Be that as it may, the result is there and it must be put up with.

Against what is enormous and crushing shall be raised what is little and subtle, like the wren in the story who triumphs over the big animals with the help of a mosquito. I have always been struck, while going through the pages of the *New Yorker*, by the subtlety of its spirit, by its liking for what is small and delicate. There is a cult of the vignette in it, which is rather curious. Besides the humorous drawings proper you always find in each number at least half a dozen drawings that are of a poetic order—landscapes, houses, shops, animals, flowers, objects; there are also women, men, and children. In these vignettes things and people are seen with charmed and softened eyes, as if a kind truth stood forth from their ways of being every time. The covers of the magazine often have a similar inspiration—they are swarming with a Lilliputian crowd. You have the impression that littleness here expresses less the humiliation of a subdued humanity than a resort to an almost invisible world, a secret and innocent world in which, through necessity or play, you can enter into mouseholes or fly away like sparrows.

The sentimental vignettes do not hinder the work of those gentlemen and ladies the caricaturists (there are formidable women on the *New Yorker*)—or the humorists, if you prefer. In fact, their drawings reveal the humorous and the comic at one and the same time; they make fun of society and the individual equally. The individual—you do not see who, in their eyes, can deserve that title. They are humorists rather because of the gentle manner that they take in general in order to say the cruelest things. Thurber goes about his slaughters with the effusions and gambols of nice dogs. Helen Hokinson and Mary Petty laugh at the persons of their own sex and put them in a box with pretty bows of ribbon. But the most fearsome of them all is assuredly Steinberg, and that, we have said, with the craft of a lace maker.

The Steinberg exhibition that took place last April at the Galerie Maeght was a discovery for many people. It won a great success—I was very satisfied. To myself, who had followed the artist in the *New Yorker*, it taught many things and gave new reasons for admiring him. He showed in it an enlarging of his manner and new inspirations in theme, some of which are frankly extraordinary, for example, the mimicry of handwriting, which begot a series entitled: diplomas, passports, identification cards, autographs, letters, and photographs. Among the other themes, likewise treated in series, I noticed these: horses, cities, the métro, the railroad, the parade, cowboys, musicians, and various women, most of whom wear furs and hats.

I shall say immediately what pleased me least. First of all, the horses; their uppish old horsewomen had already shown their hooks in the *New Yorker*. The jockeys and the horsemen who are added to them here resemble them too much, it would have you believe that horseback riding makes people uniformly ferocious; the horses themselves represent attempts at stylization that are curious but not convincing—furthermore, every time that Steinberg abandons his satirical intention and wants to make art, he gives the impression of badly seated baroque, he shows a candor that diminishes him somewhat. He must resign himself to being ill-natured. The railroads, they are not at all ill-natured; I did not understand why they took up so much room; the locomotives are like pretty toys, the stations and the viaducts are summarily made with great threads that seem to have been drawn from the web. The series on cowboys likewise seemed to me a bit too abundant in respect to the idea that it sets forth; it was very good to make fun of westerns and to put them in lace, but it seems to me that the joke turns to their glorification in this case; these brilliant drawings leave one perplexed. The best find is the cowgirl who is at one and the same time a vamp and a Venus de Lespugue sporting a male costume over her enormous charms.

Now that I have made my reservations, I can say that all the rest enchanted me, particularly the compositions based on handwriting. It was an idea of genius, these diplomas, passports, autographs, and photographs. Steinberg shows here, under the cloak of a terrifying patience and humility, an originality that is without precedent; he is a philosopher in his manner—oh! very somber: the human being that he exposes could not be more ridiculous. His spirit is related in a certain manner to Fargue's. The author of *Vulturne* would have enjoyed, I am sure of it, that succession of painstaking and unreadable scripts, ornamental scrolls, imbecile flourishes, that are almost akin to his spiritualist's tables:

> I am a kind of little splendor.
> . . . .
> To be an officer, that is everything.
> . . . .
> I am of an elegance superior and brave as a sword.
> . . . .
> I am an im-pec-cable little transactional element.

The passports and the diplomas, more imposing than real ones, make you think of Kafka also. The man who is kept waiting in the consulates, the victim of *The Trial*, is here well avenged. But it is not only the official and bureaucratic world that is aimed at. Is there anything more cruel for one and all than those family photographs in which the heads are nothing but indefinite spots? As for the autographs, they are well done, at one and the same time for those who ask for them and for those who give them—*vain writing*, as Pierre Reverdy says.

The series on parades is magnificent. There are processions of military people, decorated people, disguised people, which are Steinberg at his best. In certain groups you find again the obsession with flourishes—rather let us say with scrawls: heaps of little gentlemen march along, brandishing over their heads, like emblems or lassos, monstrous signatures.

The cities are ravishing. Steinberg must be happy when he goes for a walk. I noticed a big street in which the people come and go bustling like insects, you see little groups of passers-by who are going in one direction while others are coming from the opposite direction, and who at the moment of their meeting form a droll little animal that stirs its paws; in the front of the picture there is a whole row of phantomlike cats, they are doubtless the spirits of cats who are behind the windows and who would themselves also like to walk in the street. The covered galleries of Milan and Naples are a great success; they are swarming with a minuscule crowd that is speaking and gesticulating; the hands, which are almost as big as the bodies, stir like the pincers of scorpions—those scorpions that Fabre admired because they were able to live almost without eating, by simply absorbing the warmth of the sun. The Paris métro has inspired in Steinberg two charming images, one of which carries us back to a faraway 1900; where did he see that modern-style entrance, contemporary of the Exposition?—it seemed to me that it had been replaced everywhere by something more simple.

The series on women, the greater number of whom bear in the catalog the simple title "Furs," enter into the epic genre. They are not women but idols of sorts, with masks comparable to those of certain African or Oceanian tribes. You think of the Moundang gods that Gide saw in the Congo, personages covered all over with black algae, with the crests of porcupines, and also of the mask called "the shoemaker's wife," which Michel Leiris describes in *L'Afrique fantôme* as being a cowl of fiber overlaid with little shells that are called cowries, or again of the wickerwork masks of New Guinea. They are terrifying but are without moral responsibility; Steinberg seems certainly to have seen them as social products; they are for the most part old gambling women whose faces (if you can call them faces) show all kinds of striations under hats that without their playful plumes would be ecclesiastical.

There were some moving works in this exhibition: the violinists drawn on music paper, sad men and surely unhappy at home, but well sheltered in their art. Finally, I do not want to forget that ravishing page where you looked upon broods of notes that were little birds. Yes, Steinberg loves at least two things—walking alone and listening to music.

From *Dernières Gazettes et Ecrits divers*; first published in *Les Lettres Nouvelles* (September 1953).

The Paul-Emile Bécat Exhibition

From December 15, 1926, to January 25, 1927, at La Maison des Amis des Livres, Paul-Emile Bécat is exhibiting portraits drawn in lead pencil. Almost all of the portraits are those of writers: Paul Claudel, Georges Chennevière, Georges Duhamel, Luc Durtain, Edouard Estaunié, Léon-Paul Fargue, André Gide, Ricardo Güiraldes, Havelock Ellis, James Joyce, Valery Larbaud, Robert McAlmon, Jean Paulhan, Guy de Pourtalès, Jules Romains, Jean Schlumberger, Fernand Vandérem, and Paul Valéry.

Here are some notes on the portraitist:

Paul-Emile Bécat is forty-one years old; he is the son of a miniaturist and enameler. When he was six years old his father put a pencil between his fingers and began to inculcate in him the principles of drawing. In those days M. Ingres reigned and one did not trifle with the principles; when a child proved to be intractable it was the purpose of a good box on the ear to open him to understanding. So Bécat learned to draw in the most classical manner and was also initiated into the crafts of miniature and enameling; as a young man he copied with his father the beautiful enamels of Limousin. At the Ecole de Beaux-Arts, which he did not enter until he was twenty, he studied painting and by simple contagion contracted the idea of becoming an artist. But, the gods be thanked, it is really an artisan that he has remained; neither the teaching of Gabriel Ferrier nor the discussions that he had later on with his cubist comrades impaired in him that wonderful craft of drawing, which is the very key to the art of portraiture.

The pencil portraits of Bécat have often been compared to those of Ingres, and not without reason. But Ingres drew more finely. No doubt he was also more of an artist, which is to say that he communicated to his models a style that was his own, he based them upon a convention that was full of skillfulness—this word is used with everything that it includes of good and bad. I am not speaking here of his portraits of women: he was too sensual not to be aroused.

Bécat has more freedom and more truthfulness; he does not see his model in one fashion or another, he sees it, and through the virtue of his craft alone, which is to record rigorously the most frequent lineaments of a face, he succeeds naturally in doing the work of a psychologist. He does not wait for your rare or inspired moments, but for your very human and very average states, those in which your face is self-reflective and self-consistent. I have always thought that he is very much related to the portraitists of the fifteenth and sixteenth centuries, for he has both their adroitness and their naturalness.

I keenly recovered this impression some days ago in the course of a visit that I made with my friends the Hoppenots to the conservation department of the Louvre. Here I should speak parenthetically about this department, in which is kept a magnificent and imposing collection of drawings whose existence is too little known about. At the very top of the museum you follow long, narrow corridors that are lighted every twenty steps by a little oil lamp, you open a door and there is a square, spacious room; the walls are two-thirds covered by cases filled with cardboard boxes that have labels on their backs, like enormous books; in the frames of two large windows you see the sky and the sage profiles of the guardian angels of the place: Mme Georges Saupique and Mme André Chamson, who are bent over papers. The boxes on the walls are full of drawings from all periods. We are installed in front of an *X;* look, here are the Ingres that we were talking about. Here are the Rembrandts—secretly we place the tip of an index finger upon the spot where he signed his name. Here are the Dürers and the Holbeins, a Hieronymus Bosch that is a poem by Fargue; I find nothing by my dear Pieter Breughel, but the really velvety landscapes of "Velvet Breughel." Here are the portraits by anonymous artists of the sixteenth century, very French faces, very sensitive, with their bright everyday look. A Clouet is put in our hands, a man's head: simply the network of veins at the temples makes us want to weep—Oh, shouldn't there be in all periods artists or artisans, what does the name matter, capable of fixing a human face with the same immutable perfection!

Bécat, my friend, you have been reproached for being finicky. Well, no, you are not even finicky enough, you must not lose a single one of the slight threads that weave a human face. For others the syntheses, the adventures, the new techniques, the experiments —they are forging ahead, with good reason; for you tradition, and so many reasons.

From *Dernières Gazettes et Ecrits divers*; first published in *La Nouvelle Revue Française* (January 1927).

In the Country of Faces

Country of human faces—country that one does not leave and where one rarely goes. Because it is not easy to penetrate, it is an exploration. It is necessary to undergo polar cold there, or torrid heat. The least look means love. Quick, eyelid, lower, blow out that fire; show a little coolness. The least crease of the lips freezes. Silence. The ice would also overcome words. We are approaching the white giant of the poles, the one that Gordon Pym saw. It is the instinct of self-preservation. A measure of hate for nothing, or for almost nothing. It is better to leave.

I have come back from a voyage to the country of faces. A long voyage undertaken in the company of Gisèle Freund. It was she who was the pilot, she who held the rudder, she who operated the machine for exploring faces. This machine was an ordinary camera loaded with film sensitive to colors. The equipment also included two projectors, a screen, and a magic lantern. All that to bring them back alive.

Who alive? you ask.

Well, certainly, since it is I who am speaking, the writers, the poets, the people of language, the men of extreme situations; they occupy the most tormented sites in the country of faces, the strangest, the least beautiful according to ordinary standards of beauty—beauty abandons itself to living, or ought to have the appearance of doing so. And they do not abandon themselves to living, they cannot. For them are reserved the turbulences, the erosions, the stormy heights, the rivers of fire, all the convulsions great and small. How could a form repose in them, whose task is to express the vicissitudes of forms?

Sartre, watching all those faces pass by, among which his own appeared, accurately said, "We have the look of coming back from war."

But those faces, are they not also the most beautiful, for someone who sees them with the eyes of the spirit? It is through their defects that they attain the highest virtues. It is in suffering from what they lack that they acquire abundance. Every one of their wrinkles is precious, is a spur that puts the inner fire into play.

To think that there are photographers who conceal all that, and that great men, or men regarded as such, are the first to want that concealment—poor innocents! Have women ever hesitated to love them as they are? Hasn't genius always been for them the most powerful of attractions, even the very sign of love? Ladies who are reading me, what do you think about this?

Yes, my voyage with Gisèle Freund has been a great adventure. All the more so because she is a bold photographer and conceals nothing, not she. Tériade, looking at her portraits, said to her, "You've struck them that blow once by surprise, but they wouldn't let you try again."

Well, I wonder if they wouldn't let us try again. It's up to us to persuade them that they are handsome like this, and that we prefer them like this. The painters would have them seen very differently. No doubt the pretentious and mannered artists would arrange them nicely, but the true, the pure, would tear them to pieces for you, would gut them, would reduce them to equations; at best they would try out their vaccines of color on them. They would make subject matter out of them.

Gisèle Freund has the gift of humanity which relates her to Nadar, whom she has taken as her master, to David Octavius Hill, in whose honor she made a pilgrimage to Edinburgh. Her portraits have an incredible life.

Thanks to her, we are rich in excellent pictures of most of our best writers. It should be said that her way of projecting the photos on a screen gives very surprising results. Here light plays the role of a sculptor, which reproduction on paper doubtless would not have. The movie-star type of enlargement here finds its very reason for being.

Shall I try to describe some of the faces of these writers?

Claudel has the look of the Chinese god Lord of the Thunder. He has a little cyclone in his neck, in place of an Adam's apple. On seeing him, Mauriac exclaimed: "What a terrible look he has! That man can speak only to God."

Gide, with his pure and ascetic features, resembles a monk who has founded an order. His eyebrows are like the Burning Bush.

Valéry, whose cheeks are hollowed by deep ravines, opens eyes like the sea; they have its color and eternal youth.

Romains lifts up a face that is bitterly petrified, but the pupils of his eyes are like the tenderest sapphires.

The face of Fargue broods over and discloses *the great depths of trickery,* those on which one does not play tricks. Each of his hands is defenseless and moves like a little marionette.

Supervielle seems to have come from another planet to see the Manger—and he never ceases to see it.

From *Les Gazettes d'Adrienne Monnier*; first published in *Verve* (July–October 1939).

part four

Spectacles

The Circus

The circus—for quite a long time, really, I had not gone to it, I had not even thought about it.

There was a time when one used to go to the circus a great deal, in 1922 and 1923, it seems to me. When I say "one" I am thinking about the more or less literary tribe, for whom the circus is an estimable but not an essential thing, and who go to it only under the pressure of an influence. At that moment the visible, the very visible influence—in high relief—was Cocteau's, but underneath, deeper and from farther back, there was the influence of Copeau and Gide, who had always seriously loved the circus, and who had discovered the Fratellinis, maybe before they had discovered themselves.

I remember an evening performance at the Médrano with Gide, Fargue, Larbaud, and the beautiful Iris Tree. Gide noted that the Fratellinis no longer completely had it, that their work was becoming a bit too superficial, too easy. Naturally, their success was not diminishing, on the contrary. Clownery is like literature and the rest—it is not in bringing off one's best feats that one pleases most.

Around the same period there was also Grock, at the height of fashion, whom we went to see in the music halls.

For the last six or seven years the circus has no longer been in fashion. That is a pity. One should go to the circus, beyond any question of fashion, at least one or two times a year—I am not speaking here to the real enthusiasts, they know better than I what they have to do.

The circus is perhaps the most vital of all spectacles. It is a place full of simple and powerful charms. Charms of childhood memories. Charms of the very form of the circus, of its odor, its clamor. Charms of the ritual that presides over the entrances and the stunts. These bodily acts, these attractions that are daughters of universal Attraction take place with great ceremony. What is so moving as the roll of the drum that precedes the most perilous moment of the number and the total silence that follows it? Shall we hesitate to think of the Elevation of the Mass? And what is so noble as the hand of the gymnast, who stands up absolutely straight after his stunt, with his palm open like the very symbol of work and its fulfillment?

Here the word work has a figure, a fatality, that it does not have elsewhere. That is because it denotes only itself in a pure state. It is foreign to the human, hostile. It draws from the poor animal body efforts that are crowned by efforts; it frees it from ordinary laws only to bend it under laws that are more severe.

While the concentration of the ascetic or of the thinker seeks a state of harmony and stability in which time is abolished, the contraction of the acrobat finds only a state of supreme struggle, insufferable, which at the most will last for the time it takes to count up to ten—the ten first numbers, one by one, as solemn and terrible as the lords of existence.

One understands the liking that people of the lower class have for the circus. There they are at home. It is a world in the image of their own, to the glory of their own, a world entirely of matter, struggles, dangers, delights, illusions.

There they can see suffering rather than suffer. Those who make them laugh give and get slaps, blows, kicks without a stop; they are thrown to the ground, trampled on.

There they feel the presence of masters who do not overawe them; rather they can assert themselves of their own free will and look them in the face.

There they can enjoy themselves. One has to have seen some old workman sitting in the upper tiers, his hands propped on his knees, his head whitened and worn by the bleachings of life, follow with gently vaulting eyes the frolic of a beautiful hand-to-hand act between a man and a woman.

Yes, I had not gone to the circus for quite a long time, when the other night, as I was passing by on the Boulevard des Filles-du-Calvaire, I saw a name that was new to me on the pediment of the Cirque d'Hiver: "Bouglione." A magnificent name, above all when inscribed on the pediment of a circus. What force, what abundance in those syllables. One thought of the knots of swollen muscles, of manes, and of heavy foods slick with tomato sauce. Bouglione, Bouglione—I repeated the name to myself, as bewitched as children who learn by heart the brilliant and bizarre names of the countries of Asia or South America.

Some days later an article by Henry Thétard in *Voilà* supplied me with all the explanations I had wished for. That was the name of four brothers, descendants of a family of tamers of Piedmontese origin, themselves tamers and the present directors of the Cirque d'Hiver. The cover of *Voilà* showed their heads, worthy of their names in every respect. Thétard's article was charming, written with a great deal of zest and good nature. I remembered that this author, whose acquaintance I was making very late, had published books, one of them, *Les Dompteurs [The Tamers]*, at Gallimard's, another, quite recent, *Coulisses et secrets du cirque [Behind the Scenes and Secrets of the Circus]*, at Plon's. I read the two books in one day, with a pleasure that written things rarely give me. All at once I was seized by an immense appetite for the circus. I made an examination of my conscience. What, I had not gone to the circus for three or four years! Why? It's true, the last time we had gone we had remarked that it was very tiring for our hands; every artist seemed to us worthy of so much interest, of so much encouragement, that we forced ourselves to applaud with all our might, the more so because the public showed itself rather indifferent. The tragic side of the circus had appeared to us that evening with a great deal of intensity. We had watched the clowns with the eyes of Henry Church and Rouault. *Poor Pagliacci*, the celebrated aria by Leoncavallo (another beautiful name), the beloved *lamento* of Queen Victoria and Burgin, beat against our heads like the heavy waves of a ground swell. It was a day like that. We could not stop at this point.

I went to the matinée performance of the Cirque d'Hiver last Thursday. The house was full of children. It was ravishing.

The first part of the show was devoted to the "integral circus"; good numbers. I regretted that there were no trapezists, there should always be trapezists. The second part was composed of a "great magical and nautical spectacle": *The Queen of the Sierra*, a piece in five scenes by the Bouglione brothers themselves, if you please. I was hoping very much to see the four brothers, whose heads had pleased me so much on the cover of *Voilà*. There was only one of them: Joseph. Doubtless the others were traveling with their large itinerant circus. At any rate, I was satisfied. It is a well-assembled show. There is something in it for every taste. It begins as an operetta. I was a bit disturbed, I must say, but I was quickly reassured. In the second scene we were with the cowboys, we were present at their games as sons of the prairie. Then there were Indians, the Beaver tribe to be precise. Ah! the shouts of the kids when they saw the first Indians appear, crawling on their bellies, their ears glued to the ground. Very good attack on a stagecoach. At the Beavers' camp we had "ritual ceremonies," incantations to the god Mava, a dance with tomahawks and shields, and no less than two stakes—one for the heroine Juanita and the other, more comical, naturally, with a turnspit, for the excellent clown Beby. The most beautiful part, of course, was the end. We saw Indians on horseback arrive on the flooded track while others scaled the sides of a glowing waterfall and were received on top of the rocks by Joseph Bouglione himself, who caught them in his arms and cast them into the torrents. A fireworks display crowned the whole thing. As the program said in capital letters: Apotheosis—Finale.

From *Les Gazettes d'Adrienne Monnier*; first published in *La Nouvelle Revue Française* (March 1935).

La Revue Nègre

This review has a great success, well deserved it seems to us. The New Yorkers are astonished by our raptures; first of all they find that it isn't black so much as it is yellow, "too yellow," they say, too many mulattoes and not enough blacks; they also say that the review is not well made, that it is an assemblage of scenes that are disconnected and without great interest, that the dances and the songs are overfamiliar to them. But for us these stale things are new, and then doesn't Josephine Baker all by herself give the liveliest pleasure, the most amazing that can be imagined? With her get-ups, her grimaces, her contortions she kicks up a shindy that swarms with mocking enticements—she's a Queen of Sheba who turns into a frog, into a mischievous chicken with its feathers plucked; she passes from an enamored expression to a frightful squint; she even succeeds in "squinting with her behind," as Claude Soudieux says. To compensate for the insufficient darkness of his partners the dancer Louis Douglas appears in blackface; that gives him a physiognomy whose expression changes only slightly, but by other means he is often as funny as Baker and he lavishes choreographic wonders as much as she herself does.

From *Les Gazettes d'Adrienne Monnier*; first published in *Le Navire d'Argent* (December 1925).

Folies-Bergère-Folies

Why are the Folies-Bergère called "Folies-Bergère?" They are not located in the Rue Bergère but in the Rue Richer. Obviously, they cannot be called the Folies-Richer. The Rue Bergère is not far away, but it is not immediately adjoining. It pleases me to think that the one who baptized them (who was he?) did not have the Rue Bergère in mind so much as a type of shepherdess, and not so much a type of shepherdess as a kind of nature. Girl-animals, girl-things, girl-flowers. "A rose is a word of love." Let everything here throb without soul in the universal soul. Colors, forms, rhythms, so many sensational effects, are the sentiments of a great female being, an enormous Astarte who shows her thin plucked eyebrows to the new moon.

"Folies-Bergère"—certainly the name deserved to make a fortune, to bewitch the largest district of the largest city; on Broadway everything is "folies": "Folies-Bergère" is the very name that is given to our "spectacular revues," to their "Ooh-la-la shows."

The other night, while attending *Femmes en folie,* the aerodynamic (not bad) revue that is presently playing at the Folies-Bergère, it occurred to me that if the Americans owe us something, we owe them a great deal also (I am not speaking of the war debts, set your mind at rest). The idea of the spectacular revue, the fairy-tale show for adults only was born among us, but it seems to me that formerly the Orient had us more in its clutches. The beauties who undulated on the stage were all Egyptian dancing girls more or less, for remember, they all undulated with a broad submarine sway to the sound of pernicious music that went by the names of "Salome," "Cairo," "Arabia." Perfumes were called "Nirvana," "Yavana"—

When it was not the Orient it was the Mediterranean, everything that lies to the south: Spain, ancient Rome, Venice, the Sahara Desert (it is still in fashion, the Sahara Desert, we cannot do without mirages). The naked women had the broad haunches, the opulent breasts of *gôpis;* when they wanted to give an appearance of firmness to them they held their arms stretched out behind or arched above their heads. They were arranged in bunches, in festoons. There were living fans, beautiful crucifixions, giant bells girdled by brunettes distraught with passion. Among these scenes, these masses of flesh devoted to Venus, one saw the chorus girls march past, servants of Vulcan; their dry, electric rhythm, their chain dances, were a graceful symbol of machinery, of which only the benefits were being experienced at the time.

It is curious that now, while there are chorus boys still, and more than ever, there are no more chorus girls: they have become "Bluebell's Beautiful Ladies," the "Spark Ballet," the "Helena Stars," or even simply "Ballet."

Parisians have not yet been told what they owe to the great New York producer Ziegfeld and his follies (with two *l*'s). Morand rightly mentions him in his *New York*. We owe him the sporting blondes, perfect, with the breasts of goddesses. Remember our first amazement in front of Gertrude Hoffman's girls; they did not come from Ziegfeld's company, but they were the daughters of his genius. Go to see, now, the naked women of the Folies-Bergère: they come onstage with a natural walk, their arms at their sides; everything takes place in light colors—white, pink, cream, azure. Formerly the idea of the Black Mass was always more or less present; colors were purplish, sulfurous, red dominated. Freudism, nudism, physical culture, sun bathing, have passed that way. Two scenes in *Femmes en folie* have a church for their setting: "A Big Marriage in Hollywood" and "The Altar of the Vamps"; but the light is dazzlingly bright, nothing is repressed anymore, it is even too pure, or else it is I who am jaded.

In the scene about the marriage in Hollywood there was a little ballet that seemed remarkable to me. The program says they are the wedding guests—all in white, very girlish, in long organdy dresses with frilly flounces; but the costumes have little importance, what is good is the movement of the ballet itself. They flutter, they felicitate, they stamp, their antennae flicker, they go to eat, they eat, their agile paws rub their corselets, he, she, we laugh, we exult, wing cases rustle, there, there, look at them there.

After having witnessed the ravishing evolution of the female nude at the Folies-Bergère I had the desire to go to see how things were doing at the Casino de Paris (I had not gone into these two establishments for seven or eight years, even Cécile Sorel had not made me budge). I remembered that if the costumes were always ingenious and often very beautiful at the Casino de Paris, the total nude was more rare there. In general the women had covered or at least very well-supported breasts, at the price of showing other morsels of their bodies more generously. So I made it my duty to go to the *Parade de France*, a big tourist revue mounted with good taste and good feelings. It is almost a family show, with the exception of two or three rather ooh-la-la numbers. There is "The Naked Bath at Midnight" by Arabelle, and what seemed more interesting to me, the very indecent dance of a black woman, a so-called Martinican. She arrives on the stage making the cries of the possessed, she frisks about in a thousand and one ways and, before leaving, she hurls into the house the sharp bleat of a voo-doo goat—it makes one shudder.

Arabelle aside, nudes are not richly represented. It was to be expected; that has never been their specialty.

Upon leaving the Casino de Paris I told myself that it would be completely virtuous to go to the Alcazar de Paris to see *La Revue nue: A la manière des burlesques de New-York*, "sumptuous and magnificent nudes," the advertisements say. What stopped me was the price of the seats. They were not expensive enough: from five to eighteen francs! No, they cannot give sumptuous and magnificent nudes in the New York manner for that price, certainly not!

From *Les Gazettes d'Adrienne Monnier*; first published in *La Nouvelle Revue Française* (June 1935).

At the Opéra with Francis Poulenc

It was Eluard, Poulenc told me, who baptized my ballet. He had thought at first of the title: *A la lueur de l'homme [To the Gleam of Man]*; that was very beautiful, but not ballet. *Les Animaux modèles*, I said, is ravishing.

Now that I am acquainted with Poulenc's ballet I find the title less successful. The composer took the *Fables* of La Fontaine for the theme that inspired him, but above all he tried to make the humanity of them stand out. In short, it has to do with an homage to La Fontaine, and even, by his own admission, with an homage to the France of the seventeenth century and to her peasantry. A "model" peasantry because it is of the past, seen entirely through the paintings of Louis Le Nain, who did not hide from us the fact that the clothing of the peasants was full of patches and often in rags, but who gave a religious light to his figures. Is there, in French art, a more beautiful face of a virgin mother than that of the woman who pensively gets ready to lift toward her lips the glass that contains "a very little bit of precious wine"?

Francis Poulenc, in composing his ballet, made a very beautiful thing. The overture, which illustrates the departure to the fields of a troop of peasants, shows a solemnity, a nobility, a piety, that have great style; he wanted it to express the love that he has for the people of our soil; it is a magnificent piece.

Yes, I believe that *Les Animaux modèles* is a masterpiece, in the old sense of the term, rather, since now, as Robert Rey has written in his essay on painting, one no longer wants to recognize anything in art but genius, that is to say, invention at any price, the beauty that is necessarily bizarre, according to Baudelaire's expression.

Poulenc is not, up to now, an innovator, but he is a perfectly original composer. In his review of *Les Animaux modèles*, Arthur Honegger correctly writes that the influences that have worked upon him, Chabrier, Satie, Stravinsky, are now completely assimilated. Listening to his music you think—it's Poulenc.

If I had to describe Poulenc's style, I would speak about the particular nuances of his playfulness, of his piety, of his melancholy.

Besides these qualities that belong so essentially to our composer, we should note, in *Les Animaux modèles*, the presence of a remarkable vigor. The episode of "Les Coqs rivaux" ["The Rival Cocks"] shows a brilliance, a violence that go far beyond the resources of the minor masters.

Nothing is more French than the playfulness of Poulenc; I do not hesitate to relate it to his piety. In my essay "The Nature of France," I said, not without having thought about it very much, that in its highest form French gaiety touches faith, that it went with the grace that has "the gaiety of the fawn of the doe," according to the expression of Saint Bernard. Poulenc's first ballet is called *Les Biches*, its music is of the most graceful kind— When you think that he was only twenty-four years old then!

Poulenc's playfulness, like all real playfulness, comes from the feeling of Unity. Because of this feeling you are not a child lost in life, you laugh at your own misadventures; all forms of sociability are embroidered upon this feeling.

I do not know anybody who is as good-natured, laughing, sociable, as Poulenc.

But nothing in him charms me more, perhaps, than the tone of his melancholy. Remember, to speak only of his more recent works, the air of the Duchess de Langeais, who is waiting in the rain. In *Les Animaux modèles*: the air of Elmira, who picks up her lover's hat and presses it against her heart—the air of the man between two ages—the air of the woodcutter and death. There is, in Poulenc's melancholy, what Henri Michaux would call "an internal distance," with the magic that it always brings in. Satie was full of that magic.

Gaiety is forgetfulness of the self, melancholy is memory of the self: in that state the soul feels all the power of its roots, nothing distracts it from its profound homeland and the look that it casts upon the outer world is gently dismayed. It is the revery of children, with no other object than its own enchantment. I was speaking just now about the woman with a glass of wine in the painting by Le Nain—there is, right behind her, a little girl who is standing near the hearth, lost in daydreaming, while the fire just brightens the edges of her white cap. What a marvel!

It is true—as much as being an homage to La Fontaine, Poulenc's ballet could be an homage to Le Nain, and that is certainly how it was understood by Brianchon, who made the scenery and the costumes.

The costumes of the peasants are very beautiful, they are those that you see in the paintings of Le Nain; a group of children, at the beginning, is particularly successful. The stage is occupied by a noble Burgundian building. The backdrop is thick greenery, a crowd of trees with rich foliage. Colette found the backdrop overwhelming for the characters, lacking air and perspective; her point of view seems to me most valid, but the idea did not come into my mind, and I found that backdrop excellent.

Brianchon did not try to represent the animals; he gave to the amorous lion, to the grasshopper and the ant, a human shape and the beautiful costumes of the epoch, conforming to the wish of Poulenc, who also wanted death to appear to the woodcutter as a beautiful masked woman. Only the bear is really a bear. The cocks and the chickens are neither human nor natural; in fact they recall their models in the manner of costumed monkeys at fairs (this is not a criticism that I am formulating here, I find the costumed monkeys at fairs very successful). The chickens have those provocative tutus that make you think that the costumer let himself be led astray by the word *chicken*.

Serge Lifar's choreography is intelligent and perfectly pleasing; it goes well with Poulenc's gaiety and with his desire to go back to the seventeenth century; for the rest, one cannot demand from dance what it cannot give. As Lifar himself has nicely written, concerning the bear and the two companions, "Just try to express in dance a sentence like: 'He told me that one must never / Sell the skin of a bear one has not felled.' "

The company of dancers, with Mlles Lorcia, Schwarz, and Chauviré, and MM. Lifar, Peretti, and Efimof in the leading roles, performed wonders, naturally.

I have no need to say that the success of *Les Animaux modèles* was most lively, and that everybody considered that the Opéra had been enriched by a ballet that would become a classic.

But the interpretation of the score on the piano by the composer touched me more than that beautiful performance. Dazzling though the orchestration is, you know that Poulenc is an admirable pianist, and then the work was presented to us under particularly favorable conditions.

This interpretation took place at the house of Georges Salles, the author of that book that I love so much, *Le Regard [The Look]*, in the presence of Hélène de Wendel and Jean-Claude Fourneau.

The house of Georges Salles, perched on the Butte, at the foot of Sacré-Coeur, is a little museum; the rarest objects are to be seen in it. Among others, there is old pottery by French peasants that has a color, a form, and even a mystery that set you to dreaming.

It was there, one afternoon in July, that we were invited, Sylvia Beach and myself, to hear the ballet that the Opéra was to give shortly.

Our Poulenc, in order to begin on the piano, took off his jacket and rolled up his sleeves to above his elbows. First he gave us some explanations. Then, lowering his nose to the keys, he seemed to absorb himself in a brief prayer.

And he set about playing his music, and as he played we did not cease to be moved or ravished, or both at the same time.

A presence, it seemed, joined our own—that of Raymonde Linossier, our friend who had too quickly vanished, to whose memory Francis Poulenc dedicated this work.

From *Les Gazettes d'Adrienne Monnier*; first published in *Le Figaro Littéraire* (1942).

The Ballet Mécanique

On Friday the 13th last November George Antheil told us that they were going to give his *Ballet mécanique* at the Conservatoire, and that it was Benoist-Méchin who had made the arrangements.

But perhaps I should present George Antheil and Benoist-Méchin to those who do not know them.

George Antheil is American. He has been living in Paris for three years. As soon as he arrived Sylvia Beach and Robert McAlmon adopted him as a brother. He is twenty-four years old, but he appears to be fifteen. He has the look of a young faun; although he does not have the pointed ears and the slanting eyes of the classical faun, his face still has the ingenuousness, the stupefaction, and the easy hilarity of a new creature for whom the whole world is new.

He lives above Shakespeare and Company; when he comes home late at night, so as not to awaken his concierge, who would not fail to give him a lecture the next day, he gets back to his room (he lives on the entresol) by climbing up the wall, like Harold Lloyd in "Monte là-dessus."

When he plays his music he is terrible; he boxes with the piano; he riddles it with blows and perseveres furiously until the instrument, the public, and he himself are knocked out. When he is finished he is red, he sponges his forehead; he comes down from the ring with his forehead lowered, his shoulders rocking, his brows knitted, his fists still clenched tight. After a quarter of an hour he is in his right mind again; he laughs, he has forgotten everything.

The first time we heard his music was at the Théâtre des Champs-Elysées in the course of a kind of evening performance-bazaar with several functions: Hébertot was offering it as a bonus to his season-ticket holders; Poiret was parading his dresses; Georgette Leblanc was preparing scenes for her film *L'Inhumaine*, using the public that was present. And it was precisely in regard to this that they had engaged George Antheil. Georgette Leblanc, back from America, knew through her friend Margaret Anderson that Antheil's music always caused a scandal; and if it caused a scandal in New York, what was it going to be like in Paris!—In fact, as soon as the first bars were played the whole audience was standing up and howling. In the meantime, the cameramen were shooting the scene. Antheil had believed that they had seriously asked him to play his most "advanced" music; when he saw the trick, he was not angry, he had a lot of fun. Immediately after his number they needed an audience delirious with enthusiasm; as they had not found the work that would surely produce this effect, they simply requested the public to please applaud with all its might at a given signal and cry bravos. Beforehand they were going to take the audience at rest. The people did not know at the time of Antheil's recital that they were going to be filmed; once they knew what was expected of them, all the women put on powder and rouge again, took suggestive poses; the men, without seeming to be concerned, arranged the knots of their neckties and, pretending to pick up their programs, rearranged the creases of their trousers. When enthusiasm was commanded of them, some climbed up on their seats, some were to be seen gesticulating like windmills, a hero in the second balcony suspended himself in the void—

But let us come back to Antheil. A little while after this evening performance his friend the American poet Ezra Pound organized some concerts for him, serious this time, in the house of the Conservatoire and at Pleyel's. Both times only friends were there, the initiated, and they gave real acclaim to the young composer--I remember that sitting behind me at the Pleyel concert was Jean Cassou, who told me that this music struck him like the first versions of the first dramas of Claudel.

There was also the recital of a quartet at Miss Barney's. Florent Schmitt, who was present, was not so scandalized and even found the thing interesting.

On Friday the 13th last November we did not know what was going to happen; we simply knew that Benoist-Méchin would present the *Ballet mécanique* and would perform some fragments of it — The *Ballet mécanique* was composed by Antheil especially for Pleyel's player piano— We had already heard it ourselves in the company of Joyce at Pleyel's; Joyce had said that he discovered something of Mozart in it; Benoist-Méchin had also thought of Mozart; the connection is very subtle or very technical, and it does not seem that the public will make it for a good while yet.

So we arrive at the Conservatoire toward ten o'clock. The *Ballet mécanique* was going to go on at ten thirty. We are given a ground-floor box. We fall upon the strangest little tribe imaginable: a session of "Living Music," it appears; mamas and their young ladies, soldiers on leave, retired officials; no people on our side, none; all the same, we see Jules Supervielle in the balcony.

A very congenial gentleman, M. Léon Vallas, was announcing to the public that the designer André Hellé was going to relate the memories that he had preserved of his collaboration with Debussy for *La Boîte à joujoux [The Toy Box]*—Hellé gave, in fact, a charming little talk—then M. Vallas announced Benoist-Méchin and gently prepared the public for the operation of the *Ballet mécanique.* Benoist-Méchin entered onstage with a resolute air; he sketched a short biography of George Antheil; above all he made it clear that his friend had a perfect musical training and a really overwhelming technical knowledge. Then he put the player piano into action. As soon as the first notes were played, three people stood up crying out with fright and pain and made for the door, which they slammed with all their might. The rest of the public began to brood upon revolt, here and there groaning and protesting. M. Vallas, judging that the situation was critical, tried to anesthetize his public: "What," he told them, "haven't you preserved the memory of the tumults that greeted the first productions of Wagner, of Debussy, of Stravinsky? I am not telling you that M. Antheil will someday equal these masters, his music presently makes me as completely sick at heart as it does you, but after all, you never know—And remember that the situation is even harder for me than it is for you. It's not funny for a critic, you know, to pull to pieces somebody whom he will someday perhaps be obliged to praise to the skies. Once again, I'm not saying that M. Antheil—But really now, ladies and gentlemen, calm, I beg you, patience, it won't last much longer."

When the session was finished, we asked Benoist-Méchin how he had had the courage to continue in the presence of such a hostile public. "Ah!" he told us, "that's because at the player piano it's not the hands that play but the feet, so that I had the impression I was escaping by running away, and that the people were treading on my heels. I couldn't stop; I thought that I would have fallen under their blows."

George Antheil certainly has genius. I do not believe that he has arrived at the definitive formulation of his art. What he is presently giving us are rather his studies, his researches, which are very close to those of Picasso: without concession, as far as he can in a domain that is often arid. However, I have already been permitted to enjoy the absolutely new pathos of it, the uprooting rhythm, a joyful drunkenness of contradiction, a private discovery such as children sing to themselves—It seems to me that his music has a great and salutary influence upon the body; Jean Prévost accurately compares it to sports. Like the Tibetan and Mongol rhythms that Antheil has studied a great deal, it drives out demons and fixes gods without asking them for their opinion.

From *Les Gazettes d'Adrienne Monnier*; first published in *Le Navire d'Argent* (January 1926).

Gian-Carlo Menotti

I do not know if I am glad or sorry to share, for once, the feeling of Jean Cocteau: I like Menotti very much—his music and the way he has of making an opera or a film of it. I will not say that he fills me with enthusiasm, but I keenly appreciate him. It does not seem that there is an artist among our contemporaries who seizes so many things at once and so clearly, so practically. Menotti utilizes the genius of others while bringing to it all kinds of personal devices. His productions are neither beautiful nor agreeable, they are not moving, although they are dramatic, they have nothing elevated about them—but they are astonishing. There is an intelligence in them that knows all the tricks and that makes use of them with such dynamism, such brio, that one is taken in spite of oneself, carried away beyond the protestations and criticisms that one would like to formulate without knowing exactly what to blame. They give in their way the enjoyment of thrill rides at fairs—whirling, jolting, rocking at every rate of speed, as in the play of matter in motion. It is an art of sensation that deserves to the highest degree the favorite adjective of the American press: sensational.

In certain respects Menotti the composer recalls Kurt Weill, whose *Mahagonny* we have liked so much, but the German Jewish composer, in my opinion, has greatness—which is not the case with Menotti—and a more profound, more attaching originality. If I bring them together it is because they both of them draw their inspiration from a tragic mood of the epoch; they like what is unhappy and sordid, they are without prejudices and full of vigor; their works are coherent and give the satisfaction of what has been finished.

The influences that appear in Menotti's music have been enumerated more or less. Fundamentally it is very Italian, sprung from the same stock as Verdi, the verists, and Puccini above all, whose impassioned vocalism it has.

I have always had a weakness for Puccini, like everybody I must say; I never tire of listening to the great arias from *Tosca, La Bohème,* and *Madame Butterfly* on the radio. I do not know if I would take the trouble to go to listen to them in the theater, but on the radio it is perfect. If I were in Italy, in Milan, I would not fail to go to La Scala on the evenings when they are given with all the opera that is about. What a pleasure it has been for me to hear Michel Leiris say, upon his return from Italy, that he had discovered Puccini.

Puccini is the master of the great pathetic aria in which the voice swells and lets out all its sail and reaches toward the heavens of the flesh. It means something, the thunder of bravos that breaks out with the last note of "Upon the Calmed Sea" or "And Never Loved I Life So Much."

Like Puccini, like the Italians, Menotti has the gift of song and theater that with them are inseparable from life; in his case there is an extraordinary mixture of these gifts since it is he that does the plays completely before covering them over with music and turning them into operas or films.

The subjects that he takes are typically Italian-American. In the United States there are all the elements possible for drama and tragedy, but the multifarious life rapidly mingles them and carries them away; the artists who want to express them draw very little profit from them or simplify too much; only the journalists are good at their business, and the authors of detective stories, naturally. I do not see how a Frenchman can put up with it over there, but I see fairly well how an Italian can work there boldly and succeed there; his strong instincts of the Mediterranean man—sometimes favored but never spoiled—helping him to take and be satisfied, to stop or not let himself be stopped.

Kafka has been spoken of in regard to *The Consul*, not without reason, for the situation of the heroine is Kafkaesque: she is forced to leave her country and does not succeed in leaving it. But it is above all a drama of emigration treated by an Italian who seizes hold of it and gives it a verist high relief, with Stravinskian props to begin with and a Wagnerian content to end with—the pyre here being a gas stove.

The subject of *The Medium* is likewise a mixture of Italian and American elements. In Italy, as in the United States, traffic with the beyond finds a favorable climate, as much through the credulity of the masses as through the liking or the need for an intense and thorough exploitation. But while in Italy the Church lets almost nothing go astray, because it is strong in its unity, the American churches, in spite of their number, are incapable of responding to the diversity and the strangeness of the demand, their divisions being above all good for begetting other divisions. The European who settles for a certain time in the United States, in New York in particular, is often less subjugated by the largeness of the crowds or the height of the buildings than by the extraordinary importance that sects, prophets, and charlatans take on there—the individual, and above all the immigrant, lost in a heterogenous mass, looks for a personal aid, a precise refuge, and a sort of encampment.

A man like Jules Romains is naturally among the most sensitive to such phenomena, as he has shown with the creation of the "Brothers of the Universe" in *Violation de frontière* and of Mr. Hicks in the *Entretiens avec Dieu [Interviews with God]*. I know of another example, that of the Danish writer, Johannes V. Jensen, who has also stayed in the United States and who has brought back a novel from it, *Madame d'Ora*. That is a story about spiritualism to give one a nightmare; it is an imperfect but very curious youthful work.

The heroine of *The Medium*, Madame Flora, such as Menotti has conceived her, is exceedingly picturesque and dramatic; her costume is a success all by itself—at once middle-class and mountebank, with noble draperies and cascades of jewels. She lives with Monica, her daughter, and Tony, a mute young gypsy whom she has taken in and whom she often mistreats; the two of them serve as assistants in the practice of her strange profession—apart from that they are children who are in love with each other. Madame Flora is a false medium, her speciality is to evoke, for inconsolable parents, the children that they have lost; when she is in a trance the young dead show themselves only through a vague glimmer, but they clearly communicate with their parents through speech, or rather through song, since it is an opera, by borrowing the melodious voice of Monica. The medium, in the course of one of her séances, feels two hands squeeze her neck; she has the horrible impression that it is a spirit, then she suspects Tony, but as she cannot make him confess anything, terror seizes hold of her; we see her take to drink; in the end she kills Tony.

Here I am only sketching the story, which is complicated but plausible, the film explains it perfectly. I do not know, not having seen the opera, if that is superior; I do not believe so, the subject suits the cinema perfectly and Menotti has obtained in this area all the success he could hope for.

I am not in a position to judge the technical qualities of the film; it appeared to me as well made as another, with all kinds of personal merits. One of the greatest is certainly its interpretation. One would not have believed that they were possible, such good singers who are at the same time such good actors. Menotti has a lot of luck—when you think of the admirable Patricia Neway in *The Consul!* Marie Powers, the medium, is extraordinary, both her voice and her acting; it is as a perfect tragedian that she goes to pieces under the influence of terror, that she alternately shows fear and cruelty in regard to Tony (the scene in which she spills upon him the burning drops of a lighted candle has a great effect—one knows where the inspiration for it comes from). Monica has a ravishing voice and acts with grace; Tony has a beautiful expressive face, although his characterization includes a bit too many grimaces to my taste. But the outstanding interpreters are surely the two women and the man who play the roles of the parents in mourning; their faces are credulous and poignant, their voices are very much in agreement with their feelings. It is they who give the film what truth and humanity it can have; the scene in which they believe that they are communicating with their children is profoundly pathetic.

Shall I say that the scenery of the film and its atmosphere made me think of Atget, that old man of the theater who became a photographer, who around 1900 made photos of Paris, and who no less than Fargue was a marvelous stroller. Berenice Abbott, the American photographer, was taken with these photos and had a collection of them, for which Pierre Mac Orlan wrote a beautiful preface, published by Jonquières in 1930.

Atget's photos fondly portray shops such as one used to see in the quarters of Les Halles and Le Temple, with displays of astonishing dummies; old, sad streets; the courtyards of dilapidated houses; the rooms of humble people in which the mantelpieces are altars devoted to souvenirs and popular art. These photos, although they are all very simple, are very mysterious; few characters are to be seen in them, the places are almost always deserted, but they are charged with a sort of presence—it is sometimes hallucinating. Looking at *The Medium* you would not imagine that you were in New York or in the United States, but in an old quarter of I do not know what city.

Another one of Menotti's merits is his having chosen a subject that is so unusual and at the same time so human. Madame Flora is an exceptional being, but we put ourselves without difficulty in the position of the people who seek her out. Nothing is more heart-breaking than the feeling of being separated forever from those one loves; what would one not do in order to obtain were it only a sign from them! But the mystery of death is well kept; those who aspire to force the gates of the beyond do not do so without danger to their intelligence, above all if they want to materialize *spirits*, which is possible—if it is possible—only by drawing upon the substance of a living being; the phantom leaves the very body of the medium. The imitation is perhaps more exhausting than the production of the real phenomenon, just as it is more difficult to compose a poem outside of the state of inspiration. It is possible that professional spiritualists may be exposed to more dangers than those whom they abuse, who are protected by their credulity. Like faith, credulity—as long as nothing comes along to undeceive it—gives power and protection, above all when it is supported by a disinterested feeling. One of Menotti's most intelligent features is to show those who have been duped by Madame Flora holding on to their illusions and not wanting, in spite of her declarations, to recognize to any degree that they have been duped.

The subject of *The Medium*, as you see, is painful and full of risk; its treatment in the form of an opera-film is not less so. It is natural that the work makes many people uncomfortable, as much because of the nervous disorders that it supposes as because of the esthetic derangement that it entails. In short, Menotti is one of the most estimable moderns: he undertakes an "accursed part," as Georges Bataille would say, and even two of them, since he commits the sacrilege of giving over the opera in all its vocal pomp to the Baal of the cinema.

The proposed value remains to be discussed: opera-film. There would be a great deal to say. I shall be satisfied to present a few observations.

We are accustomed, in opera houses, to see conventional and mediocre scenery, singers who are rarely beautiful or expressive—it even happens that the best may have distressing physiques. Often, as much at the opera as at symphony concerts, we shut our eyes so as not to spoil our listening to the music. It would be a contradiction to shut one's eyes in front of a film, and recorded music is more or less denatured. There can be no question then of adapting to the cinema an opera with great or beautiful music; the works of Mozart, or Mussorgsky, or Wagner, or Debussy would not be treated thus. At the performances of such works the best placed spectators are surely those in the gallery, who see as little of them as possible.

Menotti, in being Menotti, does not reveal the highest values, he does not aspire to the sublime. His music, as we have said, is above all an intelligent combination; it is akin to the medley that is the inevitable sauce of the cinema. It seems that the Hollywood composers may be able to try some very interesting things after him. The juxtaposition of speech and music is a more arbitrary convention, upon reflection, than that of singing employed directly. Doubtless someone who is capable, as he is, of undertaking everything, who has a knowledge of voices and instruments that is as well applied to dramatic representation, will not soon be found. In this respect, Menotti's music is model: it underlines the action and blends into it, together with noises it creates masterpieces of collage, it makes marvelous use of the rhythmic power of the gong and the tom-tom.

It seems that the opera-film will not have a great choice of interpreters—unless, like Gershwin, the composers have recourse to blacks, who are always so alive, above all when they sing. It will be difficult to make use of dubbing, which is infinitely more delicate for singers than for instrumentalists.

Well, we shall see. *The Medium* represents an exciting attempt; it is a success that will beget imitation. If what comes in its wake is arguable, we shall at least have the pleasure of arguing.

From *Dernières Gazettes et Ecrits divers*; first published in *Les Lettres Nouvelles* (April 1953).

Liesbet Sanders

Liesbet Sanders—who is going to sing in Paris on the 20th of this month—is the interpreter of songs of international folklore.

I heard her for the first time around three years ago, in the salons of the *Revue Musicale*. She has since given some concerts in Paris and each time the number of her admirers and her friends has grown. When she made her first appearances she was warmly supported by Charles Vildrac, Jules Romains, Luc Durtain.

She has told me that she was attracted by the art of storytellers more than by any other—those Oriental storytellers who sit in marketplaces and hold beneath their words a group of people who have the faces of nurslings who are suckling. The sand of time flows away and the whole sun lies like a cloak upon the shoulders of the storyteller.

Liesbet Sanders precedes each one of her songs with a little story. She tells what she is going to sing: the moving, comic, or fairy-tale adventures of a woman in love, of a sailor and a cook, of the tailors of a town, of three little children, of a poor Jew, everything that peoples folk songs—a Lilliputian crowd—and already, as soon as she begins the story, we are taken by the charm of it, our eyes grow big, our lips part, we become like children.

This admirable artist speaks a precise and ravishing French, and sings besides our own language, in English, German, Yiddish, and Dutch, which is her native language. She is Dutch, of Russian parents, Hasidim. We know, thanks to the book by Jean de Menasce, *Quand Israël aime Dieu [When Israel Loves God]* that Hasidism is a mystical Jewish sect, full of interest for whoever loves not only God, but Man.

When Liesbet Sanders sings her Jewish songs you undergo an intense emotion, you are truly overwhelmed; it comes from so deep that your soul is laid bare.

Her art of singing is incredibly perfect. I do not know how to describe it. It is not popular in the manner of Yvette Guilbert's, no; even while remaining simple and human, it is extremely fine and precious; it is accompanied by a mimicry that is delectable—that is the word. Each one of her songs makes you think of a little figure of gold.

It was the singer herself who collected her songs, traveling in many countries, everywhere attentive to what is sung by children, old women, the artisans of towns, and fishermen on the shore of the sea.

She knows French songs that we do not know.

Everywhere she goes the fairies hasten to meet her and whisper to her the minuscule and immense truths that come and go in the minds of the folk on the wings of song.

From *Dernières Gazettes et Ecrits divers*; first published in *Vendredi* (May 15, 1936).

Maurice Chevalier

In my note on Dranem I had written: "I tenderly love X. Y. Z, and even Chevalier." That *even* gave rise to very different reactions. Some people said to me, "Why *and even Chevalier?* You are very difficult. What better do you need?" Others, among the pure, said to me, "What, you love Chevalier! But he isn't a comic." The argument was serious. I was interrogated.

Obviously, I understand very well what Chevalier can be reproached for. He's a handsome kid, he knows it, he makes use of it—how do you think it could be otherwise? He prefers himself to the business of making people laugh, which is for the dogs. He doesn't consent to the sacrifice. His great idea is to have English chic. He accepts being amusing, but he sets store by remaining distinguished. He likes better to be whimsical than comic. In recent years he has played the part of the nice fellow: one who doesn't worry, who lets himself live, who lets himself love, who gives himself in a friendly way to the comedy of love, but who doesn't want to put a strain on his temperament, oh, no, of course not! Rather the Chéri type, very much attached to his upkeep and preservation, with— and I don't find anything better—the facets of the jovial companion and leader of the fun. He has bet upon his smile, his straw hat, and some attitudes—excellent, besides.

You must see him, when he plays the part of the scamp, go down an imaginary sidewalk with little gliding steps.

He comes onstage like a conceited seahorse.

His head is charming, lit by a perfect smile, by a smile to illustrate the word "smile" in a dictionary.

A romantic, winking eye that suggests suburban flirtations.

A mouth that is deliberately sensual, impudent, but well heightened by drollery.

Good round cheeks of the classic good young man.

A high, intelligent brow. He can be tricked, it happens to everybody, even and above all to the sharpest, but not for long, he straightens up quickly, he gives the steering wheel a good turn.

I saw Chevalier many years ago at the Alhambra. He was wearing a little jacket of the Dranem kind. He worked damned hard. He was excellent. He was the gawky kid of the suburbs who goes around with the gamines, and for whom a number of mature women in small businesses are ready to grant big favors. On occasion he will certainly accept an apple from the fruit seller, but as for the rest, not for me. Between each of the stanzas of his songs he struggled about a lot with his arms, his legs, his torso, in the manner of the eccentric English dancers who were beginning to be popular. In his case, it made you think of somebody running down a hard road after all the phantoms of fortune. He slips, he regains his balance, he stretches out his neck, he gets out of the way, he will catch it, won't catch it, he arrives, he starts off again. It was not yet a question of the impeccable tuxedo.

My brother-in-law had the good fortune to see him when he was fifteen years old (Bécat himself was about the same age) at the Palais du Travail in Belleville. It appears that he was very promising. He had already abandoned the peasant bumpkin's blouse of his first appearances (you know, don't you, that he made his debut in the café-concert when he was twelve years old) and he was wearing the little Dranem jacket in which I saw him in 1912 or 1913.

I remember a very chichi evening performance at the Chatelet. I believe that Chevalier had just returned from his first voyage to America. A short while before he had founded his dispensary for artists. He had reason to believe that it had succeeded. In fact, what had not succeeded? Hadn't he been, during the years that followed the war, the very smile of Paris? Everybody had rushed to rediscover the creator of "Avec le sourire," "Dans la vie faut pas s'en faire," "Je glisse," "Quant on est deux."

How disappointed one had been! Why? Still, he had been nice, talented, gay, a good kid. But there was something wrong. The Chéri side had taken the upper hand. He primped too much.

This impression had stayed with me a bit, and that is what had made me write my *even*. Following the little argument I mentioned at the beginning of the article, I went to the Casino de Paris to judge as a last resort.

I returned enthusiastic. Reading the program I had started a bit when I saw "Our national Maurice Chevalier." Well, I now admit, I ratify that.

The present Chevalier is a mature man with a beautiful sportive air, sparkling with health and good humor. He sings as he has never sung; his craft reaches perfection. Not a sentence, not a word that is not touched with life, swollen with sap. That tension which an artist must have in order to hold his audience, to produce his electricity— he has it without a break, without apparent effort. He makes you laugh with a good laugh that cleans and refreshes. He reveals a wisdom that on its own level touches Montaigne's—a wisdom made up of much observation, numerous reflections, the acceptance of himself and others, amusement in the face of life, which unfolds its spectacle only for the detached and thoughtful man. Equilibrium has been found, therefore the promise of endurance. Chevalier can get older, and that will be like a good wine that ages in the bottle.

Nothing comes by chance anymore, nothing is given, everything is earned by the sweat of his brow—that is literally the truth (you have to see the labor of the comedian, it makes him sweat as much as a harvester in August). No, nothing is given to the artist, whoever he may be—poet, musician, painter, or music-hall singer. Rather it is he that gives himself, in a mystery that is sometimes as terrifying as that of the pelican. Pain of living, of giving life, joy of living.

From *Les Gazettes d'Adrienne Monnier*; first published in *La Nouvelle Revue Française* (January 1936).

Portrait of Jean Gabin

When I think of Jean Gabin a name imposes and superimposes itself upon his own: Sigurd.

At the same time as this name, I see the eyes of Gabin, raised a bit, strangely resolved, as if they were fixing their look far away on a brother star: the polestar like a beautiful idea of death, limit of the journey and of the sacrifice, well-earned repose.

The films of Gabin always seem to me to belong to a kind of saga. Every time he has a fatal "maiden" to rescue, various evildoers to beat or to kill, and at the end he finds liberating death.

Even in *Pépé le Moko*, which at first sight seems far removed from this theme, there is, as a last resort, his departure from his retreat, which is one of his most beautiful, one of his truest moments. He is going to rejoin the woman whom he loves, with the certainty that he will be killed. Do you remember, when he sets out, the cold and joyous light of his look, his superbly easy gait? He consents to death and even aspires to it.

No, for me it is not the workingman's position, in which he is admirable (we shall return to this), that forms the basis of his character; it is the theme of the Germanic or Frankish hero of Scandinavian origin: Siegfried or Sigurd.

There is nothing astonishing about the fact that he seemed to us in his most recent film, *Remorques*, so well cast in the role of the ship captain. It was necessary for him to display his valor, his sense of duty, his need for justice, his incapacity to let a woman's appeal for help go unanswered. He found here an element that is new in the history of his films (*Le Quai des brumes* gave only an indication of it), the element that is profoundly in agreement with his myth: the sea, the North Sea, his far away homeland—a tragically peaceful sea, streaked with high, radiant ice floes like the eyes of Michèle Morgan. And it is perhaps for this reason that the passage about "the star of the sea" is so troubling. Furthermore, Jacques Prévert has marked this instant with the truest seal of poetry.

But how, you will perhaps ask, can this Nordic theme be made to agree with the popular and principally working-class roles which are generally assigned to him, and in which he is without an equal?

I think that they go together very well. The face of Jean Gabin seems to me to be animated by an essentially socialist spirit. Socialism is at one with the genius of the North, that is to say, cold, which brings men together in a group and obliges them to accept a mutual dependence. The genius of the South disperses: when the weather is warm, one likes to be free of certain restraints, for the sun assures creatures of a rather easy self-preservation, they depend little upon one another and try to depend as little as possible. Individualism is natural in southern countries, where the important thing is not to tear out the goods of an impoverished soil together, but to act cleverly in such a way as to acquire the goods of a capricious or prodigal soil before the others.

In fact, Jean Gabin hardly seems possible outside of the socialist idea. And we were keenly aware of this when the popular parties were in power; his face took on then a singular intensity and all the value of a symbol. His central role, founded upon vindication and responsibility, conferred upon him the majesty of a chief. A barbarian chief, a child, like the heros of the *Eddas*, committed to the good and bad luck of primitive people, those who are beginning, who do not yet know very much, who struggle against things that are stronger, that is to say, older, more experienced than themselves.

From the North (I come back to my North) he derives reserve, a horror of idle talk, modesty about his feelings, and a zealous spirit. And all that sometimes makes up the magnificent character of a kind of French worker.

His great role, it seems to me that he found it in *Le Jour se lève*. Here again one must speak of Jacques Prévert and praise him for the exceptional qualities of the dialogue, a dialogue whose realism is admirable, in which the silences are as well handled as the words, where everything is said, and nothing is said more than is necessary. It should be added that the three artists who perform the drama by the side of Gabin are completely up to the mark. Arletty shows her intelligence and her sensibility as in no other role. Jules Berry is incontestably extraordinary as the dog trainer—an old goat. He pits himself against Gabin with a kind of viperish intensity that is hallucinating; besides, it is his venom and his sinuosity that make the drama.

Here Gabin is an ordinary worker, performing a tiring, rather unhealthy job; he is aware of this without revolt. He tells himself that after all his work is paid for and assures him of his bread and butter. He knows that by sleeping well his forces are sufficiently restored, and at the factory he does not fail to drink milk, an antidote for the poison that infiltrates his lungs. He has the wisdom, the good humor, and the good instinct for preservation that are common to most French people. He again shows himself very French in his manner of expressing amorous tenderness—with force and restraint, with that slight raillery that is one of the signs of virile modesty.

Never, I believe, has he given me so much pleasure as in the scene where he meets the little florist for the first time at her place. His face, his voice, and his manner of acting could not be more expressive or more finely shaded—The somewhat heavy muscles of his face, his mouth with their well-joined lips, the subtle rays of his eyes, like the play of light in a mirthful sky—His way of looking at the bed, of lowering his voice so as not to awaken the girl's employers, of joking, of growing curious, urgent, reasonable— Everything is wonderful in this graceful scene.

What a contrast to the face that appears behind the pane starred by gunfire after the murder to which he has been led as inevitably as in an ancient drama. We discover again a tragic Gabin, more tragic than ever, prodigiously static. His features are almost immobile under the assault of his struggling feelings. His look is polar. He fixes death, which he is about to deal to himself, having dealt death to another, with a feeling that is full of courage and justice. (There are people who find the films of Gabin immoral or unhealthy; someday they will have to explain themselves.)

And the final scene, how can one help but think with emotion of the poetic and profound spirit that conceived it? What glory there is above that stretched-out body—The sound of the alarm clock, the smoke of tear gas like a curtain of incense, the day that is breaking, that makes the fragments of shattered glass flare up—The sacrifice has been consummated, the Mass has been said. Beyond the gates of one life lies life like the sea.

From *Les Gazettes d'Adrienne Monnier.*

Jean-Louis Barrault

Four years ago Barrault presented his first production at the Atelier. It was a kind of play, *Autour d'une mère [Around a Mother]*, that he himself had taken from Faulkner's novel *As I Lay Dying*.

Barrault, I knew him well. He frequented my bookshop assiduously and amazed me with his readings. He read as a poet, as a young philosopher. He knew Milarepa—and the *Bhagavad-Gita*, which he took out of his pocket the day I began to talk to him about it. He cherished Thoreau's *Walden*, in which he seemed to find a personal forest full of murmurs and hiding places.

I had also seen him act in several pieces mounted by Dullin—small roles, but done to perfection.

I knew he was poor. I often spoke about him with Madeleine Milhaud, his comrade at the Atelier.

When he confided in me his project of mounting a play at his own expense, with *his* savings (obtained by means of senseless privations), I thought to myself: the poor child.

How would it have been possible to imagine the surprise he was preparing for us? *Autour d'une mère* was a revelation in the full sense of the word.

In a setting of vague, drab hangings, surrounded by supernumeraries, dressed in tawdry old rags, our Barrault burst forth with a natural genius, very much "the poet at seven." He acted in a frenzy. Some of his interpretations had a truly magical force, like the one about the horse, and the one about crossing the river. Almost naked, he succeeded in dancing as well as Shankar, in fact.

At that time I was contributing notes to the *N.R.F.* I wrote to Paulhan asking him to let me speak about Jean-Louis Barrault. Paulhan answered that Antonin Artaud, himself very much carried away also, had rushed to see him the next day in order to propose a report to him. Artaud's article when it appeared satisfied me completely; he was most generous, I could not have done better.

Obviously, those two must have understood each other. Artaud found in Barrault "the pure theatrical language" that he had called for in *Le Théâtre et son double*.

A year later Barrault mounted *Numance*, which he had fished out of the so little-known plays of Cervantes. It was good work and it rated him highly; everybody was saying, "Here is a worthy successor of Copeau, Dullin, Jouvet." For myself, it was not equal to *Autour d'une mère.* It did not have the same great acting.

Since then I have often thought that he should attack *Tête d'or,* at least the Prologue, whose panic humanity and pre-Christian and post-Christian dread he would express like nobody else. Why shouldn't he attempt an interpretation of "Le Bateau ivre" ["The Drunken Boat"]? And "Le Soldat" ["The Soldier"] by Paul Terrace? I have the impression that there is something here for him.

In the meantime, Barrault is acting in many films; there is nothing to regret; he creates his roles in a remarkable fashion, he always finds a means of showing us signs of intelligence in them. And then, one certainly has to live.

The play that he presented to us last May at the Atelier delighted me. We will never forget his Hamlet: it was a great creation. First let us acknowledge that Charles Granval had adapted it with uncommon intelligence and care. From the moment he entered onstage, Barrault was gently prodigious, yes, as in a copperplate engraving. There was not one of his gestures, not one of his intonations, that did not fill you with satisfaction; everything swarmed with subtle flashes.

For myself, Laforgue was living. He spoke to me with the voice and the face of Roger Blin, who impersonated him in the Prologue. I felt full of joy and remorse. Remorse? Yes, here's why:

When I was a student, I of course owned my Laforgue; he was one of my favorite poets. Then had come my acquaintance with the living great, and Laforgue had been piled in the rear to make room for them. When René Lalou's *Histoire de la littérature* appeared, I was so happy to see him do justice to the best contemporaries that I did not hold it against him for having treated Laforgue with disdain. And nevertheless those about me were very dissatisfied. Fargue and Larbaud found that grave, very grave. Ricardo Güiraldes boiled over with indignation; he had measured better than anybody Laforgue's immense influence on South American literature. Larbaud himself knew what that influence was on English poetry, upon T. S. Eliot in particular. I had not been swayed, and so great was their anger that in order to defend Lalou I even lent myself to his reasons.

Thanks to Barrault, Laforgue takes his place again in the first rank, right next to the Gide of *Paludes [Marshlands].*

La Faim, a drama taken by Barrault himself from the novel by

Knut Hamsun, is a magnificent attempt. It has been much criticized. At the first performance I had found also that it was perhaps a bit too long, and that the first act exhausted the intensity. I saw it a second time with increased pleasure and with an interest that did not weaken for an instant.

It is full of astonishing finds. The passage about the bench with the two gentlemen who are shouting at each other in an unintelligible fashion is devilishly funny. As in *Autour d'un mère*, it's great acting. One burns with Barrault. Perhaps one has to be sitting rather close to him (I had discovered already, in the case of Shankar, the importance of not being too far away).

The expressions "sacred fire," "altar of art" recover, for this artist, their original meanings. He officiates; one communes in a mystery that is all the more effective because he does not look for greatness, but the measure of flame and of breath. We live, we feel ourselves living in the heart of an essential drama. The actor is a poet in the immediate. I have often thought of the significance of applause. It might be said that our hands gather time and press it together into a wafer for the Fates, an eternal present—that time which unwinds throughout the length of the work as it takes shape, those hands that meet as in a prayer before things of beauty. Everything must break out into a single burst of flame!

He has a droll little head, that Barrault. I don't see how it can be described. It has a shape that burns the paper just as you try to trace it down. Everything says—spirit, trace of the spirit.

From *Les Gazettes d'Adrienne Monnier*; first published in *La Gazette des Amis des Livres* (July 1939).

The Latest Incarnation of Pierre Fresnay

This latest incarnation of Pierre Fresnay, in *Le Défroqué*, doesn't it seem that it was inevitable, that after having done the *curé* so well he could not escape it? The first time I saw him dressed in the cassock was before the war, in *Le Duel*, a film taken from the play by Lavedan. He played the role of an *abbé* in it, opposite Raimu, who himself was a missionary father; I remember a scene between them that was so moving it brought tears to my eyes; I have forgotten what prompted their dialogue—and the whole story besides. There was also a passage in which Fresnay was supervising boys who were playing in a schoolyard, so much an *abbé* in his gestures and expressions that it seemed astounding to me, almost inconceivable. I was struck in particular by the way the cassock behaved in regard to him, exactly the way it does for a real priest. I often observe the *curés* who pass along the Rue Saint-Sulpice, near my street; it is always with interest and even compassionate tenderness that I look at their long black gown, sister of my gray gown, its manner of stirring about their legs, like waves about a pier, and above all the movement of their heels that regularly raise the lower part of the skirt behind, and form two little waves like those that the sea sends to play at the edge of the beach.

Some years later Fresnay appeared as a pastor in *L'Assassin habite au 21 [The Murderer Lives at Number 21]*, but the role was light, if not comic, and marked a regression in the ecclesiastical sense, something that was all the more curious because the artist is Protestant and is not absolutely detached from his confession, if I am to believe what is said.

It was with *Monsieur Vincent* in 1947 that what Claude Mauriac was not wrong to call a miracle became manifest; there was really, in fact, a kind of miracle, and at the same time a sort of sacrilege. It seems to me that the unbelievers were more sensitive to the sacrilege than the believers—the latter having the illusion that I denounced in a recent gazette: that the film would be edifying and good for the others, more than for themselves. They did not see it so much as they had it seen. Personally, not having the Catholic faith, but being among those who are most sympathetic to the spirit of charity, having also kept a great deal of affection for the religion of my fathers, I was less shocked than I was filled with enthusiasm. A single person among my literary friends shared my admiration— that was Henri Michaux, who, however, does not allow himself to admire very much, who is ordinarily intransigent. We know that he loves the saints, but he could only be more demanding precisely because he does; I consider that his approval is the rarest homage that Fresnay can be proud of. It was Michaux who at that time reported to me that Orson Welles looked upon Fresnay as the greatest French actor—an opinion that the French themselves manifested on the occasion of I do not know what inquiry.

What troubled me most in that reincarnation of Monsieur Vincent was Fresnay's look; I sought to define it and this is what I found: the look of a clothes snatcher who asks you for a handout before tearing off your coat. In fact, there is an infernal glittering in the eyes of the actor, which he often strives to deaden by a play of his eyelids, as one covers a fire, but which only seems all the more disturbing because he does not lower his eyelids, he puckers them; one eye remains wider open than the other and shows its little globe impudently; yes, what he darts toward us is the look of a wizard or a demon.

A demon that it is entirely natural to find there, a demon of the theater—the desire to surpass others, to be admired, to triumph, to provoke a thunder of applause; an energy that is concentrated to the highest heating point, to the point of transmutation.

A demon that it is almost as natural to find among clergymen. It was he that was the first to whisper to Lacordaire, upon his descent from the pulpit, that he had delivered a beautiful sermon, that gave the preacher his "fiery eloquence," his "flaming look"—the look that appears so well in the portrait by Chassériau.

Every time Fresnay looked at us full face it was impossible to think that we had the saint in front of us, or even someone who could pretend to represent him; it was as if we saw a cloven foot sticking out from under the robe. And at the same time the impostor fully deserved to play the saint, and precisely that very saint; he had won the right to, gained the power at the cost of an exemplary labor, through the most noble reflection, through the elevation of his heart, through the patient training of his body, through the total mastery of his art. When the terrible eyes stopped fastening themselves to our own, we were carried away, overcome, always on the verge of tears, when we did not break into them. I am speaking, naturally, for those who gave themselves up to the emotion, and not for the strong-minded.

Nothing made such an impression on me as the scene in the galleys: when Monsieur Vincent, sitting next to the officers, suddenly sees one of the convicts collapse upon his bench, when he leaves his seat, passes along the gangway, goes to take the place of the man who has fallen, and himself begins to maneuver the heavy oar, his whole poor body stretching out like a hymn. It is here, it seems to me, that the genius of the actor best approaches the vigorous charity of the saint and brings us to closest communion. I very much liked also the passage in which he washes the rags of the sick; furthermore, he is admirable every time he is in motion. His arrival at the beginning in the frightful Châtillon is comparable to the first bars of a symphony; as soon as we see him move bravely forward, as soon as we hear his excellent voice that the accent of the Landes imbues to such good effect—it is as husky as new wine, as freshly drawn milk—we are won over, ready to follow him wherever he will lead us.

Certainly, I was among those who went along, and yet at the bottom of my adherence I rediscovered the infernal eye that tormented me all the more because this "good" film had I shall not say made me Christian, but had made me sensitive in a Christian way. The believers were much obliged to pass over that and even to declare they were satisfied by it—like someone who has a daughter to marry off and who tries to make what is a defect pass for a virtue —but the unbelievers are more fastidious. It occurred to me that the Church, which is now all indulgence, which celebrates a special Mass for actors who have died during the year, that this very Church in former times used to condemn theater people and refuse them the sacraments. I had the curiosity to look up Bossuet's opinion; I read the *Lettre sur la comédie [Letter on the Theater]* addressed to Father Caffaro and the *Maximes et réflexions sur le théâtre [Maxims and Reflections on the Theater]*. The Church, he says,

> condemns actors and thereby presumes to prohibit the theater: its decision is taken up in the rituals, its practice is constant; those who act in the theater, if they do not renounce their art, are deprived of the sacraments, both in life and death; they are passed by at the Communion table as public sinners; they are excluded from holy orders as infamous persons; as an unfailing consequence, ecclesiastical burial is denied them.

Elsewhere he appeals to Plato:

> The very Art that trained an actor to create so many different characters appeared to him to introduce into human life a quality of frivolity that was unworthy of a man and directly opposed to the simplicity of his morals.

Here, no doubt, it was above all a question of actors who put their art at the service of profane works, but Bossuet in no place makes an exception for the benefit of those who, for example, incarnated the characters of the Passion, as they did in the Middle Ages. If he had allowed that instance, no doubt he would have specified that the "miracle" or "mystery" could be produced only in certain circumstances, in consecrated places, and not in the setting of a theater where temptations naturally arise—what would he have said about cinemas, in which the obscurity favors the most pernicious one of all? It is by laying stress on the authority of the Fathers that he blames the theaters:

> They [the Fathers] blame in games and theaters the uselessness, the prodigious dissipation, the disturbance, the commotion of the spirit that is hardly suitable for a Christian, whose heart is a sanctuary of peace; they blame in it excited passions, vanity, adornment, the great embellishments that they put in the rank of the displays that we abjured through baptism, the desire to see and be seen, the unhappy encounter of eyes that look for other eyes, the too great occupation with vain things, the bursts of laughter that cause to be forgotten both the presence of God and the account that must be made to Him of one's slightest actions and of one's slightest words; and finally the whole seriousness of Christian life.

(The sentence: "the unhappy encounter of eyes that look for other eyes" gives me such pleasure that I really believe it was in order to quote it that I brought in all the rest.)

I shall not Bossuetize any longer, but I must say, yielding to his voice, the Fathers' and above all Plato's, that I found it distressing, almost scandalous, that Pierre Fresnay, after having been Monsieur Vincent, could take up common roles again. No doubt it was good that he returned to his place, Christian humility in person commanded him to do so; it would have been ridiculous if he forever took himself for a saint and did not want to come down from that height. He was an actor after all! My feeling, when I think it over, seems idiotic to me, but it is there. I will be told that there are numerous actors who have played saints, male and female, the Virgin Mary, Christ and His apostles, and that we feel no need to forbid them profane roles afterward. That is because, most of the time, it is never anything but theatrical, they do not emerge from their condition as actors, we have in regard to them the indulgence we have for children who want to play at being grown-ups, all the more indulgence because they do not attain their object, because they make us aware of the distance that exists between them and their models—their art, in a certain sense, is intended to make this distance evident. It is when "reality" appears that we change our manner of seeing. The greater the reality, the more we are inclined to react as we would in life, that is to say, with an instinct of defense that is infinitely more active than the one that is exercised in the presence of works of art. When Pygmalion's statue comes to life and turns into a woman we treat it as a woman. It is Pierre Fresnay's perfection that gives rise to our demand, it is his truthfulness that makes us scrupulous; to the degree that he appears to be a saint, we consider him as a saint and we do not accept the possibility of a lapse. We suffer, then, in *Monsieur Vincent*, as we see his actor's eye gleaming, and we suffer afterward, when he plays other roles, as we see that same eye, not redeemed on these occasions by the superabundant merits of which he gives proof in order to reach at one and the same time the summit of his art and a summit of morality.

He must have told himself all that, bitterly perhaps. His theatrical and motion-picture career, beginning with *Monsieur Vincent*, shows a zigzag between that order of thought and the reasonable desire to go beyond. We see him in roles that have nothing edifying about them, whose oddities and frivolity he heightens as he pleases: the publisher in *Vient de paraître*; M. Barjas in *Les Oeufs de l'autruche [The Ostrich Eggs]*; and finally Offenbach, the father of the cancan, whom he has speak with a discreet German Jewish accent that is surprisingly successful. We understand that Fresnay was seduced by the role of this man, who had "the nature of a bird," a spirit that was "lucid and mocking," whose look, like his own, was so sparkling and so strange that some of his contemporaries detected black magic in it; our friend Kracauer, his excellent biographer, on the contrary sees in it "white magic, that which disperses phantoms and allows one to contemplate the image of a better human homeland."

As the Gulf Stream flows across the high seas, so in the midst of these eddies of Parisian life there passes a current of virtuous characters who are more or less priestlike: the rector of the Île de Sein; the entomologist Fabre; a great master of surgery; Dr. Schweitzer—among these the Breton rector was the only one who gave us any pleasure at all; the story, which was taken from the novel by Henri Queffélec and adapted as a motion picture under the title *Dieu a besoin des hommes [God Needs Men]*, somewhat recalls *Cromedeyre-le-vieil* by Jules Romains. If I remember correctly, it has to do with a sexton who is forced to play the part of a *curé* by the common agreement of his island. Fresnay and Madeleine Robinson, who acted with him, were admirable in it because of their emotion and successful picturesqueness. Yes, it was an excellent film, not at all banal; the others left us unsatisfied, above all those that were inspired by the lives of Fabre and Schweitzer; the latter, in spite of the exploits of the interpreter, was frankly unacceptable;

it is always dangerous to bring to the stage or screen human beings who are still living or too close to us, unless the intention is to make caricatures of them—when it is not funny it is painful. After these scholastic labors Fresnay must have felt the need to take a vacation; he was happy, there can be no doubt about it, to go back to the fold of the Michodière and play the carefree hero of *Le Moulin de la Galette* opposite Yvonne Printemps, who on this occasion found one of her best roles.

Before coming to *Le Défroqué*, which is so important in Fresnay's career, let us stop a little at *La Route Napoléon*, whose subject, like that of *Dieu a besoin des hommes*, seems to have been inspired by Jules Romains: this time by *Donogoo-Tonka*—unsuccessfully, alas!

Let us note, in passing, that the great writer and the great actor have some common traits; their latest photographs even heighten an indefinable physical resemblance, when they are caught at a three-quarters angle or in profile, with their eyes lowered, for their look is not at all similar. You see on their faces nuances that are very close to an affable condescension, to a will that is strong but not devoid of good nature—of that good nature which makes them say to others: "You, my good man . . ." Nevertheless, if Romains, in his *Hommes de bonne volonté [Men of Good Will]*, has put eighteen clergymen onstage (it seems to me that this is the right number, according to the index)—the Abbé Jeanne being his Monsieur Vincent—he has not had to don their cassock, and so he has not been shown cutting the figure of a defrocked priest.

To come back to *La Route Napoléon*, let us say that the film is ambitious, clever, but disagreeable from one end to the other. Under the cover of a satire directed against improper advertising (it is proven at the same time that it is creative), Fresnay denigrates himself in it, himself and his station, in a manner that has something furious about it; he plays the entertainer, but we are too much aware of a real bitterness; his roundness is that of a porcupine. Perhaps that phase was necessary to bring him to the great creation of *Le Défroqué*, a creation that is not and cannot be a success, in the sense in which the word is generally understood. Truly, there is nothing more shocking, more cruel than this film. One wonders to what public such a work can be addressed—to the priests, no doubt, to make them see how frightful it is to lay aside the religious habit once it has been put on. The afternoon when I was at the Madeleine, there were several young *abbés* in the house, and women, a great many women, not young, who had come in couples to exchange their impressions; most of them were scandalized. One of them said as she was leaving: "When they want to show a film like that, they should give a warning!"

Some years ago I had a conversation with a priest of liberal mind; at that time the students of the Sorbonne were manifesting I no longer know what discontent; Sartre and Camus were then at the most brilliant point of their fame and their influence—Sartre, I believe, had just published his *Age de Raison [The Age of Reason]* and Camus was on the verge of publishing *La Peste [The Plague]*. We remarked that youth was difficult to handle, intractable even; Father M. said: "In order to be heard by them, one would have to have the voice of Sartre or Camus; it is only by taking on their manner that one would be able to bring them to reason."

Le Défroqué, filmed with the help of a religious adviser—an authentic priest—has almost nothing to envy Sartre for the acrimony of the tone and the audacity of the situations; lovers of strong emotions will find that it is their meat; yes, of course, but as it is devoid of eroticism, it does not at all produce the same effect. With Sartre, the gore, the vomit, go together with sex, they reinforce it, provoke it; they give the reader or the spectator "a funny tickle in the small of the back," as it is said in *Les Mouches [The Flies]*. This tickle is totally absent from the film that Léo Joannon has taken from the novel by Hervé le Boterf—I have seen the book in the windows of the bookshops of the Rue Saint-Sulpice, I have not read it. The film, in any case, is very intelligent, solidly constructed; it is exciting for a brain-worker, for an amateur of moral questions, for someone, above all, who takes delight in the problems of religion and the priesthood. Personally, it strongly interested and moved me. I cannot sufficiently admire Pierre Fresnay, who has lived the passion of Maurice Morand, the defrocked priest, with so much perception and pathos.

It seems that while composing his character he thought of Abbé Loisy, who was a professor of the history of religions at the Collège de France (the hero of the film teaches at the Sorbonne). Paul-Louis Couchoud gives a portrait of him in his book *Le Dieu Jesus [The God Jesus]*; he shows him undertaking the dissection of an evangelical text "with the gestures of an officiating priest but with a sharp smile that did not leave his thin lips, and a perpetual sparkling of his little eyes . . . ; he had a playful, almost ferocious manner of entering upon the subject." Further on Couchoud says: "Loisy did not open his heart. He was sealed, stiff, always kept his game secret, trusted nobody. . . . He discouraged friendship. His thin smile quickly became grating. . . . He had the somber pride of the recluse, whom one wounds whatever one does." Wouldn't you believe, reading these lines, that you saw Fresnay's face in this role —which he played to the life, without making up at all, while keeping his eyes wide open this time, so as, it would seem, to let the demon come out at its pleasure. His voice is perfect, that voice "upon which he practices a kind of restraint by imposing upon it a curious shift of direction through the nasal cavities," as Albert Dubeux says rightly in the study that he has devoted to him; for the occasion he has slightly accentuated the nasality of it in such a way as to mark positively the aggressiveness of his character. Couchoud also says that Abbé Loisy was "innocently malicious, candidly rancorous," he had "a certain sharpness of character and a secret venom gland." Here Fresnay differs from the man who has perhaps served him as a model; Maurice Morand is frank, with a violence that is contained up to the moment when it savagely explodes; he strikes his mother's confessor with all his might; in a transport of furious madness he strangles his friend Gérard, the young *abbé* who wants to bring him back to the Church (Pierre Trabaud acts like an angel). This atrocious scene closes the film; it is while clasping the dying body of his friend, whose mouth vomits blood, that the defrocked priest rediscovers his belief; he then puts on the cassock of the man whom he has killed; he takes the corpse in his arms the way one carries a child; he surrenders to the policemen who have come by and declares to them: "I am a Catholic priest." Nothing more overwhelming can be imagined. I am not sure, however, that such a denouement attains its object—supposing that this object is to be edifying. Finally, Fresnay really had to find, in this cruel consummation of his ecclesiastical career, an occasion to act with an open look and to put to use his "strangler's hands."

It's curious, the first time I observed his hands I was struck by their resemblance to those of the higher apes: accustomed to prehensile gestures, showing uncouth fingers, elementary nails, quadrumanous thumbs. (Let us not forget that in ancient Egypt the ape represented Thoth, the god of the arts and sciences.) I leaned toward Sylvia, who was sitting next to me, and told her my observation; she answered me: "That's what we call the histrionic hand."

From *Dernières Gazettes et Ecrits divers*; first published in *Les Lettres Nouvelles* (May 1954).

Concerning Michel Simon

There is no ugliness among men, that is to say, among the portion of humanity that is male and not female.

Everything that makes for ugliness in a woman—disproportions of features or forms, marks of age or care, unevenness of the skin—counts for little in evaluating the figure of a man. A man is often noble because of what deforms him; he is heroic to the degree that he accepts the deformation and, better, looks for it. The essential nobility of a woman is to remain, in spite of everything, sleek, uniform—to remake herself without end. "Forever virgin mothers . . ."

What is demanded of a man first of all?—power, health, or what resembles them, the good humor that is the sign of them. He has no need of correcting his body in order to be loved, but we like correctness in his clothes, proof of his good social condition and of his moral conformity, which has been obtained with great difficulty, like the sleekness of women. The impeccable crease in his trousers, that is what corresponds mysteriously to the pure line of an eyebrow.

An ugly man is always a weakling or an invalid, and even in that case he is less ugly than he is ridiculous or pitiable. What really makes the ugliness of a man is the feeling that he has of being ugly and his manner of suffering from it. Satisfaction with oneself sets almost everything to rights, when there is not too much to be set to rights. An ugly man who uses his ugliness to advantage has something about him that tickles one and raises an appetite, like the smell of cheese.

These reflections came to me concerning Michel Simon, whom I have just seen as Jo and seen again as Clo-Clo. His two best roles perhaps, two roles in which he is truly gay, and because of that irresistible.

If ugliness existed among men (but we have just proved that it does not exist), Michel Simon could be considered as a model of ugliness. Few faces are as inordinate as his own. His cheeks and his chin heave ponderously like molten lava; his short thick tongue butts up against the crooked paling of his teeth; his nose collapses timidly behind a menacing mustache.

A face that is at once violent and infantile, like a big mumbling bud. A pirate of the nursery. A character out of Shakespeare. The face of a primitive god—the very face of Bes, whom the Egyptians honored as the god of laughter and of childhood.

But what astonishes me most about Michel Simon is that his voice and his gestures are so much in agreement with his physiognomy. He finds the means, this strange-natured man, of being natural, that is to say, in harmony with others and with himself. It is the accomplishment of a very good actor, of an actor who shows a zeal that is equal to his gifts; he is more than a comic—who thinks too much about others; better than an artist—who thinks too much about himself. His acting swarms with sweetnesses—something like the earth from which light mists escape—an immense effort that finds grace.

I do not know what Michel Simon thinks of himself. Let him say to himself, in any case, that a face, that an art like his own are as precious, are as necessary to the City as the beauty of beautiful women. And of the same order.

From *Les Gazettes d'Adrienne Monnier*; first published in *La Nouvelle Revue Française* (March 1937).

Fernandel

I saw Fernandel for the first time, like all Parisians, in *Le Rosier de Mme Husson [The Rosebush of Mme Husson]*. Before seeing the whole film I had had a glimpse of him in some scenes that accompanied the advertisement of the preceding week. The final scene had already shown him descending the staircase of a bordello, singing: "Now I know what it is." That immediately had been a revelation. What a mug—a bit homely, it must be said, what hilarious power, what charm! The charm of a big domestic animal, one that is good and submissive, but whose thought, or what takes the place of it, remains as free as Caliban's. A creature who is deliciously empty of understanding and deliciously full of a secret understanding with the whole of things. A way of having it known, when his person is wronged, that God is listening and will perhaps do what is necessary. Think a bit of his manner of saying, in *Les Gaîtés de l'escadron [The Gaieties of the Squadron]*: "It'll be all right," when calamities have happened and are going to happen. That "It'll be all right"—meditative, resigned, and rebellious at the same time—

did not count for nothing. It was the only living and authentic thing in the whole film.

To come back to our Rosier, I would like to say a word or two about his way of descending the staircase of the place already named. He descended it with a certain ritual, a bit like the people for whom staircases count professionally and who draw dignity from them: the concierge of a great house, pages who are past childhood, restaurant waiters who serve on the second floor—with a free and easy, potential air, his feet not descending but treading on the steps, his shoulders speaking, his torso well set upon his hips. And in his look, what dazzling, pop-eyed satisfaction; he knew what it was, for sure!

The second time I saw Fernandel was in song numbers at the Bobino. My admiration increased even more. It was not without surprise that I saw him come onstage in the classic infantry outfit: scarlet pants, epaulettes, and kepi; his head almost unrecognizable; a mouth and a chin that were almost normal, little eyes blinking behind the red cheekbones of a clodhopper. In short, the type who is fatheaded and weasel-eyed at the same time, of which every self-respecting barracks has at least one specimen. A repertory that was no less classic, going back to Polin, not going beyond Bach, with a monologue of the most stereotyped kind: "He has it soft." But with a striking subtlety and perfection. The slightest words, the slightest feelings, re-created, diminished, or strengthened according to an impeccable esthetic. Vulgarity caught at its source—life. Infrared life, in which each thing, even and above all the most lost among trillions, bursts out with zest, irradiates, swaggers, twirls about in its own circle, its very own, like a star.

It was with those song numbers that Fernandel had won over Marseilles before being the Rosier. To some who asked him why he adopted a genre that was so out-of-date he answered, I believe, with Valérian reasons: the liking for a tradition, for a discipline, the feeling that nothing should be changed, or almost nothing, the better to be able to remake everything. I am afraid that they may have succeeded in discouraging him.

What more is there to say about this Fernandel? Now glory has come to him, the glory of the capital. He has performed at the side of Mistinguett. A military farce without him can no longer be imagined. In *Angèle*, for all that its roles are brilliantly played, he makes a star attraction out of Saturnin, whom another would have left in the middle distance or even in the background—he "steals" the film, as they would say in America. The public expands with enjoyment when he appears on the screen. It is not worth the trouble composing a text for him; like all the really great comic actors he makes you laugh with trifles. He is irresistible. He is a nature rather than a type, "a rich nature," like Dranem; less farcical and inventive, but more direct and intense. He is moving. Yes, he moves, even while remaining comic. He is human, a bit in the manner of dogs, through his aspiration toward the human (he has a way of speaking words as if he were sucking on them); when I say that, it is not to belittle him, on the contrary; if he were human like men he would be neither funny nor kind.

From *Les Gazettes d'Adrienne Monnier*; first published in *La Nouvelle Revue Française* (February 1935).

Laughter and Women

Women laugh easily, but they hardly know how to provoke laughter, except through the communicative warmth of their own. They quickly grasp the funniness of things, but they do not have much capacity for calling it into existence—if not involuntarily— and giving it a form; nothing is less feminine than vaudeville and farce. That is because comic works are above all products of the intelligence, and the feminine intelligence, as everybody knows, is infinitely more understanding than it is creative.

The heart is a stranger to comedy. Bergson brought that out very well; laughter is ordinarily accompanied by a lack of sensibility. Swift said: "Life is a comedy for one who thinks and a tragedy for one who feels." That does not mean that women basically have a greater sensibility than men; the very fact that they laugh more easily than men sufficiently proves that they do not, but nature obliges them to live through their hearts above all, that is to say, through that part of the intelligence that is closely bound to the body. It should furthermore be noted that those of the feminine sex who laugh are most often little girls, girls, and women who are still young. A woman who is old, or who feels herself growing old, almost never laughs; if she does happen to laugh, it is at herself, somewhat bitterly; in the course of life the mood of the heart has little by little absorbed the strength of the intelligence; everything that has befallen her, even what she has thought, has become transformed, often in spite of herself, into feelings, that is to say, into things that have their roots in her flesh.

Yes, a woman is terribly bound to matter. Nothing is more difficult for her than to see the world with detachment, an essential condition for comedy. She experiences a kind of internal responsibility with regard to every creature, a responsibility that completely commands her being when her children are concerned. It has been said, and nothing is more true, that her real task is to give life and to preserve it. In this respect particularly, she is as far removed as possible from comic works, which are always critical, negative, destructive. Laughter is invigorating because it cleanses, relaxes, corrects; but in its strong states it is akin to bursting apart, to explosion. It is irreconcilable with beauty, which is conformity with the outlooks of the spirit and the promise of every act of generation. Laughter produces, at least momentarily, grimaces and contortions that are deformities; it is provoked by them and it provokes them. For these reasons a woman is physically less laughable than a man, and her manner of laughing is more noisy than it is facially expressive. It is such an obligation for her to be beautiful, to respond through her body and through her face to the requirements of her soul that her ugliness afflicts more than it amuses. Her dress, her character will be ridiculed, hardly ever her physical appearance. An ugly woman must have a very mean streak or a very joyful manner for one to be able to laugh at her wholeheartedly. While one laughs readily at an ugly man, above all if he is weak and good, and often his sadness only makes him more ridiculous.

There are few women indeed who are expert in the art of provoking laughter. There are no women caricaturists, no women clowns. There are many good comediennes; they are easily playful, they are sometimes funny, but very rarely are they side-splitting. At café-concerts, where comedy must be exaggerated, women excel above all in romantic and dramatic songs; on the stage of a theater they can be carried along by the whole production, but in song numbers, where one appears alone, their incapacity for provoking laughter is clearly revealed.

From *Les Gazettes d'Adrienne Monnier*; first published in *Vendredi* (1936).

A King of Humor: Alec Guinness

Alec Guinness deserves the title of "King of Humor"; he answers truly to the general idea that one has of humor, which would have no meaning if there were not equally a very particular incarnation of it. For though one can be English, or Italian, or Chinese without personal character, with only the distinctive traits of one's race or of one's country, one can belong to the country of humor only if one is a clear-cut, and even a very clear-cut, individual. It is because one is an individual and because one is conscious of what distinguishes oneself, of what opposes oneself to others, that one manifests humor.

Humor is the contrary of the comic as it is current among us French; it is eccentric while our comic spirit is concentric. These two states are hostile to each other but they are never at war, and an incalculable number of exchanges and mixtures takes place between them. Both of them are intelligent forms of vital elasticity. The first acts in favor of the individual, it liberates him, it relaxes him in the midst of a rigorous society; the second is practiced to the profit of a tolerant society against someone who goes too far, it brings him back to the mean. Laughter, above all loud laughter, polices; the "individual" is always more or less a delinquent in its eyes, it intervenes to reestablish what it believes to be order. Humor introduces disorder, a disorder that is as regulated as punches in boxing. The supreme rule is impassivity—phlegm—in inverse proportion to the inner racket.

One easily understands why humor is distinguished and why the comic spirit is vulgar. It is out of the question, here and elsewhere, for people of a certain level to laugh or make others laugh at the top of their voices; we keep to irony, which is a well-bred or studied amusement; we joke, we banter, we make clever remarks—that's wit! We never laugh loudly but we sometimes pretend to laugh loudly, like actors. Irony resembles humor superficially, it hardly goes beyond smiling (very often humor does not even smile), but the basis of it is different; it is the comic spirit refined.

Humor is in fashion at present; here there is an influence from across the Channel, like romanticism, which came from that direction and from Germany. Now it is antiromanticism that has disembarked. Fundamentally romantic temperaments, that is to say those that like to set themselves tragically against society, have invented black humor—which is certainly their right.

Before putting an end to these hasty reflections, I shall add this in favor of our comic spirit, as much for the coarse as for the subtle kind: that it goes together with equilibrium and taste. Humor, we have said, is eccentric, it tends toward the arbitrary, it judges and does not allow itself to be judged; but though it can help the individual to put up with life and have the advantage in many ways, it does not, taken in its pure state, give him what he needs in order to be in harmony with those whom a cheerful person willingly calls his fellow men.

Alec Guinness brings us an extremely droll and charming form of humor. I do not know who, at the moment, can entertain us better than he. Like Charlie he represents a type of eccentric common man, but while Charlie is a royal tramp from the bottom of society, Alec Guinness is an inspired little man from nowhere at all, an employee, a nondescript penpusher (I use the terms *royal* and *inspired* in regard to the types that they play and not in regard to their talent, for it is obvious that Charlie is inspired to the bursting point). There is a story by Joyce, included in *Dubliners*, which makes me think a bit of Alec Guinness. It's "A Little Cloud," the hero of which is a modest clerk who dreams of becoming somebody by writing poetry. Maybe someday the actor will show us the comedy of a man who wants to reign by means of words, but in his roles up to now he looks for tangible goods that are endowed with a total and immediate power: wealth, a great invention, everything that can make a considerable person of you, what is called "a lord of the earth." He has asserted himself in this direction in the three most recent films that we have seen here: *The Lavender Hill Mob*, *The Man in the White Suit*, and *The Card*. He achieves success only in the third, in which his aims are a bit more reasonable. In the other two he inevitably fails, his ambition and his undertakings being too extravagant by far. But it should be noted that even in defeat he is not defeated. At the end of *The Lavender Hill Mob*, handcuffs on his hands, he exults for having fulfilled himself in a singularly daring robbery, for having left the humdrum existence in which he was vegetating, and for having been a Farouk for a while even so. In *The Man in the White Suit* he does not remain crushed for long by public derision; after so many misadventures that should have taught him a lesson, he proudly sets out again toward new feats with the music of his demon within him and before him.

For he has a demon. An ingenuous demon who contrary to Socrates' does not check him in action, but pushes him into it and holds him to it. Before the vainglorious or dramatic events that he sets in motion, he effaces himself with an incandescent modesty, his look proclaiming: "It isn't I, it's he!"

There is something ineffable in the face of Alec Guinness—this good young man inhabited by Puck in person. Puck, who at times fixes us with his sparkling eyes, which look out of a face that is gentle and a bit soft, like morning mists.

I have pronounced the name of Puck—is this name not among those that stand for the god of humor? Kipling says that he is the most ancient of the ancient inhabitants of England, the only one who is left of the local gods, but in my opinion he deforms him by reducing him to the role of a hardly mischievous historian (see *Puck of Pook's Hill* and *The Return of Puck*), for if Puck can be treated in a joking fashion as someone who touches History to the extent that it is influenced by Literature, it is not for him personally to narrate the noble deeds of heroes, even if they are more or less mythical.

Puck is spirit, inspiration, fantasy—he troubles brains; he makes sport of louts, ninnies, and sleepers; he brings a thousand disorders, which shake the individual and oblige him to act and react. He is an agent of energy, hence of conquest: of himself and others.

It was in *Kind Hearts and Coronets* that the name of Alec Guinness appeared to us for the first time in all its brilliance. His power of transformation in it was such that I did not perceive (and it was the same in the case of many people) that he was playing the ten roles of the Acoyne d'Ascoyne family all by himself; when I read the poster after I went out I did not believe my eyes. Every one of the members—the old banker, the clergyman, the admiral, the general, the duke, etc.—were revealed in caricature with such perfect and particular truth that it was impossible to think that only one person could play so many types, all deeply marked by their profession or their condition, with only a slight resemblance such as one sees in families among them. If the admiral and the general were the most exaggerated and consequently the most frankly comic, the banker and the clergyman remained human; they were very finely drawn, above all the banker, with strokes that were rather touching and so all the more droll. As for Lady Agatha—we should have loved to see more of her. Simply her way of walking like a determined feminist set you to rejoicing. An actor like that—he's a devil!

Before *Kind Hearts and Coronets* we had had glimpses of Alec

Guinness that should have given us cause to reflect. In *Oliver Twist* he played the role of Fagin and in *Great Expectations* the role of Herbert Pocket. In the first case he portrayed an abominable old scoundrel, in the second a very young man who, according to Dickens, gives the impression with each of his looks and with each of his intonations that he is naturally incapable of doing anything whatever that is devious or mean. What kept us from noticing him as he deserved in these two so completely opposite roles was first of all that they were episodic, and also that he embraced the spirit of Dickens so much that it was to the novelist that he forced us to pay homage.

His latest film, *The Card*, had less success with us than the preceding, it seems. The public laughed at it heartily—myself first of all—but the critics were hard to please. As for the story, it is doubtless less original in its invention and it has a rather local interest, but it abounds in entertaining episodes, and Alec Guinness is exquisite in it. His friskiness at the end of his waltz with the countess (whom he had the cheek to invite to dance with him after having had the cheek to invite himself to the ball, himself, his tailor, and two girlfriends) is a magnificent bit of fun.

I had the curiosity, after having seen the film, to refer to its namesake, the novel by Arnold Bennett that inspired it. I could not believe that the novel was so cynical and that it could, in this respect, develop completely to the glorification of an impudent and fraudulent young man, even if he had the decent look of Alec Guinness. I told myself that there was a moral laxity about it that does not go with the idea that we have of England: the adapters must have forced things in a direction that is—modern. Must we see in this film a new attitude that corresponds to the crisis that the English are undergoing, and that would be like an encouragement to the go-getters, an unctuous allusion to the virtues of the ancient Normans, who were skillful in disembarking far away from their homes and in making themselves the masters of the property of others?—Well, no, the film has not falsified the intentions of the novelist in any way at all. He gave all his sympathy to Denry Machin, he even made him one of the typical characters of the Five Towns. An invented province, the Five Towns correspond to five real towns in Staffordshire, which are the most important centers in England and in the whole world for the manufacture of pottery. These are the Five Towns without the help of which you cannot pour tea into a cup or eat with decency, as it is said in *The Old*

Wives' Tale. Arnold Bennett had the freedom of judgment of an honest man; he was not a hypocrite, and he was well acquainted with the ways of the world. Moreover, his hero always shows himself to be scrupulous even in his unscrupulousness; he is never really dishonest; he behaves like a good citizen in that he gives his town an extensive commercial growth. From the moment when, thanks to him, it becomes a brilliant sports center, he perfectly deserves to be its mayor. There is, it seems, a sequel to this story: in *The Regent* one sees how the fortunate and impudent Denry conquers London after the Five Towns. Perhaps it might be possible to show us this sequel. We ask nothing better than to applaud the total triumph of a character who, on top of all his good luck, has the good luck to be interpreted by a great actor like Alec Guinness.

From *Dernières Gazettes et Ecrits divers*; first published in *Les Lettres Nouvelles* (August 1953).

With Vittorio de Sica

Leaving my reflections on ancient Mexico, my spirit heavy from its bloody rites and its black sun, I took a vacation with Vittorio de Sica, a man of Italy. It is not that he is the herald of a sun that is forever bright and that he does not carry in himself a source of melancholy moods that are quick to become our own, but right at this moment he is showing his most cheerful humor, the most likely to entertain us, in three films.

It was *Shoeshine*, it seems to me, in 1948, that acquainted us with the name of Vittorio de Sica. He appeared to us then as the director of a new, an overwhelming film, so lyrical that it has remained in our memory not as something that belongs to the cinema, but as a work endowed with the power of music. While in the theater or on the screen it is the actor who imposes both his power and his limitations at the same time, in *Shoeshine* there was the freedom of life itself, a freedom that appeared in a pure state in the eyes and the bearing of a young boy, in the spirited body of a horse. The great prison full of ardent and silent kids made you think of a book by Jean Genet; it was the ideal illustration of it at an earlier stage, when the rose, as the song says, is still on the rosebush and when even the rosebush has yet to be planted.

The Bicycle Thief, which we saw a year later, increased our admiration for Vittorio de Sica and brought him the fame that he deserved. It was then that we took into account his manner of working, which consisted essentially of having the roles in his films played by people picked up in the street, who had been long sought for and observed. The new work did not have the singular beauty of *Shoeshine*, but it was no less original, with a bitter realism, even while remaining poetic and amusing in the manner of an epic novel in which the adventure of one man unites with the greater history of the world—like *Dead Souls*, which Gogol called not a novel but a poem.

Thinking of Gogol, I wonder if he has not more or less influenced this film and others of the same school, thus giving back to Italy what she had given him; we know that he lived there almost entirely for five years and that he wrote there a good part of *Dead Souls*; Dante, whom he read with passion at that time, renewed his inspiration and communicated his fire to him. He loved Rome above all: "It is only in Rome," he used to say, "that one finds happiness and joy." The movement of the Eternal City helped him to manage his action, to combine its episodes, which are like the intensely living streets that are cut up by solemn ruins and crowned with basilicas. There is no doubt that the gay genius that courses through *Dead Souls* owes a part of its power and accomplishment to Italy. From his first works Gogol had shown a propensity to satire and buffoonery; he used to laugh, he said so himself, without rhyme or reason, but he dropped that jesting tone only to become exasperated and full of pain. It was Italian humor that allowed him to have access to that high comedy which results from the comprehension of life. Tchitchikov was a thief, just as much as the kids in *Shoeshine* and the poor bicycle thief who steals after having been stolen from; he was even a great thief, although his manner was subtle. Writing that I suddenly see the relationship that can exist between stealing and flying away; the quickness to desire and to seize is not without a resemblance to the wings of birds—besides, don't we say that a thief "takes off"?

In *Miracle in Milan*, which takes place among the poverty-stricken, that is to say, those who can possess what they covet only by dreaming about it or by stealing it, we see toward the end, when things take a turn for the worst, the poor buggers straddle broomsticks like those of witches' sabbaths and quit the earth in order to go to the country where it is Sunday every day. Beyond the cathedral, they trail through the sky like a flight in a drawing by Meryon—extraordinary vision! There was really a miracle there— a miracle of direction.

Certainly, after *Miracle in Milan* the name of Vittorio de Sica was at its zenith for us. Only Charlie before him had shown us films as poetic, as human; but Charlie's films displayed the genius of a single man who imposes his figure upon us in a Christlike fashion, if I may say so, while, with the Italian, the genius of the earth is summoned to appear through all men and all their actions; there is a magical realism in his films—nothing to do with surrealism, which leaps above the real and seizes hold of its coarsest effects at the least expense. For Vittorio de Sica the transformation starts from a patiently observed reality. He takes the trouble to think about creation before creating in his turn.

To our praise for Vittorio de Sica it is right to add our praise for Cesare Zavattini—the author of all those scenarios directed by him and by others, like Blasetti, Mattioli, Castellani. It is to Zavattini that we owe in particular the theme of *Four Steps in the Clouds* and *Primavera*, which pleased us so much. He should be known. Nino Frank devoted a report to him in the *Mercure de France*, in which he gives the broad outlines of his biography, shows his importance in Italian literature, and above all throws into relief his strong influence on the young film makers down there. Jean Quéval, the excellent film critic of the same review, never fails for his part to pay him the homages that are his due. Thanks to them, I know who Zavattini is. Jean Quéval relates him to our Prévert and underlines the Franciscan nature of his inspiration; from his book for children, *Toto il buono [Toto the Good]*, comes the Toto of *Miracle in Milan*, "who proves to himself the goodness of the world through the practice of his own kindness." Under the title of *Un Certain Bat*, Nino Frank translated the most characteristic fragments of his works: *I Poveri sono matti [The Poor Are Mad]*. I have read these fragments; they show an art of intense modernism that one is tempted to call futurist. Facts and feelings appear in them as in the state of gestures, of movements, without ever taking on a solid body; the characters in them have monosyllabic names: Bat, Suc, Gim, Dod, Sem, Zan, Das—They appear as silhouettes, blend together, disappear; they are marionettes or rather the carcasses of marionettes, which the puppeteer moves over the surface of a thought that is entirely penetrated by a sense of the fleetingness of things—Yes, the heart is Franciscan, but the head is Buddhist. I shall not say, like Nino

Frank, that there is "a somewhat invertebrate humor in it," but rather a lyricism that is made of vertebrae, without flesh. In any case it is a very evocative art that awakens the complementary work of a novelist, of a film maker, and even of another poet, just as abstract painting is made to be clothed in literature.

So, after having read the reports of Nino Frank and Jean Quéval, I knew a bit more about the person of the effaced Zavattini than I did about that of the illustrious Vittorio de Sica, until last April, when an article by Alfredo Panicucci that was devoted to him appeared in the *Nouveau Femina*. That article was a blessing! We learn from it that Vittorio de Sica is Neapolitan; that the film *Umberto D.* was based upon the life of his father; that his father, at first a prompter, then an employee in a bank, was mad about the theater and destined him from his childhood to be an actor; that he sings the songs of his country ravishingly well and that Maurice Chevalier is making plans to perform with him; that the films he directs are hardly enjoyed in Italy and that it is as an actor above all that he is successful there. He lives, it appears, in a hotel, in the center of Rome, on the second floor when he conforms to the likings of others, but higher, right up to the roof when he wants to do what he pleases.

It is true that the director and the actor in him are different men. The director is comparable to those legendary kings who mingle with their subjects in order to see how they can be made happy, and thus discover what they prefer to keep hidden. With the actor the king abdicates and becomes the equal of his subjects, divested of supreme power but free to live as he wishes, no longer distinguishing himself except through his nobility of soul and his personal charm—it would certainly be a pity if we did not know that charm.

Let us say more simply that Vittorio de Sica is one of the most accomplished actors of this time, and surely the one who possesses the most natural qualities. He recalls our Victor Boucher, whose subtlety and seductiveness he has, with the brilliance of the people of his country—a brilliance that shines through even in the melancholy that is marvelous with him. After having seen him in *The Earrings of Madame De . . .* , in which he plays the role of the Italian diplomat who is the hero of the story, I said to myself that we must thank Louise de Vilmorin for having furnished him with the pretext for an incarnation that is so perfectly in agreement with his character. He appeared to me there to have a strong resemblance to Count Mosca, whom I have always personally preferred to Fabrizio. He even has a physical resemblance to the first. Mosca, like himself, is over forty; he had, Stendhal says, "large features, no vestige of importance, and a simple and gay manner that predisposed you in his favor"; "despite his light manner and his brilliant ways [he] did not have a soul *in the French fashion;* he did not know how to *forget* his sorrows." He was "open and easygoing"; he loved Sanseverina for her "soul that was always sincere," because she never acted "with prudence" and gave herself "completely to the impression of the moment." It has not been said, moreover, that Louise de Vilmorin, who like all of us is extremely fond of *La Chartreuse de Parme [The Charterhouse of Parma]*, may have thought about Count Mosca while drawing her character.

After *The Earrings of Madame De* . . . there was the ravishment of *Good Morning, Elephant.* This film, despite a certain puerility, is captivating, in the manner of Saint-Exupéry's *Petit Prince [The Little Prince]*. We saw it twice and Sylvia went two more times in secret, not daring, almost, to confess such a strong weakness.

I do not know if *Good Morning, Elephant* pleased the Italians; in Paris it had only a slight success. That is probably because Vittorio de Sica is so perfectly adorable in it that one can hardly bear seeing him struggle with so many difficulties, which he never escapes from except through a miracle or rather through a series of little unstable miracles. The French, in general, do not have a liking for miracles, above all for those that do not arrange things conclusively; they prefer chance or, if need be, a reward for merit. In addition, they can hardly admit that such a charming man can be the father of a large family and, into the bargain, a friend of animals. Finally, it is difficult for them to imagine that most people are so poor in Italy. Yes, the story of that schoolteacher upon whom fortune never smiles except to entangle him, to whom nothing good happens except his own good humor, is sad, despite its comic incidents and the fairy-tale element that is brought in by the Hindu prince— Charlie's misfortunes are those of men, they make us laugh while bringing us back to humility; here it is our fellow, our friend, who is in trouble, and our hearts are torn all the more because he does everything in the world to amuse us. Besides, he very often does. When the little elephant appears at the window on the fifth floor of the house, and when we see him take with his trunk a tomato placed on the food box of a neighbor, we are so satisfied that we want to clap our hands. My favorite passage is the one in which Vittorio de Sica takes refuge during a shower, he and his elephant, under a street arcade; a tart is sheltered under a nearby arcade; seeing only the man at first, she makes eyes at him; through a play of his features and gestures he has her understand that he is in company and that he cannot follow her; he has her understand this in as kindly a fashion as possible, so as not to wound her; the tart leans over and sees the elephant's behind, she cries out sharply and escapes into the rain. A little while later we are shown that if prostitutes are afraid of elephants—above all of those that can take a customer away from them—the good sisters are not afraid of them and laugh like the blessed when they have the chance to see one of them come into their convent.

Bread, Love, and Dreams, it appears, is a film made to please the public of all countries. Luigi Comencini, who is its author, deserves the greatest compliments. In his Italy humor and reality combine to give the spectator a continuous pleasure. The action takes place in a small town in the South, doubtless in Calabria, since the region is mountainous and subject to earthquakes; the people are poor there, but in a picturesque way, so as not to distress us. The film is destined to have a long career; as everybody has seen it or will go to see it, I do not want to describe it. Vittorio de Sica, in his role as a chief of police, dazzles with his drollery and kindness, showing by turns a profound goodheartedness and the total decorum that befits his post—with which Caesar would have been satisfied, since he is first in this small town. I took so much pleasure in this film that I saw it three times, once in a French version. I strongly advise you to go to hear it in Italian, for although the dubbing in is perfect, the protagonists themselves speaking French, the gesticulation goes poorly with our language's deadened sonorities. Since I saw it I often happen to laugh when I am all alone, thinking about the *marechalo.* How really well everybody acts in his company: Gina Lollobrigida, the *bersagliera,* more delicious than ever—the policeman who is her smitten lover—the charming midwife who resembles the figures of Simone Memmi—the priest—the dealer in homespun cloth from Sorrento, like the police chief, which puts the latter in an expansive mood—and all the others, all so, so sympathetic, as Caramela says, the authoritarian old servant, a character whose flavor is that of plums cooked in red wine.

After *Bread, Love, and Dreams* I went to see *The Lovers of the Villa Borghese* and *Secrets of the Alcove,* two very successful films made up of sketches in which Vittorio de Sica plays roles in the company of other actors who play, it must be said, with a perfection that is equal to his own. But in the case of the great Italian artist there is only the fact of playing. He is as little an actor as he is a good actor: everything in him unfolds in order to put us in communion with life, in order to give us a happiness that is like friendship.

From *Dernières Gazettes et Ecrits divers*; first published in *Les Lettres Nouvelles* (July 1954).

part five

A Time
with Shakespeare

On the Performing of Shakespeare

The theater of Shakespeare, when you think about it, appears to be among the least actable, but at the same time the one that it matters most to see acted. You quickly arrive at the idea that it is made to be read, but you do not read it well until after you have seen it acted, I shall say almost no matter how. It seems that it essentially has need of theatrical incarnation, as the soul has need of the body. After having written that, and not knowing too well what might strengthen my statement, I found in the *Journal* of Jules Renard this notation, which made me leap for joy:

> Read Julius Caesar yesterday evening. I had read and forgotten it. After Antoine's production and this reading, I explained to myself why I used not to like Shakespeare. He is perhaps the one great man of the theater who has the greatest need to be acted in order to be understood. It is enough to read Victor Hugo, but nothing of his on the stage has taken me like *Julius Caesar*. Shakespeare is therefore more a man of the theater than Victor Hugo.
>
> One does not discover him: one discovers oneself; one awakens in oneself an admiration for him that was sleeping.

The performance of a play by Shakespeare, it does not matter which, always leaves a feeling of imperfection, even when it is given under the most favorable conditions. But this feeling is more nourishing, more fecund than the pleasure that one experiences in seeing a good comedy played with *brio*. One suffers from the imperfection only because of the glimpsed at, the divined perfection. It is the very virtue of Shakespeare's plays that they put us, in regard to life and its representations, in a critical mood—critical and lyrical as well, for they do not draw sterile reproaches from us, but lead us to a vast exploration in which the spirit has such a road to travel over, in the visible and in the invisible, that it inevitably takes wing.

This impossibility and this necessity of acting Shakespeare, nobody has felt them as much as Gordon Craig. In his essay "The Art of the Theater," he wrote that the plays of Shakespeare were not made to be acted but to be read. He categorically quotes Goethe, who was of his opinion that Shakespeare belongs by right to the history of poetry, that it is only accidentally that he figures in the history of the theater, and that the very manner in which Shakespeare carries out his plays makes their execution on the stage to a certain extent unrealizable.

Despite this affirmation, which was written in 1908, Gordon Craig undertook the staging of *Hamlet* for the Moscow Art Theater in 1911. He came out of the experience thoroughly persuaded that the plays of Shakespeare cannot be acted.

Nevertheless, it is his practice that the good present-day directors of Shakespeare have followed. Gordon Craig fixed once and for all, it seems, what the Shakespearean stage should be: a place empty of all realistic scenery, but in which space is made more palpable by plays of light and by great architectural lines; a place in which height and depth can reign, in which our spirit finds an incentive to climb, to descend, to pervade.

The cinema, which is not obliged to confine itself to symbol and synthesis, and which even has the duty of using the material of life, does not seem to me to be excluded. Goethe, who wanted a real elephant for the big carnival of the second part of *Faust*, and who, in fact, eliminated Shakespeare from the theatrical domain on account of settings and crowd scenes that are impossible to realize upon a stage, would not at all have scorned the cinema. The cinema can show cities, palaces, armies—all imaginable people and animals—it can do so with magnificence and even with art. *Henry V* was a very beautiful thing and *A Midsummer Night's Dream*, which did not have a great success with us, displayed a truly magical fairyland, to which Paul Valéry was extremely responsive; he was struck as much as I was by the apparition of Oberon, whose face sparkled marvelously.

But when everything has been well considered, it seems to me that settings should not count so much, not any more than they did in the time of Elizabeth, when the plays were mounted anyhow. As for the staging, it is perhaps desirable that it always falls short of the action or rather of the words that express it. The true producer in Shakespeare is speech.

No, the great and almost the only problem is to find actors capable of playing the roles of this theater that is at one and the same time both central and peripheral—a sun that flares beyond all its flames. This problem certainly admits of a better solution in England than in France, where because of translation the text loses much of its formal beauty. Also, in England there are traditions that help put things in place, and naturally the actors there are more suitable for embodying the characters, who even when they are not national, as in the historical plays, always remain marked by the English genius.

Once that has been said, it can happen that in France, thanks to an exceptional actor, Shakespeare may be played better than he would be in England. Tradition has both good and bad aspects, it often smothers life to the advantage of style. In Shakespeare it is the fire of life that ought to manifest itself through forms—life and its profound reflection in the human spirit. Here we arrive at a dilemma: the characters must, even in the most intense action, remain thinkers and dreamers—the common man takes his time to pronounce sayings and proverbs, the original man secretes and molds his thoughts, like Richard II in his prison—To be or not to be— There is a bit of Hamlet in every Shakespearean character.

Yes, what must first of all be asked of the actor who wants to interpret Shakespeare, particularly the great figures that sustain or inspire his plays, is that he be human, that he be so through his spirit as much as through his heart (the heart being in its enduring states a product of reason, and in its crises an effect of the imagination); he must, at the very start, take for his motto the saying of Pascal: "Man is a reed, the most feeble in nature, but he is a thinking reed." This quality of being a thinker, he must make it felt even when abandoned to passion, even when blinded by murder; there is the true pathos of Shakespeare, the chiaroscuro that is a brother to Rembrandt's. At the moment when the drama takes shape completely and draws the body downward, the intelligence must be drawn upward even more. It is not possible, I truly believe, to expect all that of an actor, as great as he may be;

all that he can give us, and sometimes does give us, is to make us think about it for a long time and allow our brains to labor with his own.

From *Dernières Gazettes et Ecrits divers*; first published in *Les Lettres Nouvelles* (January 1954).

Memories of Antoine and de Max

It is to Antoine and to de Max that I owe my most beautiful Shakespearean memories—my most beautiful because the oldest. I was twelve years old when I saw *King Lear* at the Théâtre Antoine and fourteen when de Max played Mark Antony at the Odéon.

De Max was not, properly speaking, a thinker, but he was such a great artist that he made everything he touched sublime; he brought to his roles a dimension that was completely his own, and that had, if I may say so, something of the fourth dimension—he made the past and its mythical heroes live again, he was the hierophant who opens the doors of mystery; in the bronze of his voice arose a whole procession of anterior lives. He was handsome, astonishing, unbelievably marvelous. His shoulders, like those of the Hindu gods, had the form of an elephant's head. Really, when he showed such shoulders, when he stretched out in a cross his perfectly muscled arms, lifted beneath his abundant black hair a nobly troubled brow, and above all when there issued from his mouth that ample voice that added overtones to our language—a voice that was foreign, as one is foreign to the earth—that voice of which he made a religious use, the entire public participated in the enthusiasm. Thought—you were beyond that, you were soaring!

It does not seem to me that he often interpreted Shakespeare; I saw him act in I do not know how many roles opposite Sarah Bernhardt; the classics aside, it was in rather shoddy plays—Rostand and Sardou reached their maximum—but the two of them, Sarah as much as himself, had the art of changing lead into gold. I have not preserved a precise and really unforgettable memory in the Shakespearean domain except of his creation of Mark Antony in *Julius Caesar* at the Odéon, then under the management of Antoine. The moment when he appeared at the top of the stairway of the Forum, when he tore from his shoulders an immense purple cloak that he cast down to the bottom of the steps to cover the body of Caesar, like an eagle opening its wings—that moment, which he himself invented, there can be no doubt about it, was as prodigious as could be hoped for. I still hear his beautiful Rumanian voice, in which the muffled R's rolled like distant drums, speak the famous line: "For Brutus is an honorable man . . ." At the end of the speech there arose in each of the spectators an inflamed citizen who wanted to tear up everything and set fire to the buildings.

That was all very beautiful, and very worthy of illustrating Shakespearean speech. However, it is to Antoine, Antoine the actor, that I owe, more than I do to de Max, the almost perfect communion with Shakespeare.

Antoine was forty-six years old when he staged *King Lear* in his theater in 1904 and took upon his shoulders the crushing role of the old king. He already had behind him a long history of struggles, and he was going to have to struggle still, without respite; he was resigned to nothing, his faith remained whole, but his whole face bespoke weariness and care. He was not a very good actor, except when he had roles that suited him well, like that of Lafont in *La Parisienne*; then he gave more than the most talented actor would have given. Like all theater managers who take a hand in acting, he had authority; in his case this authority was veiled by a kind of severe timidity that doubtless came from what was conscientious and discontented in himself. In short, when I saw him it was rather late in his life; I was not acquainted with the heroic period of the Théâtre Libre. In 1892 he already passed, in the eyes of Henri de Bornier, for example, for a very vicious "wolf" who, at the head of his pack, was getting ready to pillage the "sheepfolds" of the Théâtre-Français and the Odéon. Yes, said the author of *La Fille de Roland [The Daughter of Roland]*, "They will wallow in our blood with the calm ferocity of wolves who have fulfilled a duty . . ."

Thus he came to Shakespeare with a Shakespearean past. And the fact is that I never saw anything as extraordinary as that performance of *King Lear*. In it Antoine showed himself pathetically human: weak and violent, not very sure of himself, like the absurd king; the mad scenes were transported to the innermost part of yourself, with that power of contagion that nervous derangements have. The horror scenes fully benefited from the desire for realism that animated the house; never were the eyes of Gloucester more ferociously torn out, never were the cries and the curses more frightful. The Grand Guignol could not have done better and, at the same time, the intelligence of the dramatist did not cease to be manifested, as much in the words of the Fool (whom Signoret interpreted remarkably, very much helped by his physiognomy) as in the whole cast, which Antoine animated with genius, like a great orchestra conductor. He was aware that he was filling that role of an orchestra conductor. He made note of it in his memoirs. But he was more than that, I declare it to his ghost: he was the very man whom our inner Shakespeare might have chosen.

From *Dernières Gazettes et Ecrits divers*; first published in *Les Lettres Nouvelles* (January 1954).

Charles Dullin

Surely it is vain to stage a play by Shakespeare without the actor who is capable of assuming its essential role: the one that plainly shows the creature and the creator at the same time. That actor will have more or less of a resemblance to the great Will, which is to say that he will possess, in variable proportions, the gifts of an interpreter, a manager of a company, and even an author—an author who will not write, perhaps, but whom he will contain potentially and whose critical spirit he will all the better possess.

Doubtless the title of manager of a company that I give here to Shakespeare will be contested; but according to the few sure bits of evidence that exist, and of which Martin Maurice has made an inventory in his precious work, he did not appear only as an actor, but also as the shareholder-founder of two theaters, the Globe and the Blackfriars. Besides, it is difficult in my opinion to conceive of an author-actor who, performing in his own plays, is not to a certain extent the caster and the director.

Charles Dullin was certainly one of those who can and even ought to look for the characters in the plays of Shakespeare that suit their temperament, that await, as he says in his *Souvenirs*, "the accomplice who will bring them back to life again on the stage of the world." Among these characters two above all were offered to him: Shylock and Richard III— He must often have thought of *The Merchant of Venice*. I can imagine easily enough the reasons that turned him away from this play when he took the Atelier; the first, perhaps, is that it had been put on by Gémier at the Théâtre Antoine, with a staging that could not be surpassed.

In addition, he had already played Smerdiakov and Harpagon, roles that belong, more or less, like Shylock, to the family of the accursed (he had seen Harpagon as tragic). Obviously, the nature of his talent and his build above all obliged him—it could even be said condemned him—to such roles, but the important concern was precisely to discover in them unforeseen variations that would bring something new to himself and to the public.

As early as 1921, the year that he took possession of the Atelier, he thought seriously not only of Shakespeare but also of the Elizabethan theater in general. I have a personal proof of that: he sent Antonin Artaud to take out a reading subscription at my bookshop (October 1, 1921), with the sole purpose of reading everything of that theater that had been put into French. Fortunately I possessed the five volumes translated by Ernest Lafond in 1865, two tomes of which contained the plays of Ben Jonson. With a thousand bits of advice, but without hesitating too much, I entrusted to Artaud, one by one, the precious volumes that, on principle, were not supposed to circulate. I did not have to repent of my trust, the volumes were returned to me at appropriate intervals, in perfect condition.

It was in Ben Jonson that Dullin was to find the two roles that suited him well, which even while preserving beautiful tones of black added the lively ones of outright drollery that he had need of in order to change—the role of Morose in *The Silent Woman*, adapted by Marcel Achard, which he played in 1925, and that of Volpone, in the adaptation by Stefan Zweig and Jules Romains, which he played three years later—with so much brilliance and success!

Nevertheless, it was Shakespeare's *Richard III*, performed in 1933, that allowed him to reach a height equal to that of Smerdiakov. It is the most perfect thing that I have seen in that domain where, as we have said, perfection is as if forbidden. I have never reread the play without seeing before me Dullin's sardonic face, his piercing look; without hearing the sound of his voice, hunched like his whole person; it is almost hallucinating. When you think about it, furthermore, this character lends himself better than others, in spite of his extreme particularity, to a complete interpretation—because he is absolutely determined, without internal divisions. At the very moment he enters onstage he presents himself like a proverb out of hell:

> I, that am curtail'd of this fair proportion,
> Cheated of feature by dissembling nature,
> Deform'd, unfinish'd, sent before my time
> Into this breathing world, scarce half made up,

> And that so lamely and unfashionable
> That dogs bark at me, as I halt by them;
> . . . .
> I am determined to prove a villain . . .

He follows this determination rigorously until the end of the action, without ever experiencing the slightest hesitation, even before the most horrible crimes, like that of the murder of Edward's children in the Tower of London. He has only impatience when things do not go quick enough to his liking, and sarcasm for those whom he succeeds in tricking through his hypocrisy—God, that Dullin was astonishing in the scenes with Lady Anne and Queen Elizabeth, who, coming to him with their mouths full of insults and curses, were bit by bit ground beneath the millstone of his will and forced to accept—the one by becoming his wife, the other by giving her daughter to this man—him, Richard, who has had their relations assassinated. How can one forget Dullin's voice in the epilogue that follows Anne's submission:

> Was ever woman in this humour woo'd?
> Was ever woman in this humour won?
> I'll have her; but I will not keep her long.
> What! I, that kill'd her husband, and his father,
> To take her in her heart's extremest hate;
> With curses in her mouth, tears in her eyes,
> The bleeding witness of my hatred by;
> Having God, her conscience, and these bars against me,
> And I no friends to back my suit withal
> But the plain devil and dissembling looks,
> And yet to win her, all the world to nothing!

Of Elizabeth, whose husband, brother, and sons he has killed and who consents to grant him her daughter, he says simply: "Relenting fool, and shallow changing woman!"

The truth is that there is not, in the theater of Shakespeare, a criminal who is better realized than Richard III, totally proof against pity and remorse, soberly leading his life of crimes, the master of himself and of evil, which he makes into something that is rational. The ghosts of his eleven victims, which appear to him after the battle of Bosworth, have not issued from his brain, as it most often happens, but have been produced by a collective spirit, since they appear at the same time to his adversary Richmond in order to give him confidence—Richmond, who is to kill him and become king in his place. He must hear repeated eleven times: "Despair and die!" before his conscience awakens in him, against which he struggles bravely moreover, and almost as drolly as Père Ubu:

> Give me another horse! bind up my wounds!
> Have mercy, Jesu! Soft! I did but dream.
> O coward conscience, how dost thou afflict me!
> The lights burn blue. It is now dead midnight.
> Cold fearful drops stand on my trembling flesh.
> What? do I fear myself? there's none else by:
> Richard loves Richard; that is, I am I.
> Is there a murtherer here? No. Yes, I am:
> Then fly: what! from myself? Great reason: why?
> Lest I revenge. What? myself upon myself?
> Alack! I love myself. Wherefore? for any good
> That I myself have done unto myself?
> O, no: alas! I rather hate myself
> For hateful deeds committed by myself.
> I am a villain. Yet I lie; I am not.
> Fool, of thyself speak well: fool, do not flatter.

Excellent Richard—excellent Dullin who, because of his humanity, was able to give life to this monster and make him understandable. It seemed that the role was one of the easiest for him, so natural was he in it, and, in some fashion, tranquil. However, he says in his *Souvenirs* that he did not succeed in possessing it from one end of the play to the other, and that it sometimes spurned him throughout a whole scene. I saw him two times in this role and I never had the impression of a break in the unity— That Jean Vilar had difficulties to resolve in his Richard II, as he has said so well in the article he published last November in the *Lettres Françaises*, that is understandable, but Richard III appeared to remain completely under Dullin's skin. I wonder how one can incarnate such a character without remaining marked for life by him. I remember having seen Dullin at a concert of the Pléiade during the Occupation; he was so stooped—really bent in two—and his face was so ravaged, despite makeup applied as thickly as for the stage, that he gave me a kind of fright and I restrained myself from approaching him.

This memorable creation unarguably ranks Dullin among the great interpreters of Shakespeare. He did not stop there; three years later he produced *Julius Caesar*, in which he took the role of Cassius and developed it fully; never has the character, with his envious and subtle spirit, better displayed himself; Brutus was only a plaything in his hands. The performance as a whole did not delight me, with the exception of the scenes that take place in Brutus's tent; the apparition of Caesar's ghost has remained in my memory as the best that can be seen.

In 1945, at the Théâtre de la Cité, Dullin made a worthy effort to stage *King Lear*. I was disappointed. He did not appear convincing to me in the role of the old king, which he played, it seemed, with the remnants of himself. It must be said that the company as a whole was not brilliant; the performance, I do not know why, had something provincial about it; the settings and the costumes have left me with a rather painful memory, the performers were badly matched with one another. I will confess, furthermore, that I have never much liked Dullin as a director, with the exception of certain details that he saw like nobody else. I believe that he was marvelously apt in developing the personality of his students—Artaud and Barrault are the proof of it—but that he did not know very well how to impose upon them the spirit of the whole; anarchy always reigned more or less at the Atelier; most of the performances there gave the impression of being surprise parties. That was not disagreeable, far from it!— Still, in the teaching of his art, nobody has shown himself to be as great or as generous as Charles Dullin. His *Notes de travail [Work Notes]* are the most beautiful and effective that I know of. Doubtless Jouvet wrote more brilliantly and more abundantly (a very good writer, Jouvet!) but the little book by Dullin remains like a gem; in it he says the essential without mystification; it does not seem possible to me that his *Conseils à un jeune élève [Advice to a Young Student]* can be surpassed.

From *Dernières Gazettes et Ecrits divers*; first published in *Les Lettres Nouvelles* (February 1954).

Jean-Louis Barrault and Shakespeare

It was in the power of Jean-Louis Barrault, a student of Dullin, to give us an exemplary Hamlet. He had already well prepared himself for it by staging Laforgue's *Hamlet*, adapted by Charles Granval, in which, as I said in my gazette of that time, he was gently prodigious; more Shakespearean perhaps through Laforgue than in a translation of Shakespeare. In his *Réflexions sur le théâtre* he says that it is the monologue "To be or not to be" that has most often given him "the marvelous sensation" of becoming "one" with the public. I gladly believe it, for nobody, to my knowledge, has ever spoken the famous monologue so well, not even Laurence Olivier, who is the prisoner of his admirable diction.

It was at the Comédie-Française, during the Occupation, that Barrault appeared to me to perform his role best. He played, however, with actors most of whom remained curiously foreign to the action; the settings were dull; in the midst of all that, which was a bit hostile to him, he showed himself more alive, more intelligent than ever; his performance in the first act, when the ghost appeared, had a nervous excitement that enchanted me—I discovered there again the little horse of *Autour d'une mère [Around a Mother]*.

When he put on the play again at the Théâtre Marigny, in Gide's translation, this time with beautiful, brand-new settings by André Masson, it seemed to me that there was a diminution on his part. He had become more composed, he was less agitated, but at the same time he was less intense; the "To be or not to be" was less profound. I could only admire the manner in which he had renewed himself, also admire, and how much, the performance as a whole, but while still regretting the sublime moments that he had reached at the Français. It seems to me that the presence of Gide and his translation ought to bear the responsibility for that "less." Gide, who was always haunted by the theater, had very little sense of it, or rather he had it in his own fashion. His beautiful prose, so carefully worked, was more at ease in his mouth than in the mouths of actors called upon to recite it—yes, to recite it and not to live it. Besides, he very much preferred to be read silently rather than aloud. In ordinary conversation he kept a reader's tone of voice. One could have returned him the compliment that he had addressed to me and told him, "We hear you speak less than we read you."

At the rehearsal of his translation of *Antony and Cleopatra*, which Barrault staged so remarkably at the Comédie-Française (the bacchanal on the galley had a magnificent movement, one could not stay in one's seat), Jacques Prévert was horrified by the faults of Gidian speech in the theater. Personally, the faults of the two protagonists horrified me even more; the climate of the Comédie-Française is decidedly worth nothing for Shakespeare.

To come back to Gide and his theater, which is far from being without theatrical value—*Saül*, in addition to its great beauty, has a real dramatic vitality—he could not, like Shakespeare, accommodate himself to ordinary actors, not even to those endowed with talent; he needs, he himself needs as well, interpreters whose spirit has a kinship with his own; in his case that kinship is founded above all upon the critical sense, that sense being the promoter of his vitality.

From *Dernières Gazettes et Ecrits divers*; first published in *Les Lettres Nouvelles* (February 1954).

Jean Vilar

I chanced only once to be happy about the performance of a play by Gide: that was when Jean Vilar acted Oedipe. My happiness was all the greater because Vilar, through a kind of miracle, brought to life not only the figure of Oedipus, but also that of Gide, who had died a short time before; the play of his features and his voice evoked those of the great writer in a striking manner; his personal art, in which the lyricism is always controlled, gave the piece a scope that suits its virtues, which are comic and tragic at the same time.

No actor, I really believe, has a critical sense equal to Jean Vilar's; this sense is so developed with him that he must often, if he wants to act, approach what appeared to him at first to be unacceptable and even reprehensible. The author whom he potentially contains is irritated by the too famous author who obliges him, an actor, to submit; as a compensation he has a need to carry to the heights we shall not say the first person who comes along, but the person who is not the best one to come along, and who in any case would not be able to do without him.

Jouvet as he acted took to judging men—there was a moralist in him. Vilar takes to judging the texts and the ideas that they express; by dint of moving words around in his mouth, of learning them by heart, of cramming his brain with them, he comes, like Melville's Pierre, to measure "the everlasting elusiveness of Truth; the universal lurking insincerity of even the greatest and purest written thoughts. . . ." Even more than Pierre writing his book, he can experience the feeling, as he acts, of cheating in one more game, a poor weary game.

Then he will again dream of a language that is original and capable of acting upon the public—what Artaud was looking for in his last works, what Pichette had tried to do in *Les Epiphanies*—and even though that work displeased him strongly (he said himself that during the performance he was "ready to howl"), he will stage *Nucléa*, by which attempt he will be impoverished, but where he will find for himself a negating role that at the very least will divert him, and will divert us also, even if that should be only through the resemblance, at once trifling and precise, that he should show to Monsieur Teste—the precision coming from himself.

Surely there is an imperative need to create in Jean Vilar; if this need sometimes drives him to make attempts that are risky, but that are also profitable, when everything is considered, it often guides him wonderfully in the shows that he organizes. It is to his creative spirit that he owes his mastery over his company and the power that he has to maintain its unity even while allowing everybody his complete individuality; better still—while forcing everybody to be himself to the highest degree. He is certainly the best caster and director that we have at present; perhaps, even, we have never had anybody as strong as he. Like many people I was filled with enthusiasm by the performances of *The Prince of Hombourg* and by *The Death of Danton*: it seems to me that it was with these two plays that he gave the full measure of himself and showed his originality and his mastery in the most striking fashion. Nobody could stage Shakespeare better than he—it does not matter what play by Shakespeare—provided, however, that for the most important he has at his disposal the principal actor, who might be himself in some cases.

I have never been able to console myself for having missed, in 1948, the performances that he gave of Richard II at the Théâtre des Champs-Elysées. Cournot and Saillet were carried away; never, to listen to them, had anybody witnessed anything like it.

I saw the play last November at the Palais de Chaillot; I must admit that I was a bit disappointed. I can imagine how it was possible for Vilar to be perfect in this role, whose complexity agrees well enough with his own, enough at the very least to make him capable of communicating life to it. The first criticism to address to him now is that he is no longer young enough to play Richard II, who came to the throne while he was still a child and died at around thirty. He lacks the youth, not so much physically as morally; I find him handsome and sufficiently young in appearance for the role—he resembles a figure in a stained glass window. But in recent years there has been produced in him a hardening as of a man of war, which forbids him certain shades of feeling; he sweats authority through all his pores; his gestures, most often, are those of a leader who calls people to order with sharp raps on the table; when he indulges in humor he makes you think of a professor who parodies on occasion the grimaces of his students. During the first part of the action his interpretation is excessive and not very accurate. His hasty and as if agglutinated delivery adds even more to the uneasiness. Doubtless Richard II was authoritarian, and possibly vigorous, but there was also much indecision and dreaminess in him. Poetry would have been needed to make him live—poetry, in which contraries are reconciled. Jean Vilar has felt perfectly all the personages that clash together in this character, but he has felt them in such a fashion as to remain divided himself, like the earth in a time of dryness. It must be said that he recovers his equilibrium and his effectiveness in the final scenes, particularly in the prison monologue, in which he is moving and meditative; his acting then agrees very well with what is indicated in the text; he is striking in his depiction of a man who kneads his thoughts and sees them appear like the minutes of a human clock. It is so Melvillian —Melville, as we know, was haunted by Shakespeare.

There is no doubt that Jean Vilar has shown himself to be, in regard to his Richard II, his own best critic, since he has passed on the role to Gérard Philippe. We are going to see what he will bring to it, he, the preeminently poetic actor.

From *Dernières Gazettes et Ecrits divers*; first published in *Les Lettres Nouvelles* (February 1954).

Marlon Brando as Mark Antony

It was because of Marlon Brando that I went to see the film *Julius Caesar*. After *Viva Zapata* and *A Streetcar Named Desire* I had promised myself not to miss him in any role. He had seemed astonishing to me as the young Pole in *Streetcar*—the ingenuous and cunning brute who has a heart at bottom, very much at bottom, but who does not intend to waste the streaks of intelligence in his dull drinker's brain. His way of brandishing the *Code Napoléon*—at one and the same time the *Code* and the fact of knowing it—was high comedy. Seeing him in *Viva Zapata* I thought of a Hemingway hero—virile and modest, a man-child chock-full of his secret, as savory as a pineapple under his natural cuirass.

As Mark Antony he shows himself perfectly up to the role; he brings to Shakespeare the blood that is needed to make him live—besides, has a vitality equal to his own ever been manifested in the theater or in the cinema? His diction is superb, supple and powerful, as noble as much as it is common—the dreamed-of voice for a tribune. The character finds in him a naturalness that is unexpected but immediately impressive, with such an organic unity that it is Shakespeare who yields to the actor and abandons his Antony to him. With Marlon Brando he in fact seems to be a young man about twenty years old, rather the favorite of Caesar, of the Antinoüs sort, yet with something of the filial about him. It is very much in this sense that the feelings of Marlon Antony are manifested—he is affectionate like a good son, provided with the hopes of one who is bound to have the inheritance, so sure of his right that all means are justified in regard to the opponent. I was struck, for example, after the murder of Caesar, to see the frank looks that he addresses to the conspirators, the firmness of the handshakes that he gives them with an apparent loyalty, while he is electrified by a hatred that helps him to deceive his adversaries by a kind of mimicry. In the famous speech in the Forum the refrain "is an honorable man . . . all honorable men . . ." bursts out with the defiant notes of children who proclaim the prohibited words while remarking that they forbid them to themselves. We are far from the practiced cunning of a de Max. No, here it is a primitive world in which trickery is a natural weapon, in which the tragic is a mask more than a feeling.

The youthfulness of Marlon Brando is manifested again through a very curious act. In the scene with Lepidus and Octavius, when he is alone, he turns the bust of Caesar toward him, smiling with the air of telling him: now I have you, your power is mine, Caesar!—This stage direction is not indicated in Shakespeare, but it is very beautiful and in any case it agrees with the exotic Antony.

After the film, back in my own place, I took up Plutarch again and I saw to what point the creation of Marlon Brando was personal and far from the historical truth. At the moment of the action fixed by Shakespeare, Antony is thirty-nine years old and Caesar is fifty-six. My Plutarch being illustrated with reproductions from busts and medals, I was able to ascertain the physical difference between the ancient model and the present actor. No resemblance, in fact. Antony had a head as round as a ball, the typical face of a great Roman politician—an aquiline nose, a strong and thrusting chin, a well-formed mouth with the powerful lower lip of those who are attached to the goods of this world and whose hearts do not bother them; the broad and rather low brow, swollen above the eye sockets, is that of bold and realistic men. Marlon Brando's brow, lofty and with its prominences placed high up, is that of a willful and stubborn intellectual.

In the opinion of his contemporaries, Mark Antony was a handsome, very important man who resembled Hercules, from whom his family said it took its origin. He loved pomp, above all Asiatic pomp, which is more spectacular; harnessing lions to his chariot when he passed through cities; mad about what the translator of my Plutarch calls comedians and buffoons, and in a general fashion all the partisans of the god Bacchus, whom he prided himself on imitating. He was a braggart but a good-hearted man, putting up very well with the jokes that were made at his expense, himself loving nothing so much as to spice his remarks with coarse humor. With his soldiers he showed himself simple and familiar, of an incredible generosity in regard to them, and in regard also to no matter who could give him a cause for pleasure. He thus bought a popularity that he certainly needed in order to have himself pardoned for his faults and for his disorderly life.

To come back to Marlon Brando, it must be agreed that he has nothing of Mark Antony about him; even his tribune's vulgarity is without kinship to that of the general, the merrymaker and good pal. When it is necessary, his voice has the heavy ground swells of popular speech, but he himself remains distant and secret; the tears he shows to the crowd, like the loyal looks he addresses to his enemies, depend upon fakirism. It is true that mimicry and fakirism are part of the gifts of an actor, but it must be added that with Marlon Brando they reach an exceptional point; there is something of the sorcerer in him; one does not succeed in understanding how he can stir up such strong feelings while keeping his equilibrium, while even allowing a glimpse at a strange irony, which goes very far. It seems that it may be as the incarnation of Zapata, which is a "sacred" role, that he gained that degree of superior interpretation in which one can judge life while yielding oneself to its fire, in which one plays in the full sense of the term—which is the Shakespearean degree.

From *Dernières Gazettes et Ecrits divers*; first published in *Les Lettres Nouvelles* (March 1954).

A View of Cleopatra

While I was reading Plutarch I was amused to notice the part that discusses Cleopatra. She was an astonishing person of whom it does not seem that a just and complete portrait has been made—I must confess that I have not read the works that are devoted to her. Shakespeare painted her in the light of her passion for Mark Antony and gave little account of her mind. I am thinking above all of that passage in which the historian says that Cleopatra, "perceiving that his raillery was broad and gross, and savoured more of the soldier than the courtier, rejoined in the same taste, and fell into it at once, without any sort of reluctance or reserve." I began to dream about the comedy that this sentence might inspire; Bernard Shaw could have done it, and did not do it; he preferred to put a woman-child opposite Caesar, and nevertheless Shaw loved intelligent women—but of course those who let themselves be "guided." (All the greatness of Socrates is necessary to render to Diotima what is due to her.) Cleopatra had no need of being guided; her face had less charm than her conversation; she knew a great number of foreign languages and could do without an interpreter, while the kings of Egypt, "her predecessors, scarcely gave themselves the trouble to acquire the Egyptian tongue, and several of them quite abandoned Macedonian."

Her love affairs with Caesar and with Antony are above all political. She would have been perfectly content to be able to present them with Octavius for a successor, if he had let himself be seduced; but the star of the future Augustus was more brilliant than her eyes of a woman of thirty-nine who had become, of necessity, a vamp. It was natural that the Romans should execrate her and blame the one among their leaders who ruined himself in her company, but she was a good custodian of the interests of her country and was concerned for her greatness. She used her feminine attractions with virility, that is to say, with a total lucidity. If she took a thousand pains to divert Antony, to dazzle him with senseless luxury, to make him drunk with inexhaustible pleasures, it was because there were no other means to flatter him, to please him, to hold him—and to hold Rome through him. Doubtless she would have preferred less material pleasures, for when one has intelligence one likes to make use of it, and she would have found different ways of leading an "inimitable life" if Mark Antony had been a philosopher or simply a rational man, but he had not awaited their meeting to become a great fool.

From *Dernières Gazettes et Ecrits divers*; first published in *Les Lettres Nouvelles* (March 1954).

The Shakespeare Memorial Theatre

You can well imagine that at the point where I found myself with my reflections on Cleopatra and Mark Antony, the announcement that the company of the Shakespeare Memorial Theatre was coming to Paris, precisely to act *Antony and Cleopatra*, gave me an immense pleasure and even seemed to me like a sort of personal favor.

Sylvia, without having these heroes especially in mind, but ever devoted to the great Will, was no less pleased and hurried to reserve seats for us as close to the stage as possible, inasmuch as we are both a bit hard of hearing. She had seen Peggy Ashcroft act in London in Henry James's *Heiress*, and she had been amazed. I am ashamed to confess it, but outside of *The Blue Bird* of my youth, and naturally the films that I always go to listen to in their original sound tracks, I myself had never attended a performance given in English, even when the Old Vic came to us. It must be said that my knowledge of English is too imperfect for me to be able to follow the text; and I am still less able to grasp the beauties of it. For the same reason I avoid reading poetry and literary prose in the original. Besides, nothing seems to me more difficult than to know a language thoroughly and to be able to speak it correctly. You must expend as much effort on it as for making yourself the master of an art or of a craft; you find yourself in the presence of obstacles that are greater, sometimes, and more irreducible; there are subtleties and particularities that forever escape you, unless you devote an entire lifetime to them, and more! Whatever may be the seriousness of the remarks you may wish to make, they become funny because of faults of pronunciation; these faults, furthermore, are an inexhaustible mine of comic effects for those who want easy laughs: chansonniers, vaudevillists, clowns, etc. Shakespeare himself did not disdain these coarse means, in particular in *Henry V*, in which you find all the hodgepodges of accents, not only English-French but even English in Welsh, Scottish, and Irish arrangements. Here is certainly the type of play that it would be impossible to act among us, in French, without profoundly shocking our taste and our patriotism at one and the same time. I remember that Gide, after having seen the beautiful color film made with so much care by the English, Gide, who yet cannot be accused of chauvinism, showed annoyance and said that it was very disobliging to us.

With *Antony and Cleopatra* they did not risk displeasing us, it is the play that the greater part of the French enjoy most, for it is one of the best paintings that have been made of amorous passion between a man and a woman who are both interesting because of their eminent position, their spirit, and even their age. Nothing is more interesting, in fact, than seeing the effects and the components of passion among people of a mature age, while their life is solidly constructed, their characters entirely formed, while they can judge well what happens to them, and while it all crackles and flies into pieces with great flames, thus presenting a beautiful and captivating spectacle to those who have the privilege of witnessing it. In addition to this, *Antony and Cleopatra*, having been translated by Gide and acted often enough, like *Hamlet*, is well known to the French public, who can follow the action in English, even with an imperfect knowledge of the language, their memory subtitling the scenes easily.

I shall say without further delay that I was enchanted by that performance; I should never have imagined that so much robust and zestful life could ally itself with tradition. Among us tradition does not agree with life except on the level of comedy, and then the life that we show is finely stylized; our naturalness is elaborated from the first to the last movement, and it is no less sincere for that, it is even the more sincere because it is more refined, as our sincerity does not content itself with the first truth that comes along, and wants what is closest to the ideal. Writing this I think above all of Marivaux, who is played so well at the Comédie-Française and so divinely with Madeleine Renaud and Jean-Louis Barrault. The performance of *Fausses Confidences* at the Théâtre Marigny gives an almost overwhelming delight; in the presence of such a comedy, played by such actors, you understand what the genius of our country is, and that God, according to all the evidence, is French, French because of His discretion, which forces us in no way at all but leaves us the joy and the merit of discovering Him in the little things where He resides more willingly than in the great. But these perfect pleasures, in order to be felt to the point where they refresh the heart, have need of contrasts; if we were to limit ourselves to them they would enervate us; other admirations do not diminish them, on the contrary; the consideration of foreign geniuses is always salutary. Nobody, perhaps, is more strengthening than Shakespeare, because of the vigor of his humanism and the generosity of his language; with the same light step he crosses over happiness and unhappiness, as one passes from day to night, from night to day. He is the universal poet, preeminently—a truth that has been told a hundred times.

I realized, on the occasion of the performance of *Antony and Cleopatra*, that it was not useless to absorb such a text in its original form, even if it remained nearly unintelligible to you. It produces, in this case, a very interesting phenomenon; the poetic word, deprived of meaning, does not bring ideas and feelings to mind, but acts in a physical manner, a bit like music—a music that does not have wings but feet; it is completely just to speak of the feet of poetry. Its sonority and its rhythm become more perceptible and efficacious. It seems that the English language demands of those who speak it a greater bodily effort than French or the Latin languages (that is perhaps one of the reasons why the English habitually keep silent). But well spoken, by good actors who communicate to it their vital breath, its physical action upon the hearer is notably stronger than any other; it can do without music; it does without it, in fact, since England, with the exception of Purcell alone, does not have any great composers, as compared to so many poets and writers of genius. Yes, the English language, in addition to its gymnastic quality, seems to me as nourishing as bread that is whole, not deprived of its germ and its salts, that is rich with all its vitamins. Naturally, it is in the theater that such a virtue is manifest; in the cinema there is no real presence, therefore no communion.

A moving film—for example, *Monsieur Vincent* with Pierre Fresnay or *Moulin Rouge* with José Ferrer—always has something sacrilegious about it, and the more so because it puts itself at the service of religion or art; it does not leave us with a peaceful conscience, we think rather strangely that it might be good for others, but it is not good for us, unless we add to it an intense personal labor of revivification, unless we give it our own substance. In short, films, even the most successful, impair us, they turn us into fetuses that are carried off by the currents, while the theater, which is charged with humanity, restores us. On the other hand, a bad film afflicts us infinitely less than a bad play.

Peggy Ashcroft is a magnificent and surprising tragedian; she is very beautiful, with the great hollow eyes of a drinker of absinthe or gin; I rather see her as the queen of Piccadilly, animated by an inextinguishable Eros, less in the flesh than in the spirit—oh, no, she is not sensual, unless in a Baudelairian manner. Her voice, a bit like Yma Sumac's, is by turns contralto and soprano: is she not also a daughter of the Sun? She has a way of laughing that makes you shiver, very appropriate for a queen whose femininity is mingled with State policy. I do not see who could play Cleopatra like her, and better elate us with the drama that was the end of her life—a drama assuredly less sad than a badly prepared old age would have been.

Michael Redgrave is perfect as Mark Antony; he has all the qualities that are needed in order to make the great Roman general live, to make a solid, high-colored Englishman of him. With him you can recall Plutarch (although his head is rather romantic, as Jean Adrian has remarked), and you can above all hear Shakespeare, whose lines he speaks with great style, without ceasing to be lively and zestful. You think, listening to him, to him and to Harry Andrews, who plays the part of Enobarbus, that the good actors of the Elizabethan epoch could hardly have been different. This impression is unbelievably warm, more moving than can be said.

From *Dernières Gazettes et Ecrits divers*; first published in *Les Lettres Nouvelles* (March 1954).

part six

Places

Memories of London

I was seventeen years old when I made my first journey to London in 1909. I had never until then left my family, where I was as happy as one can be at that age of torment, with a mother and a sister who were ideally companionable. The three of us lived in a state of perpetual enthusiasm for everything that seemed beautiful to us, in whatever domain it might be. Debussy and Maeterlinck were our gods. That year, 1909, had brought us the dazzle of the Ballets Russes.

I think that it was because of Debussy that I went to London. More exactly because of his *Demoiselle élue*, which had led me to the Pre-Raphaelites, to Rossetti first, then to Burne-Jones. These now discredited painters then enjoyed a great vogue, above all among the lovers of *Pelléas*; reproductions of their work were found in the Rue de Seine and at Plume's, opposite the Sorbonne. I surrounded myself with their pictures, the enchantment they brought me was mingled with that of Eros. I do not say this lightly, you are going to see why.

Among my schoolmates there was a girl named Suzanne, whose face strangely resembled one by Rossetti, the very one that he painted in all of his pictures, with a strongly modeled mouth and a long neck that swelled at the base—a beautiful face that might have been virile without the sweet animality of its look and its tresses. Was it possible for me not to be smitten with that face?

I was not on very good terms with Suzanne, she mocked what I admired to the point of making tears spring to my eyes—her gods were Mendelssohn and Musset—but I was not able to live far from her. Our examinations over, she had decided to go to London in order to learn English there by taking a place in a school or working for a family in return for room and board; I made this project my own. Her friend Zélie lived in London, with a family where she was a governess, and was doing very well there. Zélie had been the passion of her fifteenth year; she no longer had such ardent feelings for her, but by her own admission she loved her better than she did myself, who often bored her to death. There was a time when they used to spend their nights writing letters to each other—which they would send to each other the next day. It was Suzanne who told me that, which I found staggering, for I would have been completely incapable of doing as much, I who slept like a log, even with the fires of passion in my heart; but I had only more strength to torment myself during the day.

Zélie was Protestant, and because of that Suzanne felt very much attracted by Protestantism. It was understood that when we went to London we would stay in a family pension run by a French minister in Soho Square and that from there we would try to find places for ourselves. Suzanne left for London in the middle of September and rather quickly found a post in an Enfield school. I could not leave Paris until the end of the month; my mother had had a great deal to do getting my clothes ready, she had taken infinite trouble to make me a dress of royal blue cloth, with a long jacket that was elegant and proper at the same time. It was not without difficulty that I had arrived at persuading my parents, my father above all, about the usefulness of this journey. I had never until then shown inclinations to study the English language, so little that I had had to learn Italian in a few months in order to be able to take my examination for the *brevet supérieur*. After the examination I had had to demonstrate to them throughout the length of a whole day that without a knowledge of English I would not succeed very well in earning my living. Of Suzanne, naturally, it was never a question.

My voyage to England was made via Dieppe-Newhaven. I was seasick. In the train that carried me off to London I experienced my first delight when I caught sight of some cottages, and above all when I saw the color of the grass, which was so limpidly green, a slightly bluish green that appeared supernatural to me.

When I arrived at Victoria Station I found Suzanne, who helped me claim my suitcase; then we took a cab that drove us to the house of the minister of Soho Square. There Suzanne introduced me, and after we had spent an hour quarreling and weeping in my room she returned to Enfield. We were going to meet again on Sunday, at I no longer know what Methodist Church, where Suzanne attended the service in the company of Zélie.

For the first time in my life I could not fall asleep. I spent the night feeling tumultuous sensations: my solitude in an unknown and immense city, the uncertain future, my unhappy love, freedom and its mirages, everything that I was going to be able to do and everything that could happen to me. The wind from the open sea blew stronger than worry or sorrow, I was intoxicated.

The very next day I went to a nearby agency to ask for employment. I had arrived late in the homecoming season and they told me at once that there was nothing interesting to hope for in the category of nursery governess or lady's companion, above all for a beginner. It was only after ten days that they found something for me, not in London itself, where I should so much have liked to stay, but in Muswell Hill, on the northern outskirts. I was to speak French to a girl who lived with her mother in a flat and keep her company. The secretary of the agency apologized less for proposing Muswell Hill to me—very close to London and well connected to the center, with the magnificent Alexandra Park nearby—than for sending me into a family that lived in a flat, for in the eyes of the English a true "home" can only be a private house.

So I had ten days to walk about in London as I pleased. Soho Square was well located, in the most alive part of London, two steps from Piccadilly. From there I was able to go on foot to all the important museums; with a map that was not too difficult. I did not consider taking long walks, as I did not very much like walking. I had no desire to become acquainted with the whole city of London, which would have obliged me to use means of transportation, the bus or the underground, something that appeared impossible to me because I did not speak English and above all could not understand what was said to me. I sometimes happened to ask a policeman what way to take: I looked in the direction in which he stretched his arm, I followed it for a moment, then again asked another policeman. So it was on the day that I wanted to go to the Tate Gallery, which was located at a spot that was rather distant from Soho. The route was simple, however; but the fever I was in complicated matters. Besides, I needed them to be complicated and difficult. For just imagine: the Tate Gallery, the very temple of Pre-Raphaelitism. To arrive there called for trials, and the more there should be, the greater would be the benefit.

However, it was not to the Tate Gallery that I went first of all. The day after my arrival I was content to stroll up and down Oxford Street, which was the nearest and most attractive thoroughfare, a model of a street—broad, bright, with substantial and well-patronized shops. I did not take long to discover a fascinating shop window there, the very one that I should have wanted to find, furnished almost entirely with reproductions of Pre-Raphaelite paintings; it was there that I saw Watts's *Hope* for the first time. There was also a Burne-Jones with which I was not acquainted: *Aurora.* That was a young woman with cymbals in her hands, who advanced along a canal bordered by high, gray walls. This picture gave me an unspeakable delight; from that day onward, and for several years, it accompanied the movements of my thoughts and signified their awakening.

Aurora, that is also the title of a book by Michel Leiris. I wonder if he was struck like myself by this picture; in any case, the name perfectly bewitched him—read his book and see for yourself. There is a staircase in it that is not without an analogy to the canal in Burne-Jones's painting. Besides, surrealism in many respects is a dynamited Pre-Raphaelitism (yes, Pre-Raphaelitism rather than symbolism); it starts from the marvelous and it is always to the marvelous that it returns when it wants to take a rest after its exploits outside of literature. That is very clear in André Breton's *Arcane 17*; it is apparent in the allegorical and ornamented poems of René Char; it is very evident among women—temperamentally less inclined than men to be dynamiters—like Valentine Hugo and Leonor Fini.

Watts's *Hope*, I was to see it again often—in all the houses, in fact, that I was able to enter. As you perhaps know, it is a woman with blindfolded eyes who is seated on a globe of the world; she holds a lyre whose strings are broken, except one, which she still strums. The reproductions, unless it is a matter of simple post cards, are almost always in color, doubtless because of the blue of the sky that is its background, and that is very sweet to look upon. The truth is that it is a devotional picture. It occurs to me that the importance of Pre-Raphaelitism in England is in part related to its having brought in an imagery that the Protestant religion had put a stop to; it restored the sacred feminine world that had been banished for such a long time—angels and saints, sibyls and goddesses, that world and the ample decor of hieratic vegetation that accompanies it. Even at the time when we loved it here it had infinitely more significance over there; it represented a genuine renaissance for the English; it extended not only to poetry and to painting, but also to architecture, to furniture, and to everything that belongs to the decorative arts: tapestries, stained-glass windows, fabrics, wallpapers, book illustrations and decorations. It was, under the influence of Ruskin and William Morris, a new humanism; the artists of the group had a community ideal, and they gave themselves the name of brother; they wanted to honor the hand as much as the spirit; their liking for the Middle Ages of legend and above all for the Quattrocento did not prevent them from being resolutely modern: it must not be forgotten that it was they who created the Modern Style or Art Nouveau. And as the present-day art dealers say to reluctant art lovers: "Whether you like it or not, it counts!" Somebody should write the history of the Pre-Raphaelite movement; Georges Duthuit, for example, would do it marvelously.

But let us come back to London and my seventeen years of age. We are in Oxford Street in front of the famous window. Although my purse is very light and although they have advised me above all to avoid useless expenses, I decide to behave foolishly. I enter and point my finger at *Aurora* and *Hope*, and also at the reproduction of a painting by Rossetti, *The Day Dream*, which I am likewise seeing for the first time—it is a woman who really resembles Suzanne, seated in a tree. In front of me I find a file containing post cards; I leaf through them and take everything that there is of my two painters. I articulate as best I can a "how much," out of which, for fear of dropping the "h," I make a kind of little sneeze. I come to paying: it is not difficult, you give a sovereign and they give you the change. After that you have only to leave with your head on fire, pass up the sunny street again to Marble Arch, and go to refresh your mind in Hyde Park, where at this still early hour you see only strollers who are little different from those of the Tuileries. In the afternoon, a visit to the agency, then a letter to the family, with a special chapter for mother and sister, and naturally post cards.

The next day I went to the National Gallery, which is not very far distant from Soho, just Charing Cross Road to go down and you emerge in Trafalgar Square with the museum well in view. The immense square, with Nelson's Column in the center, for me produced the effect of a little seaport; what intoxicated me most, I really believe, were the calls of the bus conductors, for whom Charing Cross is an important starting point. The sound of those voices, which were gallant and a bit rusty like the chains of ships, their manner of barking the names of the stations, that all gave me a pleasure so keen that even now it happens some mornings that I rediscover those voices in my head and try to imitate them while accentuating the words that dominated the others: *Tottenham Court Road*, the name of the first station after Charing Cross.

The museum could only overwhelm me with its rich collection of painters from the Quattrocento. There were marvelous Botticellis there; my favorite, the one that really brought tears of happiness to my eyes, was *The Nativity*, with the angels who are embracing the shepherds on earth while other angels are rejoicing in heaven. I was very responsive to an *Annunciation* by Carlo Crivelli, with a virgin and a Gabriel that had exquisite faces and with a sumptuous setting that recalled those of Burne-Jones. I passed in front of admirable portraits by Rembrandt, not indifferent but almost terrified by such a strong and bitter humanity. The English school of the eighteenth century charmed me a great deal; in those portraits by Reynolds, by Gainsborough, by Romney, what grace, elegance, and also what freshness and tenderness. It seemed to me that I had never seen women so kind, so happy to be mothers—and how could they not have been with such beautiful children! It was not at the National Gallery but at the Wallace Collection that I saw the painting by Reynolds that charmed me most: the portrait of Mrs. Richard Hoare and her little child; I immediately sent the reproduction to my mother, not doubting that she would be as much delighted as myself by the sweet and luminous maternity of it. Paul Valéry must have thought of this painting when he wrote *La Jeune Mère [The Young Mother]*, for his prose seems adapted to describe it, he gives the essence of it in the closing lines:

> She is like a natural Philosopher and Sage who has found his idea and who has built for himself what he needed.
> She wonders whether the center of the universe is in her heart or in the little heart that throbs between her arms, and which in its turn makes all things live.

Yes, I saw wonders at the Wallace Collection. I shall return to it, but I want to speak first about my visit to the Tate Gallery, which prepared me, in some fashion, to enjoy the celebrated collection better. I said above that it was with great emotion that I started on my way to the Tate Gallery, since I was aware that it was there that the greatest number of Pre-Raphaelite paintings were to be found grouped together. I had the disappointment of finding there very few paintings by Rossetti and Burne-Jones. I learned afterward that the most important groups were to be found in the museums of Manchester and Liverpool, or even in private collections. I had to be satisfied with *Beata Beatrix* and *Sancta Lilia* for the first, and with *King Cophetua and the Beggar Maid* for the second. I had a curious impression in passing from the reproductions to the originals; until then I had had the pictures in my hands, pictures that were closely bound to my readings and my reveries, pictures in black or brown whose colors I could imagine. I found myself now in front of something that did not disappoint me, of course—nothing in me would have admitted disappointment—but that all the same did not give me the joys I was expecting. I am trying now to analyze that impression: it seems to me that Rossetti's colors have something that is indefinably feverish and weary about them, they are like tarnished cushions upon which one has too often leant to dream. Burne-Jones is much more a painter; his stylization is more sure, his color is more independent, and his execution is much better. Today it is rightly found that they both of them lack "subject matter," and in fact we cannot expect from them the gratification that the real plastic artists know how to give; they are too literary. I also was too literary at that time, I loved them with a love that was in my head.

Such as they were, they clearly surpassed the other Pre-Raphaelite painters: Millais, Watts, Holman Hunt, and Ford Madox Brown. In the Tate Gallery there is a whole room devoted to Watts; *Hope* is an oasis there. His symbolism is puerile but not objectionable, and the general color, in which, as I have already said, a sky blue predominates, is very agreeable. The other compositions produce the uneasiness that one experiences in front of the works of Gustave Moreau; that belongs even more to nightmares, because a stronger materiality of execution is applied to a slighter imagination, a materiality that does not correspond to a beautiful subject but to a realistic and limited manner of treating legends and dreams. There is a minotaur there that is as painful, I suppose, as certain hallucinations due to opium.

I did not much enjoy the religious and historical paintings of Holman Hunt and Ford Madox Brown. On the other hand, Millais interested me a great deal; there is a theatrical truth in his works, particularly in *Ophelia*, that causes a sensation; his *Knight Errant* with a feminine face and solid armor, who with a sword and a pensive air is freeing a completely naked, beautiful blonde woman bound to a tree, the whole thing life-size, could not fail to captivate me. I was not unresponsive to the beauty of Turner, of whom there is a full room, but I was not very responsive either; there were, however, astonishing fairylike landscapes; their mists should have charmed me, but at that time I was moved only by figures.

After the Tate Gallery I went to visit the Wallace Collection. A great adventure happened to me there: I discovered the French eighteenth century. I believed, however, that I knew it well, our eighteenth. In Paris a Sunday never passed that I did not go to a museum, and it was to the Louvre most often. That century seemed frivolous to me, remote from and even the enemy of poetry; it was mingled for me with the gallantry that is the opposite of ideal love. Only Watteau escaped my disdain, obviously Verlaine and Debussy had been inspired by him; but I believe I would have perceived his poetic essence even without that. It must also be said that I despised the eighteenth because of the middle-class infatuation that was attached to it, above all at that time: there was not a salon that was not Louis XV, and so many stupid and cumbersome knickknacks! —the Wallace Collection resembles a museum less than a town house; there is a quantity of beautiful pieces of furniture and precious objects there, arranged as if the surroundings were lived in; one rediscovers there a bit of the atmosphere of Chantilly, along with something more personal. I crossed without stopping the rooms full of all kinds of weapons. I was dazzled when I entered room eighteen, where a great number of French paintings of the eighteenth century are to be found. After the Tate Gallery, where I had been satiated by tenacious visions whose colors were raw or overcooked, I now experienced the gratification that fine cooking gives. God! the beautiful, the perfect paintings. So, the artists I had despised were there: Fragonard, Boucher, Pater and Lancret, and Watteau, whose tender enchantment I saw better than ever. I understood at last the sense of lightness and elegance, and that here too there is a soul, but discreet and modest, even in immodesty. The thunderbolt was delivered to me by Fragonard's *Hasards de l'escarpo-lette [Hazards of the Swing]*, very well placed besides, in a corner, with a special lighting. On seeing the mischievous face of the lady who is swinging and, like a rose in full bloom, the flight of the flounces of her pink skirts, I felt as much delight, I think, as any son of Albion.

And yet the next day I hurried to the Victoria and Albert Museum to contemplate there other Burne-Joneses (I had seen from certain post cards that some were to be found there). I finally discovered them in a little room on the third floor: there was *The Mill*, which is a very charming composition, and another disappointing painting, *Merlin and Nimuë*, with sketchy figures and a blurred background—not at all the habitual finish of the artist. I no longer know if it was in the same museum that I saw, likewise by Burne-Jones, *The Chariot of Love*, an immense unfinished canvas depicting men and naked women harnessed to a chariot upon which stands an androgynous being, rather male from his musculature; the chariot has the wheels of a locomotive and is crowned with frenzied drapery.

The weather was very beautiful during those first two weeks of October; I do not remember a single day of rain. I spent most of my mornings in the museums—I did not return to the Tate Gallery, but I made several visits to the National Gallery—or else I set out in search of the great monuments: Westminster Abbey, Parliament, Saint Paul's Cathedral, Buckingham and Saint James palaces. I did not fail to go to see the famous Horse Guards of Whitehall. I went one day as far as London Bridge, but I was satisfied to look from a distance at Tower Bridge, which raises its two churchlike structures in the middle of the river, and the imposing group of bulky medieval towers that form the Tower of London, and behind them, surpassing them in height, the four Moorish turrets of the Mint, with the little triangular standard floating in the midst. Very "return of the Crusades," this whole effect. The Thames appeared to me to be what it really is, an arm of the sea; you cannot imagine that it has its source in the land. It has all the ships and gulls that are needed to put you on the open sea. I never saw it in the evening at low tide when it uncovers its wreckage; I would not have been able to say, like Verlaine when he wrote to Edmond Lepelletier, "Besides, the Thames is superb, imagine an immense whirlpool of mud, something like a gigantic, overflowing latrine."

In the afternoon I walked in the streets; at five o'clock I took tea in one of the Lyons shops, where I discovered with delight buns, muffins, scones, and crumpets. Even the pastry made with beef fat pleased me, and I remember a mulberry cake that seemed delicious to me. I never went very far in my walks for the reasons that I have already mentioned, but because I was put up in the very center I could visit the most agreeable and bustling districts; a day never passed that I did not go to Piccadilly Circus; from there I went down to the end of the broad Piccadilly and up again to Oxford Street by way of Regent Street or Old Bond Street, two very elegant thoroughfares, equivalent to our Rue de la Paix, but with more reserve.

Piccadilly Circus always gave me an immense pleasure. The intersection appears very small because of the width of the streets that open into it; the buildings that surround it are covered from top to bottom by enormous advertising signs that overwhelm the eyes. In the center there is a bronze fountain that resembles a piece of wrought gold; it is topped by a sprightly Eros; the fountain rests upon an octagonal platform with two levels of steps. I remember having seen flower girls there whose dress struck me very much; they wore shawls as women of the people among us wear kerchiefs about their shoulders, and black straw hats. Their faces, above all those of the young, recalled to me the women of Burne-Jones—little hollow faces with a beautiful open look, like Christmas roses that bruise as soon as you pick them, but whose golden stamens remain full of life. I was no more in a position to see the traffic in prostitution that takes place there, it appears, than I was to see the bottom of the Thames; but I can easily believe it, for there is a kind of constriction in that place, a contrast of brutality and delicacy that are really rather orgastic. More than once I passed through Saint James Street and Pall Mall, the center of the clubs, and the Strand, with its theaters and its hotels and its shops of all kinds. Because of Oscar Wilde I did not fail to stop in front of the Savoy; as I read the *Mercure de France*, above all the old numbers, I knew something about that story, which for me was on a level with the theory of androgyny and Pre-Raphaelite art.

In those days there were horse cabs, which gave a great deal of character to the movement of the streets. I was astounded, like all Parisians, by the lowness of the dwellings, which seldom go beyond four stories. When I chanced to leave the central streets and see the long and monotonous rows of those houses, like interminable suburbs, I quickly retraced my steps and plunged back into the business districts. Among the shops, three kinds appeared to me to be without rivals. First of all there were the tobacco shops, which have a splendor that we have no idea of; the word *shop* does not suit them, they are little palaces, all more or less worthy of being run by Prince Florizel, the hero of the Suicide Club, who became, as you know, a tobacco seller in London (there is a charming book that should certainly be reprinted). In the second place, I was dazzled by the book-and-stationery shops. In general, they have two shop windows: one that displays a staggering choice of letter paper and desk articles, and, at the approach of the season, Christmas cards that do not for a second allow you to have the idea that you can forgo them; in the other window, hardbound books in dust jackets (which were not to be seen at all in France at that time), very well arranged, giving an impression of color, elegance, and variety, as if fashion were there rather than in feminine dress; and always plenty of children's books and fairy tales illustrated by Rackham and Walter Crane, and also by other artists working with finely drawn pictures and delicate colors.

The third kind of shop that charmed me comprised the confectioneries, which do not have our candy-box coyness, with beautiful packages and pretty bags, but which pile up incredible stacks of candy and cookies to the height of the shop window; all that with brilliant colors and a kind of savage fervor certain to drive a child wild with excitement. Looking at them I thought of the witch's house in *Hansel and Gretel*, with its walls of nougat, its roof made of gingerbread with candied fruit, its doors made of chocolate, its windows with posts of barley sugar, and, on the ground, instead of pebbles, bonbons and still more bonbons. It was in these shops that I saw hazelnut chocolate for the first time, not in bars but in enormous paving stones; they sold them to you for sixpence, splintering the bulky pieces with special little tongs.

I must not forget to note, among the things that struck me most, the letter boxes that stood upon the sidewalks like round posts, of the most beautiful vermilion. And the buses that in those days were covered with advertisements and resembled enormous newspapers.

But above all, like everybody who goes to London, I was bewitched by the smell of the city. I often wondered what it could really be that composed it. It smelled strongly of anthracite smoke, with a foundation of iodine and tar that told of the sea. In the fashionable districts it was mingled with the light smell of blond tobacco. It lay hold of you, it rocked you in its waves. You forgot everything except the pleasure of walking, of going as far as possible, with the intoxication of solitude, as if some great thing were promised to you alone. You had no notion of being happy or unhappy, you were in the kingdom of a god who communicated to you his breath and his greatness.

It was toward the middle of October that I arrived at Muswell Hill. I have a rather vague memory of that place, which was not very remarkable yet showed even so a certain little local character: it was calm, very middle-class, with shops that were well kept if not elegant, rather like Auteuil, while being more airy because it was on a height. There were two churches, of which one was a Wesleyan chapel where beautiful music could be heard on Sunday evenings.

Confectioneries were not lacking, and it was there that I bought "sixpence of broken nut chocolate" every day, both to finish off the somewhat frugal meals and brighten the dull hours. And then I could spend all day Thursday in London; I had a bus that drove me directly to Charing Cross in less than an hour. When I arrived at my destination I found myself again at a spot that I was well acquainted with, and I started forth again on nearly the same walks that I had taken at the beginning.

One Thursday, from Highgate, I saw the fog stretched out over the outskirts. I was very satisfied, it had been promised and I was looking forward to it. Even in London it seemed ideal to me, everything was more beautiful and more mysterious, it was like music. When the mists became more dense a week or two later I found the matter less agreeable, and that was still not it, they told me, the famous pea soup. I became acquainted with it once and for all, and it was even more terrible than I could ever have imagined it to be. In the afternoon the fog became thick and reddish, then really black; the passers-by, who at first were phantomlike, melted away completely, you could distinguish nothing anymore but the feeble halos of the streetlights, which far from guiding you led you farther astray. Although I had made an effort not to wander away from my familiar streets, I was incapable of finding Charing Cross and the station of the bus that was to carry me back to Muswell Hill. I have no idea of the length of the time during which I wandered with increasing anguish. I was lost, and this feeling, which at first transported me close to Mélisande and Golaud—"I shall never be able to get out of this forest"—bit by bit became the very feeling of death. My will to live was dissolved, I was resigned, it seemed to me more easy to pass away into the other world than to remain in this one. I do not remember what saved me: I must have gone up again toward the north, following Tottenham Court Road, then Euston Road; it is beyond doubt that, knocking into a passer-by, I was able to make him understand my distress and that he helped me to reach King's Cross Station, for I am sure that I went back by train. I see myself again seated in a railway compartment, recovering my appetite for life with little gulps.

Such a day, fortunately, did not occur again; the fog proved to be mild until December 15, the date on which I came back to France.

A bit before my departure I had the good fortune to attend a performance of *L'Oiseau bleu,* which was being acted at the Haymarket Theatre. The play was not produced in Paris until the year after. As I understood spoken English very poorly, I had bought the book—a beautiful volume bound in mauve cloth that had appeared at Methuen's, it was the ordinary edition—and I had studied it with great help from the dictionary. I had reserved my seat, which was for a Saturday matinee, a long time in advance: a seat in the balcony, first row center. My mother had sent me the money in secret, not telling my father, so that I would be equal to the occasion. Was it not miraculous to be in London just at the moment when they were performing *L'Oiseau bleu?* It was a sign that was at least as surprising and favorable as the canary that came to rest in Gide's hand when he was fifteen years old. And as an additional stroke of good luck, Haymarket Theatre was located between Piccadilly Circus and Trafalgar Square, in the part of London that I knew best.

I have a clear enough memory of that performance. It was much more familiar and charming than it was in Paris. At the Théâtre Réjane, where I saw it later with Georgette Leblanc, they had wanted to create art, and in fact they had not done badly, but it had become cold. In England the symbols of this exquisite fairy tale found natural and as if everyday clothing, they were touching and profound with simplicity; the text was solidly established by the honest, rugged voices of the men who acted—the dog barked to perfection. The spirit of Maeterlinck, which reveals treasures of humor and poetry in this work, was happily married to the English spirit, which gave it vigor. Yes, it seems to me that I saw an excellent performance there; my idolatry for the author of *Serres chaudes [Greenhouses]* was not increased by it, for that had reached a peak that could not be surpassed, but I derived from it all possible satisfaction and pride.

I spent my last full London day in Oxford Street doing Christmas shopping: candy and toys for my little cousins. There was a big store in this street that was called, I believe, Peter Pan; in any case, its Christmas windows were done after the adventures of Peter Pan. How gay it was, seen through a benevolent fog, the windows decorated with lights, with all the children in front of them! In this store, where I generally went shopping, it was a pleasure to pay and to see how they gave you the change: the saleswoman folded your money in a piece of paper upon which she had written the expense, she put the whole thing in a copper box that slid along a pulley and went I do not know where; the change came back to you by the same system.

When I arrived in Paris, at the Gare du Nord, the first thing that struck me was the outward appearance of the men of our country; that has changed a great deal since, but how many beards and mustaches there were then, how many bellies and trousers twisted like corkscrews. It was only then that I got a clear idea of the physical beauty of Englishmen and of the style and elegance of their clothing. In my walks over there I did not look at them any more than they looked at me, but I had really seen them even so.

From *Rue de l'Odéon*; first published in *Les Lettres Nouvelles* (May 1953).

Return to London

You will be astonished, perhaps—and I am the first to be astonished—that I stayed for so long without going to London: I did not return to it until 1948. That was because from the moment I opened my bookshop I was not able to leave the Rue de l'Odéon except in the month of August, when I went to take a rest in the mountains. Sylvia Beach shared the same fate. Before the establishment of Shakespeare and Company she was a traveler. Like Valery Larbaud she had made long stays abroad, she was well acquainted with the great cities of Europe. The day when she settled in Paris, full of experience and wisdom, she knew what she was doing—but certainly she did not suspect the subjection into which Joyce was going to put her. At the present moment the publisher of *Ulysses* is in the act of rediscovering her country; she writes to me from New York, where she spent the Easter holidays, which are very spirited over there, that everything is so full of life, so amusing, that she is dumbfounded. On March 17 she saw the Saint Patrick's Day parade, a parade that lasted a day and a night because of the blacks with trumpets and drums who had joined the Irish.

So, Sylvia could not dream of leaving Paris any more than myself. Even at Easter we were kept there, for then England came to us. When the Parisian students went away, it was the English students who stopped in front of our shop windows and the young professors of Oxford and Cambridge who crossed our thresholds in order to ask us what poets they should read. I remember an extraordinary thing: in 1925, when I had the idea of putting together an issue of the *Navire d'Argent* devoted to William Blake (the idea came to me in the spring and several months were necessary in order to carry it out), one morning when I was thinking about Blake intensely an unknown young man entered the bookshop and asked me if I could send him books in England. When I asked him his name he answered: William Blake—Like the poet?—Yes, like the poet—Such occurrences were not rare at the bookshop; it happened rather often that a passer-by would come in to ask for precisely the book I was musing about or that I was in the act of talking about with a friend, but nothing ever gave me so much pleasure as that greeting from the beyond.

During the months that followed the Liberation we had visits from several English friends. First to come was Monica Sterling in uniform. In January, when it was so cold, we saw Cyril Connolly; he was staying at the Embassy, but he had pitiable shoes whose soles were soaking up the snow on our streets in great draughts. Spring brought us Stephen Spender. On Victory Day itself T. S. Eliot paid us the honor of coming to have tea with us. A bit later the Stuart Gilberts came back to live in their apartment on the Ile Saint-Louis. When we questioned them, our friends told us about the sufferings that the English, and the Londoners above all, had undergone during the war. They told us about what the bombardments had been like, and about the terrible ruins that they had left. I learned that nothing remained of the City. Alas, I had hardly seen it at the time of the journey of my youth, and I had promised myself so much to visit it in the company of Sylvia!

The desire to return to England was decidedly imposed upon us after we read *Beowulf* by our dear Bryher. Like very few works, this novel about a London teahouse during the war has the gift of putting one in sympathy with its characters. They are not exceptional human beings, but brave and simple people, real English people whom the author has portrayed faithfully. There appears in this book the face of English goodness, which is masculine even among the women. It is a book that helps one to penetrate to the heart of the Great Island and that gives one the feeling of not being foreign to it. *Beowulf* had appeared in the *Mercure de France* in April 1948; on May 28 of the same year the two of us took the plane for London.

I had promised myself upon leaving Paris to take again the walks of former times and above all to see Soho and Muswell Hill again, which I remembered so vaguely. In the meantime I had read Paul Morand's *London*, and I had learned very interesting things about that Soho neighborhood that I had passed through blindly. But the week that we were to spend over there quickly ran out, all the more so because we took two days in order to visit Oxford and Stratford-on-Avon.

That week we saw more friends than streets and monuments. Fortunately, for the city with its rationing and its gaping wounds caused great sorrow. We stood horror-stricken before the ruins of the City and at the same time we marveled to see above these ruins the dome of Saint Paul's, more imposing than ever, preserved as by a miracle—hardly a Christian miracle, since it let the houses of men be annihilated. There was a biblical vision here: one thought of the voices of prophets thundering out during calamities.

I was struck, during this journey, by London's resemblance to a book, to the world of books. The walks there resemble readings. Ideas are superior to what one sees, just as if they started from print. Things and people compose a text, they do not distract one's looks but make them thoughtful. The passers-by are concentrated, contained by what they signify. The monuments do not show figures, their embellishment is typographical. The bright red mailboxes make beautiful pages. With the red buses, and above all when one sees several of them at a time, the page is overloaded.

One follows the long streets like the sentences of a long novel, often too long, but never completely empty because there is always the sense of an action and the appeal of one does not know what distant tribal rhythm. More than in any other place, one feels in London the presence of the invisible world. The English must never have been afraid that the sky might fall upon their heads, for the sky is close to them, blended with the smokes and the fogs of the earth and the waters. Cigarette smoke has a meaning in their cities that it does not have elsewhere: it climbs up like incense toward gods who are close by; it joins the ancestors whose souls are always ready to blend themselves with those of the living.

It is not in the places prepared to receive them that the souls of the ancestors show themselves best. Doubtless it occurs to them to slip over to Westminster and to Saint Paul's just as the fog slips into the houses, but they do not stay there. Great men hardly like their statues, which are officially consecrated to them and which equalize them under the idea of national greatness. Of course they know that it is good to have them, for they are a guarantee against total oblivion all the same. From time to time they come to see if they are still there; on solemn days, theoretically, they must occupy them, but most of them send in their stead secondary spirits who demand only that. Their pleasure is to move about searching among the living for those whose brains can serve as wombs for their posterity.

The statues of famous men are like ghosts—made to torment the ignorant and some unbelievers. They rear up before those who are not familiar with the names on the pedestals and oblige them to bow down or to raise their heads, they give them an uneasiness and a profound discouragement. Westminster Abbey, what ghostly bric-a-brac! We visited it for a long time one morning of bitter sunlight when it was a pleasure to be swallowed up by its porch. Sylvia, obviously, did not risk being tormented, at least by the poets, she was even able to guide and protect me. In regard to historical personages, Shakespeare, her patron, had armed her with a sprig of the Golden Bough. Seriously speaking, let me say that this visit was very agreeable; the statue of Handel amused us very much, we could not tear ourselves away from it—poor Handel, such a great musician, condemned to that contorted appearance—and it was a French sculptor who made it, somebody named Roubillac!

While moving around among the statues, busts, and medallions, I thought about phantoms, of which England is the land of choice, as one knows. What is the difference, I wondered, between a phantom and a ghost? Many people believe that they are the same thing, but not at all. A phantom is a spirit in the scantiest attire—a sheet negligently thrown over a skeleton that is generally invisible with the exception of the skull, whose eye sockets are very hollow, and sometimes, in ball-and-chain cases, the tibia to which they are attached. A ghost resembles in a more blurred fashion the dead person from whom he emanates, he wears one of his familiar costumes and can, like Hamlet's father, be armed from top to toe. In short, a phantom does not come especially for somebody, he haunts a place and terrifies automatically, so to speak, those who inhabit it. A ghost does not take the trouble to appear without a reason: he wants to communicate with a specific person, whether to disturb him, or to reassure him, or, as it is in the case of Hamlet, to reveal a secret to him and charge him with a mission. By way of concluding, let us say that statues are related to ghosts, of which they are the solidified forms, but that they are as limited as phantoms, whose powers they are far from having.

We were put up, during this stay, in a charming hotel of

Grosvenor Gardens, very close to Buckingham Palace and Hyde Park. One of our first concerns was to go to Basil Street in order to see the site of The Warming Pan, whose story Bryher told in *Beowulf.* As it is said in the book, the neighborhood has been bombed, and piles of stone arise on the spot where the house of Selina Tippett was.

As for museums, we went only to the National Gallery. There we had a great surprise upon seeing the cleaned-up canvases. The effect of the Rembrandts is amazing; many details appear that were formerly hidden. All the same we regret the patina, which was as if bound to a certain experience of life and to their magnificent bitterness. On the whole, the paintings benefit from the treatment. The landscapes of Claude Lorrain are more radiant still, but Poussin loses his distinction, his nymphs are now too pink—Gide would not have liked that. It was with great pleasure that upon entering the museum we saw the *Blue Umbrellas* by Renoir.

Our longest walk was in order to visit The Temple. We were accompanied by two friends of Sylvia—Miss Ball and Miss Topalian, who were her companions during her captivity at Vittel. They were the ones who had decided that I must see this extraordinary spot, the most beautiful in London in their opinion. It is very sad that I was not able to go there before the war, for it is now terribly damaged; the precious round church of the Templars, dedicated to the Virgin, was burned twice in the course of the bombardments, and there are many other ruins besides these. In spite of everything I could feel the enchantment that they had promised me. It is really a little village consecrated to Justice; there and nearby, in Chancery Lane, are found the Schools of Law, the Courts of Justice, and the attorneys' offices. One sees an assembly of long and noble buildings that have the look of palaces made to be set around a larger one. That is invisible, but in its place there are gardens with beautiful trees that go down to the Thames. Into the calm and somewhat monastic atmosphere of these places is blended a gracious courtly spirit; I thought as I walked there of the music of Purcell.

We spent four fine evenings in the homes of our London friends, one of which was in the home of the two charming women I have just named, one at Robert Herring's place, one at Cyril Connolly's, and one at T. S. Eliot's. We went to Chelsea twice, but it was at night, and we did not see very much. I had in mind the exquisite description that Larbaud has given of this neighborhood in *Beauté, mon beau souci [Beauty, My Beautiful Care].* I should have loved to visit it thoroughly; I have the impression, however, that it is not enough to pass through it, and that one must stay there for a long while, as did the author of *Barnabooth*.

Robert Herring properly lives in Chelsea; he has a little house that is very gracefully arranged, even though he is a bachelor; but over there men like domesticity, they even bring a certain stylish charm to it. It was he who had prepared the dinner, he had even taken a great deal of trouble to make numerous dishes, most of which were based on canned foods. The kitchen being located in the basement, as is the custom in private houses, he had a lot of trouble merely bringing up the dishes. When the moment came for coffee, which was delicious, we were very happy to see him finally at ease and to be able to have a nice chat with him. He is one of the most sympathetic young men. He is marvelously well acquainted with the Elizabethan authors, of whom he possesses a large number of original editions. He is presently preparing a work on Shake-speare to which he intends to devote two years of labor. We know Herring through Bryher: he was the director of her review throughout the whole time it lasted, about fifteen years. This review, it gives me pleasure to recall, was particularly devoted to French literature; some writers, I believe, were translated in it for the first time: Aragon, Jean Cassou, André Chamson, Louis Guilloux, Henri Michaux, Jean Prévost, J. P. Sartre. It was there that Sylvia published the translation of Paul Valéry's *Littérature,* which she had done with the help of the author.

Cyril Connolly's house is plainly bigger. It is situated in the surroundings of Hyde Park. He too is a domestic man; he has beautiful furniture, precious knickknacks, and pleasing paintings, two of which are by Balthus. The double curtains of the windows of his living room are made of red damask; he drew them open at a favorable moment and we saw outside a magnificent tree, doubtless a plane tree. It was Madame Lys, so very nice, who had devoted herself to the cooking; there was only one dish, but it was so good and so well put together that we could desire nothing else. We found within it bits of fresh salmon, all kinds of vegetables, and slices of hard-boiled egg. The kitchen is in the basement, naturally, but a little adjoining room serves as a dining room, which is much more convenient. To get to the dining room one passes through the kitchen, and this gave me pleasure, for I adore kitchens and everything that is inside of them. In this one there was a superb piece of furniture for silver plate that had the look of being out of its element.

Cyril Connolly loves France very much and greatly appreciates our literature, as he has shown very well in his review *Horizon*. His compatriots must find him too Frenchified, for he is epicurean and irreverent, but he is a true Englishman at bottom, very Restoration. Even though the English seventeenth century resembles our eighteenth century in some respects, he is wrong, in my opinion, to believe that he could have been Chamfort, he is much closer to Samuel Pepys; one can easily imagine Pepys with a face like his own. When I think of him a passage from *Alice in Wonderland* comes to mind, the one in which Alice cradles in her arms a little pig that she at first takes for a baby; when she understands her mistake she tells herself that it would have become "a dreadfully ugly child" if it had grown up but that it was "rather a handsome pig" such as it was; and, thinking about the children that she knows who would make ravishing little pigs, she concludes, "If one only knew the right way to change them—" Well, for Cyril they have found the way: his face is charming. Add to this that he has a devilish wit and one of the liveliest sensibilities. He has written a book, *The Unquiet Grave* (translated into French by Michel Arnaud and published by Robert Laffont as *Le Tombeau de Palinure*), in which he has portrayed himself well. It is a curious work that mixes into the most personal reflections and witticisms an incredible amount of quotations that are for the most part taken from French authors. One also finds in it cities and landscapes that are drawn with deft, light strokes like those of Chinese painters, portraits of animals and fruits—no people—his Quince is as beautiful as a king. The author says, furthermore, that he is no longer concerned with anything but the vegetable world, and he seems to have wanted to present in this book the fruit of a mind that has arrived at ripeness. We are baffled, we French, to find so many quotations in a work whose ambition is apparent; we would never have shown such honesty or such humility; we would have plagiarized or taken the time that was needed to digest and transform; here the "connoisseur" has harmed the creator. And nevertheless what a pleasure it is to find at the head of a chapter this sentence from Flaubert, which Connolly calls an illumination: "Melancholy is only a memory that does not know itself."

From *Dernières Gazettes et Ecrits divers*; first published in *Les Lettres Nouvelles* (June 1953).

The Coronation of Elizabeth II

We leave Paris, Sylvia Beach and I, the morning of Thursday the 28th. Sylvia had come back from New York only a week before; she was supposed to stay over there for three months, but she hastened her return in order to go the coronation. In New York, she had told me, the crown was all the rage; it decorated dresses and even underwear, it served as the theme for all kinds of jewels. One saw it on handkerchiefs, neckties, and the heels of nylon stockings; some of the big stores that were displaying wedding gowns simply replaced the classic crown of orange blossoms with the crown of the coronation.

In the motorcoach that drives us to Orly I observe our traveling companions. It seems that there are as many English people as there are French; among the first I distinguish several middle-aged couples with a well-off appearance. On their knees the wives have hat boxes or bags that they protect carefully; the husbands have newspapers that they are reading and in their mouths or in their hands pipes that they are not smoking. There are some girls, doubtless students, who are returning to their country for the occasion. On the French side there are also girls, in groups of two or three, little different from the English ones; only one is all alone, she is going to London for the first time by plane, she is charming and excited—less excited, however, than her father, who accompanied her to the Gare des Invalides. Those four men who are exchanging animated remarks, they are probably journalists; they have the good raincoats, the leather briefcases, and the determined faces of the profession. Sitting behind us are two young men of good family, we do not doubt it: they are well dressed, their English is correct, and their French is existentialist, that is to say, based on the derivatives and the annexes of the word, as one knows. But the most remarkable of our contingent are a half-dozen serious ladies of sober elegance who speak English exquisitely and know how to show off the facets of their education to good purpose; two of them are accompanied by their daughters. My kind neighbor is probably a professor of English in a *lycée*.

Upon our arrival at London Airport around noon we take the motorcoach that is to carry us to Waterloo Air Terminal. A journey of an hour and a half through I do not know how many suburbs that are cut up at the beginning by scraps of country. All of the houses (those long lines of little houses squeezed against one another) are bedecked with tricolored festoons and streamers with the inscription *Long Live the Queen*, which is often printed on simple little posters stuck to the panes. It is also in the form of a poster that one sees almost everywhere the national flag with beneath it a medallion of the face of the queen, flanked by the Lion and the Unicorn. Astonishing, the liking of the English for what is printed: the fronts of their shops present more to read than our own, and in bigger letters—I like their shops very much.

At Waterloo we take a taxi in order to go to our lodgings; this is not a hotel but a room in the house of the friend of a friend, at the top of Fulham Road at the edge of Chelsea. Now we have broad views of the city, the stands that have been set up and the street decorations. Around Westminster the stands are immense. They are covered over with roofs, the inside surfaces of which are decorated with the arms of the cities of England; along the bases bordering the pavement one sees the names of the Commonwealth countries in big letters.

Our room delights us, it is furnished in the English style, the good English style, as is the whole house, which our hostess has us visit. The beds are excellent; I shall be able to come and go in the kitchen without fear of disturbing the mistress of the house, who leaves for her office in the morning and does not come back until the evening. We have brought butter, which we immediately put in the refrigerator.

In the afternoon we go to have tea at Bryher's place. What a joy to see her again in London, in her city, for she lives in Switzerland most of the time. I have brought her a painting by Michaux—she had expressed the desire to own one of them when she saw mine. These are "Emanglons"; I held them in my hands throughout the journey, protecting them just as the English women protected their hats.

That evening we are to make a motorcoach tour of the city, which is being illuminated for the first time. It is a tour organized by the International Services, which have taken the initiative this year of showing "London at night." This agency, one of the best I know, is directed by two very congenial women, Miss Winsor and Miss Molesworth.

Fortunately, we made this tour on the day of our arrival, because from the next day onward bus and taxi traffic were forbidden along the route of the procession on account of the congestion, which is unimaginable. All of the English provinces, all of the suburbs of London must be there; people are packed together like sardines; there are whole families with babies in their arms. Most of the women do not wear hats, and the men are also bareheaded with the exception of some, not so rare, who wear bowlers. These men are by themselves. As the evening advances we do not see any more at all; they must have gone home. Such a crowd does not permit a gentleman to walk with dignity.

Our tour begins rather early, at eight o'clock. We start out from Haymarket, next to the theater, where at the moment they are presenting *The Apple Cart* by Bernard Shaw, with Noël Coward. Until the time of the illuminations, at nine o'clock, we can make headway and see the decorations in the great thoroughfares very well. On the whole, these decorations are inspired by the Middle Ages; they give the streets the look of tournament lists. This style agrees admirably with the city, with its low and rectangular houses. Streamers with the colors of manuscript illuminations are stretched out at every story; one sees nothing but blazons, pennons, and banners everywhere. The most successful ones of this kind are undeniably in Pall Mall and Piccadilly. Athenaeum Court, in Piccadilly, is like a picture. One sees stands everywhere, in front of the houses when the width of the sidewalks permit, or on the inside of shops instead of window displays. In general the stands are as high as the ground floor; they are covered with draperies or painted, spangled with heraldic motifs. This Thursday evening the workmen are still on the job; in many places they are putting boards together, hammering nails, painting, stretching cloth. The stands are fashioned by means of metal frameworks; the benches are thick boards, not wide—they are going to be solid, but nobody is going to be very well seated. How many trees had to be cut down for so many benches and palings! But the wood will be very useful afterward. The stands that are raised not in front of dwellings but in open spaces are often higher than the houses; on each side of Waterloo Place there are two that are formidable: seven-story structures supported by metal beams and equipped with steep ramps—one thinks of Piranesi's prisons. Regent Street is decorated with large motifs inspired by the Thistle˙ and the Rose; the buildings are covered with great stucco eglantines that will soon be glowing. At the entrance to Old Bond Street there is an enormous crown from which the trumpets of heralds of arms shoot out in rays. Along the street, hooked to the windows, hang red oriflammes; in the middle, crossing the roadway like a bridge, there is an immense blue standard with the initials of the queen. The Dorchester Hotel in Park Lane is among the most remarkable: entirely hung with draperies of old blue with a row of real, smoking torches in front. In Oxford Street, Selfridge's stores have done things well—gold and white banners in every window; above the main entrance, life-size, the queen on horseback passing her troops in review, and behind her the portrait of Elizabeth I; along the front, up at the second story, a series of panels representing personages that looked Shakespearean to me—being in a vehicle I did not have the time to take a good look. The Liberty stores make less of an effect but show a more refined taste: their windows display dummies dressed in magnificent old costumes. The decorations in Whitehall please me very much; they are inspired, not without humor, by the demeanor of the Horse Guards in their helmets with astonishing plumes and chin straps; a group of silhouettes cut out of metal, modern in spirit and fabrication, rears up every hundred steps. It is the most daring thing I have seen.

The streets of the City and of Saint Paul's are decorated in a single fashion: with festoons of white roses (paper ones, naturally) stretched above the roadways, and every sixty-five feet or so, where the festoons cross over, a banner with the arms of the City, almost like Savoy's—a cross, but red upon a white ground with, in addition, a sword in the upper left-hand corner. Fleet Street, the famous street where newspapers occupy almost all of the buildings, is the most flowery and beautiful.

As we return by way of Regent Street, our motorcoach can no longer make headway. A great number of buses (those big buses the color of boiled lobsters) have been appropriated for tours of our kind in the bedecked and illuminated streets. These buses advance single file, at a walking pace, like the crowd that presses against their sides. Our guide advises us to get off a little before Piccadilly Circus and go back by way of the underground. It is already eleven o'clock at night, and we get off. Before being swallowed up by the subway, we cast a glance at the Circus; the enormous glowing signs eclipse all other illumination. But what have they done with the Eros in the center of the Circus? They have put him in a high gilded cage, rounded at the top like certain parrot cages. Sylvia says that it is a crown, I myself say that it is a cage. The pretty fountain that serves as a pedestal is completely hidden by a makeshift octagonal construction whose panels are alternately white and dark green—it resembles a box. There, in a cage or a box, is the Coronation Eros.

This is the first time in my life that I am going down into the London subway; I truly believe that it amazes me more than the temporary splendors that I have just seen. What depths, what a kingdom! One after the other, escalators more vertiginous than those of the Palais de Chaillot, each with four rows, take you far down under the earth; I was oppressed by them. One is completely surprised to find seats of brown velvet in the cars, in good condition, really; I should never have thought that velvet was so deserving. There is no question of sitting down on it, there are too many people. Just as I grip one of the handles for standing passengers a man kindly gives me his seat. I shall not say, like Duhamel (the matter has been brought up in the *Observer*), that "courtesy is not dead—it has simply taken refuge in Great Britain," no, because in Paris gentlemen and even girls often offer me their places in the subway.

We spend all Wednesday walking in the center of town, looking at the stores, buying post cards and souvenirs. We go up Piccadilly again on foot. The itinerant fruit sellers have turned their carts into genuine little altars that the image of the queen dominates like a Holy Virgin. There is a crown in every store, one or several, treated with reverence, more or less; sometimes it is placed in the center with befitting majesty, sometimes it enhances fabrics, hats, objects of all kinds; I saw one upon which shoes had been placed—I was shocked. The prettiest are the ones that we saw when we were in the motorcoach: these are fine wicker baskets displayed in a shop almost opposite the Victoria and Albert Museum; we shall go to buy one.

We sit down on the grass in Saint James Park; we write post cards; then we go on foot to Buckingham Palace. The crowd is gathered in front of the railings at every hour of the day, it seems. Three superb soldiers from Pakistan mount guard; their high turbans of khaki gauze whose wings stream and twist in the wind give them the look of bird-men, as Rebecca West says. All eyes converge upon them; their faces are as impassive as those of idols.

Saturday, a visit to Chelsea, which is next door to us: we have only to go down Sydney Street and we are in King's Road. This street and the one we are in, Fulham Road (which is still a part of the district of Kensington), must count among the longest of the capital; not less than an hour is needed to go the length of each of them, above all if one strolls; they are very pleasant, with well-frequented shops and charming antique stores. The displays of confectionery and smoking supplies, often together in the same place, are less exuberant than those that had enchanted me in my youth. In short, the London of my seventeen years of age, as it is fixed in my memory, was bedecked to the utmost.

Chelsea is very calm, with the exception of King's Road, its principal thoroughfare, where all the shopkeepers are gathered. It is less a neighborhood than it is a little province that has very much its own particular history and physiognomy; it takes pride in having been inhabited by many poets and artists; Henry VIII had had a castle-nursery built here for his children; the little Elizabeth, the future queen, walked here in the beautiful gardens that go along Cheyne Walk. Today there is an extraordinary liveliness in the streets; Sylvia bought at a newsdealer's a "Chelsea Souvenir Programme" (these two words *souvenir* and *programme* have also been adopted by the official publications of London). We saw that a great procession was announced for the afternoon, with historical floats illustrating the epochs of the sovereigns: Elizabeth, Anne, Victoria, and the present queen; there would also be floats representing the events of the week. We shall have to see it. After lunch, a walk along the Thames, which is very beautiful at this spot, with its flock of swans and some placid large factories on the other side. The weather lends itself poorly to revery, with a cold wind and an acid sun. It is impossible to remain seated on the benches or leaning on one's elbows against the embankment; we have to walk. We go up Cheyne Walk again, looking at the houses that bear plaques; first of all the one in which Turner lived and worked—he did not die in it, we know why: his case is a bit like Dr. Jekyll's, though much less tragic, fortunately—then those of Whistler, Henry James, Swinburne, Rossetti, George Eliot. We get back to King's Road just in time to see the procession. The floats are numerous, large and well furnished with characters who perform their roles conscientiously; the costumes are made of inexpensive materials of the mid-Lent sort. There is a parade of old vehicles and velocipedes. I see nothing that might apply exactly to what the Souvenir Programme calls "the events of the week." The two military bands are playing a tune that has something to say to me. I need a moment or two in order to recognize in that martial fanfare punctuated by beats on a big drum our *Jean de la lune.* The second group of musicians is made up of girls in uniform who are valiantly playing bugles; they have as much wind as the men, my word, only one seems to be a bit flushed in the face; they are preceded by a drum majorette who brandishes her baton—I'll say no more!—but the chief attraction is a motorcoach full of old people, men and women, with good faces, whom we see are all lively and laughing.

Sunday morning Bryher comes looking for us in a taxi; we are going to visit the City, or rather its ruins, and to see the decorations of the neighboring districts. We get off very close to Saint Paul's Cathedral and go along the devastated streets, where we see only earth, stone, and scrap iron; at the most, sometimes, foundation walls emerging from the ground. Things have remained almost in the state that they were in five years ago; certain spots have simply been transformed into squares of greenery; grass and flowers are covering up the expanse bit by bit; it seems, Bryher tells us, that a great number of different and rather unexpected flowers have been found—she told me the number, but I do not remember. We go to Silver Street, where Shakespeare lived. Coming back we go along the London Wall, which is the ancient Roman rampart, of which vestiges remain. Some distance away, in the courtyard of an old half-destroyed house, we stop in front of a little monument surmounted by the bust of Shakespeare; it is the monument raised to the memory of the actors John Heminge and Henry Condell, who seven years after the death of the dramatist published the folio of his complete works, half of which were as yet unpublished. On the pedestal we read the declaration that they put at the beginning of the edition: it is touching and it does them much honor; I shall remember their names.

Monday we decide to make a rehearsal of the course we must take the next day in order to get to our seats in Haymarket. It is very simple, we take the subway to Leicester Square, as the Piccadilly Circus station is going to be shut, and we have a five-minute walk before coming to the street that will allow us to reach from the back the building in which our seats have been reserved. According to our tickets we must be there a little before seven o'clock in the morning. Sylvia having decided to go sooner than I (I was afraid for a moment of the fatigue of the journey), we are not in the same spot, but close to one another; she is in Haymarket House and I am at the International Services, which have installed a stand in the embrasure of a large window of their offices. In Leicester Square we see that they are showing a film with Charles Laughton, *Young Bess*, in which he is again playing the part of Henry VIII; but we are even more tempted by *Abbott and Costello Meet Captain Kidd*, posted up at the London Pavillion. Laughton as Captain Kidd—we will hurry to it when they show it in Paris.

One more time we go up Piccadilly, mixing with the crowd. A bootblack has set up business on the sidewalk with his dog, who is stretched out on a blanket, covered by his master's overcoat, which is arranged in such a way as to show the belt (I really mean the belt, not the collar) of tricolor flowers with which he is decked out. The names of this nice couple are written on a piece of oilcloth spread out in front of the dog: *Trixie and Sailor*; but which is Trixie and which is Sailor?

Along Saint James and Green Park we see people installed behind the metal barriers that border the sidewalk—it is two o'clock in the afternoon. Some are already solidly encamped there: newspapers and blankets on the ground, baskets and hampers with thermos sticking out. There are many girls and young boys with boy-scout knapsacks; but there are also some aged women—I see two of them who have white hair. We are told that people have been installed since the night before at Trafalgar Square, where the procession will pass three times.

Tuesday, June 2—it's the great day. We get up at five o'clock and are at the South Kensington subway station at six. A long line in front of the gate. Gray weather, a little rain is falling. The people —good middle-class people—are in Sunday dress, with umbrellas rather than raincoats; the women are wearing pert hats, the men bowlers or beautiful felts; there are three top hats, one of which is gray. We do not stand in line for more than ten minutes, we get our tickets quickly thanks to automatic distributors; the cars are packed, like our own during the Occupation; we have trouble getting in; I am squeezed against an old gentleman in a top hat, the velvet collar of his overcoat is frayed. The ride is interminable, the train stops two or three times between each station. At Leicester Square the rain is falling rather heavily, fortunately we have raincoats. At the end of Coventry Street there are great wooden gates that shut off access to Piccadilly Circus; Sylvia takes Oxendon

Street, and I Shaver's Place, and here we are at our destination.

I enter by the back door of the restaurant Chicken Inn, which occupies the ground floor of the building in which the offices of the International Services are located. I am to have breakfast, lunch (with a half-bottle of champagne), and "television facilities" in this restaurant. The people I see are, like the ones in the subway, very joyful about the news communicated by the morning newspapers: Everest has been conquered by a man of the Hunt expedition, the New Zealander Hillary. It is certainly a good omen. I take my seat on the stand; I look at the compact crowd on the sidewalks of Haymarket; the first row is occupied by people who have spent the night there and who have blankets and baggage with them. They are standing propped against the metal barriers. I am lucky to have a roof and walls. Only the triple window, from which the panes have been removed, is open; it is not warm, but I am well clad. I have a remarkable woman for a neighbor: Miss Agnes Latham, a professor of literature at Bedford College; she speaks French a little and understands it rather well; for once it is an Englishwoman who speaks her own language least willingly; she has a very shrewd look, shy and sly at the same time. We try to exchange ideas about royalty, I tell her that I find it very good in England, but that with us it would not be possible to go backward, and that furthermore it would not suit us. She agrees and adds: it is unfortunate that during the time of your kings you did not have a queen. I agree with her; obviously, we have had queens, morganatic as well as legitimate, but they were not consecrated. Yes, it would have been interesting to see what an absolute woman sovereign would have done in France; I cannot come to the point of imagining such a thing. We are really comfortable in these offices, where we can come and go without remaining seated for hours on a bit of board; when we arrived our kind directresses offered us tea. At 8:30 we shall have a complete breakfast in the restaurant, and at 10:20 television. We go to take a look at where the television will be: it is in the basement, with a large screen and comfortable chairs.

Let me say immediately that television that day was a revelation and an enchantment, for myself as for everybody. To think that one could be present at such a ceremony at the very moment it was taking place! that one was seeing, better than the privileged people at Westminster, the succession of acts that composed it and the actors who assumed its roles! It is not irreverence on my part to call them actors: the queen, the archbishop, and everybody who surrounded them. The spot in the cathedral where the rites take place is called the *theater*; and we know how many rehearsals were necessary in order to arrive at an impeccable performance. The fact that it was a queen and not a king increased the interest and the emotion, above all among the women. We all watched Elizabeth II with the eyes of mothers and sisters, trembling lest she be not completely at her best and proud to see her endure the trial valiantly. When she arrived in the nave and moved forward with an air of meditation, we felt that she was thinking intensely of her father, and of the ancestors to whom he had joined her. It was with lowered eyelids that she received each of the consecrated things that made her queen after them. Her resemblance to George VI, slight at first, became striking toward the end of the ceremony—everybody called attention to it.

I remained for three hours in front of the screen, motionless, absolutely fascinated by the concentration and by the magical slowness of the spectacle. The faces that appeared made one think of the faces of ghosts, come from the past as if with difficulty on waves that stage by stage reached back to the imperceptible; ancient times rose toward us, thanks to the most modern invention. I do not believe that those who witnessed this will henceforth be able to make light of a tradition capable of having us reach such a "mother-center"—it is completely equal to what can be seen in Tibet or among the Tarahumaras.

There is also the tradition of not wanting tradition; it is less heavy but more tiring—it is very fine to walk, but still it is necessary to take the time to sit down and recover one's breath, if only to be able to start off again.

For all their scepticism the French have at bottom a truer and more demanding religion than the English, who put themselves less at the service of God than they put Him at their own service. With us, the pure suffer from naming Him as from an immodesty, they detest "the frightful abuse" that can be made of Him; they do not make the task easy for themselves, that is for sure. In the end, all is well this way and it can hardly be otherwise. It is magnificent that England is what she is, and it is no less magnificent that we are what we are, even with our governmental "infirmity." Their queen is a bit our queen, and our Revolution is a bit their own. It is thanks to us, thanks to democracy, that they should have perfect sovereigns who make us almost envious, and whom we are in any case obliged to respect. It was not so much Victoria who installed an era of virtue and conformism as it was the universal suffrage that was established under her reign; a royal family in our time can be only a model family. It must be admitted that Queen Elizabeth II, with her radiant smile, with everything that one senses in her of vitality and kindness, is one of the most charming women one could hope to see. And what a very handsome and very sympathetic man the Duke of Edinburgh is. And little Princess Anne and bonnie Prince Charles are darlings.

The television session lasted until two o'clock in the afternoon. Then we had the lunch, which included, according to a healthy logic, fresh salmon from Scotland and chicken from Surrey, and very good apple pie. France was represented by champagne and frosted petits fours. After that there was hardly anything to wait for except the procession; it was to be at Piccadilly Circus at 3:30. Hail fell, it seems, while we were watching television; feeble rays of sunshine alternate with showers; the crowd massed on the sidewalks in their streaming raincoats has the look of a people of Neptune arisen from the waters. The soldiers who are lining the way take off their raincoats all at once, fold them, and place them in little heaps behind them. Here we are. Not exactly, a quarter of an hour still passes before we hear the full clamor that precedes the arrival of the first contingents. Here are the bands—four of them belonging to different army corps. Then comes the Commonwealth parade: Southern Rhodesia, Ceylon, Pakistan, South Africa, New Zealand, Australia, and Canada. Each group is greeted with vigorous cheering, New Zealand above all, naturally. The armies of the United Kingdom, which begin with detachments of the Royal Air Force, are not less acclaimed. A parade of English soldiers is really an astonishing thing, their march is as measured as the movement of a loom, the regular swing of their arms gives the impression of a weaver's shuttle. The crowd continues roaring with varying intensity. The weak moments do not at all correspond to a lesser enthusiasm but to the drawing of breath. It is always the classic hurrah, of which only the second syllable is pronounced—rah— with an "r" that starts from the depths of the breast. Yes, a real lion's roar, as Edith Sitwell has rightly noted in her book on Queen Victoria.

The vehicles that follow convey the colonial sovereigns and prime ministers. They are almost all covered landaus; from the third floor where we are we cannot make out their faces. We should have loved to see Sir Winston. The imposing Queen Salote of Tonga, who shows herself in an uncovered carriage, has a deserved success, which she accepts with a face and with gestures as open as the flowers of her island.

The Queen Mother Elizabeth and the Princess Margaret are cheered with special ardor. We wonder how it will be possible for the uproar to be stronger for the queen. It happens, nevertheless; when the gilt coach arrives, with its eight pearl-gray horses, its equerries, and its picturesque escort of yeomen of the guard, it is like an atomic bombardment. I do not see the queen, but the whole street is lit up by her smile. The people who see her best are those who are in the first row on the sidewalks. It is justice itself, they have well deserved their places.

I was astonished to read the next day in the *Evening Standard* that the coronation ceremony had been long and tiring for the royal family and for the attendants, and that it could perhaps have been cut down; but even supposing it had been shortened by half an hour or an hour, the good English people would still have waited a day and a night, if not twice that long, for the passage of the queen. The patience and the devotion of the sovereign must correspond to the patient and devoted love of the people. And that is exactly how Elizabeth II understands it. *Long live the Queen!*

From *Dernières Gazettes et Ecrits divers*; first published in *Les Lettres Nouvelles* (July 1953).

In London with Jacques Prévert and Izis

It was as poets more than as tourists that Jacques Prévert and Izis saw London, but as poets who are not content to dream in their corner. Sound on their feet and with good eyesight, they passed through the streets of the City that is

> Four times larger than any other
> and maybe four times as lost

in order to discover its secrets and to learn *the true first names of its beauty.* They did not linger in front of the celebrated monuments; you will not find in their *Charmes de Londres* the sort of thing that fills the pages of a *Blue Guide*, except Tower Bridge seen through a window (this is on the cover) and Piccadilly Circus. It would seem that the book was not made for those who do not know London, but to wink at those who do know it.

An unexpected thing—the book is enjoyable from the beginning to the end. It has nothing of the sourness of Vallès or the somewhat special curiosities of Verlaine. They have not looked for the counterpart of "the nice children of Aubervilliers," which would have been easy. They recalled that William Blake had already written the Prévert poem in *Songs of Experience.* You know that "London," about the hellish side of the city, which was translated by Auguste Morel:

> I wander thro' each charter'd street
> Near where the charter'd Thames does flow,
> And mark in every face I meet
> Marks of weakness, marks of woe.

Since it's been done, no need to do it over again, eh, Jacques? Rather, like sailors on shore leave they go looking for pleasure. And first of all they are going to say hello to all the animals possible: dogs, cats (beautiful, the black cat in the fog), rabbits, the goat, the donkey, horses—real ones, wooden ones, stone ones—and birds: pigeons, gulls, swans. No, of course not, they won't overlook Father Thames who *lunches with one of his friends among the birds,* or the little boy who is giving bread to the pigeons in Trafalgar Square.

Then they will go to greet the beautiful trees:

> Trees
> great trees of London
> like the last bison you are placed
> far away behind the bars
> of your great private parks.

In Chelsea they will not set out in search of Carlyle's house, but they will look at the little fruit seller:

> Passing by
> somebody said of her
> So fresh so pretty a flower you'd say
>
> Why say you'd say
>
> Just as in those boxes all those fruits are fruits
> that girl is a flower
> a flower of life.

Naturally, they will see many children who love one another, here as elsewhere.

Among the pages that I enjoyed, poems or photos, I shall mention: the views of the Thames, with their ships, their gulls, and their swans that are sailing around a mattress spring at low tide.

Excellent, the snapshots of gentlemen: a view from behind of top hats and tail coats in the Saint James neighborhood; two men who are strolling in Hyde Park—you believe you are hearing the sound of their voices.

Superb, the organ grinder and the poor fiddle scraper with his "Songs of Caruso."

Nice, the fine old people on wooden horses:

> Emigrants from childhood
> in spite of themselves well on their way to the
> promised lands of longevity.

Striking, the clarinet amateur in Whitechapel:

> A charmer with the face of a mongoose
> haggles over a cobra.

Look at the milk wagon in Gordon Square:

> Already
> the sound of the first bottle placed upon the
> fresh and naked stone has awakened the whole street.

Beautiful, the houses and streets caught in the fog. And beautiful too the clouds of factory smoke that have the look of issuing from the boilers of hell:

> When the devil does the cooking the good Lord
> sits down at table
> and the poor world cleans the stoves.

For an epigraph the volume carries a musical phrase taken from Handel's *Water Music*. The poems are almost all very successful; their nonchalance, if you please, is elegance itself—the knot of a necktie brought off with the first stroke.

From *Dernières Gazettes et Ecrits divers*; first published in *Les Lettres Nouvelles* (June 1953).

A Cavalier View of Venice

I saw Venice this summer for the first time. I was not disappointed. The gondolas gave me much pleasure, and they appeared to me to be up to their legend. And I experienced a feeling that I was not expecting—that of the future. I understood why futurism was born in Italy. This city, with its weighty past, its small outlines, its strong odor, reveals in essence such wide perspectives that we are outside of time in it. We find here, better than elsewhere, the proof that difficulties are the best artisans of great destinies. Most cities have taken convenient sites, of easy access. Venice, built upon water, a mobile element and treacherous for man, has found in water the principles of a perpetual youth. In this city where everything is preserved and restored in an excellent manner, there is no ruin; the present here is simply the reproduction of the ancient; but it is alive and very much present exactly because the idea of being satisfied with what is, without introducing new elements, makes it seem that nothing is old.

Something did disappoint me, however: the famous palaces of the Grand Canal. These palaces in front of which the names of Byron, Wagner, and a number of others are pronounced, display an architecture that is without distinction. The eternal rosette that adorns almost all of them is the sign of little spirit; some have an indefinably fairlike look.

Yes, Venetian architecture as a whole is rather mediocre; its uniform surfaces have need of gold, mosaics, bas-reliefs, statues. There is all of that in profusion in the Piazza San Marco. But strange to say and even to think, the Piazza San Marco could do without it. What makes the beauty of the Piazza San Marco is that it approaches the sea as one approaches a divinity—while listening, expanding, rising up. It is governed by a few simple and happy motifs: the immense rectangle of the piazza; the three masts that stand in the background; the domes of the basilica lifted up like breasts; the sustained ascent of the campanile with its mute stones; the insurgence against the sky of the Mori, like corsair-workmen; the atomic vibration of the pigeons—and its Piazzetta, which talks to the sea.

It is this magnificent European place that gave me the sensation of being in a city of the future, a Utopian city after Wells, where a major element—light or water—has been mastered by man and transmutes its rhythm to him. Men live more simply, more subtly, less unhappily. I thought, I do not know why, for in fact there isn't any relationship, of certain Soviet films. I saw everywhere the small, pressed in, joyously busy crowd, like the population of the pigeons.

From *Les Gazettes d'Adrienne Monnier*; first published in *La Nouvelle Revue Française* (November 1936).

Tignes in the Winter

I recently made the acquaintance of Tignes. It is a Savoyard village situated at an altitude of about 5,400 feet, to which ski enthusiasts go especially. The arriving visitor sees first of all only a rather ordinary aspect. Twenty houses are clustered together, as everywhere, around a bell tower. Four hotels equipped with modern conveniences and two or three family pensions attract attention with their signs. Two times a day a motorcoach service carries travelers there and supplies the hotels. The village square is almost invaded by the civilized life. One of the hotels displays its façade here. Next to it a bar, the pleasure spot of the place, announces on a cotton streamer a 1900 ball with La Goulue and Valentin le Désossé. Two groceries with their windows full of souvenirs evoke a nondescript provincial town. At the far end a sports and photo shop occupy attractive quarters. To complete the picture, a food shop promises (it's painted on the window) oysters and snails. Inside you see neither oysters nor snails, but enormous Bresse chickens, oranges, all kinds of dried fruits, and, precious provender here, salad. The ladies in the hotels prize this salad most, which for the country people is only grass after all.

All the same, there along the sides of the square, look at the sleighs harnessed to mules, which are already providing more local color.

Many people during the time of their stay here become acquainted only with that aspect of Tignes which has been created for them, and with the vast surroundings, which offer them its snowfields. At the other end of the village you notice the place where the ski lift is, like a sheet swarming with fleas. You can be satisfied with this, but you can also, whether by chance or by merit, be initiated into the life of the country people. Generally, the initiation begins by way of the shoemaker's house. A shoe or a sealskin needs repair, or you need a pair of laces. You have to go to the shoemaker's place. You go there and discover with ravishment that his livestock and his farmyard animals live in the same room as himself. The same room forms a stable, a chicken coop, and a complete place of habitation for people. Look at the beds, the stove with its fat kettles, the dining table; in the embrasure of the window the shoemaker has installed his work table. The whole length of one wall is occupied by four cows and two calves, whose tails have been carefully lifted up and attached to the ceiling by strings (it's so that they won't trail in the urine when the animals are lying down). You hear "moo," "moo," "moo." Where are the sheep? They are under one of the beds. The bed, placed high like a Breton bed, rests upon a little stall in which two sheep are lodged. The front of the stall is formed by a large wooden bench with a back. The board of the seat has been removed, and it is the very framework of the bench that serves as a manger for the sheep, whose heads can be seen lower down. The number of pairs of shoelaces the shoemaker sells in one season cannot be imagined, for that is the reason that tourists generally give for going to see him. It was to his place that the ministers Pierre Cot and Léo Lagrange went recently. They certainly saw the cows, but did they see the sheep under the bed?

There are still other means for penetrating into the homes of the inhabitants. The grocery-tobacco shop sells beautiful woolens of the region. Most of the countrywomen know how to knit very well. You have a pair of stockings or a pullover made, and there is a reason for going many times into the homes of the people of Tignes. Their houses, it should be added, are often very clean. A gutter hollowed into the floor marks the limits of the animals' corner, and by means of this gutter the manure and the urine are carried away outside. Many of the country people burn aromatic plants after the thorough morning cleaning. Some maniac housewives always have a broom within hand's reach and sweep away the droppings as they are produced. To tell the truth, the good people are embarrassed in front of strangers, unkind remarks have been made to them so many times. And nevertheless, their manner of living shows intelligence. If they lodge their animals with them in this way, it is in order to procure heat for themselves. The winters are very harsh, the region is very sparsely wooded, and they are often too poor to buy coal. Once the fine days have come, they send their livestock into the pastures that surround the lake of Tignes, which is situated at an altitude of about 6,600 feet.

When you enter a house you are at first suffocated by the odor, but you get used to it very quickly, and after a moment you feel invaded by a well-being that to me, personally, seems magical. Yes, in some of these interiors there is a fairy-tale atmosphere. If the animals do not speak it is because they do not see the use of it. Life is here, very much stronger than that need to represent it that troubles man. There is a source of marvels here and the heart bathes in it without any other desire than to be a lamb of God.

I shall not forget my visits to a woman who lives in one of the hamlets that surmount Tignes. This woman lives alone with her animals. Her dwelling is the smallest, the darkest, and the most peopled that I have ever seen. She has four cows, three calves, a donkey, two sheep, two goats, and chickens, without counting the cat and the bitch Estelle. Each kind has its place, but as in a workbox where things stay badly in place in their compartments and overlap a bit. Some pieces of furniture huddled against one another around her deep, narrow window have the air of enchanted animals. How good one felt in this house! How warm and reassuring it was—was it not a little hollow of eternity—and the woman of the place showed a face whose features were finely fringed with light, like those of hermits.

From *Les Gazettes d'Adrienne Monnier*; first published in *La Nouvelle Revue Française* (May 1937).

Italian Men

At our departure from Paris for Savoy there were a dozen Italian men, all big and handsome, standing in the corridor of our coach, the compartments of which were full. A family got off at La Roche and three of them were able to install themselves in our compartment; two had brown hair and energetic features and one was a superb blond, a kind of Apollo with a low forehead and a broad gaze in which strength and sweetness radiantly told of the wedding of Jupiter and Latona.

This Olympian installed himself opposite me like a great bull—wasn't Apollo also the god of herds?—obliging a priest who occupied the corner to huddle up even more. There, with his legs stretched out and spread wide apart, displaying the bulge of his sex as women show off their breasts, with his thick arms that were bare to the elbows encircling his temples in the manner of the Young

Fate, he fell asleep, his mouth slightly open. On his belt, hung from a string, he wore a medal of the Madonna. The priest, an elderly gentleman who like ourselves had hoped to make himself a bit comfortable after the exit of the family at La Roche—it was there that he had got his corner—was not one of those who practice the unctuous manner: as cross as he was crowded, he absorbed himself in reading his *Figaro*.

A bit before Dijon, around noon, our young man woke up; as he had to wait for the third service in order to have lunch, he took out of his pocket a large bar of milk chocolate, which he ate after having kindly offered it around. Sylvia, who knows Italian a little, began to chat with him. He informed us that he was from Turin and that he had just participated in a soccer match that had taken place in Orléans—that was what explained the beautiful sporting look of these men. His neighbor on the left, who was from Sorrento, found himself sitting next to a charming young woman who was accompanied by an old governess and two children: a pretty and boisterous little girl and a baby who had been placed at the start in a hammock hung from the bars of the racks. Next to the governess there was the third companion, whom we did not ask—I do not know why—for the name of his town; looking at him you thought of a centurion, laughter marked his face after the manner of care. So, the young mama was surrounded by the three Italians. While the blond was still sleeping the two brown-haired men had taken it on themselves to entertain and help her, very much in harmony with each other, like dancers, each one proceeding in turn. The centurion noticed first of all that the baby was turned against the netting of his hammock and that the strings were cutting into his face; in fact, the cheeks and the forehead of the baby, whom he put right again, were as checkered as a waffle. He laid him carefully on his back, but as the baby unceasingly returned to his favorite position, which was on his side, a bit on his belly, which inevitably set his face against the netting, his nose sticking through the mesh, the two men in turn kept placing him on his back again, brushing his tangled hair from his forehead and straightening his clothes. That was all accompanied by smiles that were like a mama's; they did not speak French, but their smiles were only the more eloquent for it. They were those of the possible lover, and also those of the husband and of the father. They paid just as much loving attention to the little girl, it was a question of which of the two men could better make his hands dance before her with no end of *ciaos*. That word, which to us sounds Chinese—*tchao,* I never thought that it could be used otherwise than to say "goodbye"; I had heard it for the first time, it seems to me, in *The Bicycle Thief;* but it no doubt happens that it is said to little children to start them playing, as we say "look," or "watch" to them. In any case the word is apt, and it deserves to be in the first rank of the esperanto of childhood.

Coming back from the diner our Italians discovered in a neighboring compartment another perfectly pretty and graceful little girl and her mother, who was just as young and charming as our own. As the little girl was going to and fro in the corridor, it was not difficult for them to attract her toward them; she did not go inside but remained in the doorway, taking her part in making little marionettes and *ciaos* with her hands, and laughing like an angel; her mama came to join her and remained standing for a long time to enjoy her daughter's pleasure; toward her too, naturally, arose a whole flock of gallant and honest smiles.

Our Turinese followed things and participated in them from time to time, rather like a spectator, he too smiling, but at himself as much as at the others.

After Bourg was passed, a middle-aged man came to pay a visit to the three companions and even sat for about a quarter of an hour in the seat that one of them gave up to him. We understood that he was their manager; he was very much the *maestro,* well dressed and appropriately corpulent, with a face whose eyelids were a bit heavy and whose mouth showed a wry intelligence—the face of somebody who has nothing more to learn about the game of life.

These men, like all self-respecting Italian men, were very smart, with gold chains on their wrists, wristwatches with straps of white leather, artfully arranged hair, and well-cut clothes, which were also made of a fabric that was more "fancy" than it is with us. Watching them I thought once again about the kindness of Italians and in particular about their naturalness, which is life at its source and at the same time all of its theater. They are, no doubt about it, the most practical and the most artistic people on earth. Nobody knows the shape of the genius of mankind as well as they do or better gives it the display that becomes it. The gallantry of the men is exemplary; insistent though it may be, it rarely abandons a certain moral depth in which the idea of the *paterfamilias* always remains present along with what it includes of authority, responsibility, and protection. Anglo-Saxon men also have this sense of protection in regard to women (on condition, however, that women accept being protected). With Frenchmen it is more complicated, we shall put them aside this time. But nobody has the brilliance of Italian men—which is that of the love that establishes households.

During the Occupation there was a performance at the Palais de Chaillot at which we were shown Italian documentary films, all remarkable, above all one that displayed horses at the time of their mating. We saw stallions paying court to mares—their manes were suns, their eyes seemed like stars, their neighing rang out like great laughter, fire flowed throughout their bodies and leapt from their hooves. Nothing more beautiful, more fabulous could be imagined; the camera had fixed an aspect of the divine ardor that Italian artists have expressed so many times in their painting and in their music.

Our journey in the company of the friendly soccer players recalled another one to me, one that took place very long ago, but that has never ceased to be present to me.

We were coming back from vacation, mama, my sister, and myself, by the train from Modane, which we had taken at Chambéry; mama was a young woman and the elder of her little girls—that was I—was eight or nine years old. In our compartment there happened to be an Italian, also young, who was coming to France for the first time. He spoke French a little and immediately began to converse with us. Throughout the whole journey he did not stop surrounding us with attentions, offering us fruit and candy and trying to entertain us, all the while heaping tender looks upon mama, who blushed now and then. Naturally he asked many questions about Paris and the life that was led there; mama strove to answer him, the two of them laughed at their difficulty in making themselves understood. Upon our arrival in Paris, after having set down the baggage and set down the children, he remained next to us on the platform until the moment when my father came to meet us; my father stared at him, wrinkling his eyebrows deeply. There was a very embarrassing silence, but the Italian, without saying anything, made a gesture toward him that meant: here is your treasure, and he plunged into the crowd. After this encounter mama experienced long moments of revery. Until the end of her days she never put anything above Italian men.

From *Rue de l'Odéon*; first published in *Les Lettres Nouvelles* (October 1953).

A Sketch of Les Déserts

Here we are in this mountainous place where we spend our vacations.

It is a place in Savoy; it is called Les Déserts; Françoise Sollier, our maternal grandmother, was born here. We have been coming here every summer since childhood.

Les Déserts is not only a village, it is a veritable region that occupies the entire eastern slope of the massif that reaches from the summit of Nivolet to that of Revard. It is a very extensive commune that includes at least twelve distinctive hamlets that are distant from one another and satisfied with their differences. These hamlets are arranged in tiers upon a vast slope. Those at the bottom have an altitude of about 3,000 feet, those at the top an altitude of about 4,250 feet. Between about 3,950 feet and 4,250 feet the slope spreads out into a wide circular plateau surrounded by forests. Upon this plateau, which is called La Féclaz, most of the inhabitants of Les Déserts come with their animals to spend the three summer months in chalets, to which they carry up cooking utensils, tools, and some clothes.

This plateau is one of our homelands, one of the faces of our soul.

In front of us, in the distance, the Belledonne chain spreads out a range of mountains of equal height, covered with snow. To our left, very near, Mount Margériaz rears up rather abruptly and lords it over us—not very much, though, as it is hardly better favored than ourselves; its height doesn't bother us. At the end of its slope, in the back, the massif of the Bauges displays three solid and gentle backs. To our right the pass of La Féclaz has the look of an immense eagle; its wooded slopes open like wings. It is above these wings that the Shepherd's Star appears—prima donna of the evening, borne up by the violins of the sky, she suspends all listening nature on the strand of her diamondlike voice.

Our altitude is middling, to be sure, but the expanse around us is free and springing; the distant summits do not crush us, they melt upon the horizon. We are not so much upon a mountain as in the mountains—a high, serene place swept by pure air, with perspectives like vast thoughts.

Beyond the western forests the slopes start up again more boldly; the earth is covered with nipplelike hills. Stretched out here and there, an Allobrogian goddess and her heavy daughters turn their haunches and their breasts toward the sky. They guard the approaches of the long terrace that goes from Nivolet to Revard. When you have scaled them all you find yourself facing the void. You dominate the valleys of Chambéry and Aix-les-Bains. Here you see Lake Bourget encased in the earth like a turquoise out of a Tibetan legend.

On the other side of the lake, opposite us, a long mountain stretches out parallel to our own. Its line, which is uniform and monotonous for a great extent, hollows deeply toward the end and gives way to a pass. Immediately beyond the pass lies the Ain country.

To the left, in the direction of Nivolet and behind Chambéry, there is a beautiful circular massif that includes La Grande Chartreuse; seven or eight mountains lift up noble brows of almost equal height there and seem to hold counsel.

To the right, in the direction of Revard and Aix-les-Bains, the heights slowly level off toward the plains. Those in the distance stretch out into a blue mist that resembles good hope.

You never tire of lingering before these spaces that have nothing terrifying about them, that give bright vistas to the soul, inclining it toward easy renunciations. These towns at our feet are no more than geometrical forms, lines arranged by chance. The sign of life is a little upside down V, for as many roofs as there are. The roads are like veins of milk. Nature, when seen from a bit high up, but not from too high up, is unaware of men, just as we are unaware of the organic world of our bodies.

—Still, from a magic, invisible village, which is projected into a kind of interior space, arises the sound of a bell, the cry of a cock, and the bark of a dog that no other dog answers.

From *Les Gazettes d'Adrienne Monnier*; first published in *La Nouvelle Revue Française* (September 1935).

A Little Promenade

First days after our return from vacation. We sulk at Paris and Paris sulks at us. However, we are still going to have to begin to understand and love one another again.

How can we touch the heart of the city, and what can we do so that it will touch our own heart?

Last year I imagined a ritual promenade, a little pilgrimage that succeeds rather well for me. I am going to go to the Seine and to the two islands that she enfolds in her arms, to pay homage and to ask for support. I am going to tell you about it.

Good. You know that I live in the Rue de l'Odéon. I start on my way one beautiful morning; I reach the Place Saint-Michel. Here I am on the quais; I turn right. Quai Saint-Michel. And first of all, I embrace Notre-Dame de Paris with an encompassing look. I am not Catholic, but you know that I honor goddesses, and she is a great goddess. I needn't take the trouble of going into her house, I know it by heart, and I have only to think about it in order to be there.

The two Gibert shops. The same sales as before vacation. Nothing new except a Rabelais in modern French that presents itself decently enough. When I was a very young girl I knew old man Gibert; he was a bespectacled little hunchback, shy, really honest, and devoted to his work. It was from him that I bought my schoolbooks, which I sold back to him again. He took them back at reasonable prices and never failed to compliment me on their remarkable neatness. It is true that they were little enough worn, for I made very little use of them—I was not a good student. What a concern those Gibert bookshops have become since then, almost a trust!

Messein. Look, a photo of Verlaine that I did not know about. Still the same numbers of Men of Today. That's really funny, that *Leda* over the portrait of our good Royère.

Chacornac. Occult sciences. Chacornac—the name is excellent: it contains the black cat of the witches, the horns of the Evil One, and that snickering "nac." The *Veil of Isis* is still there, faithful at its post. In the place of honor, a novelty: *L'Astratarot.* It's a kind of game, like the *jeu de l'oie,* whose compartments are occupied by tarot figures. It is consulted by means of dice and costs twenty-five francs. The advertisement says that it is "a sincere friend." The fact is that anything is friendly that lets us make use of it, and sincere because it is not interested in lying to us, like people. If it answers it doesn't matter what to us, aren't we it doesn't matter who?

Ah, but that Bookshop-Post Cards, the devil if I had ever noticed it. It's very neat and pretty. They have nothing better at the Palais-Royal.

Here we are at the Square Saint-Julien-le-Pauvre—we don't call it the Square René-Viviani, isn't that so?—the Pont au Double, but

I am not going to cross it, I am going to go along on the Seine side; on the houses side there is nothing diverting anymore except the names of the streets: Rue du Haut-Pavé, Rue des Grands-Degrés, Rue Maître-Albert. The spire of Notre-Dame is being repaired; they have covered it with delicate scaffolding, it looks like a pagoda.

The stalls on the quais are almost all shut. Many fishermen. Few tramps. Seine, Seine, what shall I call you? In the song about the Mississippi they say, "old man river," but you, you are not old! You are young, like all the waters that flow through cities. It is our cities that are old as soon as they are born, with their gray faces, the furrows of the streets, and the passers-by. But the waters remain young and fear nothing of fate, they will always have the advantage.

Pont de la Tournelle. Sainte-Geneviève. I love that stiff Geneviève; with her long, straight folds she is like a lifted finger. It was a good idea to put her there. Shall we cross the bridge? No, let's wait for the next one. But let's rest our elbows for a moment on the balustrade of the entrance. Over there is the Tour Saint-Jacques. The barges are passing by, as if in the song that a young fellow is humming at my side. It's a langorous, eddying tune that can suit a number of emotional states, from the slight stirring of the soul to piercing regret. It's a really banal refrain, besides.

The Halle aux Vins. What a discreet, silent place, how little like the markets for solid foods. The wines sleep in the barrels while awaiting the time when they will lead a wild life.

Crossing the Pont Sully. On the right hand, cranes and factory chimneys. On the left hand, Notre-Dame and Sainte-Geneviève. Let's not take the Boulevard Henri-IV. We are going to go along the beautiful flank of the Ile Saint-Louis up to its prow. The houses along the Quai de Béthune have a meditative air, their simple alignment is moving. At the corner of the Rue Bretonvilliers an old pink house with a little gilded balcony is like a tender memory. The Polish Library, Rue Budé, Arvers. Let's stop at this bend of the Quai d'Orléans. The Seine opens her arms and enfolds the Ile de la Cité. Let's say nothing more, it's too beautiful. The city and the river sing in unison. The winter can come.

Now let's go toward the prow where a group of trees is standing, one of them all bent down. Here are the three benches meant for lovers. The barges follow the bend of the island. Their wakes widen and the waves reach the other arm of the river. The air is full of idle and solemn words murmured there, carried away by the waters, carried back by the waters. It is a place of motionless departures. The soul trembles gently at its roots—

Let's shake ourselves, enough emotions for this morning. We are going to take a turn in the bazaar of the Hôtel de Ville; it is one of my passions.

Would you believe that the one-sou counter still exists? It exists mystically, even, fully conscious of what it represents. It is maintained only by a certain artifice, though. It occupies only a little corner of the five-sou counter, and it contains only very few things. You see there minuscule cooking utensils, blackboard sponges, wooden tokens, three kinds of whistles, and, occupying the most space, clothespins—ten sous the dozen. Poor little toys for kids, all mixed up with homework and mama with her terrible washing, beside herself, her hair in her eyes, her hands itching from slaps.

There is no two-, three-, or four-sou counter.

When you go to the bazaar you must see the "fantasy subjects" and the art objects. They fill no less than four counters. The most beautiful things there are the imitation bronze or wood statues in plaster. The subjects have their titles engraved on little plaques of copper fixed to their bases: *Mignon, Old Salt, First Cigarette, Kabyle Chief, Enraged Tiger, Old Laborer, Watchdog, Woman Reading*, etc. Beside Houdon's Voltaire, a mask of Mistinguett. Two spaniels made of real metal are marked "unique piece" and are worth 360 francs. At the smokers' supply counter I notice with disappointment that they are no longer making the little tobacco pots, *Jean Weeping* and *Jean Laughing*.

The bookshop is very up to date. Upon a little device high up are exhibited: *Sainte Anne d'Auray* by Henri Ghéon, *Samouraï 8 cylindres* by Maurice Dekobra, *Conversations dans le Loir-et-Cher* by Paul Claudel, *Le Troisième Sexe* by Willy, and *Lucie-Paulette* by Jean Prévost.

The radio sends out passionate and lulling waves. We are in the crowd as if in the water. Now that we have bathed ourselves thoroughly let us leave.

Rue de Rivoli. We are going to follow it to the Tour Saint-Jacques. Although it is hardly eleven o'clock in the morning, the crowd is so heavy that we have trouble advancing. The café Aux Armes de la Ville announces on all its windows that "the sweet white wine has arrived"; that would go well with the neighboring brioches of La Lune; you simply need the stomach for it.

The Tour Saint-Jacques. We love it, it is beautiful. It is inhabited by a powerful genie, may he be favorable to us!

Place du Châtelet. The Théâtre du Châtelet is alternately presenting *Michel Strogoff* and *Au temps des Merveilleuses,* "the two celebrated successes in different genres." At the Théâtre Sarah-Bernhardt, *Le Courrier de Lyon* with Rozenberg. All is well.

Quai de la Mégisserie. Flowers, birds, fish. Let's pass quickly in front of La Belle Jardinière and La Samaritaine, "too much genius," as Gide said of Claudel. A genuflection in front of the Pont Neuf, which would be worth a mass all by itself.

Quai du Louvre. Fish take the advantage over birds and flowers. Au Bon Vieux Chic, it's an antique shop that specializes in armor. As a matter of fact, it was good old chic, perhaps it could be worn again.

But here we are at one of the essential stages of our promenade: the Pont des Arts, launched between us and the Institut like Allah's bridge of paradise, frail and terrible above no one knows what abysses! And why, my God? In order to have oneself received by an insipid Republic armed with a sword whose point is downward, attended by four consternated lions?

For us, simple onlooker, this will be, of all the bridges, the one that we shall cross most slowly, because, on both sides, Paris is gentle and magnificent, because we are here at the threshold of the islands, because we can sit down for a moment on a bench, our look lost in the fascinating and mocking look of the young woman river.

From *Les Gazettes d'Adrienne Monnier*; first published in *Vendredi* (1935).

part seven

Reflections

The Swastika

I recently asked the German writer Walter Benjamin, who was passing through Paris, for explanations about the swastika (which here we more ordinarily call the *croix gammée*), the emblem of present-day Germany. Did he know who, exactly, had proposed or imposed it, and for what reasons?—No, he did not know exactly. Hindenburg had already adopted it, before Hitler. As for the reasons, they no doubt had their origins in the worship, so widespread over there, of everything that passes for being Aryan.

It is generally acknowledged that the swastika is a symbol with an essentially Aryan origin, but there is almost no part of the ancient world, even the non-Aryan, where it has not served as a magic or religious ornament, with much variety in its form. The modern redskins still make use of it; it is associated with the thunderbird, as our friend Durtain was able to observe in the course of a long journey in America, which he novelized in *Frank et Marjorie*.

Archaeologists are not in agreement about the meaning that should be given to the swastika. Some see in it a symbol of the sun, or of fire, or of water, or of the four cardinal points; others see a symbol of the phallus or, quite the contrary, the feminine sex; still others see a simple ornament, a craft mark, a flying bird, an octopus, etc. I personally see in it, without difficulty, a symbol of the sun in motion. The form adopted by the Germans, which has diagonal and not vertical and horizontal arms like the classic swastika, is particularly animated. It really has the look of running —its head is thrown back, its knee is raised high.

Walter Benjamin told us that there were some very interesting ideas about the swastika in Bachofen—but who is Bachofen? He is a Basel philosopher who flourished in the latter half of the nineteenth century; he wrote a very extensive work about matriarchy, whose influence has been great if rather underground—we should become acquainted with this Bachofen, of whom we are almost totally ignorant in France.

Well, Bachofen maintains that in very ancient times the swastika had arms that were turned toward the left, as a sign of the predominance of the feminine forces; the moon then had superiority over the sun and the night was more honored than the day. In the course of a very great war, like the one that the *Mahabharata* relates, the son of the sun brought about the triumph of the masculine forces and turned the arms of the swastika toward the right. Things are still in that state. The right-armed swastika still passes for having a fortunate influence while the left-armed one is inauspicious. The side that is directionally sinister, on the left, has become sinister as an omen. The right one and the right of the law are identical. The fortune-teller, who more or less has to do with the devil, cuts her cards with her left hand.

This manner of seeing would certainly not be that of the Chinese, for whom the left, the honorable side, is attributed to men and the right to women, as we have just read in the beautiful work by Marc Granet on Chinese thought.

At any rate, the Germans have opted for the right, their swastika turns to the right. But look out! The use of a symbol calls for reflection. The swastika that decorates their flags certainly goes toward the right, but the one that they put on their chests or their arms carries them away toward the left. In fact, contrary to a person, an inanimate object takes the direction of the spectator; it is understood that the right and the left of the image that I look at are on the same sides as my right and my left; but if, instead of having the object facing me, I put it upon me or next to me, the side called right corresponds to my left side, and the side called left to my right side.

Yes, the Germans had better not put so many swastikas on themselves. God knows where that might lead them. But God knows where we are all going, with or without the swastika!

From *Les Gazettes d'Adrienne Monnier*; first published in *La Nouvelle Revue Française* (August 1934).

On War

Some years ago I happened to think a great deal about war; it was the principal theme of my readings and my reflections for several months. That was in 1933, at the time when the correspondence between Einstein and Freud, *Why War?*, appeared at the International Institute of Intellectual Cooperation.

Naturally, this text was my first reading, and the first question that I put to my own mind was the very one that Einstein put to Freud: "Does a means exist for freeing men from the menace of war?"

Freud's answer gave me little reassurance and did not surprise me. I was very much expecting to read sentences of this kind:

> We suppose that man's instincts can be reduced exclusively to two categories. On the one hand are those that want to preserve and unite; we call them erotic. On the other hand are those that want to destroy and kill; we include them under the name of the aggressive or destructive impulse. In short, as you see, this is only the theoretical transposition of the universally recognized antagonism of love and hate, which is perhaps a form of the polarity of attraction and repulsion that plays a role in your own province. But let us not pass on too rapidly to ideas of good and evil. Each of these impulses is just as indispensable as the other; from their combined or antagonistic action spring the phenomena of life.

I cannot quote the whole text, which could however be quoted completely. Here again is a passage that seemed important to me:

> I should like nevertheless to deal with a further problem, which you do not raise in your letter but which interests me especially. Why do we rise up so energetically against war, you and I and so many along with us, why do we not choose to accept it as one of the innumerable vicissitudes of life? For it seems to conform to nature; it is biologically very well established and practically it is almost inevitable. Do not be scandalized by the question that I am asking here. For the needs of an inquiry it is perhaps permissible to put on the mask of an impassivity that one hardly possesses in reality. And this is what the answer shall be: because every man has a right over his own life, because war destroys human lives that are full of promise, places the individual in situations that disgrace him, forces him to kill his neighbor against his

own will, annihilates precious material values, products of human activity, etc. It can also be added that war in its present form no longer gives any occasion for displaying the ancient ideal of heroism and that the war of tomorrow, as a result of improving the machines of destruction, would be equivalent to the extermination of one of the adversaries or perhaps even of both of them.

Freud then studies the influence of culture upon the individual and demonstrates that it is culture that makes him pacifistic. Here is his conclusion:

> Among the number of psychological characteristics of culture there are two that seem to be most important: the consolidation of the intellect, which tends to master the instinctive life, and the internal reversion of the aggressive tendency, with all its favorable and dangerous consequences. But the psychic conceptions toward which the evolution of culture draw us often find themselves struck up against in the most violent way by war, and it is for this reason that we must rebel against it; we can no longer just simply put up with it; it is not only an intellectual and emotional repugnance, but it is also, among us pacifists, really a constitutional intolerance, an idiosyncracy that in some way has become magnified to an extreme. And it truly seems that the esthetic degradations that war involves do not count for much less in our indignation than the atrocities that it instigates.
>
> And now how much time will still be needed so that the others may become pacifists in their turn? We cannot say, but perhaps it is not utopian to hope for the action of these two elements—the cultural conception and the justified fear of the repercussions of a conflagration to come—to put an end to war in the near future. By what direct or roundabout ways we cannot guess. While waiting we can tell ourselves: Everything that works for the development of culture also works against war.

There is a little hope in that last sentence even so, a hope that shines "like a bit of straw in the stable." And a person who has put himself, as I have, in the service of culture, receives from it a confirmation of his faith.

When I had finished and thoroughly meditated this text, I entered upon other readings. I shall name for you two books that impressed me as being stupendous and beautiful of their kind: the *Maximes sur la guerre [Maxims on War]* by René Quinton and *La Guerre, notre Mère [War, Our Mother]* by Ernest Jünger. Here are some of Quinton's maxims:

Men can dream that they do not love war. Nature loves struggle and death.

War does not transform men; it returns them to their natural end; war is the natural state of males.

In the universe service to the species imposes the burdens, the risks of maternity upon females. It imposes upon males of the same blood fratricidal struggle, combat among themselves, and death if necessary. What instinct imposes the animal accepts naturally. Males are organized to die, at least to accept the risks of death in struggling.

Nature does not desire fecundation; she desires essential fecundation. The first mission of males is not to reproduce themselves but to kill among themselves. Throughout the whole living world their slaughters are preludes to love. The female propagates the species; the male, through his death, exposes it to the process of selection. Nature, which benefits thereby, creates males for the sake of mutual destruction; she gives them the liking for it and the strength to take risks.

I must say that such sentences, to use a common expression, bowled me over. I was terrified, obsessed, amazed by them. I remember that one day while I was chatting with Fargue I read him the sentences in question and asked him: "Now, what do you think about it, what do you have to say to that?" He answered me laconically: "Soldiers are cuckolds." Naturally, that did not satisfy me at all. Besides, as I now think, if soldiers are cuckolds on the home front, they make cuckolds on the war front, so it comes out even. No, something else had to be found. I turned Quinton's assertions over and over again in my head; at last I saw a ray of light. And I simply said to myself: but that takes place among insects, and not among men.

With Ernest Jünger it is not a matter of insects but of rats.

The perception of animal nature of the two authors in question reassured me on one level but not on all. For when everything is well considered, what proved to me that man was truly human, that he was not simply "in the state of a rough draft," as Paul Valéry wrote recently?

I made a new series of reflections in this direction: supposing man is only a kind of animal subjected to the same laws as the other animals, is war really the natural state of males?

To be sure, the struggle for life appears at every level of existence.

It should not be said that nature "loves struggle and death," she *is* struggle and death at the same time as she is union and procreation.

Nevertheless, if one observes the various species of living beings, one sees, granting there is always struggle among them, that this struggle does not necessarily end in the putting to death of the adversary; the death foreseen by nature seems really to be *natural* death, that is to say, the one that is brought about by the wearing away of individual organisms.

Furthermore, of all the vital operations, putting to death is the one that is the object of the strictest regulation. Among animals this regulation is inseparable from instinct.

Of course, it seems to be acknowledged that each animal species has the right to kill and to eat other animal species, but they are almost never its fellow creatures. It can even be said that most beings are careful to choose their victims in the clans of life that are the farthest removed from their own. There must be an extreme necessity in order for them to become resigned to eating one another, and even then they most often do not become resigned.

(From this observation may follow the fact that among men preparation for war always involves the disparagement of the enemy; to induce a human being to kill other human beings it is necessary to make him believe that the latter are not his fellow creatures, but creatures of an inferior race, who have nothing in common with him, and that he is therefore permitted to destroy them.)

Primitive peoples, who show so much spirit when they give battle to their enemies in other respects display feelings that are very remarkable. They feel real scruples about killing the animals and the plants upon which they feed; they are afraid of angering the spirits of their species and never fail to give them marks of respect in the form of propitiatory practices; sometimes they even pay honor to the animal that has been killed. Read Levy-Bruhl's work on this subject: *Le Surnaturel et la nature dans la mentalité primitive.*

It seems obvious to me that the instinct of preservation inclines each being to preserve not only himself but all other beings to the extent that they do not stand in the way of his existence. He does not kill of his own free will except in cases of legitimate defense. There is not a living being that does not feel in the depth of himself that the act of dealing death exposes himself to death. Human justice is only the translation of Justice.

What I have just said is applicable to defensive warfare; but, you will think, there is the offensive kind. The enemy is not only he that attacks you, but likewise the one whom you want to attack. In what case does one want to attack?

One attacks those who possess things that one does not possess. The attack is all the more savage because the one who attacks is destitute and the one who is attacked is well provided. The one who attacks always considers himself to be in the position of legitimate offense.

Some primitive forms of war are so cruel only because man is placed in the most cruel conditions of life. When one speaks of tribes with a particularly warlike disposition, one must first of all observe that these tribes live upon frightfully barren ground. It should not be said that there are plunderers, it should be said that there are beings in this world who can live only by plundering.

No doubt you will ask me what I make of the famous slaughters by males that are "preludes to love." But these slaughters are observed in all their beauty only among certain insects, as we said above. Of course, we see many dogs, and sometimes even men, fight for their fair one; but if there is a struggle there is very rarely a crime; that doesn't even take place except by accident; the desire to deal death is very exactly counterbalanced by the fear of dealing death. Between these two feelings how many games there are! Dogs know better than anybody how to look proud and dreadful; their barking makes you think of Homeric challenges and outcries. I can never see dogs fighting without being terrified, and still I must remark each time that our jolly dogs pull through without great harm, above all if there are no men to astonish.

Civilized man has more than one means of ousting his rival; among these means the act of ridiculing is certainly one of the most subtle and one of the most effective. Laughter is among the destructive energies; it is in this sense that our Rabelais could say that laughter is proper to man. In fact, it is not only a characteristic of man but also, let us say, playing upon the words, the proper way (that is to say, the least dirty) that man has of destroying what troubles him in and outside of himself.

I have just spoken about the destructive energies, which brings me back to Freud's "aggressive or destructive impulse." I am going to try to express a series of reflections that I made on this subject.

Doesn't this impulse manifest itself continually? Isn't it the condition of all existence? It represents the negative pole; no doubt it is the one that is present in the electrons of the atom and that stimulates them to make incessant movements of repulsion relatively to one another. On the human level it is the very field of consciousness; there is, as Freud says, the "internal reversion of the aggressive tendency." The more conscious a being is the more he experiences intimate struggles; a cultivated being never stops pulling out his weeds, and this operation counts no less than sowing and watering. Among the most conscious individuals, among the saints, there is perhaps a kind of radioactivity, that is to say, a disintegration of the positive. Ordinary beings lay the blame on others; superior beings blame only themselves.

It is through a mastered destructive impulse that we make order prevail. To straighten out a room, to criticize a book, to scoff at an oddity, to think before having children, and even simply to think—that all depends on the negative energy of the universe.

This energy certainly receives, it seems, all the satisfactions it desires, for antipathy shows many more forms than sympathy. To resort again to the atom, I shall say that for any positive, calm, benevolent, and almost inoperative nucleus in each being there is always around this nucleus a flock of restless and quarrelsome electrons.

Don't you see what I am driving at? This is what I am driving at:

If struggle exists in a permanent state, if it is *legion,* like the devils of our forefathers, if it is the very fabric of life, why add more to it? War is useless.

It is too easy to say that war puts everything out of order, it is better to say that it puts nothing in order. It is a superstition, an illusion, the great illusion, as Norman Angell says—and Jean Renoir after him. What is gained by it is always retaken. Once it escapes certain limits it is unorganizable, inorganic. It is through its most restrained expressions that it becomes identified with the vital *no.* To assent to it, to let it expand, is to make of it some monstrous derangement of the planet, it is to return to the unleashed elements, that is to say, to the very thing that it did not want, since according to its principle it is the critical spirit.

No doubt there are some men and some animal species that cherish struggle and death; they belong to the caste of warriors; they are the *ksatriyas,* as the Hindus call them; they become identified more or less with the forces of destruction. It is good that this is so; for them there is more than one profession: they can be policemen, boxers, killers of vipers, toreadors—and soldiers, as long as it is believed that armies are necessary.

But, on the whole, if men are shaken by an infinite number of aggressive and destructive impulses, if during childhood their games give full vent to these impulses, precisely because they are children, it is certainly true that once they become adults their combative instinct diminishes: they accept fighting only under the pressure of necessity; one must be able to tell them: "They are coming into our arms to cut the throats of our children, our helpmates."

It is logical that at certain stages of humanity war might have seemed beautiful and praiseworthy, while the fighting was among *ksatriyas*. And the world being a child, the warlike temperament abounded. It was less a question then for the hero to deal death than it was to receive it or to run the risk of it; the fact of dying for the homeland was not at all a cessation of life but an identification with a cause, the passage of a little individual life into a much broader life—that of the *Pitris*. The warlike spirit is so intoxicating that it can easily be understood why men should still be haunted by it. But this spirit is good no longer except for display, for ornament. It began to lose its meaning when the little homeland became larger, when things ceased to be clearly defined, when responsibilities came into the question.

Today men can no longer hope to preserve their children and their helpmates through war, since modern war exposes them even more than the combatants. And it is known that war would bring about not the extermination of one people but the destruction of the whole of Europe—these are truths that have been said many times.

Please consider my reflections as a slight sketch of the philosophical work that would have to be done on a subject that quickly disheartens reason—here I have simply attempted the *reduction* of a few appearances.

From *Les Gazettes d'Adrienne Monnier*; first published in *Les Gazettes des Amis des Livres* (July 1938).

On Anti-Semitism

I have thought many times about the Jewish question these recent years. Since the beginning of German anti-Semitism I have been striving to understand and to see clearly. I am going to try to entrust you with my reflections on this subject.

And first of all I must say that I like Germany. It has been easy for me, since the time she took it, to greet her with the name of Great Germany. Europe owes her some of its most splendid geniuses; it seems that it has been reserved for her to reach the summits of philosophy and music. Bach, Goethe, Kant, Hegel, Beethoven, Wagner, Nietzsche are a part of our substance, they are ourselves; they have modeled I do not know how many faces of our spirit and they do not cease shaping the human temperament, in harmony with the other geniuses.

And I like the German people, who are brave, good-natured, wonderfully applied to their tasks, as if they were forever helped by a crowd of little familiar spirits. German civility, which often seems stiff to us, shows an attentive and touching respect for the person that I often prefer to our offhandedness. I am not saying that we ought to imitate them—each people has its character, and this diversity delights the soul; it tells its own true country to it.

And the Germans, in spite of what certain people claim, are no more liars than we are; they have their own manner of being sincere, which is not ours; we remain faithful to principles without often being concerned about their obsolescence; they are natural. Yes, like nature they are simple and complicated, immutable and changing, but they are never at a loss to make themselves understood. When they are not driven to the end of their naturalness (and in that case they become baroque, like nature when she has too much or not enough material), they show a certain good sense, a good sense that is undoubtedly more solid than our own, because they leave it in all its thickness, instead of doing as we do, who refine, plane away, until nothing much is left. . . .

. . . We were speaking of Germany. It was concerning her anti-Semitism that the problem of anti-Semitism was posed for me. I do not believe I had ever seriously thought about it before. The Dreyfus affair, which had taken place when I was a little girl, had not disturbed me. And still, at the time of the affair my parents were living at the Place Saint-André-des-Arts and the students used to pass by under our windows crying "Spit upon Zola!" My grandfather, an anti-Dreyfusard, and my Dreyfusard father, used to wrangle at every meal; I used to see them rise up over the table, ready to throw themselves upon each other, and the women bustle about them in order to get them to sit down again. But I was only five years old, and I was plunged all day long in reading or revery, to such a point that the external world did not count. I am sure that at the same age our friend Bryher would have fully participated in the event, she who had a political sense so precociously, as we know through her delicious "Paris 1900."

Later I never heard the Jewish question spoken about. I read, while a girl, some novels by Gyp that appeared disgustingly stupid to me and that, precisely because they were, shelved the question.

When I established my bookshop in 1915 and because of that fact was put in relations with a large and various public, I often happened to hear expressions of this sort (I am quoting the mildest): "He's a Jew"; "He's really a Jew, that one"; "With Jews everything goes well for a while, but one day or another something goes wrong somewhere." This last remark, uttered by one of my best friends, struck me a great deal. I observed, in fact, that with Jews something always occurred, at a given moment, that could be criticized.

I could just as well have observed that there was no human being who did not sooner or later offer himself to our criticism.

The Jews are victims of the strongest of collective suggestions. The truth is that they are neither better nor worse than others, but what comes from them is underlined, exaggerated, made responsible for all evil. They seem to have perpetually to fulfill the function of the scapegoat. Is there something in them that lends itself to this? The rite of the scapegoat is a part of their ancient customs, but so it was for many ancient peoples. Christianity seems to have fixed the role by dividing it in two: on the one hand there is Christ, who voluntarily atones for the sins of the world; that is the redeemer, that is no longer the goat but the lamb. On the other hand there is the Jew, the "unclean goat," who is obliged to atone for the sins of the world.

I am not sure that Christ would have been very satisfied to foresee that He would be looked upon principally as a *redeemer* and nailed forever upon the cross by human ignorance. It seems to me that He above all desired to bring men a message of truth, that He wanted to heal them of their faults by making an appeal to all their energy; He shook them as much as He could, He did not seek to spare them the trouble. But men had the advantage from all points of view; if the saints take care to relive the passion of their Master, ordinary people adopt the cross as a convenient myth that exempts them from effort; with the same stroke it frees them from the obsession of original sin and from all responsibility; as a children's song says: "It was for you, it was for me, that Christ died upon the cross"—after that, one can live as one pleases.

Nor am I sure that the Jews are very happy to be ceaselessly reduced to the role of the scapegoat. I have heard people say, with an astonishing lack of awareness, "Basically they like that." No doubt they are resigned by the very force of circumstances, but how many reasons they would have to scorn us! How could they help but laugh at us, to the point of being consoled, were they to think about the prodigious destiny of their books.

Our Western world is built upon the Old and the New Testaments. While the Greek sages created a moral code for the elite alone, who were incapable of extensive benefactions, Judaism and Christianity introduced a spirit that is truly democratic in the sense that their spiritual leaders have never separated themselves from the mass of people and have taken its education for the essential goal. . . .

From its first verses the Bible rises up toward the Eternal, the essential synthesis, toward the Supreme Being from which it has all beings flow forth with a fecund constancy.

In my opinion what distinguishes the Bible from the other books is its sense of time. Its first concern is to establish a calendar. Then it traces a genealogy. It imposes rhythms, it orders, it operates, it does not abandon the earth where its destiny must be fulfilled and whose own destiny must be fulfilled by it. Its history will be that of men and not of idle gods. The whole spirit must become incarnate and explore the possible. The books of India, the *Bhagavad-Gita* apart, are almost without history, they abound in repetitions, their variations are monotonous; it is true that they promise the highest summit, but for one who cannot reach it there is nothing to do but go around in a circle or stay put.

The Bible is the opposite of this immobility. It shows the most various and the most free advances of thought, the most poignant figures, the most necessary experiences. When you think about it a bit, the myths of Genesis astound with their beauty and their intelligence; there is a psychological truth in them that it seems cannot be surpassed. The destiny of humankind is portended and portrayed as it was not in any part of the world. The great traits of our Western life are there: the need for knowledge that comes before animal happiness, the law of work that springs from it. Adam and Eve became our father and mother forever.

Yes, by establishing its history Israel marked the first steps of our own.

It was a small people, born in one of the most arid and the most uninhabitable corners of the earth that, looking for something better, ascending toward the north, opened our march forward.

But, you will tell me, that was Israel, not the modern Jews. You will not deny their shortcomings? Certainly not, I shall not deny them, but I see only too well their causes and our own part of the responsibility, the part that belongs to us, so-called Aryans.

I do not want to enter here into the details of questions that have already been very well discussed. I refer my readers to two excellent books: *Israël parmi les nations* [*Israel among the Nations*] by Anatole Leroy-Beaulieu and *Antisémitisme* by Bernard Lazare. This latter work has the drawback, for a simplistic reader, of being marked by too many scruples. Bernard Lazare is like some of my Jewish friends, the Ordo group, for example, who think, naïve people that they are, that the Jews have numerous faults and that they must take the greatest part of the responsibility for the wrongs that weigh them down. In the eyes of a heroic morality they are right, but it is not their improvement that will put things in order, in my opinion. It is rather the improvement of others.

How shall we not be touched by this, which I notice in Leroy-Beaulieu's work:

> Throughout two thousand years learning is the only distinction acknowledged in Israel. To the scholar fall all honors. "The scholar," says the Talmud, "comes before the king; the bastard scholar before the ignorant high priest."
> —What a contrast to our barbarians of the West, Franks, Goths, or Lombards. Israel has been faithful to this maxim through all its humiliations. When enemy hands shut its schools in Christian or Moslem countries, the rabbis crossed the seas in order to go and reopen its academies far away. Like the wandering Jew of the legend, the wavering torch of Jewish learning has thus passed from the East to the West and from the South to the North, emigrating, every two or three centuries, from one country to another. When a royal edict would give them three months to abandon the country where their fathers were buried, where their sons were born, the treasure that the Jews took the greatest care to carry away with them was their books. . . .
> Let us picture to ourselves who these scholars of Judah were, and what their learning was. The rabbis and the *hakkam* were not scholars of the study, shut up in their academies or in their schools, isolated

from the mass of their coreligionists, and all the more honored by their people for being less understood by them. Not at all, in every epoch they have been in close and intimate relations with the main body of Israel; they have quite truly formed its soul and shaped its intelligence. They were really its guides, its counselors, its masters, its leaders. The whole of Israel was impregnated by their doctrines, becoming impassioned over various rival schools. It could be said that all Jews were scholars more or less, were literate more or less. The absolutely illiterate Jew, the *inalfabeto* as the Italians say, has always been rare. Education in Israel has always been compulsory.

And how shall we not be ashamed when we think of the tortures that we have made the Jews undergo, of the constant degradations that we have imposed upon them, through religious fanaticism, through stupid and sterile national pride, through vulgar envy. . . .

Jews are not a foreign element in Europe; they are, on the contrary, in many respects, a basic element in it. As Leroy-Beaulieu says, their race is "the most anciently cultivated in our Mediterranean world." (They are a foreign element only when they are driven from their native lands.)

As it is known, there is no European race, as that race has been overlaid by Aryan immigrations and only the Iberians can claim to be indigenous. Are not the Aryan places of origin, in fact, more distant from the European continent than the Semitic places of origin? I shall ask those who protest that the Aryans were the first occupants what they think about the case of England and America. . . .

What hindered assimilation was the separatism that the Jews evinced at the beginnings of European history and their refusal to adhere to triumphant Christianity. Originally the nature of the complaint that was made against them was of a religious and not a racist order. It must further be observed that, even when they held fast to their faith, they never tried to impose it on others through violence. And can they be reproached for having held to their faith?

But isn't that all very ancient history?

From the day that the Jews were emancipated (as you know, it is one of the glories of the French Revolution that they were), they have proved that they could be national elements of the first order. . . .

From *Les Gazettes d'Adrienne Monnier*; first published in *La Gazette des Amis des Livres* (December 1938).

On Pre-Columbian Mexico

The memory left by the great exhibition of Mexican art that took place in 1952 at the Musée d'Art Moderne has been happily revived by Gisèle Freund's album *Mexique précolombien*, which has just appeared in the "Collections des Ides photographiques," directed by Richard Heyd.

Paul Rivet has written for this album a masterful preface in which he presents the basic ideas that are indispensable to an understanding of Pre-Columbian and even modern Mexican art; what he says about the artists of today, whose humanism is at once Indian and Mediterranean, creates an understanding and an appreciation of their works. The history of Mexican art is far from being simple, and it is difficult to find one's way in it at first; it includes the contributions of twelve civilizations, the first of which, the archaic, goes back to 1500 B.C., and the last of which, the Aztec, stops at 1521, the date of the Spanish conquest. Besides the succession in time, it takes account of the different peoples of which they were characteristic: Olmec, Toltec, Zapotec, Mayan, Aztec. Some civilizations have received a geographical name, those of the Gulf and of the West, for example; under these titles are grouped the productions of peace-loving peoples who did not impose their name through conquests, but who nonetheless left evidence of art and skill that have a personal character.

It was in the civilization of the West that a place was occupied by the Tarascans, whose statuettes of clay are enlivened by a gay and familiar spirit that seems to belong to them alone on Mexican soil. They did not sculpt terrible gods or raise huge monuments; it must be said that they occupied beautiful fertile regions and that, except when they had to defend themselves against invaders—which they did very well, considering their number—they were able to give themselves over to living. In 1952 Paul Hartmann published an album composed solely of reproductions of Tarascan works in terra cotta, almost all of them belonging to the collection of Diego Rivera; this album, which was arranged by Gilbert Médioni, is extremely refreshing. The finds of our avant-garde sculpture are trifles next to these little figures that are so free, whose strong deformations are always intelligent and sensitive. It is true, for example, that if our sculptors had done *The Helmeted Man with His*

Hand Open (that open hand makes one think of Henri Laurens) they would not have been satisfied with the fifteen-by-ten-inch dimensions that were enough for the primitive artist, oh no!

Gisèle Freund's album is a much more important and complete thing, since it gives the essential works of all the Pre-Columbian civilizations; as Paul Rivet says, she has made her choice "with a refined taste and incontestable artistry." The most beautiful and the most distinctive pieces of the exhibition are to be found again here, beginning with a little woman with two faces who is devilishly Picassoesque. It was an excellent idea to have the views of the teocallis alternate with the reproductions of statues and objects.

The teocallis are temples, always so imposing, model temples one might say, because with their form of a truncated pyramid and their terraces they give better than all others the idea of a gradual ascent toward the upper world; their ornaments, when they have any, are classic in a universal manner: has one ever seen more powerful plays of lines, a more beautiful variety of geometrical motifs? Some have ten terraces, like those of the Nuns of Uxmal; they almost all have four vertiginous stairways, whose steps have a depth of less than six inches, says Constantin Balmont, who after having painfully climbed them, had a great deal of difficulty going down the stairways of the formidable Mayan Castillo.

The contemplation of Gisèle Freund's photographs drew me into all kinds of reflections on ancient Mexico and its religion. The authors who have studied this religion, particularly that of the Aztecs (the best known because it prevailed in Anahuac, that is to say, the valley of Mexico City, when the Spanish arrived), have not failed to call attention to the atrocities that characterized it. Nowhere, in fact, has human sacrifice been pushed to such a degree; some claim that twenty thousand victims were sacrificed each year, two thousand five hundred of them in Tenochtitlán alone, the capital, which is now Mexico City. What is known on this subject comes from the conquistadors and from the ecclesiastics who accompanied them; Cortez himself drew up reports for Charles V and proved himself to be an attentive observer of religious acts, all the more because he used their cruelty as a warrant for giving full vent to his own. We know how much he and his companions were horrified by what they saw and by what they experienced. In his memoirs Bernal Diaz described the impressions of their first visit to the great temple of Mexico City, to which they went accompanied by the king, Montezuma, and his priests. In the hall that contained the altars of the supreme gods, Uitzilopochtli and Tezcatlipoca, which gods appeared to them to be frightful devils, they saw the hearts of Indians who had just been sacrificed burning at the same time as incense. "There was such a layer of blood on the walls and the ground was soaked with it to such a point that the slaughterhouses of Castille do not emit a stench that can compare."

I do not want to multiply quotations of this kind. I shall be satisfied to recall that ritual murder included several varieties, which they adopted according to the god whom they wished to please. The most important was the one that consisted of stretching the victim out upon the sacrificial stone; four priests held his limbs in position while a fifth opened his chest with a knife of obsidian (that is a brilliant black stone, there is a whole showcase full of it in the Musée de l'Homme), quickly inserted his hand into the wound and tore out the still quivering heart, which he then offered to the gods named above, who both symbolized the sun. The first, the hummingbird god, lorded it over the months of fine weather; his festival was celebrated three times a year, in May, July, and November—when you pronounce his name, Uitzilopochtli, don't you see the hummingbird fluttering with his swift and brilliant little wings? The second, Tezcatlipoca, that is to say, Brilliant Mirror, was the harsh sun of the cold season, when there is no rain and when the ground is barren; it was he who was feared most, he sent men the greater part of their misfortunes, he was often called Necoc Yaotl, which means "the enemy on all sides"; he had triumphed over Quetzalcoatl, the Plumed Serpent, and had compelled him to retreat to the eastern part of the country, to Tlapallan, the region of the dawn. The serpent-god was of Mayan origin, he was the true good God, the friend of humans and of peaceful labors; he stopped his ears, it was said, when he heard war spoken about. Legend asserted that he would come back one day, and Montezuma at first believed that Cortez, arriving from the east, was none other than he.

It was for Tezcatlipoca, the pitiless, the retributive, that they sacrificed each year the most beautiful young man who could be found. For an entire year this young man personified the god and led a blissful life; he was covered with flowers and precious jewels, he was dressed in the richest fabrics, his face and his body were painted black, which made the bright colors of his attire stand out wonderfully. They married him to four beautiful and well-bred girls, but only twenty days before putting him to death, doubtless so that he would know them only on a honeymoon. On the fatal date, everything was stripped from him. In his hands they left only flutes, which he broke one by one as he climbed the steps of the temple, upon whose height they tore out his heart, according to the custom.

Tlacoc, the god of rain, had for a hieroglyphic sign a cross with arms of equal length, symbolizing the four cardinal points from which rain may come. For him young children with curly hair who could not yet walk were thrown in the lake; earlier they were carried in procession through the city, perched upon litters, after having been covered with precious stones and flowers and fitted with paper wings. If the children cried a great deal that was a good sign, it meant that the rains would be abundant; but if a dropsical person was met with, that was bad: Tlaloc would keep his rains to himself. The drowning was preceded by a sacrifice of adults, so numerous that the first to be immolated were called "the base of the others," because their corpses supported those that came afterward.

Another great form of ritual murder was beheading followed by flaying. That is what they did for Centeotl, the goddess of corn and agriculture, whom they preferred to call Toci, "our grandmother." For her they took a woman, they pampered her for a long time before the festival; on the day of the sacrifice the priestesses said to her, "Don't worry, lovely friend, you will spend tonight with the king, rejoice." At midnight she was deftly beheaded and flayed; the Toci-priest covered himself with her skin, with the exception of the skin of her thighs, out of which a young priest made a mask for himself. That was all accompanied by processions and by ritual dances in which figured "the dance of arms," a mimicry of vegetation.

For Xipe-Totec, "our lord of the flayed," the patron of goldsmiths, they naturally flayed many victims, after having disemboweled them, and the priests always dressed themselves in their skin.

Xiuhteculi, the god of fire, profited from the most atrocious holocaust; for him they made "human broils." While in the other cases death was promptly dealt and the refinements that followed had only an insensible body for object, his victims were thrown upon an enormous, fiery brazier. "There was then for some moments," we read in Réville, "an indescribable jumble of sputtering, crackling, cracking human flesh, contortions, howls that filled those who were present with terror. The priests alone were calm as they performed their monstrous functions, and equipped with long hooks they harpooned the wretches, drew them out of the brazier before they had given up their last gasp, and threw them three-quarters broiled upon the sacrificial stone, where they finished them off in the ordinary manner. Soon a pile of smoking hearts was rising before the idol of the god of fire."

Before making an outcry as we read such things, it behooves us to remember the hell of our own religions, a hell that some among the greatest artists strove to describe and paint, a hell to which we truly believed sinners were consigned for eternity. Dante tells how the devils held the damned in boiling pitch with long forks, in the manner of cooks. Hieronymus Bosch in his paintings prepares human meat in a thousand and one ways, each more frightful than any of the others. It will be said that it is the devils who find their pleasure this way, and not ourselves, but aren't the devils the offspring of our brains?

Joyce, in *A Portrait of the Artist as a Young Man*, reproduces in full the sermon of Father Arnall, who is preparing for the retreat of the students at the Jesuit college where he was educated. The preacher creates for his "dear little brothers in Jesus Christ" a picture of hell that is so thorough, so precise, particularly in what concerns the horrible details—tortures, stench—that after the sermon poor Stephen leaves the chapel on shaking legs, idiotic with fear.

For his own part, hasn't our contemporary, Claudel, brandishing a *crêpe flambée* on the end of a fork, declared to the son of Francis Jammes that Gide would burn that way in hell?

All that, it can still be said, takes place in the imagination and not in reality; but the men of Europe and Asia have never been wanting in effective and often very elaborate cruelty. Without citing Chinese or Hindu torments, the games of the Roman circus, weren't there tortures and burnings among us? Doesn't every war give full vent to sadism? The subject is immense, I do not want to speak complacently about it. What I simply want to try to prove is that despite strong appearances the ancient Mexicans were no worse than the others. When you really think about it you even see that they were not cruel, properly speaking; that is to say, they did not endeavor to torture the victims and did not derive pleasure from their sufferings; they immolated them to the gods in the manner that seemed most suitable, most propitious to them. For example, if they flayed people in honor of Toci or Xipe it was through analogy to the earth, which it was necessary to flay so that the corn might sprout, with the metal that it was also necessary to flay in order to transform it into objects and jewelry. They thought that the heart was the very seat of life, the inner altar of every breast; that blood was the essential fluid that bound men to the higher powers; it seemed natural to them, if one wanted to be on good terms with these powers, to shed blood and offer them hearts that were still warm—during the sacrifice they beat an enormous drum covered over with snakeskin, whose sound could be heard five miles away.

(It seems to me that such rites issue from an excessive poetic vigor while the esthetic sense is lacking. A liking for beautiful forms moderates manners and customs.)

Blood was not drawn only from consecrated victims; everybody was called upon to give more or less of his own, according to his piety. At the basis of the ancient Mexican religion there was an extraordinary austerity, a spirit of demanding and continual sacrifice that leaves the hair shirts, scourges, and other Christian mortifications far behind. The Aztecs were trained from their early childhood to practice scarifications of the tongue, the ears, the legs, and the chest. For Quetzacoatl, who was a peace-loving god as we have said, victims were not killed, but it was still necessary for everybody to give a bit of his blood. These practices naturally went very far for the priests, who in many circumstances were obliged to pierce their tongues and their ears with slender rods; they inflicted the same penance in an attenuated form upon people who had sinned and confessed their faults—for confession existed among the Aztecs, and Communion as well, in the form that we shall discuss further on. The little pieces of wood in the ears of Père Ubu come perhaps from this source; Jarry probably knew the works of Bernal Diaz and Sahagun, who have both been translated into French. It seems that there were four priests in Teotihuacán who surpassed all the others in austerity: sleeping upon the bare ground, eating only two ounces of bread and a bit of mush every day, keeping watch at night by turns, and bleeding themselves with prickles of the agave plant. These priests in particular passed slender rods of hard wood through the lobes of their ears, every day; after a month they had thirty of them in each ear. They then drew out the bloody sheaves and started over again, so that at the end of the year there was a total of two thousand eight hundred and eighty, which they burned in the course of a ceremony.

There were very many convents in ancient Mexico; they took the place of schools, as much for the men as for the women; all the boys from six to nine years old entered sacerdotal establishments to be educated there. The girls remained in the convent until the age of fifteen; their hair was cut and they were bound to chastity; throughout all this time they were taught to sew, to weave, to embroider, and to make the sacred cakes, which for the most part were kneaded with blood. They underwent frequent fasts, often slept without undressing, and had to get up three times a night, by turns, to renew the incense that burned before the gods. Many of them, at the age when they could leave and marry, preferred to embrace the religious life; it was from among the nuns that were recruited the convent directresses and the priestesses who attended to the domestic upkeep of the temples.

Yes, in Pre-Columbian Mexico, as much as in Spain, there were many good sisters and priests; the latter were dressed in black, like the Catholic ones, but in a style that was pushed farther, with their long hair smeared with blood and their cadaverous odor. In fact, the poor people rarely escaped from their labors of slaughter. I have not found any details about the particular apprenticeship that they necessarily underwent in order to learn how to kill in several ways, to flay, to tear out the heart—all that demanding strength and skill. They also had to be cooks, they had to cook not only the hearts that were destined for the altars but also the flesh of the victims, which they ate and gave the faithful to eat; it was in this form that Communion was taken. The Aztecs, we see, practiced cannibalism, but only in a sacramental fashion, never in any other case, since at the time of the siege of their capital by the Spaniards they preferred to let themselves die of hunger.

In the presence of all these facts that I have just mentioned, commentators hesitate to attribute a moral sense to the ancient Mexicans; they see an attenuation of their "savagery" only in the fact that they always took prisoners of war or criminals for victims. That was furthermore the excuse that Montezuma made to Cortez when the latter wanted to remonstrate with him: "We have the right to kill our enemies in war, and you do the same as we; why then should we not put to death and offer to our gods people who otherwise would have been killed?"—Personally, I do not exactly praise them for this trait, which appears to me rather to diminish them; if they believed in the efficacy of human sacrifices it would have been noble and meritorious to offer their own persons or those of their children for their holocausts—that could have been decided in the form of drawing lots. It is true that the Aztecs, who were extremely warlike, could consider that the fact of going bravely to war and confronting death put them in a totally sacrificial position;

and then it was also very necessary to make the best use of prisoners of war; wasn't it less cruel after all to immolate them rather than to shut them up in camps, feeding them like dogs, or reduce them to slavery?

It was all the less cruel—here we come to one of the most important ideas—because every victim sacrificed to the gods became consubstantial with them and enjoyed their paradise and their festivities throughout eternity. The soldiers who fell on the field of battle and the women who died in childbirth made up a part of the number of the elect; the little children drowned in honor of Tlaloc rose directly to the gardens of the god of rain and frolicked there joyfully forever; it even happened that devout people heard the rustling of their wings. Yes, contrary to the Christians, the Aztecs never imagined that an eternity of torments and tortures was possible; they never placed their enemies there, or those who are very arbitrarily judged to be sinners. For them the kingdom of Mictlán, the god of the dead, was made up of great spaces that were dark and sad, which one reached after a very wearisome journey; everybody except the elect submitted there to the same fate, which was to suffer tedium; there were nine divisions that one crossed like the rooms of an empty house; come to the end of the ninth division, one fell asleep at last and slept eternally.

For those who would still like to quibble about the moral sense of the ancient Mexicans I offer these lines, which come as a conclusion to an Aztec father's counsels to his children:

> Strive to live in peace with your neighbor and treat him with respect. If someone speaks evil of you, do not answer him; be friendly with everyone without going as far as familiarity; do not slander anyone; be patient and return good for evil, the gods will make amends to you for the wrongs suffered. Lastly, my children, do not waste either your goods or your time, for both are precious. In every period pray to the gods and draw your inspiration from them; apply yourselves to what is useful.

This text is quoted in *L'Histoire de la civilisation indienne* by Paul Radin, who unfortunately does not give precise details about his subject. I also read with great interest *La Vie des Mayas* by Jean Babelon; there are many curious details in it about Mayan mortifications, which are in no way second to those of the Aztecs. But it was from Réville's excellent work, *Les Religions du Mexique, de l'Amérique Centrale et du Pérou*, that I drew the greater part of my information, because he makes use of all the documents that have authority in the matter. After leaving these readings I relaxed in the company of two poets: one, Mexican, was Alfonso Reyes, "our noble friend," as Valery Larbaud has called him; the other was Antonin Artaud, who loved and understood the genius of Mexico to the highest degree.

Yes, I reread *Au pays des Tarahumaras*, the thin volume put out by the Age d'Or, and the complementary pages that appeared in the *Arbalète* and the first number of this review. How beautiful it is!—After these transcendent texts I took up again the poem by Alfonso Reyes that Larbaud translated in 1929 for number twenty of *Commerce*. This poem, which is entitled "Les Herbes du Tarahumara" ["The Herbs of the Tarahumara"], gives an intimate idea, and how precious it is, of the Indians of that region; we see that they come down from the mountain when the year is bad and that they go to Chihuahua to sell magic herbs that cure all kinds of ailments. Sometimes, Reyes also says,

> Sometimes they bring gold from their hidden mines,
> And all day long, sitting in the street,
> They break the auriferous lumps
> Among the politely dissembled envy of the whites.

The people of Chihuahua are happy to see them; they rejoice in the inclemency of the weather that has obliged them to come down, these "worthy inhabitants of the snows" who are on familiar terms with everybody and who

> Always answer thus the required question,
> "And you, isn't your face cold?"

Why shouldn't a collection be made of the poems of Alfonso Reyes? In it would be placed the "Vision de l'Anahuac," translated by Jeanne Guérandel, which appeared in 1927 in the *Nouvelle Revue Française* with a preface by Larbaud. And the poem "Tropique," translated by Marcelle Auclair and Jean Prévost, which is to be found at the beginning of the twelfth and last number of my *Navire d'Argent*. And "Les Herbes du Tarahumara," naturally. And everything it would be possible to translate well.

I read the "Vision de l'Anahuac" with enchantment. There are descriptions in it that set you to dreaming: the one of the great valley with its high central plateau where "the vegetation is harsh and heraldic, the landscape orderly," where, in a resplendent light, "things stand out in extraordinary relief"; the one of the market of ancient Mexico City that amazed Cortez and his companions, a prodigious market where there were "all the things that can be found everywhere on earth," things to eat and ornamental or useful things. Alfonso Reyes quotes Gomara, the chaplain of Cortez—it is with this delectable description that we shall leave Mexico:

> The most beautiful things in the marketplace are the works of gold and those of feathers that counterfeit every thing and every color. The Indians are such good workmen in these materials that they can fashion with feathers a butterfly, an animal, a tree, a flower, grasses, and even rough stones; they bring so much exactness to it that their work is similar to what is natural and living. And it happens that they do not eat for a whole day, taking up the feather, laying it aside, and taking it up again, looking at it on all sides in sunlight, in shadow, in half-light, to see if it is better in its regular direction or "counter-feather," placed lengthwise or crosswise, or even on the wrong side; they let it leave their hands at last only after they have brought to it the utmost perfection.

From *Dernières Gazettes et Ecrits divers*; first published in *Les Lettres Nouvelles* (June 1954).

part eight

The Nature of France

Occupation Journal: May 8 to July 10, 1940

May

Wednesday 8—Yesterday evening *Quasimodo* with Charles Laughton. *Atrocious* and prodigious. One could become ill, have a miscarriage from it. Looked at it wide-eyed, with a terrible desire to weep all the time. It's what brings me back to Joyce and saves the situation for this *Gazette*, which will be able to come out end of May.

Sunday 12. Pentecost—Rocfoin. Mama gives me letters Dr. Jean Bernard and Claude Roy (a gem of good grace, on the *Very Rich Hours of the Duke de Berry*) for *Gazette*.

Introduction: the idea of publishing this talk came to me while listening to Dr. Marc Klein and Claude Roy speak to me about *Ulysses*—"How is it that a person as rational as yourself could bowl that monster between our legs?" (Claude Roy)

For the Beautiful Books of the World, it's promising and even too promising. Wants to become something important, a real profession of faith like the preface of 1918 and no. 1 of the *Gazette*. Mama in complete agreement that I work on it for a month: double number (opening and bibliography) printed in 2,000 copies, of which 1,000 besides subscription with advertisement in *Bibliographie de la France*.

Monday 13. Pentecost—Return to Paris, having read that leaves have been canceled. At noon, on arriving, we learn that refugees of German origin have been put in camps; no exception, even for *prestataires* and *libérés*.

Afternoon at the shop. Telephone call from Hoppenot concerning our friends Benjamin and Kracauer, as well as Kaminski and Koestler: he has already intervened, they do not have to move.

Tuesday 14—Incredibly exceptional favor for these writers. Benjamin can't get over it. Even those who were exempted at the time of the first concentrations in September are now obliged to obey the summons. To thank Hoppenot Benjamin is going to make him a present of *Anabase*, the original edition that Rilke had sent him just before he died, asking him to translate this poem, which he no longer had the time to translate himself.

Wednesday 15—After lunch, reading *Le Seau à charbon [The Coal Scuttle]*—with a pleasure, an amusement that are almost continuous —unexpected arrival of Stéphane [Hessel].
In the afternoon, visit from the Kracauers, Mo. and his daughters, Koestler.

Thursday 16—In the morning went to reserve two seats for *Ondine*, the Athenée shut since the day before. Saw Benjamin's *Anabase*. In three places shows beginnings of translation written by Rilke in pencil.

Friday 17—I earned while spending this evening at the shop that Mlle Gobillard went up to the apartment in the afternoon. Valéry poorly recovered from his grippe. They leave for Brittany.

Saturday 18—Benjamin and Kaminski at Membré's. There is a means of sleeping at Rue Pierre-Charron. Tériade and Angèle [Lamotte] for dinner.

Sunday 19—Tea at [John and Estelle] Rewald's.

Monday 20—Proofs Joyce and the French public 18 pages. With the Benjamin on Georges Salles and Bryher, am very short of space. Drop letters D., S., and part St., or put back in July. That works out very well.

Tuesday 21—Kracauer and woman friend Koestler. With Benjamin went over old note on Scheerbart to replace study on Bachofen.

Wednesday 22—Hoppenot lunches with us. As agreed, Koestler comes to see him at the apartment after lunch.

Thursday 23—Koestler spent the night on the sofa. Four-leaf clover falls on him out of *Le Rouge et le noir* right between his eyes!

Friday 24—Telephoned to Membré, still agrees to have our friends sleep at Rue Pierre-Charron.

Saturday 25—Koestler has his visa and can leave this evening for Limoges.

Sunday 26—Rocfoin.

Monday 27—Visit Carcano with young attaché cousin of Adelina [Güiraldes]. Asks me plan for Library University of Buenos Aires, the one supplied by D. worthless. Big job but not tiresome.

Heart heavy and oppressed. Impossible to think of the Beautiful Books of the World.

Tuesday 28—Capitulation of the King of the Belgians.

Wednesday 29—Telephone call from Koestler in Limoges for lodging certificate and certificate of good life and morals. We go to the police station of the 14th, Benjamin and I.

Thursday 30—Saillet requests news about Thomas, Lévesque, and Malacki for Gide. Gide still in Nice, would go to Aude "but for my kidneys, which are breaking down"(?). Matisse told Tériade that he was spending his time with Simon Bussy doing strategy on maps.

Friday 31—Rinette comes to hang her embroidery [called "Fable"]. Hoppenot, whom I had invited for lunch tomorrow, telephones me that Hélène and Violaine [Hoppenot] are returning this evening from Touraine.

Evening. Charlie show at the Ursulines.

[?. End of May or beginning of June]—Visit from Céline [Oerthel], who is very upset. In the vestibule knocks into Benjamin, who takes fright and runs off. I tranquilize her concerning Lucien and Maurice and send her to pray Sainte-Geneviève.

Young woman, friend of Groethuysen and Alix [Guillain], tells me why Paulhan did not come on the day agreed to. Germaine [Paulhan] more and more tired and oppressed. It seems that the no. of *Mesures* that ought to appear and that is printed at Abbeville is shot to hell.

June

Saturday 1—At noon, lunch with the three Hoppenots. Hélène urges Gisèle [Freund] to leave Paris.

In the afternoon, John Rewald telephones Gisèle that Estelle [Rewald] has come back from Aix.

Sunday 2—In the afternoon, visit from Rinette, from the Rewalds, whom I do not see. In the morning, Mo. and his daughters.

Monday 3—Wrote this morning to Saillet and Stéphane [Hessel]. After lunch: alert. Stayed in the apartment. Loud noise of planes roaring over our heads. Raid: 200 planes, numerous victims. Passy very much damaged, etc.

Tuesday 4—At 8:00 in the morning receive cablegram from Victoria [Ocampo]: "Say if safe am with you all." Coupon for the answer—what to answer?

Sending out *Gazette*, which the book sewer brought this morning.

In the afternoon I send Gisèle to look for the iron trunks at Rinette's—In the evening to the Ursulines, *Italian Straw Hat*.

Wednesday 5—Prepare departure Gisèle for Cusset.

This evening dined with Tériade and Angèle [Lamotte] in the Grill-Room [Médicis]; we began with asparagus.

Thursday 6—Fargue comes to spend a full hour with us, very funny and nice. Gisèle, who is leaving for Cusset, receives advice from Bomsel to go to Lot instead; she goes to the railroad station immediately.

Also visit from Le Masle, offers to help me, badly received: cannot keep his "reliquary" of Saint François de Sales and Saint Jeanne de Chantal—horrible as a suppuration of the fingertips—that he had given me in memory of Larbaud (?); comes back at the end of the afternoon with the son [of] Tiffeneau.

Friday 7—Morning at 7:40 departure Gisèle Gare d'Austerlitz. Rose at 5:00, alert at 5:10. Came back from station on foot, passing in front of Saint-Geneviève.

In the afternoon, visit from Michaux, whom I had come up to the apartment, Rinette being there. We were talking about him when Ida came to announce him. We tell him that he should be given a Bureau of Fabrications (Tériade told me the day before yesterday that he was thinking about it). In fact, he maintains that he could find tricks as good as those of the Germans and that he could make millions of Germans neurotic on the radio; that he does not want to create literature but only practical things. How introduce him to Information? We say that Julien Cain is very intelligent and very advanced. At that moment Ida comes back and tells me that Mme Cain is downstairs. We all three of us go down. Mme Cain has come to see the embroidery, having received the *Gazette*. Michaux, invited by Mme Cain to go to see her husband, says that first he is going to leave Paris for two weeks.

Saturday 8—In the morning, went to see Rinette at her place to tell her that I was not going to Rocfoin. I accompanied her to the station. Afterward went to the Rue de Grenelle to the house of Hélène Grund [-Hessel], where the concierge was not in; waited for her more than twenty minutes.

Cablegram to Victoria [Ocampo]: "Victoria be with us. Long live the Argentine Republic."

In the afternoon, to the shop, not a soul. Paul-Emile [Bécat] takes away tome I of the *Histoire des Gaulois*.

In the evening, dinner at the Grill-Room with Hélène Hoppenot. Extremely friendly atmosphere. She lets me understand that Paris will be involved in the battle. She gives me a bottle of plum brandy.

Sunday 9—Lunch with Sylvia. Chicken and peas. The *"Aux armes citoyens"* that precedes the news on the radio: dampened plumage. Cry of the cock wounded to death.

At night, very heavy cannonade. We think seriously of putting mattresses in the cellar to sleep on.

I fill my bathtub with water every night.

Monday 10—In the morning, Hoppenot comes to say goodbye to me at 11:45; he lets me understand that Paris will not be involved in the battle. Then, visit from Philippe Fontaine.

In the afternoon, Tériade and Angèle absolutely want to take me away. She says that if I stay it will be believed that I am one of those who want to come to terms with the Germans. He, very worried because he has no visa for leaving Paris; tell him to go immediately to Information, which Julien Cain should be leaving, it seems, at 5:00.

Visit from [?] who requests a testimonial of loyalty to the Allies.

Departures everywhere, above all in cars, on bicycles and motorcycles.

Read meditations on the destruction of Paris (*Secret Grande Pyramide*).

Tuesday 11—Visit, in the morning, from Mo. and Imo., who are leaving. They tell me that Russia, Turkey, and Egypt are at war, that people are hugging one another in the Métro. All Paris believes it. The matter has not been confirmed.

In all the streets a ceaseless stream of evacuees. The Rue de l'Odéon is upside down. Saw Thévenet at noon. Advise her to return to Cusset. At any rate, impossible to leave because of the condition of the roads, where people cannot advance, it seems. In spite of everything, a contagious desire to get away.

In the afternoon, second visit from Mo. Visit from Paul-Emile. Very anguished atmosphere.

Wednesday 12—Personal longing to leave and go to Rocfoin. Prepared my catalogs, which Sylvia would have carried on her motorcycle. Sent Sylvia Gare Montparnasse to see if there are any trains. Tell Thévenet and Ida useless to come to the bookshop until the end of the week, to provide themselves with necessities and see if they do not really want to leave (Marcel left this morning for Cusset).

Rinette comes after lunch, entreats me not to leave, that we should live such moments here, witnessing the stream of evacuees. Wrote letter to mama. Went with Rinette and Sylvia Boulevard Sebastopol, then to Porte Centrale; had coffee opposite the Magasins du Louvre. Returned by way of Rue du Bac. Bon Marché, which was closing (6:00). Came back Rue de Buci, bought two pounds of butter, which I melted in the evening with two pounds bought yesterday.

Thursday 13—In the morning, Sylvia's desire to leave. She went to the American Embassy.

Saw the young ones at quarter to twelve. Ida tells me that there is a herd of cows Place Edmond-Rostand.

We learn at noon that Paris is open city.

In the afternoon, went with Rinette to the Gare Montparnasse, to the Bon Marché, then to the Dôme (Coupole and Rotonde shut, Milk Bar open), then Rue du Bac to Vita Nova (shut).

Black rain.

Friday 14—First day of the Occupation. It is said that we must stay shut in for forty-eight hours.

With Sylvia observe from my windows the procession of motorcycles and trucks on the Boulevard Saint-Germain.

At noon begin to see people on the sidewalk.

In the afternoon, visit from Paul-Emile, who saw the procession

of the first German battalions this morning at the Place de l'Etoile.
In the evening, great depression.

Saturday 15—Second day of the Occupation. We learn that we
can go out from 7:00 in the morning to 9:00 in the evening,
German time.

Morning: Halles. Sylvia came for me at 9:00. Nortier, Batten-
dier, Varraz (wretched meat and fish). Sole.

Afternoon, went out with Rinette. Got meat at Adrien Brunel's.
Deux-Magots, Flore, and Lipp shut. People's tension slackening:
"What if the Germans are here, there will at least be order." It is
said that they have supplied the evacuees with milk.

Sunday 16—Lunched with Sylvia. Broiled sirloin, tomato salad,
potatoes with butter sauce.

Afternoon to Rinette's. Plum tarts.

Monday 17—In the morning, went to the Samar., bought soap.
Many German soldiers at the jewelry counter.

At twelve thirty, Pétain declaration. Sylvia lunches with me.
Sirloin cold mayonnaise cauliflower.

Reopening of the bookshop (2:00 to 6:00). Saw three subscribers.
Sold only one book: *Gone with the Wind.*

Thévenet and Ida tell me that many people when they see the
Germans refrain from fraternizing with them.

Saw Paul-Emile and Rinette. Paul-Emile gives the 11th arrondissement's impression of Russia. Many people wept listening to
Pétain.

At 6:00 went out with Rinette, had tea at the Dôme; the
Rotonde has reopened. Coming home, found nice tomatoes at the
Russian restaurant. As I crossed the Luxembourg, the pink and red
(?) flowers [crossed-out word] me; never saw so much variety in
shades of pink.

Gloomy evening. I feel defeat and that it's going to be fascism.

Tuesday 18—Hitler's and Mussolini's answer is being awaited.
Toward noon ventured as far as the Pont des Arts. Eco has
reopened. No meat, no butter, only a bit of pork.

Dr. May came to change his books. Most reasonable ideas. He
says that the Germans are doing "armored tourism" in France. If
Germany can bring about European unity, let her do it, he says; we
might as well try in good faith to come to an understanding with
Germany and Italy.

At 4:00 in the afternoon Mme Allier comes to tell me that Sylvia, who left this morning around 9:00 on bicycle, has not yet come back. Seriously worried. Telephoned the American Embassy, tell Mme Allier to go to the police station. Around 6:30 Marthe Lamy arrives on bicycle (she is feeling the Spanish blood rising), tell her my worry about Sylvia; she telephones the Hôpital Marmottan, where they bring those who are injured in street accidents, and the Hôpital Américain. Around 7:00 Sylvia arrives. She had gone to Carlotta [Briggs's] apartment on the Boulevard Suchet, then to the American Embassy.

This evening, message on the radio by Pomaret, the minister of the interior, who, in a stentorian voice, enjoins the French to stay where they are and not to take flight on the roads, that all cities of more than 20,000 inhabitants have been declared *open cities.*

Yesterday, Charles Baudoin, the minister of foreign affairs, declared that if an honorable peace is not offered to France she *will perish completely in order to bequeath her soul to the world.*

I am resigned to defeat and fascism.

Wednesday 19—Morning, around 11:00, went in Métro to the Etoile, took a stroll around the Place, went down the Champs-Elysées. Fouquet's open with great style. The Triomphe and various other [cafés] of lesser importance also open. At the level of the Rue Pierre-Charron, big procession of troops (military transports and personnel: little wagons with six seats, vans, men on horseback and on foot), a procession that was a half-hour long, at least. Went down as far as the Rond-Point: there, orchestra composed chiefly of drums, brass instruments, and Chinese bells. Rather monotonous march.

Went down as far as the Concorde: in front of the Hôtel Crillon another orchestra playing somewhat lighter marches. Took Rue . . . (American Library), then [Rue du] Faubourg Saint-Honoré: all the shops shut.

Rue Royale, Weber shut. Trois Quartiers reopen tomorrow.

Grands boulevards, everything shut. Place de l'Opéra, Café de la Paix open with terrace; many Germans at the tables.

Avenue de l'Opéra, everything shut. At the level of the Rue Saint-Anne, meeting with Léautaud, who is going up the avenue, I going down, with shopping bag. I salute him, making the French military salute. He brings his hand to his hat and says to me, pointing to the street, in which German motorcycles and sidecars are circulating: "Well, that's nice." I answer him without stopping, while laughing in spite of myself: "Yes, it's great."

Lunched at the Danish Pâtisserie, which never shut.

Came back by way of the Place du Théâtre-Français. Stock open; the Régence and other cafés open. Went down Rue de Rivoli, Saint-Germain l'Auxerrois, Pont des Arts, Rue de Seine.

The Seine has never been so beautiful; it is green, like some mountain lakes. Splendid weather.

Struck, while looking at the soldiers who were marching past, by their sweetness. Average height, short noses, strong chins, light eyes, very childlike. Saw three or four like girls—very much Schumann's *"nussbaum."* Some, squarer faced, are very medieval. On the whole, Grimm's fairy tales. They march past with a modest manner, intent upon bearing themselves well.

In the evening, took Sylvia to the Luxembourg to see the borders of pink flowers. Went to Montparnasse, to the Milk Bar. Met Burgin with her dog. Sylvia asks her if she has made drawings of her dog. No, she answers, only when he is dead.

Thursday 20—In the morning Sylvia comes for me in order to go to the market in the Rue Mouffetard. We find superb escarole and even tarragon and chives. A bit of beef at the butcher's. No butter or potatoes. Oranges and American "Delicious" apples at 6 francs 50 centimes a pound. The big bakery-pâtisserie in the Rue Racine has reopened; they are not making croissants anymore.

In the afternoon, Rinette. Rue de Rivoli, Place Vendôme, Rue de la Paix. Went to the Café de la Paix. Coming back, saw Maxim's open. The obelisk has been entirely cleared of its sand bags, only the framework at the base is left. Boulevard Saint-Germain, met the Chambrillacs.

Dined with Sylvia. This afternoon she saw a patron who questioned her a great deal, bought various magazines, etc. Sylvia, in return, questioned her no less. Conversation: the English are going to settle in Canada and lord it over North and South America, as they have done in Europe. The old mother.

Friday 21—Heard this morning on the radio (Toulouse) what Rinette told me yesterday: that England has proposed that we merge our two countries into one, with a single Parliament, etc.

To the shop in the afternoon, visit from Thérèse Bertrand-Fontaine and Andrée Brunel.

At the end of the afternoon, stroll in the Luxembourg with

Sylvia. Been to buy sugar shortbread cookies in a bakery in the Rue [blank]. Sylvia finds very ripe and very fresh cherries. At noon I'd had excellent strawberries (11 francs 50 centimes a pound), two small, very good lamb chops, a tomato in a salad.

Sylvia, who went to her Embassy this morning, tells me that Keeler Faus has invited us to have tea at his place Sunday. "You understand," she says, "he would never have dared to invite you at an ordinary time, but he thinks that with the Occupation one can do things that are completely unusual."

Feeling of the Embassy people [American], completely isolated, as if on an island, with the German police next to them (quartered in the Ministère de la Marine).

Saturday 22—The newspaper [the *Matin*] describes the Compiègne interview: railway car, etc.

Been to see Rinette this morning to tell her that I shall not go to her place tomorrow afternoon. Bought some peas and heads of lettuce at her market; only one provisions van, with a line in front of it.

While coming back from her place on foot met Mlle Mercoiret. Bon Marché.

After lunch, visit from Louisette [Bécat].

Sunday 23—In the morning, vegetable market null. At the butcher's, beef and mutton. Lots of legs of mutton at Eco's; people are buying few of them, I think, because the gas is too weak to cook them thoroughly in the oven.

Sylvia has migraine: yesterday she had tea at the house of a secretary of the American Embassy and ate two pieces of chocolate cake.

In the afternoon, tea at Keeler Faus's; a Mr. Moran was there, agent for the interests of the Republic of Liberia (!), charming—Faus's home ravishing; books in profusion, fine old furniture, etc.

While coming back, saw an interminable procession of vans and artillery pieces Boulevard Saint-Germain. A working-class man near us said: "The game isn't over; if the English were to beat them, that would give me pleasure, *really*."

Bought *Paris-Soir*: very sound article on the evacuees.

Tuesday 25—The order for "cease fire" was given this morning at 1:35 along the whole front [the *Matin*]. The armistice with Italy was signed yesterday at 7:35 P.M.

Wednesday 26—This evening, on the English radio, message from Rosamond Lehmann: "In no country, it seems, is it as easy to be happy as in your own. . . . We know how much you have suffered. . . . We have so much to learn from you. . . ."

In the afternoon, talked with subscribers (Mlle Doré, Mlle Saulet): astonishingly intelligent and kind.

Thursday 27—Went this afternoon with Rinette to Hédiard's (cashews, ginger) and to the House of Honey. Bought sweets, nougats chiefly. At Foucher's found chocolate with whole hazelnuts, not milk chocolate. Had tea at the Danish Pâtisserie.

This evening, while listening to the German radio, which tells about the steps taken in Rumania against the Jews (forbidden to occupy official posts), I am seized by despair. I call upon the gods of Israel and beg them to make themselves known, so that their own may not suffer new wrongs and torments. I weep wholeheartedly, it does me good.

Friday 28—Sylvia goes to Nortier's (she had been told that there was butter). No butter, but she brings back a piece of superb Comté Gruyère, the like of which I have not seen since the beginning of the war. No meat. Almost nothing on the market. People are falling more and more upon canned food. Yesterday bought half-pound of mushrooms. I eat a dish of rice with mushrooms and Gruyère that makes me ashamed of myself, it's so good.

In the morning, received letter from Stéphane [Hessel] written the 8th! It's the first letter that I've received from the armed forces for quite a long time.

Met M. Myon, who had tried to join his wife in Burgundy. Like everybody else, he found no assistance except on the part of the Germans; brought back to Paris by a German ambulance. At Mehun-sur-Yèvre, a German went as far as Bourges to look for beer to drink with him.

Saturday 29—Cotton sheets at 125 francs a piece at the Bon Marché, the smallest size, so 250 francs a pair. Found same size at 59 francs at the Magasins du Louvre.

New subscribers, two young fellows, students of Sartre. Conversation in the evening with Mme Lebobitz. The workers, she says, are very ready to be Hitlerites, because the German soldiers tell them that Hitler will immediately let them have pensions for the old.

This evening, on the German radio, they tell the "French

listeners" that they have been duped by literary people and journalists: Wladimir d'Ormesson, Geneviève Tabouis, Duhamel, Maurois, the Tharaud brothers. Attacks confirm the *Epoque* and the *Oeuvre*.

Sunday 30—Nothing at the market, no meat. Still no butter or potatoes. At noon ate peas bought yesterday at the Bon Marché; the most tender of the year, the Telephone or Senator variety. A few raspberries, like yesterday, jellied.

July

Monday 1—After lunch, went out with Rinette. At the Gare Montparnasse we learn that we can go without restriction as far as Rambouillet or Chartres; no stop at Maintenon. Rinette decides to leave tomorrow morning.

At the end of the afternoon, visit from Rose Celli and Charles Mauban.

Tuesday 2—In the afternoon, visit from Marthe Lamy, who tells me that on the first day of the Occupation working-class people, men and women, in the 15th, at Billancourt, fraternized with the Germans, who told them: "We like you very much. We must be allies."

At Nortier's this morning saw more than a hundred people lined up for a quarter of butter. A great many beautiful raspberries on the vans.

Wednesday 3—This morning met Blaise Briod while going to Corcellet's. He had left with his wife. Caught several times in the bombardments. Is with a man, a worker who, he says, saved their lives, his wife's and his own. He accompanies me to Corcellet's and introduces me to the manager: M. Chauveau, charming, decorated, very well read, it seems. They sell me two half-pounds of [coffee], Palais-Royal mixture, as a favor, for they are not supposed to sell any until the afternoon.

While coming back saw unbelievable lines in front of the few shops where they have received a bit of ham, bacon, or sausage.

The daughter-in-law of the concierge, her daughter, and their boys, have been back since yesterday evening. They went as far as the outskirts of Sancerre, found a village where the people showed them a good deal of kindness, gave them beds, bread, milk.

It's the first time that I see people who were not received like dogs.

They came back in a truck, a truck in which 21 persons had been piled up at 200 francs per person. The fellow wanted to take 400 francs. The people went to see the mayor, who compelled him to reduce his price by half (about 155 miles from Paris).

Saturday 6—Bought a leg of mutton for 91 francs 80 centimes at Mme Allier's from a woman who brought it from a butcher of [blank]. The woman, the widow of the composer Letorey, had come some time ago to the shop, wanting to read the letters of Pliny the Younger.

During the day we find a bit of butter at the dairy shops, generally bad (mixed with fat).

Sunday 7—Lunch with Paul-Emile and Rinette. Sylvia went to the Régence to look for cakes: rather good tarts with flaky pastry, but the fruit (pears, cherries) is hardly sweetened.

Wednesday 10—This afternoon, went to the House of Honey, for honey, which is becoming scarce. Bought a pretty dotted red ribbon for a tie and very pretty metal buttons at the Galeries [Lafayette].

Coming in, I find at the concierge's a line from Thévenet, who tells me that Fargue is in Paris, that he telephoned in the afternoon.

This evening arranged my food cupboard.

From *Trois Agendas d'Adrienne Monnier.*

A Letter to Friends in the Free Zone

February 1942

You ask me, dear friends in the Free Zone, how things have been going in the Rue de l'Odéon? We are holding out, we are holding on, and not too badly.

In spite of my gourmandise I am putting up with the rationing rather well. Better than I had supposed. Doubtless because I knew what food represents. I honored flavors as much as genies. I loved fats; I was not afraid of becoming fat; I saw in them one of the effects of the goodness of the world; in the fashion of the Hindus, I would mentally anoint my gods with them every morning. I did not say: this is only vulgar matter. I knew that it was also of the spirit.

Just as it is easier to do without love when one has a good conception of it and when one perceives its essence, it is easier to do without good things when one has fixed them in ideas. I see with surprise and amusement the annoyance of so many people who scorned Eating and its rites, in words at least; they're suffering now, they're learning.

Myself, I am learning to love the vegetables that I used to disdain. When one eats them with care their humble flavors shine a bit more; they have to be encouraged. Oh, it's never very exciting. Valéry grates a little nutmeg on the dishes that they serve him—classic—do you like nutmeg?

Spices are much in fashion. I tried hard for a while to make wide use of them, but I gave them up quickly. In a general manner, they must be used in homeopathic doses. The one great type of the family is pepper. It does not transform flavors so much as it exalts them, it makes them exhilarating. A pinch of pepper and a hint of garlic—that's what makes a delicious combination out of a modest stew of turnips and potatoes. Alas! we are often short of the most ordinary vegetables. You are thinking, perhaps, that I can get some from the little estate of my parents in Eure-et-Loir, but they are too old and too tired to cultivate them; no, nothing from that direction. Imagine, a kind friend, Marguerite Clerbout, sends them to me when they are in short supply here; she who was a poet has become a farmer. I discovered in my neighborhood a fruit and grocery store run by a young lady who is a poet and mystic herself as well, who knows her business better than anybody I am acquainted with. Her clients adore her and kindly call her by her fist name: Mademoiselle Michèle. That's marvelous, isn't it?

Hardest to put up with, we are all of the same opinion, is the cold. In the bookshop, where I have had a wood stove installed, it is livable, but my apartment, like those of most people, is glacial; I can neither read nor write. Every night I light my kitchen stove, and it is while installed next to this dear stove that I am writing to you today.

The *Gazette*? I don't even think about it.

The bookshop is giving us tremendous work. Fortunately, I have Saillet. Provisions for it are becoming almost as hard to find as food supplies. We often have to stand in line at the publishers, and most of them give us copies of the good titles one at a time. I do not know how many among the best works are completely out of stock. The sales that have hampered us so much in recent years have been almost wiped out, and that is not a misfortune! Something is happening that has not happened for a long time, have I even seen it at such a point? People are buying books. And they are not buying it doesn't matter what. They must have beautiful books, the most beautiful books possible, those that they believe to be the best servants of the spirit. It matters little to them that the form be more or less luxurious, they accept bad or mediocre paper without grumbling too much. It is the texts that they search for above all, whose possession they want to secure for themselves or for those close to them. How many books are sent to prisoners or kept against their return! They know that because of the paper shortage many works, in the English and American fields above all, are going to disappear for a time, for a time that will perhaps be long, and even risk disappearing forever.

Have you ever consulted the publishers' catalogs of the last century or read carefully the backs of the covers of Hachette's red series (the ones that cost a franc)? How many names of authors, how many titles which we do not even have an idea of anymore and which perhaps had the popularity of *Gone with the Wind* or *The Rains Came!* Most of these authors are not to be regretted—novelists, they have been replaced by other novelists; they were only the vegetation of little societies that were closed in upon themselves; one read them the way one chats, to say nothing, to pass time, to be stylish, to change the air, to lead a polite existence instead of living. Novels, they are the real leaves of grass. The pages they are printed on are leaves indeed! Once a civilization arrives at the stage of the novel—and it is the middle-class stage at its most characteristic, the one in which people no longer act, in which they no longer want to risk acting, the one also in which everybody becomes reflective and ceases from action—yes, when a civilization arrives at this stage, we can say that it makes more fodder for brains than for animals. But even so, it is in the midst of all this fodder that great works are hidden, those from which they will begin to clear away the weeds after a century or two, or more.

People have bought or completed their classics. That was their first concern, even. Since the beginning of the Occupation, since their return to Paris, they have turned toward them with piety. They have relished the *Fables* of La Fontaine, the *Caractères* of La Bruyère, the *Maximes* of La Rochefoucauld. They have discovered or rediscovered Ronsard and the poets of the Pléiade, forever green. They have sought out the clearest, the most concise, the most elegant, and the wisest works that our genius offers, in order to wash themselves in them and quench their thirst with them. Some, not without a certain spirit of penitence, have gone as far as the never-read Boileau, and have regretted nothing. They have gone still farther with Racine, with Corneille, and with Molière. They have reread the hundred-times-read Montaigne, Descartes, and Pascal.

Yes, it is to these sixteenth and seventeenth centuries that we have all gone with the same urge to find once more the person of France, to take her in our arms and weep upon her shoulder. It seemed to us, and doubtless we were not wrong, that never had she been so completely herself, that never had her speech filled her mouth so worthily—so it seemed to us, who were less ashamed of our defeat than we were of all the vain and braggart words that had led us to it.

Not less than toward the classics, the fervor of the literary public has turned toward poetry in general. They had neglected the poets during those years of crisis, they are remembering them now with the strong feeling that they are the surest guardians of a country. A country is above all a language.

Naturally, it is Péguy who has been summoned first of all, who had written *Notre Patrie [Our Country]*, who is so profoundly rooted in our soil. His repetitions resemble the slow speech of countryfolk, who, in order to set forth their idea very clearly, imagine it under all its aspects; they also make you think of roots that embrace the earth and draw the sap from it with so many little arms stretched out in all directions.

After Péguy they have demanded Apollinaire, he who is almost without roots, baroque and subtle, like spices, which must not be abused, as I have said, but which are necessary to our fine cooking.

And then the whole nineteenth century has passed by, beginning in reverse with Mallarmé and Rimbaud.

Among the living, Claudel and Valéry are in the lead, as you surely must think. Henri Michaux is almost up to them, much thanks to Gide's lecture.

They are demanding the young with insistence. As the poets have hardly found publishers these recent years, there are few volumes or little books to offer them. Even so, fortunately, there is Jean Paulhan's collection *Metamorphoses*.

I opened my purgatory at once: it is the corner of the library in which I shelve the little books (most of them printed at the author's expense) that I receive, and that calmly await there, with their slim backs pressed together, the coming of a last judgment. Saillet has tried hard to pronounce it, this judgment, but he is not good Lord enough to come to the end of his task; he has been content to withdraw from limbo a number of dozens of souls; he has handed them over to *Jeune France*, which is preparing to provide them with a destiny.

—You ask me how Sylvia Beach is doing. She is still in Paris, which she never left. She had to shut her bookshop a few days ago. Now that she has leisure she is going to start her memoirs. Dear Sylvia! It's thanks to her, to friends that she has in Touraine, that we receive a rabbit almost every week. She was even able to procure a Christmas turkey for us after a year of maneuvering.

From *Les Gazettes d'Adrienne Monnier*; first published in *Le Figaro Littéraire* (1942).

A Letter to André Gide about the Young

April 1942

I would like to give you an idea of the young people that I am seeing nowadays—the ones who come to the bookshop and with whom I happen to talk.

By young I mean those who have not gone to war and who may be from about fifteen to twenty years old—the students.

I believe that they are rather different from those that you have been acquainted with. Nevertheless, in '39 and even in '38 many of the young people already had the reading interests and the ideas that they have now: they were already at what we shall call the Sartre point. But their behavior has changed, that's logical.

First of all, their physical appearance. Their dress is at one and the same time more fanciful and rudimentary; a sweater usually replaces waistcoat, jacket, and necktie; all colors are worn, above all in the scarves, which often display bold tones—I should add that these are the ones that have been least quickly sold out in the stores. They wear their hair long, but not too long. It doesn't resemble in any way at all the style of the show-off artist with long, stiff hair—the dauber of before '14. No, it aims at being a mane, it's lion type, with a patch of long hair at the nape in a beautiful well-ordered disarray. The hair of the girls still falls to their shoulders, which is charming, but they have lately adopted a high bouffant that is seldom becoming and that I do not like.

They have a very carefree air, which does not seem blameworthy to me. So much preaching to correct them and the excess of hardships that crush us have carried them back to the devilry and the lightheartedness of childhood. But above all it is an appearance, and at bottom they are reflective and studious in their fashion. They have, I believe, a great appetite for bravery, and at the same time they want to see clearly and not let themselves be duped. They know that for the moment any serious enterprise is hardly possible; they are taking a vacation. For lack of everything that is missing for them, they are *swing*.

Perhaps you are going to ask me what it is to be swing; it seems to me that in the Free Zone you do not know about that.

To be swing, obviously, requires a liking for swing, which comes from jazz, which is—nobody is unaware of it—American Negro music (you can imagine that serious people have no trouble at all berating it). However, when one thinks about it a bit, it is the result of the liking for Negro and primitive arts; perhaps Rimbaud is the cause of all that—or the prophet. I assure you that Duke Ellington and *Les Illuminations* go very well together in their minds—"I am an animal, I am a Negro—Hunger, thirst, cries, dance, dance, dance, dance!—"

Swing, real swing, as it is defined by Panassié, who is an authority on the matter, is of Negro origin: the essential element of jazz music, "it is a kind of swing in rhythm and in melody that always calls for great dynamism." In the case of hot jazz, which is much more swing than the straight, there is a constant improvisation. Music played with swing is distinguished by an imperious rhythm —at bottom it's the tom-tom—but this rhythm must be produced without effort, it must be as natural as the beating of the heart, it is thus that it calls for and favors inspiration. The players in a hot jazz orchestra are all of them, if you wish, creators—one appreciates their "burning spontaneity."

That's not bad, what do you think about it? Doesn't it seem that one catches a glimpse, through these definitions, of a humanity whose unconstrained order tolerates and even approves of individual expression?

I remember a big Duke Ellington concert that took place around three years ago, to which I went with Saillet. I assure you that for him it was an event, something like the *Pelléas* of my youth; he was so moved that he could hardly eat dinner before setting out; it was because he had read Panassié's book and had listened to the records; and he knew what it all represented for many youths of his generation.

The concert began with a sort of overture that seemed extraordinary to me. One had the impression of a city all in smoke, from which escaped the moans of women in labor and the whimpers of newborn babies; one also thought of the cries that are emitted by factory chimneys, steamboats, or trains. It was a world being born, in which the very excess of despair took the place of hope, like a creature who comforts himself while weeping as hard as he can, the explosion of energy creating its passage and its outlet.

I have never forgotten this impression; it is bound up with the novels of Faulkner and the first theatrical expressions of Barrault. Kurt Weill's *Mahagonny* had also given us the idea of a lowly and heartrending people drifting toward high and resplendent shores.

And already in *The Rites of Spring* there was the panic and the ordering rhythm of terrible actions.

I believe that the young people of today are well acquainted with this climate. I found it recently in the poetry of Pierre Emmanuel. His *Tombeau d'Orphée [Tomb of Orpheus]* is an outcry from beginning to end. One might say with Valéry that it lacks "gray parts" and, because of that, fatigue comes easily and damages the emotion. But have you, like myself, singled out the poems that begin with these lines: "A man descended the slopes of his death" and "A man returned to the depths of his life"? I find them truly beautiful.

But, you will tell me, how do you reconcile this lightheartedness you spoke about above and this dramatic mood?

I believe that they are joined together just as the mask of ancient comedy is joined to the mask of tragedy. In both cases the feelings are played out more than they are lived—true life being almost absent in these unhappy days: it is a very small flame that must be endlessly relighted, one extinguishes it in wanting to communicate it, like a match in a draft of air.

We see very well why our dear Michaux pleases the young so much. He has this mixture of irony and despair, his manner is so detached and so droll! I am thinking above all of the admirable poem "Clown," which is in *Peintures [Paintings]*.

One must also speak of Jacques Prévert, who does not cease to enchant our young men. The "Déjeuner des têtes" ["Luncheon of Heads"], which unfortunately is contained only in a number of

Commerce, gives them complete satisfaction. Saillet widely circulates this text, which he cares for passionately, and wins for it all the friends he wants.

Melville's *Moby-Dick* has been read with enthusiasm, you easily understand why. The book has appeared at a good moment. There too, what a tragic spirit, what humor, what bewildering lyricism— and what sweetness—the story of Queequeg is ravishing!

I spoke to you at the beginning about the Sartre point. Isn't there an important notion here? Sartre has made a definition on the moral plane that for the young, and perhaps for us, represents the greatest effort of lucidity. It is the opposite of being falsely optimistic, and still there is a certain mystique in it, and a certain joy. Think of the end of *La Nausée [Nausea]*. There too we come again upon Negro light.

What more is there to tell you?

I return to my affirmation that our young people are studious. It is true that they read with more application than ever, not only what suits them, but also their great French and foreign elders.

The questions of craft, of technique, seem to me to inspire a rather new interest in them; they are more sensitive than they were yesterday to the lessons of a Valéry; some of them attend his lectures at the Collège de France with thoughtful respect.

Claudel and Péguy often satisfy them without their letting themselves be stopped, like the surrealist generation, by the Catholic sentiment. I believe that they find happiness as much as I myself do in reading in *La Ville [The City]*:

> . . . If there is no garbage or mud from which
>   knowledge cannot draw a profit,
> I believe that there is no being so vile or so mean
> That he is not necessary to our unanimity.

Such an affirmation agrees perfectly with the work of Joyce, with all deference to Claudel. Yes, *Ulysses* still has a high rating; they read it from the beginning to the end, without beginning at the end as they used to do at first.

As for yourself, dear great Friend, do not doubt that they love you as intensely as ever. Our young people run all over Paris in order to find your *Journal*, which has been out of stock for about a year. And those who can offer themselves your complete works in a deluxe edition, what a rank they have in the eyes of their pals!

From *Les Gazettes d'Adrienne Monnier*; first published in *Le Figaro Littéraire* (1942).

A Christmas Letter

I received for Christmas a beautiful letter from Marc Klein. Marc Klein is a professor of biology on the faculty of Strasbourg. I knew him before the war. When he came to Paris he used to visit the Rue de l'Odéon and we talked about our books and our favorite authors, above all about Joyce, whom he liked in particular.

During the Occupation he took refuge with his family in Clermont-Ferrand. In spite of his friends, who advised him to leave France, he considered that his duty was to stay, even at the risk of being deported. In 1943 he was in fact taken by the Gestapo and sent to Auschwitz; his family, by a miracle, was able to hide and escape search. By a miracle that was no less great he came back from captivity in a satisfactory state of health—he is only, he says, a bit more nervous than before.

About two months ago he gave a lecture before teachers of German in Paris about the camps to which he went: he knew Auschwitz and Buchenwald. As his lecture is going to appear in the *Revue des Etudes Germaniques* I shall not talk about it for the moment. It deserves a serious review, given the importance of the message that it carries. I shall only say that he spoke for two hours and that never in my life have I felt so interested and so moved. However, he did not lay stress upon the "horrors." No, it was through his perfect humanity, his astonishing energy that he won us over. We left so astounded that we could hardly say a word.

Here is the essential passage of the letter that I received:

> I am going to celebrate Christmas this year with my wife and my four children. It is a great joy, but I shall have trouble not to recall the Christmas at Auschwitz. In the center of the camp they had raised a gigantic Christmas tree that was lit up every night from December 23 to January 6. And one night, before the whole assembled camp, in front of the tree glittering with lights, they hanged four Polish patriots who had taken part in a conspiracy and who right up to the end cried out, "Long live liberty, down with tyrants!" And I shall have trouble forgetting that for the same Christmas I had the most precious gift that I have ever had: a ball of bread that a comrade had set aside for me bit by bit and that he deprived himself of so that I might eat my fill during the holidays. But time heals all wounds, and it is possible that in a few years a relative forgetfulness may bring me peace again.

Thank you, Marc Klein, for having shared with me, like blessed bread, the memory of the ball of bread that had been given to you. Nor shall I myself be able to forget your Christmas at Auschwitz.

At the time of your last visit you told me that some tragic experiences, and often some of the most tragic, were quickly changed into songs, into stories, and into games. You mentioned the case of *Les Dragons de Vilars [The Dragoons of Vilars]*, an opera that is set in the time of the persecution of the Huguenots. And you also said, with well-justified indignation, that you had already seen in the window of a cheap shop a children's game entitled "the Gestapo and the deported prisoner." There is certainly good ground for thought here.

Would you believe that the account in your letter was changed almost immediately in my mind into a fairy tale? When one thinks about it, fairy tales are woven out of facts taken from lives that are unhappy in an archetypal manner and that have become stars of sorts.

That glittering of your Christmas tree, which still brightens you, was something like the fairies, the lively powers, who sang to make you forget the frightful present and to give you courage. That's it, "the choir of little voices."

When the stuff of life is all torn apart, and when nothing but the threads of it are left, those threads become the strings of a great living harp that makes out of sorrow arpeggios that are at once music and light. Very poor people experience such hallucinations in their reveries.

I am thinking of poor Ireland's harp. There is also a memorable vision of a harp in the hell of Hieronymus Bosch. Do you remember that body which is crucified and pierced through by the strings of the instrument?

Forgive me for this vague poetic mood that I have applied to such moments of your life. I find solace and even happiness in letting myself go.

Ah yes, if men derive stories and games from the blackest experiences, it is no doubt in order to follow an undefined and forever to be poorly defined tendency of the instinct of preservation: Art, in fact.

It is, as ordinary people say, in order to be able to put up with life —not to lose the liking for it.

From *Dernières Gazettes et Ecrits divers*; first published in *Terre des Hommes* (January 5, 1946).

Americans in Paris

To tell the truth, I have never been without Americans in Paris. At the very time when so many people were totally deprived of them and were awaiting them while being devoured by impatience during the past four years, I myself had my requirement, almost.

And first of all Sylvia Beach, my dearest friend, was there. Sylvia and a small number of her countrywomen who, having settled in Paris, never wanted to leave it. They shared our sufferings and privations with love and underwent a more or less long captivity.

But yes, I did know a time of bitter privation: it was the long months that my American friends spent at Vittel.

Besides Sylvia there was Sarah Watson, the directress of the International Students' Hostel. There was a magnificent type of American woman, a true spiritual daughter of Benjamin Franklin. It should be told in full how she and her assistant, Marcelle Fournier (one of the noblest Frenchwomen that I know) succeeded, as a result of firmness and cleverness, in saving the house from the Germans who wanted to seize it; how, in spite of all kinds of difficulties, they made sure that there would be meals every day for their little group; how, without neglecting the international equity that is the rule of the hostel, they were able to establish an active center of resistance where I do not know how many patriots, French and foreign (Czechs in particular), found help and friendship.

There was Katherine Dudley, who has so much charm and wit, a friend of Picasso, herself a painter of great talent.

The angelic Mabel Gardner who sculpts graceful figures in wood.

Dru Tartière, beautiful and brave, who hid five American aviators in her house in Barbizon—and that is only the most obvious of her exploits.

Camilla Steinbrugge, who is one of the most accomplished women I know.

Mary Dixon, the daughter of a famous evangelist preacher, as keen and sensitive as a heroine of Hawthorne.

This choir of friends was brought to me by Sylvia.

Sylvia, so American and so French at the same time. American by her nature—"young, friendly, fresh, heroic . . . electric" (I borrow the adjectives from Whitman speaking of his fellow citizens). French through her passionate attachment to our country, through her desire to embrace its slightest nuances.

There are people who are afraid of the American influence. They think that someday it could bring us skyscrapers and make our cities shake the way their own do. These people have never been much in the company of Americans.

They appreciate above all in France and in Europe what they do not have at home: what is calm, old, graceful, and made by hand. In Paris they live on the Ile Saint-Louis, in the Rue de Seine, in the Palais-Royal.

If we were ever to want to return to the past, they would be rather glad about it. We may be sure that they have to try hard to listen to the voice of reason at certain moments, so as not to want us to have kings, fortified castles, sedan chairs, thatched roofs, oil lamps, etc. But no, let's not be afraid of that any more than of the skyscrapers. They will certainly impose a little oil lamp upon us occasionally ("And at the same time," Keeler Faus tells me, "we will bring you a refrigerator that will help you a lot without spoiling the decor"), but they will never bring the kings back to us. They are people who know how to reason with themselves, and who have democracy in their blood; it is their tradition, their reason for being, the voice that speaks to them stronger than any other. When we are tempted to cast doubt upon the democratic idea, let us listen to them: they have felt it and expressed it better than anybody. And at this point I cannot refrain from quoting from a text that is, in my opinion, the most beautiful thing that has been written about democracy. It is from Melville, a passage from *Moby-Dick*:

> But this august dignity I treat of, is not the dignity of kings and robes, but that abounding dignity which has no robed investiture. Thou shalt see it shining in the arm that wields a pick or drives a spike; that democratic dignity which, on all hands, radiates without end from God; Himself! The great God absolute! The center and circumference of all democracy! His omnipresence, our divine equality!

When I read these lines I feel that I am an American, just as the Americans feel that they are French when they live in Paris.

But until now I have spoken only of my companions of the Occupation. There are so many other friends who lived among us before this war, who had come after the other war, or who had even been Parisians "for ages," like our dear Carlotta, like Gertrude Stein and Jo Davidson.

There were the writers, the professors, who used to pay us a visit every year during the vacation months. At that time the French hardly troubled themselves about their young poets and their little reviews. The Americans were almost the only enthusiasts of the surrealist "revolutions," of the *Minotaures*, of the *Documents*, without ever forgetting the latest Gide and the latest Valéry.

No doubt we shall see Katherine Anne Porter, Thornton Wilder, and Archibald MacLeish as soon as the war is over.

Alas, we shall not see either Sherwood Anderson or Scott Fitzgerald again.

What will become of Ezra Pound? Poor Ezra who was a zealous fascist propagandist in Italy. There is a man who made liberal use of "the right to error" that Jean Paulhan demands for writers.

George Antheil must already be packing his suitcases. It appears that he has just won a big success in New York with his latest symphony. What has become of the ruckus of the *Ballet mécanique*?

Will Grace Flandrau come back again to delight in the rough cobblestones of the Cour de Rohan?

Shall we see Louis Bromfield again in his Passy apartment full of potted flowers—ravishing flowers from the gardens of other times, which he takes care of himself?

Will Bob McAlmon take his lodgings again in Montparnasse, and will he start to publish *Contact* again?

Will Bill Byrd come back to live in his mill and enjoy our wines, which he knows better than anybody?

Will Janet Flanner again be sending her witty "Letters from Paris" to the *New Yorker*?

Shall I finally make the acquaintance of Pearl Buck?

Will Faulkner and Steinbeck, whom I have not yet met, pass by in the Rue de l'Odéon?

But with the Liberation some of them have already arrived, in jeeps, naturally: Eugène Jolas, who edited the avant-garde review *Transition* in Paris, you remember; Bravig Imbs, who is Mr. Pipper on the radio; the poet George Dillon, who directs the magazine *Poetry* in Chicago and who is something like the guard of the Eiffel Tower over here.

I do not know how many newcomers there are, each of them more Joycean than the rest, who want to meet Sylvia Beach and even "Miss Monnier," to whom they come to ask for the translation of *Ulysses* in order to "practice" their French.

We have made the acquaintance of Helen KirkPatrick, the famous war correspondent.

We have clasped Adelaide Massey, ace of the American Red Cross, in our arms.

We have seen our friend Justin O'Brien, who has become a lieutenant-colonel, in uniform.

Our dear Keeler Faus has come back. He lived with us during the first months of the Occupation, then followed the embassy to Vichy, to Baden-Baden, to the United States.

But do you know who was the first to pay us a visit, at the very time of the Liberation?—Ernest Hemingway. His arrival in the Rue de l'Odéon was so remarkable that I must describe it.

It was Saturday the 26th, the day of the assassination attempt on General de Gaulle. We had left the house with the intention of going to Notre-Dame, but the gunfire caught us on the Boulevard du Palais and obliged us to turn around and go back the way we came. The way back was punctuated by splendid bursts of fire from the rooftops.

Our street was not one of the calmest. As we went up it with cautious steps, keeping close to the walls, we saw in front of number 12, that is to say, Shakespeare and Company, four little cars (not jeeps), marked B.B.C. in the back, in large white letters. We hardly paid them any attention.

When we were back again on our fifth floor, we heard after a moment a voice coming up from the street: "Sylvia! Sylvia!" We ran to the window and there we saw Saillet in front of the door, shouting with his hands cupped around his mouth: "Sylvia! Hemingway is here!" Sylvia ran down the stairs four at a time and my sister and I saw little Sylvia down below, leaping into and lifted up by two Michelangelesque arms, her legs beating the air. I went downstairs myself. Ah, yes, it was Hemingway, more of a giant than ever, bareheaded, in shirtsleeves, a caveman with a shrewd and studious look behind his placid eyeglasses. He was with a soldier who was carrying his helmet and field jacket, a Frenchman named Marceau, whom he introduced to us as his affectionate bodyguard. The four automobiles were his own, the Hem division, sixteen men in all, half of them American, half of them French, dressed in the same uniform; the French were members of the Maquis, whom he had joined, fighting all along the way from Brittany. A few days before they had taken Rambouillet all by themselves; the night before they had stormed the Ritz and naturally they had installed themselves in the best rooms. For the moment, hardly in a hurry to put down their arms, they had come to purge the Rue de l'Odéon of its snipers on the roofs. They had already climbed to the top of several suspect houses, which the onlookers vied with one another to point out to them; but really they had not yet found anything. As my building had not yet been visited, it would be a good idea for them to climb up and also to refresh themselves.

I went toward the men, who were standing around the little cars or sitting inside, awaiting orders from their captain, and I invited them to come and drink the wine I had kept for them, like every good, self-respecting French person. But others had already given them so much to drink that they excused themselves after heartily shaking my hand. Only the stalwart Marceau agreed to accompany Hemingway, he and a young American who came along out of politeness and as a delegation for the others; they were content to moisten their lips with the wine.

Hemingway, his brow wrinkled, blazed a path through the thicket of our questions and his answers to one idea: to find some laundry soap so that he could wash his shirt that night in his washbowl at the Ritz. I gave him, without hesitating too much, my last piece. (Let's be frank, it was the next to the last.)

Another idea was preoccupying him: Hadn't I, Adrienne, during those years of the Occupation, been brought to the point of collaborating a little?—In which case he offered to draw me out of all possible danger. (Obviously, he must have thought, that fat gourmand couldn't endure the rationing; she must have weakened at one moment or another.) I seriously examined my conscience. No, I swear, I had not "collaborated." He drew Sylvia off into a corner and repeated the question to her: "Are you sure, Sylvia, that Adrienne did not collaborate and that she does not need a little help?"—"Not at all," Sylvia answered. "If she collaborated, it was with us, the Americans." Hemingway seemed to show some regret at not being able to be the knight errant—a slight regret that flickered across his good face as it became serene again.

From *Les Gazettes d'Adrienne Monnier*; first published in *Fontaine* (1945).

The Nature of France

Letting the waves of these words—*the Nature of France*—take us where they please, and where I please, I am going to sail out with you to visit two very human places, and then I do not know how many others like them.

First of all, I am going to visit Saint Bernard. I remember the sermon in which he tries to describe to his brothers the presence within him of the Word, that Word which he can neither see nor hear, and which he recognizes only by the movement of his heart, only by his diligence in correcting his secret faults.

It is through the renewal and reform of his *inner man*, his spirit, that the Bridegroom Word reveals its infinite beauty to him.

When the Word withdraws everything languishes and becomes cold, *just as when one takes away the fire from beneath a vessel.* Nothing gives him pleasure. He calls out to it with the familiar voice of the Bride. He begs it to come back full of grace and truth—*truth with eyes as piercing as a goat's, grace with the gaiety of the fawn of the doe.*

I go next to Stendhal. Once again *The Red and the Black* runs in my veins like quick blood. The final pages make my temples throb.

Julien Sorel is in prison and he is about to die. He is not afraid of death. He has a talk with himself. He surpasses and comes into possession of himself. He perceives the operation of society in its most intimate movements. Without exaggerating, by means of a simple readjustment, he takes the measure of the age and acquires a new understanding.

—*So death, life, eternity are very simple things for one who has faculties great enough to conceive them.*

His heart longs for a true religion. But how, he asks, *can one believe in the mighty name of God after the frightful abuse of it by our priests?* Everywhere, in and around himself, he sees hypocrisy or exaggeration. He can find refuge only in the deep love that he feels for the woman who remains his good friend, and this love occupies him, not without gaiety, until his last day.

This believer and this atheist do not resemble each other so much as they form a part of the same whole. The same light shines upon both of them and makes it seem that each is contained in the other. The virtue they have in common is discretion.

Discretion, upon which, without a doubt, both taste and measure depend.

French taste, French measure.

I tremble as I write these words, for they have become as

worn-out as old clothes. Foreigners when they speak of us often use them both to praise and blame us. They find us exquisite but limited. They extol our perfection, but by way of contrast they call attention to our lack of force, of height. They say that in order to possess the finite we lose our sense of the infinite.

The truth is that at present we care little enough about taste and measure. For around a century now our spirit has been inclined toward expansion and experiment. We have invented, we are still inventing, the most novel and daring forms; we appropriate everything baroque. Ah, we are far from being exquisite and perfect, or if we are we do not know it. Too many things have been happening to us, and we do not have the leisure to classify and arrange them. But the time for classification and order will come. We shall find our taste and measure increased and renewed. After the invasions of the barbarians, after the decline of Roman civilization, came the cathedrals!

Let us return to discretion. With Saint Bernard and Stendhal we should observe that it is practiced less in regard to others than to the self, or rather to the principle that guides the self. The saint and the writer are not much interested in managing their readers or giving them pleasure. Their concern is first of all not to distend their souls, not to abuse the Word, not to dry up the source of their being.

They want to live as well as possible.

They come to expression as to the highest and most effective way of living—and the most difficult as well. There are forms of expression that govern forms in nature by making them stable or lighter. They help heavy bodies to find a spirit, and wandering spirits to find a body. They tame powerful elements and make them well disposed toward us. Such are the wonderful effects of the Word when it is treated with love and reverence. And when it is mistreated it brings calamities and disturbances.

No one who is wise and discerning willingly trespasses on serious things; he would rather be lighthearted.

The people of our country are happy to keep silent when they approach the centers of life. They do not want it to be *said*. They laugh instead.

—French gaiety—Another expression that will let the daylight through; it has been used so much. Still, it applies to one of our most enduring qualities, a daughter of our earth and sky, like the beloved lark. Obviously, we are not the only people in the world who know how to enjoy themselves. Laughter is universal: it is a manifestation of the spirit of life, a form of liberty—the most real, perhaps. Every people has its own way of laughing, and every individual has his own nuance. But it goes without saying that we have been favored!

The gaiety of the French includes every kind of laugh and smile, for our humanity comes from so many sources. An Englishman once said rather jokingly that we have wit but no humor. If he had thought carefully about the matter he would not have found it surprising. Humor arises from the reaction of the individual against society. The more severe and restrictive a society is, the more will original people show a sense of humor. Like Gulliver, they feel bound up to their necks by innumerable ties, and they make a thousand attempts to free themselves.

As French society is relatively tolerant toward the individual, it is natural that gaiety with us rarely takes the form of humor.

It is perhaps our ways of laughing that show best the universality of our spirit.

The French—Rabelais and Montaigne are good examples—are amused by human pretensions that defy the laws of nature and the order of things. If they are ordinary people, they mock the pretensions of individuals toward what for them takes the place of the order of things and seems natural—their groups, their customs, and their opinions. Our laughter is at one with morality and wisdom in all their degrees. It is what returns us to the golden mean. Contrary to Anglo-Saxon humor, it is almost always practiced at the expense of eccentrics and to the advantage of the social spirit, that is to say, of agreement and good understanding. Our motto, *Liberty, Equality, Fraternity,* is nowhere better written or more real than in the moving creases of our laughter.

In its highest form, French gaiety touches faith: it is born, like faith, from the loving perception of an order of greatnesses. These greatnesses take shape in us and arise by degrees; our mind conceives them in the same manner that they conceive us; they are familiar to us. We smile at them and they smile at us. Grace and gaiety go together.

In its most ordinary forms, our gaiety is like the roundness of the earth. Laughter is a round thing. It is a whole little end in itself. Bon mots are not without resemblance to well-made objects.

I shall certainly not say that our liking for the finite deprives us of our sense of the infinite. Rather, it derives from it. It affirms it by resolving not to be lost in it. Eternity is made of no other stuff than time.

Whenever our artists and artisans raise their heads toward the sky and follow the clouds with their look, they return to their task with greater application. It is then that they work most closely, as if they wanted to make the music of the atomic spheres leap from the bit of matter that their hands control. They strive for a polish that will make their work a mirror of the firmament.

The first time I saw the miniatures of Fouquet and the Limbourg brothers at Chantilly my delight was such that my eyes filled with tears. Before *The Hours of Etienne Chevalier* I thought I heard the reds and the blues and the heavenly white singing life and its reasons in a full voice.

Before *The Very Rich Hours of the Duke de Berry* I seemed to perceive as through a magic emerald the very nature of France: our land and its people dressed in bold colors; gestures of work, as pure as those of the Mass; women in flowerlike dresses; fanfares of leisure; living water, branches; desires and loves; beautiful castles in the distance; a comforting sky; our animals near us; our days colored with hope and finely woven.

It is not without reason that the stroke of strong admiration brings tears to the eyes. The sight or sound of perfect things causes a certain suffering. In the case of these miniatures, is it not as if one were burned by a fine rain of fire? Such works are like the focus of a lens that gathers the light of all space into one intense point. With a passionate concentration they draw from the world of forms a kind of jewel, a fairy-thing.

I have often thought that a talisman resides in the work of Fouquet and the Limbourg brothers. France, as we know, has many talismans. This one is perhaps the most active. In any case, it is the best conceived.

And do we not owe this talisman largely to discretion? For it is discretion that obliges the longest reasonable time to occupy the least reasonable space, thus forming a supernatural reserve of life.

The virtue I call Discretion, to give it its most discreet and thus most invulnerable name, how can I describe its features a bit more? It has the smile of the angels in our churches. According to the first definition, it is doubtless the quality of discernment. It is also the power to keep secrets—secrets of the appetite for life. The truth is that these secrets keep themselves without us. They are hidden in reality in numberless and limitless ways. We can keep them simply by knowing that they escape us, by not boasting that we are their masters, and by finding attraction in them.

Art of living, of knowing how to live—that is what I have tried to make you see in a saint and in a writer. Which you may see as well in so many other people of our country, wherever the waves of these words may take you—*the Nature of France.*

From *Les Gazettes d'Adrienne Monnier*; first published in *Verve* (September–November 1940).

illustrations

The Rue de l'Odéon in the thirties looking north toward the Carrefour from
Adrienne Monnier's apartment. La Maison des Amis des Livres is on the
right-hand side of the street near the lamppost.

Adrienne and Marie Monnier in 1898 at the ages of six and four.

Adrienne Monnier in 1911 at the age of nineteen, after her first visit to London.

Adrienne Monnier in her bookshop in 1915. She lived on the premises from that year until 1918.

Guillaume Apollinaire

SOME EARLY FRIENDS AT THE BOOKSHOP, 1916 OR 1917

Louis Aragon

André Breton
and
Théodore Fraenkel

Pierre Reverdy

Francis Poulenc and Raymonde Linossier
"on the way to the fair,"
1919 or 1920.

SOME POTASSONS

Valery Larbaud, Léon-Paul Fargue, Marie Monnier, Sylvia Beach, and
Adrienne Monnier at the Foire d'Orsay, June 1924.

Marie and
Adrienne
Monnier in 1919
or 1920.

Maurice Saillet

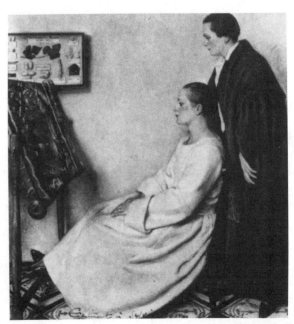

Oil painting, 1924, of Marie
and Adrienne Monnier by
Paul-Emile Bécat.

Sylvia Beach Collection

George Antheil climbing to his apartment above Shakespeare and Company, 1922 or 1923.

F. Scott Fitzgerald and Adrienne Monnier on the threshold of Shakespeare and Company, 1928.

Adrienne Monnier in her apartment around 1925, the time of the *Navire d'Argent.*

Jean Prévost, Monnier's partner on the *Navire*, around 1925.

Clovis Monnier and Sylvia Beach with Mousse, his dog. Rocfoin, around 1925.

James Joyce and Clovis Monnier, with Adrienne Monnier, Philiberte Monnier, and Sylvia Beach standing behind them. Rocfoin, around 1928.

Sylvester Beach, Clovis Monnier, and Adrienne Monnier. Rocfoin, 1928.

Adrienne Monnier cutting Sylvia Beach's hair, with Juliette Monnier, a cousin. Rocfoin, around 1930.

Maurice Saillet

Family group at Rocfoin on Adrienne Monnier's birthday, April 26, 1935.
Behind her and her father and mother are Sylvia Beach, Paul-Emile
Bécat, Marie Monnier, and Juliette Monnier.

Adrienne Monnier with her father, 1935, and her mother, 1938, at Rocfoin.

Venice, Piazza San Marco, summer 1936.

Shopping at the market in the Rue de Buci, 1938.

Picking flowers, 1938.

With Sylvia Beach at Shakespeare and Company, around 1935.

A meeting of the staff of the review *Mesures* at the home of Henry and Barbara Church in Ville d'Avray in 1936 or 1937. Sitting around the table from left to right are: Sylvia Beach, Adrienne Monnier, Germaine Paulhan, Henry Church, Barbara Church, and Jean Paulhan. Behind them are: Henri Michaux, Michel Leiris, and Vladimir Nabokov.

T. S. Eliot reading at Shakespeare and Company, June 6, 1936.

James Joyce, Sylvia Beach, and Adrienne Monnier at Shakespeare and Company, 1938.

Joyce and Monnier in the Rue de l'Odéon on the same occasion.

Paul Valéry reading *"Mon Faust"* at Adrienne Monnier's apartment, March 1, 1941.

Victoria Ocampo reading her *Impressions parisiennes* at La Maison des Amis des Livres, October 1946.

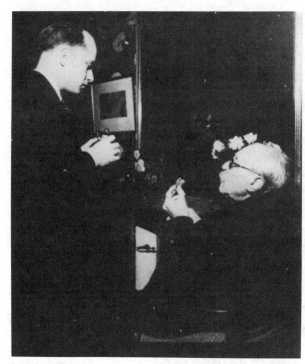

Keeler Faus and Paul
Valéry at Sylvia Beach's
apartment, late 1944 or
early 1945.

Henri Michaux and Adrienne Monnier on the same
occasion.

Adrienne Monnier in her kitchen with Sylvia Beach in 1944, just after the liberation of Paris. Sylvia had written on the backs of both photos: "Nothing to cook!"

Maurice Saillet

Maurice Saillet

Sylvia Beach and Adrienne Monnier at Les Déserts in 1953 or 1954. Sylvia is seen in front of her chalet.

Adrienne Monnier dedicating her *Gazettes* at La Maison des Amis des Livres, late 1953 or early 1954.

commentaries

VALÉRY IN THE RUE DE L'ODÉON

(page 75)

Adrienne Monnier describes her first impression of Paul Valéry, who she believes was brought to her bookshop by Paul Poujaud, a collector and amateur of art, with a metaphor taken from his short prose work *La Soirée avec Monsieur Teste [The Evening with Monsieur Teste]*. "He had *killed the marionette*," Valéry says of his hero, who incarnates pure intellect. "He did not smile, did not say either 'good day' or 'good evening'; he seemed not to hear 'How do you do?'" Monsieur Teste (his name has the old spelling of "tête," or "head") has abolished from his ruthlessly cerebral personality all merely polite social gestures and phrases. Though Monnier discovered the work in Paul Fort's review, *Vers et Prose*, it first appeared in 1896 in the *Centaure*, which, with the *Conque*, published a number of Valéry's early poems.

The year of this first meeting, 1917, brought the publication of the first important poem that Valéry wrote after many years of self-imposed silence, *La Jeune Parque [The Young Fate]*, a long, musical, interior monologue in alexandrine verses that recall those of Racine. *The Oxford Companion to French Literature* says: "It may be the monologue of a young Fate torn between the serenity of the immortals and the conflicts and responsibilities, and also the dark ecstasies, of mortal life; or it may signify the mind struggling to free itself from the fetters of the body." Another critic, Henry A. Grubbs, says that "the real subject" of *La Jeune Parque* is "thought conscious of itself"—a succinct statement of a typical Valérian activity, contemplative self-analysis. When questioned by his friend Dorothy Bussy, the translator of André

Gide, Valéry himself disarmingly said: "The subject of *La Jeune Parque*? It's the physiology and the psychology of a girl."

The publication of the poem reawakened an interest in Valéry's earlier work and established his reputation, which was further enhanced by the reading that Monnier describes in the present article and by her own publication of his *Album de vers anciens* in her Cahiers des Amis des Livres in 1920. André Breton heard the poet himself read *La Jeune Parque* at the home of Jean Royère, the director of the *Phalange*. Monnier also mentions readings by Fargue at Arthur Fontaine's and Jeanne Muhlfeld's. Fontaine, who was the friend of many writers, artists, and composers, was active in the field of labor legislation; Mme Muhlfeld presided over an influential literary salon that had strong ties with the Académie Française. Monnier herself first heard the poem read at another prominent salon, that of Mme Aurel, the wife of the playwright and critic Alfred Mortier; she refers to Valéry's late arrival after "his business" as the private secretary of Edouard Lebey, the director of the press association Agence Havas. Daniel Halévy, who described Fargue's introductory speech at the Valéry reading of April 12, 1919, as "militant," was an essayist, critic, and social historian. Most of the poems that were read on the occasion were collected in *Charmes* in 1922.

FIRST ENCOUNTERS WITH LÉON-PAUL FARGUE

(page 78)

This detailed, almost microscopic physical—and psychological—portrait of Léon-Paul Fargue on the verge of middle age in 1916 shows the darker, the heavier side of his personality, which "frightened" Suzanne Bonnierre, Adrienne Monnier's partner, and made Monnier herself regret at the time she wrote this article, many years later, that she had not known him when he was younger, as he appears in a photograph of 1907 in the 1927 issue of the *Feuilles Libres* that was devoted to him as an homage. She herself contributed her "Fargue and Words" to this issue. As she says, between the time of the photograph and her first encounters with the poet, he had become embittered. Both his father, whom he loved dearly, and his close friend, Charles-Louis Philippe, who is best remembered for his novel *Bubu de Montparnasse*, died in 1909. The "glassware factory that had done very well in his father's time" declined under Fargue's mismanagement. Beginning in 1910, he made a number of trips around France with Valery Larbaud, in a chauffeured limousine provided by Larbaud's mother. Having "dissipated all the money inherited from his father" in the course of his travels, he could not hope to keep up with his wealthy friend. Monnier alludes to "grave disappointments in his affections." According to his biographer, Louise Schub, Fargue courted at one and the same time—only to lose both of them—the ex-wife of a friend of Paul Valéry, who later married the actor and director Charles Dullin, and a Cuban heiress. The "powerful and fortunate" friend who "had made game of him" may be Gaston Gallimard, the publisher, who informed the heiress's family about the existence of the other woman.

The "priceless little book," *Tancrède*, a collection of prose and verse that shows the influence of the symbolists and of Rimbaud in particular, appeared originally in a German literary review, *Pan*, in 1895. In 1911 Valery Larbaud had it printed as a gift for Fargue by A. Raymond, a printer of Saint-Pourçain-sur-Sioule, a town in the department of Allier near the country estate of Larbaud's aunt. A great deal has been written about the "mystery" concerning the epigraph. What is certain is that the line, though Fargue assigns it to Gide, is actually by himself: a slightly different version of it opens his first published prose poem, *Ouvertures de tragédie [Tragic Overtures]* (1894). Gide, in his literary satire *Paludes [Marshlands]* (1895), attributes the line, as Monnier says, to his "young friend Tancrède," by whom he meant Fargue, who gave this pseudonym, possibly invented by Gide, to his own work, which appeared several months later.

PIERRE REVERDY

(page 83)

In this memoir, an excerpt from her "Mémorial de la rue de l'Odéon" that follows a passage on Fargue, Adrienne Monnier evokes the essential somberness of the poetry of Pierre Reverdy, who is no doubt the most austere of the generation of French poets whose work began to appear in Paris just before World War I. One of his critics, Michel Manoll, notes that "the poetry of Reverdy is neither diverting nor anecdotal, for there is nothing to describe to human beings except their misery and dereliction." He felt close to the cubist painters, in part because like himself "they claimed no affiliation, no solidarity with schools or traditions." He shared the spirit that made them prefer "the most simple objects: the package of tobacco, the stringless guitar, the matchbox, the unfolded newspaper, which replace, in their works, the faiences of Chardin, the coppers of Rembrandt, the precious consoles of Boucher."

Reverdy was born in Narbonne, near the Mediterranean, in 1889. Some of his forebears had been sculptors, but he himself early chose to be a poet, and in 1910 he moved to Paris, where he worked as a proofreader and lived in Montmartre. Here he became acquainted with the cubist painters—Picasso and Braque among them—and with the poets who were their friends, such as Guillaume Apollinaire, Max Jacob, and Pierre Albert-Birot, who founded the review *Sic* in 1916. Paul Dermée, according to Philippe Soupault in a memoir of the poet, was one of Reverdy's "awkward imitators, . . . whose good will disarmed him." Vincent Huidobro, a Chilean poet, wrote in French as well as in Spanish.

Reverdy's review *Nord-Sud* appeared in sixteen issues, between March 1917 and October 1918. Among its contributors, besides those whom Monnier mentions, were Braque—the magazine published reproductions of drawings as well as literature—Tristan Tzara and Jean Cocteau. In his biography of Cocteau, Francis Steegmuller says that the review was "named after the Paris subway line—now called simply 'No. 12'—that connects two artists' quarters, Montmartre and Montparnasse."

Apollinaire's "genuine lettrist manifesto in an early form," "La Victoire," from *Calligrammes* (1918), declared, "Let everything have a new name," and called for "new sounds new sounds new sounds." Monnier refers to these lines in her memoir on André Breton. Lettrism, according to the succinct definition of a French encyclopedia, is the "poetic theory that would have poetry consist solely of the sonority of letters arranged in a more or less arbitrary fashion."

Reverdy published several volumes of poetry besides *La Lucarne ovale [The Oval Attic Window]* (1916) and *Le Gant de crin [The Horsehair Glove]* (1927); they include *La Guitaire endormie [The Sleeping Guitar]* (1919), illustrated by Juan Gris, *Flaques de verre [Puddles of Glass]* (1929), and *Le Chant des morts [The Chant of the Dead]* (1948), which contains lithographs by Picasso. He also published a novel and much criticism of literature and art. In 1926 Reverdy retired from Paris to the village of Solesmes, the site of an ancient Benedictine abbey; he died and was buried there in 1960.

ANDRÉ BRETON

(page 86)

In this account, also taken from the "Mémorial," of her early relationship with André Breton, founder of the review *Littérature* with Philippe Soupault and Louis Aragon in 1919 and later an exponent of surrealism, Adrienne Monnier opposes an outlook that is essentially conservative—in the best sense—to Breton's "need for violent novelty." "The spirit is always new" is the statement of one who neither rejected the enduring works of the past nor dismissed the promises of the future. As she says toward the end of the "Mémorial," she felt that surrealism represented "very valid steps toward a new humanism," and she tried to see the movement in the broadest literary context. She acknowledges that the surrealists themselves recognized their debts to other writers, to contemporaries like Apollinaire and Reverdy and to earlier masters as well: "They have inscribed in their heaven the names of Poe, Hugo, Baudelaire, Mallarmé, Rimbaud, Lautréamont, Jarry." But she believes that they were "excessively unjust toward masters to whom they owed a great deal." She came to realize that their own success and welfare depended upon their not being "too respectful." When she first knew them, however, "the absolutism and the violence of Breton and his friends were insupportable" to her, and she was indignant because of their attitude toward Gide, "who marked them so strongly," and toward Claudel, whose first dramas "can hardly be appreciated without adopting the surrealist esthetic."

It was a quarrel concerning Claudel, in fact, that cooled the friendship between Monnier and Breton. In the issue of *Littérature* that came out after the reading of May 30, 1919, that she offered in honor of Claudel at the Théâtre du Gymnase, there appeared a parody of the poet, presumably by Breton, that enraged her. "We had, Breton and I, a big fight. I remember that he said this to me: 'You support Claudel because he is your friend.' To which I answered that I had a great deal of affection for him, certainly more than for Claudel, but that I did not like what he was writing. His eyes sparkled, I saw tears appearing in them. After that, naturally, we were hardly on good terms." After the seventh issue of *Littérature*, the notice on the back of the cover—"For sales, address La Maison des Amis des Livres"—was suppressed and the magazine was placed elsewhere.

The friendship suffered another setback when Monnier showed little enthusiasm for *Les Champs magnétiques [The Magnetic Fields]* (1920), which Breton wrote in collaboration with Soupault. However, she admits that when his *Manifeste du surréalisme* appeared in 1924, she "was almost awestruck by the success of the work. Even now this manifesto appears to me to be one of the masterpieces of satire; some pages have the verve and the loftiness of tone of Swift or Erasmus. Posterity often demands no more." Referring to his address, which is given in French at the end of this memoir, she concludes: "Breton can sleep peacefully, there will always be a room for him in the Hotel of the Great Men."

JEAN COCTEAU

(page 90)

In her "Mémorial" Adrienne Monnier introduces the present passage on Jean Cocteau with the remark that she is about to give satisfaction to her "aggressive impulse" by telling the story of "a little meeting" at La Maison des Amis des Livres "of which I was never very proud." Yet, her description of Cocteau's underhanded way of arranging for his reading of his *Cap de Bonne-Espérance [Cape of Good Hope]* at the bookshop—it took place in February 1919—is not at all unkind, and her assessment of his work is fair-minded. André Breton and Philippe Soupault, as she notes toward the end of her anecdote, were themselves hostile toward him, and Breton was determined that he should not contribute to *Littérature*, as he wished to do. Louis Aragon, the third editor of the review, was at first friendly toward Cocteau, as she says later in her memoir, "but the two others put things to rights and succeeded in setting them at odds." Cocteau's biographer, Francis Steegmuller, referring to Monnier's remarks about Breton's rebellion against "the despotism of a bourgeois milieu" and his search for "violent novelty," suggests that it was Cocteau's social ease and early successes that "irritated him beyond endurance."

Born into a wealthy bourgeois family, Jean Cocteau (1889–1963) did in fact have a charmed youth. His first volume, *La Lampe d'Aladin*, mannered verse in the postsymbolist vein, was published in 1909, a year after a reading given by famous performers and sponsored by the actor Edouard de Max. *Le Prince frivole*, which appeared in 1910, was a collection of stylish pieces in which the poet, as the title shows, unabashedly assumed the affectations of a dandy and esthete. However, Steegmuller notes, "one aspect of *Le Prince frivole* is the rather dutiful-sounding insistence that beneath the frivolity there is anguish. . . ." *La Danse de Sophocle* (1912) shows the influence of the exuberantly romantic style of the Comtesse de Noailles, whose acquaintance Cocteau had recently made. The book takes its title—presumptuously, according to a review of the work that appeared in the *Nouvelle Revue Française* and in which Steegmuller detects the "feline" judgment of André Gide, Cocteau's rival "fellow homosexual"—from the legend that Sophocles, when young, danced in the games of Salamis: the implication of the title was that great works were to come.

As Monnier notes, Cocteau renounced these early works and plunged into modernism, taking for his model, in *Le Cap de Bonne-Espérance*, Stéphane Mallarmé's *Coup de dés [A Cast of the Dice]* (1897), which also influenced Guillaume Apollinaire and "led to all the fantasies of the ideograms," his experiments with pictorial typography. Cocteau based *Le Cap* upon the exploits of his friend Roland Garros, a fighter pilot in World War I and the first aviator to fly the Mediterranean. Written throughout the war, *Le Cap* was published in 1919; Garros died in the same year in a plane crash. The lettrist passage to which Monnier refers is an extensive series of vowels spaced two by two. Pierre Albert-Birot, the director of *Sic*, employed a similar technique in a poem published in the November 1918 issue of that review.

WITH GIDE AT HYÈRES

(page 93)

The present selection is a private journal in which Adrienne Monnier describes several days that she spent with Sylvia Beach in the company of André Gide at a small hotel on the Mediterranean coast near the town of Hyères in September 1921. According to Sylvia, who gives her own account of the occasion in her *Shakespeare and Company*, Gide arrived a couple of days after they had settled at the hotel, which she believes had been recommended to them by Jules Romains, who dropped by with his family a few days later while they were on their way from the town of his birth, Saint-Julien-Chapteuil, to their house in Hyères.

Mlle Elisabeth Van Rysselberghe, another visitor, was the daughter of the Belgian painter, Théo Van Rysselberghe, and his wife, Maria. Known by her intimates as "La Petite Dame," Maria Van Rysselberghe was one of Gide's closest and oldest friends; she was his biographer as well, for from 1918 until his death in 1951 she kept a meticulous, frank, and hardly interrupted journal of his life as she saw it—a journal of the journalist, who remained unaware of its existence until he was on his deathbed, when she told him about it. The Van Rysselberghes had a house in the town of Saint-Clair, not far from Hyères, where Jacques Copeau, the founder of the Théâtre du Vieux-Colombier, was visiting them at the time of this writing.

Elisabeth Van Rysselberghe, whom Sylvia describes as "a handsome, rather boyish girl," was to become the mother of Gide's only child, Catherine Lambert Gide. "Elisabeth was an excellent swimmer," she continues. "As for Gide and myself, it would have been hard to tell who was the worse. Adrienne didn't swim at all. In a cork jacket and lifebelt, she simply floated upright close to the shore. Gide rowed me in a boat far out, where he wanted me to dive. . . . He watched me as I went off the end of the boat and flopped flat on the water; *'pas fameux!'* was his comment." She gives other glimpses of Gide, and like Adrienne Monnier, she describes him at the piano, "an instrument that was somewhat affected by the sea air," playing "with great feeling," but not, in her own opinion (with allowances made for the defective piano) very well.

Some of the references in this brief journal of Monnier have to do with ancient gossip probably beyond recall; others, as for example those to Gide's work, will no doubt be familiar to the reader; a few need clarification. Sylvia had brought Fielding's *Tom Jones* to Hyères precisely because Gide had mentioned it in a preface he had recently written for Stendhal's *Armance* and which had appeared in the *Nouvelle Revue Française* in the preceding month, August. The "curious letter written by a German baroness, the idol of Greenwich Village," which Gide lent Mlle Van Rysselberghe, was no doubt by Elsa Von Freytag Loringhoven, an eccentric figure in the literary and artistic circles of New York and Paris, who was a friend of Margaret Anderson, the editor of the *Little Review*. The telegram from Pierre Louÿs was probably a practical joke: Gide was a Protestant; Saint Bartholomew's Day is the anniversary of the massacre of the Huguenots in 1572. Monnier surmises that one of Gide's motives for cutting short his visit was to avoid "offending Copeau," who was waiting for him at Saint-Clair. His play *Saül*, for which he was concerned, was produced at the Théâtre du Vieux-Colombier in June 1922, with Copeau in the title role. Gide himself mentions his stay at Hyères in his *Journal* and describes his visit with Elisabeth Van Rysselberghe to the Salins de Pesquier, "an extraordinary little village near the old saltworks . . . that one might have called Polynesian: sheltered, hidden, buried under the trees and breathing such a strange felicity that immediately one wished to live there, to end one's days there."

RAYMONDE LINOSSIER

(page 98)

Raymonde Linossier, lawyer, Orientalist, and "the Youngest *Potasson* in the World," was born in 1897, the daughter of a well-known physician. Francis Poulenc, to whom she dedicated her

Bibi-la-Bibiste, was her best friend. Sylvia Beach says: "She had grown up with him, and their tastes and their ways of seeing things were identical. She divided her time between her poets in the Rue de l'Odéon and her musical friends in the group known as 'The Six.'" She often visited Shakespeare and Company, where she could be found "assisting, encouraging, and even at times replacing its proprietress." At one point she helped to type an episode for the manuscript of *Ulysses*. Léon-Paul Fargue, as Adrienne Monnier says, was "the poet whom she preferred," and according to Sylvia, "she possessed everything he wrote, including most of his manuscripts."

Bibi-la-Bibiste, supposedly written by "the X sisters," was entirely the work of Raymonde Linossier. Her sister Alice, who became a physician and was known after her marriage as Dr. Alice Ardoin-Linossier, helped pay for its printing in 1918 by the Birault Press. Ezra Pound had it published in the September–December 1920 issue of the *Little Review*, along with a note in which he said that it had "all the virtues required by the academicians: absolute clarity, absolute form, beginning, middle, and end." "Bibi" in French slang means "I," and the title of the work, as translated by Sylvia Beach, is: "One's Self the One's Selfist." "Bibism," then, would be the doctrine of "selfism." But Raymonde Linossier, as Monnier shows, had very little of the "selfist" about her.

The Musée Guimet, with which she was associated, specializes in Oriental art. René Grousset, whose article in the *Débats* on her activities came as a revelation to her friends, was an eminent Orientalist, the author of a history of Genghis Khan and his successors and of a history of China. His article was reprinted as the preface to *Etudes d'Orientalisme [Studies in Orientalism]*, published by the Musée Guimet in 1932 and dedicated "to the memory of Raymonde Linossier." The work, in two volumes, contains studies by Linossier's colleagues and teachers, and two contributions by herself as well: a catalog of a collection of Tibetan paintings and an uncompleted translation from a work in Japanese. Grousset writes: "Those who have not assiduously frequented Orientalist circles will be unable to imagine the delicate soul that was hidden in that young archaeologist, scrupulously honest. When we asked her to let the works that she had been preparing for a long time appear at last, . . . she was astonished, she refused, ignorant of the mastery for which she was recognized everywhere. Indeed, this girl had the temper of true scholars."

Raymonde Linossier died on February 1, 1930, after a brief illness whose nature was kept private by her family. Her death, as Monnier says, came as an overwhelming shock to the circle of the *potassons*. Her sister proposed to publish a collection of writings in her memory, but this was not realized. It is very probable, however, that it was in view

of this posthumous homage that Fargue wrote his poem on Raymonde Linossier, "Une Violette noire" ["A Black Violet"]. This prose
poem was collected in his *D'après Paris [After Paris]* in 1931. He writes:
"I think of Raymonde as of someone who can be seen tomorrow,
today even. She is going to come with her true look, her secret
seriousness, with her sober and tender eyes." And he addresses her:
"Every time I feel that I am in difficulty, . . . I think of you,
Raymonde, . . . I have a need to speak to you." The poem ends:

> If we meet each other again elsewhere, we shall look for a wall that
> resembles that wall on the Boulevard de Port-Royal, which we passed
> along, where you consoled me when I was sad.
> We shall also try to find a road like that road at the very end of
> Neuilly, where we went walking one vacation day, with Adrienne
> Monnier, and where you said, turning toward us with such a wise air: "I
> am happy . . ."

ANGÈLE LAMOTTE

(page 103)

Angèle Lamotte, born Angèle Lang, was the wife of the painter
Bernard Lamotte, who was a friend of Saint-Exupéry. She became
the close friend of E. Tériade and the codirector of his magazine,
Verve. She died of cancer in 1945. The present memoir was published
that year at the end of the November issue of *Verve*, which was
devoted to the work of her friend Henri Matisse. Two drawings of her
by Matisse accompany Monnier's article.

WHITMAN AT SYLVIA BEACH'S

(page 106)

From April 20—not March 1, the date that is given in the present
article—until June 20, 1926, Sylvia Beach presented an exhibition on
Walt Whitman at Shakespeare and Company. She agreed to donate
her admission receipts to a fund of the Walt Whitman Memorial
Committee of New York's Authors Club, which was trying at that
time, as Adrienne Monnier says, to have a monument to the poet
raised in the city—a statue, which the sculptor Jo Davidson had been
commissioned to execute. This was intended for Battery Park, near

the harbor, but the city's Art Commission refused to allocate a site there, and subsequently several other spots in the city were refused by various groups. Davidson did not make his statue until the end of the next decade, when he was assured of a location for it to the north of the city in Bear Mountain Park, where it was set up after being shown at the New York World's Fair in 1939. However, he did make a model of his project shortly after receiving his commission, and this was exhibited in the bookshop along with several rare photographs of the poet that he had found in New York.

Among the other items on display besides the "rough manuscript drafts" that Monnier describes were a copy of the original 1855 edition of *Leaves of Grass*, annotated by the author; a copy of *Feuilles d'herbe* (1919), the French translation of the work by Léon Bazalgette, a member of the French Whitman committee, and his study, *Walt Whitman, l'homme et l'oeuvre [Walt Whitman, the Man and the Work]* (1908); and a copy of *Oeuvres Choisies [Selected Works]* (1918), a volume of French translations of Whitman's prose and poetry by Jules Laforgue, André Gide, and by other committee members—Jean Schlumberger, Valery Larbaud (who also wrote the preface of the book), and the president, Francis Vielé-Griffin, who was an American by birth, as Monnier says, but was of French descent and lived in France from childhood on. Among his translations from Whitman is "Thrène pour le President Lincoln" (1908), his rendering of the elegy "When Lilacs Last in the Dooryard Bloom'd." Sylvia Beach also exhibited two pages of the proofs of Whitman's *Eighteenth Presidency*, which she and Monnier translated for the March 1926 issue of the *Navire d'Argent*. As Monnier says in her "Letter to Larbaud," it was discovered by the Whitman scholar and committee member Jean Catel, the author of *Walt Whitman: La Naissance du poète [Walt Whitman: The Birth of the Poet]* (1929), and a study (1931) of the rhythm and language of *Leaves of Grass*.

A LETTER TO LARBAUD

(page 108)

This letter to Valery Larbaud appeared in the Gazette of the March 1926 issue of the *Navire d'Argent*, which was devoted to American writers—Walt Whitman and four contemporaries: William Carlos Williams, Robert McAlmon, Ernest Hemingway, and e. e. cummings. It was at once personal and a literary composition. It was followed by an excerpt from a recent letter to Adrienne Monnier from Larbaud himself, who at the time was staying in Lisbon, where he delivered two lectures on the sixteenth-century poet Maurice Scève.

Whitman's address appeared in its French translation as *La Dix-Huitième Présidence*. Jean Catel published the original English text, *The Eighteenth Presidency*, in 1928. In a notice that follows the address in the *Navire*, he writes that it is probable that Whitman delivered it. As Monnier notes, she and Sylvia Beach translated from proofs made by the poet himself, who was a printer by trade. Catel believes that possibly Whitman intended to distribute the printed speech to his audience after the meeting. According to its subtitle, the address was intended for "each young man in the nation, north, south, east, and west." Whitman calls upon his audience to exercise their democratic power against corrupt politicians, whom he heartily abuses. *Collect*, in which appears "Origins of Attempted Secession," whose "polite expressions" remind Monnier of the invective of the address, is a volume of Whitman's prose works that was published in 1882. In the election campaign of 1856, the date of the address, Whitman sided with John Charles Frémont, the antislavery candidate of the newly formed Republican party; Frémont was defeated by the Democratic candidate, James Buchanan, but drew more support than Millard Fillmore, the leader of the "Know Nothing" party that succeeded the Whigs.

For literary quality, the address cannot be remotely compared to the great passages of *Leaves of Grass*, and it is a pity that Monnier did not have better access to the work in English. It appears that she was acquainted mainly with the translation, *Feuilles d'herbe* (1919), by Léon Bazalgette. Whitman's eloquence reminded her of Paul Claudel's play *Tête d'or [Head of Gold]*, about a power-mad general, a regicide and usurper, who is brought to humility by defeat. In her *Shakespeare and Company* Sylvia Beach herself describes the labor of translating from the minuscule print of the address: "I came near blinding myself working on it. I went to Joyce's oculist. That same day, Joyce's birthday, I attended his birthday party, and behold! both Joyce and his publisher wearing a black bandage over one eye."

In the same number of the *Navire* appeared "Agence de publicité," their translation of Robert McAlmon's slangy, conversational short story "Advertising Agency." Williams was represented by fragments of his *Great American Novel* (1923), translated by Auguste Morel, the translator of *Ulysses*, under the title *Le Grand Roman américain*. In his autobiography Williams calls it "a satire on the novel form in which a little (female) Ford car falls in love with a Mack truck." This is followed by "L'Invincible," a translation by Georges Duplaix of Hemingway's short story "The Undefeated." The selection from

American writers—"les Etats-Uniens" Monnier called them—ends with a translation, also by Duplaix, of "Sipliss," from e. e. cummings's *Enormous Room* (1922).

JOYCE'S *ULYSSES* AND THE FRENCH PUBLIC

(page 112)

The providential encounter of James Joyce and the two women with whom he was to find "a place favorable to the appearance of his work and the establishment of his reputation," as Adrienne Monnier says in the first of the two articles that she wrote about his work, took place at the house of the poet André Spire on July 11, 1920, only three days after he and his family had arrived in Paris from Trieste, where they had been staying since the fall of 1919. Joyce had earlier lived in that city from 1905 to the middle of 1915, when World War I compelled him to move to Zurich. He returned to Trieste after the war with the hope of resettling there, but finding it impossible to resume his former life, he left the city with the intention of going to London. His visit to Paris was to have been very brief, but in fact he was to live there for the next twenty years.

While Monnier was having her "little discussion with Julien Benda"—he was attacking Gide, Claudel, and Valéry in particular, while she was robustly defending them before a group of interested onlookers—Sylvia Beach approached Joyce. As she says in her *Shakespeare and Company*, "Trembling I asked: 'Is this the great James Joyce?' 'James Joyce,' he replied. We shook hands; that is, he put his limp, boneless hand in my tough little paw—if you can call that a handshake." Joyce visited her bookshop the next day, and in a short time he became the presiding genius of the place.

At this period Joyce was having great difficulty in finishing and publishing *Ulysses*, which he had begun in 1914. In March 1918, the New York-based *Little Review*, under the courageous direction of Margaret Anderson and Jane Heap, had begun to put out the novel in installments. Despite attacks by censors and a ban by the U.S. Post Office that led to the burning of four issues, the editors continued to present *Ulysses* until the September–December issue of 1920. The July–August issue of the review, which contained the "Nausicaa," or Gerty MacDowell, episode, brought charges of obscenity against them, and they were tried and found guilty in February 1921. The verdict seemed to rule out the possibility that the book could ever appear in the United States. In England, Harriet Weaver had earlier tried to present the work in installments in her review the *Egoist*. A few sections had appeared there in 1919, but trouble with her printers and public and official disapproval had forced her to give up her enterprise. In August 1920 she was also forced to abandon a plan to publish *Ulysses* as a book. Weaver, the heiress of a wealthy Quaker family, a woman of almost incredible kindness and generosity, helped Joyce financially during much of his career. The *Egoist* had published his *Portrait of the Artist as a Young Man* in serial form between February 1914 and September 1915. She was able to publish this novel in England as a book in 1917, through agreements with an American publisher.

One day in April 1921, when the last possibility for the American publication of *Ulysses* had to be abandoned, Joyce came to Sylvia's shop and told her about his discouragement. "It occurred to me that something might be done," she says in her memoirs, "and I asked: 'Would you let Shakespeare and Company have the honor of bringing out your *Ulysses*?'" Joyce eagerly accepted her offer, and Adrienne, who was to publish the French translation of the book, enthusiastically approved of it. She recommended her own printer, Maurice Darantière, of Dijon. It was agreed that a thousand copies were to be printed; costs, it was hoped, would be paid for with money from subscribers, and a prospectus was drawn up to attract them. In the following months Joyce labored to finish *Ulysses* and corrected the galleys as they were sent to him, increasing the text greatly as he did so, to the despair of Darantière but with Sylvia's approval. The first copy of the book was delivered to Joyce on his birthday, February 2, 1922. Subsequently the book had to be smuggled out of France to English-speaking subscribers, and a number of shipments to New York were confiscated. When the first thousand copies of *Ulysses* were exhausted, Harriet Weaver was able to publish an edition of two thousand copies under the imprint of the Egoist Press. Many of these were seized and burnt by the authorities in England, and others were intercepted in New York. The first legal acceptance of the book came in December 1933, when the United States District Court of New York declared that it was not obscene. *Ulysses* was published by Random House in 1934.

In her "Translation of Ulysses," Adrienne Monnier describes in more detail than here the work that preceded the presentation of Joyce to "the French public"—it would be more accurate to say to the elite of the Rue de l'Odéon—at the December 7, 1921, meeting at her bookshop. In his biography of Joyce, Richard Ellmann gives the gist of Larbaud's talk, which "was necessarily introductory." After describing the writer's life and notoriety, he "took up each of Joyce's books in turn, and showed that each had supplied an element for

Ulysses to combine. . . . The key to the book was *The Odyssey*, the hero being like Ulysses and his adventures paralleling those described by Homer. . . . Larbaud hinted at the extraordinary organization of each episode in terms of hour, organ, and the like, but understandably did not dwell upon it." Larbaud was helped in his work by consulting Joyce's scheme of the book, which Joyce sent to him early in November. The lecture was published in the *Nouvelle Revue Française* in April 1922.

Monnier's present article was first delivered as a speech in her bookshop on March 26, 1931, on the occasion of her reading the French translation of "Anna Livia Plurabelle" from Joyce's *Work in Progress*, which became *Finnegans Wake*. She touches upon the job of translating the episode in her article on *Waiting for Godot*.

Among her references to the various critics of *Ulysses*, Monnier quotes at length the objections of Ernst Robert Curtius, a professor at the University of Bonn, who was a German specialist in French literature and the author of several works on the subject.

THE TRANSLATION OF *ULYSSES*

(page 126)

From the moment that Joyce arrived in Paris, Adrienne Monnier and Sylvia Beach were eager to establish his French reputation. They felt that Valery Larbaud, with his knowledge of English literature and his concern for new writing, might, if interested, be willing to help him. Accordingly they arranged a meeting between the two writers on Christmas Eve, 1920. There was cordiality on both sides, and Larbaud expressed curiosity about *Ulysses*. He was sent the copies of the *Little Review* in which installments of the novel had appeared. After several weeks of silence he wrote to Sylvia Beach in English on February 15, 1921: "I am reading *Ulysses*. Indeed I cannot read anything else, cannot even think of anything else." He wrote her again on February 22 that he was "*raving mad* over *Ulysses*." It was "wonderful! As great as Rabelais: Mr. Bloom is an immortal like Falstaff." He then proposed to write his article for the *Nouvelle Revue Française* and suggested that it be read in public before being published.

Joyce labored throughout most of that year to finish the novel, and Larbaud's reading of his article and fragments of *Ulysses* was able to take place on December 7 before a paying audience of about two hundred and fifty people, as many as could be crowded into La

Maison des Amis des Livres. Larbaud was accompanied by an American actor, Jimmy Light, who read portions of the "Sirens" episode in English. "Joyce himself," Ellmann notes, "was hidden behind a screen, but was obliged, much against his will, to come forward afterwards in response to enthusiastic applause. Larbaud fervently embraced him, and Joyce blushed with confusion. On the whole he felt that the séance had gone well. Subscriptions flowed into Shakespeare and Company."

As Adrienne Monnier says, Jacques Benoist-Méchin, who was the first to translate parts of *Ulysses* into French, was "carried away" by the installments that had appeared in the *Little Review*. Reporting an interview with him in 1956, Ellmann says that "he remarked that, though he had met several geniuses in his lifetime, Joyce always seemed to him to give the strongest impression of human genius he had ever encountered. . . . He looked . . . like a Shakespearean prince, a Prospero." Larbaud's "lecture on Samuel Butler," at which Benoist-Méchin "performed on the piano," was given at La Maison des Amis des Livres on November 3, 1920.

The review *Commerce*, which published the first portions of the French translation of *Ulysses* by Auguste Morel and Valery Larbaud in its opening number in August 1924 was supported by the American-born Marguerite Caetani, Princesse de Bassiano, who during the 1950s in Rome sponsored the international literary magazine *Botteghe Oscure*. Larbaud also published an article, "Ce Vice Impuni, la Lecture" ["That Unpunished Vice, Reading"], in the same issue, to which Paul Valéry, Léon-Paul Fargue, and Saint-John Perse were the other contributors. The translations from *Ulysses* included the opening of the first episode, "Telemachus," fragments of "Ithaca," from the third and last part, and the closing pages of "Penelope," the soliloquy of Molly Bloom, which ends the book. It should be noted in passing, in regard to the typographical presentation of "Penelope," that Monnier is obviously mistaken when she says that the English language does not include apostrophes.

The translation of *Ulysses* continued under Morel alone. In 1927 Stuart Gilbert, an Englishman who had been a judge in Burma and who was to make numerous translations from French into English and write *James Joyce's Ulysses*, an indispensable key to the work, came to live in Paris with his French wife. One day, in the course of a visit to Beach's shop, he noted and called her attention to several errors in an installment of *Ulysses* that had appeared in a recent issue of a review that she had shown him. At her request he brought them to Joyce's attention, and while acknowledging Morel's competence, he asked to be allowed to participate in the work of translation. Joyce was happy to accept Gilbert's offer, but Morel was understandably upset, and Larbaud, Ellmann writes, "who had agreed to oversee Gilbert, the overseer, was several times embroiled with Adrienne Monnier and Sylvia Beach; they seemed to wish to diminish his role." It was agreed, however, that Larbaud was to be the "final arbiter." Monnier published the French *Ulysse* in February 1929. On June 27 she gave a somewhat belated luncheon to celebrate both the publication of the book and the twenty-fifth anniversary of Blooms-day, June 16, the day during which the action of the novel occurs. In 1937 she sold her rights to the French version to Gallimard.

BENOIST-MÉCHIN

(page 133)

The distinction of Jacques Benoist-Méchin in the life of the Rue de l'Odéon was to have translated the first fragments of *Ulysses* for Valery Larbaud's lecture of December 7, 1921. At that time, and at the time of this sketch, which follows "The *Ballet Mécanique*," Adrienne Monnier's description of George Antheil and his work in the *Navire d'Argent*, it appeared that Benoist-Méchin's own career, like Antheil's, was to be in music, but in fact, he entered politics. During World War II he sided with the French Fascists and became a minister in Pétain's Vichy government. In 1947 he was condemned to death for collaboration, but his sentence was commuted to life imprisonment shortly afterward. He was pardoned in 1953. Benoist-Méchin, a baron, has written many historical and political works, among them a history of the German army, books on the Middle East, and an account of Napoleon in Egypt. He has also done studies on Proust and a bibliography of Claudel, and has translated German works. His *Verdun* was a translation of Fritz von Unruh's antiwar novel *Opfergang*, written in 1916, which appeared in English as *The Way of Sacrifice*, a literal translation of the German title, in 1928. In describing Benoist-Méchin's devotion to the bookshop, Monnier refers to a mystical and philosophical work by Friedrich von Hardenberg (Novalis), the setting of which is the ancient Egyptian delta city of Sais; it is known in Maurice Maeterlinck's French translation as *Les Disciples à Saïs [The Disciples at Sais]*.

READINGS AT SYLVIA'S

(page 134)

The homeward exodus of American writers during the Depression, which also hurt the French economy, seriously threatened the existence of Sylvia Beach's bookshop, although by this time, paradoxically, it had become famous. She notes in her *Shakespeare and Company* that "it was even pointed out to American Express tourists as they passed—in buses that stopped in front of No. 12 for a couple of seconds." According to Sylvia, the first idea of Gide and other friends who wanted to save her business was "to petition the French government to subsidize Shakespeare and Company. The petition was signed by the writers and also by eminent professors at the Sorbonne, but funds were lacking, especially for the support of a foreign enterprise such as mine." In a letter of October 27, 1935, Gide wrote to her that it had been decided that the best thing to do "would doubtless be to form a group of friends of Sylvia Beach (since there is no ground, it seems, for hoping for any ministerial or official help)," and he promised her his own support. The appeal by Jean Schlumberger that Adrienne Monnier mentions here, drawn up after "a decade at Pontigny"—a small town near Auxerre, in the department of Yonne, where intellectuals met for ten-day conferences on various topics—declared that the bookshop, to which the Paris literary community owed a debt as "a place where letters are loved for their own sake, are honored and served," must be saved, and that "it would be enough, to permit it to live, if fifty people, hearing our appeal, agreed to form a group of friends contributing three hundred francs each year. Their gift would cover the deficit and their presence at the gatherings, which we would hope to organize four or five times a year, would create a renewal of life around the enterprise." The meetings succeeded and Shakespeare and Company was saved. After mentioning a double reading by Hemingway and Stephen Spender, Sylvia writes, "By this time we were so glorious with all these famous writers and all the press articles that we began to do very well in business."

NUMBER ONE

(page 136)

As its title indicates, the present article composed the entire first number of Adrienne Monnier's *Gazette des Amis des Livres*. This review, which apart from readers' correspondence and occasional quotations, was written entirely by herself, appeared irregularly in ten short, simply printed issues from January 1938 to May 1940, just before the fall of Paris. As the very voice of La Maison des Amis des Livres, it was her vehicle not only for expressing herself directly to her own public on whatever topics she chose, but also a means of disseminating a bibliography, which she published serially from the second issue through that of July 1939, the last before the outbreak of the war.

In both ways the review continued "the only personal part" of the *Navire d'Argent*, as Monnier says toward the beginning of "Number One": the section of the *Navire* known as the Gazette, and the bibliographical sketches of foreign literature that appeared in most of its issues. The subtitle of the bibliography, which was never resumed, announced that it would be devoted to "the countries of the world, ancient and foreign," that it would deal with "their history and their civilization" and with "their literature translated into French." It was intended to be the second volume of her *Catalogue critique de la bibliothèque de prêt [Critical Catalog of the Lending Library]*, under that main title; the first volume, on "French Literature and General Culture," according to its own subtitle, appeared in 1932. Monnier completed her survey of books on history and civilization and went on with her list of foreign works in translation, beginning with English literature; the bibliography breaks off with an entry for Charles Dickens.

Though the bibliography is noteworthy as an example of Monnier's work as a propagator of books, the chief interest of the *Gazette des Amis des Livres* lies in its articles, several of which, in addition to "Number One," appear in the present collection: "On War"; "On Anti-Semitism"; "Jean-Louis Barrault"; *"Verve"*; "Our Friend Bryher"; and "Joyce's *Ulysses* and the French Public," the text of Monnier's speech at La Maison des Amis des Livres and the only piece not written especially for the review.

In keeping with its small circulation—it seems that the review at no time had more than a thousand subscribers—the tone of the *Gazette des Amis des Livres* is intimate throughout, even in the bibliography.

Furthermore, Monnier not only addressed a small group of readers with congenial interests, but also invited their comments, as at the end of "Number One"; a fair portion of the pages of the *Gazette* is given to correspondence. An inscription on the cover of the review, below the title, reads: *"Rédigée par Adrienne Monnier et par les Amis des Livres"* ["Drawn up by Adrienne Monnier and the Amis des Livres"].

Monnier began to write "Number One" toward the end of 1937, after giving up, as she says, the administration of the review *Mesures*, which she had assumed in 1934. Two references in the article to French publishing practices call for clarification: when she speaks of "author's copies" available for half the marked price, she is referring to the custom, now fallen into disuse, of printing a certain number of books especially for the sake of the author and his friends; "the first thousand copies not marked with the edition number" are those that are printed on special paper without a serial number, and that are therefore more expensive than regular copies; nowadays the number is less than a thousand.

Upon reading this opening article of the *Gazette*, André Gide wrote to Adrienne Monnier in a letter of April 15, 1938: "Dear friend, it is *excellent*. One does not read you so much as one hears you speaking, for you have been able to give the most natural tone of your voice to your sentences. All your reflections are pertinent, sagacious, and find an immediate echo in my heart and in my brain. I applaud, I agree, and hope to be able to help you."

SAINT-EXUPÉRY AND *LE PETIT PRINCE*

(page 155)

Noble through heredity, again noble through his achievements as a writer and aviator, Antoine de Saint-Exupéry, who was born in Lyons in 1900, "was one of those blessed 'children of the Gods,' as Thomas Mann liked to call them," says his American biographer, Curtis Cate. He was fascinated by aviation at an early age, and after World War I he was trained as a military pilot. In 1926 he became a commercial aviator on the air-mail route between Toulouse and North Africa. His literary career began in the same year when Adrienne Monnier published his "Aviateur" in the April issue of the *Navire d'Argent*, with a note by the review's codirector, Jean Prévost, who introduced him as "a specialist in aviation and mechanical engineering." The work was composed of eight fragments of a now lost novella, *L'Evasion de Jacques Bernis [The Escape of Jacques Bernis]*. Bernis became the hero of

Saint-Exupéry's first novel, *Courrier sud [Southern Mail]* (1929), which was based on his first experiences as a mail pilot. *Vol de nuit [Night Flight]* (1931), his next novel, followed from an assignment, again as a mail pilot, in South America, where he was sent after a period as the director of an airfield at Cape Juby in North Africa.

In 1932 Saint-Exupéry returned to Europe, where he continued his career as a pilot and was also a journalist and a representative of Air France. In 1935, while attempting a record flight between Paris and Saigon, he crashed with his copilot in the Libyan Desert. *Terre des hommes [Wind, Sand and Stars]*, written in 1936 but not published until 1939, contains a description of their ordeal; but like all of his writings about aviation, *Terre des hommes* is more than an account of physical adventure and hardship. Flight, as Adrienne Monnier shows in the present article, provided Saint-Exupéry with the images that he needed in order to express his meditations on spiritual values, which alone could give a meaning to existence. The book was dedicated to his close friend Henri Guillaumet, another pioneer in aviation, who was killed in 1940 while on a flying mission.

After the outbreak of World War II in 1939, Saint-Exupéry served as a captain in the French air force. *Pilote de guerre [Flight to Arras]* (1942), dedicated to his commander, Henri Alias, describes his experiences as a reconnaissance pilot at the time of the defeat of France. Saint-Exupéry lived in exile in the United States from the end of 1940 until the spring of 1943, when he rejoined his flying unit, by that time under American direction, in North Africa. He disappeared during a reconnaissance flight over southern Europe on July 31, 1944, and was declared missing in action. *Le Petit Prince [The Little Prince]*, his story for children, was written in New York in 1942 and published the next year. *Lettre à un otage [Letter to a Hostage]* (1943), was addressed to his friend Léon Werth, and, through him, to the French people under the Occupation. Saint-Exupéry's posthumous works include *La Citadelle [The Wisdom of the Sands]* (1948); and *Un Sens à la vie [A Sense of Life]* (1956), a collection of miscellaneous writings that opens with "L'Aviateur."

ALICE IN WONDERLAND

(page 158)

The film version of *Alice in Wonderland* that Adrienne Monnier and Sylvia Beach are on their way to see during the course of the present dialogue was released in 1933 by Paramount Films. It was acted by a famous cast that included the child star Charlotte Henry as Alice, Cary Grant as the Mock Turtle, Gary Cooper as the White Knight, and W. C. Fields as Humpty Dumpty. The book appeared as *Alice aux pays des merveilles* in a French version by Michel J. Arnaud. *Through the Looking-Glass* was translated as *La Traversée du miroir* by Paul Gilson. *Bardol Thödol*, to which Monnier refers in passing, is better known as the Tibetan *Book of the Dead*. "Little Diana Jane Mowrer," who was "scandalized" by the liberties taken with Carroll's text, was the daughter of Edgar Ansel Mowrer, the foreign correspondent and author.

FARGUE AND WORDS

(page 160)

The review *Feuilles Libres*, under the direction of Marcel Raval, devoted its entire issue of June 1927—"the most beautiful number in homage that has ever been published," Monnier calls it in her "First Encounters"—to Léon-Paul Fargue. It contained critiques like the present article and reminiscences of the poet as a friend by Colette, Valéry, the Comtesse de Noailles, and many others; posthumous letters to Fargue from writers such as Rilke, Apollinaire, and Proust; illustrations by artists, among them Paul Klee, Marie Laurencin, Giorgio di Chirico, Marie Monnier, and Paul-Emile Bécat, whose finely drawn full-figure portrait of Fargue is the frontispiece; musical scores by Maurice Ravel and other composers; and photographs, including one of Fargue as a young man in 1907, described by Monnier in "First Encounters": "How sympathetic he was then, how direct his look seemed!" The issue also included a fragment of the French translation of *Ulysses*, which Joyce contributed, as he says in an introductory note, *"en hommage à mon ami Léon-Paul Fargue."* The *Feuilles Libres* was published from February 1922 to June 1928. Some of the best writers, artists, and composers of the time appear in its index.

At the beginning of her article, Monnier quotes from "De la tendresse—et de la tristesse" ["Of Tenderness—and of Sadness"], which appeared in *Poèmes* in 1912. Fargue's "decisive interview with his muse," which appeared in a work that opened the June 1924 issue of the *Feuilles Libres*, is presented here in a fairly literal translation. "The Cartesian languages," "the flexuous languages," and the rest would seem to refer to conventional poetry. "The new Mexico" (not to be confused with the state) remains rather obscure, as do a few other references: for example, "the one-eyed man on roller skates" (*"roulettes"* might also be translated simply as "rollers" or "little wheels"). The poems of "a Fargue in the second manner" that appeared in the opening issue of *Commerce* in August 1924, composed a suite in prose called "Mirages"; they were collected in *Epaisseurs [Densities]* in 1928, along with "Nuées" ["Clouds"], the "versified" poem that Monnier describes. Her article appeared in the *Feuilles Libres* as "Les Poèmes de *Commerce.*"

WAITING FOR GODOT

(page 164)

Samuel Beckett's *En attendant Godot [Waiting for Godot]* had its première performance in Paris at the Théâtre de Babylone on January 5, 1953. It was directed by Roger Blin, who had enthusiastically accepted the play after it was rejected by several others. Both the public and the press confirmed his own enthusiasm. "It had the effect of a bomb," he said. *En attendant Godot* ran for some three hundred performances, and it has since had a worldwide success in many languages, including English, in Beckett's own translation. "The lamentable story of Vladimir and Estragon"—acted by Lucien Raimbourg and Pierre Latour—is that of two *clochards,* or tramps, of uncertain age who on two successive nights, at twilight, on a lonely country road, await a mysterious Godot, who has arranged a rendezvous with them. As the name suggests, Godot represents the absolute, an all-powerful and all-knowing being whose existence—if it can be proven—will relieve the absurdity of a world in which, as Adrienne Monnier remarks, "man drags himself along under the burden of having been born." At the end of each of the play's two acts the tramps are told by a boy messenger that Godot will not come that night, but tomorrow. In each of the acts Vladimir and Estragon are joined by another couple—Pozzo, who was played by Blin himself in the original production, and Lucky, who was played by Jean Martin. The first is a cruel master with a whip, the second is a slave led on a leash and burdened with Pozzo's belongings. Monnier prefers "the realistic interpretation" of this symbolic essay in the theater of the absurd to the farce suggested by the bowlers, which reminded her and her friend Katherine Dudley of the ones that were worn by the Frères Jacques, a quartet of comedians.

Samuel Beckett, for whom "Joyce had a great deal of esteem and affection," and who became his close friend and associate, was born near Dublin in 1906 of Protestant parents. He was educated at Trinity College, where he received the degree of Bachelor of Arts and taught Romance languages. He made his first contacts with France in the 1920s and has lived there since shortly before World War II, during which he participated in the Resistance. Beckett, perfectly bilingual, has written in both French and English and has translated the original versions of many of his works, including plays and novels, from one to the other of the two languages. In 1969 he won the Nobel Prize. The translation of "Anna Livia Plurabelle," upon which he collaborated, was eventually published in the *Nouvelle Revue Française*, in May 1931, and not in *Bifur*, for which it had been intended. During its short life—from May 1929 to June 1931—Joyce was a foreign adviser for this review. Several of his *Pomes Penyeach*, translated by Auguste Morel, appeared in its issue of September 1929.

A LITTLE SPEECH ADDRESSED TO

VICTORIA OCAMPO

(page 167)

The present homage to the Argentine writer and editor Victoria Ocampo was delivered by Adrienne Monnier at a reception in her honor at La Maison des Amis des Livres on October 7, 1946. Ocampo, who was born in 1891 into a wealthy family of Spanish, Basque, and also Irish ancestry, passed part of her early years in France. "Her spirit is French as much as Argentine," Monnier wrote of her in her July 1939 issue of the *Gazette des Amis des Livres* on the occasion of a visit to France at that time. "From childhood, she has spoken our language. Our words have nourished her thought." Her "essay on Colonel Lawrence"—Lawrence of Arabia, which Monnier mentions in her speech—was published in Buenos Aires in 1942; it is available in an English translation by David Garnett which appeared in 1963. Among other works, Ocampo has written *La Mujer y su expresión* [*Woman and Her Expression*] (1936), *Virginia Woolf en su diario* [*Virginia Woolf in Her Diary*] (1954), and a series of collections of essays, largely literary. In 1931—Monnier suggests an earlier date—she founded the still extant literary review *Sur*. She also supported the *Lettres Françaises* (1941–47), a French literary review that was based in Buenos Aires and edited by the poet Roger Caillois; it was especially important as a place of publication for French writers in exile during the war.

Ocampo's lecture in the issue of *Sur* that was "devoted to Paul

Valéry in October 1945," shortly after his death, is followed there by her "appeal for solidarity," which was delivered on the same occasion. Ocampo recalls that Valéry, in a letter of April 1942, asked her for a badly needed pair of shoes and remarks: "In this state was found one of the first writers of France and of Europe, if not the first. Not much imagination is needed to figure what the lot of the others must be." Monnier, as she wrote at the time to a friend, was "very anxious" to assure "a fair distribution" of the provisions that were being sent to her bookshop. The commemorative issue of *Sur* includes thirteen letters from Valéry to Ocampo and Spanish translations from his *Charmes* and *"Mon Faust"* as well.

LUST

(page 169)

Paul Valéry composed *"Mon Faust"* *["My Faust"]*, of which the comedy *Lust* is the first part, during the summer of 1940, at the beginning of the Occupation, while he and his family were staying at the seacoast town of Dinard in Brittany. In a letter he wrote at the time to a friend he remarked that he believed he "would have died of rage and despair" if he had not had the work to keep his mind from the thought of the defeat of France. And to Victoria Ocampo he wrote, "The civilization that was our reason for living is struck at the heart of the very country that sustained it as well as it could. . . . However, despite my despair I cannot help feeling flashes of spiritual power, brief signals of energy that direct me toward the goal of employing myself to bring the light of my country back to life again." Valéry returned to Paris toward the end of September. *Lust* was to have had four acts, but the last was not written. The second part of *"Mon Faust"*—*Le Solitaire; ou, les Malédictions d'univers [The Solitary One; or, the Maledictions of the Universe]*—is another play, of which Valéry completed only the first two of three projected sections.

There is a note of ironic modesty in Valéry's use of the personal adjective in his title, as of one who comes late to a long tradition, but comes to mock it a little, just as Faust in the first part of the work mocks Mephistopheles, who is, as Adrienne Monnier says, "rather old-fashioned, very out of date." He tells him, for example, in the first act: "The whole system of which you were one of the essential pieces is nothing anymore but ruin and dissolution. You must yourself admit that you feel bewildered, and dispossessed as it were, among all these new people who sin without knowing it, without attaching importance to it, who do not have any idea of Eternity, who risk their lives ten times a day, in order to enjoy their new machines, which produce a thousand marvels that your magic has never dreamed of accomplishing, and which are put within the reach of children, of idiots."

Monnier devotes most of her observations to Faust's secretary, Lust, whom she compares to Emilie Teste, the wife of the super-intellectual hero of *La Soirée avec Monsieur Teste [The Evening with Monsieur Teste]*, which she discusses in "Valéry in the Rue de l'Odéon," and to the heroine of *La Jeune Parque [The Young Fate]*, who appears in the same article; she also quotes Madame Roland, the celebrated woman of letters and victim of the French Revolution. Another character of the play, whom she mentions in passing, is Faust's Disciple, who falls in love with Lust and spurns the temptations of the devil. Valéry's *L'Idée fixe*, which, as she says, resembles *"Mon Faust"* in manner, is an intellectual dialogue that appeared in 1932. Gallimard's limited edition of *"Mon Faust"* was published early in 1945. The hero of the title of its second part, *Le Solitaire*, which Monnier does not discuss, carries the intellectual characteristics of Faust and his creator to an extreme degree, annihilating the claims of the world and the devil.

"UNKINDNESS"

(page 173)

André Gide's *Journal 1889–1939* was published by the Librairie Gallimard in their Pléiade collection in the latter year, of which, Wallace Fowlie says in his *André Gide: His Life and His Art*, it was "the outstanding literary event." In his entry for October 16, 1926, Gide writes: "Conversation with Adrienne Monnier, who does not like *Les Faux-Monnayeurs [The Counterfeiters]*." This work, the only one of his fictional creations that he called a novel, had appeared earlier in the same year. In the next paragraph he continues: "Adrienne Monnier speaks to me for a rather long time and eloquently about the fundamental coldness and *unkindness* that this book reveals and that must be the basis of my nature. I do not know what to say, what to think. Whatever criticism is addressed to me, I always acquiesce."

Gide's *Journal 1939–1949* was posthumously published in 1954 in a second volume of the Pléiade collection, along with a number of other works that have an affinity to it, including his autobiography of the earlier part of his life, *Si le grain ne meurt [If It Die]* and *Nunc manet in te [Madeleine]*, a memoir of his wife, Madeleine Rondeaux, that was gathered from unpublished portions of his *Journal* and pages that he wrote after her death in 1938.

BEOWULF

(page 174)

In 1948 the Editions du Mercure de France published Bryher's novel *Beowulf* in a French translation by Hélène Malvan, with this article as a preface. The American edition of *Beowulf*, published by Pantheon Books in 1956, is dedicated "To Sylvia Beach and the memory of Adrienne Monnier."

In her *Days of Mars*, Bryher remarks that "the English refused to publish *Beowulf*," which was written in 1944. "They do not want to remember. It was a documentary . . . of what I saw and heard during my first six months in London. It sold steadily if not brilliantly after the war in America. I loved my characters, especially Rashleigh, Ruby, and Selina." She describes the genesis of the novel in 1940: "The raids were heavy throughout October. I went out gloomily one morning with my basket to get our rations and saw a huge crater at the end of Basil Street. Somebody had fetched a large plaster bulldog, I assume from Harrods because they were then on sale there, and stuck it on guard beside the biggest pile of rubble. At that moment *Beowulf*, my war novel, was conceived." The plaster bulldog Beowulf, named by one of the characters of the novel after the hero of the Anglo-Saxon epic, becomes in its pages, as Monnier says, "an emblem of English tenacity and good sense." Bryher declares that "those plaster bulldogs were standing proudly about the streets in 1940," but that when she tried to buy one years later "to serve as a model for the book's jacket" she was told by a salesman at Harrods that "they had never stocked anything so vulgar. 'There wouldn't be any demand for it,' he said, 'I've never been asked for one.' 'Of course not,' I could not resist replying, 'it was merely a national emblem.' "

AN AMATEUR OF SURREALISM

(page 179)

Besides the works that Adrienne Monnier mentions, Henri Parisot, the "amateur of surrealism" of this article, presented editions of Guillaume Apollinaire and Jean Cocteau, among other writers; he also directed the Age d'Or, which published a series of collections that included Antonin Artaud's *D'un voyage au pays des Tarahumaras [About a Journey to the Country of the Tarahumaras]*, mentioned by Monnier in her reflections "On Pre-Columbian Mexico." The *Cahiers G. L. M.*, whose question on poetry is the starting point for her present discussion, was a magazine with surrealist tendencies that appeared nine times between 1936 and 1939; it took its name from the initials of its director, Guy Lévis Mano. Each of its issues centered around a specific topic: there was one on automatic handwriting; another, assembled by André Breton, the high priest of surrealism, was concerned with dreams. Monnier refers to the issue of October 1938, which was devoted to an inquiry on indispensable poetry. Contrary to what she says, the "little prodigy" of the surrealists, Gisèle Prassinos, continued to write after her precocious career as a child; long after the date of this article she published novels, short stories, and poetry.

LES AMIES DES LIVRES

(page 183)

Among the names mentioned in "Les Amies des Livres," that of the "bibliophobe" novelist George Sand (1804–1876)—whose collected work fills 105 volumes in a standard edition—and that of the critic Sainte-Beuve (1804–1869) hardly need comment, while others that are likely to be unfamiliar, especially to non-French readers, are sufficiently identified by Adrienne Monnier herself. Mme Emile de Girardin (1804–1855), a poet and novelist of the Romantic epoch, was as famous for her beauty as for her writings. The wife of the journalist Emile de Girardin (1806–1881), the founder of *La Presse*, to which she contributed a gossip column, she was born Delphine Gay, the daughter of Mme Sophie Gay (1776–1852), a novelist of society

life. Chrysale is the henpecked husband of the blue-stocking Phila-
minte in Molière's *Femmes savantes* (1672), a satire, like his *Précieuses
ridicules* (1659), of the intellectual and literary affectations of Parisians
of his time. Both Paul Valéry and Léon-Paul Fargue wrote in praise
of the work of Marie Monnier (Bécat).

A LETTER TO A YOUNG POET

(page 186)

"A Letter to a Young Poet" appeared in the Gazette of the *Navire
d'Argent* for May 1926, a poetry number, as its subtitle announces, and
the last of twelve. Like the first number of the *Gazette des Amis des
Livres*, the next decade's more modest successor to the *Navire*, and like
her essay "La Maison des Amis des Livres," the letter is a manifesto of
faith in literature and the spirit. Unlike Rainer Maria Rilke's letters
to a young poet, to which she refers in her memoir of him, Adrienne
Monnier's own open letter was not addressed to a specific person; but
the supposed recipient is less a fiction than a kind of generalization of
the young poet in search of publishers and readers: Adrienne
Monnier saw a great many of them and gave shelter to a number of
publications made at the authors' own expense. She refused, however,
to publish such books.

Some of the names that have a bearing on Monnier's discussion are
not well known, but most of these are sufficiently identified by their
context or by the author herself. At least one needs further mention:
Hroswitha, or Hrosvitha—to whom she refers when she speaks
ironically of the "little value" that, as a woman, she was taught to
attach to her mind—was a German abbess who flourished in the
latter half of the tenth century at Gandersheim; she wrote verse and
also plays in praise of virginity. In an address to the readers of her
collected plays, whom she calls "men full of learning and discourse,"
the abbess apologizes for "the rusticity of my paltry productions."
The address and her preface to the collection were published in
French in the April issue of the *Navire*. Hence, Monnier would more
or less have expected her readers to understand the reference without
further identification.

RAINER MARIA RILKE

(page 195)

This memoir of the great Austrian poet appeared for the first time in 1942 in a commemorative volume, *Rilke et la France*, to which Valéry and Gide, among others, also contributed. Though Adrienne Monnier's acquaintance with Rilke was slight, as she herself indicates, it was based on a true communion between poets whose natures were essentially mystical. Pierre Klossowski, who introduced them, was the son of Polish friends of Rilke; in 1923 the poet brought him from Germany to Paris and helped establish him there. In the Gazette of the February 1926 issue of the *Navire d'Argent*, Klossowski, who was to become a novelist and translator—he was only twenty-one years old at the time—contributed a note on Rilke's German translation of Valéry's *Charmes*, which had appeared in Germany the year before, and also referred to Rilke's fictional autobiography, *The Notebooks of Malte Laurids Brigge*. Three fragments of this work—on Beethoven, Ibsen, and Duse—appeared in the *Navire* of April 1926, in a French translation by Maurice Betz, who published the whole book in the same year. *The Notebooks* reveal the extreme sensibility of the poet, whom Monnier compares to the nineteenth-century Hindu yogi Ramakrishna. Rilke's volume of French poems, *Vergers* [*Orchards*], which Monnier suggests were written to give him "the distance that he needed so as not to be destroyed in the act of living," appeared in Paris in the summer of 1926.

On that June day when Monnier received her copy of the book, Rilke was at his home in Muzot, Switzerland, fatally ill with leukemia; he died at the end of the following December. The full dedication of *Vergers* with its quotation from her "Letter to a Young Poet," which appeared in the final issue of the *Navire* in May, reads as follows, translated from Rilke's French: "To Mademoiselle Adrienne Monnier, Poet, and who lives in the spirit: 'To see . . . no matter what object in its felicity . . .' Adrienne Monnier ['Letter to a Young Poet']." It was followed by the brief poem, "Le Grand Pardon" ["The Great Pardon"], in which the poet speaks of "the unexpected healings between things, which called us to witness without our ever having known how to name them." Monnier's copy of *Vergers* is now in the Bibliothèque Littéraire Jacques Doucet, in Paris, which possesses most of the books and letters addressed to her by writers. Rilke's own letters to a young poet (there was not one, as she says, but several) were written to Franz Xaver Kappus between 1903 and 1908.

LUNCH WITH COLETTE

(page 196)

Of Colette herself, *"notre grande Colette,"* "our great Colette," as Adrienne Monnier calls her and as she is known in France and perhaps everywhere her books are read, nothing need be said. Monnier's acquaintance with her was slight, for the two women moved in different worlds, the Right Bank that was represented by Colette and the Left Bank represented by Monnier. She herself remarks, in a note in the July 1939 number of her *Gazette des Amis des Livres*, "At bottom, what am I for her: a little provincial of the Left Bank!" A far too modest judgment, for she goes on to tell about a cordial chance meeting with Colette at the home of mutual friends, where the novelist had come to look at color photographs by Gisèle Freund: "She said nice things about my portrait in blue. I saw her peck at strawberries. I heard her, her, a master, call Valéry 'master.' " And in a letter to Sylvia Beach in the following month she describes how Colette visited her own apartment and praised the work of her sister.

Paulette Gauthier-Villars, who with Monnier's other friend, Marthe Lamy, arranged this lunch, was the niece of Colette's first husband, Henri Gauthier-Villars, known as "Willy"; he collaborated with her on her early novels. Thérèse Bertrand-Fontaine, though she is mentioned here only in passing, was one of Monnier's dearest and most admired friends. A famous physician, she came from a family of eminent scientists and was the daughter-in-law of the art patron Arthur Fontaine, whose name appears in "Valéry in the Rue de l'Odéon."

A VISIT TO T. S. ELIOT

(page 200)

After her stay there as a girl, as she says in her "Return to London," Adrienne Monnier did not revisit the city until 1948. On May 28 of that year, she and Sylvia Beach, with Bryher's novel *Beowulf* very much on their minds—it had appeared the month before —set off together by plane for "the Great Island." During their stay they saw a number of English friends: she mentions a visit to two women whom Sylvia met during her internment at Vittel and describes evenings that they spent with Robert Herring and Cyril Connolly. The present article, which follows "Return to London" in her *Dernières Gazettes*, was reserved for Eliot, who, as she remarks in *Lust*, visited them in Paris in May 1945, on the day peace was declared in Europe.

That was the first time Eliot had seen them since June 1936, when he gave the poetry reading at Shakespeare and Company that Monnier describes in her "Readings at Sylvia's," in which she invited Jean de Menasce to translate *Murder in the Cathedral*. In fact, as she notes in the following discussion of the French translations of Eliot's work, it was Henri Fluchère who translated the play; it was published in 1946. She refers to two productions by Jean Vilar—the first in 1945, the second in 1952, when the play was performed by the company of his Théâtre Nationale Populaire at the Palais de Chaillot. She and Sylvia Beach, as she says, translated "The Love Song of J. Alfred Prufrock" for the June 1925 opening issue of the *Navire d'Argent*. Only one French translation of Eliot's poetry seems to have appeared before this date: Saint-John Perse's adaptation of the first part of "The Hollow Men," in the winter 1924 issue of *Commerce*. Pierre Leyris published his translations of Eliot's poetry, *Poèmes 1910–1930*, in 1947 and his translations of *Four Quartets* in 1950.

In his reminiscence "Miss Sylvia Beach," from the volume of tributes to her memory that was put out by the Mercure de France, Eliot recalls the dinner that Adrienne Monnier gave at her apartment on the occasion of his visit, remarking that "Gide and Schlumberger were there also." Schlumberger, like Monnier, was an admirer of the Tibetan guru Milarepa, but Gide, as she says, was indifferent to Oriental philosophy as a whole. In the "amusing letter" to which she refers, dated April 24, 1931, Gide says that Milarepa gave him "an immeasurable ennui, and that same kind of sterile torpor, stupor, that I experience upon each new contact with Asia."

Cyril Connolly, who attended Eliot's own dinner with his close friend Madame Lys, founded *Horizon: A Review of Literature and Art* in 1939 and was its editor until it ended in 1949. The issue that Monnier discusses, which published "The Case for Responsible Literature" by Jean-Paul Sartre, the founder of the *Temps Modernes*, was entitled *News Out of France*. In his editorial comments Connolly calls it an "introduction to contemporary French literature." Besides Sartre's contribution and the critic John Russell's article on the existentialist theater, the issue also included an English translation of a part of Valéry's *"Mon Faust,"* and an article by Stephen Spender, "Impressions of French Poetry in Wartime." Monnier discusses Connolly's rapport with France in more detail in "Return to London." John Hayward, a close friend and associate of Eliot, will be remembered as an editor and anthologist.

OUR FRIEND BRYHER

(page 204)

Adrienne Monnier's praise for "our friend Bryher" is answered by Bryher's own affectionate memories in her autobiography, *The Heart to Artemis*. She recalls that after they were introduced in May 1921, "I was shy with Adrienne Monnier at first, my British accent got in my way and I also knew directly I looked at her round forehead and deceptively placid blue eyes that she was a thought reader. It was an instinctive gift and . . . I felt . . . that she was part of that timeless nucleus that has, as its purpose, the transmission of a wisdom that cannot be written down, even in poetry." It was because of Monnier, she says, that she "kept consistently in touch with modern French literature for forty years. She sent me regularly parcels of what she considered to be the best books published every season."

Bryher, whose first husband was Robert McAlmon, the publisher of Contact Editions, married Kenneth Macpherson in 1927, when they established *Close-Up*. *Life and Letters To-Day* appeared in September 1935, with the manifesto that it would be devoted "to living literature," and that "any bias we have is not towards experiment for its own sake, but to unrecognized achievement." Bryher recalls in her *Days of Mars: A Memoir, 1940–1946*, that "Adrienne Monnier sent me material by Henri Michaux and other French writers and until the post ceased in 1940, we always stressed our connection with France." The review was discontinued in 1950. In her "Return to London" Monnier affectionately recalls a dinner for her and Sylvia Beach at the house of its editor, Robert Herring, and describes its French leanings.

The excerpt from Bryher's article on her initiation into French literature in "Our Friend Bryher" was somewhat longer in the original version of this memoir that appeared in the *Gazette des Amis des Livres*, and the postscript to the present version was added before it was published in *Les Gazettes*. "Friendship" and "faith" endured throughout the war, but the latter was not without its trials. In her memoir Bryher recalls how the thought of Adrienne and Sylvia haunted her in October 1940 during the course of a visit with the Sitwells: "I kept thinking of Sylvia Beach and Adrienne Monnier in

Paris until it was almost as if they were waiting in another room."
Later in the book she recalls asking herself, "Where was Sylvia?
Where was Adrienne? I had heard nothing of them since June 1940,
when a letter had reached me posted just before the Germans entered
Paris. 'Don't worry about us,' Sylvia had written, 'it's only the time
between one holiday and the next, we shall soon be together again.' "

In her autobiography Bryher says of her final separation from
Adrienne: "When the time came she showed us how to die and hardly
a day passes now when I do not miss her."

FARGUE AS A TALKER

(page 207)

In spite of his erratic habits and his legendary latenesses, Léon-
Paul Fargue was "accepted everywhere, even sought after and fought
over," says his biographer Louise Schub, for his company was
"dazzling, enchanting," and his conversation was "a perpetual verbal
creation, . . . living poems." He excelled, as Adrienne Monnier says
in the present article, in "the spirit of caricature," and his victims
were quick to resent his descriptions of them. An explanation of a
couple of metaphors that she offers will show why. " 'He resembles an
anemic gendarme, a swimming teacher,' " refers to a rather pale
photograph of Paul Claudel, showing him naked to the waist, that
hung in the bookshop. "A sheep's foot in *sauce à la poulette*"—which is
made with cream and egg yolk and is flavored with lemon or vinegar
—describes another writer, whose identity cannot be revealed, and
was meant to suggest the soft side of the person and his soured
character. The metaphors that Monnier takes from *Vulturne* (1928)
occur in a passage of apocalyptic invective with Parisian images.
Schub calls the work "a cosmic and absurd nightmare, . . . suggested
thanks to a rich, sparkling vocabulary. . . . Valéry found this poem
'extraordinary.' " It was collected in *Espaces* in 1929.

Fargue "adored the songs of Dranem and the adventures of Colonel
Ronchonnot." Dranem, the stage name of Armand Ménard (he
reversed his last name), was a comedian much admired by Fargue
and the other *potassons*. Monnier wrote a brief appreciation of him
that is quoted in the commentary to her article on Maurice
Chevalier. Colonel Ronchonnot (literally, "Colonel Grumbler") is the
hero of Georges Frison's *Aventures du Colonel Ronchonnot* (1886), a sort of
vaudevillesque military chronicle.

Impossible to translate—they have been left in French—are two spoonerisms, one from the "classics" and one that is Fargue's own invention. The term "spoonerism" itself is only an approximate translation of *contrepéterie*—a word play in which letters or syllables of one expression are transposed to create a new expression with an entirely different and often comic meaning. The English term derives from the name of a nineteenth-century Oxford clergyman, the Reverend William Spooner, who made such transpositions unintentionally, as for example when he said, "We have a very queer dean," when he meant to say, "We have a very dear queen." The homophonic French language offers great possibilities for *contrepéteries*, and they abound in Fargue's poetry. According to the formula for delivery, the correct expression is given, and is followed by the distortion. Monnier's example: *"Dites, j'ai mangé une excellente tourte aux cailles à l'enseigne du congre debout"* is followed by *"Ne dites pas, j'ai mangé une excellente tarte aux couilles à l'enseigne du bougre de con."* To translate: "Say, I have eaten an excellent quail pie at the signboard [inn or restaurant] of the upright conger eel; do not say, I have eaten an excellent tart of *couilles* [testicles] at the signboard of the *bougre de con* [roughly, imbecile, fool—but the French expression has an untranslatable coarseness]." Fargue's own invention, *"Je suis venin* [poison], *calme orphelu* [non-sense]," derives from *"Je suis venu, calme orphelin"* ["I have come, calm orphan"], the first line of Paul Verlaine's poem "Gaspard Häuser Chante" ["Gaspard Häuser Sings"].

In closing her article Monnier refers to the memoir of Fargue, published in 1947, by his close friend André Beucler.

A VISIT TO MARIE LAURENCIN

(page 210)

Marie Laurencin (1885–1956) established herself as a painter during the decade preceding World War I in the literary and artistic circle that centered around Picasso and Guillaume Apollinaire. Adrienne Monnier's brief but apt description of her work in the present article perfectly evokes the manner she had adopted by the mid-1920s and in which she continued to paint during the rest of her life, as the portraitist of "girls with the eyes of does and does with the fears of virgins," in the words of her friend the poet André Salmon, who added that "there is something of a fairy wand in the brush of Marie Laurencin." Other critics have been less favorable and have regarded these portraits, some of which resemble herself as a young woman, as hardly more than decorative. It is certainly true that some of her earlier work has a force that is lacking in the pastel colors and vaguely delineated forms of her later paintings—and well might Adrienne Monnier have feared for her nose when Marie Laurencin offered to do her portrait. Laurencin also designed scenery for Sergei Diaghilev's Ballets Russes and the Comédie-Française, and illustrated books, including André Gide's *Poésies d'André Walter* and Lewis Carroll's *Alice in Wonderland*, as well as Marcelle Auclair's novel *Changer d'étoile [Change of Star]*, of which "La Coquetterie guérit l'amour" ["Coquetry Cures Love"] was a selection published in the December 1925 issue of the *Navire d'Argent*.

Marcelle Auclair, who spent much of her childhood in Chile, has written in Spanish as well as in French. In 1926 she married Adrienne Monnier's partner on the *Navire d'Argent*, Jean Prévost, with whom she translated poetry by Federico García Lorca. Her life of Saint Teresa of Avila won great success in 1950. In 1937 she founded the magazine for women *Marie-Claire*.

VERVE

(page 213)

Between December 1937, when it appeared under the short-lived sponsorship of *Esquire*, until 1960, when it ceased publication after some twenty-five issues with a collection of illustrations for the Bible by Chagall, *Verve* realized the desire of its only director, E. Tériade, "to bring together the best in literature and art," as the *New York Times* wrote on the occasion of an exhibition of work from the magazine that was given in his honor at the Grand Palais in Paris in June 1973. With its fine paper of ample size, its excellent typography, and above all its accurate techniques of reproduction, *Verve* was a physically beautiful medium for the transmission of the beauty of its words and images.

With some exceptions—Joyce, Hemingway, and Dos Passos are among them—the writers who appeared in *Verve* were French, and of these most were deservedly famous or were to become so. Adrienne Monnier's roster of the contributors to its issue on the human face—to which she might have added her own name as the writer of "In the Country of Faces"—typifies both the French orientation and the literary excellence of the magazine. However, presumably because of its American readership, *Verve* appeared largely in English translation until 1943.

"Shocks of icicles against the stars," Monnier's quotation from Rimbaud's *Illuminations*, aptly describes the almost hallucinatory effect of *Verve*'s art, its "mixture of the old and the modern," its presentation together of contemporary artists—the designers of the covers whom she lists also contributed to its pages—earlier masters, and photographers. Furthermore, whole issues of *Verve* were often devoted to the works of single painters, as for example the closing number on Chagall, the Matisse number of November 1945 and another of October 1948, and the Picasso numbers of April 1948 and October 1951.

Perhaps the most outstanding artistic achievement of *Verve* was its publication of French miniatures of the fifteenth century, among them the *Calendar* of the Limbourg brothers' *Very Rich Hours of the Duke de Berry*, to which its number of April–July 1940 was entirely devoted; *The Life of Jesus* from the same work, which appeared in its tenth issue; and the miniatures of Jean Fouquet, including his own *Life of Jesus* from *The Hours of Etienne Chevalier*, which was published in March 1945. In her "Nature of France" Monnier describes the work of the Limbourg brothers and Fouquet as being epitomes of the genius of France. It is also as an epitome of this genius, in one of its greatest periods of flowering, that *Verve* itself will be remembered.

THE HENRI MICHAUX EXHIBITION AND

THE PAINTINGS OF HENRI MICHAUX

(pages 217 and 220)

The poet and artist Henri Michaux was born in Namur, Belgium, in 1899 and spent most of his early life in Brussels. The critic René Bertelé describes his childhood as having been "solitary, all withdrawal and distance, constraint and refusal, in the midst of a father, a mother, and an elder brother who were always to remain strangers for him." Michaux himself has said that from the very beginning he "clenched his teeth in the face of life." Bertelé believes that "it is really in this first refusal, without remission, of what is external to himself, and in the intense internalization which results from it that the key to the character and to the work of Henri Michaux must be sought first of all." The act of writing became "his struggle to safeguard the singularity of his otherness," and imagination "a means of salvation." He is among those poets whose purpose is "to call the world in question with words, to try to invent another one that obeys other laws: those of the imagination, of dream, of various relations, associations, and correspondences that arise from the profound claims of a condition that can be called primitive, infantile, or magical." Michaux is "one of those rare poets" who have succeeded in creating "a world that does not resemble the one we know, and yet imposes itself upon us with the same evidence." This created world, however, is "above all one of *little reality,* little consistency, emptiness, and lack," in which "there are only forms looking for a substance, ideas, qualities, or feelings in search of an incarnation."

According to Bertelé, the poet who calls reality in question is questioned in turn. He becomes guilty of "the greatest crime, perhaps; in all cases, the one that society pardons with the greatest difficulty: *the crime of poetry,* that is to say, the one that consists of refusing the organized world" in favor of one that is "unique, irreplaceable, and irreducible, made in the image of his most intimate dreams." Guilt is part of the atmosphere of Michaux's universe, which Bertelé compares to Kafka's. With Michaux, however, in contrast to Kafka's resignation, there is a violent reaction against authority, accompanied by humor, which is a means of catharsis and through which "man creates his liberty." "His universe is that of Kafka revised and corrected by Swift and Voltaire."

Though Michaux has been related to the Dadaists and the surrealists, he has remained apart from all schools. His work, written in many genres, includes lyrical poetry, poems in prose, narratives, maxims, and essays. As an artist as well—and it is as an artist first of all that Adrienne Monnier considers him in these two articles—he escapes classification.

As a youth Michaux showed religious and mystical tendencies and wanted to enter the order of the Benedictines. Instead, when his father objected, he went to sea as a sailor and began to write after his return. One of his first works, "Les idées philosophiques de *Qui je fus*" ["The Philosophical Ideas of *Who I Was*"], was published in the Brussels review *Le Disque Vert* in 1922. *Fable des origines [Fable of the Origins]* and *Le Rêve et la jambe [The Dream and the Leg]* appeared in Belgium in the following year. In Paris in 1924, Michaux made acquaintances among the surrealist writers and among the painters as well, including André Masson. In 1927, as Monnier notes in "The Paintings of Henri Michaux," he contributed a drawing to the Fargue number of the *Feuilles Libres.* Later that year he published *Qui je fus,* one of the "seven perfectly admirable volumes" that had appeared by 1936. Among the others were two books based upon journeys "to the equator and to Asia"—*Ecuador* (1929) and *Un Barbare en Asie* (1933)—*Un Certain Plume* ("Plume," or "Pen," is a fictional alter ego or persona of the poet) in 1930, and *Voyage en Grande Garabagne* in 1936, the account of a journey to an imaginary country whose absurdly cruel customs reflect the irrationality of the real world, a country inhabited by the Rocodis, Nijidus, Arpèdres, and

Vibres—among other tribes—that appear at the end of "The Paintings of Henri Michaux."

Entre centre et absence [Between Center and Absence] (1936), a collection of prose poems with illustrations, contains "Un tout petit cheval" ["A Very Little Horse"], to which Monnier refers in the same article, that lives in the room of the narrator and undergoes frightening metamorphoses that illustrate the insubstantiality of Michaux's world: "In less than an hour see how his head swells, swells; his back curves in, buckles, unravels and flaps in the wind that comes in through the window." In "Clown," from *Peintures [Paintings]* (1939), the poet longs to be "nothing and nothing but nothing," to be "drained of the abscess of being someone," to be "lost in a faraway place . . . , without a name, without an identity."

Between 1937 and 1939 Michaux was the editor in chief of *Hermès*, a review with an interest in mysticism. Two collections of poetry, *Exorcismes* (1943) and *Labyrinthes* (1944), both illustrated by the author, were written while he lived in wartime exile in Le Lavandou, a town on the Mediterranean. The Vichy government regarded him with suspicion and called his work "degenerate." He returned to Paris with his wife a few months after the liberation of the city and resumed his life there. *Mouvements* appeared in 1951. More recent works include a collection of essays, *Les Grandes Epreuves de l'esprit [The Great Trials of the Spirit]* (1966), and a collection of poems, *Moments* (1973). Michaux has published in a great many reviews, including *Commerce*, *Mesures*, and *Verve*.

THE DRAWINGS OF STEINBERG

(page 225)

Saul Steinberg, who was born in Rumania in 1914, studied philosophy at the University of Bucharest and then architecture at the Reggio Politecnico in Milan, where he practiced as an architect between 1939 and 1941. Earlier, from 1936 to 1939, he was a cartoonist for the Milanese magazine *Bertoldo*. In 1941, after the outbreak of World War II, he left Italy and went to Ciudad Trujillo in the Dominican Republic; the next year he moved to the United States, where he settled and, in 1943, became an American citizen. Since 1941 he has been a free-lance cartoonist, notably for the *New Yorker*. His work is represented in the collections of the Museum of Modern Art and the Metropolitan Museum, among other places.

Steinberg has published numerous books of his drawings, including *All in Line* (1945), *The Passport* (1954), *The New World* (1965), and *The Inspector* (1973).

THE PAUL-EMILE BÉCAT EXHIBITION

(page 229)

Adrienne Monnier very much prized the work of her brother-in-law, Paul-Emile Bécat, who was a consummate craftsman in the classical manner, with a strong affinity, as she says, to Ingres. Bécat was born in Paris in 1885. He studied at the Ecole de Beaux-Arts and won the Grand Prix de Rome. From 1913 he exhibited at the Salon des Artistes Français. He was noted not only for his drawings of writers, many of whom appear on Monnier's list in the present critique, but also for his portraits in oil of figures familiar to the Rue de l'Odéon: of Monnier and her sister, his wife Marie Monnier-Bécat, together (see page 432); of Valery Larbaud; of Léon-Paul Fargue, a close friend of the Bécats, at work; and of Sylvia Beach. His pictures have been reproduced in a number of books about the literary life of Paris between the wars; to Monnier's list might be added the names of Archibald MacLeish and Sherwood Anderson. Paul-Emile Bécat died in 1960.

IN THE COUNTRY OF FACES

(page 231)

One Sunday afternoon in the spring of 1939, at La Maison des Amis des Livres, Adrienne Monnier exhibited a collection of photographs of writers by her friend Gisèle Freund. These were in color and were projected upon a screen. In the introduction to her *James Joyce in Paris*, which is illustrated with pictures of Joyce and his friends, including Monnier and Sylvia Beach, she says that she had begun her collection some time before the show with a photograph of André Malraux and had continued with other writers who, like Malraux, wanted illustrations for their books. "All the authors who frequented the Rue de l'Odéon dropped in to see the portraits. They were projected life-size or even larger, and for some people this was a startling experience." In her preface to the same book, Simone de

Beauvoir notes: "The place was crowded with famous writers. I don't remember who was there; what has stayed eternally in my mind, however, is the sight of the chairs lined up in rows, the screen glowing in the darkness, and the familiar faces bathed in beautiful color. . . . All the consecrated authors as well as the new talents with a still-uncertain future drifted across the screen before our eyes."

"In the Country of Faces" appeared in the issue of *Verve* devoted to "that subject of subjects, *the human face*," as Monnier says in her article on the magazine. This issue also included an essay by Freund on David Octavius Hill and photographs by him from her collection.

THE CIRCUS

(page 237)

Some of the figures whom Adrienne Monnier mentions in regard to what is "perhaps the most vital of all spectacles," the circus, have become a part of its history. Grock, whom she and others of the "literary tribe" saw in the music halls, was a clown of Swiss origin, Adrien Wettach by name, the son of a watchmaker. He entered the circus while very young and settled in France. He was renowned for his acrobatic skills and his musical ability. The Fratellinis, whom Gide had discovered "maybe before they had discovered themselves," were three brothers of Italian ancestry: Paul, François, and Albert. They were famous for their pantomime, and like Grock they were accomplished musicians. Jacques Copeau, the actor and director, admired them as much as Gide and wrote a preface to their biography, *Les Fratellini: Histoire de trois clowns* (1923) by Pierre Mariel. In his *Journal* for April 13, 1916, Gide notes that he met Copeau at the Cirque Médrano and talked with the eldest of the brothers, Paul. Jean Cocteau, like Gide and Copeau, was also interested in the circus, and from farther back than Adrienne Monnier would have it seem. He describes his childhood enthusiasm for it in his book of reminiscences, *Portraits-Souvenir* (1935). In 1915 he had the intention—not to be realized—of staging Shakespeare's *Midsummer Night's Dream* at the Cirque Médrano, with the Fratellinis in the roles of Bottom, Flute, and Starveling.

The Cirque Médrano, founded in 1873, one of the most famous Parisian circuses—Toulouse-Lautrec, Picasso, Modigliani, and Derain drew inspiration from it—was originally known as the Cirque Fernando, after the name of its founder. Jérôme Médrano, the clown "Boum-Boum," took over its management after 1897 and gave it his own name. Since 1963, when it was acquired by the junior members of the Bouglione family, it has been known as the Cirque de Montmartre. The original Bougliones, as Monnier notes, were four brothers—Alexander, Joseph, Firmin, and Nicolas—of Italian descent. The Cirque d'Hiver, another famous circus, opened under their management on November 17, 1934. Founded in 1852 and originally known as the Cirque Napoléon after Napoléon III, the Cirque d'Hiver took its present name at the beginning of the Third Republic. The Bougliones liked elaborate spectacles and equestrian pantomimes of the kind that Monnier describes, and they put to good use a *piste nautique,* a track that could be flooded, which had been installed shortly before they assumed direction of the circus.

LA REVUE NÈGRE

(page 240)

"She made her entry entirely nude except for a pink flamingo feather between her limbs; she was being carried upside down and doing the split on the shoulder of a black giant. Midstage he paused, and . . . swung her in a slow cartwheel to the stage floor, where she stood . . . in an instant of complete silence. She was an unforgettable female ebony statue. A scream of salutation spread through the theater. . . . Within a half hour of the final curtain on opening night, the news and meaning of her arrival had spread . . . up to the cafés on the Champs-Elysées. . . ." So writes Janet Flanner in the introduction to her *Paris Was Yesterday* about the debut of the American singer and dancer Josephine Baker in *La Revue Nègre,* which was staged in 1925 at the Théâtre des Champs-Elysées. Baker, who was born in St. Louis, Missouri, in 1906 had earlier performed in the United States in a traveling theatrical company and in a Broadway musical, *Shuffle Along,* in 1923, but her appearance in Paris marked the beginning of her fame. She soon after became a star of the Folies-Bergère and as her career advanced she won an international reputation. A French citizen from 1937, she participated in the Resistance and was a member of the Legion of Honor. Called "La Belle Dame sans Années," seemingly ageless, Josephine Baker appeared as recently as 1974 at Carnegie Hall and at the Palace Theater in New York City. She died in the following year.

FOLIES-BERGÈRE-FOLIES

(page 241)

The famous music hall in the Rue Richer, which still thrives, has known three periods in its career since its founding in 1869. Its early years were promising, but it failed in 1885 after its first director tried to present classical music to audiences that preferred popular songs. Between 1886 and 1918 the Folies-Bergère was famous for its singers, among them Yvette Guilbert, Mistinguett, and Maurice Chevalier. At the end of World War I the house entered its present era as a showplace for spectacular revues featuring nearly naked dancers. According to the tradition of the house, as a charm against bad luck —of the kind that deliberately challenges it—the titles of the spectaculars are composed of thirteen letters, as was *Femmes en folie,* the "aerodynamic revue" that Adrienne Monnier describes in the present article. In her remark on Florenz Ziegfeld she refers to *New York* (1930), one of several travel books by Paul Morand. The actress Cécile Sorel, whom Monnier would not go to see at the Casino de Paris, was associated at first with the Théâtre de l'Odéon and later with the Comédie-Française. She appeared at the Casino in a decorous role in 1933, the year of her retirement from the Comédie.

AT THE OPÉRA WITH FRANCIS POULENC

(page 243)

Francis Poulenc's ballet *Les Animaux modèles*, based upon six fables by Jean de La Fontaine, was presented at the Paris Opéra during the Occupation, on August 8, 1942, in response to an invitation of long standing by the theater's director, Jacques Rouché. The idea for the ballet came to Poulenc in the summer of 1940, as he struggled to affirm his faith in France after her defeat. He turned for his subject to the beginning of the seventeenth century because, he said, referring to the past of his own country, "no other historical epoch has been more specifically French." Above all the other poets of that century he preferred La Fontaine, some of whose verses, he said, were enough "to quench his thirst." His biographer Henri Hell notes that "the better to make the hidden meaning stand out—through an operation inverse to that of the fabulist—he gave back their human appearance to the characters" in the pieces that he chose. His intention was realized, as Adrienne Monnier remarks, by the painter Maurice Brianchon, who designed the costumes and the scenery. Thus, Hell says, the grasshopper in the fable "The Grasshopper and the Ant" "becomes a prodigious dancer: after her hour of success, stripped of resources, she comes back to her home country to 'touch' a childhood friend," the ant, who is represented as "an old maid asleep on her bags of gold." Death, in the fable "Death and the Woodcutter," appears to the poor peasant "in the costume of a great lady of the court. She arrives masked and takes off her mask only for several seconds, which explains the terror of the woodcutter." The setting of the ballet is a Burgundian farmyard on a sunny morning. It begins with the departure of the peasants for the fields and ends with their return for their midday meal. "The curtain falls," Hell remarks, "while they recite the Benedicite grouped around a long table as in a painting by Le Nain." The painting by Louis Le Nain that Monnier herself recalls is *The Peasant Family* in the collection of the Louvre. In describing Poulenc's gaiety, she refers to his early ballet *Les Biches [The Does]*, ordered by Diaghilev and produced in 1924, with choreography by Nijinska and scenery and costumes by Marie Laurencin.

The private performance of the score by "our Poulenc" in the house of the art connoisseur Georges Salles, for her, Sylvia, and other friends, and in the imagined presence of the spirit of Raymonde Linossier, appealed to Monnier more than the official presentation at the Opéra, as it must have recalled to her the intimacy of the early years of the *potassons*. After her own death, Poulenc said in his homage for the memorial issue of the *Mercure de France* that "Adrienne Monnier wrote, in regard to *Les Animaux modèles*, some of the most pertinent sentences that have ever been written about my music."

THE *BALLET MÉCANIQUE*

(page 247)

George Antheil, the composer of the *Ballet mécanique*, was born in 1900 in Trenton, New Jersey, where his father, says Sylvia Beach in her *Shakespeare and Company*, "was the proprietor of the Friendly Shoestore. . . . The younger Antheil's interests lay in music rather than in shoes; and at eighteen, all his father's efforts to train a successor having failed, young George had set off for Philadelphia to seek his fortune in music." He studied there, according to other sources, at the Curtis Settlement School, the precursor of the Curtis Institute of Music, which Gian-Carlo Menotti attended later. Although he wrote music, Antheil originally planned to be a concert pianist; but after a performance of his First Symphony by the Berlin Philharmonic while he was touring Europe in 1922, he decided to become a full-time composer, and he moved to Paris, where he soon gained notoriety for several avant-garde works. Adrienne Monnier heard his music for the first time on October 4, 1923, on the riotous occasion she describes, when he played three piano pieces as a prelude to a performance of the Ballets Suédois [Swedish Ballets] at the Théâtre des Champs-Elysées.

In 1925 Antheil married Elizabeth (Boski) Markus, a niece of the Austrian playwright Arthur Schnitzler. The couple lived in a one-room apartment above Shakespeare and Company. Confirming Adrienne Monnier's remarks on his homecoming habits, Sylvia Beach says: "If George had forgotten his key and Boski was out, he would climb up, with the help of the Shakespeare sign, and hoist himself through his window. . . ." Sylvia's devoted concierge, Madame Tisserant, "liked Americans. She said, 'We Americans,' and thought we were almost as amusing as the races. . . . She was especially fond of George Antheil, except when he came home late at night and she had to let him in."

George Antheil was helped by Ezra Pound, as Monnier remarks, and it was he that introduced him to the American writer and hostess Natalie Clifford Barney, at whose home in the Rue Jacob his string quartet was performed in the presence of the composer Florent Schmitt.

Sylvia says that "Adrienne and I were in on the *Ballet mécanique* from the beginning. Antheil had no piano at the time he was working on it, so she let him use the one in her apartment, since she was in her bookshop all day." The player piano, for which it was composed, calls for the use of rolls of perforated paper, the perforations determining what notes are struck on the keyboard, which is operated by pressure of the feet and is not touched by the hands. Here Monnier describes his performance of fragments of the *Ballet* at the Paris Conservatoire in November 1925. In his autobiography, *Bad Boy of Music*, Antheil says that the *Ballet* was "given a number of semiprivate premières, several with Jacques Benoist-Méchin," who began the French translation of *Ulysses*. Monnier's article on Benoist-Méchin immediately follows "The *Ballet Mécanique*" in the *Navire d'Argent*.

The full performance of the work took place at the Théâtre des Champs-Elysées on June 19, 1926, after the date of this article, under the direction of Vladimir Golschmann. According to *The World of*

Twentieth-Century Music, the *Ballet* was scored for "machines, anvils, bells, automobile horns, player pianos, and percussion." The performance was attended, Sylvia says, by all of the friends—she calls them the "Crowd"—of the Rue de l'Odéon. "There were the Joyces in a box. There was our rarely seen T. S. Eliot, so handsome and so elegantly attired, and with him was Princess Bassiano. Up in the top gallery . . . was Ezra Pound to see that George Antheil got a fair deal. In the orchestra, a distinguished-looking lady in black was bowing to everybody very graciously. Royalty, it was whispered. 'It's your concierge,' Adrienne exclaimed." The public's reaction was violent. "The music was drowned out by yells from all over the house. . . . You saw people punching each other in the face, you heard the yelling, but you didn't hear a note of the *Ballet mécanique*." However, "these angry people suddenly subsided when the plane propellors called for in the score began whirring and raised a breeze that, Stuart Gilbert says, blew the wig off the head of a man next to him and whisked it all the way to the back of the house."

The *Ballet* caused another storm when it was performed in Carnegie Hall in New York City on April 10, 1927; but a much later performance in 1954 in the same place "fell flat completely," says *The World of Twentieth-Century Music*. Yet, the *Ballet* "was a pioneer not only in exploring the possibilities of non-musical sounds within serious contexts, but also in the use of rhythmic processes."

Antheil returned to the United States in 1933. His later work, which includes operas, symphonies, chamber music, and piano and violin concertos, became progressively more traditional in form. In 1936 he moved to Hollywood, where, though he was not closely associated with the motion-picture industry, he wrote scores for films. His autobiography, *Bad Boy of Music*, appeared in 1945. He died in New York City in 1959.

GIAN-CARLO MENOTTI

(page 250)

Jean Cocteau, with whom Adrienne Monnier says that she must for once agree, described the film version of Gian-Carlo Menotti's opera *The Medium* (1951), which the composer himself directed, as "motion-picture perfection." *The Medium* appeared on Broadway in 1947, along with a shorter work, *The Telephone*. Marie Powers sang the title role, as she did in the film. To Monnier's commentary it is necessary only to add that Madame Flora, "under the influence of terror," confesses to her clients in the second of the opera's two acts that she is a fraud. Unwilling to abandon their comforting illusions, as Monnier notes, they refuse to believe her. *The Medium* had great international success in both its original form and as a film, and added to Menotti's already substantial reputation.

Menotti, who was born in Italy in 1911, attended the Milan Conservatory between 1923 and 1928, when he moved to the United States. He continued his studies at the Curtis Institute of Music in Philadelphia, where his first mature work, the one-act opera *Amelia Goes to the Ball*, had its première in 1937. In 1939 he presented *The Old Maid and the Thief*, which had been commissioned by the National Broadcasting Company.

The Consul opened in New York in 1950. An immensely popular work at home and abroad, it won a Pulitzer Prize and was produced at La Scala. Suicide by the "gas stove," which Monnier mentions in the present article, is the final recourse of the opera's heroine, Magda, after continually frustrated attempts to acquire a visa that will allow her to leave her police-state country. "The admirable Patricia Neway," the American soprano, sang the role of Magda in the United States and during an extensive tour in Europe.

Menotti's *Amahl and the Night Visitors* was performed on television in 1951. *The Saint of Bleecker Street* (1954), won a second Pulitzer Prize for the composer. Later operas are *Maria Golovin* (1958), *The Last Savage* (1963), and *The Most Important Man in the World* (1970).

The German-born composer Kurt Weill, whom Monnier likens to Menotti in certain respects, died in New York in 1950. His *Rise and Fall of the City Mahagonny*, a fictitious town in Alabama where every form of vice is tolerated but where lack of money is a crime, was produced in Germany in 1930, against the protests of the Nazi party, which regarded the work as decadent. Actually a bitter satire of materialism, "the song play," as it has been called, consists of popular tunes, ragtime, and jazz set to a libretto by Bertolt Brecht. Weill fled Germany when the Nazis came into power and later moved to the United States, where he became an American citizen.

The scenery and atmosphere of *The Medium* remind Monnier of Jean Eugène Atget's photographs of Paris in the early years of the century. Atget, who died in 1927, had little success during his lifetime. His work owes its posthumous fame to the photographer Berenice Abbott, whose *World of Atget* was published in 1965. In 1970 she issued a collection of her own work, which includes a photograph of Adrienne Monnier and one of Sylvia Beach as well.

MAURICE   CHEVALIER

(page 256)

Maurice Chevalier (1888–1972) began his career while still only a young boy, performing at café-concerts in Belleville, the working-class quarter of Paris where he was born. He won the favor of the demanding patrons of the concerts, who called him their "p'tit Jésus," their "p'tit Chevalier," with imitations of some of the famous comedians of the time, including Armand Ménard (1869–1935), or Dranem, as he was known by his reversed last name. In her note on Dranem, which she mentions at the beginning of the present article, Adrienne Monnier wrote, speaking in particular of herself, Léon-Paul Fargue, and Valery Larbaud, "We had, we poets and friends of poetry, great reasons for cherishing him. He was the contemporary of certain symbolists, alchemists of language . . . ; he had their verbal intoxication; like them, he labored upon the material of words." Dranem was celebrated for his delivery of comic songs. Like Groucho Marx and W. C. Fields, he was a specialist in the absurd; his costume consisted of a tiny hat placed upon a perfectly bald head, a tight, checked jacket (the "little Dranem jacket"), and much too wide, much too short pants that revealed laceless shoes that were much too large.

Moving to the boulevard theaters after his local successes, Chevalier began his slow transformation from grotesquely comic roles into the character of the suave, sophisticated man of the world, for which he is remembered internationally. In the years before World War I Chevalier had great success performing at the Folies-Bergère and the Casino de Paris, and in the decade following the Armistice he was, in Monnier's words, "the very smile of Paris." From 1929 to 1935 he played in a dozen or so romantic comedies in Hollywood, from which he returned to France on visits between films. His triumphant engagement at the Casino de Paris in 1936 proved that he had not lost the favor of the French public despite his years abroad, and his career continued to flourish. After the last war he was accused of having let himself be used for propagandistic purposes by the Vichy government and the Nazis, but charges against him were dropped. In the late 1940s and thereafter Chevalier performed at the Théâtre des Champs-Elysées. In another article, "Bravo, Chevalier!" published in the *Figaro Littéraire* in 1948, Monnier describes him as having the appearance of "a business man who has succeeded very well and at the same time remains a charming fellow." As he aged, Chevalier's pace became slower; monologues gained in importance over singing. He attained his sentimental apotheosis at the Théâtre des Champs-Elysées in 1968, with a celebration of his *quatre-vingts berges* [eighty years].

PORTRAIT OF JEAN GABIN

(page 259)

Jean Gabin, who was born Jean-Alexis Moncorgé in 1904 into a family of performers—his mother was a singer, his father a music-hall actor—was, in his early years, an "ordinary worker" of the kind that Adrienne Monnier describes in this article. He began his theatrical career as an extra in the Folies-Bergère and as a cabaret entertainer. His period of great fame as a film actor began in the mid-1930s. In 1936 he appeared as a gangster trapped in the Casbah of Algiers in Jean Duvivier's *Pépé le Moko*, and then as a prisoner of war in Jean Renoir's idealistic film about World War I, *La Grande Illusion*. In *Le Quai des brumes [Port of Shadows]* (1938), by the poet Jacques Prévert and the director Marcel Carné, he played a deserter of the colonial infantry who is shot by gangsters in Le Havre as he tries to escape to Venezuela. In this film, as in *Remorques* (1941), he performed with Michèle Morgan, who in both pictures appeared as a woman with whom he shares a fated love. After the fall of France, the Vichy government banned the film, which it considered demoralizing. It is possible that Monnier refers to the official disapproval when she speaks of the "people who find the films of Gabin immoral or unhealthy." In any case, her own article was banned by the censors and was not allowed to appear in the *Figaro Littéraire* in 1942.

In *Le Jour se lève [Daybreak]* (1939), one of the most successful collaborations of Prévert and Carné, Gabin played a factory worker who befriends two women who are dominated by a sinister dog trainer—the young assistant of a florist and the trainer's former mistress. Acting out of impulse, he shoots the trainer dead and then, besieged in his room by the police, himself. Monnier refers to the final scene, when he lies sprawled on the floor as an alarm clock rings at daybreak. Like other works by Prévert and Carné, including their *Enfants du paradis [Children of Paradise]* (1943), *Le Jour se lève*, which has an industrial suburban setting, is charged with an atmosphere that is at once bitterly realistic and poetic:

JEAN-LOUIS BARRAULT

(page 262)

Abandoning early plans to become a painter in favor of a theatrical career, Jean-Louis Barrault entered the Atelier, the theater-workshop of the actor Charles Dullin, in 1931, when he was twenty-one years old. He was, as Adrienne Monnier remarks, very poor during his early years as an actor, but at the end of its 1934–1935 season he was able to rent the Théâtre de l'Atelier and stage a drama in pantomime based on William Faulkner's novel *As I Lay Dying*, which had obsessed him throughout the year. The work was enthusiastically received, especially his pantomime of the character Jewel breaking in his horse and fording a river on its back. Monnier compares him to the Indian dancer Uday Shankar, whom Joyce greatly admired. Antonin Artaud, himself a disciple of Dullin, later the exponent of "The Theater of Cruelty," praised the play for its magical power of transformation and its "sacred atmosphere." Barrault's *Numance* (1937) attracted the attention of Paul Claudel, several of whose plays he was to direct and act in later in his career, including *Tête d'or [Head of Gold]* (1959 and 1968), which Monnier recommends in her article. In 1939 he appeared in both *La Faim [Hunger]* and the adaptation that the actor and director Charles Granval made of Jules Laforgue's prose work on *Hamlet*. In 1940 he played Rodrigue in Corneille's *Le Cid* at the Comédie-Française, where he was to remain as a director and actor until 1946, when he and his wife, Madeleine Renaud, founded La Compagnie Madeleine Renaud–Jean-Louis Barrault at the Théâtre Marigny, opening with a production of André Gide's translation of *Hamlet*. Among the plays staged at the Marigny were Marivaux's *Fausses Confidences* (1946), *Le Procès* (1947), an adaptation of Kafka's *Trial*, and Claudel's *Partage de Midi [Break of Noon]* (1948). In 1959 Barrault became the manager of the Odéon, renamed the Théâtre de France, where he continued to present a wide repertory that included Eugène Ionesco's *Rhinocéros* (1960) and Racine's *Andromaque* (1962). He gave up his position at the theater in 1968. Barrault has appeared in many films, including *Les Enfants du paradis [Children of Paradise]* (1943).

THE LATEST INCARNATION OF PIERRE FRESNAY

(page 264)

Pierre Fresnay, whose real surname was Laudenbach—his family was of Lutheran, Alsatian origin—was born in 1897 on the Left Bank of Paris in the neighborhood of the Rue de l'Odéon, where he spent his childhood. He frequented the Théâtre de l'Odéon, then under the management of André Antoine, and very early decided to become an actor. He appeared onstage for the first time in 1912 at the Théâtre Réjane. In 1914 he entered the Conservatoire, where he was a brilliant novice, and early in 1915, helped by the wartime shortage of young male performers, he was admitted to the Comédie-Française. At the end of that year he acted the title role in Racine's *Britannicus* at the side of Edouard de Max, who was making his own debut with the company as Nero.

Except for a period of military service during and for a short time after World War I, Fresnay acted in the Comédie-Française until 1927, when he resigned his position—he had become a *sociétaire*, or full member, of the company in 1924—after disputes with the management. Thereafter, he pursued an independent stage career, notably at the Théâtre de la Michodière, of which his wife and partner, Yvonne Printemps, became the director in 1937. From 1930 onward he appeared in motion pictures, including those that Adrienne Monnier mentions in the present article and many others, among them Marcel Pagnol's *Marius* (1931) and *Fanny* (1932) and Jean Renoir's *Grande Illusion* (1937).

Monsieur Vincent (1947), which Monnier discusses at length along with his latest role at the time, *Le Défroqué [The Defrocked]* (1954), was based upon the life of the saint Vincent de Paul (1581–1660), who dedicated himself to the service of the poor and oppressed and founded the orders of the Lazarists and the Sisters of Charity.

Monnier says that she was troubled by "an infernal glittering in the eyes of the actor," which seemed to belie the saintliness of the character that he was playing. Fresnay himself said, in an interview: "Look at the portrait of Vincent de Paul . . . ; that is certainly not a naïve and tender face. That eye is the most watchful one that I know; that gaze is the least burdened by illusion. It's a lucid understanding, total and without indulgence, of the weaknesses of humankind that inspired pity in Vincent and awakened in him the spirit of charity. He might have been a great sceptic." Monnier detects "a demon of the theater" in the actor's look, a demon that "it is almost as natural to find among clergymen." As an example, she mentions a portrait by Théodore Chassériau of the nineteenth-century Dominican preaching friar Jean Lacordaire, who was famous for his eloquence in the pulpit, as, for that matter, was the seventeenth-century prelate Bossuet, whose invective against the theater she quotes at length.

Pierre Fresnay died in 1975. His later career as a stage actor included roles in adaptations of Paul Valéry's *"Mon Faust"* (1962) and his *Idée Fixe* (1966).

CONCERNING MICHEL SIMON

(page 273)

"A misanthropic humanist in the great tradition," as one French critic has called him, Michel Simon (1895–1975) was born in Geneva. In 1911 he left Switzerland for Paris, where he began his career as a clown and acrobat. He returned to Switzerland in 1914 and for a while served in the army. In Paris again in 1920, he made his theatrical debut in the company of the director Georges Pitoëff, playing a bit part in Shakespeare's *Measure for Measure*. He left the company in 1923 . and became a vaudeville actor in boulevard theaters. In 1929, in Louis Jouvet's company, he won great success in a production of Marcel Achard's *Jean de la Lune*, in which he acted the comic role of the heroine's brother, Clo-Clo. He went on to act in plays by Shakespeare, Shaw, Pirandello, Wilde, and Gorki. His motion-picture career began in 1925 in the silent films, one of which was Theodor Dreyer's *Passion of Joan of Arc* (1927–28) in which he played the role of a judge. His immense popularity as a film actor began with the advent of sound. He played in innumerable films, notably in a version of *Jean de la Lune* (1930), in which he re-created his original role, in Jean Renoir's *Boudu sauvé des eaux [Boudu Saved from Drowning]* (1932), in Jean Vigo's *L'Atalante* (1934), *Quai des brumes [Port of Shadows]* (1938), *La Beauté du Diable [Beauty and the Devil]* (1949), and *Le Vieil Homme et l'enfant [The Two of Us]* (1966).

FERNANDEL

(page 274)

The comic actor Fernandel (1903–1971) was born Fernand Contandin in Marseilles. He began to act at an early age in vaudeville and the theater; in 1930, after working for a time as a bank employee, he made his motion-picture debut in *Le Blanc et le noir* *[The White and the Black]*, a film based upon a play by Sacha Guitry. He won popular success in 1932 in *Le Rosier de Mme Husson [The Rosebush of Mme Husson]*, the film in which Monnier first saw him, for his role as a chaste if moronic young man who, upon winning an annually awarded cash prize for virtue from his village, in default of a suitable candidate among the young women, spends the money in a bordello.

Fernandel appeared in numerous films besides this and the others that Monnier mentions. Among them are Marcel Pagnol's *Fille du puisatier [The Well-Digger's Daughter]*, in which he played next to the great Raimu, *Un Chapeau de paille d'Italie [An Italian Straw Hat]* (both 1940), and the popular series in which he created the character of the Italian priest, Don Camillo.

LAUGHTER AND WOMEN

(page 276)

"Laughter and Women" first appeared in the weekly review for writers of the left-wing Front Populaire, *Vendredi*, to which Adrienne Monnier also contributed her "Little Promenade," and "Liesbet Sanders." It formed the first part of an article on the French comic actress Marie Dubas; the second part, which has not been translated here, follows the present selection in *Les Gazettes*, with her name as the title. Monnier's thesis in "Laughter and Women," though it contains valid observations, may be too categorical, as when she says that "there are no women caricaturists, no women clowns." As she notes, her statement that "the heart is a stranger to comedy" follows Henri Bergson, who regarded laughter as having an essentially critical function. As *The Oxford Companion to French Literature* says, he proposed in his study *Le Rire [Laughter]* that "at the root of the comic element is a certain rigidity or inadaptability to circumstances or to the conventions of society, . . . and that laughter is the means by which society tends to correct this defect." The Bergsonian definition would seem to underlie Monnier's discussion of the comic spirit in "The Nature of France" and in her article on Alec Guinness. The remark that she attributes to Swift was in fact made by Horace Walpole in a somewhat different form.

Marie Dubas, Monnier says in the second part of her article in *Vendredi*, appears to be an exception to the rule. She is "the only woman who can lay a claim to real comedy, who can rival artists like Chevalier, Fernandel. . . . She is boyish. . . . Her shoulders and her arms, her shoulders above all, have something virile about them; they offer a remarkable mixture of grace and power. Her face is incisive, strangely bold. Her chin is accentuated like that of a mask of ancient comedy." She concludes that the actress, whom she calls a *garçon manqué* (tomboy), "is a prodigiously accomplished woman, a woman who is charming and comic at the same time, which is as much as to say, a white blackbird."

A KING OF HUMOR: ALEC GUINNESS

(page 278)

Alec Guinness, born in 1914, began his acting career in the theater with a walk-on part in 1934 and in the years immediately following he established his reputation in the company of John Gielgud and with The Old Vic. A versatile actor, capable of an immense range of transformations in both comic and serious roles, he has appeared notably in plays by Shakespeare, Chekhov, and Sheridan. Internationally he is best known as an actor in films, of which *Great Expectations* (1946), adapted from Dickens's novel, was the first. *Oliver Twist* followed in 1948. In *Kind Hearts and Coronets* (1949), he appeared as the several members of an aristocratic English family who are murdered off one by one by an Italian count who is determined to succeed to the title of the family, to which he is related on his mother's side. In *The Lavender Hill Mob* (1951), Guinness played the part of an unremarkable employee who is charged with the delivery of gold bullion to the bank. With the collaboration of a souvenir maker—their plan is to smuggle the gold out of England in the form of miniature Eiffel Towers—he becomes a resourceful and almost successful thief. In *The Man in the White Suit* of the same year he portrayed a nondescript scientist who discovers a miracle fabric that cannot soil or wear out, and who thus becomes the enemy of both big business and labor. Though the cloth falls apart in the end, "he proudly sets out again toward new feats," as Monnier says, "with the music of his demon within him and before him." As the son of a Midland laundress in *The Card* (1952), he begins a resourceful and successful career with a minor forgery of his school marks. Later films in which Guinness has appeared include *The Bridge on the River Kwai* (1957), *The Horse's Mouth* (1959), *Lawrence of Arabia* (1962), *Dr. Zhivago* (1966), and *The Comedians* (1967). More recently, proving his capacity for transformation to the utmost, he played Adolf Hitler in *The Last Ten Days* (1973).

WITH VITTORIO DE SICA

(page 282)

Consulting the article by Alfredo Panicucci in the *Nouveau Femina*, which Adrienne Monnier herself read, and other sources as well, we learn that the great Italian actor and director Vittorio de Sica (1901–1975) was born in Sora di Frosinone, a small town between Rome and Naples, and that he was the elder of the two sons of Umberto de Sica, an employee in the Banca d'Italia. "Mad about the theater," as Monnier says, his father wanted him to become a singer, and in 1914 he took him to Rome for an audition. Here, during World War I, de Sica sang Neapolitan songs before wounded soldiers in hospitals. At the end of the war, deciding upon a banking career in the interests of security for his family, he entered the University of Rome, from which he received a degree in accounting. In 1923, after serving in the army, he joined the company of a noted Russian actress, Tatiana Pavlova, with whom he remained briefly. He then toured Italy with acting troupes and went on to establish a reputation as a singer.

He knew his first great success in a Milanese review in 1931, by which time he had appeared in drama, vaudeville, and musical comedy, and had played his first motion-picture roles. Between then and 1940 he acted in over twenty films and at least forty stage shows; but most of these were musicals in which he had romantic, sentimental parts that left him dissatisfied despite his growing popularity, and he decided to become a director. Backed by the publisher Angelo Rizzoli, he made several comedies, including *Teresa Venerdi* (1941) with Anna Magnani. In 1942, collaborating for the first time with Cesare Zavattini, whom he had known since 1935, he made his first serious film, *I Bambini ci guardano [The Children Are Watching]*, a study of the effects of a broken marriage upon a child. Using a documentary approach and actors who were most of them nonprofessional, the film was an early contribution to the neorealist Italian cinema, of which de Sica was to become one of the leading directors. It was followed after the war by *Shoeshine* (1946), *The Bicycle Thief* (1947), *Miracle in Milan* (1950), and *Umberto D.* (1951).

These films were well received abroad, but not so well in Italy: de Sica's realism, his dwelling upon poverty, depressed Italian audiences, who preferred him as a lighthearted actor. In 1952 he briefly and unsuccessfully visited Hollywood. Throughout his career as a director he continued to appear in films, some directed by himself, some by others. Among those that he directed after the date of Monnier's article are: *Gold of Naples* (1954), *Two Women* (1961), *The Garden of the Finzi-Continis* (1970), and *A Brief Vacation* (1974).

Cesare Zavattini, who worked also with the other directors whom Monnier names—Alessandro Blasetti, Raffaele Mattioli, and Renato Castellani—was educated as a lawyer but became a journalist early in life and then a writer of fiction. Monnier refers to articles about him by Nino Frank and Jean Quéval that appeared respectively in the August 1951 and January 1952 issues of the *Mercure de France*.

ON THE PERFORMING OF SHAKESPEARE

(page 291)

This article introduces a series of writings that center chiefly around the performing of Shakespeare; all of them were collected in their present sequence in *Les Dernières Gazettes*, where they were given the general title *Petite Randonnée Shakespearienne*, or *Little Shakespearian Ramble*. These reminiscences are especially remarkable for the span of time that they cover: Adrienne Monnier began to attend the theater as a young girl, and her interest in it was sustained throughout the rest of her life. Above all, she loved Shakespeare—the presiding spirit of Sylvia Beach's shop, their "great Will."

The writer Jules Renard (1864–1910), whose judgment of Shakespeare she embraces in this opening article, was a founder of the *Mercure de France*. He is probably best remembered today for his bitterly satirical autobiographical novel *Poil de Carotte* (1894), and for his *Journal*, which he kept from 1887 until his death as a form of "daily prayer," so he said. Monnier quotes from his entry of December 4, 1906, after he saw a performance of André Antoine's production of *Julius Caesar*, which she herself recalls in the next article.

To this excerpt she might have added other comments entered on the same day. He says, for example, that he felt Shakespeare for the first time at that performance, and that such an evening "is the reward for our classical studies." Later he remarks, "The imagery of Shakespeare is less literary than that of Victor Hugo, but it is more human. With Victor Hugo it happens that one sees only the imagery; with Shakespeare one never ceases to see the truth, the muscles and the blood of the truth." He continues: "Shakespeare should be loved only very late, when one is disgusted with perfection."

The actor, director, and stage designer Edward Gordon Craig (1872–1966), whom Monnier also consults, was the only son of the actress Ellen Terry. She also refers to Laurence Olivier's film of *Henry V* (1944), and to Warner Brothers' production of *A Midsummer Night's Dream* (1935), directed by Max Reinhardt, in which James Cagney played Bottom and Mickey Rooney played Puck.

MEMORIES OF ANTOINE AND DE MAX

(page 294)

This reminiscence of early theatergoing brings together the names of two actors who were at the height of their fame when Adrienne Monnier was a girl—André Antoine (1857–1943), founder of the Théâtre Libre and later manager of the Théâtre Antoine and the Théâtre de l'Odéon, and the Rumanian-born Edouard Alexandre Max, called de Max (1869–1924). De Max began his career in 1891 at the Odéon and acted in several theaters thereafter, often in collaboration with Sarah Bernhardt, with whom he sometimes performed, as Monnier notes, in the highly theatrical plays of Victorien Sardou, the author of *Tosca*, and Edmond Rostand, who is best remembered for his *Cyrano de Bergerac*. In 1915 de Max was engaged by the Comédie-Française. He was much admired by Antoine, for whom he created several roles. *Julius Caesar*, in which he played Mark Antony, was the first work that Antoine produced at the Odéon after assuming its management in 1906.

Born into a poor family of Limousin origin, André Antoine struggled to educate himself in the intellectual and artistic milieus of Paris. Obsessed by the theater above all, he began to act in an amateur theatrical group made up of artisans, shopkeepers, and office workers. In 1887, after the performance of a controversial play based upon a story by Zola, Antoine and a number of fellow performers, favoring realist and naturalist works that opposed the prevailing bourgeois theatrical conventions of the time, broke with the group and founded the Théâtre Libre under his management. In the years that followed, moving from theater to theater, the company presented a wide repertory that included the unpublished works of young writers as well as works by Zola, Eugène Brieux, Georges Courteline, and Henry Becque, in whose *comédie rosse,* or "cruel comedy," *La Parisienne,* Antoine excelled, as Monnier says, in the role of the lover, Lafont. Besides French plays, the Théâtre Libre introduced foreign works by Tolstoy, Ibsen, Strindberg, and Gerhart Hauptmann. Despite opposition by a reactionary press, the Théâtre Libre eventually won wide recognition and helped to renovate the French theater.

In 1896 the Théâtre Libre was disbanded and in the following year Antoine took over the management of the theater that had been its last home, which he renamed the Théâtre Antoine. Here he continued to present the repertory of the Théâtre Libre and modernized the classics through innovations in staging and direction. In particular, he was interested in presenting Shakespeare, often mutilated in France, in faithful translations. His production of *King Lear* in 1904 was enthusiastically received and the Théâtre Antoine prospered.

In assuming the management of the Odéon in 1906, his purpose was to make of that house a theater that would be comparable to the state theaters of other European countries. *Julius Caesar* had a great success, but brought a deficit, and Antoine was unable afterward to overcome completely the reluctance of the hidebound Parisian public to frequent the Odéon, whose Left-Bank location at the end of the street where Monnier herself was to live one day was considered out of the way. Antoine left the Odéon in 1913 and thereafter devoted himself to theatrical criticism and to the writing of his memoirs.

CHARLES DULLIN

(page 296)

The actor and director Charles Dullin (1885–1949) was born in Savoy, the ancestral home of Adrienne Monnier's mother's family. At an early age he rebelled against his parents' plan to have him become a priest and went to live in Lyons, where he held several poorly paid jobs and discovered his vocation. In 1904 he moved to Paris and began his acting career. He had his first great success in 1911 as the character Smerdiakov in a dramatic version of Dostoievski's *Brothers*

Karamazov. In 1913 he helped Jacques Copeau, one of the adapters of the novel, to found the Théâtre du Vieux-Colombier. Despite poor health, he was mobilized at the outbreak of World War I and fought in the army for three years. Released from service in 1917, he went to New York to join the company of the Vieux-Colombier, which was acting there at the time. He won American recognition in Molière's *Avare [The Miser]* in the leading role of Harpagon, which he was to play throughout his career. After the war he left the Vieux-Colombier and for a time collaborated with the actor and director Firman Gémier. Gémier, whom Monnier praises for his production of *The Merchant of Venice* at the Théâtre Antoine, was the manager of that house from 1906, when Antoine left for the Odéon, until 1919. In 1920 he founded the state-subsidized Théâtre Nationale Populaire, which he managed until his death in 1933. It was Gémier who created the title role of Alfred Jarry's *Ubu Roi* in 1896, playing the anarchic king who keeps his conscience shut up in a suitcase.

In 1921, as Monnier notes, Dullin established the Atelier, his theater-workshop, which he called "a laboratory for dramatic attempts." Shortly afterward the Atelier was permanently installed in its own house, the Théâtre de l'Atelier. Here, until the outbreak of World War II, Dullin taught acting and produced a broad repertory of plays by modern and classic authors. In addition to those by Shakespeare and Jonson, which Monnier mentions, he staged works by Pirandello, Marivaux, Sophocles, Molière, Aristophanes, and Marcel Achard, among many others. From 1941 to 1947 he managed the Théâtre Sarah-Bernhardt (renamed the Théâtre de la Cité). His one great success of this period is considered to be his production in 1942 of *Les Mouches [The Flies]* by Jean-Paul Sartre.

Rejecting elaborate settings, preestablished rules for performance, and what he believed to be the excessive naturalism of Antoine, Dullin favored primordial and poetic aspects of the theater, such as pantomime and dance, and found inspiration in the Japanese theater and the Italian *commedia dell'arte,* whose spirit of improvisation he admired. Jean-Louis Barrault, Jean Vilar, and Antonin Artaud were among his most famous students. In his *Réflexions sur le théâtre* (1949), Barrault gives a moving account of Dullin's teachings and pays homage to him as a man of the theater.

JEAN-LOUIS BARRAULT AND SHAKESPEARE

(page 300)

Recalling her article on Jean-Louis Barrault that she published in her *Gazette des Amis des Livres* in 1939, Adrienne Monnier again praises his performance in Charles Granval's adaptation of Laforgue's *Hamlet* in that year and his earlier pantomime in *Autour d'une mère [Around a Mother]*. In the passage from *Réflexions sur le théâtre* (1949), to which she refers, Barrault says, "When we are all only one together, I can say that I know human love, the love of a whole group of human beings, love among human beings." Barrault played Hamlet at the Comédie-Française in 1942 and at the Marigny, in Gide's translation of the play, in 1946. Gide's version of *Antony and Cleopatra* was given at the Comédie-Française in 1945. Jacques Copeau presented his *Saül* in 1922 at the Théâtre du Vieux-Colombier.

JEAN VILAR

(page 302)

Jean Vilar was born in 1912 in the Mediterranean port of Sète, which was also the birthplace of Paul Valéry. He moved to Paris in 1932 with the intention of becoming a writer, but in the following year, after attending a rehearsal of the production of *Richard III* by Charles Dullin at the Théâtre de l'Atelier he decided upon a dramatic career and became a student in the actor-director's Atelier, like Jean-Louis Barrault and Antonin Artaud before him. He stayed with Dullin until 1937, when he entered a period of military service. He returned to the theater in 1941 as a member of a company of traveling players, and in 1942 he established himself in Paris. In the following year he organized his own Compagnie des Sept [Company of Seven] and thereafter directed and appeared in many plays, including works by Strindberg, Molière, and T. S. Eliot, in whose *Murder in the Cathedral*, in French translation, he played the role of Thomas à Becket in 1945. In 1946 he acted his first important motion-picture role in Marcel Carné's *Les Portes de la nuit [The Gates of the Night]*. From 1947 to 1964 Vilar was the manager of a series of summer theater festivals in Avignon, and from 1951 to 1963 he was also the manager of the Théâtre Nationale Populaire (T.N.P.), which had been founded by Firman Gémier in 1920. Shortly before assuming this position, in April 1951, in Paris, he played the title role of André Gide's *Oedipe*, which he had created in Avignon in 1949, when Gide himself praised him for "the suppleness and the subtle intelligence" of his interpretation. Gide died in the February preceding the Paris production, which was the one that Monnier saw.

In the T.N.P.'s theater in the Palais de Chaillot, in Avignon, and in the course of numerous tours at home and abroad, Vilar presented an immense repertory of plays, French and foreign, classic and modern. To comment only on some that are mentioned in this article: *Nucléa*, a play about atomic warfare by the poet Henri Pichette—whose long dramatic poem *Les Epiphanies* had its première in Paris in December 1947—was staged in May 1952. Heinrich von Kleist's *Prince of Hombourg* was presented in the February of that year, and Vilar played the role of Robespierre in his production of Georg Büchner's *Death of Danton* in April 1953.

Gérard Philippe, "the preeminently poetic actor," was one of Vilar's closest friends and a member of his company from 1951 to 1959, when he died unexpectedly at the summit of his stage and motion-picture career. Monnier refers in passing to Louis Jouvet (1887–1951), himself one of the century's great actor-directors, known especially for his work in the theater of Molière and Giraudoux. Her Melvillian reference is to the hero of the "psychological tragedy" *Pierre; or, The Ambiguities* (1852).

MARLON BRANDO AS MARK ANTONY

(page 304)

Surely few writers have been in a position to compare two performances of the role of Mark Antony that are as far removed in time, technique, and medium, as the one that Edouard de Max gave at the Théâtre de l'Odéon in 1906 and Marlon Brando's portrayal in the film of *Julius Caesar*, which Metro-Goldwyn-Mayer issued in 1953. Brando, who began his film career in 1950 with *The Men*, had at the time of this article won recognition for his roles in the two pictures that Adrienne Monnier mentions—*Viva Zapata* and the adaptation of Tennessee Williams's play *A Streetcar Named Desire*, both of which appeared in 1952. In the light of Monnier's praise for Brando's diction, for his ability to project "the dreamed-of voice for a tribune," it is interesting to note that the studio had at first objected to casting him as Antony. His performance as Stanley Kowalski in *A Streetcar Named Desire* had typed him for roles as a brute with slovenly speech. Monnier says that he "seems to be a young man about twenty years old." In fact, Brando, who was born in 1924, was approaching thirty at the time. *Julius Caesar* was produced by John Houseman and directed by Joseph L. Mankiewicz. Other members of the cast were Louis Calhern as Caesar, Greer Garson as Calpurnia, James Mason as Brutus, Deborah Kerr as Portia, and John Gielgud as Cassius.

A VIEW OF CLEOPATRA

(page 307)

To think of Antony is to be reminded of Cleopatra. Moving naturally from the one to the other, Monnier gives a pertinent and amusing glimpse of the queen from a woman's point of view. In his *Caesar and Cleopatra* George Bernard Shaw preferred to portray the wisdom of the general, with whom he sympathized, and the youth of the queen. Monnier considers her neither as a pupil nor as the romantic heroine of Shakespeare, but as an intelligent and capable human being. She refers in passing to the perhaps legendary Arcadian priestess Diotima, mentioned in Plato's *Symposium*, who supposedly taught philosophy to Socrates. The passages that Monnier quotes from Plutarch are given in the English version by John Dryden.

THE SHAKESPEARE MEMORIAL THEATRE

(page 308)

In January 1954 the Shakespeare Memorial Theatre undertook a Continental tour, in the course of which the company visited The Hague, Amsterdam, Antwerp, and Brussels, as well as Paris, where its production of *Antony and Cleopatra* received mixed reviews that ranged from enthusiastic to disapproving. The vocal naturalism of Michael Redgrave, who is celebrated in English-speaking countries for his performances in Shakespearean roles, which have included those of Richard II and King Lear, was condemned in some quarters, one critic declaring that with such a voice he would not be allowed to perform at the Comédie-Francaise. More generously and sympathetically, Monnier notes the differences between the French and English languages and theatrical traditions, and finds reason to praise precisely where others blamed. The exquisite artifice of Marivaux and the more robust, more natural style of Shakespeare are worlds apart, but her powers of appreciation were great enough to allow her to enjoy both playwrights, and to see the traditions that they represent as complementary. In describing the voice of Peggy Ashcroft, whose career, like Redgrave's, has embraced a number of Shakespearean roles, she compares it to that of the Peruvian singer of Spanish and Indian ancestry who was in vogue at the time, Yma Sumac, whose vocal range extends from a deep contralto to a high coloratura soprano. Sylvia would have seen Ashcroft's performance in the role of Catherine Sloper, the heroine of *The Heiress*, which was adapted from Henry James's novel *Washington Square*. Like Redgrave and Ashcroft, Harry Andrews, who played Enobarbus, has a distinguished record as a Shakespearean actor. Monnier refers in passing to the English version of Maurice Maeterlinck's *Oiseau bleu [The Blue Bird]*, which she saw in London as a young woman, and to Laurence Olivier's film version of *Henry V*, presented in 1944.

MEMORIES OF LONDON

(page 315)

Her business as a bookseller kept Adrienne Monnier from traveling very much and very far aside from her yearly visits to Savoy, and after her retirement, poor health made it necessary for her to renounce long journeys—to Buenos Aires, for example, to see her Argentine friends, and to Mexico, where she had been invited by the writer Alfonso Reyes. Besides her journeys to London she made visits of short duration to Belgium, Holland, Italy, Switzerland (where she stayed with Bryher in Lausanne), and Germany, where in 1938, going as far as Berlin, she saw the families of Jewish friends in exile. She also made short trips by car in France, to Provence, Brittany, and the northern Alps.

As she says in the present article, her reasons for visiting London for the first time had less to do with her interest in the English language than with her desire to see her friend, Suzanne Bonnierre, who was later her partner during the early days of La Maison des Amis des Livres. Her feelings for Suzanne, whose face, according to her description, was that of the ideal woman of Dante Gabriel Rossetti, was mixed with her impressions of Pre-Raphaelite painting, which was in vogue in Paris toward the end of the last century; it agreed very well with the prevailing exotic taste for symbolist art, music, and literature, and also had traits in common with the popular Art Nouveau style, which in England derived from the Arts and Crafts Movement led by William Morris, who was a member of the Pre-Raphaelite Brotherhood. One of the pictures that Monnier saw at the Tate Gallery, *King Cophetua and the Beggar Maid*, by Edward Burne-Jones, had been an attraction of the exhibition of English art at the Paris Exposition of 1889.

At the beginning of "Memories of London" she declares that it was Claude Debussy's cantata *La Demoiselle élue* that brought her to the Pre-Raphaelites, but according to her memoir, "*Le Mercure* vu par un enfant" ["*The Mercure* Seen by a Child"], she became acquainted with the painters through a study in that magazine by the poet and critic André Fontainas and then "set about buying all the reproductions possible and lived among their pictures." It was also in the *Mercure de France*—she describes in her article how she used to search for back numbers of the magazine in the bookstalls along the Seine—that she read a work on androgyny by the symbolist playwright Joseph Péladan, who was an admirer of the paintings of Odilon Redon, Gustave Moreau, and Burne-Jones. "I was personally impressed by it to the supreme degree," she says, "to the degree that I despised my feminine form and pressed down my breasts, like a nun or like an amazon." And again it was in the *Mercure* that she discovered the "Défense d'Oscar Wilde" by the poet and novelist Hugues Rebell, an article that "seems timid today, and naïve, but that was unsettling then." Rebell proposed setting fire to the prison in which Wilde was confined, "as they had done for the Bastille in 1789." So, stopping in the course of her London walks in front of the Savoy Hotel, where Oscar Wilde used to stay before his public disgrace, she could say, calling to mind her childhood associations: "as I read the *Mercure de France*, above all the old numbers, I knew something about that story, which for me was on a level with the theory of androgyny and pre-Raphaelite art."

Thanks to her parents, and to her mother especially, Monnier was introduced to the theater at an early age. In 1902, shortly after her tenth birthday, she attended a performance of *Pelléas et Mélisande*, Debussy's opera based upon the play by the Belgian symbolist poet Maurice Maeterlinck, whose *L'Oiseau bleu [The Blue Bird]* she saw in London and later in Paris in the company of the poet's friend, the actress and singer Georgette Leblanc, for whom he wrote. Nothing was more likely to appeal to a girl of her sensibilities than the opera, with its story of the ideal love of the princess Mélisande for Pelléas, the half-brother of her husband Golaud, its medieval setting, its castle, its forest. She says in her "*Mercure* vu par un enfant": "What that performance was for me, I can give only a feeble idea of it here: there is too much to say. It was an enchantment that held me throughout the whole length of my adolescence and that made a perfectly mad symbolist of me." In a letter that she wrote to Sylvia Beach after Adrienne Monnier's death, Katherine Anne Porter recalled how she "told such delicious things about her childhood. I remember best about how she and her sister Marie always wept when their parents took them to hear Mélisande. 'From the first notes, we would begin to shed tears, and to sniff and sob, with people around us hissing at us for silence. We could not help it, and we wept just the same, every time. That music was *si mystérieusement émouvante!'* "

RETURN TO LONDON

(page 328)

As a girl Adrienne Monnier saw London mainly from the outside, through the eyes of a foreign tourist; many years later, with strong ties to England and in the company of Sylvia Beach, she spent the brief, belated visit that she describes in the present account seeing "more friends than streets and monuments." In her "Visit to T. S. Eliot" she recalls their evening with the poet and his friend John Hayward. Robert Herring, whom they also saw, was the director of Bryher's *Life and Letters To-day*; he and the review are described in "Our Friend Bryher" and in the commentary to the article. Miss Topalian, one of "the two charming women" whose home they also visited, is mentioned by Sylvia in her account of her internment at Vittel as being "of Armenian origin"; she did volunteer work in the kitchen of the hotel in which the British women prisoners were lodged; there is no mention of her friend Miss Ball.

Cyril Connolly, another host, was present with his friend Madame Lys at Eliot's dinner and party. In his editorial comments to his May 1945 issue of *Horizon* he gives his own impression of his visit to Paris in the winter of 1945, when, as Monnier says, "it was so cold." He recalls that though "the heavy snow and the emptiness made the city resemble Vienna or Petrograd," he was "indescribably happy." Sitting in the Café de Flore, he rejoiced at the thought of the closeness of "the sacred Rue de l'Odéon, where those two bilingual sirens who have so long enchanted us with all that is best in two literatures, Sylvia Beach and Adrienne Monnier, still decoy." He assures his readers: "Don't worry. It's all all right. Everything you love is still there. . . . The European orchestra is tuning up, and its members are as pleased to see us as we are to be with them." He believes that "France alone, if she can survive an acute attack of nationalism, is capable of a bloodless 1789, of a new proclamation to the world of the old truths that life is meant to be lived and that liberty is its natural temperature, that brains are to be used and beauty to be worshipped, and that human beings (the only animals who can laugh) are intended to be happy." Chamfort (1741–1794), whom Monnier says Connolly wanted to resemble, was a critic, dramatist, and writer of ironic maxims; his real name was Nicolas-Sébastien Roch. Connolly refers to him in his *Unquiet Grave* (1945), a miscellany of observations and citations that he assembled as a kind of therapy for melancholy and anxiety. Among his other books are a novel, *The Rock Pool* (1935), and essays about writing and writers, *Enemies of Promise* (1938). His last work, a collection of essays, is *The Evening Colonnade* (1975). Connolly died in 1974.

THE CORONATION OF ELIZABETH II

(page 335)

Adrienne Monnier visited London for the last time shortly after writing her reminiscence about her brief stay there in 1948, and again with Sylvia Beach; Bryher had invited them to the city for the coronation of Queen Elizabeth, which took place in Westminster Abbey on June 2, 1953, a few days after Edmund Hillary, a New Zealander, and his Nepalese guide, Tenzing Norkay, made the first ascent to the top of Mount Everest, an achievement that was regarded as a happy omen for the new reign. Monnier's description of London on the eve of the ceremony, of the coronation itself, and of the procession afterward is an example of consummate, circumstantial reporting, and more—for here the eye of the journalist is at the service of the vision of a poet.

IN LONDON WITH JACQUES PRÉVERT AND IZIS

(page 346)

Charmes de Londres, an album of forty-one poems by Jacques Prévert and sixty-three photographs by the photographer Izis Bidermanas, was published by Editions Clairefontaine, of Lausanne, Switzerland, in 1952. Prévert, whose satirical, iconoclastic poetry Adrienne Monnier greatly admired, has also written the scenarios of a number of internationally known films. He collaborated with Jean Renoir on his *Crime de Monsieur Lange* (1936) and with Marcel Carné on several works, among them vehicles for Jean Gabin that Monnier describes in her portrait of the actor, and *Les Visiteurs du soir [Visitors of the Evening]* (1942), which starred the actress Arletty. "The nice children of Aubervilliers" refers to a song, "Les Gentils enfants d'Aubervilliers," one of three that Prévert wrote, along with the commentary, for a documentary, filmed in 1945, about Aubervilliers, a town near Paris.

She also refers to Jules Vallès's *La Rue à Londres* (La Rue was his pen name), a series of articles on London life that first appeared in a Paris newspaper in the late 1870s while the author, a revolutionary who had been a member of the Commune in 1871, was living in exile in England. Paul Verlaine first visited London in 1872 with Arthur Rimbaud and taught in England later in that decade. Monnier may have in mind his correspondence or an article, "Un Tour de Londres," an account of a later visit by the poet to the city at the end of 1893, published in *Figaro* in January 1894. Auguste Morel's translation (in collaboration with Annie Hervieu) of "London," from *Songs of Experience*, appeared in the William Blake issue of the *Navire d'Argent* in September 1925.

A CAVALIER VIEW OF VENICE

(page 349)

Adrienne Monnier gathered these impressions of Venice during a brief visit that she made to the city in August 1936, in the company of her friend Gisèle Freund, the photographer, with whom she was traveling in northern Italy.

TIGNES IN THE WINTER

(page 350)

The town of Tignes that Adrienne Monnier describes in the present article no longer exists. It was evacuated in 1952 to make way for a hydroelectric dam; its site is now occupied by the artificial Lac du

Chevril. A new community center by the same name was established at a somewhat higher altitude to the northwest of the lake. Like the former Tignes, the rebuilt town is a center for winter sports. It lies close to the eastern, Italian border of Savoy, on the Isère River.

A LITTLE PROMENADE

(page 357)

The ceremonial promenade that Adrienne Monnier invites her readers to take with her on the occasion of this one of many homecomings to Paris has a counterclockwise circuit that centers upon the heart of the city—the Ile de la Cité with, immediately behind it, the Ile Saint-Louis, which she reaches by way of the Pont Sully at its farthest, eastern tip. She passes then along the quais on the south side of the island to its prow, where she crosses over to the Right Bank. Moving westward, first along the Rue de Rivoli and then the Quai de la Mégisserie, she comes to the Pont des Arts. Here, fittingly, she ends her narrative, at the so humanly scaled footbridge between the main body of the Louvre on the Right Bank and, on the Left Bank, the Institut de France.

THE SWASTIKA

(page 365)

The flag of the Nazi party, which displayed a black swastika with its arms bent at right angles but centered diagonally in a white circle upon a red ground, was flown for the first time in 1921. A biographer of Hitler has written that the emblem itself had been brought to Germany from Finland and Estonia by early members of the party. The public reacted strongly to the flag and Hitler, who claimed to have designed it, delightedly realized that in the swastika he had at his disposal a potent magic symbol. A universal emblem, the swastika has been assigned many meanings—Monnier lists some of them; for Hitler, as he wrote in *Mein Kampf,* it stood for "the fight for victory of Aryan man and of the idea of creative work, which in itself eternally has been anti-Semitic and eternally will be anti-Semitic." In March 1933, shortly after his rise to power, the flag bearing the swastika was flown beside Germany's national colors; it was the official standard of the Third Reich from 1935 until the defeat of Germany in 1945. The swastika in the Nazi arrangement was widely displayed, as for example on military equipment and postage stamps; it was also worn on uniforms—hence Monnier's warning concerning the reversal of the direction of its arms in relation to the bearer. Because of its associations with national socialism, use of the swastika was suppressed by Allied authorities after the war.

Johann Jakob Bachofen, mentioned by Monnier's German Jewish friend Walter Benjamin, in connection with the swastika, was born in 1815 in Basel, where he died in 1887. He was a jurist and a student of classical antiquity. His book on matriarchy, *Das Mutterrecht [The Mother Right]* (1861), propounded the theory that matriarchal social structures precede patriarchal ones in the development of cultures.

The *Mahabharata* is a vast ancient Indian war epic of over 200,000 verses; its central theme is the struggle for supremacy of two rival families. It contains many episodes, of which the *Bhagavad-Gita* is probably the best known.

ON WAR

(page 367)

Warum Krieg? [Why War?], an exchange of open letters between Albert Einstein and Sigmund Freud, was published in pamphlet form in Paris in 1933 by the International Institute of Intellectual Cooperation of the League of Nations as a part of a series of exchanges between intellectuals on urgent problems of the day. The English translation of the Einstein-Freud correspondence was made by Stuart Gilbert, who supervised the French translation of *Ulysses*. The pamphlet was printed by Darantière of Dijon, Adrienne Monnier's and Sylvia Beach's own printer. The English translation of the passages Monnier quotes in the present article is based upon her own text; presumably she had read a French version of *Warum Krieg?*.

The present essay appeared under the title "Reflections on War," the opening article of her *Gazette des Amis des Livres* of July 1938. September of the same year brought the appeasement of Germany and Italy by England and France at Munich: the Munich Pact, which allowed German occupation of part of Czechoslovakia, was intended to satisfy what Germany declared at the time to be limited territorial demands, and thus to avert war; in fact, the English and French concessions only increased Hitler's ambitions and merely delayed the war, which broke out the following September. In that same month Sigmund Freud died in London, where he had taken refuge from the Nazis after Germany invaded Austria and occupied Vienna, his native city.

"Reflections on War," like "Reflections on Anti-Semitism" (reprinted as "On Anti-Semitism," following the present article), which she published in her *Gazette* in December 1938, after the signing of the Munich Pact, reveals Monnier's own concern with the desperate state of Europe. Her own articles, together with the exchange of letters between Einstein and Freud, call to mind the lines of W. H. Auden in his "September 1, 1939," which takes its title from the date of Germany's invasion of Poland, the act that precipitated World War II:

> Defenceless under the night
> Our world in stupor lies;
> Yet, dotted everywhere,
> Ironic points of light
> Flash out wherever the Just
> Exchange their messages. . .

Einstein wrote his message to Freud at "Caputh near Potsdam," July 30, 1932. Freud answers from Vienna, September 3, 1932. As Monnier notes, Einstein begins by asking if humankind can be freed from "the menace of war." He continues (in Stuart Gilbert's translation): "Is it possible to control man's mental evolution so as to make him proof against the psychoses of hate and destructiveness?" He speaks of "the craving for power," "the power hunger" of the governing classes, and of their ability to force the great majority to commit aggressive acts that are generated by "a collective psychosis." He admits the inherent weakness of any organization for peace that cannot enforce its decrees: "law and might inevitably go hand in hand."

Monnier herself offers an explanation for war that may be simplistic: "It should not be said that there are plunderers, it should be said that there are beings in this world who can live only by plundering." She does not sufficiently consider the irrational or "psychotic" aspects of warfare, nor does she speak of the wars that are waged by the powerful against the weak; and she might have mentioned Freud's own remarks in his reply to Einstein that touch upon the possibility that war, at certain times in history, has been a means of imposing order and peace. Freud says (in the Gilbert translation): "No single all-embracing judgment can be passed on these wars of aggrandizement. Some, like the war between the Mongols and the Turks, have led to unmitigated misery; others, however, have furthered the transition from violence to law, since they brought larger units into being, within whose limits recourse to violence was banned and a new regime determined all disputes. Thus the Roman conquests brought that boon, the *Pax Romana*, to the Mediterranean lands. The French kings' lust for aggrandizement created a new France, flourishing in peace and unity. Paradoxical as it sounds, we must admit that warfare well might serve to pave the way to that unbroken peace we so desire, for it is war that brings vast empires into being, within whose frontiers all warfare is proscribed by a strong central power." He adds, however, that most often "the new-created unit falls asunder once again, generally because there can be no true cohesion between the parts that violence has welded." Also, war leads to disputes between units: "For humanity at large the sole result of these military enterprises was that, instead of frequent not to say incessant little wars, they had now to face great wars which, for all they came less often, were so much the more destructive." Here Freud describes the actual results of international rivalry in modern times; the success of the *Pax Romana* depended upon Rome's having abolished all rivals in the Mediterranean world of her time.

It was perhaps not within the scope of Monnier's article to consider these observations of Freud, who himself, in a passage from which she quotes, did not—and could not, considering the limits of the letter form—deal thoroughly with the relation between war and culture. His own observation that "everything that works for the development of culture also works against war" gives rise to many questions; as, for example, have not the greatest periods of cultural flowering occurred, in some countries, when they were also at the height of imperial glory brought about by war? That glory has even been the theme of poets, as the glory of Rome was the theme of Virgil under Augustus, the conqueror who was his patron; and Molière praised the conquests of his own patron, Louis XIV.

These attempts at criticism, these notes on notes, in the end perhaps only serve to indicate the complexity of a subject that, as Adrienne Monnier says at the conclusion of her own article, "quickly disheartens reason."

ON ANTI-SEMITISM

(page 373)

A few passages have been omitted from this discussion of anti-Semitism as being for the most part extraneous to its main theme. They contain further reflections on war, which develop out of the preceding article, remarks on certain Eastern holy books, quotations from "the great German naturalist Carl Vogt, a professor at the University of Geneva," who "courageously took the initiative for a countermovement" against a German anti-Semitic campaign of around 1880, and the summation of the article, which ends with a reference to the Munich agreement of the previous September and calls—far too hopefully, wishfully even, as it appears in retrospect—for a crusade against anti-Semitism by the French: "We have tried, at the price of a great sacrifice, to avoid war; we must now assure the triumph of good sense and of equity. By taking the lead in a worldwide endeavor, by leading this endeavor with vigor and coherence, we shall find honor again. And the German people will only esteem us more."

The persecution of the Jews in Germany would naturally remind Adrienne Monnier of the Dreyfus affair in France, which began in 1894 with the trial and conviction of the Jewish army captain Alfred Dreyfus, who had been accused of delivering military secrets into German hands, but who in fact was the victim of an anti-Semitic campaign conducted by right-wing elements of French society. Although he was not formally exonerated until 1906, Dreyfus was pardoned after a second trial in 1899, by which time it was obvious that the evidence used against him had been forged, and the affair, which had divided France into pro- and anti-Dreyfus factions and even threatened the existence of the Third Republic, effectively came to an end. Foremost among Dreyfus's literary supporters was Emile Zola, whose famous open letter to the president of the Republic, beginning with the words, "J'accuse," was published in the pro-Dreyfus paper *L'Aurore*. Gyp, whose "disgustingly stupid novels" repelled Monnier, was an anti-Semitic chronicler of Parisian high society, and of course an enemy of Dreyfus; she possibly chose her monosyllabic *nom de plume* as an escape from the length of her real name: Marie-Antoinette de Riquetti de Mirabeau, Comtesse de Martel de Janville. Bryher's "Paris 1900," in which Monnier sees evidence of her friend's political sense when she was a little girl—Bryher speaks, for example, of her awareness at the time of the difference between a monarchy and a republic—is a record of her visit to the Paris Exposition of that year; it appeared in the *Nouvelle Revue Française* in December 1937.

ON PRE-COLUMBIAN MEXICO

(page 379)

Mexique précolombien, an album of photographs by Gisèle Freund with an introduction by Paul Rivet, the founder of the Musée de l'Homme in Paris, the museum of anthropology and ethnology, was published in 1954 by Editions Ides et Calendes as number eight in their series "Collection des Ides photographiques." Rivet says that the exhibition of Mexican art which Adrienne Monnier mentions "was certainly the most resounding artistic event of the year 1952. The success was as considerable in Stockholm and in London, where the collections were transported before going ba˜k to Mexico."

Réville—Albert Réville—to whose work *Les Religions du Mexique, de l'Amérique Centrale et du Pérou* (1885) Monnier refers as the principal source for her article, was a nineteenth-century scholar of the history of religions. After her studies, as she says, she turned to work by Alfonso Reyes, "our noble friend," and Antonin Artaud. In a note that accompanies his "Tropique," which appeared in the final, May 1926 issue of the *Navire d'Argent,* Valery Larbaud describes Reyes, who was a critic and scholar as well as a poet, as one "who can guide us, better than any other, in our excursions through the contemporary literature of the Spanish-language world. . . . Alfonso Reyes has become the interpreter, at one and the same time, of Latin America in Spain, of Spain in Latin America, and of the whole of the Spanish world in Europe. . . . And that without ever ceasing to be specifically Mexican, without abandoning anything of that lofty Mexican tradition . . . that goes back to the Pre-Columbian epoch." "Tropique," like the other works by Reyes that Monnier describes, was published in French translation. His poem "Soleil de Monterrey" ["Sun of Monterrey"], also in translation, with an epigraph that reads "Pour la couronne d'Adrienne Monnier" ["For the crown of Adrienne Monnier"], appeared in the January 1956 issue of the *Mercure de France* devoted to her memory.

Antonin Artaud's *D'un voyage au pays des Tarahumaras [About a Journey to the Country of the Tarahumaras]* appeared in the collection of the Age d'Or in 1945, along with a letter from Artaud to the director of the collection, Henri Parisot. The work, whose basis is two essays that Artaud first published in the *Nouvelle Revue Française* in 1937, after a visit to Mexico in the preceding year, describes his experiences among the Tarahumara Indians—the subject of Reyes's poem as well, whom he visited in their mountain fastnesses north of Mexico City, with the hope of bringing about a reintegration of his personality—he suffered most of his life from insanity—by participating in their religious ceremonies, in which peyote was used as a means of mystical communion with the divine. A related essay, "Le Rite du peyotl chez les Tarahumaras" ["The Peyote Rite among the Tarahumaras"], came out in the review *Arbalète* in 1947. The *Lettres Nouvelles* published two other supplements in its issue of March 1953, to which Monnier contributed her article on *Waiting for Godot*. All of Artaud's texts on the Tarahumaras are to be found in volume nine of Gallimard's edition of his complete works.

OCCUPATION JOURNAL: MAY 8 TO JULY 10, 1940

(page 391)

On May 10, 1940, two days after the first entry in the present private journal, Germany put an end to the "phony war," as it has been called, the quiescent first phase of World War II, by attacking the Netherlands, the first step in its offensive against France. Belgium was invaded shortly thereafter, and on May 13 the German army crossed the Belgian border into France itself, near Sedan. On June 14, in just over a month's time, during which the Germans overcame all resistance along the way by the French and the British defenders, Paris, which had been declared an open city shortly before, fell to the enemy. By that time a large portion of the city's population had fled. "Day and night," Sylvia Beach writes in her own account of the invasion in *Shakespeare and Company*, "people streamed through the Rue de l'Odéon. People camped, and slept, in front of the railway stations in the hope of getting on a train. Some left in their cars. . . . Most of them fled on foot. . . . Meanwhile, a constant stream of refugees from the north and northeast, including Belgium—people uprooted from their farms and towns—flowed through the city toward the west. Adrienne and I did not join the exodus. Why flee?"

In most cases—Monnier gives instances in her journal—flight was futile and more dangerous by far than staying in the city. As she notes, she herself, encouraged by her sister Marie—here called by her nickname, "Rinette"—resisted the urge to take refuge with her parents at their home in the small town of Rocfoin, to the southwest of Paris near Maintenon. Her journal is in large part a record of how the daily life of the Rue de l'Odéon continued despite the catastrophe. The most commonplace facts—about shopping, eating, prices—

are set beside notations on historical events such as Henri Philippe Pétain's request for peace terms on June 17, the signing of the armistice agreement at Compiègne on June 22 in the railway car in which the German surrender of 1918 was signed, and the cease-fire of June 25.

At the beginning of the crisis, and even after the invasion of France, one of Monnier's primary concerns was her *Gazette*, the May issue of which was to be its last. She had planned to devote it to "The Most Beautiful Books in the World," but circumstances forced her to set aside the larger part of the issue to "Joyce's *Ulysses* and the French Public," the text of the speech she had delivered at La Maison des Amis des Livres in March 1931. In the same issue—as she notes in her entry for May 20—she also published her own "Our Friend Bryher" and an article by her friend Walter Benjamin on Georges Salles's *Regard*. This *Gazette* also contained several letters from friends in the army, two of whom she mentions in her entry for May 12. Claude Roy's was in praise of the seventh issue of *Verve*, which was devoted to *The Very Rich Hours of the Duke de Berry*. She preceded the article on *Ulysses* with a note that referred to observations on the work by Roy and by Marc Klein, who is the subject of "A Christmas Letter," which appears later in Part Eight.

In her entry for May 13 and others Monnier hints at the aid that she rendered some of her writer friends who, as refugees from Germany, were subject to internment when France was invaded and were in especially grave danger because they were Jewish. She successfully appealed on their behalf to her friend the diplomat-poet Henri Hoppenot, at the time the director for European affairs at the Quai d'Orsay and later the French ambassador to Washington. Then, at grave risk to herself, she hid Arthur Koestler, who had already spent time in a French detention camp, in her apartment; as he had no papers of any kind, he was in danger of being apprehended by the police. Koestler recalls the incident that Monnier notes in her entry for May 23 in his autobiography, *The Invisible Writing*, and in a letter to Gisèle Freund, October 5, 1955, where he says that when she saw the four-leaf clover that fell, as Monnier remarks, "right between his eyes," "Mlle Monnier . . . kissed me on the spot where it had fallen: 'Now,' she said, 'I know that you will come out of it safe and sound.' " Later he and others hid at the offices of the P.E.N. Club of Paris, of which Henri Membré, whom she refers to here and there, was the secretary. Finally, again with the help of Hoppenot, Monnier procured a visa for Koestler that allowed him to escape from Paris to Limoges.

The critic and translator Walter Benjamin was to kill himself in despair after being refused entry into Spain while en route to Lisbon, where he hoped to find passage to the United States. Benjamin translated Saint-John Perse's *Anabase*, which Rilke had originally undertaken, and parts of Proust's *A la recherche du temps perdu* *[Remembrance of Things Past]*, in collaboration with Franz Hessel. Monnier cared immensely for Benjamin as a man and as a writer; she wrote two brief articles on him, "Note sur Walter Benjamin" (1952) and "Un Portrait de Walter Benjamin" (1954). She says in her "Note" that it was very much while thinking of him that she set down her reflections on anti-Semitism.

Many of the other persons that Monnier mentions here will be familiar from earlier references or because they are very well known. Several can and should be identified further, following the day-to-day sequence of the entries. May 19: John Rewald, the art critic and historian, is the biographer of Cézanne. May 27: Miguel Angel Carcano was at this time the Argentine ambassador to France; Adelina Güiraldes and her husband, the poet Ricardo Güiraldes, were editors of the Argentine literary review *Proa*, which had strong ties with France. May 31: Hélène Hoppenot is the wife of Henri Hoppenot; Violaine, their daughter and the goddaughter of Paul Claudel, was active in the Resistance. June 1: Gisèle Freund, the photographer, left her native Germany at the time the Nazis came to power; she took refuge during the war in southern France and later in Argentina. She was staying at the time at Adrienne Monnier's apartment. June 7 and 11: Ida Bonetto and Léonie Thévenet were Monnier's young bookshop assistants. June 18: Mme Allier was the concierge of Shakespeare and Company; Marthe Lamy, the gynecologist, appears in "Lunch with Colette"; Carlotta Briggs, one of Sylvia Beach's closest friends, is also mentioned in "Americans in Paris." June 19: Paul Léautaud, the writer and chronicler—and notorious misanthrope—was for many years an editor of the *Mercure de France*. June 21: Keeler Faus, who appears in "Americans in Paris," is identified in the commentary to that article.

A LETTER TO FRIENDS IN THE FREE ZONE AND
A LETTER TO ANDRÉ GIDE ABOUT THE YOUNG

(pages 403 and 407)

The so-called "Free Zone," which included the southern part of France, was established at the time of the Franco-German armistice toward the end of June 1940; it remained unoccupied by the German army until November 1942. One of the friends who read her open letter in the *Figaro Littéraire* with appreciation was André Gide, whom Adrienne Monnier was to address directly in the pages of the same review. The writer had taken refuge in Nicé, and he was to remain there until the beginning of May, when he sailed to North Africa, where he lived until the end of the war. On March 4 he wrote to her, speaking for himself and his friends in Nice, among them Maria Van Rysselberghe and the novelist Roger Martin du Gard: "Your chronicle in *Figaro* is the magic wand that suddenly transports us near you. I hear everything. I see everything. . . . We send you a bundle of best remembrances from all of us, and for Sylvia, for your sister, for the friends who surround you and of whom we are a bit jealous for being near you."

Though the tone of Monnier's *Figaro* letters seems somewhat circumspect, somewhat subdued, her praise for "the person of France" is clearly felt in the present instance as she calls the roll of some of the country's greatest writers, and in the letter to Gide she insinuates more than she says directly about the mood of the moment, as in her discussion of jazz and her impressions of it. Here she refers to a definition by Hugues Panassié, a jazz enthusiast and a friend of Duke Ellington. "Gide's lecture" on Henri Michaux, which she mentions in her first letter, was banned at first by the Vichy government, to which the poet was a suspect person; permission to deliver it was eventually given, but Gide refused to do so, not wanting, he said, "to add to the divisions among the French." It was published in 1941 as a booklet, *Découvrons Henri Michaux [Discovering Henri Michaux]*. A laconic reference toward the end of this letter to Sylvia Beach's closing of her bookshop was probably as much as Monnier could permit herself to say about the dangerous predicament of her friend, who according to her own account in her autobiography, moved the contents of Shakespeare and Company into an unused upstairs apartment after a German officer, to whom she refused to sell a copy of *Finnegans Wake*, threatened her with the confiscation of her property by the occupants. The Germans eventually interned her in their camp for enemy aliens in Vittel. Sylvia's friends in Touraine, the country region southwest of Paris, who sent "a rabbit almost every week," were probably Carlotta Welles (Mrs. James Briggs) and her husband, who had a home there.

AMERICANS IN PARIS

(page 413)

Of chief interest in the present article, which is a tribute to her American friends, is Adrienne Monnier's description of the arrival in the Rue de l'Odéon of Ernest Hemingway and his military division on Saturday, August 26, 1944, the day after the German commander in Paris, General Dietrich von Choltitz, officially surrendered to General Jacques Philippe Leclerc. Despite the German capitulation, sporadic fighting continued here and there in the city, and on that Saturday General Charles de Gaulle and his entourage were shot at by snipers as they entered Notre-Dame to attend a service to celebrate the liberation of Paris. As Monnier says, the sniping along the way forced her and Sylvia Beach to abandon their own plan to visit the cathedral, and they returned to the Rue de l'Odéon. The shooting had been going on for several days, and it was to continue for several days longer, but without stopping the residents from attending to their affairs.

Sylvia Beach ends her *Shakespeare and Company* with an anecdote about Hemingway's visit that differs significantly from Monnier's minute account, which other writers say is accurate. Her statement that Hemingway "got his company out of the jeeps and took them up to the roof," after which they "heard firing for the last time in the Rue de l'Odéon," is no doubt pure invention.

The first and longer part of Monnier's article can be described as a series of salutations beginning with the "choir of friends" whom Sylvia brought to her, and who had been imprisoned, like Sylvia herself, in the German internment camp in Vittel, a hot springs resort in the department of Vosges in eastern France. Sarah Watson, "the directress of the International Students' Hostel" (the Foyer International des Etudiantes) was freed before long and returned to the hostel, where Sylvia used to visit her and her assistant, Marcelle Fournier, after her own release six months later. Katherine Dudley, a painter and a friend of Picasso, as Monnier says, was the sister of Dorothy Dudley, who wrote a study of Theodore Dreiser, *Dreiser and the Land of the Free* (1932), and of Caroline Dudley, who presented *La Revue Nègre*, starring Josephine Baker, at the Théâtre des Champs-Elysées in 1925. In her account of her internment in Vittel, Sylvia says that Mabel Gardner, the sculptor, "carved beautiful statues in the logs provided for our stoves." She also mentions Dru Tartière and

Mary Dixon, "another directress of the students' home." Camilla Steinbrugge was a close friend who was admirable to Sylvia in her last years.

Some of the other Americans in Paris, such as Gertrude Stein and the sculptor Jo Davidson, are too famous to need mention; some are identified by Monnier herself. Keeler Faus, a secretary in the American Embassy before 1940, appears in her article on Saint-Exupéry and in her Occupation journal. "Carlotta" is Carlotta Welles (Mrs. James Briggs), a childhood friend of Sylvia and a long-time resident of France; her father, she says in *Shakespeare and Company*, "represented Western Electric in Paris." Of Grace Flandrau and her love for the Cour de Rohan no record has been found. Like Bob McAlmon, who established Contact Editions, Bill Byrd was an amateur publisher; he directed The Three Mountains Press. Bravig Imbs was an acquaintance of Gertrude Stein and of George Antheil.

THE NATURE OF FRANCE

(page 417)

"This, the eighth number of *Verve*," we read in its fall 1940 issue, "devoted to the Nature of France, was entirely composed during the war, and its printing was completed in Paris June 1, 1940." Not until late in 1943, though again despite the war and the Occupation as well, did *Verve* reappear. This issue, then, celebrated the genius of France at the very moment of her gravest loss. Adrienne Monnier's tribute appeared in a splendid context, with Rouault's "Visage de la France"—reproductions of his paintings, including one of Saint Joan on horseback, with commentaries by the artist; "Réflexions" by Braque, with reproductions of his own work; a piece by Valéry that was accompanied by an etching and a drawing by the poet himself; more articles or pictures by Claudel, Reverdy, Matisse, Derain, Picasso, and others; the illuminations of the fifteenth-century *Calendar of Charles d'Angoulême*; and an introduction by Julien Cain, the general administrator of the Bibliothèque Nationale. Monnier brought to her article the same scrupulous attention for which she praises in it the work of Fouquet and the Limbourg brothers. She wrote at the beginning of her *Gazette des Amis des Livres* of May 1940: "As Tériade asked me to do a study for *Verve* on the Nature of France, I spent nearly two months thinking about it and writing it—still it's something rather short." Short, yes, as the miniatures are small, showing the same "passionate concentration," and like them "a talisman."

selected index